Autonomous Cyber Resilience

IEEE Press

445 Hoes Lane

Piscataway, NJ 08854

Autonomous Cyber Resilience

Edited by

Charles A. Kamhoua
US Army Research Laboratory
Adelphi, MD, USA

Alexander Kott
US Army Research Laboratory
Adelphi, MD, USA

Quanyan Zhu
New York University
Brooklyn, NY, USA

Nandi O. Leslie
RTX Corporation
Bethesda, MD, USA

IEEE Press
WILEY

Published by John Wiley & Sons, Inc., Hoboken, New Jersey.

For general information on our other products and services or for technical support, please contact our Customer Care Department within the United States at (800) 762-2974, outside the United States at (317) 572-3993 or fax (317) 572-4002.

Wiley also publishes its books in a variety of electronic formats. Some content that appears in print may not be available in electronic formats. For more information about Wiley products, visit our web site at www.wiley.com.

Library of Congress Cataloging-in-Publication Data has been applied for:

Hardback ISBN: 9781394215386
epdf ISBN: 9781394215393
epub ISBN: 9781394215409
oBook ISBN: 9781394215416

Cover Design: Wiley
Cover Image: © traffic_analyzer/Getty Images

To all who see in failure not defeat but design, who shape adversity into adaptation, and who turn uncertainty into understanding.

Contents

Preface

Cyber resilience has emerged as one of the defining challenges of our time. As societies, industries, and governments become increasingly dependent on interconnected cyber-physical infrastructures, the stakes of security have escalated beyond protection alone. Traditional approaches that emphasize prevention and defense are no longer sufficient; adversaries are adaptive, threats are dynamic, and the systems we depend upon are growing more autonomous and complex. In this new environment, resilience, understood as the capacity not only to withstand attacks but also to adapt, recover, and evolve, has become central to the very fabric of cybersecurity.

This book was conceived with the recognition that cyber resilience is not a singular discipline but an inherently interdisciplinary pursuit. Building resilient systems requires insights from computer science, control theory, machine learning, game theory, economics, and policy. It demands attention to both the microdynamics of adversarial interactions and the macrodynamics of organizational, societal, and systemic interdependencies. By bringing together these diverse perspectives, our aim has been to articulate a roadmap for cyber resilience that integrates foundational principles, algorithmic innovation, and strategic reasoning.

The book is organized into three parts, comprising 13 chapters in total. The first part establishes the foundations of cyber resilience, introducing concepts such as zero-trust architectures, cyber insurance, and cognitive feedback loops that enable adaptation and learning. The second part examines the vulnerabilities and defenses of machine learning systems, a domain increasingly central to both the promise and the peril of modern cyber infrastructures. The third part explores game-theoretic approaches, offering rigorous tools for understanding and shaping the strategic interactions that define adversarial environments, from intelligent transportation systems to quantum-secure communication networks.

Each chapter reflects the state of the art in its domain while also pointing forward to new directions. Collectively, the volume argues that resilience is not merely an addition to security but a dynamic property that must be designed into systems from the outset. It highlights the central role of autonomy, as systems that can perceive, reason, and act with foresight under adversarial uncertainty, and the need for transparency and explainability to ensure trust and accountability.

This book is intended for researchers, practitioners, and policymakers alike. For researchers, it offers new theoretical frameworks and open problems. For practitioners, it provides models and mechanisms to guide the design of resilient architectures. For policymakers, it outlines the institutional and regulatory dimensions necessary to sustain resilience at scale. Our hope is that the volume serves not only as a reference for today's challenges but also as an inspiration for tomorrow's innovations. The pursuit of cyber resilience is, at its core, a collective endeavor, one that requires collaboration across disciplines, sectors, and nations. By embedding resilience into the heart of our digital infrastructures, we can begin to shape a future in which security is not brittle but adaptive; not reactive, but anticipatory; not fragile, but enduring.

The editors would like to acknowledge the contributions of all the chapter authors. We also extend our gratitude to Ya-Ting Yang of New York University for providing extensive editorial assistance, to anonymous reviewers whose feedback strengthened the chapters, and to Victoria Bradshaw, Mary Hatcher, and Kavipriya Ramachandran of Wiley for their kind support in guiding this book through the publication process.

Charles A. Kamhoua
Alexander Kott
Quanyan Zhu
Nandi O. Leslie

Editor Biographies

Charles A. Kamhoua is a Senior Electronics Engineer at the Network Security Branch of the US Army Research Laboratory (ARL) in Adelphi, MD, where he is responsible for conducting and directing basic research in the area of game theory applied to cybersecurity. Prior to joining the Army Research Laboratory, he was a researcher at the US Air Force Research Laboratory (AFRL), Rome, New York, for six years and an educator in different academic institutions for more than 10 years. He has held visiting research positions at the University of Oxford and Harvard University.

He has co-authored more than 200 peer-reviewed journals and conference papers, including five best paper awards. He is a co-inventor of three patents and six patent applications. He has been at the forefront of several new technologies, co-editing four books at Wiley-IEEE Press entitled *Game Theory and Machine Learning for Cyber Security, Modeling and Design of Secure Internet of*

Things, *Blockchain for Distributed System Security*, and *Assured Cloud Computing*. He has presented over 70 invited keynote and distinguished speeches and has co-organized more than 10 conferences and workshops. He has mentored more than 65 young scholars, including students, postdocs, and summer faculty fellows.

He has been recognized for his scholarship and leadership with numerous prestigious awards, including the 2020 Sigma Xi Young Investigator Award for outstanding leadership and contribution to game theory applied to cyber security, the 2019 US Army Civilian Service Commendation Medal, the 2019 Federal 100-FCW annual award for exceptional impact on federal IT, the 2019 IEEE ComSoc Technical Committee on Big Data Best Journal Paper Award, the 2018 Fulbright Senior Specialist Fellowship, two ARL Achievement Awards (2019 and 2018), the 2017 AFRL Information Directorate Basic Research Award "for Outstanding Achievements in Basic Research," the 2017 Fred I. Diamond Award for the best paper published at AFRL's Information Directorate, 40 Air Force Notable Achievement Awards, the 2016 Florida International University (FIU) Charles E. Perry Young Alumni Visionary Award, the 2015 Black Engineer of the Year Award (BEYA), the 2015 NSBE Golden Torch Award – Pioneer of the Year, and selection to the 2015 Heidelberg Laureate Forum, among others. He has been congratulated by the White House, the US Congress, and the Pentagon for these achievements.

He received a BS in electronics from the University of Douala (ENSET), Cameroon, in 1999, an MS in Telecommunication and Networking from FIU in 2008, and a PhD in Electrical Engineering from FIU in 2011. He is currently an advisor for the National Research Council postdoc program, a member of the FIU alumni association and Sigma Xi, and a senior member of ACM and IEEE.

Alexander Kott served as the Chief Scientist for the US Army Research Laboratory until 2023. In this role, he provided leadership in the development of the laboratory's technical strategy. He was also the Army S&T for cyber resilience. Between

2009 and 2016, Dr. Kott served as the Chief of the Network Science Division, Computational and Information Sciences Directorate, US Army Research Laboratory. He was responsible for, and helped initiate, a diverse portfolio of fundamental research and applied development in network science and science for cyber warfare. In 2013, Dr. Kott served as the Acting Associate Director for Science and Technology of the ARL's Computational and Information Sciences Directorate. In 2015, he also served as the Acting Director of the Computational and Information Sciences Directorate. From 2003 to 2008, Dr. Kott served as a Defense Advanced Research Programs Agency (DARPA) Program Manager responsible for a number of large-scale advanced technology research programs. Technologies developed in programs under his management ranged from adversarial reasoning about the enemy intent to command and control of human-robotic forces.

His earlier positions included Director of Research and Development at Carnegie Group, Pittsburgh, PA, one of the world's first artificial intelligence (AI) companies, and Information Technology Research Department Manager at Allied Signal, Inc., Morristown, NJ. There, his work focused on using AI in complex problems in engineering design, planning, and control in manufacturing, telecommunications, and aviation industries. Dr. Kott received the Secretary of Defense Exceptional Public Service Award and accompanying Exceptional Public Service Medal, in October 2008. He earned his PhD from the University of Pittsburgh in 1989, where his research proposed AI approaches to innovative design of complex systems. Dr. Kott published over 100 technical papers and has served as the initiator, co-author, and primary editor of 14 books.

Nandi O. Leslie serves as a Principal Technical Fellow at RTX in the Raytheon Business Unit – this position is the highest technical honor for RTX employees. While serving in this position, she has held additional RTX roles, including the

Chief Data Scientist, Chief Engineer for the Raytheon Research and Development (R&D) portfolio, and Technical Solutions Director for Cybersecurity with global teams in the US, Europe, and West Asia. She has strong expertise in the following sectors and business functions: aerospace and defense, academia, AI, machine learning, data science, modeling and simulation, cybersecurity, and test and evaluation.

Since 2020, Dr. Leslie has also served as an Adjunct Professor at Johns Hopkins University in the Applied and Computational Mathematics Program. Furthermore, since 2019, she has served as a Visiting Professor at the African Institute for Mathematical Sciences in M'bour, Senegal. Before joining RTX in 2015, Dr. Leslie led and contributed to projects on modeling and simulation related to sensor performance (e.g., acoustic, radar, global positioning system) and cybersecurity for the Navy, Office of the Under Secretary of Defense for Research and Engineering, and other customers at Systems Planning and Analysis, Inc. as a Program Manager and Senior Operations Research Analyst starting in 2007. From 2005 to 2007, she taught at the University of Maryland, College Park in the Department of Mathematics as a Lecturer, where she was also a Postdoctoral Researcher sponsored by the National Science Foundation Vertical Integration of Research and Education in the Mathematical Sciences conducting research.

Dr. Leslie is an award-winning applied mathematician and technology leader who has written over 60 publications in journals, conference proceedings, technical reports, and edited books, and she has presented her research at over 100 international conferences, workshops, and meetings. She received the BEYA Award for Outstanding Technical Contribution in Industry in 2020.

Dr. Leslie has served as a member of the following boards and committees: (1) Princeton University Board of Trustees, (2) National Academies of Sciences; Engineering, and Medicine (NASEM) Committee on Biotechnology Capabilities for National Security Needs, (3) President's National Security Telecommunications Advisory Committee, Strategy for Increasing Trust in the Information and Communications Technology and Services, (4) NASEM Army Board on Army R&D on AI and Justified Confidence Committee, (5) NASEM on AI Test and Evaluation for the Air Force Committee, (6) Howard University, Center of Excellence in AI and Machine Learning Advisory Board, (7) Society of Industrial and Applied Mathematics (SIAM), Industry Committee, (8) SIAM Committee on Programs and Conferences; and (9) American Mathematical Society Short Course Committee.

Dr. Leslie earned her PhD and MA in Applied and Computational Mathematics from Princeton University, and she graduated magna cum laude with her BS in Mathematics from Howard University.

Quanyan Zhu received BEng (Honors) in Electrical Engineering from McGill University in 2006, MASc from the University of Toronto in 2008, and PhD from the University of Illinois at Urbana-Champaign (UIUC) in 2013. After stints at Princeton University, he is currently an Associate Professor at the Department of Electrical and Computer Engineering, New York University (NYU). He is an affiliated faculty member of the Center for Urban Science and Progress (CUSP) at NYU. He is a recipient of many awards, including the NSF CAREER Award, NYU Goddard Junior Faculty Fellowship, NSERC Postdoctoral Fellowship (PDF), NSERC Canada Graduate Scholarship (CGS), and Mavis Future Faculty Fellowships. He spearheaded and chaired INFOCOM Workshop on Communications and Control on Smart Energy Systems (CCSES), Midwest Workshop on Control and Game Theory (WCGT), and ICRA workshop on Security and Privacy of Robotics. His current research interests include game theory, machine learning, cyber deception, network optimization and control, smart cities, Internet of Things, and cyber-physical systems. He has served as the general chair or the TPC chair of the 7th and the 11th Conference on Decision and Game Theory for Security (GameSec) in 2016 and 2020, the 9th International Conference on NETwork Games, COntrol and OPtimisation (NETGCOOP) in 2018, the 5th International Conference on Artificial Intelligence and Security (ICAIS 2019) in 2019, and 2020 IEEE Workshop on Information Forensics and Security (WIFS). He has also spearheaded in 2020 the IEEE Control System Society (CSS) Technical Committee on Security, Privacy, and Resilience. He is a co-author of two recent books published by Springer: *Cyber-Security in Critical Infrastructures: A Game-theoretic Approach* (with S. Rass, S. Schauer, and S. König) and *A Game- and Decision-theoretic Approach to Resilient Interdependent Network Analysis and Design* (with J. Chen).

1

Introduction

Alexander Kott

Independent researcher

1.1 Cyber Resilience and Cybersecurity

Numerous definitions of cyber resilience have been offered in the literature – partly similar and partly conflicting. The terminology and definitions of key concepts in the field of cybersecurity continue to evolve, and the term "cyber resilience," among others, is subject to these evolutionary processes [1].

Terms such as risk, resilience, and security are often conflated. This is even more so when the word "cyber" is added. Let us begin with the dictionary definitions. Security is "the state of being free from danger or threat [2]." Note that this definition closely relates to the definition of risk: "a situation involving exposure to danger (threat) [2]." Clearly, security has much to do with the elimination or reduction of risk. Now we turn to the definition of resilience: "the capacity to recover quickly from difficulties [2]." These definitions imply a key difference between security and resilience. Security is about eliminating or reducing the risk of experiencing difficulties caused by a threat. Resilience, on the other hand, is about recovering from the difficulties caused by a threat.

Having noted the definitions of resilience and security in general, consider definitions of cyber resilience and cybersecurity. The United States National Institute of Standards and Technology (NIST) defines cybersecurity as "Prevention of damage to, protection of, and restoration of computers, electronic communications systems, electronic communications services, wire communication, and electronic communication, including information contained therein, to ensure its availability, integrity, authentication, confidentiality, and nonrepudiation [3]."

Cyber resilience is defined by NIST as "The ability to anticipate, withstand, recover from, and adapt to adverse conditions, stresses, attacks, or compromises on systems that use or are enabled by cyber resources. Cyber resiliency is intended to enable mission or business objectives that depend on cyber resources to be achieved in a contested cyber environment [4]."

In comparing the two definitions, we see at least one element that is common to both definitions, particularly the related terms "restoration" (in cybersecurity) and "recovery" (in cyber resilience). Still, the distinction is very salient: cybersecurity primarily aims to ensure that damage to the system is avoided, while cyber resilience primarily aims to withstand and recover from the damage that has already occurred.

Both disciplines – cybersecurity and cyber resilience – are important. However, conflating security and resilience is counterproductive. The difference between the two is real, and ramifications of the difference are practical. Problems that require security (i.e., risk-reducing) approaches should not be solved with resilience-focused approaches, and vice versa. Applying the wrong type of approach will result in a costly failure to solve the problem [5].

The importance of cyber resilience – as compared to cybersecurity – grows when the cyber environment is strongly contested, the likelihood of a cyber compromise is significant, and reducing that likelihood is difficult for technical or cost reasons. Furthermore, as the NIST definition of cyber resilience emphasizes, cyber resilience is particularly important when a cyber compromise is likely to prevent the achievement of a critical mission or business objective.

Here we must note that cyber resilience is not limited to technological aspects – neither with respect to the systems that require resilience nor to the systems that provide or enhance resilience. Cyber resilience often refers to the resilience of individuals, organizations, and entire societies in the face of damaging events, experiences, and behaviors occurring in cyberspace. This book, however, focuses primarily on the resilience of technological systems. Still, no consideration of cyber resilience can disregard the role of humans in any technological system – users, operators, and communities.

To a large extent, the argument for cyber resilience is economic in nature. As illustrated in Figure 1.1, organizations often find that as cybersecurity reaches a certain level, further incremental improvements in cybersecurity come at higher and higher costs. At some point, further investments in preventing and avoiding a cyber compromise become prohibitively expensive. Then, the organization should ask itself whether it would make economic sense to invest in cyber resilience, that is, withstanding and recovering from the compromise if it does occur.

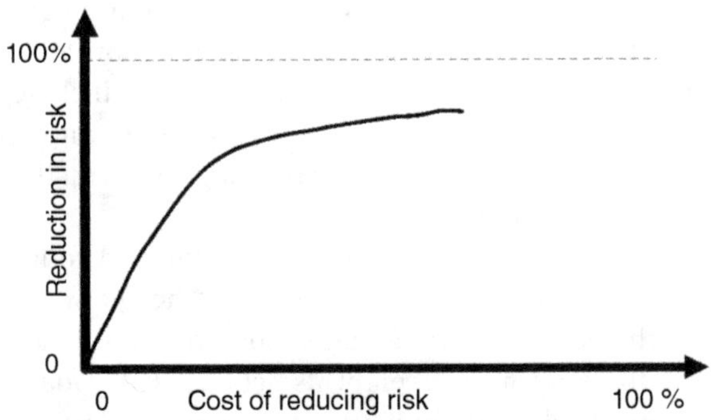

Figure 1.1 When further investments in security (reducing risk) yield ever-lower returns, investments in resilience become more attractive economically.

1.2 Autonomy and Cyber Resilience

Systems that can change their behavior in response to unanticipated events during operation are called "autonomous [6]." Clearly, the definition assumes independence (or the ability to be independent) of human control during the change of behavior. Combining this definition with the one for cyber resilience, we can offer the following definition for autonomous cyber resilience: the system's ability to withstand, recover from, and adapt to adverse cyber compromises by changing the system's behavior in response to the compromise, without the necessity of human control.

Implicit in this definition is a significant level of intelligent reasoning and independent agency of the system, or a subsystem, responsible for autonomous cyber resilience. In particular, the system must have means to perceive and understand the situation, that is, to observe, analyze, and interpret events relevant to potential cyber compromise. This includes especially the ability to observe, detect, and interpret well-concealed actions taken by sophisticated hostile malware. Traditional intrusion detection and anomaly detection must be a part of these perception and interpretation capabilities.

With the available understanding of the situation, the autonomous cyber resilience system should be able to formulate a suitable behavior, such as, for example, a potentially complex plan of response and recovery actions. A complex plan may include multiple actions directed at different elements of the cyber environment. These actions may have complex temporal relations, that is, they may be simultaneous and consecutive, in various combinations. The actions may also have conditional relations; that is, an action may only be initiated if other actions have succeeded in establishing the required preconditions [7]. Alternative plans or branches of a plan may need to be prepared as well.

In building such complex plans, an autonomous cyber resilience system should be able to assess the chances of success and possible ramifications – short-term and more strategic – of the proposed actions. These ramifications may include unintended negative impacts on functions of the cyber environment, for example, certain programs might stop working and may even have cascading effects on the physical world that depend on those functions [8].

Furthermore, the autonomous system must anticipate the reaction and counteraction of the hostile malware residing in the environment. The malware, having observed or anticipated the actions of the autonomous cyber resilience system, may attempt to destroy the system or preempt its actions. This would demand elements of game-theoretic analysis [9] or adversarial reasoning [10] on the part of the autonomous cyber resilience system.

Finally, the autonomous system should be able to execute the plan of actions while observing the effects of the actions and being ready to adapt as needed. If an action fails in its intended outcomes, the system should be able to reformulate its plan of actions or switch to executing a prepared alternative branch of the plan. Because the actions are potentially observed by the hostile malware, the system may need to execute its actions in a stealthy mode, concealing the actions and perhaps even using elements of deception directed at the hostile malware.

1.3 Autonomous Actions

Autonomy implies an ability to take actions, as mentioned frequently in the previous section. Assuming a system possesses autonomous cyber resilience mechanisms, let us consider examples of actions that such mechanisms might undertake. The discussion in this section is based largely on [11].

Available actions fall mainly in the following broad categories [11, p. 86]:

Absorption means accepting a level of damage to some of the system elements while also taking actions to reduce the impacts (or repair the damage) to other system elements.

Deflection involves transferring threat events or their effects to different system elements or to systems other than those that were targeted or initially affected.

Discarding and replacement means removing system elements if indications and the degree of damage warrant doing so. After the removal, those elements are replaced with undamaged ones, or alternatively the system is enabled to operate without them, although potentially with degraded capabilities.

Examples of more specific approaches to courses of action may include [11, pp. 93–105]:

Reconfiguration, resource reallocation, and relocation: Such courses of action may include making changes to individual subsystems or components to modify their functionality or behavior, changing the allocation of resources to tasks or functions, or changing the location of resources that provide functionality or information, either by moving the assets or by transferring functional responsibility.

Obfuscation, disinformation, and misdirection: Courses of action in this category may include hiding, transforming, or otherwise obscuring the contents, properties, or presence of information or other assets from the adversary; providing deliberately misleading information to adversaries; or creating deceptive resources or environments and directing adversary activities there.

Dynamic generation of information, services, and connections: Here the autonomous cyber resilience system may refresh information and services periodically or generate information on demand and delete it when no longer needed. It may also establish connections on demand and terminate connections when no longer needed.

Dynamic restrictions of usage, privileges, and function: These restrictions may include, for example, to define, assign, maintain, and apply usage restrictions on cyber resources based on the criticality or sensitivity of missions or business functions; elevate or decrease privileges assigned to a user, process, or service based on transient or contextual factors; and remove or disable unneeded functionality or connectivity or add mechanisms to reduce the chance of vulnerability or failure.

1.4 Approaches to Implementing Autonomous Cyber Resilience

It is useful to distinguish two broad classes of approaches to cyber resilience: resilience by design and resilience by intervention [12]. Resilience by design is characterized by tight integration, that is, strong links exist between the resilience elements of the system and those components of the system that are responsible for producing the primary functions of the system. Furthermore, in resilience by design, the decision authority for taking actions is internal to the system – it does not require the permission (or direction) of an external actor to change system properties or reorganize itself. In all cases, the qualifier “by design” indicates that the source of resilience is inherent in the structure and operation of the system.

Views on the implementation of resilience by design differ widely. Some argue that systems must be designed and implemented in a provable mission assurance fashion, with the system's intrinsic properties ensuring that a cyber-adversary is unable to cause a meaningful degradation [13]. Others envision autonomic resilience [14], where cyber resilience is provided by reflexive, no-thinking-required actions of appropriate elements within the system. Yet others [15] recommend that a system should include a built-in autonomous intelligent agent responsible for thinking and acting toward continuous observation, detection, mitigation, and remediation of a cyber degradation.

On the other hand, resilience by intervention does not require a tight integration between the resilience-producing elements and the rest of the system. The links are established occasionally and selectively based on circumstances. The decision authority for taking actions resides primarily outside of the system itself. Resilience by intervention is usually implemented by providing a system under protection with a thin client that communicates with an external service that provides monitoring, mitigation, and recovery support [16].

Both approaches have their advantages. Resilience by design, with its internal decision authority, can quickly seize opportunities to minimize or to recover from disruption. It avoids potential inefficiencies or delays from waiting for an external actor to yield permission or direction for change. In addition, it can take necessary actions even if the system's communications with the outside world are severed or degraded, which may be happening due to the interference of hostile malware or other means.

Resilience by intervention also has advantages. An external service may have stronger competence and greater resources, as compared to resilience by design mechanisms, for providing resilience to the system under its care. It may be more economical because the expenses of maintaining the service are spread over many customers. In addition, the lack of tight integration means that an external service can be easily replaced, as dictated by reasons of economy or quality of service.

To illustrate, consider a particular approach to the implementation of autonomous cyber resilience called the Autonomous Intelligent Cyber-defense Agents (AICA). Figure 1.2 depicts the functional components of the agent architecture.

The AICA Reference Architecture [17] defines the following main functions:

"Sensing" and "world state identification" allow the agent to acquire data (percepts) from the environment in which it operates, as well as from itself, in order to understand the current state of the world and self. These "sensing" and "world state identification" functions rely upon the "world model," "current state and history," "world dynamics," and "goals" components of the functional architecture.

The "planning" and "action selection" functions allow AICA to formulate one or several action proposals and perform the action selection. The latter decides on the

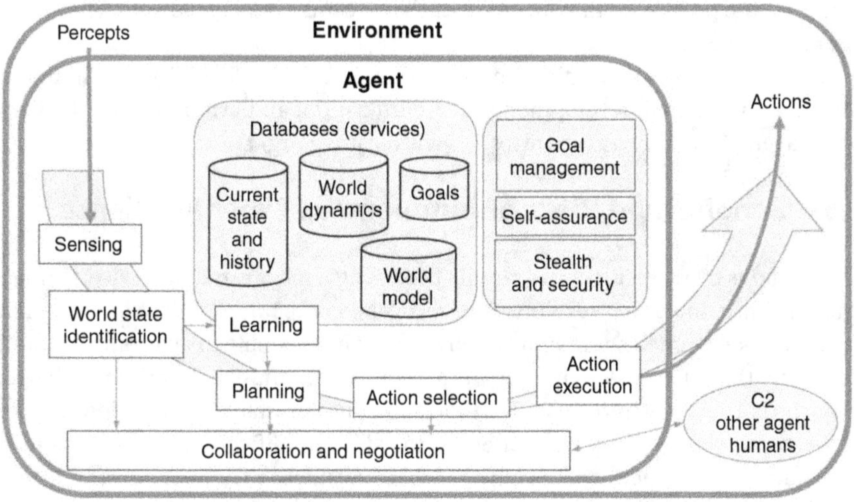

Figure 1.2 Functional components of an AICA agent. *Source*: Adapted from [17]. [17]; the figure is in public domain as derived from the US Government work.

action or a set of actions to execute to resolve the differences between the goals of the agent and the current world state identified by the "world state identification" function. This function relies in part upon the "world dynamics" component of the functional architecture.

The "collaboration and negotiation" function enables AICA to (1) exchange information with other agents, humans, and a central cyber command and control, for instance, when one of the agent's functions cannot reach satisfactory conclusions on its own, and (2) negotiate with its partners the details of a consolidated conclusion or resulting actions. In particular, this function helps the external entities to form relevant situational awareness. Negotiation with other entities may require adjustments to the goals of the agent, which is performed by the "goal management" function.

The "action execution" function enables AICA, based on the action selection's executable response plan, to monitor its execution and its effects, and provides the means to adjust the execution of the plan (or possibly dynamically adjust the plan) as needed. This function relies in part on the "goals" component of the functional architecture.

The "learning" function allows AICA to use its experience to progressively improve its efficiency and effectiveness. The "self-assurance" function helps the agent to observe its own behavior and to correct errors and deficiencies. The "stealth and security" function modulates the behavior of the agent in order to minimize the possibility that an opponent's malware would detect and degrade or disable the agent.

An international working group exists that focuses on fostering research and education, industrial developments, standardization, and evaluation methods in AICA agents' technology (see https://www.aica-iwg.org/).

1.5 Benefits and Risks of Autonomous Cyber Resilience

Autonomous cyber resilience is rapidly becoming a recognized necessity. Human cyber defense, including response and recovery, is expensive. Competent human cyber defenders are in short supply and may not be available in environments and situations that are challenging for human presence, and where cyber resilience might be particularly important. Furthermore, human analysis and actions for the purposes of cyber resilience are often far too slow. Ramifications of a cyberattack may unfold in seconds, while human cyber defenders may need days to assess the situation, formulate a plan for remediation and recovery, and then weeks to execute the plan. In short, manual and semi-manual approaches are inadequate, and autonomous cyber resilience is a clear necessity [18].

An important factor is the rapidly growing presence of autonomous systems of various sorts in our society and industry. These include purely cyber systems, such as chatbots; physical systems like self-driving cars; and cyber-physical systems, such as control systems of a manufacturing plant. The sheer number and pervasive presence of such autonomous systems make the likelihood and impact of a compromise ever more significant and threatening.

Traditional, human-based cyber defense approaches are particularly unsuitable to resilience – that is, rapid recovery – of autonomous systems. Speed of response is often paramount because a compromised autonomous system may cause extensive damage. Merely taking a system offline is often not an option because no humans are available to replace a critical function performed by an autonomous system. Human cyber defenders are unavailable because an autonomous system is intended to operate without human participation. In addition, reliance on external monitoring and recovery is dubious because a sophisticated malware will disable communication links.

In light of the above considerations, the benefits of autonomous cyber resilience are extensive. An autonomous cyber resilience can respond quickly and decisively to a cyber compromise, thereby preventing damaging ramifications of the cyberattack. It can do so without the need for expensive, unavailable, and slow human personnel. It eliminates or reduces the need for having intact communication links for external monitoring and response.

These benefits, however, do not come without risks [19]. Like any autonomy, autonomous cyber resilience raises questions regarding the related risks. Indeed, any autonomous cyber resilience mechanism, regardless of its implementation details, must take actions autonomously, and these include destructive actions such as deleting or quarantining certain software. Admittedly, such actions may cause damage, especially if the disabled software is necessary for controlling mission-critical functions of a broader system.

Developers can mitigate such risks to some extent. For example, destructive actions should be controlled by rules that prevent or minimize the potential damage of autonomous resilience actions. The effects and ramifications of all actions should be analyzed and predicted using built-in modeling and simulation tools. Propagation of autonomous resilience software to other computers should not be allowed. Under particularly questionable circumstances, autonomous cyber resilience should seek human authorization of its actions, if humans are available to respond to such a request. Continuous monitoring and measurements of cyber resilience should be conducted [20] to ensure it remains effective.

Still, residual risks cannot be entirely avoided. In general, actions taken by autonomous resilience cannot be fully guaranteed to preserve the availability or integrity of the functions and data of computers protected by the autonomous cyber resilience mechanisms. Neither, however, can human-based cyber defense offer a full guarantee of preserving the availability or integrity of computing systems. Lack of foolproof guarantees – an inevitable fact of any practical technology – should not be discouraging. We must accept the residual risks because alternatives are even worse. Benefits of autonomous cyber resilience far outweigh the risks.

1.6 The Preview of the Book

Cyber resilience, as explored in this volume, is not a static property but a dynamic capability: a system's ability to endure and adapt amid uncertainty, deception, and attack. This capability requires not only robust defenses but also strategic foresight, architectural flexibility, and cognitive tools that allow for autonomous, intelligent responses to emerging threats. The book provides readers with the latest theoretical insights, systems-level frameworks, and practical techniques necessary to understand and engineer resilient cyber ecosystems.

To organize this wide-ranging exploration, the book is divided into three interconnected parts, each addressing a core pillar of cyber resilience. Together, these sections guide the reader from foundational principles to cutting-edge research directions.

1.6.1 Part I: Foundations of Cyber Resilience

The first part lays the groundwork by introducing innovative mechanisms and quantitative frameworks essential for establishing resilient cyber systems. Given the inherently adversarial nature of cyberspace, game theory serves as a key methodology to model strategic interactions between defenders and intelligent adversaries. Chapter 2 illustrates this in the context of Intelligent Transportation Systems (ITS), highlighting how game-theoretic approaches can proactively mitigate the impact of data manipulation attacks and enhance systemic robustness.

Equally pivotal is machine learning, which empowers systems with real-time decision-making and adaptive response capabilities. Chapter 3 introduces the CYBER-MIRA framework, combining hypergame theory and subjective Bayesian modeling to assess mission impact resilience in ML-based tactical systems. Chapter 4 advances the discussion by integrating topological data analysis and ML to model the resilience of autonomous networks under adversarial conditions, offering a novel perspective on networked system robustness.

Resilience mechanisms also include architectural innovations. Chapter 5 examines the zero-trust paradigm, emphasizing continuous trust evaluation and adaptive access control as central to modern cyber defense. Chapter 6 turns to cyber insurance as a socio-technical mechanism that complements technical defenses by addressing residual risks and enabling recovery from financial impacts. Chapter 7 explores cyber deception through honeypots, demonstrating how their effectiveness is topology-dependent and can be strategically enhanced to mislead adversaries and gather intelligence.

1.6.2 Part II: Resilient Machine Learning

The second part returns to machine learning, one of the two conceptual pillars of this volume. While ML offers transformative capabilities for cyber resilience, it is itself vulnerable to various attacks. This part explores how to defend machine learning systems against threats that compromise integrity, confidentiality, and availability.

Chapter 8 addresses decision-time adversarial attacks, analyzing their implications for malware detection and image classification systems. It contrasts feature space and realizable attacks to assess effective defense strategies. Chapter 9 focuses on privacy-preserving machine learning, introducing federated learning as a framework to mitigate vulnerabilities such as model inversion and membership inference. Chapter 10 presents a moving target defense approach based on random deep neural network ensembles, which increase resilience by disrupting the attacker's targeting ability without sacrificing accuracy.

1.6.3 Part III: Game Theory for Network Resilience

The final part returns to game theory, underscoring its central role in modeling adversarial dynamics, designing incentives, and formulating adaptive defense strategies in increasingly complex and interconnected systems.

Chapter 11 models poisoning attacks in federated learning for next-generation (NextG) wireless communication systems as a non-cooperative game between malicious and benign agents. The chapter introduces a defender-side admission control strategy informed by game-theoretic reasoning. Chapter 12 extends game-theoretic analysis to quantum communication networks, particularly addressing vulnerabilities in quantum key distribution systems caused by insecure relay nodes. It proposes redundancy-based strategic configurations to enhance end-to-end confidentiality and availability.

Chapter 13, the concluding chapter, synthesizes the themes, techniques, and insights presented throughout the book. It connects the three parts, articulating a vision for future research that combines unsupervised learning, explainable artificial intelligence, dynamic game theory, and emerging technologies such as quantum computing and blockchain. This integrative outlook forms a roadmap for building autonomous, scalable, and trustworthy cyber systems.

References

1 A. Kott and I. Linkov, Eds. *Cyber Resilience of Systems and Networks*. New York, NY: Springer International Publishing, 2019, pp. 381–401.

2 Oxford English Dictionary. Oxford University Press, 2015. https://en.oxforddictionaries.com/definition.

3 NIST Computer Security Resource Center. *Cybersecurity*, n.d. https://csrc.nist.gov/glossary/term/cybersecurity.

4 NIST Computer Security Resource Center. *Cyber resiliency*, n.d. https://csrc.nist.gov/glossary/term/cyber_resiliency.

5 I. Linkov, B. D. Trump, and J. Keisler, Don't conflate risk and resilience. *Nature*, 555(7694): 27, 2018.

6 D. P. Watson and D. H. Scheidt. Autonomous systems. *Johns Hopkins APL Technical Digest*, 26(4): 368–376, 2005.

7 A. Kott, R. Budd, L. Ground, L. Rebbapragada, and J. Langston. Building a tool for battle planning: Challenges, tradeoffs, and experimental findings. *Applied Intelligence*, 23: 165–189, 2005.

8 A. Kott, J. Ludwig, and M. Lange. Assessing mission impact of cyberattacks: Toward a model-driven paradigm. *IEEE Security Privacy*, 15(5): 65–74, 2017.

9 E. J. M. Colbert, A. Kott, and L. P. Knachel. The game-theoretic model and experimental investigation of cyber wargaming. *Journal of Defense Modeling and Simulation*, 17(1): 21–38, 2020.

10 A. Kott and W. M. McEneaney, Eds. *Adversarial Reasoning: Computational Approaches to Reading the Opponent's Mind*. CRC Press, 2006.

11 R. Ross, V. Pillitteri, R. Graubart, D. Bodeau, and R. McQuaid. *Developing Cyber-Resilient Systems: A Systems Security Engineering Approach*, Publication SP 800-160, Vol. 2, Rev. 1. National Institute of Standards and Technology, 2021.

12 A. Kott, M. S. Golan, B. D. Trump, and I. Linkov. Cyber resilience: By design or by intervention? *Computer*, 54(8): 112–117, 2021.

13 K. Jabbour. The post-GIG era: From network security to mission assurance. *The Cyber Defense Review*, 4(2): 117–128, 2019. https://cyberdefensereview.army.mil/CDR-Content/Articles/Article-View/Article/2017729/the-post-gig-era-from-network-security-to-mission-assurance.

14 S. Hariri, M. Eltoweissy, and Y. Al-Nashif. BioRAC: Biologically inspired resilient autonomic cloud. In *Proceedings of the 7th Annual Workshop on Cyber Security in Intelligent Research*, page 1, October 2011, no. 80. https://doi.org/10.1145/2179298.2179389.

15 A. Kott and P. Theron. Doers, not watchers: Intelligent autonomous agents are a path to cyber resilience. *IEEE Security & Privacy*, 18(3): 62–66, 2020.

16 A. Kott and C. Arnold. The promises and challenges of continuous monitoring and risk scoring. *IEEE Security & Privacy*, 11(1): 90–93, 2013.

17 A. Kott, P. Théron, M. Drašar, E. Dushku, B. LeBlanc, P. Losiewicz, A. Guarino, L. Mancini, A. Panico, M. Pihelgas, and K. Rzadca. Autonomous intelligent cyber-defense agent (AICA) reference architecture, release 2.0. *arXiv preprint arXiv:1803.10664*, 2018.

18 A. Kott. Intelligent autonomous agents are key to cyber defense of the future army networks. *The Cyber Defense Review*, 3(3): 57–70, 2018.

19 A. K. Ligo, A. Kott, and I. Linkov. Autonomous cyberdefense introduces risk: Can we manage the risk? *Computer*, 54(10): 106–110, 2021.

20 A. Kott and I. Linkov. To improve cyber resilience, measure it. *Computer*, 54(2): 80–85, 2021.

Part 1

Cyber Resilience

2

Game-theoretic Foundations for Cyber Resilience Against Deceptive Information Attacks in Intelligent Transportation Systems

Ya-Ting Yang and Quanyan Zhu*

Tandon School of Engineering, New York University, Brooklyn, NY, USA

*Corresponding Author: yy4348@nyu.edu

2.1 Introduction

The increasing complexity and interdependence of Intelligent Transportation Systems (ITS) make them particularly vulnerable to cyber threats. Modern ITS integrate a network of technologies, such as automated vehicles [1], intelligent traffic management [2, 3], and communication systems [4], to ensure smooth operation. However, this interconnectedness means that a cyberattack on one component can ripple across the entire system [5]. For example, an attack on a traffic control center can disrupt communications, traffic flow, and logistics in a region. Addressing these interdependencies through robust cyber resilience measures is essential to ensure the continuous and safe operation of ITS [6].

ITS face a dynamic and growing array of cyber threats. Attackers exploit vulnerabilities in transportation systems, using ransomware to lock systems, denial-of-service (DoS) attacks to overwhelm networks, and unauthorized access to compromise sensitive data or take control of systems [7]. Such attacks are not limited to opportunistic hackers; state-sponsored actors and organized crime groups also target critical transportation infrastructure. To combat these threats, ITS must employ advanced threat detection tools, real-time monitoring systems, and proactive defense mechanisms to identify and neutralize potential risks before they escalate.

The cybersecurity of transportation systems has direct implications for public safety. Cyberattacks on automated vehicles, traffic signals, or transportation control systems can lead to accidents, injuries, or even fatalities. For instance, a compromised automated vehicle system could malfunction, putting passengers and other road users at risk. Similarly, a failure of emergency response networks could delay critical assistance during accidents or disasters. Ensuring cyber resilience [8] is not just a technical challenge but a public safety priority, critical to maintaining trust in transportation systems and protecting lives.

The economic impact of cyberattacks on ITS can be significant. Transportation systems are vital to global commerce, enabling the movement of goods and people. A cyber incident could disrupt supply chains, delay deliveries and cause financial losses for businesses and consumers [9]. For example, ransomware attacks on freight logistics systems can halt deliveries and impact industries reliant on timely supply chains. By building resilience into ITS, agencies can prevent such economic disruptions and ensure that transportation continues to support economic stability and growth.

The adoption of advanced ITS technologies, such as automated and connected vehicles, depends heavily on public trust. Users need to feel confident that these technologies are safe and reliable [10]. A high-profile cyberattack that compromises safety or disrupts operations can erode public trust, slowing the adoption of these innovations. Cyber resilience is therefore essential not only for preventing attacks but also for demonstrating a commitment to security, fostering confidence among users, and encouraging the widespread adoption of advanced transportation technologies.

With the growing emphasis on cybersecurity, regulatory bodies are mandating stringent standards for transportation systems. Frameworks like the NIST cybersecurity framework [11] and strategies like zero-trust architectures [12, 13] require transportation agencies to adopt comprehensive security practices. Compliance with these standards not only protects systems from cyber threats but also aligns transportation infrastructure with national and international security objectives. By adhering to these frameworks, ITS operators can ensure a consistent and proactive approach to security.

Addressing the cybersecurity challenges of ITS requires a detailed understanding of attack vectors and their implications. In the first part of the chapter, we delve into deceptive information attacks, highlighting their mechanisms and potential consequences for ITS. These attacks manipulate data integrity and decision-making processes in ITS, using techniques such as data poisoning, spoofing, and phishing, which exploit system and human vulnerabilities [14]. For example, data poisoning and injection attacks compromise data servers that collect operational inputs, resulting in flawed decisions by machine learning tools. These attacks skew models, leading to unsafe or inefficient system operations. Similarly, jamming and spoofing target physical signals, affecting vehicular control, potentially causing road accidents by transmitting false GPS coordinates or disrupting V2V (vehicle-to-vehicle) and V2I (vehicle-to-infrastructure) communications. Phishing attacks, often part of sophisticated advanced persistent threats (APTs) [15, 16], exploit human vulnerabilities. Such attacks may lead to the installation of malware that traverses both IT and OT networks, compromising critical assets like trains, traffic signals, or control systems, showcasing the intersection between human error and technical vulnerabilities.

2.1.1 Multi-domain Threats in ITS

To understand this, we create multidomains, including intra-vehicle, inter-vehicle, transportation infrastructure, and human domains. Each domain presents unique challenges and is susceptible to specific types of attacks that exploit its vulnerabilities. The intra-vehicle domain focuses on the internal systems of a vehicle, including control units, sensors, and communication modules. Attacks in this domain, such as malware, ransomware, and adversarial machine learning, target critical functionalities such as braking, steering, and navigation. These attacks often exploit software vulnerabilities or user actions, such as connecting to unsecured networks or falling victim to phishing scams, potentially compromising the safety and reliability of the vehicle. The inter-vehicle domain involves communication between vehicles and between vehicles and infrastructure. This domain is particularly vulnerable to data injection, spoofing, and man-in-the-middle attacks, which exploit protocols such as V2V and V2I. These attacks can lead to significant disruptions, including traffic congestion, false routing information, and unsafe driving conditions.

The transportation domain encompasses the broader infrastructure that supports ITS, such as traffic management centers, traffic signals, and dynamic pricing systems. Attacks in this domain, including DoS, data manipulation, and APTs, can disrupt operations on a large scale, creating traffic chaos, financial losses, and risks to public safety by compromising critical systems.

The human domain involves the interaction between humans, such as drivers, operators, and users, and ITS. Attacks in this domain often exploit human vulnerabilities through social engineering, phishing, and cognitive manipulation [17]. For example, misleading drivers with falsified traffic updates or tricking operators into deploying malicious software can propagate malware or lead to unsafe decision-making.

The domains are interdependent, and attackers often exploit vulnerabilities in multiple domains to achieve their goals. For instance, a phishing attack targeting an operator in the human domain could introduce malware into the transportation domain, which may propagate to the inter-vehicle domain and ultimately compromise the intra-vehicle domain. A domain-specific view is essential for understanding and mitigating targeted attacks within a single domain, while a cross-domain view is crucial for identifying cascading effects and interdependencies. Both perspectives are vital to achieving the overall goal of cybersecurity and resilience in ITS.

2.1.2 Security Risk Assessment

In the second part of the chapter, we evaluate and quantify the risks associated with deceptive information attacks in ITS, providing a foundation for designing resilience mechanisms to mitigate their impact. A central approach to achieve this involves the use of game theory [18], complemented by tools from control and learning theories [8]. Together, these methodologies offer a structured framework for both assessing risks and crafting adaptive, robust defenses.

Game theory provides a systematic way to model the strategic interactions between attackers and defenders, allowing a deeper understanding of adversarial behaviors and optimal response strategies. It allows for the analysis of various scenarios, such as resource allocation for defense, the propagation of misinformation, and the cascading effects of attacks across interconnected domains. For example, Stackelberg games [19–21] can model leader-follower dynamics in which attackers initiate malicious actions and defenders respond adaptively to minimize disruptions. Control theory complements this by offering tools to stabilize systems under attack, ensuring operational continuity, and preventing cascading failures. By integrating dynamic models, control mechanisms can anticipate potential system instabilities caused by attacks and implement corrective measures in real time. Techniques such as adaptive control and fault-tolerant control play a critical role in maintaining system resilience.

Learning theories, particularly reinforcement learning [22], further improve resilience by enabling ITS systems to learn from historical and real-time data [23]. These tools can identify evolving attack patterns and adjust defense strategies accordingly. For example, learning algorithms can refine game-theoretic models by incorporating new insights, enabling ITS to adapt dynamically to emerging threats. The integration of machine learning with game theory [24] also supports predictive risk modeling, allowing systems to anticipate adversarial behaviors and proactively deploy mitigation measures. By combining these disciplines, ITS can move beyond static defenses to implement adaptive and cross-layer resilience mechanisms. These mechanisms not only respond to ongoing attacks but also evolve to address future threats, ensuring the robustness and safety of ITS in the face of complex and interdependent cyber risks.

2.1.3 Chapter Organization

The organization of the chapter is as follows. In Section 2.2, we introduce the key domains of ITS and the specific challenges and vulnerabilities they face, including intra-vehicle, inter-vehicle, transportation, and human domains. This section lays the groundwork by describing the interdependencies among these domains and how attackers exploit them to achieve their goals. In Section 2.3, we present game theory as a foundational framework for analyzing and designing resilience strategies. This section discusses how game-theoretic models, combined with control and learning theories, can be used to assess risks, predict adversarial behaviors, and develop adaptive defense mechanisms to improve ITS resilience. Key concepts such as Stackelberg games, dynamic games [25, 26], and signaling games [27, 28] are highlighted as tools to model and counter deceptive information attacks.

In Section 2.4, we use a case study to demonstrate the practical application of these theoretical frameworks. The case study focuses on the risks of misinformed demand attacks on ITS navigational systems, showcasing how game-theoretic models and resilience mechanisms can mitigate cascading failures, maintain system stability, and address both local and system-wide impacts of such attacks. This section also provides insights into the effectiveness of proposed strategies in real-world scenarios. The chapter concludes with Section 2.5, where we discuss the future directions on the deceptive information threats and the resilience mechanisms to protect ITS.

2.2 Deceptive Information Attacks

This chapter focuses on deceptive information attacks within ITS, which are designed to create misinformation [29], manipulate data [30], and compromise system integrity through techniques such as data poisoning and injection. These attacks can leverage malware (for example, APTs), man-in-the-middle tactics, or jamming and spoofing. They can occur across multiple layers of the ITS, which can be broadly categorized into intra-vehicle, inter-vehicle, and transportation system domains, as well as human interactions.

Table 2.1 provides a domain-oriented overview of representative threats, the consequences they pose, and potential resilience mechanisms. This cross-domain tabulation highlights the interdependencies among system layers and the necessity of tailored, yet coordinated, defense strategies to enhance cyber resilience in ITS.

Table 2.1 Threats, impacts, and resilience measures across ITS domains.

Domain	**Threats**	**Impacts**	**Resilience measures**
Intra-vehicle layer	Malware, ransomware, adversarial ML, infotainment exploits	Loss of control (braking, steering), system lockout, unsafe operation	Encrypted comms, IDS, OTA validation, cyber insurance, cloud fail-safes
Inter-vehicle layer	Data injection, MITM, spoofing, Sybil attacks	Route misguidance, protocol exploitation, V2X disruption	Multi-factor V2X auth, blockchain ID, 5G-aware monitoring, zero-trust edge
Infrastructure layer	APTs, DoS, controller hijack, pricing manipulation	Gridlock, financial loss, degraded services	Secure pricing, SCADA hardening, anomaly detection, redundant control
Human layer	Cognitive exploits (bias, overload), phishing, social engineering	Malware spread, misinformed actions, panic rerouting	Trust-aware HMI, operator training, cognitive-aware alerts, trust constraints

2.2.1 Intra-vehicle Domain

Vehicles, as complex control systems, are increasingly vulnerable to a variety of cyber threats, including malware, spoofing, and man-in-the-middle attacks. These threats can compromise the safety and reliability of critical vehicle functions, particularly in autonomous and connected vehicles. For instance, adversarial machine learning attacks can manipulate or poison the training data used by AI perception systems, leading to incorrect object detection or decision-making, which could undermine the functionality of features like lane-keeping, collision avoidance, or traffic sign recognition [31, 32]. In addition, ransomware attacks represent a growing concern, especially as vehicles frequently connect to external networks for software updates or infotainment services. These attacks can encrypt vehicle systems or data, rendering them inoperable, and are often facilitated by user negligence, such as falling victim to phishing attempts or connecting to unsecured networks.

An example of malware targeting vehicles is the "Jeep Cherokee hack" [33] demonstrated by cybersecurity researchers in 2015. The attack exploited vulnerabilities in the vehicle's Uconnect infotainment system, allowing remote access to critical controls such as the engine, brakes, and steering. The researchers were able to wirelessly send malicious commands through the vehicle's cellular connection, showing how an attacker can disable the brakes or take control of steering while the vehicle is in motion. This event highlighted the real-world dangers of malware

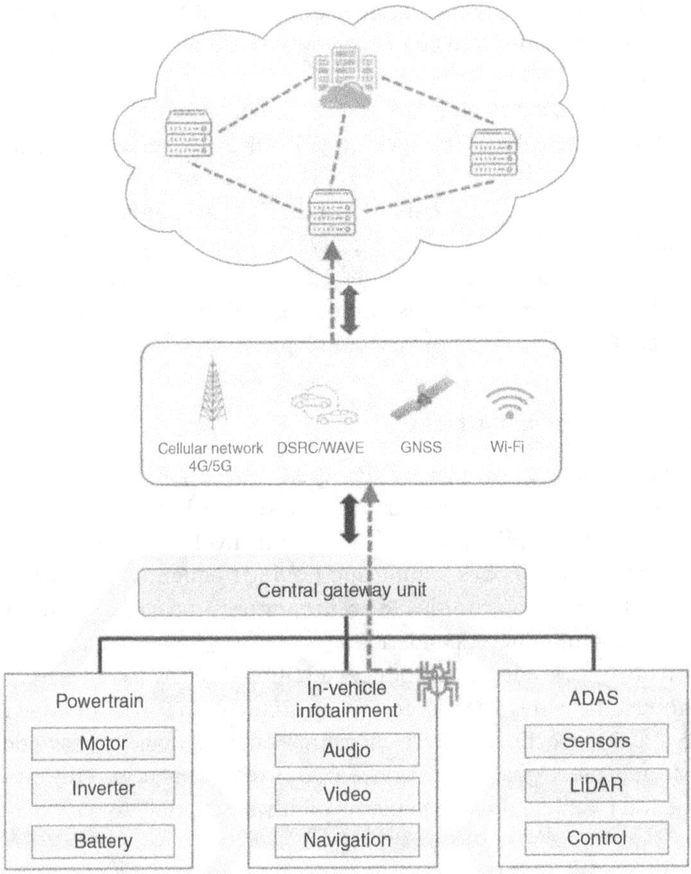

Figure 2.1 Intra-vehicle domain attacks: An attacker can exploit vulnerabilities in the in-vehicle infotainment system, such as audio, video, or navigation modules, to compromise the central gateway unit. Once the gateway is breached, the attack can propagate through vehicle-to-infrastructure (V2I) communications using technologies like cellular networks (4G/5G), DSRC/WAVE, GNSS, or Wi-Fi, potentially impacting cloud servers and disrupting critical services across the connected vehicle ecosystem.

attacks on vehicles and emphasized the urgent need for improved cybersecurity in the automotive industry.

To enhance resilience in the intra-vehicle domain, as illustrated in Figure 2.1, robust mechanisms must be implemented. Cloud-enabled backup control systems [34], such as those explored in [35–37], provide a fail-safe by allowing vehicles to revert to a secure and functional state even in the event of a cyberattack. Furthermore, deploying layered protections for vehicle control systems is critical. This includes encrypting communication channels, implementing strong authentication protocols, and employing intrusion detection systems to identify and mitigate threats in real time.

In addition to technical safeguards, organizational measures such as cyber insurance [38] and accountability frameworks [39, 40] are essential to mitigate the financial and operational impacts of attacks. Cyber insurance can help offset the costs associated with recovery and liability, while clear accountability measures ensure that stakeholders prioritize cybersecurity best practices, from vehicle manufacturers to end-users. Together, these strategies form a comprehensive approach to protecting vehicles from cyber threats, protecting their functionality, and maintaining user trust in modern automotive technologies.

2.2.2 Inter-vehicle Domain Attacks

The inter-vehicle domain, as shown in Figure 2.2, encompasses the communication infrastructure that supports cloud and edge computing, intersection management, and interference mitigation. This domain involves a vast network of highly dynamic nodes, with nodes joining and leaving frequently. Such dynamics increase risks, including opportunities for ransomware propagation and disruptions due to infrastructure interdependencies.

The adoption of 5G technologies introduces additional security concerns. There is a need for robust measures such as zero-trust architectures [41] for edge computing services at intersections. These measures must manage access control, establish trust, and meet quality of service (QoS) requirements. Without such safeguards, the inter-vehicle domain remains highly susceptible to data manipulation and other informational attacks.

To address these vulnerabilities, zero-trust architectures are essential for securing the inter-vehicle domain. This approach operates on the principle of "never trust, always verify," treating every entity within the network as potentially hostile. Key measures include fine-grained access controls, such as multi-factor authentication and continuous monitoring, to ensure that only authorized entities can access network resources. Trust can be further enhanced using blockchain-based identity verification [42] to prevent impersonation and spoofing attacks. Additionally, ensuring QoS is vital to prioritize critical applications, such as emergency vehicle coordination, and mitigate threats like DoS attacks.

Without these safeguards, the inter-vehicle domain remains vulnerable to a range of informational attacks, including data injection, eavesdropping, and manipulation. For example, attackers could inject false data into vehicle-to-infrastructure (V2I) communication [43], causing traffic congestion or unsafe driving conditions. Similarly, man-in-the-middle (MITM) attacks [44] could intercept and alter messages between vehicles, leading to accidents or service disruptions.

An example is Simon Weckert, who tricked Google Maps into creating a fake traffic jam in Berlin [45]. The attack involved Weckert pulling a wagon loaded with 99 smartphones, all running Google Maps, through a street in Berlin. The system interpreted the cluster of devices as heavy vehicular traffic, resulting in Google Maps rerouting drivers to avoid the area. While this was a benign demonstration, it highlighted the vulnerabilities in ITS to data manipulation attacks. Furthermore, in Ref. [46], researchers demonstrated a Sybil attack on Google Maps, which created a significant impact on traffic management and user experience within ITS. By generating numerous fake identities, the attacker manipulated Google Maps to display fabricated congestion, leading to misinformed traffic routing.

2.2.3 Transportation System Domain

The transportation system domain is a pivotal layer of ITS, including traffic management systems and centers that house critical infrastructure such as traffic control mechanisms, dynamic pricing systems, and other essential operational

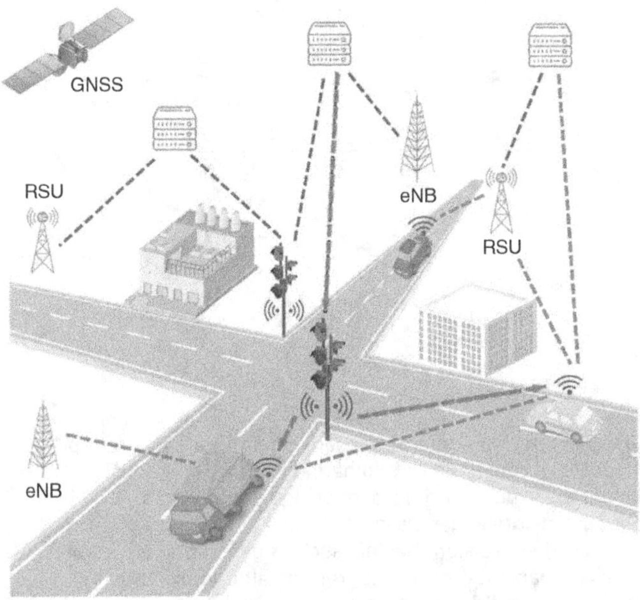

Figure 2.2 Attacks in the inter-vehicle domain: smart transportation systems rely on the integration of GNSS, roadside units (RSUs), and enhanced Node BS (eNBs) to facilitate seamless vehicle-to-infrastructure communication and optimize traffic flow at urban intersections. However, these systems are vulnerable to deceptive information attacks. For instance, an attacker can compromise an edge server, poisoning the traffic data it collects. This misinformation can then be propagated to vehicles, leading to incorrect routing decisions and the deliberate creation of traffic congestion.

components. Unlike the inter-vehicle domain, which emphasizes communication between vehicles and between vehicles and road infrastructure, the transportation system domain focuses on the overarching operation and control of the transportation network from a supervisory perspective. Figure 2.3 provides a detailed overview of the layered architecture that connects IT and OT systems in a Transportation Management Center (TMC). The framework is designed to integrate high-level enterprise management with field-level operational control, ensuring secure and efficient management of modern transportation systems.

At the highest level, the IT system encompasses enterprise and supervisory functions. Level 4 (enterprise network) includes critical systems such as web servers, email servers, and enterprise computers, which support administrative tasks, decision-making, and overall management of the transportation infrastructure. Below this, Level 3 Demilitarized Zone (DMZ) serves as a security layer, isolating sensitive enterprise systems from operational networks. It houses DMZ servers and authorized computers to mediate secure interactions between IT and

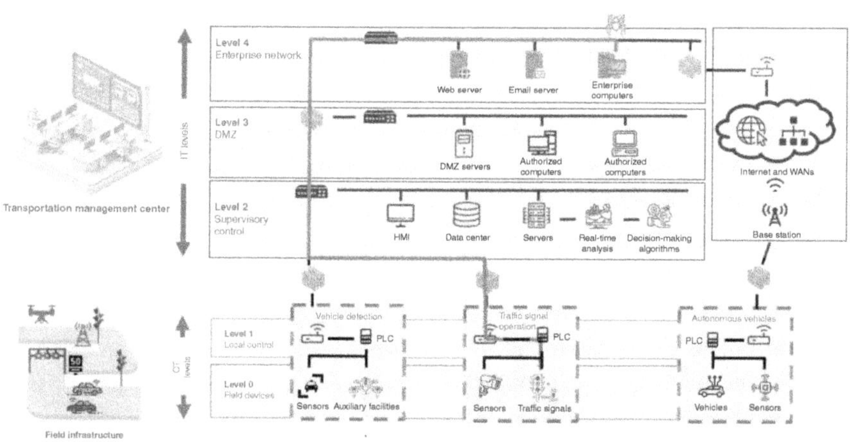

Figure 2.3 Attacks in the transportation domain: malware can infiltrate the enterprise network of a transportation control center, often originating from a compromised workstation through phishing, malicious downloads, or other attack vectors. Once inside, the malware can corrupt or poison critical databases that store and process real-time traffic data. This can lead to falsified decision-making, such as generating inaccurate traffic flow recommendations or manipulating vehicle routing algorithms, thereby causing congestion or unsafe road conditions. Additionally, the attack can escalate to the OT level, where the malware targets interconnected physical assets such as traffic light signaling systems, toll collection points, or electronic message boards. By compromising these systems, attackers can manipulate traffic lights to cause accidents, disrupt toll collection to create revenue loss, or display misleading information to drivers, amplifying the overall impact on road safety and traffic management. The cascading effects of such attacks can result in significant economic and social disruption.

OT domains. Moving further down, Level 2 (supervisory control) facilitates operational oversight through tools such as human–machine interfaces (HMIs), data centers, real-time analysis modules, and decision-making algorithms, enabling effective control of transportation operations.

The OT system focuses on field-level control and interaction with the physical infrastructure. Level 1 (local control) comprises Programmable Logic Controllers (PLCs) and similar devices that handle localized operations, such as vehicle detection, traffic signal management, and autonomous vehicle coordination. These controllers translate supervisory commands into actionable outputs at the field level. At the base, Level 0 (field devices) includes sensors and auxiliary facilities that interact directly with the physical environment, monitoring conditions such as traffic flow, vehicle positions, and signal status to feed real-time data back into the system.

There are two-way communications between the IT and OT systems for the hierarchical flow of information and control. Secure gateways ensure that high-level decisions made within the TMC translate into actionable directives for field-level systems. A red path within the diagram underscores potential vulnerabilities, drawing attention to cybersecurity risks that could compromise system functionality and safety.

Attacks can occur at multiple levels within a transportation management system, posing significant risks to both the IT and the OT components. At Level 0, field devices, such as sensors and controllers, are particularly vulnerable to compromise. Attackers can manipulate these devices to disrupt their functionality, leading to inaccuracies in vehicle detection or traffic signal operation. These disruptions can cascade, undermining the broader transportation network.

In addition to direct field-level attacks, cyber threats from the IT domain pose even greater risks. Cyberattacks, including malware, ransomware, and APTs, can infiltrate the enterprise network of a transportation control center, as illustrated in Figure 2.3. Often, these attacks originate from compromised workstations through phishing campaigns, malicious downloads, or other sophisticated attack vectors. Once inside the system, the malware can corrupt or poison critical databases that store and process real-time traffic data. This can result in falsified decision-making, such as inaccurate traffic flow recommendations or manipulated vehicle routing algorithms, which can cause severe congestion, unsafe road conditions, or even system-wide failures.

The threat does not stop at the enterprise network; it can escalate to the OT level, where malware targets interconnected physical assets. These include traffic light signaling systems, toll collection points, and electronic message boards. By exploiting these systems, attackers can disrupt real-time operations, manipulate the physical infrastructure, and exacerbate the impact of initial compromise.

The consequences of such attacks can extend far beyond localized disruptions, with the potential to cripple entire cities. For example, a compromised traffic control system can cause widespread gridlock by altering the time of the traffic lights or creating unsafe intersections [47]. Similarly, malware targeting train signaling systems can cause delays, operational shutdowns, or even collisions [48]. Furthermore, breaches in payment and pricing systems can result in stolen financial data or interrupted revenue streams for metropolitan transit authorities, compounding the economic and operational impacts [49].

These vulnerabilities indicate the critical importance of securing operational technologies within ITS. Ensuring the resilience and security of OT systems is essential to maintain the reliability and safety of modern transportation networks, protecting public safety, and supporting uninterrupted mobility and commerce. OT within ITS plays a foundational role in ensuring the seamless operation of critical transportation infrastructure. Unlike traditional IT, which focuses primarily on data processing and storage, OT systems are designed to control and monitor physical processes, such as traffic signal operations, train signaling, and road sensor functionality. Given their critical role in transportation safety and efficiency, OT systems must be not only secure but also resilient, i.e., capable of maintaining functionality and recovering quickly in the face of threats or failures [50–52].

OT resilience goes beyond conventional cybersecurity measures, as it must account for the operational continuity and physical safety of systems [51, 53, 54]. For example, while IT systems prioritize protecting data confidentiality, OT systems focus on ensuring the availability and reliability of operational processes. Any disruption of OT, be it due to a cyberattack or a physical fault, can have immediate and far-reaching impacts, such as traffic congestion, delayed emergency responses, and increased safety risks. Therefore, resilience in OT systems means equipping them with mechanisms to prevent, detect, and respond to attacks while maintaining critical operations [55]. The following gives two examples of resilience to deceptive information attacks.

1. Resilience of traffic conditions: OT systems must ensure that traffic flows remain stable and efficient even when under attack. Consider a scenario where a misinformation attack provides falsified traffic data to navigation systems [56], misleading drivers to congest specific routes unnecessarily. Resilience mechanisms such as dynamic traffic management algorithms, rooted in principles like Wardrop equilibrium, can mitigate these impacts by redistributing traffic loads in real time, ensuring optimal usage of available road capacity [57]. Similarly, in the case of data manipulation attacks targeting sensors, systems can leverage redundant data sources or anomaly detection algorithms to validate and correct manipulated inputs.

2. Resilience of traffic control systems: Traffic control systems, including pricing mechanisms and signaling systems, are particularly vulnerable to data injection attacks [58]. For instance, attackers could inject false pricing data into toll-collection systems [59], either disrupting revenue collection or causing confusion among drivers. Resilient systems can counteract such attacks by using advanced techniques to verify the integrity of data and applying real-time monitoring to detect anomalies [60, 61]. Similarly, signaling systems, such as those used for train operations, must maintain strict operational integrity. A resilient system would isolate compromised signals, revert to predefined safety configurations, and notify operators to prevent collisions or service interruptions, maintaining safety and efficiency under duress.

2.2.4 Human Aspects

Humans play a pivotal role in the ITS ecosystem, not only as users but also as decision-makers, and their responses to information – accurate or otherwise – significantly influence traffic conditions. Social networks and other communication platforms can amplify the impact of misinformation [62, 63], giving rise to information-induced DoS attacks. For example, falsified traffic recommendations or panic-inducing misinformation can lead to erratic driver behaviors, unnecessary reroutes, or even traffic jams, further exacerbating the vulnerabilities of the ITS infrastructure.

Both users and operators are susceptible to deceptive informational attacks. Users can be misled into downloading malicious software, which may compromise intra-vehicle systems. Through inter-vehicle communications, this malware can propagate across the entire transportation network, creating a systemic risk. Similarly, TMCs operators are vulnerable to social engineering attacks that trick them into deploying malware. Once inside, such malware could disrupt key operations, alter traffic signals, or corrupt routing algorithms, leading to widespread congestion and unsafe road conditions.

These attacks often exploit cognitive vulnerabilities inherent in human decision-making [64]. One such vulnerability is base rate neglect, where individuals do not consider the base rate or statistical probability of an event when making decisions. For example, in transportation networks, a driver might overreact to misinformation about an accident ahead, ignoring the statistical improbability of a major incident that affects multiple routes simultaneously. This could result in unnecessary detours or panic-induced congestion, which could compound traffic problems rather than alleviate them.

Another common cognitive vulnerability is confirmation bias [65], where individuals selectively seek or prioritize information that aligns with their preexisting beliefs, ignoring contradictory evidence. For instance, a user predisposed to distrust automated navigation systems might disregard accurate routing suggestions during an emergency, relying instead on unverified social media updates. This can lead to suboptimal route choices, further straining the transportation network.

By exploiting these cognitive biases, attackers can manipulate both users and operators, leading to cascading effects that disrupt ITS and create widespread chaos. A recent example of such exploitation occurred during a cyber-induced traffic manipulation attack, where attackers disseminated falsified traffic alerts through social media platforms and GPS navigation apps [66]. Users, influenced by confirmation bias, trusted these updates because they aligned with their assumptions about typical traffic congestion during peak hours. As a result, many drivers followed incorrect detour routes, leading to significant congestion in previously uncongested areas, amplifying delays, and frustrating commuters.

Another instance involved base rate neglect during a coordinated misinformation campaign targeting TMCs [67]. Attackers tricked operators into believing that a high-probability cyber event, such as a widespread signal outage, was underway. They achieved this by using phishing emails that mimicked alerts from legitimate monitoring systems. The operators, failing to consider the statistical likelihood of such an outage, deployed emergency protocols that unnecessarily rerouted traffic and temporarily disabled interconnected systems. This not only disrupted traffic flows but also created vulnerabilities for additional attacks.

Such examples highlight how cognitive biases are not merely abstract vulnerabilities but can be directly weaponized by attackers to cause real-world consequences. These manipulations can cripple the ITS infrastructure by overloading resources, erode trust in automated systems, and create feedback loops of inefficiency. Mitigating these risks requires integrating cognitive and behavioral insights into the design of ITS and cybersecurity protocols, ensuring that the systems are resilient to both technical attacks and human-induced errors.

Several works have focused on modeling cognitive biases and mitigating their adversarial exploitation, particularly in the context of human-centric systems such as ITS and at a broader level Human-Cyber-Physical Systems (HCPS). These efforts often integrate insights from cognitive science, psychology, and system science to create defenses against attacks that exploit human vulnerabilities. For instance, reactive and proactive attention attacks have been extensively studied, with models developed to counteract the impact of Informational Denial-of-Service (IDoS) attacks, where feint alerts induce cognitive overload [68, 69]. Techniques such as Q-learning through consolidated data and visual aid designs have been proposed to enhance attention and improve operator decision-making. Such mechanisms aim to filter critical signals from noise, reducing the likelihood of manipulation through cognitive overload.

Other approaches leverage game-theoretic and decision-theoretic models to predict and counteract adversarial strategies that exploit biases such as base rate neglect [67] and confirmation bias [65]. For example, incorporating the principles of cumulative prospect theory [70], defenses can be tailored to address how individuals over- or under-weigh probabilities during decision-making, which attackers often exploit. Furthermore, human-centered AI technologies have been developed to mitigate memory vulnerabilities and cognitive manipulation. Examples include HMIs that adapt to user cognitive states, providing explainable recommendations, and real-time feedback based on biosensor inputs such as heart rate or motion signals. These systems aim to minimize errors caused by biases, such as anchoring or framing, by offering contextual explanations and alerts during critical decision-making.

2.3 Cross-layer Resilience

Resilience in ITS cannot be effectively ensured by focusing on individual components or isolated layers. The interconnected nature of ITS, spanning vehicles, transportation infrastructure, and human interactions, demands a **holistic systems approach** that recognizes and addresses the interaction between these layers. Each layer depends on the others to function optimally, and vulnerabilities in one layer can spread throughout the system, leading to cascading failures that impact the entire transportation ecosystem.

For example, consider a scenario where malware infiltrates a single vehicle through a compromised on-board system, such as an infotainment or telematics application. Although the initial infection might appear localized, the interconnected nature of ITS means that this malware can exploit V2V and V2I communication channels to spread. This could disrupt real-time traffic management systems, disable critical infrastructure such as traffic signals, or compromise autonomous vehicle coordination. The ripple effects may include system-wide traffic congestion, delayed emergency response times, increased safety risks, and significant economic consequences for individuals and businesses that rely on transportation services.

The interplay between ITS layers amplifies risks, as failures in one area can trigger disruptions in others. For example, human behavior, such as negligence or lack of cybersecurity awareness, is often the initial trigger for attacks. A driver may accidentally download a malicious app or click on a phishing link, introducing malware into a vehicle system. This seemingly isolated event could escalate if the malware exploits vulnerabilities in the V2I ecosystem, infecting traffic control systems, and causing widespread disruptions. Similarly, compromised infrastructure components, such as road sensors or edge computing nodes, could transmit false data to vehicles, causing unsafe driving conditions or inefficient traffic flows.

These interdependencies underscore the importance of addressing resilience at a system-wide level. Ensuring that each layer is secure and resilient on its own is insufficient; the connections and interactions between layers must also be safeguarded.

2.3.1 Holistic Framework for Resilience

To effectively protect ITS from cyber threats and operational disruptions, a comprehensive resilience framework must address vulnerabilities at all layers of the system. This framework ensures seamless coordination between components and layers, enhancing the system's ability to prevent, detect, and recover from potential failures or attacks.

2.3.1.1 Layer-specific Defenses

Resilience begins with tailored security measures for each layer of ITS, addressing the unique challenges and requirements of vehicles, infrastructure, and human interactions. Modern vehicles, increasingly dependent on sophisticated software and communication systems, are prime targets for cyberattacks. Robust defenses include IDS to monitor vehicle networks for unauthorized access, encrypted communication protocols to secure data exchanges, and regular software updates to address vulnerabilities. Fail-safe mechanisms are also critical, enabling vehicles to revert to safe operating modes in the event of a system compromise.

Infrastructure components such as traffic management systems, edge computing nodes, and communication networks form the backbone of ITS. Securing these elements involves network segmentation to isolate critical infrastructure from nonessential systems, multifactor authentication, and role-based access control, and anomaly detection tools to identify and respond to potential threats.

Human interaction is another crucial layer, as human error remains a significant vulnerability in ITS. Cybersecurity education and awareness campaigns are essential to train users and operators on best practices, such as recognizing phishing attempts and securing connected devices. Additionally, user-centric design [71] can minimize errors caused by complex interfaces or cognitive overload.

2.3.1.2 Cross-layer Coordination

ITS resilience is based on the ability of different layers to work smoothly. Effective coordination ensures that a threat detected in one layer is communicated across the system for a unified response. For example, if a vehicle detects abnormal behavior, such as malware activity, it should notify nearby vehicles and infrastructure systems. This allows the broader system to isolate the threat, reroute traffic, or take other protective actions. Shared intelligence platforms where vehicles, infrastructure, and operators exchange real-time threat data can further enhance coordinated responses. Ensuring interoperability between devices and systems, regardless of the vendor or protocol, is also critical to maintaining resilience.

2.3.1.3 Proactive Threat Mitigation and Cascading Failure Containment

Anticipating and addressing vulnerabilities before they are exploited is a cornerstone of resilience. Predictive analytics can leverage historical data and real-time monitoring to identify patterns indicative of emerging threats, such as unusual congestion caused by misinformation attacks. Machine learning algorithms can detect subtle anomalies, such as a slow-moving APT, allowing timely interventions. Regular risk assessments [72] ensure that the ITS adapts to changing technologies and threat landscapes, proactively identifying and addressing weak points.

One of the greatest risks in ITS is the potential for a failure of a component to propagate across the system. Containment strategies are vital to isolate and manage these failures effectively. Redundancy in critical infrastructure, such as duplicate traffic control servers or alternative communication paths, ensures operational continuity during failures. Fail-safe systems are designed to automatically revert to a secure and functional state when compromised. For example, a compromised traffic sensor can be isolated, while redundant inputs maintain accurate traffic flow predictions. Similarly, compromised autonomous vehicles can switch to manual operation or pre-defined safe driving modes. Layer isolation ensures that issues within one layer, such as a compromised vehicle network, do not cascade into others like traffic management systems.

Consider a scenario in which malware infects a vehicle's system through a malicious app. The vehicle's IDS detect the anomaly and isolate the infected components. During the same time, it sends alerts to nearby vehicles and infrastructure systems, prompting a coordinated response. Traffic management systems reroute unaffected vehicles to reduce congestion caused by the compromised vehicle. Anomaly detection tools monitor the network for additional signs of malware propagation, while predictive algorithms assess the likelihood of similar attacks elsewhere. These coordinated efforts contain the impact, prevent escalation, and ensure the continued functionality of the system.

2.3.2 Theoretical Foundations and Design Frameworks

Game theory [24, 73] offers a robust mathematical framework for understanding and designing interactions among agents in ITS, particularly under conditions of uncertainty, adversarial actions, and competing interests. This framework is essential for creating distributed resilience mechanisms that enable ITS components, such as vehicles, infrastructure systems, and users, to make optimal decisions that balance individual goals with the overall goals of the system.

Game theory captures the strategic dynamics between different entities in ITS, such as defenders (system operators) and attackers (cyber adversaries), as well as between cooperative and noncooperative agents within the system. These interactions often involve adversarial scenarios where attackers aim to exploit vulnerabilities, and defenders must anticipate and mitigate potential disruptions. By modeling these interactions, game theory provides insights into optimal strategies for both attack and defense, helping system designers create more resilient frameworks [74, 75].

For example, autonomous vehicles might collaborate to share information about road conditions to improve safety and efficiency. Cooperative game theory helps determine how resources, such as bandwidth or computational power, are allocated among vehicles to maximize collective resilience. In scenarios where agents have competing objectives, such as prioritizing emergency vehicle routing versus minimizing congestion for general traffic, noncooperative game theory helps balance these conflicting interests. Given the inherent uncertainty in ITS environments, stochastic games can model dynamic scenarios in which agents adjust their strategies based on evolving conditions, such as unpredictable traffic patterns or emerging cyber threats.

2.3.2.1 Dynamic Games for Cyber Resilience

The complexity of ITS requires dynamic game models that adapt to changes in real time. Dynamic games, as discussed in [8], involve sequential interactions in which the actions of one stage influence the strategies and results of subsequent stages. For instance, in **proactive resilience**, defenders might reconfigure traffic management systems to reduce vulnerabilities before an attack occurs. During a **responsive phase**, the system could employ adaptive mechanisms such as rerouting traffic to mitigate the impact of a detected attack. **Retrospectively**, game theory supports analyzing attacker strategies to refine defensive measures and prevent future incidents.

Dynamic games are particularly valuable for modeling cyber resilience, as they account for the evolving tactics of attackers and the adaptive responses of defenders. These models provide a structured way to plan for multistage interactions to ensure that ITS remain resilient under dynamic and adversarial conditions [76–78].

2.3.2.2 Leveraging Asymmetric Information and Learning

In many ITS scenarios, agents operate under asymmetric information, where one party (e.g., attackers) has more knowledge about vulnerabilities or state of the system than others (e.g., defenders). Game-theoretic frameworks such as Bayesian games and signaling games are particularly effective in addressing these challenges. For instance, in a **signaling game** [79], attackers may send deceptive signals to mislead ITS components, such as providing false traffic data to divert vehicles or disrupt traffic flow. Game theory helps design mechanisms that allow defenders to distinguish genuine information from false signals, enhancing the resilience of the system. Similarly, asymmetric information games are instrumental in designing **zero-trust architectures** [80, 81], where the system continuously verifies user behaviors to dynamically assess trustworthiness.

2.3.2.3 Integration with Learning Frameworks

Game theory becomes even more powerful when combined with learning mechanisms. As attackers evolve their tactics, ITS can employ reinforcement learning to adapt their strategies in real time, continuously refining game-theoretic models with updated data [82]. This integration offers several advantages. One is **predictive modeling**, where ITS can anticipate adversarial behaviors based on historical patterns and dynamic interactions, enabling proactive defense measures. The other is **continuous adaptation**. Systems can dynamically adjust defenses to counter emerging threats, such as new types of malware targeting connected vehicles. By combining game-theoretic models with machine learning [83], ITS resilience frameworks can operate with greater flexibility and precision, addressing known and unknown threats effectively.

Game-theoretic models play a crucial role in addressing the complex challenges within ITS. These models are particularly valuable in cyber-physical security, traffic management, and resource allocation, enabling strategic decision-making that improves resilience and efficiency across the system.

In **cyber-physical security**, game-theoretic models are used to analyze and mitigate coordinated attacks on the ITS infrastructure. These attacks often exploit vulnerabilities in both cyber and physical layers, such as malware targeting traffic management servers or tampering with field devices like traffic lights. Game theory provides a framework for anticipating attacker strategies and designing optimal defensive measures. For instance, it can guide the deployment of decoy systems to mislead attackers or recommend the isolation of compromised nodes to prevent the spread of malware [84]. Furthermore, game-theoretic models help mitigate cascading failures by predicting how disruptions in one part of the system could impact interconnected components [76], thus forming strategies to contain the damage and maintain overall functionality.

In **traffic management** [2, 3], game-theoretic frameworks address conflicting objectives, such as minimizing traffic delays while prioritizing the passage of emergency vehicles. Cooperative game theory facilitates collaboration between traffic lights and autonomous vehicles to optimize signal timings, reducing congestion, and improving overall flow. In contrast, noncooperative game theory is useful when different agents, like emergency responders and civilian drivers, have competing priorities. These models help determine equitable strategies that balance the system's needs without compromising safety or efficiency. By modeling these interactions, game theory ensures that traffic management systems can operate effectively even under complex dynamic conditions.

Effective **resource allocation** is another area where game theory excels [85]. ITS rely on limited resources, such as communication bandwidth, computational power, and energy, to operate optimally [86]. Game-theoretic models enable agents to make strategic decisions about resource use, ensuring critical operations are prioritized. For example, autonomous vehicles and traffic management nodes can negotiate bandwidth allocation based on urgency, ensuring that collision avoidance data is transmitted with minimal latency. Similarly, computational resources at edge nodes can be allocated to high-priority tasks, such as processing real-time traffic data, while less critical operations are deferred. These strategies optimize resource utilization and maintain system reliability.

2.3.3 Benefits of Game-theoretic and Learning-based Design Principles for Cyber Resilience

The integration of game-theoretic models and learning-based approaches into ITS resilience frameworks provides several key benefits, particularly when these frameworks adhere to foundational design principles such as scalability, interoperability, real-time responsiveness and adaptability.

Scalability is essential to ensure that resilience mechanisms can handle the increasing complexity and scale of ITS. Game-theoretic models are inherently suited for distributed solutions, where individual components make localized decisions that collectively scale across the network. For example, a decentralized traffic management system based on cooperative games can expand efficiently from managing a single intersection to coordinating traffic throughout an entire metropolitan area. This scalability allows ITS to grow without compromising resilience.

Interoperability is critical in ITS, which encompasses diverse devices, protocols, and data sources. Resilience frameworks must seamlessly integrate these heterogeneous components [19, 87–89]. Game-theoretic strategies provide a flexible framework for collaboration between agents with varying capabilities, such as autonomous vehicles of different manufacturers. These strategies enable interoperability by establishing common rules and protocols for interaction, ensuring that the overall system functions cohesively despite technical diversity.

The real-time responsiveness of resilience mechanisms is vital to addressing dynamic threats and disruptions in ITS. Learning-based frameworks, such as reinforcement learning [90–92], complement game-theoretic models by enabling agents to adapt strategies as conditions evolve. For example, reinforcement learning can update game-theoretic models in response to sudden congestion caused by an accident or a cyberattack, ensuring that defenses remain effective. This combination of real-time adaptability and strategic foresight enhances the system's ability to manage unexpected challenges.

Finally, robustness and adaptability are the core principles of cyber resilience. Robustness ensures that the ITS can withstand known threats, while adaptability allows it to respond effectively to novel challenges [55]. A dual-layer approach that combines rule-based strategies with adaptive learning is particularly effective. Predefined game-theoretic models handle predictable scenarios, such as routine resource allocation, while machine learning algorithms refine these models to counter emerging threats. For example, if attackers develop new malware targeting V2V communication, reinforcement learning can update defense strategies to mitigate the risk [80, 92, 93].

2.4 Case Study

2.4.1 Misinformation Attacks on Recommendation Systems

One practical case study for applying resilience frameworks in ITS utilizing game-theoretic methods is the Proactive Risk Assessment and Mitigation of Misinformed Demand Attacks (PRADA) framework. PRADA, [94], addresses vulnerabilities such as those shown in Figures 2.1–2.3 for navigational recommendation systems (NRS) [95], which are critical components of ITS. These systems, such as Google Maps or Waze, guide users by providing optimal route recommendations and updating based on real-time traffic conditions. However, they are susceptible to deceptive information-based attacks that compromise both overall system efficiency in terms of travel time and user trust.

The study focuses on misinformed demand attacks, where attackers manipulate the origin-destination (OD) requests submitted to an NRS. By fabricating nonexistent demands through techniques like GPS spoofing within the intra-vehicle domain, Sybil attacks, botnets on the inter-vehicle domain, or insider threats compromising the transportation domain, attackers can alter the system's navigational recommendations. This manipulation can misdirect genuine users, causing congestion on targeted roads or benefiting specific entities, such as businesses along those routes.

For example, attackers might fabricate congestion reports or falsely inflate the demand for certain OD pairs to influence the NRS algorithm, as shown in Figure 2.4. This not only misguides users but also destabilizes traffic conditions across the network, leading to inefficiencies and potential safety concerns.

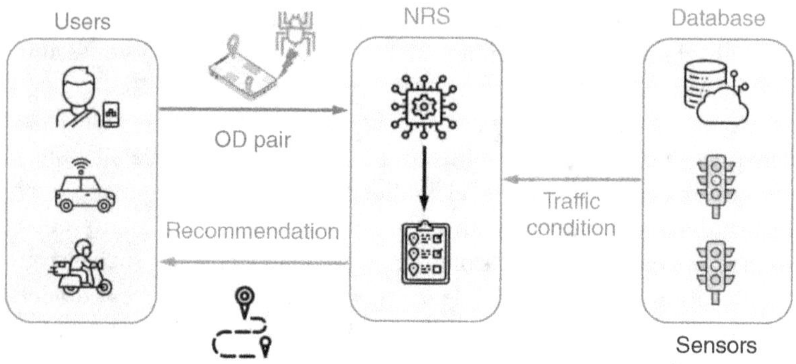

Figure 2.4 The process for navigational recommendations and where the demand attacks exist.

2.4.1.1 Game-theoretic Framework

PRADA employs a game-theoretic approach to assess and mitigate the risks associated with misinformed demand attacks on navigational recommendations and supports the cyber-informed design of resilient systems. It conceptualizes the interaction between attackers and the NRS as a Stackelberg game, a leader-follower model. In this framework, the attacker assumes the role of the leader, strategically fabricating OD demands to manipulate the system. The NRS acts as the follower, adjusting its route recommendations based on these manipulated data. This interaction forms the foundation for understanding and countering such attacks.

More specifically, the PRADA framework integrates three analytical layers to proactively and comprehensively measure the risks of possible attacks, as illustrated in Figure 2.5. The first layer is User Equilibrium (UE) Modeling in the routing game, which captures the interaction between users and the NRS. This layer ensures that the system's recommendations are incentive compatible, which means that users have no advantage in deviating from suggested paths. This compatibility fosters user adherence and minimizes unintended behavioral deviations.

The second layer involves Stackelberg game analysis, which focuses on modeling the interplay between attackers (threat models) and the NRS. This analysis examines how fabricated demands (or other deceptive informational attacks) influence navigational recommendation decisions, providing information on the attacker's strategies and the NRS's ability to counteract them. By simulating these interactions, the model identifies vulnerabilities and optimal defensive strategies.

The final layer, meta-game assessment, evaluates the broader impacts of various attack scenarios. This layer goes beyond local impacts, considering system-wide effects on traffic flow and overall resilience. By analyzing cascading effects and

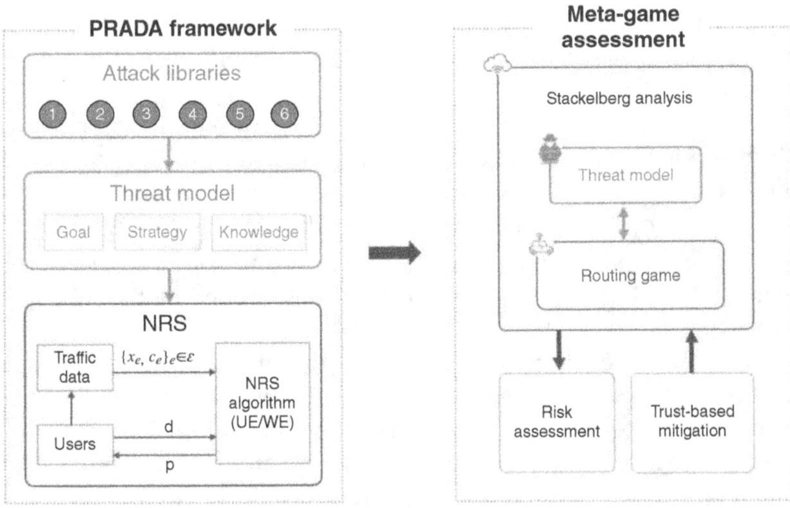

Figure 2.5 The PRADA framework is analyzed through three layers of games between users, the NRS, the threat model of the attacker, and the PRADA risk evaluator.

emergent traffic patterns, potential risks, mitigation methods, and opportunities are highlighted to improve system stability.

2.4.1.1.1 UE Modeling

Consider the urban transportation network represented by $\mathcal{G} = \{\mathcal{V}, \mathcal{E}\}$, where the set of nodes $\mathcal{V}$ corresponds to intersections and the set of edges $\mathcal{E}$ indicates the roads. Traveling along a road $e \in \mathcal{E}$ incurs a road-specific cost $c_e : \mathbb{R}_{\geq 0} \mapsto \mathbb{R}_+$ associated with the flow $x_e \in \mathbb{R}_{\geq 0}$ on road e. One usual choice for the cost $c_e(\cdot)$ is the standard Bureau of Public Roads (BPR) function

$$c_e(x_e) = t_e\left(1 + \alpha\left(\frac{x_e}{k_e}\right)^{\beta}\right)$$

for travel time costs. Here, $t_e \in \mathbb{R}_+$ represents the free-flow travel time on road e, $k_e \in \mathbb{R}_+$ signifies the capacity of road e, and $\alpha, \beta \in \mathbb{R}_{\geq 0}$ are some parameters.

The user set of NRS is denoted as $\mathcal{U}$. Each user, $u \in \mathcal{U}$, is associated with a specific origin $O_u \in \mathcal{V}$ and destination $D_u \in \mathcal{V}$ pair. We refer to the pair as an OD pair, expressed by $\theta_u = (O_u, D_u)$, and the set of OD pairs for the NRS users is $\Theta_{\mathcal{U}} \subseteq \Theta$, with $\Theta = |\mathcal{V}| \times |\mathcal{V}|$ representing all the possible OD pairs within the network. Then, user u with OD pair θ_u has the feasible path choice set $\mathcal{S}_u = \{s_{u,1}, \dots, s_{u,k_u}\}$, which is identical to the feasible path choice set $\mathcal{S}_\theta = \{s_{\theta,1}, \dots, s_{\theta,k_\theta}\}$ for OD pair θ, where $\theta = \theta_u$. Each choice $s_{u,i} \in \mathcal{S}_u$ or $s_{\theta,i} \in \mathcal{S}_\theta$ provides the user u a path from the origin to the desired destination.

To this end, the elements of the urban transportation network considered by the NRS can be encapsulated using the notation $\mathcal{R} = \langle \mathcal{G}, (c_e(\cdot))_{e\in\mathcal{E}}, \mathcal{U}, (\mathcal{S}_u)_{u\in\mathcal{U}} \rangle$, and we call $\mathcal{R}$ the "NRS component."

Consider the scenario where the NRS recommends a mixed strategy over feasible path choices to the users. Define $\mathcal{P}_u := \Delta\mathcal{S}_u$ as the simplex of $\mathcal{S}_u$. A mixed strategy for user u is $\mathbf{p}_u \in \mathcal{P}_u$ so that $\mathbf{p}_u = \{p_{u,i}\}_{s_{u,i}\in\mathcal{S}_u}$ is a probability distribution over $\mathcal{S}_u$. Each element $p_{u,i} \in [0, 1]$ denotes the probability that the NRS recommends path $s_{u,i} \in \mathcal{S}_u$ to user u, and it must satisfy the constraints $\sum_{i=1}^{k_u} p_{u,i} = 1,\ \forall u \in \mathcal{U}$. Then, letting $\mathcal{P} := \Pi_{u\in\mathcal{U}}\mathcal{P}_u$, the recommendation suggested by the NRS to all users is $\mathbf{p} = \{\mathbf{p}_u\}_{u\in\mathcal{U}} \in \mathcal{P}$.

In transportation, from a microscopic perspective, the probability $p_{u,i}$ can be viewed as the expected volume generated by the user u along the path $s_{u,i}$. This, in turn, contributes to the expected road flow (load) $x_e^r : \mathcal{P} \mapsto \mathbb{R}_{\geq 0}$ on the road $e \in \mathcal{E}$ as $x_e^r(\mathbf{p}) = \sum_{u\in\mathcal{U}} \sum_{s_{u,i}\in\mathcal{S}_u} p_{u,i} a_{es_{u,i}}$, where $a_{es_{u,i}}$ is an element of the road path incidence matrix $A_{|\mathcal{E}|\times|\Pi_{u\in\mathcal{U}}\mathcal{S}_u|} = [a_{es_{u,i}}]$, and is defined as follows.

$$a_{es_{u,i}} = \begin{cases} 1 & \text{if } e \in s_{u,i}, \\ 0 & \text{otherwise.} \end{cases}$$

Hence, a generalized travel cost $C_{u,i} : \mathcal{P} \mapsto \mathbb{R}_+$ for the path $s_{u,i}$ can be formulated by summing the costs of all roads along the path: $C_{u,i}(\mathbf{p}) = \sum_{e\in s_{u,i}} c_e(x_e^r(\mathbf{p}))$. In this context, the expected cost evaluated by user u is $F_u^r : \mathcal{P} \mapsto \mathbb{R}_{\geq 0}$, where

$$F_u^r(\mathbf{p}_u, \mathbf{p}_{-u}) = \sum_{i=1}^{k_u} p_{u,i} C_{u,i}(\mathbf{p}_u, \mathbf{p}_{-u}). \tag{2.1}$$

Note that a recommendation $\mathbf{p} \in \mathcal{P}$ can be interpreted as the strategy profile in a routing game between NRS users. Hence, the routing game addressed by the NRS can be defined as $\Gamma^r = \langle \mathcal{R}, \mathcal{F}^r \rangle$, where $\mathcal{F}^r = (F_u^r)_{u\in\mathcal{U}}$ represents the costs evaluated by the users. However, human users may choose not to follow the NRS recommendation if they find a better alternative. Therefore, the NRS must ensure that given the recommendations $\mathbf{p}_{-u}$ to users other than u, user u has no incentive to unilaterally deviate from the recommended $\mathbf{p}_u$. This coincides with the concept of UE, which is defined as follows:

Definition 2.1 ***(User Equilibrium Recommendation)***: Considering a routing game addressed by the NRS defined as $\Gamma^r = \langle \mathcal{R}, \mathcal{F}^r \rangle$, a mixed strategy profile $\mathbf{p} \in \mathcal{P}$ for all users is called a user equilibrium recommendation if it satisfies:

$$F_u^r(\mathbf{p}_u, \mathbf{p}_{-u}) - F_u^r(\mathbf{p}'_u, \mathbf{p}_{-u}) \leq 0, \forall\ \mathbf{p}'_u \in \mathcal{P}_u, \forall u \in \mathcal{U}. \tag{2.2}$$

UE recommendation can be found by gradient descent-based method [95]. Let $\text{proj}_{\mathcal{P}_u}$ represent the projection onto simplex $\mathcal{P}_u$ and $\rho \in \mathbb{R}$ denote the step size, problem (2.2) can be solved by finding a fixed point to:

$$\mathbf{p}_u^* = \text{proj}_{\mathcal{P}_u}\left[\mathbf{p}_u^* - \rho\nabla_u F_u^r(\mathbf{p}_u^*, \mathbf{p}_{-u}^*)\right], \; \forall u \in \mathcal{U}. \tag{2.3}$$

2.4.1.1.2 Stackelberg Game Analysis

Recall that $\mathcal{U}$ represents the user set of the NRS, with their associated set of OD pairs, denoted as $\Theta_{\mathcal{U}}$. For each pair of ODs $\theta \in \Theta_{\mathcal{U}}$, the aggregated demand flow of users that must be routed from the corresponding origin to the desired destination is $d_\theta = \sum_{u\in\mathcal{U}} \mathbf{1}_{\{\theta_u=\theta\}}$. For the OD pair $\theta \in \Theta \setminus \Theta_{\mathcal{U}}$, $d_\theta = 0$. As we consider the case of deceptive misinformed demand attacks, let vector $\mathbf{d} := \{d_\theta\}_{\theta\in\Theta}$ and denote the set of solutions to NRS's problem defined in Definition 2.1 associated with demand $\mathbf{d}$ as $U(\mathbf{d})$.

Consider an example of strategic attackers with local-targeted attack objectives. Specifically, the attacker intends to have a desired level of expected flow load caused by genuine NRS users on the target road $e' \in \mathcal{E}$. That is, the attacker aims to make $x_{e'}^r(\mathbf{p}) = \sum_{u\in\mathcal{U}} \sum_{s_{u,i}\in\mathcal{S}_u} p_{u,i} a_{e's_{u,i}}$ in the UE recommendation achieve a desired level $\gamma \in \mathbb{R}_{\geq 0}$.

In the case where a Sybil-based attacker generates nonexistent demands $\mathbf{d}^a \in \mathcal{D}$, where $\mathcal{D} = \mathbb{Z}_{\geq 0}^{|\Theta|}$ using Sybil (fake) users so that the user set considered by the NRS becomes $\mathcal{U}'$. Then, the NRS will need to consider an aggregated demand of $\mathbf{d}' = \mathbf{d} + \mathbf{d}^a$ when generating the recommendation. Note that for each pair of OD θ, the demand d_θ' under attack consists of $d_\theta + d_\theta^a$. Without loss of generality, we can assume that only a proportion of $\frac{d_\theta}{d_\theta + d_\theta^a}$ of the expected path flow (for OD pair θ) $\sum_{u\in\mathcal{U}'} p_{u,i}'^* \mathbf{1}_{\{\theta_u=\theta\}}$ with respect to solution $\mathbf{p}'^* \in U(\mathbf{d}')$ is caused by authentic users. In this case, the attacker aims to make the flow load from genuine users, denoted as $x_{e'}^u(\mathbf{p}'^*) = \sum_{\theta\in\Theta} \sum_{u\in\mathcal{U}'} \sum_{s_{u,i}\in\mathcal{S}_u} \frac{d_\theta}{d_\theta + d_\theta^a} \mathbf{1}_{\{\theta_u=\theta\}} p_{u,i}'^* a_{e's_{u,i}}'$, on the targeted road e' reach the desired level γ. To this end, the Stackelberg game between the attacker (AT) and the NRS can be defined as $\Gamma^s = \langle \text{AT}, \mathcal{D}, U_{AT}, (e', \gamma), \Gamma^r \rangle$, where $U_{AT} : \mathcal{D} \mapsto \mathbb{R}_{\geq 0}$ is the attacker's cost in terms of the resources spent in fabricating fake demands. The leader-follower problem is formulated as follows and can be solved by gradient descent-based algorithms [96].

$$\min_{\mathbf{d}^a} \; U_{\text{AT}}(\mathbf{d}^a) = \sum_{\theta\in\Theta} d_\theta^a \tag{2.4a}$$

$$\text{s.t. } x_{e'}^u(\mathbf{p}'^*) \geq \gamma, \tag{2.4b}$$

$$\mathbf{p}'^* \in U(\mathbf{d} + \mathbf{d}^a), \tag{2.4c}$$

$$d_\theta^a \geq 0, \forall \theta \in \Theta. \tag{2.4d}$$

2.4.1.1.3 Meta-game Assessment

To assess the risks, we introduce two metrics as the outcomes of our PRADA framework. Let $\mathbf{p}$ be the recommendation to all users without attack, and let $\mathbf{p}'$ be the one under attack.

The targeted impact metric is defined as the difference in traffic flow on each road with and without the demand attack, divided by the flow without the attack. Specifically, for each road $e \in \mathcal{E}$, the measure TI_e is given by:

$$\mathrm{TI}_e = \frac{|x_e^r(\mathbf{p}') - x_e^r(\mathbf{p})|}{x_e^r(\mathbf{p})}, \tag{2.5}$$

which can assist in measuring the percentage change in traffic flow on the specific or targeted road affected by the demand attack. A larger value of TI_e indicates the road e is influenced more, often implying higher risk under the attack.

Given the metrics TI_e, $\forall e \in \mathcal{E}$, the network impact metric is then defined as the mean of TI_e across all roads / edges within the network. The measure NI is as follows:

$$\mathrm{NI} = \frac{1}{|\mathcal{E}|} \sum_{e \in \mathcal{E}} \mathrm{TI}_e = \frac{1}{|\mathcal{E}|} \sum_{e \in \mathcal{E}} \frac{|x_e^r(\mathbf{p}') - x_e^r(\mathbf{p})|}{x_e^r(\mathbf{p})}. \tag{2.6}$$

The metric NI allows us to evaluate the percentage change in traffic flow across the entire network. It is important to note that if the demand attack primarily affects traffic flow on roads within a small area, as indicated by the TI_e values for those roads, this localized impact will be averaged out when considering the network-wide impact.

Then, the PRADA risk evaluator can measure the risk for different threat models from different types of attacks in the attack libraries, compare the targeted and network impacts, and design methods for defense or mitigation purposes. For example, if the risk evaluator aims to assess the risk considering the scenario where the attacker with local-targeted objectives performs misinformed demand attacks, the risk evaluator can adjust parameters of Γ^s in the Stackelberg game analysis layer and get insights from the framework outputs, TI and NI.

2.4.1.2 Key Insights from the Case Study

Simulation experiments conducted under the PRADA framework reveal several critical insights. One notable finding is the impact of local-targeted attacks, where attackers redirect user flow to specific roads to benefit certain entities, such as businesses or political interests. For example, attackers might manipulate OD requests to artificially increase traffic through a specific area, creating commercial advantages or political leverage. These localized manipulations demonstrate how small-scale attacks can disproportionately affect user behavior and traffic patterns. Figure 2.6 shows the risk report in terms of network-wide impact (NI) and local-targeted impact (TI) on each road/edge when the attacker targets edge (10, 17),

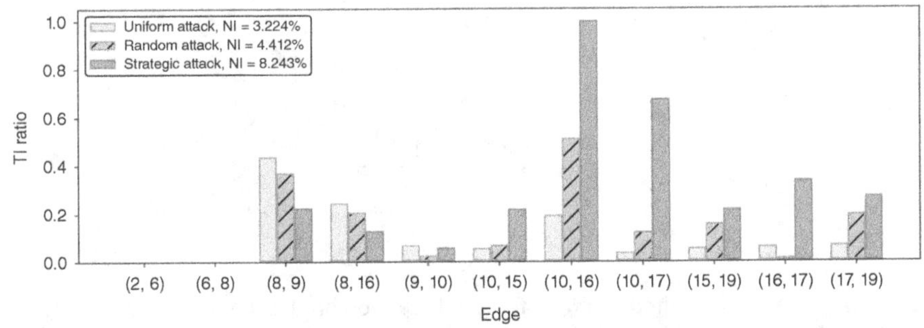

Figure 2.6 Risk report for misinformed demand attacks targeted edge (10, 17) in terms of TI (local-targeted impact on roads along users' feasible paths) and NI (network-wide impact) when encountering non-strategic (random, uniform) and strategic attackers. Here, strategic attackers refer to the ones who solve problem (2.4) while non-strategic ones manipulate demands by uniformly or randomly increasing or decreasing the number of requests associated with some OD pairs.

and we can observe both strategic and nonstrategic indeed affect genuine user's behavior and traffic patterns.

Another key insight is the system-wide risks posed by such attacks. Even localized disruptions can have cascading effects, destabilizing broader traffic networks. For instance, in Figure 2.6, a locally targeted attack for edge (10, 17) eventually leads to network-wide impact indicated by NI in the figure, and the risks posed by strategic attackers are higher compared to non-strategic ones.

Interestingly, the study also uncovers a "Fragile Paradox," where some attacks inadvertently improve traffic conditions by redistributing flow across underutilized routes. This paradox highlights the complexity of ITS dynamics and underscores the importance of proactive risk assessment to anticipate both intended and unintended consequences. We use the transportation network shown in Figure 2.7 as an illustrative example. There are 30 users who aim to go from node A to node B, and ϵ is small enough so that the cost on C-D is close to 0 even though all 30 users are passing through. Before the attack, the NRS will recommend a mixed strategy $(1/3, 1/3, 1/3)$ on paths A-C-B, A-C-D-B, and A-D-B, respectively. The overall costs on these three paths are all 4, which leads to a total travel time cost of 120 for users. Suppose that the attacker wants more "genuine users" to pass D-B by fabricating a large demand on C-D to make C-D seem congested to the NRS. The NRS will recommend a strategy $(0.5, 0, 0.5)$ on paths A-C-B, A-C-D-B, and A-D-B, respectively. The total costs on A-C-B and A-D-B are both 3.5, which leads to the total cost of travel time for the users being 105. Therefore, we can conclude that the cost under attack is "better" than the performance without attack in this carefully crafted example.

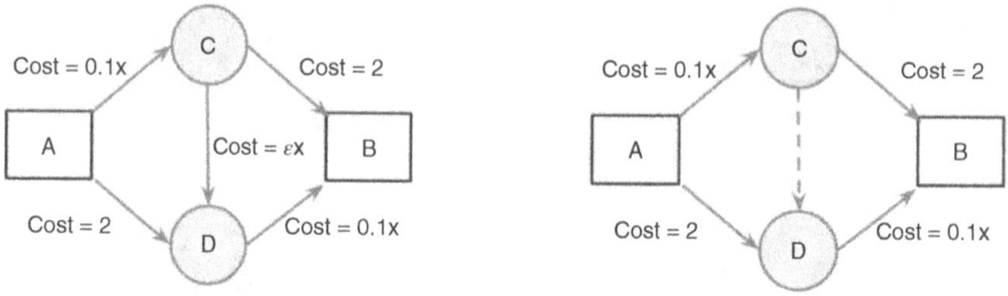

Figure 2.7 A carefully crafted example for the discussion on the "fragile paradox." Left: without attack; Right: with an attack.

2.4.1.3 Mitigation Strategies

To address the vulnerabilities exposed by these insights, PRADA introduces a trust mechanism to enhance the resilience of NRS against demand attacks. Central to this mechanism are trust scores, $T_u \in \mathbb{R}_{\geq 0}$ for all $u \in \mathcal{U}$, which quantify the user's confidence in the recommendations of the system. Based on trust scores, PRADA emphasizes trusted recommendations, which integrate trust constraints defined in Definition 2.2 directly into the NRS recommendation algorithms.

Definition 2.2 ***(Trust Constraint [TC]):*** Consider an NRS component, denoted as $\mathscr{R}$. A recommended mixed strategy $\mathbf{p}_u \in \mathcal{P}_u$ for a user u is said to satisfy the trust constraint if the distance (in terms of Kullback–Leibler [KL] divergence) between the current and previous recommended strategy $\mathbf{p}_u^o \in \mathcal{P}_u$ is less than the trust score $T_u \in \mathbb{R}_{\geq 0}$:

$$D(\mathbf{p}_u || \mathbf{p}_u^o) = \sum_{i=1}^{k_u} p_{u,i} \log\left(\frac{p_{u,i}}{p_{u,i}^o}\right) \leq T_u. \tag{2.7}$$

The trust constraints act as a regulatory mechanism, limiting how much the NRS recommendation can deviate from historical traffic patterns. Higher trust scores enable more adaptive and flexible recommendations, while lower scores prioritize consistency, reducing the system's susceptibility to manipulation. In this context, the trusted recommendation ensures that current recommendations align closely with user expectations and historical traffic conditions, thereby enhancing user adherence and the overall reliability of the system. By balancing flexibility and consistency, these mechanisms help mitigate the impact of demand attacks while maintaining the integrity of traffic management.

2.5 Conclusion and Discussion

2.5.1 Conclusion

This chapter introduces the concept of deceptive information attacks within ITS, focusing on their distinctive characteristics and critical implications. These attacks represent an emerging class of threats that exploit the interconnectedness and interdependencies of ITS, with impacts that span multiple domains. Unlike traditional attacks that often target individual devices locally, deceptive information attacks propagate through networks, manipulating data flows to trigger systemic disruptions.

The deceptive nature of these attacks allows adversaries to manipulate not only technical systems but also human operators and users, tricking them into actions that serve malicious objectives. For instance, falsified traffic updates may misdirect vehicles or induce panic, resulting in unsafe driving conditions or widespread inefficiencies. These attacks exploit vulnerabilities across intra-vehicle, inter-vehicle, infrastructure, and human domains, leading to cascading effects.

Many of these threats stem from composite attacks that traverse domain boundaries. A phishing email in the human domain may introduce malware into the infrastructure, which then compromises vehicles through V2X links. Such cross-domain propagation necessitates a holistic understanding of ITS cybersecurity. Mapping attack vectors and their interdependencies is essential to designing effective mitigation strategies.

Misinformed demand attacks on navigational systems serve as a representative case, demonstrating how adversaries can fabricate traffic data to alter routing decisions, manipulate user behavior, and trigger widespread congestion.

Addressing such threats requires a combined domain-specific and cross-domain perspective, along with integrated resilience mechanisms.

2.5.2 Discussion

Addressing deceptive information attacks in ITS requires a comprehensive analytical and methodological foundation. Game theory offers a powerful approach to model adversarial interactions, enabling systematic risk assessment and the design of decentralized mitigation strategies. Its ability to represent the objectives and actions of users, attackers, and defenders makes it especially suitable for analyzing cross-domain dynamics in ITS.

The PRADA framework exemplifies the application of game-theoretic analysis to ITS. By modeling attackers, system designers, and users in a Stackelberg game, PRADA reveals how misinformed demand attacks can exploit system dynamics. The integration of trust mechanisms further enables dynamic adaptation based on user behavior and system reliability. Combined with learning-based methods, PRADA supports proactive adjustments and continuous resilience.

The game-theoretic methodology extends naturally to a wide range of attacks. In spoofing scenarios, adversaries inject false GPS signals or tamper with V2X communication protocols. These can be modeled to reveal attacker incentives and identify countermeasures such as trust-based protocols and adaptive signal verification. For APTs, which involve stealthy, long-term intrusions, dynamic games allow defenders to evolve strategies over time. Techniques such as decoy deployment and anomaly detection can then be optimized within this framework.

The approach also scales to address other adversarial behaviors, including man-in-the-middle attacks, data poisoning, ransomware, and DoS attacks. For instance, DoS attacks can be mitigated by game-theoretic models that optimize dynamic resource allocation and system reconfiguration. Ransomware risks may be countered by predictive detection and quarantine strategies informed by adversarial modeling.

Overall, the integration of game theory with control mechanisms and adaptive learning forms a robust toolkit for ITS cyber resilience. It enables both proactive and reactive strategies tailored to diverse threats. Importantly, the adaptability of this methodology ensures that defense mechanisms evolve with the threat landscape – making it a critical enabler of long-term security and trust in intelligent transportation infrastructures.

References

1 Haozhe Lei and Quanyan Zhu. Cognitive level-k meta-learning for safe and pedestrian-aware autonomous driving. *arXiv preprint arXiv:2212.08800*, 2022.

2 Tao Li, Zilin Bian, Haozhe Lei, Fan Zuo, Ya-Ting Yang, Quanyan Zhu, Zhenning Li, and Kaan Ozbay. Multi-level traffic-responsive tilt camera surveillance through predictive correlated online learning. *Transportation Research Part C: Emerging Technologies*, 167: 104804, 2024.

3 Tao Li, Zilin Bian, Haozhe Lei, Fan Zuo, Ya-Ting Yang, Quanyan Zhu, Zhenning Li, Zhibin Chen, and Kaan Ozbay. Digital twin-based driver risk-aware intelligent mobility analytics for urban transportation management. *arXiv preprint arXiv:2407.15025*, 2024.

4 Quanyan Zhu and Stefan Rass. Game theory meets network security: A tutorial. In *Proceedings of the 2018 ACM SIGSAC Conference on Computer and Communications Security*, pages 2163–2165, 2018.

5 Teodora Mecheva and Nikolay Kakanakov. Cybersecurity in intelligent transportation systems. *Computers*, 9(4): 83, 2020.

6 Yunian Pan, Tao Li, and Quanyan Zhu. On the resilience of traffic networks under non-equilibrium learning. In *2023 American Control Conference (ACC)*, pages 3484–3489. IEEE, 2023.

7 Muhammad Usama, Ubaid Ullah, and Ahthasham Sajid. Cyber attacks against intelligent transportation systems. In *Cyber Security for Next-Generation Computing Technologies*, pages 190–230. CRC Press, 2024.

8 Quanyan Zhu. Foundations of cyber resilience: The confluence of game, control, and learning theories. *arXiv preprint arXiv:2404.01205*, 2024.

9 Anna Cartwright and Edward Cartwright. The economics of ransomware attacks on integrated supply chain networks. *Digital Threats: Research and Practice*, 4(4): 1–14, 2023.

10 Qiyuan Zhang, Christopher D. Wallbridge, Dylan M. Jones, and Phillip L. Morgan. Public perception of autonomous vehicle capability determines judgment of blame and trust in road traffic accidents. *Transportation Research Part A: Policy and Practice*, 179: 103887, 2024.

11 NIST. The NIST cybersecurity framework (CSF) 2.0. Technical Report NIST Cybersecurity White Paper (CSWP) 29. Gaithersburg, MD: National Institute of Standards and Technology, 2024. https://doi.org/10.6028/NIST.CSWP.29.

12 Yunfei Ge and Quanyan Zhu. Zero trust for cyber resilience. *arXiv preprint arXiv:2312.02882*, 2023.

13 V. Stafford. Zero trust architecture. *NIST Special Publication*, 800: 207, 2020.

14 Mikhail Buinevich and Andrei Vladyko. Forecasting issues of wireless communication networks' cyber resilience for an intelligent transportation system: An overview of cyber attacks. *Information*, 10(1): 27, 2019.

15 Linan Huang and Quanyan Zhu. A dynamic games approach to proactive defense strategies against advanced persistent threats in cyber-physical systems. *Computers & Security*, 89: 101660, 2020.

16 Ya-Ting Yang and Quanyan Zhu. When to deceive: A cross-layer stackelberg game framework for strategic timing of cyber deception. *arXiv preprint arXiv:2505.21244*, 2025.

17 Linan Huang and Quanyan Zhu. *Cognitive Security: A System-Scientific approach*. Springer Nature, 2023.

18 Quanyan Zhu. Game theory for cyber deception: A tutorial. In *Proceedings of the 6th Annual Symposium on Hot Topics in the Science of Security*, pages 1–3, 2019.

19 Yuhan Zhao and Quanyan Zhu. Stackelberg game-theoretic trajectory guidance for multi-robot systems with Koopman operator. In *2024 IEEE International Conference on Robotics and Automation (ICRA)*, pages 12326–12332. IEEE, 2024.

20 Tao Li, Henger Li, Yunian Pan, Tianyi Xu, Zizhan Zheng, and Quanyan Zhu. Meta stackelberg game: Robust federated learning against adaptive and mixed poisoning attacks. *arXiv preprint arXiv:2410.17431*, 2024.

21 Ya-Ting Yang, Tao Zhang, and Quanyan Zhu. A game-theoretic analysis of auditing differentially private algorithms with epistemically disparate herd. In *International Conference on Decision and Game Theory for Security*, pages 349–368. Springer, 2023.

22 Thanh Thi Nguyen and Vijay Janapa Reddi. Deep reinforcement learning for cyber security. *IEEE Transactions on Neural Networks and Learning Systems*, 34(8): 3779–3795, 2021.

23 Ya-Ting Yang, Yunian Pan, and Quanyan Zhu. Preference-centric route recommendation: Equilibrium, learning, and provable efficiency. *arXiv preprint arXiv:2504.01192*, 2025.

24 Fei Fang, Shutian Liu, Anjon Basak, Quanyan Zhu, Christopher D. Kiekintveld, and Charles A. Kamhoua. Introduction to game theory. In *Game Theory and Machine Learning for Cyber Security*, pages 21–46. John Wiley & Sons, Inc., 2021.

25 Juntao Chen, Corinne Touati, and Quanyan Zhu. A dynamic game approach to designing secure interdependent IoT-enabled infrastructure network. *IEEE Transactions on Network Science and Engineering*, 8(3): 2601–2612, 2021.

26 Juntao Chen, Quanyan Zhu, and Tamer Başar. Dynamic contract design for systemic cyber risk management of interdependent enterprise networks. *Dynamic Games and Applications*, 11(2): 294–325, 2021.

27 Jeffrey Pawlick, Edward Colbert, and Quanyan Zhu. Modeling and analysis of leaky deception using signaling games with evidence. *IEEE Transactions on Information Forensics and Security*, 14(7): 1871–1886, 2018.

28 Tao Li and Quanyan Zhu. Commitment with signaling under double-sided information asymmetry. *arXiv preprint arXiv:2212.11446*, 2022.

29 Ya-Ting Yang, Haozhe Lei, and Quanyan Zhu. Strategic information attacks on incentive-compatible navigational recommendations in intelligent transportation systems. *arXiv preprint arXiv:2310.01646*, 2023.

30 Yunian Pan and Quanyan Zhu. On poisoned wardrop equilibrium in congestion games. In *International Conference on Decision and Game Theory for Security*, pages 191–211. Springer, 2022.

31 Yunian Pan, Tao Li, and Quanyan Zhu. Is stochastic mirror descent vulnerable to adversarial delay attacks? A traffic assignment resilience study. In *2023 62nd IEEE Conference on Decision and Control (CDC)*, pages 8328–8333. IEEE, 2023.

32 Lijun Chi, Mounira Msahli, Qingjie Zhang, Han Qiu, Tianwei Zhang, Gerard Memmi, and Meikang Qiu. Adversarial attacks on autonomous driving systems in the physical world: A survey. *IEEE Transactions on Intelligent Vehicles*, 10(9): 4433–4454, 2024.

33 Christopher King and Dan Klinedinst. Vehicle cybersecurity: The jeep hack and beyond. Carnegie Mellon University, Software Engineering Institute's Insights (blog), May 2016. https://insights.sei.cmu.edu/blog/vehicle-cybersecurity-the-jeep-hack-and-beyond (accessed 3 December 2024).

34 Quanyan Zhu and Zhiheng Xu. New architecture: Cloud-enabled cps. In *Cross-Layer Design for Secure and Resilient Cyber-Physical Systems: A Decision and Game Theoretic Approach*, pages 19–24. Springer International Publishing, 2020.

35 Quanyan Zhu and Zhiheng Xu. Secure and resilient design of could-enabled CPS. In *Cross-Layer Design for Secure and resilient Cyber-Physical Systems: A Decision and Game Theoretic Approach*, pages 25–41. Springer International Publishing, 2020.

36 Juntao Chen and Quanyan Zhu. Security as a service for cloud-enabled internet of controlled things under advanced persistent threats: A contract design approach. *IEEE Transactions on Information Forensics and Security*, 12(11): 2736–2750, 2017.

37 Jeffrey Pawlick, Juntao Chen, and Quanyan Zhu. iSTRICT: An interdependent strategic trust mechanism for the cloud-enabled internet of controlled things. *IEEE Transactions on Information Forensics and Security*, 14(6): 1654–1669, 2018.

38 Shutian Liu and Quanyan Zhu. Cyber insurance for cyber resilience. *arXiv preprint arXiv:2312.02921*, 2023.

39 Yunfei Ge and Quanyan Zhu. Accountability and insurance in iot supply chain. *arXiv preprint arXiv:2201.11855*, 2022.

40 Ya-Ting Yang, T. Zhang, and Quanyan Zhu. Herd accountability of privacy-preserving algorithms: A stackelberg game approach. *IEEE Transactions on Information Forensics and Security*, 20: 2237–2251, 2025.

41 Yunfei Ge and Quanyan Zhu. Trust threshold policy for explainable and adaptive zero-trust defense in enterprise networks. In *2022 IEEE Conference on Communications and Network Security (CNS)*, pages 359–364. IEEE, 2022.

42 Yang Liu, Debiao He, Mohammad S. Obaidat, Neeraj Kumar, Muhammad Khurram Khan, and Kim-Kwang Raymond Choo. Blockchain-based identity management systems: A review. *Journal of Network and Computer Applications*, 166: 102731, 2020.

43 Maanak Gupta, James Benson, Farhan Patwa, and Ravi Sandhu. Secure V2V and V2I communication in intelligent transportation using cloudlets. *IEEE Transactions on Services Computing*, 15(4): 1912–1925, 2020.

44 Mahmood A. Al-Shareeda, Mohammed Anbar, Selvakumar Manickam, and Iznan H. Hasbullah. Review of prevention schemes for man-in-the-middle (MITM) attack in vehicular ad hoc networks. *International Journal of Engineering and Management Research*, 10: 153–158, 2020.

45 Simon Weckert. Google maps hacks, 2020. https://www.simonweckert.com/googlemapshacks.html.

46 Cihan Eryonucu and Panos Papadimitratos. Sybil-based attacks on google maps or how to forge the image of city life. In *Proceedings of the 15th ACM Conference on Security and Privacy in Wireless and Mobile Networks*, pages 73–84, 2022.

47 Yiheng Feng, Shihong Ed Huang, Wai Wong, Q. Alfred Chen, Z. Morley Mao, and Henry X. Liu. On the cybersecurity of traffic signal control system with connected vehicles. *IEEE Transactions on Intelligent Transportation Systems*, 23(9): 16267–16279, 2022.

48 Simon Unger, Markus Heinrich, Dirk Scheuermann, Stefan Katzenbeisser, Max Schubert, Leon Hagemann, and Lukas Iffländer. Securing the future railway system: Technology forecast, security measures, and research demands. *Vehicles*, 5(4): 1254–1274, 2023.

49 Numaan Huq, Rainer Vosseler, and Morton Swimmer. Cyberattacks against intelligent transportation systems.: Assessing Future Threats to ITS. *TrendLabs Research Paper*, 2017.

50 Craig G. Rieger, David I. Gertman, and Miles A. McQueen. Resilient control systems: Next generation design research. In *2009 2nd Conference on Human System Interactions*, pages 632–636. IEEE, 2009.

51 Craig Rieger, Indrajit Ray, Quanyan Zhu, and M. Haney. *Industrial Control Systems Security and Resiliency*. Springer, 2019.

52 Craig Rieger, Quanyan Zhu, and Tamer Başar. Agent-based cyber control strategy design for resilient control systems: Concepts, architecture and methodologies. In *2012 5th International Symposium on Resilient Control Systems*, pages 40–47. IEEE, 2012.

53 Hideaki Ishii and Quanyan Zhu. *Security and Resilience of Control Systems*. Springer, 2022.

54 Quanyan Zhu and Tamer Başar. Robust and resilient control design for cyber-physical systems with an application to power systems. In *2011 50th IEEE Conference on Decision and Control and European Control Conference*, pages 4066–4071. IEEE, 2011.

55 Quanyan Zhu and Tamer Başar. Disentangling resilience from robustness: Contextual dualism, interactionism, and game-theoretic paradigms. *IEEE Control Systems Magazine*, 44(3): 95–103, 2024.

56 Yuqiang Ning and Lili Du. Robust and resilient equilibrium routing mechanism for traffic congestion mitigation built upon correlated equilibrium and distributed optimization. *Transportation Research Part B: Methodological*, 168: 170–205, 2023.

57 José R. Correa and Nicolás E. Stier-Moses. Wardrop equilibria. In *Encyclopedia of Operations Research and Management Science*. Wiley, 2011.

58 Sultan Ahmed Almalki and Frederick T. Sheldon. Deep learning to improve false data injection attack detection in cooperative intelligent transportation systems. In *2021 IEEE 12th Annual Information Technology, Electronics and Mobile Communication Conference (IEMCON)*, pages 1016–1021. IEEE, 2021.

59 Amirhossein Adavoudi Jolfaei, Abdelwahab Boualouache, Andy Rupp, Stefan Schiffner, and Thomas Engel. A survey on privacy-preserving electronic toll collection schemes for intelligent transportation systems. *IEEE Transactions on Intelligent Transportation Systems*, 24(9): 8945–8962, 2023.

60 Quanyan Zhu and Zhiheng Xu. *Cross-Layer Design for Secure and Resilient Cyber-physical Systems*. Cham, Switzerland: Springer, 2020.

61 Zhiheng Xu and Quanyan Zhu. Secure and resilient control design for cloud enabled networked control systems. In *Proceedings of the First ACM Workshop on Cyber-Physical Systems-Security and/or Privacy*, pages 31–42, 2015.

62 Ya-Ting Yang, Tao Li, and Quanyan Zhu. Designing policies for truth: Combating misinformation with transparency and information design. In *2023 21st International Symposium on Modeling and Optimization in Mobile, Ad Hoc, and Wireless Networks (WiOpt)*, pages 127–134. IEEE, 2023.

63 Ya-Ting Yang, Tao Li, and Q. Zhu. Transparent tagging for strategic social nudges on user-generated misinformation. *arXiv preprint arXiv:2411.00825*, 2024.

64 Shuo Huang and Quanyan Zhu. Psyborg+: Cognitive modeling for triggering and detection of cognitive biases of advanced persistent threats. *arXiv preprint arXiv:2408.01310*, 2024.

65 Harsh Katakwar, Cleotilde Gonzalez, and Varun Dutt. Attackers have prior beliefs: Comprehending cognitive aspects of confirmation bias on adversarial decisions. In *International Conference on Frontiers in Computing and Systems*, pages 261–273. Springer, 2023.

66 Marcin Waniek, Gururaghav Raman, Bedoor AlShebli, Jimmy Chih-Hsien Peng, and Talal Rahwan. Traffic networks are vulnerable to disinformation attacks. *Scientific Reports*, 11(1): 5329, 2021.

67 E. Blair Cox, Quanyan Zhu, and Emily Balcetis. Stuck on a phishing lure: Differential use of base rates in self and social judgments of susceptibility to cyber risk. *Comprehensive Results in Social Psychology*, 4(1): 25–52, 2020.

68 Linan Huang and Quanyan Zhu. Advert: Defending against reactive attention attacks. In *Cognitive Security: A System-Scientific Approach*, pages 67–83. Springer, 2023.

69 Linan Huang and Quanyan Zhu. Radams: Defending against proactive attention attacks. In *Cognitive Security: A System-Scientific Approach*, pages 85–99. Springer, 2023.

70 Amos Tversky and Daniel Kahneman. Advances in prospect theory: Cumulative representation of uncertainty. *Journal of Risk and uncertainty*, 5: 297–323, 1992.

71 Linan Huang, Shumeng Jia, Emily Balcetis, and Quanyan Zhu. Advert: An adaptive and data-driven attention enhancement mechanism for phishing prevention. *IEEE Transactions on Information Forensics and Security*, 17: 2585–2597, 2022.

72 Rui Zhang and Quanyan Zhu. Flipin: A game-theoretic cyber insurance framework for incentive-compatible cyber risk management of internet of things. *IEEE Transactions on Information Forensics and Security*, 15: 2026–2041, 2019.

73 Mohammad Hossein Manshaei, Quanyan Zhu, Tansu Alpcan, Tamer Bacşar, and Jean-Pierre Hubaux. Game theory meets network security and privacy. *ACM Computing Surveys (CSUR)*, 45(3): 1–39, 2013.

74 Mustafa Abdallah, Saurabh Bagchi, Shaunak D. Bopardikar, Kevin Chan, Xing Gao, Murat Kantarcioglu, Congmiao Li, Peng Liu, and Quanyan Zhu. Game theory in distributed systems security: Foundations, challenges, and future directions. *IEEE Security & Privacy*, 23(1): 64–74, 2024.

75 Quanyan Zhu and Tamer Başar. Game-theoretic methods for robustness, security, and resilience of cyberphysical control systems: Games-in-games principle for optimal cross-layer resilient control systems. *IEEE Control Systems Magazine*, 35(1): 46–65, 2015.

76 Quanyan Zhu and Tamer Başar. A dynamic game-theoretic approach to resilient control system design for cascading failures. In *Proceedings of the 1st International Conference on High Confidence Networked Systems*, pages 41–46, 2012.

77 Juntao Chen, Corinne Touati, and Quanyan Zhu. A dynamic game approach to strategic design of secure and resilient infrastructure network. *IEEE Transactions on Information Forensics and security*, 15: 462–474, 2019.

78 Yurid Nugraha, Ahmet Cetinkaya, Tomohisa Hayakawa, Hideaki Ishii, and Quanyan Zhu. Dynamic resilient network games with applications to multiagent consensus. *IEEE Transactions on Control of Network Systems*, 8(1): 246–259, 2020.

79 Jeffrey Pawlick, Edward Colbert, and Quanyan Zhu. A game-theoretic taxonomy and survey of defensive deception for cybersecurity and privacy. *ACM Computing Surveys (CSUR)*, 52(4): 1–28, 2019.

80 Yunfei Ge, Tao Li, and Quanyan Zhu. Scenario-agnostic zero-trust defense with explainable threshold policy: A meta-learning approach. In *IEEE INFOCOM 2023-IEEE Conference on Computer Communications Workshops (INFOCOM WKSHPS)*, pages 1–6. IEEE, 2023.

81 Tao Li, Yunian Pan, and Quanyan Zhu. Decision-dominant strategic defense against lateral movement for 5g zero-trust multi-domain networks. In *Network Security Empowered by Artificial Intelligence*, pages 25–76. Springer, 2024.

82 Yunhan Huang, Linan Huang, and Quanyan Zhu. Reinforcement learning for feedback-enabled cyber resilience. *Annual Reviews in Control*, 53: 273–295, 2022.

83 Charles A. Kamhoua, Christopher D. Kiekintveld, Fei Fang, and Quanyan Zhu. *Game Theory and Machine Learning for Cyber Security*. John Wiley & Sons, 2021.

84 Jeffrey Pawlick and Quanyan Zhu. *Game Theory for Cyber Deception*. Springer, 2021.

85 Ya-Ting Yang and Hung-Yu Wei. Edge–IoT computing and networking resource allocation for decomposable deep learning inference. *IEEE Internet of Things Journal*, 10(6): 5178–5193, 2022.

86 Ya-Ting Yang and Hung-Yu Wei. A coalition formation approach for privacy and energy-aware split deep learning inference in edge camera network. *IEEE Transactions on Network and Service Management*, 20(3): 3673–3685, 2022.

87 Yuhan Zhao and Quanyan Zhu. Stackelberg meta-learning for strategic guidance in multi-robot trajectory planning. In *2023 IEEE/RSJ International Conference on Intelligent Robots and Systems (IROS)*, pages 11342–11347. IEEE, 2023.

88 Yuhan Zhao and Quanyan Zhu. Stackelberg meta-learning based control for guided cooperative LQG systems. *IFAC-PapersOnLine*, 56(2): 10120–10125, 2023.

89 Yuhan Zhao. Learning and game-theoretic paradigms for strategic coordination of multi-agent autonomous systems. PhD thesis, New York University Tandon School of Engineering, 2024.

90 Tao Li and Quanyan Zhu. Symbiotic game and foundation models for cyber deception operations in strategic cyber warfare. *arXiv preprint arXiv:2403.10570*, 2024.

91 Kim Hammar, Tao Li, Rolf Stadler, and Quanyan Zhu. Automated security response through online learning with adaptive conjectures. *arXiv preprint arXiv:2402.12499*, 2024.

92 Tao Li, Haozhe Lei, and Quanyan Zhu. Sampling attacks on meta reinforcement learning: A minimax formulation and complexity analysis. *arXiv preprint arXiv:2208.00081*, 2022.

93 Tao Li, Haozhe Lei, and Quanyan Zhu. Self-adaptive driving in nonstationary environments through conjectural online lookahead adaptation. In *2023 IEEE International Conference on Robotics and Automation (ICRA)*, pages 7205–7211. IEEE, 2023.

94 Ya-Ting Yang, Haozhe Lei, and Quanyan Zhu. Prada: Proactive risk assessment and mitigation of misinformed demand attacks on navigational route recommendations. *arXiv preprint arXiv:2409.00243*, 2024.

95 Ya-Ting Yang, Haozhe Lei, and Quanyan Zhu. Adaptive incentive-compatible navigational route recommendations in urban transportation networks. *arXiv preprint arXiv:2409.00236*, 2024.

96 Stephen P. Boyd and Lieven Vandenberghe. *Convex Optimization*. Cambridge University Press, 2004.

3

CYBER-MIRA: Cyber Mission Impact Resilience Assessment Framework for Tactical Mission Systems

Ashrith Reddy Thukkaraju,[1] Han Jun Yoon,[1*] Shou Matsumoto,[2] Jair Feldens Ferrari,[2] Donghwan Lee,[3] Myung Kil Ahn,[3] Paulo Costa,[2] and Jin-Hee Cho[1*]*

[1]*Department of Computer Science, Virginia Tech, Blacksburg, VA, USA*
[2]*C4I&Cyber Center, George Mason University, Fairfax, VA, USA*
[3]*Defense Cyber Technology Center, Agency for Defense Development, Seoul, Republic of Korea*

*Ashrith Reddy Thukkaraju and Han Jun Yoon contributed equally to this chapter. Corresponding Author: jicho@vt.edu

3.1 Introduction

A cyber mission impact assessment (CMIA) is performed to assess the impact of cyber threats or incidents on the mission. CMIA frameworks can help organizations of all sizes identify infrastructure critical to their missions and determine the potential impact of threats and vulnerabilities, allowing them to develop risk-mitigation strategies. We propose a cyber mission impact resilience assessment (Cyber-MIRA) framework that can be used to evaluate the mission's performance, particularly in the context of cyber resilience.

Mission resilience assessment is a very important part of the impact assessment process, especially for maintaining the continuity of critical missions. Although it is a very common practice for the MIA frameworks to evaluate the mission's performance using security metrics like confidentiality, integrity, and availability, using metrics for cyber resilience is essential for critical missions, as cyber resilience is an important aspect of ensuring mission success.

The traditional threat-centric CMIA frameworks use techniques like attack paths to model the attacker's behavior. These methods, however, only view the system from the attacker's perspective. To study mission systems with both adversaries and defense mechanisms, we need to introduce interaction models. This is particularly important for the cyber resilience assessment because defense strategies play a crucial role in the mission system's cyber resilience. To address this problem, in Cyber-MIRA, we propose a hypergame-theoretic enemy behavior modeling module that not only helps model the impact of the attacker's presence but also the attack–defense interactions using hypergame-theoretic interactions. This would help model the defense's interactions with the mission system, which is essential for system failure recovery, a key metric of cyber resilience.

We propose using the three traditional cyber resilience metrics: fault tolerance, adaptability, and recoverability, and also introduce another metric, "transformability," which measures the system's ability to learn from the past. These metrics, together coupled with the hypergame-theoretic enemy behavior model will help assess the impact of the threats on the cyber resilience of the mission.

3.1.1 Motivation and Challenges

Cyber resilience is the capacity of a cyber entity to consistently deliver the expected output in the face of unfavorable cyber occurrences. It helps an organization or a business to prepare for the worst-case scenario and minimizes the damage to the mission system and its services caused by unfavorable cyber occurrences. These unfavorable cyber occurrences, also called threats, constitute intentional cyberattacks on the mission system and unexpected system component failures. The cyber entities or assets are the mission system devices that provide services and tasks essential for the successful completion of the mission. These cyber assets are the primary targets for the attackers trying to compromise the mission, since damaging these devices directly impacts the mission outcome.

Ensuring the intended outcomes are delivered even in the face of adversity is the ultimate goal of cyber resilience. The most significant distinction between cyber resilience and cybersecurity is that cyber resilience assumes the attackers are equipped to infiltrate and damage the mission system and then studies how effectively the system performs under those circumstances. It studies the response and recovery effectiveness of a breached mission system. On the other hand, cybersecurity is all about designing security mechanisms to ensure the safety and robustness of mission systems and networks against attacks in the first place.

There have been many developments in newly emerging IT technologies over the past two decades. By utilizing this, both attackers and defenders could develop more advanced, sophisticated, and intelligent methods of launching attacks and defending them. When assessing mission impact, the focus is usually on the attackers and their strategies. However, the defender's responses to the attacks, the interaction between the attackers and defenders, and their impact on the mission are an unexplored area. Particularly, how the relationship between the key components of the mission, like the assets, their capabilities, and vulnerabilities, as well as the attacker and defender capabilities, helps understand the resilience of a mission system better.

Lastly, although machine learning (ML)/deep learning (DL) has been substantially used in mission systems, their resilience has not been investigated and quantified by the existing assessment tools. We consider an IoT-based object detection mission system and propose a Mission Impact Resilience Assessment framework, CYBER-MIRA, for tactical mission systems.

3.1.2 Research Goal

In this chapter, we aim to develop a cyber mission impact resilience assessment framework called CYBER-MIRA to analyze the efficacy and performance of an IoT-empowered tactical ML-based mission system. We will look into the relationships between the essential parts of a mission system, their weaknesses, how attackers can take advantage of them, and the defenses against the attacks. The proposed CYBER-MIRA will measure the resilience of the tactical ML-based mission system as a function of the system's fault tolerance, adaptability, recoverability, and transformability in the presence of adversarial attacks and network dynamics in distributed, resource-constrained tactical environments. In addition, the CYBER-MIRA will consider how efficiently the mission can be completed with the minimum resource consumption and overhead generated while providing seamless services under highly contested network environments.

3.1.3 Key Contributions

In this chapter, we made the following key contributions:

1. We propose a conceptual tactical mission resilience assessment framework called CYBER-MIRA, which is a thorough package that can be used in other mission scenarios as well. CYBER-MIRA-MIRA provides a template to model the mission system using Concept Models, Business Process Modeling and Notation (BPMN), Impact Dependency Graphs (IDGs), and strategies to implement various other components of the framework.
2. CYBER-MIRA uses a belief model called Subjective Logic (SL) [1] to propagate uncertainty aware-resilience of a given system through the IDG. Although the Bayesian Networks (BNs) technique has been widely used in the literature [2–10] for mission impact assessment (MIA), subjective Bayesian networks (SBNs) [1] allow us to consider uncertainty in the belief propagation (BP) to make effective decisions under uncertainty.
3. We propose a game-theoretic enemy behavior model. We model the attacker and the defender interactions as a hypergame and also propose methods to model the costs and the effectiveness of the strategies using the vulnerability scores (Common Vulnerability Scoring System [CVSS]) that allow performing a particular strategy.

3.1.4 Structure of This Chapter

The rest of this chapter is organized as follows:

- Section 3.2 provides the overview of the related work in terms of the methodologies of CMIA, MIA frameworks, and cyber resilience assessment.
- Section 3.3 describes our system models, including the mission model, asset model, network model, attack model, defense model, and vulnerability model. In addition, we discuss the assumptions made in our work.
- Section 3.4 provides a detailed description of the architecture of the proposed CYBER-MIRA. Leveraging the key skeleton of the Cyber-ARGUS [10], we describe the key modules of our CYBER-MIRA in terms of mission scenario, topology discovery, vulnerability discovery (VD), game-theoretic attack behavior modeling, specification of the relationships of the key modules, and asset importance, reasoning model generation using uncertainty-aware IDG (UA-IDG), and metrics to measure mission performance.
- Section 3.5 discusses the limitations of the proposed CYBER-MIRA.
- Section 3.6 concludes the chapter and suggests our future work directions.

3.2 Related Work

In this section, we provide an overview of the existing related works in terms of the methodologies of CMIA, MIA frameworks, and cyber resilience assessment.

3.2.1 Methodologies of CMIA

There are two primary methodologies for assessing the impact of cyber missions: the *threat-centric* and *mission-centric* approaches. The *threat-centric MIA* involves estimating impact from the perspective of the enemy or threat. Notable works employing threat-centric approaches include the Network Risk Assessment Tool (NRAT) [11] and Mission-Oriented Risk and Design Analysis (MORDA) [12]. These frameworks analyze system security considering the attributes of potential attackers but are not designed for state-based analyses portraying dynamic full attack vectors.

An alternative method is the Adversary View Security Evaluation (ADVISE) [13], which is an alternative technique that employs quantitative metrics for trade-off assessments along with multistep attacks. However, it is suitable only for planning and not for real-time scenarios. Commonly applied in Terrorism Risk Management [14], these techniques help understand attacker actions and assess the impact of attacks on crucial infrastructures and individuals. In cases where information about the attacker is insufficient, as seen in events like the September

11th attacks, the protection offered by threat-centric approaches proves ineffective. Despite their simplicity, the need for detailed knowledge of the attacker's actions, behavior, and goals renders threat-centric approaches unsuitable for real operations.

The *mission-centric MIA* was initially introduced to conceptualize the evaluation of mission impact by understanding key requirements to achieve mission objectives, as detailed in the CMIA framework [6, 7, 15, 16]. Using a business process language, the CMIA method describes an objective and the actions required to fulfill it, along with any limitations (such as dependencies, infrastructure, and services). Finding the most important resources for the accomplishment of the task is the framework's main concept. Additionally, monitoring helps comprehend the consequences of changes to these assets on the mission. However, a significant limitation is its inability to analyze cascading effects, making it unable to capture the collective impact of simultaneous attacks.

Another drawback is the framework's offline mode, which lacks awareness of immediate impacts, posing challenges in resource prioritization during mission execution. Moreover, the lack of detailed guidance on implementing CMIA stages raises uncertainties about its practicality and ability to deliver promised results. Despite these limitations, CMIA's focus on consequences marks a noteworthy advancement in quantifying cyber impact, facilitating impact assessment for zero-day attacks. The mission and cyber domain mapping also contribute significantly, enabling mission analysts to understand the impact of the events happening within a cyber mission. However, the absence of real-world scalable implementations in CMIA research is attributed to its emphasis on system architecture design.

3.2.2 MIA Frameworks

To detect and deliver relevant data on asset criticality, threats, and vulnerabilities, Carnegie Mellon University developed the Operationally Critical Threat, Asset, and Vulnerability Evaluation framework, or OCTAVE [2]. In order to control information risks and put preventative measures in place for organizational information assets, this information was used. But OCTAVE was mostly concerned with locating information risks inside businesses.

To understand the impacts of cyberattacks, MITRE presented an integrated strategy called "Analyzing Mission Impacts of Cyber Actions" (AMICA) [3]. Process modeling, simulation, dynamic representations, and attack graph-based dependency modeling are all combined in AMICA. It combines the mission process execution with tactics, techniques, and procedures (TTPs) related to defense and cyberattack. Furthermore, to improve cyberspace mission assurance, MITRE unveiled the Cyber Command System (CyCS) tool [4], which maps mission operations to network activities. With the use of effect analysis and situational awareness, CyCS offers MIA and pertinent data on danger, vulnerability, and consequence management. In 2015 [5], MITRE responded to a Request for Information (RFI) by offering solutions for the Cyber Defense Situational Awareness (CDSA) capacity of the NATO Communications and Information Agency (NCIA). The CMIA instrument, which represents cyber resources, procedures, and incident repercussions, was created by them [6, 7]. Dependencies between asset vulnerabilities and attack or defensive impacts, however, were not taken into consideration by CMIA.

An extensible, layered data model guaranteeing cyber situational awareness (CSA) was introduced by Komarkova et al. [8]. The missions, assets, networks, devices, threats, detection and mitigation capabilities, and access control inside an organization's network are all monitored by the CRUSOE data model. Although the paper did not carry out simulation studies to validate the framework, it did provide ontological relational viewpoints for seven distinct levels.

In 2012, Barreto et al. [9] introduced the Framework for Evaluating the Impact of a Cyberattack on a Physical Mission (FEICAPM). To provide decision-makers with essential information, FEICAPM entails mission modeling, network topology development, relevant information collecting, and impact evaluation. The 2019 Cyber-ARGUS mission assurance framework, a Command and Control (C2) support system, was built using this architecture. By integrating tools and technology, Cyber-ARGUS offers a logical mapping between operations and the cyber environment. It builds a BN for impact assessment using a knowledge base (KB); however, it ignores the strategic relationships between attackers and defenders. In order to establish the best attack and defensive techniques, the proposed CYBER-MIRA framework takes into account these interactions and applies game theory.

3.2.3 Cyber Resilience Assessment

Cyber resilience is a system's ability to recover from the effects of a cyberattack. One widely used definition of resilience is "the ability to prepare and plan for, absorb, recover from, and more successfully adapt to adverse events" [17].

Previous work in this domain has used a variety of approaches, both for qualitative and quantitative assessment of cyber resilience. Ligo et al. [18] developed a qualitative framework that uses a cyber resilience matrix based on the comprehensive set of resilience measures, including the resilience abilities: *plan* and *prepare*, *absorb*, *recover*, and *adapt*. Each of these abilities corresponds to a cyber measure in one of four domains: *Physical*, *Information*, *Cognitive*, and *Social*. These qualitative measures provide an in-depth understanding of a resilient system from various perspectives. However, the qualitative measures are not enough to obtain an objective assessment or compare different systems' resilience.

Ligo et al. [18] also discussed a quantitative cyber resilience measure using the *area under the functionality curve*. The question is not only how much a system's functionality decreases due to a cyberattack. It is also about the amount of time it takes to recover functioning. The main challenge with this approach to measuring cyber resilience is determining the *functionality* of cyber systems. It is even more difficult with multiple autonomous attackers and defenders performing and detecting the attacks continuously. We do not have a single source to deduce the functionality curve from. The heterogeneous sources that constitute a system's resilience make it harder to find a numerical way of understanding the functionality of a system.

Cho et al. [17] described a number of system-level resilience metrics that capture *fault tolerance*, *adaptability*, and *recoverability*. In addition, the authors elaborated how each of such resilience properties can be measured in terms of their sub-attributes, such as *fault tolerance* with robustness and diversity, *adaptability* with autonomy, learnability, and reconfigurability, and *recoverability* with recovery delay, recovery effectiveness, and recovery cost.

Another approach to measuring cyber resilience is through *simulation and modeling*. A quantitative measure for cyber resilience is the Resilience Index [19], which is defined as the percentage of Monte Carlo simulations in which the mission essential functions (MEFs) performance goes below the acceptable threshold in the presence of adverse cyber events (ACEs). Since we cannot define the likelihood and the duration of the attacks, we can consider all these variables in the simulation as uniform random variables. Performing this over various runs in the simulation ensures capturing the general performance and likelihood of the mission and attacks, respectively.

Eisenberg et al. [20] also proposed an alternative way to measure cyber resilience in terms of mission completion. The mission system and its dependencies are considered when measuring cyber resilience in mission completion. For instance, an attack that slows or stops a system but does not significantly disrupt the mission or services it supports has a smaller impact on resilience than an attack that can successfully compromise a mission. However, the main challenge with this is the mission dependencies and their complex relations, making understanding mission completion difficult.

3.3 System Model

In this section, we discuss the details of the network, mission, attack, defense, and vulnerability models used in our work. In addition, we describe the assumptions made in this work to design our CYBER-MIRA framework.

3.3.1 Network Model

Regarding the network model, it functions in an Internet-of-Things (IoT) environment that includes servers and a variety of IoT devices, including mobile sensors like cars, laptops, portable devices, and security cameras. Sensor nodes gather information (pictures) and send it to servers on a regular basis so they may process it further and identify objects. Each node in the network belongs to its Virtual Local Area Network (VLAN) and provides unique functionalities and services. VLANs may have one or more servers, depending on their functionalities for IoT device communication. Edge servers gather data and send it to the closest multi-access edge computing (MEC) server, which does object detection and uses edge devices to send the findings back to IoT devices. Training takes place in the Cloud Computing System (CCS), where cloud servers update global models in the MEC on a regular basis. Figure 3.1 shows the IoT network model.

3.3.2 Attack Model

MITRE ATT&CK is a framework that captures malicious behaviors attackers use in real-world cyberattacks at various phases. ATT&CK stands for Adversarial Tactics Techniques and Common Knowledge, and it contains thorough descriptions

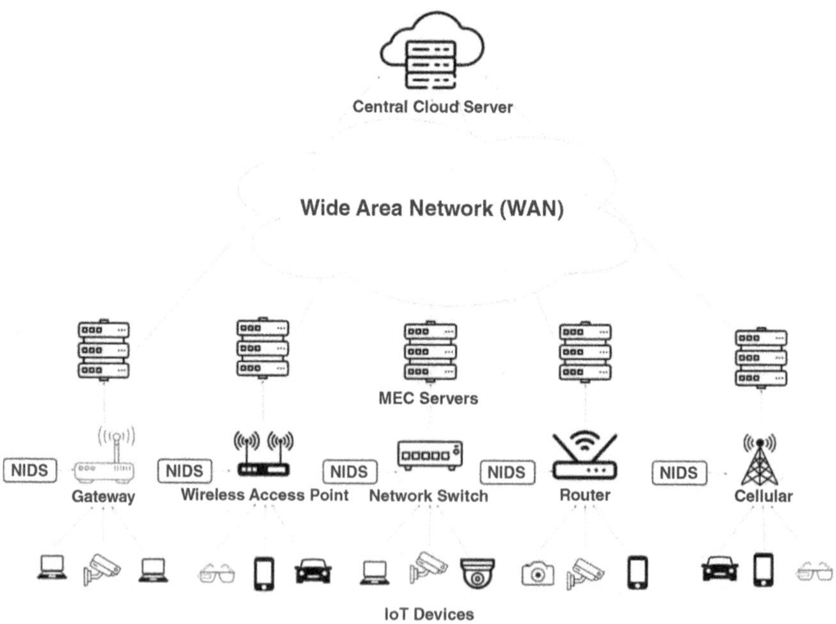

Figure 3.1 IoT network model.

of these groups' observed TTPs. Attackers behave differently depending on the target of their attack. They use distinct TTPs to compromise the enterprise system than they would to mobile devices or industrial control systems, for example. MITRE ATT&CK has organized attack tactics and techniques, including 14 tactics, 185 techniques, and 367 sub-technologies. Reconnaissance, initial access, execution, and collection are examples of tactics used by attackers to achieve attack targets, and techniques define methods for achieving tactics such as man-in-the-middle and phishing attacks.

For this work, we consider some of the most common attacks in the IoT environment. These sets of attacks are chosen from the list of MITRE's ATT&CK framework and chosen so they target each of the security requirements (CIA security goals, including Confidentiality, Integrity, and Availability).

- **Active Scanning (T1595):** Active Scanning attack comes under the class of reconnaissance attacks in MITRE's framework. In an active scanning attack, an attacker gathers information about the system using the network traffic. Usually, the attacker performs scanning on the network to collect the necessary information to plan the infiltration process and impact the mission in the future. A subtype of this attack that we want to focus on in this work is *Vulnerability Scanning* (T1595.002).
  - **Vulnerability Scanning (T1595.002):** In a vulnerability scanning attack, the attacker can use various tools and resources to gather information about the configuration of the victim machine. More specifically, the attacker scans for the software services available and their version numbers to potentially target them using known or crafted exploits.
- **Phishing (T1566):** Phishing is a form of social engineering where the adversary uses electronic means like emails, messages, and malicious file attachments, typically with the intention of infiltrating the victim's device. These attachments usually have hidden malware that runs malicious code on the victim's system. After infiltration using phishing, the attackers could perform various attacks to impact the mission outcome.
- **Data Manipulation (T1565):** After infiltration into the victim machine with the ability to execute remote code, the attacker can manipulate the contents of the local file system. The attacker can also manipulate the network traffic and the data that needs to be transmitted to other machines.
  - **Stored Data Manipulation (T1565.001):** The adversary can poison the data that is present in the victim machine and breach the integrity of the mission. This would directly impact the integrity of the mission outcome.
- **Network Denial of Service (T1498):** Denial of Service (DoS) is one of the most common attacks in any network environment. In this attack, the attacker could flood the network or a particular system in the network with

huge volumes of traffic to inundate the victim and impact its normal functionality. This would impact the availability of a service to genuine users. A variation of this attack is *Distributed Denial of Service (DDoS)*, in which the attacker floods the victim machine with traffic from multiple machines using botnets.

3.3.3 Defense Model

The defense model consists of all the possible defensive mechanisms that a defender can choose from. According to MITRE's D3FEND framework, a model can accurately list the capabilities of the cybersecurity defense mechanisms. It is a comprehensive knowledge graph with over 500 defensive mechanisms from the literature. It defines five defense tactics: Harden, Detect, Isolate, Deceive, and Evict. These five classes of tactics are further classified into 17 defense techniques.

MITRE's D3FEND framework uses digital artifacts (Files, Network traffic, Software, and other Top-level artifacts) to map its ATT&CK framework to its D3FEND framework. This is very useful since once the attack is identified, we have a limited number of defensive mechanisms to choose from to defend against the said attack.

For this work, we consider the following subset of defense mechanisms from the set of defenses specified in MITRE's D3FEND framework.

- **Message Encryption (D3-MENCR):** This most common way to ensure confidentiality of the messages sent over the network is to encrypt the messages. Symmetric (i.e., shared secret key) and asymmetric (i.e., public and private keys) cryptography can be used depending on the context. When the key is known to the attacker or when the attacker can break the encryption, the quickest fix would be to change the encryption key or the encryption algorithm used.
- **File Encryption (D3-FE):** File Encryption is very similar to message encryption in terms of the encryption mechanisms used. The encryption is applied to the files on a local file system. Encrypting the files in the local file system would make it harder for the attacker to read or manipulate the data in the compromised victim system.

- **Local File Permissions (D3-LFP):** Restricting the access of files to a set of users would make it difficult for the attacker to read, write, or delete even after infiltrating the victim's machine. However, the attacker could achieve privilege escalation and get permission to modify or manipulate the data.
- **Multi-factor Authentication (D3-MFA):** Multi-factor authentication uses two or more ways to authenticate the user of a service. This is essential because usually, the attacker gets hold of one or a few of the user credentials but not all of them. Hence, this ensures that the adversary cannot misuse the services even after being able to deceive the victims to gain their user credentials. Usually, the credentials in MFA are chosen based on something you know (passwords, pins), something you have (smartphones, smart cards), and something you are (e.g., biometrics, fingerprints).
- **Message Authentication (D3-MAN):** A digital signature or a Message Authentication Code (MAC) is a common method for message authentication. When the recipient receives the message or the file, they can simply perform the predetermined hashing method using the shared secret key to ensure their integrity.
- **Network Traffic Community Deviation (D3-NTCD):** Identification of statistically deviant communications in a predefined network community helps capture peculiar network traffic patterns. A Network-based IDS (NIDS) is a tool that monitors the network traffic for aberrations from a predefined rule set. These rules are to capture the patterns in malicious network packets.
- **Network Traffic Filtering (D3-NTF):** The objective is to control the flow of data originating from a specific network or device or directed toward a particular network or device. To address packet flooding attacks such as SYN Flooding, DoS, and DDoS, the practice of either blacklisting or whitelisting network traffic is employed.
- **Rekeying Encryption Keys:** Attackers require breaking encryption or phishing confidential information like passwords from the users to decrypt encrypted messages. Changing the encryption keys for the local files and messages and the keys for authentication mechanisms is an instantaneous response to such attacks.
- **Software Update (D3-SU):** Most vulnerabilities that the attackers use as a means of infiltration are usually in the software services provided by the victim machines. The software vulnerabilities are often patched in the newer versions, while the device might not have the updated version installed. Hence, a simple defense mechanism to prevent attackers from infiltration is to keep the software and services up to date.

3.4 CYBER-MIRA Framework

Most existing approaches in this domain use attacker strategies and system vulnerabilities to create a framework to assess a system's cyber resilience. The advances in cybersecurity technologies lead a mission system to be equipped with defenses in place to detect and respond to adversaries. This necessitates considering the impact of defense mechanisms and the interactions between the attack and the defense mechanisms on the system as a whole when assessing the cyber resilience of a complex system. The interaction between the attackers and defenses in a system or a network plays a significant role in cyber resilience. No prior work has considered the interactions between the attackers and the defense mechanisms when designing a resilience framework to the best of our knowledge. Game theory has been extensively utilized in cybersecurity to model the attacker(s) and defender(s) strategic interactions. We shall provide models of game-theoretic interactions that can describe the attacker's and the defender's strategic decision-making, as well as the influence of their strategic decisions on the system or the network state, including its performance and efficiency.

We will define the attacker as well as defender strategies as a list of choices for each of the attackers and the defender agents can choose from at any point in the game. For the attacker, we will consider different types of attacks, including common cyberattacks (e.g., DoS, message modification/forgery, or jamming attacks). For the defender agent, we can choose defense strategies ranging from Intrusion Detection Systems (IDSs) to detect the attacks happening in real time, Intrusion Prevention Systems (IPSs) to prevent the attacks from happening in the first place, and Intrusion Response Systems (IRSs), which provide a course of actions after intrusions are detected by the IDS.

Studying the cyber resilience of a system with a defender model to protect, identify, detect, and respond to attacks happening in real time would induce more complexities into the framework compared to ones that only consider the attacker capabilities and strategies and the system vulnerabilities. This would also make our framework a comprehensive, one-of-a-kind cyber resilience assessment tool for ML-based mission systems. Further, we will leverage the concept of a SBN to investigate the interdependence of the key system components. Using the SBNs will allow considering relationships between key system components and conditional inferences of the relationships under uncertainty based on a belief model called SL. This chapter will culminate in a concept model of the CYBER-MIRA that evaluates a mission system's resilience capabilities by considering the interdependencies among its essential components.

3.4.1 Architecture of CYBER-MIRA

The CYBER-MIRA framework for mission impact resilience assessment contains six essential components: Mission Modeling module, Vulnerability Module, Mission Monitoring Module, Metrics Module, Belief Module, and Enemy Behavior Module. The CYBER-MIRA framework aims to assess the resilience of any given mission system based on the interdependence of the main components of the mission. This section clearly describes each one of these components and how they combine to help us assess the impact resilience of any mission. For this work, we chose the IoT device-based object detection mission scenario. Figure 3.2 depicts the architecture of the CYBER-MIRA framework.

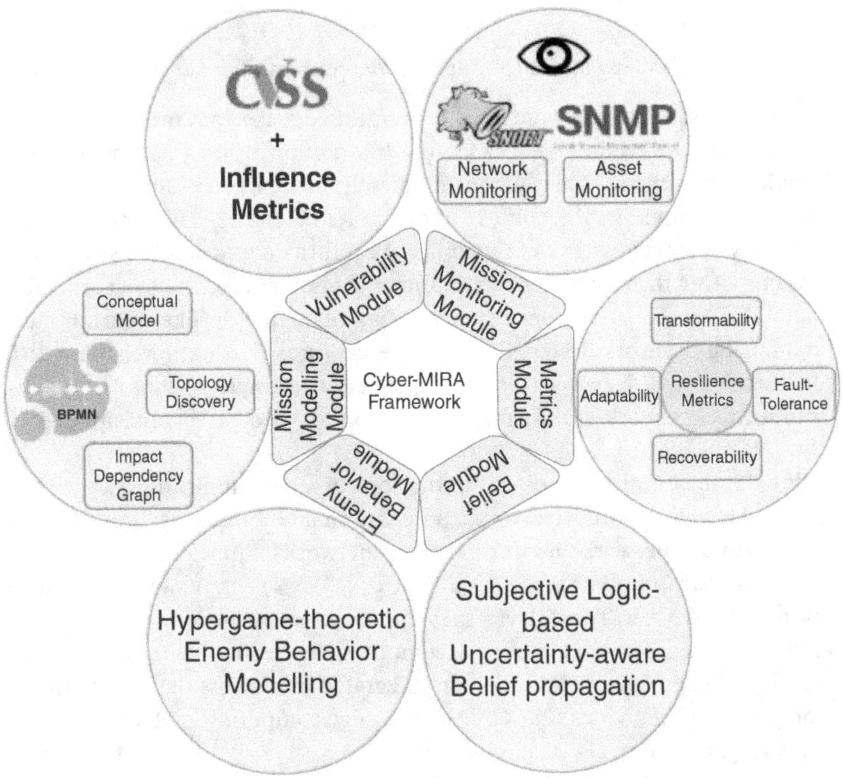

Figure 3.2 CYBER-MIRA framework.

3.4.1.1 Mission Description

3.4.1.1.1 Mission Scenario

A considered mission is to perform an object detection task on the images received from the IoT devices at the edge devices while training the object detection model at the Central Cloud Server (CCS). The IoT devices will capture the images of various objects in the environment, forward them to the edge server they are connected to, and execute the object detection task. The task of the edge devices is to perform the object detection on the received image using the model available at the edge device. The CCS is where the training takes place. After that, the CCS will send the updated detection model to the individual edge device at regular intervals to improve the performance of object detection at the edge devices.

3.4.1.1.2 Asset Model

We consider the following assets for our considered mission system:

- **IoT devices:** IoT devices are small computing devices that may collect data and connect with other devices via the Internet or inside a particular communication network. They are outfitted with sensors, processing power, and software features. In the context of our mission, the sensors embedded in IoT devices must possess the capability to capture images or video streams of objects within the designated environment. Examples of such devices include laptops, cameras, surveillance cameras, handheld devices like smartphones, and various sensors designed for image capture. Furthermore, these IoT devices should be capable of connecting to either a single- or multi-hop communication network to transmit information to the edge servers situated in their VLAN.
- **Edge devices:** Hardware placed at the edge of a communication network is referred to as an edge device. Its purpose is to enable communication between devices in one network and those in other networks. Firewalls, routers, routing switches, and other Wide Area Network (WAN) components are examples of edge devices. These devices essentially act as entrance or exit points for network traffic. The advent of edge computing has led to the development of intelligent edge devices that include integrated processors that can perform computational activities. The ability to do edge computing enables the use of lightweight ML models.
- **Multi-access edge computing (MEC) server:** MEC servers are the computing devices directly connected to the network edge devices. These intelligent servers have computing processors that allow us to run ML and other applications to provide services closer to the user to reduce network congestion. Usually, these servers help cellular and other such networks provide edge computing abilities.

- **Cloud central server (CCS):** The CCS is where the training of the object detection model happens. It is assumed to be trusted and out of reach from the attackers. The CCS, at regular training steps, forwards the updated model to the edge servers, which they use to perform the task of object detection in real time on the images received from the IoT devices.

3.4.1.1.3 Concept Model for a Mission System

Figure 3.3 illustrates the concept model to describe the entire mission, the concepts involved, and the relations between them. This concept model provides relevant information about the mission and its key components. We use this concept model as a template to store the mission-relevant information in the KB. In the concept model, the mission has a goal to be achieved by the services the mission assets executing tasks provide. The assets have the capacity (e.g., functionality such as training a model, predicting a result, and detecting intrusions) and vulnerabilities. Attackers can exploit the vulnerabilities to launch an attack on the assets, indirectly compromising the mission. We also have a *performer* in our mission in the form of defenders, whose goal is to provide defense mechanisms to protect the mission assets by mitigating their vulnerabilities.

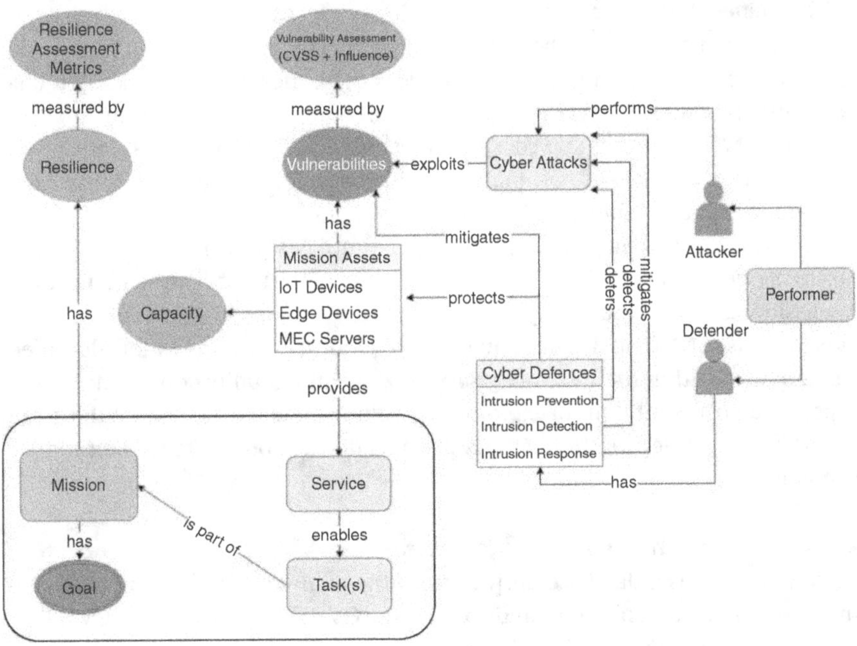

Figure 3.3 Concept model.

3.4.1.1.4 BPMN for a Mission System

With its extensive usage to model mission systems in previous works, BPMN has become the standard modeling notation. To model the process flow of our mission, we chose the BPMN [21]. BPMN has a simplistic notation system that makes it easier to model and understand the processes. The BPMN diagram helps the system designer as a blueprint for implementing the mission system. Figure 3.4 shows the BPMN for our object detection mission process.

3.4.1.2 Topology Discovery

Network topology discovery (NTD) is to find and map the devices in a system and their links. NTD is essential to monitor the network for normal functioning and failures. We can discover the network's topology using a preexisting KB that contains the information about the service hosted in the cyber assets, their logical and physical addresses, and the connections between these assets.

If a KB is not at our disposal, we can use NTD protocols, such as Simple Network Management Protocol (SNMP), Internet Control Message Protocol (ICMP) [22], or Link Layer Discovery Protocol (LLDP) [23]. SNMP-based discovery tools [24, 25] are majorly used in practice because most of the IT devices are SNMP enabled.

3.4.1.3 Vulnerability Discovery

VD in any system is a process that involves analyzing the devices within a network, as well as the software and hardware services they offer, to identify known disclosed vulnerabilities. VD is crucial for comprehending potential paths an attacker may take to infiltrate assets and compromise a mission. The VD process for a given mission system consists of two main steps: constructing a network model and aligning it with vulnerability databases.

Topological Vulnerability Analysis (TVA) [26] utilizes tools like Nessus [27] to acquire the network model and simultaneously scan for known vulnerabilities in the mission assets. Vulnerability databases, such as the NIST National Vulnerability Database (NVD) [28], are employed to obtain impact scores for identified vulnerabilities within the system. By scrutinizing vulnerability dependencies and the pre- and post-conditions of exploits, all potential attack paths within the given network are generated, outlining the routes an attacker could take to compromise the mission.

3.4.1.3.1 Common Vulnerability Scoring System

The NIST's NVD is a database derived from the analysis of vulnerability disclosures (Common Vulnerabilities and Exposures [CVEs]) reported in the CVE Dictionary. It assesses these vulnerabilities using the CVSS [29]. CVSS consists of three metric groups: Base, Temporal, and Environmental. The metrics in the Base Metric Group encompass features of a vulnerability that remain constant over time

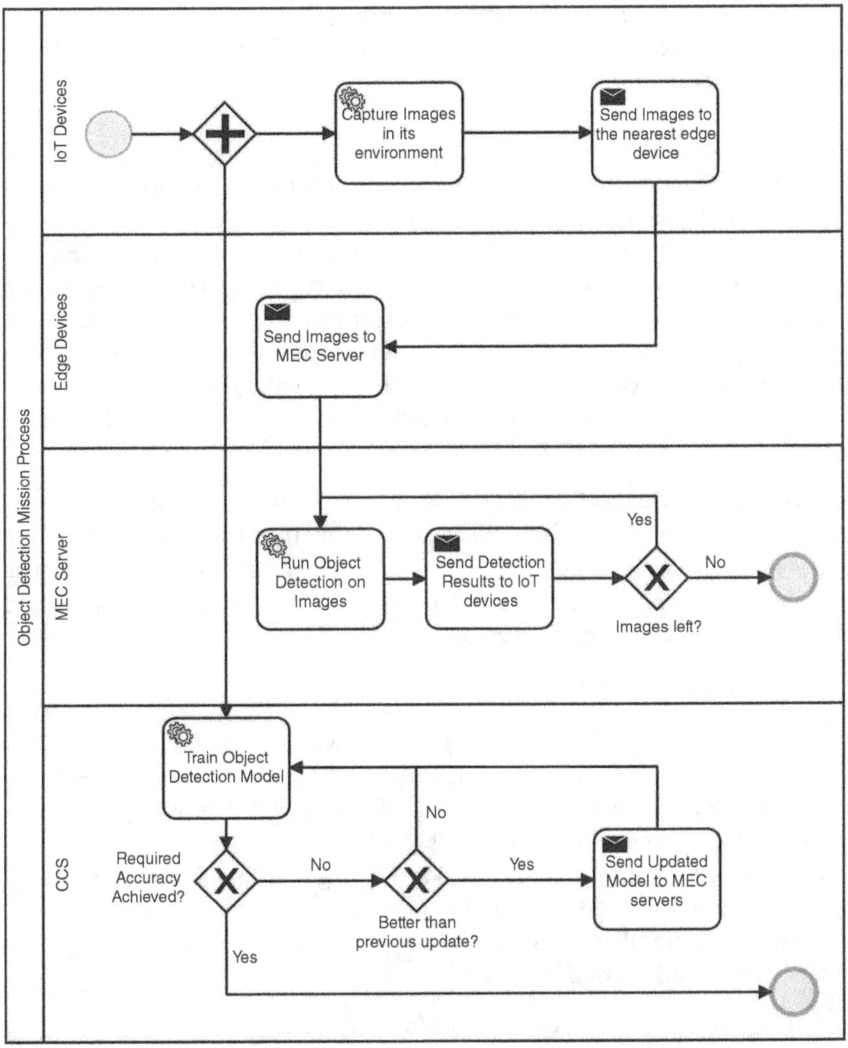

Figure 3.4 Business Process Model and Notation.

or in a particular environment. This group includes *Exploitability metrics*, describing the ease of performing an attack, and *Impact metrics*, detailing the consequences of a successful exploit. The Temporal Metric Group covers metrics reflecting the vulnerability's characteristics that change over time, typically diminishing after the vulnerabilities are patched. The Environmental Metrics Group outlines metrics describing the security controls required to mitigate some or all consequences of an attack, along with explaining the relative importance of the vulnerable system in its environment.

3.4.1.3.2 Influence Metric

When evaluating the vulnerability of nodes within a network, it is essential to consider the centrality of nodes. Centrality metrics have been proposed to gauge node influence in various scenarios [30]. Evaluating the algorithmic complexity (Big-O) and performance of each metric is crucial, particularly in terms of their impact as an attack targeting a node, measured by the network's connectivity, specifically the size of the giant component. A smaller giant component size signifies a higher impact of a centrality metric as a basis for targeting a victim node. Several promising centrality metrics for measuring node influence in a network are addressed as follows:

- **Eigenvector Centrality [31]:** Eigenvector centrality, also known as Bonacich's degree centrality, considers not only the centrality (degree) of a node but also its power. Nodes connected to other influential nodes receive higher scores than those connected to less influential ones. The computation of eigenvector centrality is given by:

$$\mathrm{EVC}(u) = \frac{1}{\lambda} \sum_{v \in N(u)} A_{uv}\, \mathrm{EVC}(v), \tag{3.1}$$

  where λ is the eigenvalue of the adjacency matrix A and $N(u)$ is the set of all neighbors of node u with an incoming edge toward it. The asymptotic complexity of the eigenvector centrality is $O(n^3)$ [30].
- **PageRank [32]:** The founders of Google, Sergey Brin and Lawrence Page, developed this metric. It is very similar to the eigenvector centrality in that it considers the number of inbound nodes as well as the corresponding importance. PageRank is computed by:

$$\mathrm{PR}\,(u, \alpha, \beta) = \alpha \sum_{v \in U, v \neq u} A_{vu} \frac{\mathrm{PR}(v, \alpha, \beta)}{\max(k_v^{\mathrm{out}}, 1)} + \beta \tag{3.2}$$

  where α is a damping factor that ensures that every node (even those with no incoming edges) obtains a PageRank value. The β is a free score that all nodes receive irrespective of their centrality, and k_v^{out} denotes the number of outgoing nodes from the node v.
- **Dynamic Influence [33]:** The Dynamic Influence centrality metric incorporates system dynamics and network structure to quantify a node's dynamic state, particularly its impact on diffusion processes like the spread of a computer virus. This metric considers a system with n time-dependent variables

$x = [x_1, x_2, \ldots, x_n]$, a corresponding $n \times n$ real linear dynamics matrix $\boldsymbol{M}$, and an update function $x' = \boldsymbol{M}x$. The largest eigenvalue $\mu_{\max}\boldsymbol{M}$ determines the dynamics classification. When $\mu_{\max}$ is negative, $x(t)$ converges to a fixed solution, growing indefinitely large when $\mu_{\max}$ is positive. Assuming a non-degenerate $\mu_{\max}$ for $\boldsymbol{M}$, the scalar product $\phi_c = c.x$ is a conserved quantity. Here, c is the left eigenvector of $\boldsymbol{M}$ for the eigenvalue $\mu_{\max}$. The final state can be computed from the initial state $x(0)$ as:

$$\mathrm{DI} = x(\infty) = \lim_{t \to \infty} x(t) = \frac{c.x(0)}{c.e} e, \tag{3.3}$$

where e refers to the right eigenvector of $\boldsymbol{M}$ for $\mu_{\max}$. We refer to c_i as the ith element's dynamical influence (DI) on the dynamics under equation. This equation implies that the $x(0)$'s projection onto c is all that the system considers about the initial state when deciding about the state $x(\infty)$.

3.4.1.4 Mission Monitoring

Mission monitoring is a technique to track physical assets in the mission remotely and the network using specialized technology and software. This technique is required for us to track the status of the assets in executing a mission in real time. We can use asset monitoring tools and software to obtain the status information of a given mission, such as whether the given mission asset is available and active without being compromised. System monitoring can be classified as network attack monitoring and asset monitoring.

3.4.1.4.1 Network Attack Monitoring

Network monitoring allows the system or the network administrator to determine if there is any malicious activity detected in a network. To this end, we will use a Network-based IDS (NIDS). An IDS is a monitoring system that can detect cyberattacks and generate alerts in real time for the administrator to take the necessary actions. We use a signature-based NIDS to monitor network attacks. NIDS can be strategically placed in the network to passively monitor the network traffic to match with predefined set of attack signatures. We assume that an NIDS is placed at each edge node to analyze the traffic flowing to and from its corresponding VLAN. We may consider NIDS tools, such as Snort [34], Zeek [35], or Suricata [36].

3.4.1.4.2 Asset Monitoring

Asset monitoring keeps track of the status of mission assets in terms of whether they are available and operating correctly. This monitoring status can ensure optimal mission performance and enable an administrator to take the necessary actions to keep the mission performance intact in the presence of expected or unforeseen events. For the IoT-based mission scenario, the IoT devices are already equipped with the necessary sensors to give real-time asset information to the administrator. For the other devices, such as the edge devices and the MEC servers, we can use tools based on the SNMP. SNMP helps discover the network topology and provides the functionality to probe the devices for information about their performance, availability, and status. The SNMP manager at the CCS can regularly poll the devices in the network for a status update. Moreover, the devices can also send unsolicited SNMP trap messages to the SNMP manager when a critical event is detected.

3.4.1.5 Game-theoretic Attack Behavior Modeling

We represent the interplay between the attacker and the defense as a two-player game in game theory. There is often ambiguity in real-world circumstances, and every participant has a unique viewpoint on the game. As a result, we choose to use hypergame theory to illustrate the attacker–defender game. (G, G_A, G_D) is the definition of a hypergame, where G is the real game, and G_A and G_D are the attacker's and defender's perceived games, respectively. The hypergame reduces to normal game theory when these three games, G, G_A, and G_D, coincide.

3.4.1.6 First-level Hypergame

The simplest case is where we have two players p and q with V_p and V_q as the actual preferences of players, respectively. For this case, the game can be defined as $G = \{V_p, V_q\}$. Although, in reality, this assumption might not be valid since each player p and q might have their view about the game and their own perceived preferences. For such a case, player p's game is based on the perception of q's preferences, V_{qp}, and player q's game is based on the perception of player p's perception, V_{pq}, as $G_p = \{V_{qp}\}$, $G_q = \{V_{pq}\}$, respectively. The First-level Hypergame can be formulated as:

$$H^1 = \{G_p, G_q\}. \tag{3.4}$$

3.4.1.7 Hypergame Normal Form

The Hypergame Normal Form (HNF) characterizes the hypergame by incorporating players' beliefs and opponent strategies, consisting of four key elements: Full Game, Row-mixed Strategies (RMSs), Column-mixed Strategies (CMSs), and belief contexts.

A **Full Game** is a matrix encompassing both row and column strategies along with their corresponding utilities, denoted as $ru_{11}, \ldots, ru_{mn}$ and $cu_{11}, \ldots, cu_{mn}$. The matrix U of dimensions $m \times n$ is represented as:

$$\mathbf{U} = \begin{pmatrix} (ru_{11}, cu_{11}) & \cdots (ru_{1n}, cu_{1n}) \\ \cdots & \cdots \cdots \\ (ru_{m1}, cu_{m1}) & \cdots (ru_{mn}, cu_{mn}) \end{pmatrix}. \tag{3.5}$$

The **RMSs** are strategies derived from how a row player perceives the strategies of a column player. As both players confine their strategy scope based on their perceptions, the subgame chosen by the row player, denoted as κ, results in RMSs within the subset κ":

$$\text{RMS}_\kappa = [r_{\kappa 1}, \dots, r_{\kappa m}], \qquad \text{where} \sum_{i=1}^{m} r_{\kappa i} = 1, \tag{3.6}$$

where each strategy i represents an estimate based on the row player's knowledge gained from prior experience. In any given subgame, the player selects one strategy to play. All the strategies not in the chosen subgame will have a zero probability (i.e., $r_{\kappa i} = 0$).

The CMSs are the strategies based on how a column player perceives a row player's strategies. Suppose the column player chooses to play a subgame κ, the CMSs of the subset κ are:

$$\text{CMS}_\kappa = [c_{\kappa 1}, \dots, c_{\kappa n}], \quad \text{where} \sum_{i=1}^{n} r_{\kappa i} = 1, \tag{3.7}$$

where each strategy i represents an estimate based on the column player's knowledge gained from prior experience. In any given subgame, the player selects one strategy to play. Even for the column player, similarly to RMSs, $c_{\kappa i} = 0$ if the strategy i is not a part of the subgame.

The action space for the attacker consists of all the attack strategies $A_{\text{actions}} = \{A_1, A_2, \dots, A_i\}$ and the action space for the defenders $D_{\text{actions}} = \{D_1, D_2, \dots, D_i\}$ are the set of their defense strategies against the specified attacks.

Belief contexts are the probabilities of each subgame κ being played based on the row player's belief.

$$P = [P_0, \dots, P_K], \quad \text{where} \sum_{\kappa=0}^{K} P_\kappa = 1, \quad \text{and } P_\kappa = \frac{\rho_\kappa}{\sum_{\kappa \in \mathbf{AT}} \rho_\kappa},$$

where P_0 is the probability of playing the full game, and for all other i's P_i is the probability of playing the ith subgame. **AT** is the set of attackers in the game, and ρ_κ is the number of attackers in the subgame κ. When the player is unsure about which subgame to play, it plays the full game.

The belief of the row player that the column player takes the strategy j is S_j, and it is given by:

$$S_j = \sum_{\kappa=0}^{K} P_\kappa c_{\kappa j}, \quad \text{where} \sum_{j=1}^{n} S_j = 1. \tag{3.8}$$

We denote $C_\Sigma = [S_1, S_2, \dots, S_n]$ by the set of row players beliefs that the column player takes all n strategies.

3.4.2 Hypergame Expected Utility

According to hypergame theory, the hypergame expected utility (HEU) guides each player's decisions. The expected utility EU(·) and perceived uncertainty g, which indicate the player's degree of ambiguity regarding their understanding of the game and their opponent's strategy, are used in the computation of HEU. The estimated perceived uncertainty of the player affects how they observe the opponent's actions. In this case, the attacker does not know the defender's strategy, and the defender does not know the attacker's plans or if an attack has been carried out. In the event that a player lacks assurance, g is set to 1, and in the case of complete certainty, it is set to 0 [37]. According to Vane [38], the HEU for a row player's strategy rs_i under a certain uncertainty g is computed.

$$\text{HEU}(rs_i, g) = (1 - g) \cdot \text{EU}(rs_i, C_\Sigma) + g \cdot \text{EU}(rs_i, \text{CMS}_w),$$

The expected utility of the row player in this scenario, when the column player chooses any of their tactics, is denoted as $\text{EU}(rs_i, C_\Sigma)$. Conversely, when the column player chooses the worst-case strategy—that is, the plan with the least utility versus the row player—$\text{EU}(rs_i, \text{CMS}_w)$ denotes the expected utility of the row player. In both definite and uncertain conditions, the row player's EU is calculated as follows:

$$\text{EU}(rs_i, C_\Sigma) = \sum_{j=1}^{n} S_j \cdot u_{ij}, \tag{3.9}$$

$$\text{EU}(rs_i, \text{CMS}_w) = n \cdot S_w \cdot u_{iw}. \tag{3.10}$$

The HEU value can take both positive and negative values. To normalize HEU to take a positive value between 1 and 10, we use the min–max normalization method [39].

We model the perceived uncertainties of the attacker and the defender in a subgame as the following:

$$g_t^A = e^{-\lambda t}, \quad g_t^D = e^{-\mu t}. \tag{3.11}$$

The value of these functions decreases as time t (the time for which the attacker and defender have monitored the target system) increases. In other words, the more time monitored, the more certain the attacker and the defender are about the system. In the above equations, λ and μ are parameters that control the attacker and the defender's risk-taking ability. The higher these values are, the more steeply the uncertainties of the attacker and the defender's perception decrease, meaning that the player's confidence increases initially.

In a hypergame, each player considers themselves a row player and the opponent a column player. The **utility** when a row player chooses a strategy p and the column player chooses the strategy q can be computed as the difference between the gain and the loss.

$$u_{pq} = G_{pq} - L_{pq}. \tag{3.12}$$

Since we model the hypergame as a zero-sum game, one player's gain is the opponent's loss, and one player's loss is the opponent's gain. The gain and loss can be calculated by:

$$G_{pq} = r_p^{\text{impact}} + c_q^{\text{cost}}, \qquad L_{pq} = r_p^{\text{cost}} + c_q^{\text{impact}}, \tag{3.13}$$

where r_p^{cost} and r_p^{impact} are the cost and impact, respectively, of the row players strategy p, and c_q^{cost} and c_q^{impact} are the cost and impact for the column players strategy q. In our case, we need to model the cost and effectiveness of the attacker's and the defender's strategies.

For the attacker strategies, we can use the prior information about the exploitability to model the cost and impact to model the effectiveness of the strategies. We can leverage the Exploitability Sub Score (ESS) and the Impact Sub Score (ISS) of the CVSS base metric of the reported vulnerabilities that correspond to a particular kind of attack to get an estimate of the cost and the effectiveness of the attack strategies.

Let $a_{p\alpha}^{\text{cost}}$ be the cost of the attacker for choosing a strategy p on an asset α. We model this by the sum of the ESS of all the reported vulnerabilities of the set $V_\alpha(p)$ for a given asset α that allows the attacker to perform a particular attack strategy p. The $a_{p\alpha}^{\text{cost}}$ can be computed by:

$$a_{p\alpha}^{\text{cost}} = \omega \times \left(\frac{\sum_{i \in V_\alpha(\mathbf{p})} \text{ESS}(i)}{||V_\alpha(p)||} \right) + (1-\omega) \times \delta_p, \tag{3.14}$$

where $V_\alpha(p)$ is the set of all the vulnerabilities of an asset α that allow the attacker to perform the attack strategy p. The δ_p refers to an extra cost for each attack strategy p based on prior knowledge about the attack complexity and other factors. The range of δ_p is expected to be [0–10]. The value δ_p is assigned by an expert for each attack, and it is the same for a given kind of attack p irrespective of the asset. ω is the hyperparameter that helps us perform the weighted average of the two terms to get a better estimate of the attack cost. The value of ω must be in the range [0,1].

The impact $a_{p\alpha}^{\text{impact}}$ of an attack strategy p on a particular asset α can be defined as the sum of ISS of all the reported vulnerabilities of the set $V_\alpha(p)$ for a given asset α that allows the attacker to perform an attack p. The $a_{p\alpha}^{\text{impact}}$ can be computed as:

$$a_{p\alpha}^{\text{impact}} = \omega \times \left(\frac{\sum_{i \in V_\alpha(p)} \text{ISS}(i)}{||V_\alpha(p)||} \right) + (1-\omega) \times \gamma_p, \tag{3.15}$$

where ω is the hyperparameter for weighted sum. γ_p refers to an extra impact for each attack strategy p based on the importance and centrality of the compromised nodes in the given network. The γ_p is modeled as the sum of the product of importance and centrality of each compromised node because of the attack strategy p divided by the total number of nodes in the network. For a given set of compromised nodes C_p because of the attack strategy p, the γ_p is given by:

$$\gamma_p = \frac{\sum_{\alpha \in C_p} \text{importance}_\alpha \times \text{centrality}_\alpha}{N}, \tag{3.16}$$

where C_p is the set of nodes compromised because of the attack p. The N is the total number of nodes in the network, and importance_α can be a predefined value at the beginning of our mission, representing how important the given asset is in completing a given mission. The centrality_α can be estimated by one of the centrality metrics defined in Section 3.4.1.3. Here, we assume γ_p is normalized to be in the range [0–10].

The **cost of the defense** mechanisms can be defined as an integer between [0 and 10], and this value can be assigned to the defense strategies based on the prior knowledge from the literature and experts about the complexity and the financial cost required to deploy and use a particular defense mechanism. We denote this defense cost by d_q^{cost} scaled in [1, 10] for each defense strategy q.

The **impact for the defense** for a given strategy q can be modeled as the failure of the corresponding attack strategy. This can be calculated as:

$$d_q^{\text{impact}} = 10 - a_{p\alpha}^{\text{impact}}, \tag{3.17}$$

where p is the strategy picked by the attacker and the defender, respectively, for an attack on an asset α.

When an attacker picks a strategy p and the defender picks a strategy q, the attackers utility u_{pq}^A can be computed as:

$$u_{pq}^A = G_{pq}^A - L_{pq}^A,\ G_{pq}^A = a_p^{\text{impact}} + d_q^{\text{cost}},\ L_{pq}^A = a_p^{\text{cost}} + d_q^{\text{impact}}. \tag{3.18}$$

Similarly, the utility for the defender u_{qp}^{D} in this case can be computed as:

$$u_{qp}^{D} = G_{qp}^{D} - L_{qp}^{D},\ G_{qp}^{D} = d_{q}^{\text{impact}} + a_{p}^{\text{cost}},\ L_{qp}^{D} = d_{q}^{\text{cost}} + a_{p}^{\text{impact}}. \tag{3.19}$$

From Eqs. (3.18) and (3.19), we can clearly see that $u_{pq}^{A} + u_{qp}^{D} = 0$. This means that the game between the attacker and the defender is a zero-sum game.

In a given subgame κ, the **Belief Calibration** can be computed based on the frequency of the strategies taken in the past. At the beginning of a subgame, both the players make random decisions. However, as time progresses, the players have a more shaped probability distribution to choose their actions. The probability of row player choosing a strategy p in a subgame κ at t is denoted as $r_{\kappa p}^{t}$ and the column player choosing a strategy q at the same time t in the same subgame κ as $c_{\kappa q}^{t}$. The $r_{\kappa p}^{t}$ and $c_{\kappa q}^{t}$ can be estimated by modeling them as a Dirichlet distribution by:

$$r_{\kappa p}^{t} = \frac{\gamma_{\kappa p}^{t}}{\sum_{p \in \mathbf{RS}_{\kappa}} \gamma_{p}^{t}},\quad c_{\kappa q}^{t} = \frac{\gamma_{\kappa q}^{t}}{\sum_{q \in \mathbf{CS}_{\kappa}} \gamma_{q}^{t}}, \tag{3.20}$$

where $\mathbf{RS}_{\kappa}$ and $\mathbf{CS}_{\kappa}$ are the set of row and column player's strategies, respectively. At a time t, γ_{p}^{t} and γ_{q}^{t} represent the cumulative amount of evidence both the players gathered in the time interval $[0 - (t - 1)]$.

Hence, in a subgame at a time t, for every player i who chooses a strategy p, HEU can be computed by:

$$\text{HEU}(rs_{ip}) = \text{HEU}(p, g_{i}^{t}), \tag{3.21}$$

where g_{i}^{t} is player i's uncertainty at time t.

3.4.2.1 Reasoning Model Generation

Impact dependency graph: In this section, we propose how we infer the mission resilience impact on the mission system. To achieve this, we need to model the mission as an IDG. We then use the IDG to propagate the belief using the SBN. For the IoT-device-based object detection mission system, the IDG is demonstrated in Figure 3.5.

SBNs-based inference: Our SBN-based impact inference extends the current framework for probabilistic models called *UnBBayes* [40]. To employ SBN-based inference on the IDG, we apply mapping between binomial opinions and the Beta distribution, stochastic simulation (SS), junction tree (JT), and BP. We discuss each technique in detail as follows.

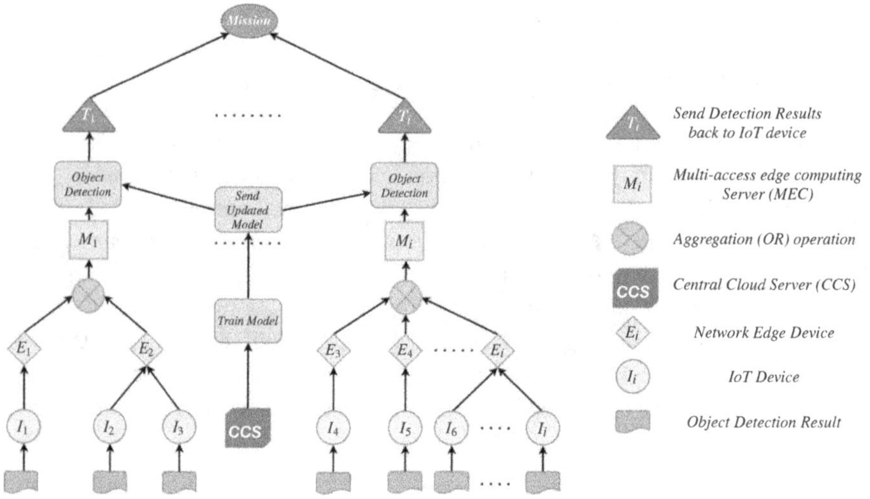

Figure 3.5 Impact dependency graph.

3.4.2.1.1 Mapping Between a Binomial Opinion and a Beta Probability Density Function (PDF) [41]

In the context of SL, $\omega = b, d, u, \boldsymbol{a}$ denotes a binomial opinion related to a specific random variable, such as whether an asset is compromised or not. This binomial opinion comprises four components: b for belief mass, d for disbelief mass, u for uncertainty mass, and $\boldsymbol{a}$ for the prior over the belief and disbelief masses. It is essential to note that the sum of belief, disbelief, and uncertainty masses must equal 1, represented as $b + d + u = 1$. The assignment of values to the binomial opinion arguments b, d, and u is achieved by mapping evidence in the following manner:

$$b = \frac{r}{r + s + W}, \quad d = \frac{s}{r + s + W}, \quad u = \frac{W}{r + s + W}, \tag{3.22}$$

where r, s, and W denote the amount of positive, negative, and uncertain evidence, respectively. Since the binomial opinion follows Beta distribution, α, β, and the expected probability, $E(X)$, can be obtained as follows:

$$\alpha = r + aW, \quad \beta = s + (1 - a)W, \quad E(X) = \frac{r + aW}{r + s + W}. \tag{3.23}$$

Given a binomial opinion, ω, we can obtain the projected probability of supporting X or not supporting X (i.e., $\overline{X}$) by:

$$P_X = b + u \cdot a, \quad P_{\overline{X}} = d + u \cdot (1 - a). \tag{3.24}$$

Utilizing binomial opinions derived from historical data or expertise of domain specialists, a bijective mapping rule is employed to establish a connection between a binomial opinion and a Beta Probability Density Function (PDF). This mapping allows the transformation of binomial opinions into the parameters of the Beta distribution, denoted as α and β. When the posterior Beta distribution is transformed into a posterior opinion after aggregating all sampled BNs – obtaining the mean and variance of the posterior probability for a representative BN – the same bijective mapping rule is applied to convert the Beta distribution back into the form of a binomial opinion. It is important to note that in this process, we assume the default non-informative prior weight W is set to 2. This assumption is made to ensure that a vacuous opinion aligns with a uniform Beta PDF.

The opinion ω_x and the Beta PDF $Beta^e(p_x, r_x, s_x, a_x)$ can be mapped to each other using the following mapping rule. The bijective mapping is defined as:

$$\begin{cases} b_x = \dfrac{r_x}{W + r_x + s_x}, \\ d_x = \dfrac{s_x}{W + r_x + s_x}, \\ u_x = \dfrac{W}{W + r_x + s_x} \end{cases} \Leftrightarrow \begin{cases} \text{For } u_x \neq 0: & \begin{cases} r_x = \dfrac{b_x W}{u_x}, \\ s_x = \dfrac{d_x W}{u_x}, \\ 1 = b_x + d_x + u_x \end{cases} \\ \text{For } u_x = 0: & \begin{cases} r_x = b_x \cdot \infty, \\ s_x = d_x \cdot \infty, \\ 1 = b_x + d_x \end{cases} \end{cases}. \tag{3.25}$$

3.4.2.1.2 Stochastic Simulation [42]

Upon converting a binomial opinion into the parameters of the Beta distribution (α, β), these parameters are used as inputs to sample a Beta distribution, thereby generating a BN with conditional probability tables. Subsequently, the JT and BP methods are applied to derive the posterior probability or belief for each sampled BN. This simulation process is iteratively executed until a representative sample BN is attained through aggregating the mean and variance of posterior probabilities from numerous rounds of simulations.

3.4.2.1.3 Junction Tree

Junction tree (JT) [43] generalizes the BP algorithm to a non-tree structure. A clique is a subset of vertices of an undirected graph, such as Markov Random Field (MRF), such that every two distinct vertices in the clique are adjacent. JT is designed to eliminate cycles to output a tree with no cycle. With JT, we can convert a non-tree structure into a tree-like structure, and message passing protocol can then be performed on the JT. The first step in constructing a JT is to connect nodes with common children and make the network an undirected tree. Second, the variable elimination (VE) algorithm [44] adds fill-in edges based on elimination to generate a triangulated graph such that each clique in the original non-tree network is transformed into a single cluster node in a JT. Until this point, we generated the so-called *junction graph* (JG). After that, we build a maximum-weight spanning tree to have a JT. Based on the JT, BP is performed for the inference of random variables. BP calculates the marginal distribution for each unobserved node (i.e., dependent or outcome variable) conditional on any observed nodes (i.e., independent or predictor variables). A JT has three properties: (1) There must be exactly one unique path between each pair of clusters; (2) For every clique in an original network, there is some cluster (i.e., variables clustered into a single node after VE) in the JT, such that some cluster in the JT contains a clique from the original network; and (3) If two clusters (i.e., a set of variables in a single node), for instance, B and C, contain variable i in common, each cluster on the unique path between B and C should also contain variable i.

3.4.2.1.4 Belief Propagation in JT

We employ belief propagation (BP) for inference once the JT [45] is created using a series of steps described in Section 3.4.2.1.3. BP in the JT is similar to that for trees, except that each node in trees, in general, corresponds to a variable, while one node contains a set of variables in a JT. Each edge in the JT corresponds to some subset of variables that the two nodes share in common. In this conceptual work, we use the *Hugin algorithm* [46], which is the updating form of a belief, which refers to the posterior probability based on new observations.

To exchange messages between nodes, *Hugin algorithm* collects and distributes evidences. For instance, the root node V requests all its neighbors to send it a message (i.e., evidence). If they are not permitted to do so, they keep asking all neighbors for a message except the one from which the request came. After then, V sends messages to all its neighbors, who keep sending messages to all neighbors except the one from which the message came. Rules to follow in the Hugin algorithm can be summarized as follows [47]:

- The root node initiates the message-sending process to its neighbors only after it has received messages from all of them.
- Each non-root node sends its message to a specific neighbor only after receiving messages from all of its neighbors.
- Upon readiness to send a message to a particular neighbor, a node calculates the message by marginalizing its current potential with the intersection of this potential with the neighbor's and subsequently transmits the message to the separator between them.

- Upon receiving a message (denoted as B) from one of its two nodes, a separator divides the message by its existing potential (denoted as A), sends the quotient $\frac{B}{A}$ to the other node, and updates A with B.
- When a node receives a message, it replaces its current potential with the product of the potential and the received message.

By performing evidence collection, which is followed by distribution, all messages are passed; thus, belief is updated based on the rules. ψ_f is referred to as the initial potentials at the clique nodes. At the end of the propagation, the potentials on all the nodes (i.e., a set of all cliques), F(T), and separators, S(T), are marginals of the posterior joint P $\propto \otimes\psi_f$. Given F(T) and S(T) in the JT, at any step in the BP, the following expression should be met:

$$\mathrm{P} \propto \frac{\left(\otimes_{\mathrm{f} \in \mathrm{F(T)}} \psi_{\mathrm{f}}\right)}{\left(\otimes_{\mathrm{s} \in \mathrm{S(T)}} \psi_{\mathrm{f}}\right)}. \tag{3.26}$$

3.4.2.1.5 Practical Implementation Guidance

This chapter introduces a systematic and formalized framework for modeling cyber mission resilience using SBNs. While real-world validation is not included at this stage, the chapter aims to establish the theoretical foundation necessary for future empirical deployment. Although CYBER-MIRA is currently presented as a conceptual framework, its design is intended to support future operational deployment. To assist organizations and practitioners in integrating CYBER-MIRA into real-world systems, we provide a set of initial implementation guidelines:

- **Integration with system design:** CYBER-MIRA can be embedded into early system design phases by modeling mission assets and their interdependencies using the proposed concept model and BPMN. These models enable structured identification of vulnerabilities and system dynamics, supporting risk-aware architecture planning.
- **Tool compatibility:** The framework's modular design allows alignment with widely used cybersecurity assessment tools, such as Nessus for vulnerability scanning, Snort or Suricata for intrusion detection, and CVSS databases for modeling exploitability. These tools can provide the inputs necessary for instantiating CYBER-MIRA's reasoning engine.
- **Reasoning under uncertainty:** By using SBNs, the framework supports decision-making in the presence of uncertain or incomplete information, which is common in mission-critical and tactical environments. This enables a more robust assessment of mission resilience over time.
- **Organizational use cases:** CYBER-MIRA is particularly suited for military, defense, and critical infrastructure organizations operating distributed,

IoT-based mission systems in adversarial environments. For example, tactical object detection missions using edge computing and MEC servers can leverage CYBER-MIRA to assess resilience under cyber threats by modeling interdependencies, propagating risk through SBNs, and capturing attacker–defender dynamics via hypergame theory. The framework is also applicable to cybersecurity agencies and tool developers seeking to integrate mission-level resilience metrics into intrusion detection, vulnerability analysis, and system monitoring platforms.

The framework contributes to the development of autonomous resilience by enabling adaptive reasoning under uncertainty, modeling intelligent attack–defense interactions through hypergame theory, and integrating resilience metrics such as adaptability, recoverability, and transformability.

3.4.3 Resilience Assessment as a Measure of Performance

To assess a system's resilience, which refers to its ability to predict, absorb, and adapt to disruptions, we choose the following metrics: *fault tolerance, adaptability, recoverability* [17], and *transformability*. Each metric attribute is described in detail as follows.

3.4.3.1 Fault Tolerance

Fault Tolerance is a measure of the system's ability to be functional and provide normal services in the presence of threats (attacks and failures). This can be measured as a function of robustness and the diversity of the system as follows:

- **Robustness:** Robustness is the ability of a system to be robust and healthy. It can be classified into survivability and reliability.
  - **Survivability:** Survivability measures how long a system can function normally in the presence of threats. It can be measured using the Mean Time to Failure (MTTF) metric [48]. MTTF is the time that the system takes to reach a failure state based on the amount of system functional entities. However, this can be variable based on the type and intensity of the threat. The percolation threshold [49] is another metric to measure the survivability of a mission system. It is defined as the proportion of nodes that may be nonfunctional without a network failure.
  - **Service reliability:** A system's ability to deliver proper services without delays and hiccups is referred to as service reliability. Some of the metrics that can measure reliability are service failure frequency and response time of the services. Service failure frequency measures the amount of instances where the expected standard is not achieved by a service. Response time of a service measures the speed with which a desired service is provided.

Network delay, algorithmic complexity in software, and hardware capacity all have an impact on this.

- **Diversity:** Diversity measures the degree of variance in system components and security procedures.
  - **Diversity in system components:** Multiple devices in a system running the same software and hardware components could lead to massive damage. When an attacker infiltrates one system, he can easily propagate through the network and compromise other similar devices. Hence, it is vital to measure the diversity in system components. This is achieved by counting the number of different software and hardware component versions enabling the same service and the degree of similarity between them.
  - **Diversity in security mechanisms:** Various security mechanisms could increase the likelihood of a threat being detected and mitigated. Measuring the diversity of security mechanisms can be a good indicator of the system's fault tolerance.
  - **Redundancy of same functionalities:** Having redundancy of the same system component functionalities in various forms can increase a system's reliability and fault tolerance [50].

3.4.3.2 Adaptability

Adaptability is a system's ability to reconfigure itself to ensure providing normal services in the presence of threats or changes in the environment. This can be measured as a function of the Autonomy, Learnability, and Reconfigurability of a system.

- **Autonomy:** Autonomy is defined as a system's ability to function well under uncertainty without any external intervention. This can be measured by the degree of local decisions, the degree of intelligent decisions, and the degree of automation in the system.
  - **Degree of local decisions:** The extent to which an entity can make decisions based on local information without needing centralized decision-making is a good measure of autonomy [50].
  - **Degree of intelligent decisions:** This metric refers to the ability of a system to make rational decisions to maximize the system's efficacy and ensure the mission's success.
  - **Degree of automation:** The extent to which a system can make decisions without human intervention can measure the autonomy of a system.
- **Learnability:** This metric is defined by a system's ability to learn from past performance to make better decisions to improve the present performance. It can be measured as a function of learning defense strength, attack patterns, and system vulnerabilities.

- **Learning defense strength:** This can be measured based on the efficiency of the defense systems as well as the cost of employing them. A way to study the effectiveness of the defenses would be to count the ratio or the number of uncompromised nodes in the system. The cost of the defense can be the financial cost or the time and resources required to employ the defense.
- **Learning attack patterns:** Attack patterns include the tactics, intent, types, cost, and power of an attack. Attack tactics are the strategies the attacker uses to breach the system by evading defenses. The attacker's intent refers to the attacker's ultimate goal. Studying this would help us understand the key targets and help us better defend them. The attacker can perform different attacks, each having a different cost, which can be measured by the time, resources, and financial cost required to perform the attack. Attack power is the ability of an attacker to exploit the system and achieve his ultimate goal.
- **Learning system vulnerabilities:** Identifying known and exploited vulnerabilities in various system components helps us understand the risk and their impact.

- **Reconfigurability:** This metric measures the ability of a system to reconfigure to a state and to provide expected functionalities in terms of changes in the environment and threats. This can be obtained by:
  - **Reconfigurability delay:** Measures the time it takes for a system to achieve a state reconfiguration and gives an estimate of the Reconfigurability of a system.
  - **Accuracy of reconfiguration:** Estimates the performance and reliability of the reconfigured state of the system.
  - **Flexibility of reconfiguration:** Estimates the availability of alternate states to reconfigure to provide normal functionality in the presence of threats.

3.4.3.3 Recoverability

A system's recoverability refers to its ability of recovering from failure(s) and quickly returning back to its normal state that can provide the normal services. This can be measured by the following metrics:

- **Recovery delay:** This metric estimates the time a system takes to go from a failure state to a normal functioning state and can be obtained by:
  - **Mean Time to Full Recovery (MTTFR):** This metric calibrates the time a system takes from the moment it starts degrading from its normal functioning state to when it fully recovers back to its normal functioning state. Hence, this metric measures the time the system does not stay in the normal functioning state.

  - **Mean Time Between Failures (MTBF):** This metric estimates the amount of time elapsed the system has not been in a failure state divided by the total number of failures.
  - **Mean Time to Repair (MTTR):** This metric refers to the average time a system goes from a failure state to a fully functioning normal state. This metric represents a direct estimate of the system's recovery delay.
- **Recovery effectiveness:** This metric indicates how much the system has recovered back to a normal state, which is commonly measured by the following indicators:
  - **Degree of recovery from system degradation:** This metric refers to the difference between the system's functionality when it starts degrading and its current functionality at a given time t.
  - **Degree of recovery from system failure:** This metric estimates the difference between the system's functionality when it goes to failure based on a system failure threshold to the system's current functionality at a time t.
  - **Resilience curve:** The resilience curve evaluates the system's best possible performance as a function of the disruption in the worst-case loss scenario (e.g., multiple components simultaneously degrading or failing) [51].
- **Recovery cost:** This cost metric refers to the cost for a system to recover from a failure state to its normal functioning state and can be measured by the following:
  - **Intrusion response cost:** This metric estimates the response cost to a detected attack. For example, rekeying cost can be measured by the communication and computation cost to change an encryption key. Patching costs for known vulnerabilities can be estimated by the communication cost to disseminate the patches.
  - **Replacement cost:** This metric can include financial cost, time, and the complexity of replacing the damaged or affected hardware and software.
  - **Cost for physical storage repair:** This measures the cost of repairing or replacing damaged physical infrastructure in a system.
  - **Cost for user training:** This estimates the cost of providing cybersecurity training to users, such as the security and reconfiguration of the system software or hardware after the recovery and replacement.

3.4.3.4 Transformability

Transformability is a system's ability to learn and perform better than before after the attack or system failure. This can be measured as a function of the transformation's effectiveness and cost.

- **Transformation effectiveness:**
  - **Degree of trasformation:** This captures the difference between the system's current resilience and the system's resilience before the previous attack.
  - **Failure frequency:** This is computed by the number of times the system goes into a failure state divided by the total elapsed time. When the system becomes more resilient due to a transformation, the failure frequency should also naturally reduce.
  - **Total system vulnerability score difference:** This metric obtains the change in the total system vulnerability score according to the vulnerability score in the CVSS before and after the transformation. This is designed to measure the effectiveness of the transformation after the threat occurred in the system.
- **Transformation cost:** This gives the cost (e.g., time and financial cost) required to transform the system configuration or take the necessary intrusion response steps after the attack to achieve better resilience than before the attack.
- **Transformability score:** This metric can be measured by the transformation effectiveness divided by the transformation cost. The higher the transformability score, the better the transformation.

3.5 Limitations

This chapter proposes a conceptual CYBER-MIRA Framework that focuses primarily on the resilience perspective of the mission system. Although this chapter discusses all the critical components of the framework and how they work together, we plan to implement it and test it on an IoT device-based object detection environmental setup. The concept model proposed in this chapter is mainly used to understand the mission system from a resilience perspective. With some modifications, we can include other metrics, such as agility, trust, and security [17]. This chapter is the preliminary effort toward designing a robust interdependent mission impact assessment (iMIA) framework that overcomes all these limitations.

3.6 Conclusion and Future Work

3.6.1 Summary of the Key Contributions

We proposed the CYBER-MIRA framework, aiming to assess the cyber resilience impact of a mission system in real time in the presence of cyber threats, where the system has defense mechanisms in place. With the help of various modeling tools, we can understand our mission scenario and the details of the mission process. Hypergame-theoretic modeling of the enemy behavior allows us to incorporate the uncertainty in the attacker's and the defender's beliefs while choosing the optimal strategies at each step of the mission. Using the cyber resilience metrics, including fault tolerance, recoverability, adaptability, and transformability, we can analyze the resilience of a mission system in real time. We use the SBN to propagate the uncertainty-aware belief through the IDG defined to understand the resilience impact of the system in the presence of uncertainty.

3.6.2 Future Work

This chapter primarily focuses on the resilience aspect of a mission scenario. We plan to extend the MIA that considers other security aspects, such as Security, Trust, and Agility, in our ongoing iMIA Framework development. Moreover, we plan to implement and experiment with the conceptual CYBER-MIRA framework on an IoT-based object detection mission system experimental setup. Furthermore, we would like to extend the reasoning model to include the trust aspect between the nodes by combining the SBNs-based reasoning with the Subjective Trust Networks (STNs). Lastly, we will implement the iMIA framework and evaluate its performance compared to other counterparts, such as Cyber-ARGUS [10].

References

1 A. JØsang and L. Kaplan. Principles of subjective networks. In *2016 19th International Conference on Information Fusion (FUSION)*, pp. 1292–1299. IEEE, 2016.

2 C. J. Alberts, S. G. Behrens, R. D. Pethia, and W. R. Wilson. Operationally critical threat, asset, and vulnerability evaluation (OCTAVE) framework, version 1.0. Pittsburg, PA: Carnegie-Mellon University, Software Engineering Institute, Technical Report, 1999.

3 S. Noel, J. Ludwig, P. Jain, D. Johnson, R. K. Thomas, J. McFarland, B. King, S. Webster, and B. Tello. Analyzing mission impacts of cyber actions (AMICA). In *NATO IST-128 Workshop on Cyber Attack Detection, Forensics and Attribution for Assessment of Mission Impact*, 2015.

4 The MITRE Corporation. *Cyber command system (CyCS)*. [Online], (2015). Available: http://www.mitre.org/research/technology-transfer/technology-licensing/cyber-command-system-cycs

5 T. Moye, R. Sawilla, R. Sullivan, and P. Lagadec. Cyber defence situational awareness demonstration/request for information (RFI) from industry and government (co-14068-mncd2). *NCI Agency Acquisition*, 2015.

6 S. Musman, M. Tanner, A. Temin, E. Elsaesser, and L. Loren. Computing the impact of cyber attacks on complex missions. In *2011 IEEE International Systems Conference*, pp. 46–51. IEEE, 2011.

7 S. Musman and A. Temin. A cyber mission impact assessment tool. In *2015 IEEE International Symposium on Technologies for Homeland Security (HST)*, pp. 1–7, 2015.

8 J. Komárková, M. Husák, M. Laštovička, and D. Tovarňák. CRUSOE: Data model for cyber situational awareness. In *Proceedings of the 13th International Conference on Availability, Reliability and Security*, pp. 1–10, 2018.

9 A. Barreto, P. C. G. Costa, and E. T. Yano. A semantic approach to evaluate the impact of cyber actions on the physical domain. In *7th International Conference on Semantic Technologies for Intelligence, Defense, and Security (STIDS 2012). CEUR-WS. org*, 2012.

10 A. B. Barreto and P. C. Costa. Cyber-ARGUS - a mission assurance framework. *Journal of Network and Computer Applications*, 133: 86–108, 2019.

11 B. Whiteman. Network risk assessment tool (NRAT). *IAnewsletter*, 11: 4–8, 2008.

12 D. L. Buckshaw, G. S. Parnell, W. L. Unkenholz, D. L. Parks, J. M. Wallner, and O. S. Saydjari. Mission oriented risk and design analysis of critical information systems. *Military Operations Research*, 2: 19–38, 2005.

13 E. LeMay, M. D. Ford, K. Keefe, W. H. Sanders, and C. Muehrcke. Model-based security metrics using adversary view security evaluation (ADVISE). In *2011 Eighth International Conference on Quantitative Evaluation of Systems (QEST)*, pp. 191–200, 2011.

14 D. C. Daniels, L. D. Hudson, K. B. Laskey, S. M. Mahoney, B. S. Ware, and E. J. Wright. Terrorism risk management. In *Bayesian Networks: A Practical Guide to Applications*, pp. 239–262, 2008. https://onlinelibrary.wiley.com/doi/book/10.1002/9780470994559

15 S. Musman, A. Temin, M. Tanner, D. Fox, and B. Pridemore. Evaluating the impact of cyber attacks on missions. MITRE Corporation, Technical Report, 2010.

16 S. Musman, M. Tanner, A. Temin, E. Elsaesser, and L. Loren. A systems engineering approach for crown jewels estimation and mission assurance decision making. In *IEEE Symposium on Computational Intelligence in Cyber Security (CICS)*, 2011.

17 J.-H. Cho, S. Xu, P. M. Hurley, M. Mackay, T. Benjamin, and M. Beaumont. STRAM: Measuring the trustworthiness of computer-based systems. *ACM Computing Surveys*, 51(6): 1–47, 2019. https://doi.org/10.1145/3277666

18 A. K. Ligo, A. Kott, and I. Linkov. How to measure cyber-resilience of a system with autonomous agents: Approaches and challenges. *IEEE Engineering Management Review*, 49(2): 89–97, 2021.

19 T. Llanso and M. Mcneil. Towards an organizationally-relevant quantification of cyber resilience In *Proceedings of the 54th Hawaii International Conference on System Sciences (HICSS-54)*, pp. 7065–7074, 2021.

20 D. Eisenberg, K. Plourde, T. Seager, J. Allen, and A. Kott. Resilience metrics for cyber systems. *Environment Systems and Decisions*, 33: 471–476, 2013.

21 J. Roj and M. Owen. BPMN and business process management. *Popkin Software*, 2003.

22 H. Yan. The study on network topology discovery algorithm based on SNMP protocol and ICMP protocol. In *2012 IEEE International Conference on Computer Science and Automation Engineering*, pp. 665–668, 2012.

23 V. Z. Attar and P. Chandwadkar. Network discovery protocol LLDP and LLDP-MED. *International Journal of Computer Applications*, 1(9): 93–97, 2010.

24 SNMP Monitor. https://www.paessler.com/snmp_monitor.

25 Data dog SNMP monitoring. https://www.datadoghq.com/dg/monitor/snmp/.

26 S. Jajodia and S. Noel. *Topological Vulnerability Analysis*, pp. 139–154. Boston, MA: Springer US, 2010.

27 Nessus. https://www.tenable.com/products/nessus.

28 Nist, National Vulnerability Database (NVD). https://nvd.nist.gov/.

29 CVSS. *Common vulnerability scoring system* [Online], (2015). Available: https://www.first.org/cvss/specification-document.

30 Z. Wan, Y. Mahajan, B. W. Kang, T. J. Moore, and J.-H. Cho. A survey on centrality metrics and their network resilience analysis. *IEEE Access*, 9: 104773–104819, 2021.

31 P. Bonacich. Factoring and weighting approaches to status scores and clique identification. *Journal of Mathematical Sociology*, 2(1): 113–120, 1972.

32 S. Brin and L. Page. The anatomy of a large-scale hypertextual web search engine. *Computer Networks and ISDN Systems*, 30(1–7): 107–117, 1998.

33 K. Klemm, M. Serrano, V. M. Eguíluz, and M. S. Miguel. A measure of individual role in collective dynamics. *Scientific Reports*, 2(1): 1–8, 2012.

34 Snort. https://www.snort.org/.

35 Zeek. https://zeek.org/.

36 Suricata. https://suricata.io/.

37 R. Vane. Advances in hypergame theory. In *Proceedings AAMAS Workshop on Game-Theoretic and Decision Theoretic Agents*, 2006.

38 R. R. Vane. Hypergame theory for DTGT agents. In *American Association for Artificial Intelligence*, 2000.

39 J. Han, J. Pei, and M. Kamber. *Data Mining: Concepts and Techniques*. Elsevier, 2011.

40 S. Matsumoto, R. N. Carvalho, M. Ladeira, P. C. Costa, L. L. Santos, D. Silva, M. Onishi, E. Machado, and K. Cai. Unbbayes: A java framework for probabilistic models in AI. In *Java in Academia and Research*, p. 34, Australia: iConcept Press, 2011.

41 A. JØsang. *Subjective Logic: A Formalism for Reasoning Under Uncertainty*. Springer, 2016.

42 E. Zio. Monte carlo simulation: The method. In *The Monte Carlo Simulation Method for System Reliability and Risk Analysis*, pp. 19–58. Springer, 2013.

43 D. Kahle, T. Savitsky, S. Schnelle, and V. Cevher. Junction tree algorithm. *Statistics*, 631, 2008.

44 N. L. Zhang and D. Poole. A simple approach to bayesian network computations. In *Proceeding of the Tenth Canadian Conference on Artificial Intelligence*, 1994.

45 K. P. Murphy. *Machine Learning: A Probabilistic Perspective*. MIT press, 2012.

46 S. K. Andersen, K. G. Olesen, F. V. Jensen, and F. Jensen. Hugin-a shell for building bayesian belief universes for expert systems. In *International Joint Conference on Artificial Intelligence (IJCAI)*, vol. 89, pp. 1080–1085, 1989.

47 G. Shafer. *Probabilistic Expert Systems*. SIAM, 1996.

48 J.-H. Cho. Tradeoffs between trust and survivability for mission effectiveness in tactical networks. *IEEE Transactions on Cybernetics*, 45(4): 754–766, 2015.

49 A. Barabási. Network robustness. In *Network Science*, pp. 270–319. Cambridge: Cambridge University Press, 2016.

50 R. Dove. Fundamental principles for agile systems engineering. In *Conference on Systems Engineering Research (CSER)*. Hoboken, NJ: Stevens Institute of Technology, 2005.

51 D. L. Alderson, G. G. Brown, W. M. Carlyle, and L. A. Cox Jr. Sometimes there is no "most-vital" arc: Assessing and improving the operational resilience of systems. *Military Operations Research*, 18(1): 21–37, 2013.

4

Modeling Autonomous Network Resilience in Adversarial Environments Using Machine Learning and Topological Data Analysis

*Nandi O. Leslie**

Raytheon, RTX, Arlington, VA, USA

*Corresponding Author: nandi.o.leslie@rtx.com

4.1 Introduction

It has become increasingly difficult to structure impenetrable computer networks and quickly repair them from cyberattacks and the resulting failures. In many cases, networked devices (e.g., mobile phones, laptops, autonomous vehicles) are vulnerable because it is challenging to monitor dynamic attack surfaces and thwart adaptive attack types (e.g., botnets, data exfiltration). Moreover, network monitoring can be further complicated by factors, such as autonomously generated attacks that leverage adversarial machine learning techniques, including poisoning and evasion attacks, and advanced persistent threats (APT) that may collaborate in adversarial coalitions and remain undetected for extended periods of time [1, 2]. An additional challenge is that disruptions to network functionality can persist for long periods of time (e.g., several weeks to months) following an attack or network failures until their initial detection by automated network intrusion tools. Network resilience modeling approaches that examine these phenomena fall into three phases: the avoidance phase explores the proactive measures; the survival phase provides information for corrective measures; and the recovery phase examines restorative measures [3]. Despite the growing body of literature in these areas, challenges increasingly impact the resilience of a variety of network types in each of these phases [3].

Traditionally, network monitoring has been performed with signature-based solutions, such as signature-based intrusion detection systems (IDS), endpoint detection and response (EDR), and security information and event management

(SIEM) solutions, each of which suffers from high false-negative rates. These solutions are still often used instead of anomaly-based approaches for IDS, EDR, SIEM, and extended detection and response (XDR) systems, which leverage probabilistic and/or artificial intelligence (AI)-based modeling techniques to monitor network traffic and recover from cyberattacks. Certainly, it is well known that machine learning algorithms can play a crucial role in monitoring a network and detecting attacks, yet they are less prevalent than other probability-based approaches and signature-based systems (e.g., IDS, SIEM) [4–6]. In either case, anomaly-based machine learning systems tend to have high false alarm rates [4, 5].

It is reasonable to study whether there are network topologies that are more resilient to attacks than others. Recently, topological data analysis (TDA) has emerged to understand how various types of attacks impact network resilience and robustness [7–9]. These studies characterize networks as weighted graphs, extract simplicial complexes, and present topological summaries of the simplices to describe network vulnerability [7–9].

In this chapter, I explore the role of machine learning and TDA in modeling and assessing autonomous network resilience problems during the avoidance and survival phases. I explore both supervised and unsupervised learning approaches for intrusion detection and autonomous network resilience modeling, and I consider TDA in the interest of understanding the impact of the adaptive shape of networks on cybersecurity and measuring resilience. Anomaly-based IDS/EDR are powerful tools for monitoring networks to detect cyberattacks [4]. These approaches have the capacity to distinguish efficiently (in terms of computational resource utilization) and effectively (e.g., high accuracy) between benign and malicious activities. To address the high false alarm rates often suffered by anomaly-based models, I explore methods for pre-processing the data and feature extraction, which may help to improve prediction performance. In particular, I define concepts from algebraic topology and TDA, such as simplicial complexes, persistent homology, and Betti numbers. In addition, I describe how topological invariants are useful for machine learning-based approaches (e.g., feature extraction). I show how these computational topological approaches, combined with machine learning may, with further study, continue to advance the understanding of autonomous network resilience.

4.2 TDA Concepts

There is a growing body of recent research that shows how augmenting the feature space with topological signatures, which measure the shape of the data, may be beneficial as input for machine learning algorithms [7–9]. Specifically, in this chapter, I will define a dominant TDA technique, persistent homology, and explore how it can be used to inform our understanding of data partitioning; for example, whether there are clusters and how many, and what the topological structure of these partitions is (e.g., existence of n-dimensional holes) [10]. For this purpose, it is necessary to explore a *cover* of the dataset, which is a collection of open sets over the point cloud, and then construct a set of simplicial complexes. In this process, one builds a nested sequence of simplicial complexes called a *filtration* to understand the persistence of such topological features, or their lifetime. These topological features are also useful for understanding and measuring network resilience, as discussed in further detail in Section 4.3 [9].

4.2.1 Simplices, Simplicial Complexes, and Filtration

In this section, I share some formal definitions from algebraic topology to explore certain topological invariants in networked systems and explore how to promote autonomous cyber resilience with computational modeling. According to Rockafeller [11], M is called an *affine set*, if all lines through any two distinct points in M also lie in M such that $(1-\lambda)x + \lambda y = \lambda(y-x) \in M$, where $x, y \in M$ and $\lambda \in R$. Similarly, a set is referred to as *convex* if $(1-\lambda)x + \lambda y = \lambda(y-x) \in C$, where $x, y \in C$ and $0 < \lambda < 1$. Therefore, all affine sets are also convex sets [11]. A convex combination of $x_1, x_2, \ldots, x_m$ is a vector sum, $\lambda_1 x_1 + \cdots + \lambda_m x_m$ if $\lambda_i \geq 0$ and $\lambda_1 + \cdots + \lambda_m = 1$, which gives the coefficients similar properties to those of probabilities. Furthermore, Rockafeller [11] defines a convex hull of $S \subset \mathbb{R}^n$ as the intersection of all convex sets containing S, and it is referred to as conv S – this is the smallest convex set containing S.

A *p-simplex* is a geometric object defined as the convex hull of a set formed by a collection of affinely independent points, $\{b_0, b_1, \ldots, b_p\}$, and b_i are also called the vertices of the simplex [11]. The p-simplex has $p+1$ vertices. Some familiar examples of p-simplices also depicted in Figure 4.1 are the following:

1. A point is a 0-simplex.
2. A line segment is a 1-simplex.
3. A triangle is a 2-simplex.
4. A tetrahedron is a 3-simplex.

A face of a p-simplex, σ, is a sub-simplex, σ', generated by a nonempty subset of the vertices of σ – it is also a simplex. For example, a $(p-1)$-simplex spanned by the vertex set of σ' is also a face of σ.

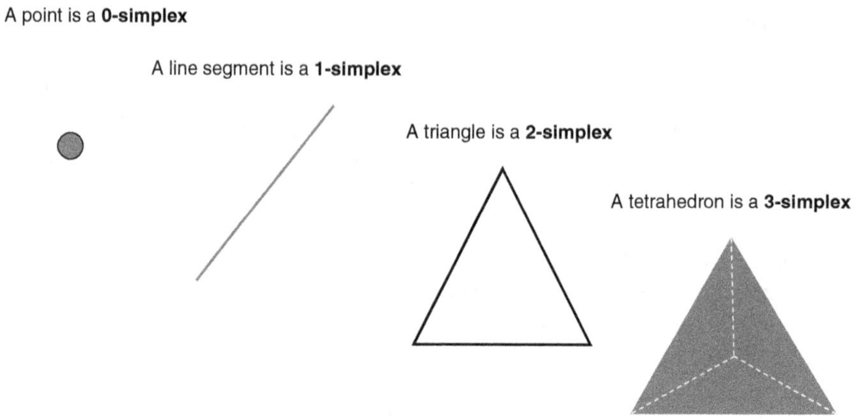

Figure 4.1 Examples of n-dimensional simplices that can be visualized in three-dimensional space.

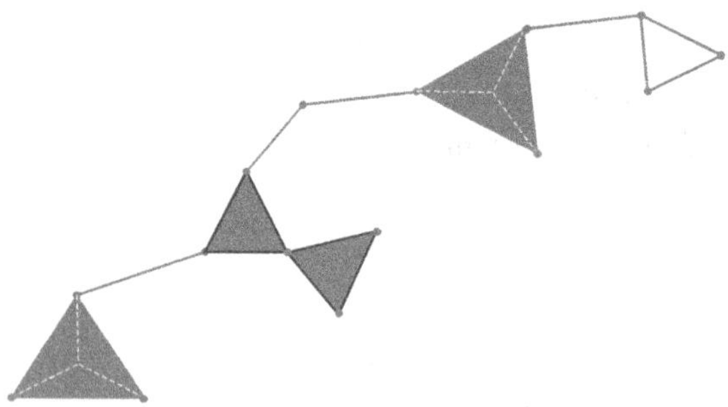

Figure 4.2 An example of a simplicial complex.

A *simplicial complex*, K, is a finite set of simplices that is closed under the face relation, satisfying the following two conditions: (i) if σ' is a face of $\sigma \in K$, then $\sigma' \in K$; and (ii) if $\sigma', \sigma \in K$, then $\sigma' \cap \sigma$ is either empty or a face of both simplices [12]. Figure 4.2 presents an illustration of a simplicial complex. A subcomplex is defined as a subset of a simplicial complex K, and it is also a simplicial complex.

The Vietoris–Rips (VR) complex is an example of a simplicial complex that is frequently used in TDA to obtain geometric and topological information for a better understanding of the space; such data may be a point cloud, such as a feature space representing the network topology, and some of its other characteristics, which can collectively serve as the input domain for machine learning algorithms, for example. Topological information, such as the VR complex, may present keys to unlocking information about the data that may be otherwise inaccessible with other methods. Of particular interest in this chapter is that it may improve the prediction performance of machine learning approaches.

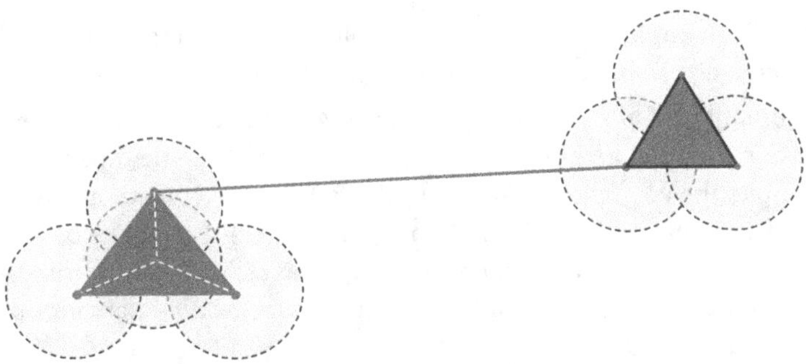

Figure 4.3 An example of a VR complex of a point cloud with a tetrahedron on the left spanned by four vertices and faces and a triangle on the right spanned by three vertices and its faces.

Given a metric space, (X, d), the *VR complex* for X is defined as the simplicial complex with a vertex set $X = \{x_0, x_1, ..., x_p\}$ spanning a p-simplex, *sigma*, such that $d(x_i, x_j) \leq \epsilon$ for all $0 \leq i, j, \leq p$ [13]. The VR complex is denoted by $VR(X, \epsilon)$, and an example is presented in Figure 4.3.

Other examples of simplicial complexes include the Delaunay, *Čech*, and witness complexes. Dey and Wang [14] provide a detailed explanation of these topics related to simplicies and simplicial complexes.

4.2.2 Persistent Homology

A useful notion for understanding changes in topological features is the persistent homology. Intuitively, homology studies the n-dimensional holes of a space, where a hole in a space prevents it from being reduced continuously to a single point. This intuition can be used when grouping mathematical objects into different categories because a cluster is a zero-dimensional hole – indeed, clustering algorithms form the basis of many unsupervised learning approaches. For example, a one-dimensional hole is a loop, and a two-dimensional hole is a void. There are many combinations, such as adding a one-dimensional hole to a two-dimensional hole to obtain a torus.

Several studies examine network resilience in terms of TDA methods and build on persistent homology to help describe the shape (e.g., vertices, holes) of the high-dimensional data, such as feature spaces that are inputs for machine learning algorithms, and the conditions under which those shapes change. To explore these relatively new approaches to network resilience modeling, I briefly introduce chains, cycle groups, and boundaries to define simplicial homology groups. I then present persistent homology and Betti numbers; I describe Betti numbers to measure network characteristics with topological invariants from TDA, and, in turn, with these methods, explore network resilience in the event of attacks or failures.

Let K be a simplicial complex that contains p-simplices, of which there are m_p, $\{\sigma_0, \sigma_1, ..., \sigma_{m_p}\}$. Then, a p-chain, $c \in K$, is an algebraic structure that lies in K; it is the linear combination of p-simplices, $\sum_{i=1}^{m_p} \alpha_i \sigma_i$ [14]. The α_i are coefficients that belong to a ring; they can be integers, or they can belong to some other vector field. For example, the coefficients may lie in the field $\mathbb{Z}/2\mathbb{Z}$, which only has the elements 0 and 1, where addition is modulo 2 – that is, $1 + 1 = 0$. The σ_i are p-simplices. If the coefficients α_i lie in a group, G, such as $\mathbb{Z}/n\mathbb{Z}$ with n prime, then the group of all p-chains with the addition operation forms a p-chain group and is denoted by $C_p(K)$ or C_p.

Moreover, a $(p-1)$-chain, C_{p-1}, can form the boundary of a p-chain, using the homomorphism $\partial_p : C_p \to C_{p-1}$, where ∂_p is referred to as the *boundary operator* or *boundary homomorphism*. C_{p-1} is a subspace of the p-dimensional simplices [14, 15]. A p-chain c with 0 boundary is a called a p-cycle, and the collection of all p-cycles forms the p-cycle group, $Z_p = Z_p(K)$. Z_p is the kernel of ∂_p, which is defined as a subgroup of p-chains, C_p, such that for $z \in C_p$, $\partial_p z = 0$. B_p is the *pth boundary group*, $B_{p-1} = \partial C_p$. B_p is a subgroup of the p-cycles, Z_p [15].

Two p-cycles are called *homologous*, if they differ only by a boundary [14]. Formally, the *pth simplicial homology group* of the simplicial complex K, $H_p(K)$, is the quotient group, $H_p = Z_p/B_p$, where H_p are vector spaces. Intuitively, H_p measures the frequency of k-cycles that are not k-boundaries [12].

The dimension of H_p is the *pth Betti number*, denoted by $\beta_p := \dim H_p$. The measure β_p can be interpreted as the number of p-dimensional cavities in the simplicial complex K. To illustrate this concept, given the simplicial complex K, β_0 is the number of its connected components, β_1 is the number of one-dimensional holes or its circular structures, and β_2 is the number of two-dimensional holes.

A persistent homology extends the homology group to evaluate high-dimensional data across multiple scales using the notions of filtration and persistence modules, by capturing critical information while reducing the dimensionality of the data. Informally, this concept from algebraic topology conveys that the homology group structure is long-lived or persists. Given a filtration of a simplicial complex, we can define a homology module. More formally, a *filtration* of K is a nested sequence of subcomplexes $\emptyset = K_0 \subseteq K_1 \subset K_2 \subset \cdots \subset K_m = K$, where $K_{i-1} \subset K_i$ [16]. The simplicial complex is a filter of a filtration K – it is a sequence of simplices. An example of a filtration is the VR filtration of a metric space (X, d) for $\epsilon \leq \epsilon'$ that satisfies the following property: $VR(X, \epsilon) \subseteq VR(X, \epsilon')$, where ϵ and ϵ' are called filtration parameters [14].

Functors and categories are formal notions that bridge the concept of filtration to persistent homology: informally, functoriality describes the relationship with continuous maps between topological objects, where maps between objects can be invariant; and a *category* is a set of objects together with a set of morphisms (e.g., homomorphisms, isomorphisms) between every pair of set objects such that "composition" is defined [13, 14, 17]. Specifically, let X and Y be topological spaces and let A be an abelian group. Suppose that $f : X \rightarrow Y$ is a continuous map. Then, *functoriality* of a homology is defined by the following two conditions: (1) the existence of an induced homomorphism $H_p(f, A) : H_p(X, A) \rightarrow H_p(Y, A)$; and (2) $H_p(f \circ g, A) = H_p(f, A) \circ H_p(g, A)$ and $H_p(Id_X, A) = Id_{H_k(X,A)}$ [13, 16].

Using the condition of functoriality of homology, we define persistent homology in terms of the algebraic concept, persistence module, as the filtration progresses. That is, given a simplicial filtration F, a homology module is $H_pF : 0 = H_p(K_0) \rightarrow H_p(K_1) \rightarrow \cdots \rightarrow H_p(K_i) \xrightarrow{h_p^{i,j}} \cdots \rightarrow H_p(K_j) \rightarrow \cdots \rightarrow H_p(K_n) = H_p(K)$. The *pth persistent homology group* $H_p^{i,j}$ is the image of the homomorphism, $h_p^{i,j}$, where $0 \leq i \leq j \leq n$ [14]. A nontrivial homology class $\xi \in H_p(K_a)$ is "born" at $K_i, i \leq a$, if $\xi \in H_p^{i,a}$ but $\xi \notin H_p^{i-1,a}$; conversely, $\xi \in H_p(K_a)$ is said to "die" as it enters the simplicial complex K_j for $a < j$, if $h_p^{i,j-1}(\xi)$ is nontrivial, and $h_p^{a,j}(\xi) = 0$ [14, 16]. Persistent homology is a TDA tool for exploring the filtration and the "birth" and "death" of homology classes in the persistence module as the filtration progresses [14]. Typical topological features derived from persistent homology are Betti numbers, barcodes, and persistence diagrams [13–15].

A *barcode* is a finite set of intervals that are bounded below; namely, there is a fixed number that serves as its greatest lower bound. In the context of persistent homology, the infimum of the barcade can represent the birth of a topological feature (e.g., homology class), and its supremum represents its death [18]. The length of a barcode shows the importance of the topological attribute that can persist despite perturbations to the functions that generate the filtrations of the complex [14].

A *persistence diagram* plots the barcodes as points in $\mathbb{R}^2$. That is, the birth and death of homology classes in a persistence module can be presented in the persistence diagrams in $\mathbb{R}^2$, where the x-coordinate represents birth, and the y-coordinate represents the death time in the filtration [20]. Persistence diagrams are often compared by examining the p-Wasserstein or bottleneck distance between them to determine their similarity [7, 9, 20].

Figure 4.4 provides numerical illustrations of two-point cloud datasets for "clean" and "noisy" depictions of the infinity sign. I compute and present their respective filtered simplicial complexes and persistence diagrams to visualize how, by adding noise, one can substantially change the "shape" of the data [19].

4.3 Network Resilience Modeling

Resilience examines whether and how quickly the functionality of a system recovers from disruption, whether that event is the result of benign and maliciously induced failures, even if that recovery is marginal or suboptimal. A related notion

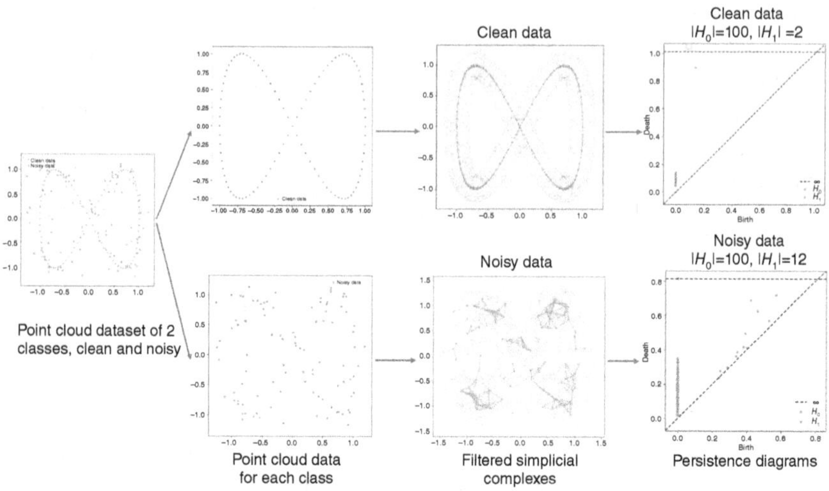

Figure 4.4 Computation of the filtered simplicial complexes and the persistence diagrams of point cloud datasets. *Source*: Ref. [31] / DOI Foundation / CC BY 4.0.

to resilience is robustness, as it explores the ability of the network to maintain its functionality in the face of disturbances. These disturbances cause network security and functionality failures that may go undetected for some fraction of the time. Moreover, even once detected, degradation levels of network functionality can vary depending on a number of factors, including whether the attacks induced random, targeted, or cascading failures – each of which has varying degrees of impact on network functionality.

Several autonomous cyber agility approaches have been introduced to (1) proactively mitigate the impacts of cyberattacks on network resilience and robustness and (2) respond to them, such as node/edge deletions or additions to ensure there are dynamic network adaptations for reinforcements, moving target defense (MTD), network redundancy, and diversity. These cybersecurity and agility approaches impact whether failures occur, the types of failure, how long they are likely to last, and the fault tolerance of the network. Figure 4.5 depicts this relationship between network resilience, types of failures, and dynamic cyber agility approaches. Here, I also depict the degree of impact on network functionality of these cyberattack-induced failures and the agility approaches with the grayscale aspect of the diagram (see [21] for the graphic in epidemiological research that motivated this figure).

Traditionally, the network resilience modeling literature has focused on graph-theoretical and complex systems approaches, where cyberattacks are represented

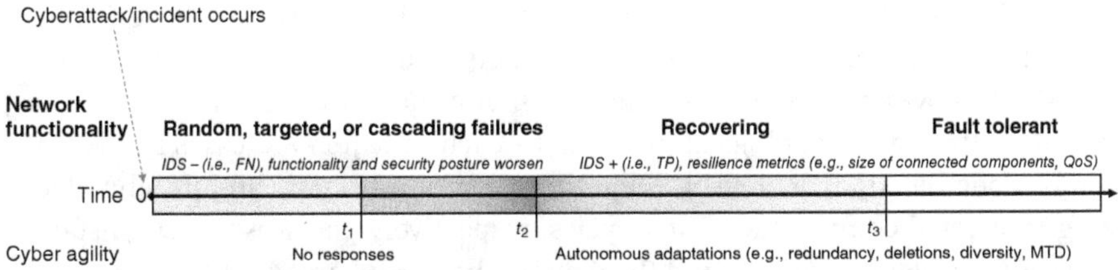

Figure 4.5 An illustration of the interplay of network functionality and agility. At time 0, unauthorized network access occurs, which can subsequently result in random, targeted, and/or cascading failures that precede recovery to some degree – ideally, in response, the network becomes more fault-tolerant. Cybersecurity and agility approaches, such as accurate IDSs, autonomous node or edge additions/deletions, network redundancy, diversity, and MTD, can each reduce the amount of time that unauthorized users have access to the network and network downtime.

as node or edge deletions and/or edge weight reductions. In particular, supposing that a network is defined as a graph, bond, and site percolation are useful approaches from complex systems theory for assessing the impacts of these attacks or failures on the size of the largest or giant connected component [3, 9, 22–27]. Additional graph-theoretical measures of network resilience are network motifs (i.e., recurrent subgraph patterns) and patch size distribution, which help to analyze network interconnectedness, thereby supporting the characterization of the robustness of the local graph structure [28, 29].

Similarly, machine learning is often also used to explore the dynamic impacts of cyberattacks and agility approaches on network resilience. For example, a generative adversarial network (GAN) is a type of generative AI algorithm that has been shown to enhance anomaly-based IDS, in that GANs can generate adversarial samples in settings where the prevalence of malware is low in a sea of benign network traffic and log data [1]. Furthermore, GANs can be useful for exposing network vulnerabilities [1].

Recently, efforts to leverage TDA for machine learning have focused on manifold learning, including nonlinear dimensionality reduction, generating features for existing machine learning approaches, topological uncertainty, and the development of novel clustering algorithms [30, 31]. These TDA applications in machine learning have emerged as viable solutions to improve prediction performance, computational resource utilization, and prediction reliability assessment [30–33].

During the past decade, TDA has been applied to network resilience and robustness problems [9, 34]. Several studies characterize the vulnerability of power grid networks under targeted attacks as well as intrusions into other types of networks with topological summaries, such as persistence diagrams, barcodes, and Betti numbers defined in Section 4.2.2 [7, 9, 33, 34].

With the recent expansion of TDA to network resilience, studies have found a link between network vulnerability and the persistence of one-dimensional holes [9, 34]. Moreover, the increased fragmentation of networks of various types has been measured with topological invariants – each of which increases as the fraction of node deletions increases, including Betti numbers, β_0 and β_1, characterizing connected components and 1-cycles, respectively, the Wasserstein distance between persistent diagrams, and the distance between barcodes [7, 9, 34].

A few recent studies indicate that TDA techniques can inform the machine learning pipeline, including feature pre-processing needs, such as feature space dimension reduction and feature selection. To this end, persistent diagrams and other topological or algebraic measures have been transformed to features for machine learning applications (e.g., image classification, network intrusion detection) with various vectorization or featurization techniques, including kernel methods, persistence diagrams/landscapes, and using persistent diagrams more directly (Figure 4.6) [20, 33].

In addition, TDA has been recently integrated with adversarial learning approaches, such as GANs for image analysis to autonomously learn the topological features of images and inform a GAN loss function to measure the proximity of real to synthetic images [35]. However, the integration of TDA into machine learning remains an emerging approach to understand network resilience problems [33].

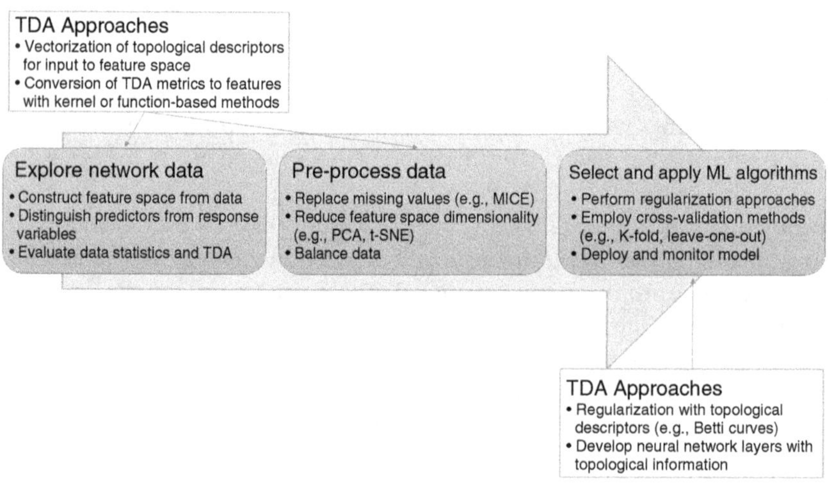

Figure 4.6 Overview of example TDA approaches that can be included in a machine learning operations process.

4.4 Conclusion

In this chapter, I have explored TDA and machine learning approaches, and how they may be developed to understand network resilience in the proactive phase. In addition, machine learning serves as an important methodology for enhancing network intrusion detection to reduce the negative impacts of cyberattacks on network functionality, including the amount of time an APT has undetected, unauthorized access to a network. Furthermore, anomaly-based IDS can improve prediction performance, the assessment of node and edge failure rates, the prediction of triggers for cascading failures in networks in spatiotemporal environments, and the forecasting of cyberattacks [36, 37]. Specifically, I have considered how machine learning combined with TDA can provide viable solutions to autonomous cyber resilience problems. Although using TDA in the machine learning pipeline is an understudied area, there are practical examples where its exploration may yield enhancements to network resilience.

References

1 Dule Shu, Nandi O. Leslie, Charles A. Kamhoua, and Conrad S. Tucker. Generative adversarial attacks against intrusion detection systems using active learning. In *Proceedings of the 2nd ACM Workshop on Wireless Security and Machine Learning*, pages 1–6, 2020.

2 Thai-Hoc Vu, Senthil Kumar Jagatheesaperumal, Minh-Duong Nguyen, Nguyen Van Huynh, Sunghwan Kim, and Quoc-Viet Pham. Applications of generative AI (GAI) for mobile and wireless networking: A survey. *IEEE Internet of Things Journal*, 12(2): 1266–1290, 2024.

3 Liudong Xing. Cascading failures in internet of things: Review and perspectives on reliability and resilience. *IEEE Internet of Things Journal*, 8(1): 44–64, 2020.

4 Varun Chandola, Arindam Banerjee, and Vipin Kumar. Anomaly detection: A survey. *ACM Computing Surveys (CSUR)*, 41(3): 1–58, 2009.

5 Nandi Leslie. An unsupervised learning approach for in-vehicle network intrusion detection. In *2021 55th Annual Conference on Information Sciences and Systems (CISS)*, pages 1–4. IEEE, 2021.

6 Hongpo Zhang, Chase Q. Wu, Shan Gao, Zongmin Wang, Yuxiao Xu, and Yongpeng Liu. An effective deep learning based scheme for network intrusion detection. In *2018 24th International Conference on Pattern Recognition (ICPR)*, pages 682–687. IEEE, 2018.

7 Paul Bruillard, Kathleen Nowak, and Emilie Purvine. Anomaly detection using persistent homology. In *2016 Cybersecurity Symposium (CYBERSEC)*, pages 7–12. IEEE, 2016.

8 Binghui Li, Dorcas Ofori-Boateng, Yulia R. Gel, and Jie Zhang. A hybrid approach for transmission grid resilience assessment using reliability metrics and power system local network topology. *Sustainable and Resilient Infrastructure*, 6(1-2): 26–41, 2021.

9 Dorcas Ofori-Boateng, Asim Kumer Dey, Yulia R. Gel, Binghui Li, Jie Zhang, and H. Vincent Poor. Assessing the resilience of the Texas power grid network. In *2019 IEEE Data Science Workshop (DSW)*, pages 280–284. IEEE, 2019.

10 Elizabeth Munch. A user's guide to topological data analysis. *Journal of Learning Analytics*, 4(2): 47–61, 2017.

11 R. Tyrrell Rockafellar. *Convex analysis*, Vol. 18. Princeton University Press, 1997.

12 Cecil Jose A. Delfinado and Herbert Edelsbrunner. An incremental algorithm for betti numbers of simplicial complexes on the 3-sphere. *Computer Aided Geometric Design*, 12(7): 771–784, 1995.

13 Gunnar Carlsson. Topology and data. *Bulletin of the American Mathematical Society*, 46(2): 255–308, 2009.

14 Tamal Krishna Dey and Yusu Wang. *Computational topology for data analysis.* Cambridge University Press, 2022.

15 Herbert Edelsbrunner and John Harer. Persistent homology-a survey. *Contemporary Mathematics*, 453(26): 257–282, 2008.

16 Herbert Edelsbrunner and John Harer. *Computational topology.* Duke University, 2008.

17 Ib H. Madsen and Jxrgen Tornehave. *From calculus to cohomology: de Rham cohomology and characteristic classes.* Cambridge University Press, 1997.

18 Gunnar Carlsson, Afra Zomorodian, Anne Collins, and Leonidas Guibas. Persistence barcodes for shapes. In *Proceedings of the 2004 Eurographics/ACM SIGGRAPH Symposium on Geometry Processing*, pages 124–135, 2004.

19 Nathaniel Saul and Chris Tralie. Scikit-tda: Topological data analysis for python, 2019. https://doi.org/10.5281/zenodo.2533369.

20 Peter Bubenik. Statistical topological data analysis using persistence landscapes. *Journal of Machine Learning Research*, 16(1): 77–102, 2015.

21 Joshua S. Weitz. *Asymptomatic: the silent spread of COVID-19 and the future of pandemics.* JHU Press, 2024.

22 Réka Albert, Hawoong Jeong, and Albert-László Barabási. Error and attack tolerance of complex networks. *Nature*, 406(6794): 378–382, 2000.

23 Duncan S. Callaway, Mark E. J. Newman, Steven H. Strogatz, and Duncan J. Watts. Network robustness and fragility: Percolation on random graphs. *Physical Review Letters*, 85(25): 5468, 2000.

24 Jin-Hee Cho and Terrence J. Moore. Percolation-based network adaptability under correlated failures. In *IEEE INFOCOM 2018-IEEE Conference on Computer Communications*, pages 2186–2194. IEEE, 2018.

25 Alexander A. Ganin, Emanuele Massaro, Alexander Gutfraind, Nicolas Steen, Jeffrey M. Keisler, Alexander Kott, Rami Mangoubi, and Igor Linkov. Operational resilience: Concepts, design and analysis. *Scientific Reports*, 6(1): 1–12, 2016.

26 Jianxi Gao, Xueming Liu, Daqing Li, and Shlomo Havlin. Recent progress on the resilience of complex networks. *Energies*, 8(10): 12187–12210, 2015.

27 Paul Erdos and Alfréd Rényi. On the evolution of random graphs. *Publications of the Mathematical Institute of the Hungarian Academy of Sciences*, 5(1): 17–60, 1960.

28 Asim Kumer Dey, Yulia R. Gel, and H. Vincent Poor. Motif-based analysis of power grid robustness under attacks. In *2017 IEEE Global Conference on Signal and Information Processing (GlobalSIP)*, pages 1015–1019. IEEE, 2017.

29 Martí Rosas Casals and Bernat Corominas Murtra. Assessing European power grid reliability by means of topological measures. *WIT Transactions on Ecology and the Environment*, 121: 527–537, 2009.

30 Gunnar Carlsson, Rick Jardine, Dmitry Feichtner-Kozlov, Dmitriy Morozov, Frédéric Chazal, Vin de Silva, Brittany Fasy, Jesse Johnson, Matt Kahle, Gilad Lerman, et al. Topological data analysis and machine learning theory. In *Proceedings of BIRS Workshop*, pages 1–11, 2012.

31 Théo Lacombe, Yuichi Ike, Mathieu Carriere, Frédéric Chazal, Marc Glisse, and Yuhei Umeda. Topological uncertainty: Monitoring trained neural networks through persistence of activation graphs. In *IJCAI 2021-30th International Joint Conference on Artificial Intelligence*, 2021.

32 Adélie Garin and Guillaume Tauzin. A topological "reading" lesson: Classification of MNIST using TDA. In *2019 18th IEEE International Conference On Machine Learning And Applications (ICMLA)*, pages 1551–1556. IEEE, 2019.

33 Nandi O. Leslie. Cyberattack detection with topological data, December 21 2023. US Patent App. 17/844,429.

34 Umar Islambekov, Asim Kumer Dey, Yulia R. Gel, and H. Vincent Poor. Role of local geometry in robustness of power grid networks. In *2018 IEEE Global Conference on Signal and Information Processing (GlobalSIP)*, pages 885–889. IEEE, 2018.

35 Fan Wang, Huidong Liu, Dimitris Samaras, and Chao Chen. Topogan: A topology-aware generative adversarial network. In *European Conference on Computer Vision*, pages 118–136. Springer, 2020.

36 Nandi Leslie and Michael De Lucia. Network-resilience modeling and intrusion detection. *Resilience and Hybrid Threats*, pages 94–101, 2019.

37 Alexander Kott and Igor Linkov. *Cyber Resilience of Systems and Networks*, Vol. 1. Springer, 2019.

5

Game-theoretic Frameworks for Zero-trust Authentication in Autonomous Cyber Resilience

Yunfei Ge[*] *and Quanyan Zhu*

Department of Electrical and Computer Engineering, New York University, Brooklyn, NY, USA

[*]Corresponding Author: yg2047@nyu.edu

5.1 Introduction

The world we live in is becoming more interconnected each day. With the advent of cloud services, data communications, and automation technologies, we can now operate with greater flexibility and efficiency. But with this progress comes a new set of cyber risks that threaten not just one entity or industry, but all private and public sectors. First, the increased connectivity inevitably enlarges the attack surface and enables the attacker to access the system from multiple entry points. Second, modern networks, especially massive Internet of Things (IoT) networks, consist of heterogeneous devices, diverse applications, and third-party services, and not all of them are accompanied by regular security updates [1]. Moreover, recent trends such as remote work and bring your own device (BYOD) exacerbate the need for a trustworthy environment to provide proper access and authentication mechanisms for external connections from unknown or uncertain environments [2]. As IoT networks continue to grow in size and coverage, it becomes increasingly difficult to defend against all vulnerabilities and manage their security. It is imperative that we take proactive measures to keep our systems safe from cyber threats.

Traditional perimeter-based defense, e.g., firewalls, intrusion detection systems (IDS) and virtual private networks (VPN), aims to keep the attacker outside the security perimeter. As illustrated in Figure 5.1, the traditional security architecture divides the networks into trusted and untrusted zones by establishing a defensible boundary between internal assets and the outside world. However, they become insufficient to defend against sophisticated adversaries, including insider

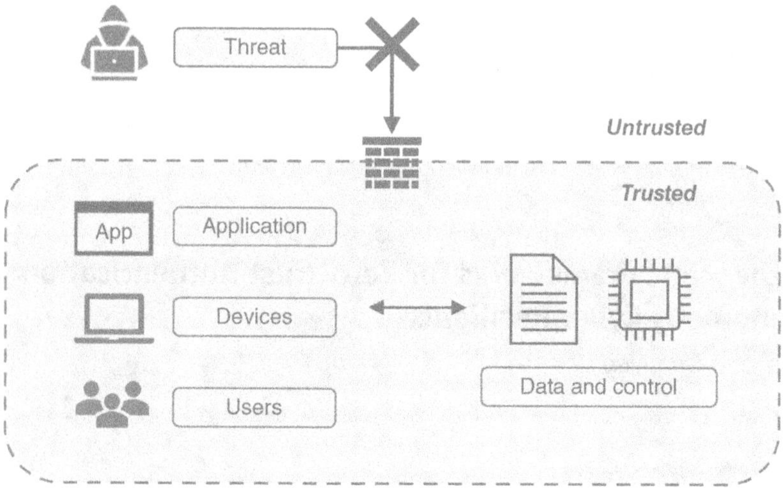

Figure 5.1 Traditional perimeter-based security architecture divides the network into trusted and untrusted zones by establishing a boundary between internal assets and the outside world. It assumes that anything inside the perimeter is trustworthy. However, this model fails to address insider threats or lateral movements by attackers who gain access using stolen credentials. Once an attacker breaches the perimeter, they are treated as a trusted entity, which creates a major vulnerability in modern, highly connected networks.

threats [3] and advanced persistent threats (APTs) [4, 5]. In these attack scenarios, the attacker can evade traditional protections, obtain privileges as an insider using stolen credentials, and move laterally in the network toward the primary target. Once attackers breach the perimeter, they will be inherently trusted and unhindered to achieve their goals. Modern networks must transform from static and perimeter-based defenses to a strategic and dynamic trust-based security framework that focuses on the identity and integrity of individual components in the network at present.

The complexity in network structure and the sophistication of the attack model lead to an emerging security solution, **zero trust**. Zero trust is a new security concept that forfeits the assumption that everything behind the security perimeter is safe [6]. With the principle "never trust, always verify," zero trust eliminates implicit trust and continuously validates the identity and integrity of each entity. Regardless of the physical location (inside or outside the network), any request for access to critical data or services would first be verified through the zero-trust engine, locally distributed or in the cloud, before granting access. The zero-trust engine would verify the user, device, and application associated with the request based on fine-grained access policies. Once the zero-trust engine decides the access attempt will be approved, it dynamically updates the network configuration to accept the request. It aims to prevent data breaches and limit internal lateral movement (Figure 5.2).

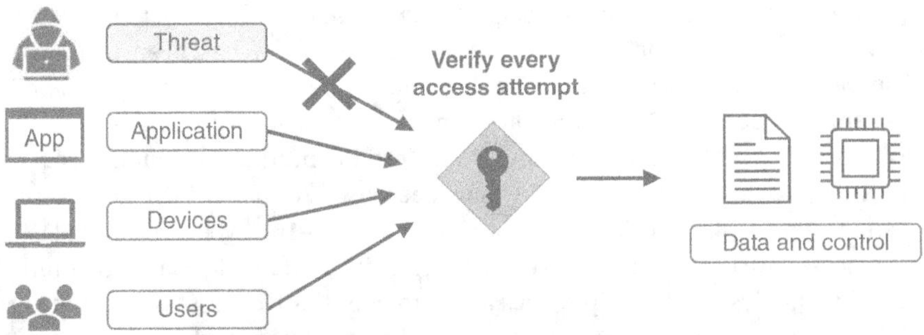

Figure 5.2 Zero-trust security architecture replaces perimeter-based assumptions with the principle of "never trust, always verify." It treats every access request regardless of origin as potentially hostile, requiring verification of users, devices, and applications each time access is requested. The zero-trust engine dynamically evaluates the trustworthiness of each entity based on historical data and contextual analysis, enabling fine-grained, adaptive, and continuous access control that improves the system's ability to detect, prevent, and recover from cyber threats.

Zero trust plays a major role in building cyber resilience, as it provides additional layers of protection to withstand unpredictable threats and limit impact if an unauthorized entity does gain access. It enables fine-grained security policies based on the trustworthiness of the network component. With accurate trust evaluation (TE), the system can quickly identify suspicious components in the system, agilely implement proper defense against potential threats, and efficiently respond to cyber incidents after the attack. Besides, it can incentivize compliant behaviors of the network users and reduce the temptation for insiders to abuse or misuse the network [7], as they need to be sufficiently trustworthy in order to accomplish their missions. The security posture of the system can be more efficient, visible, compliant, and cost-efficient with trust-based defense.

However, several challenges arise from the design of zero-trust security models. First, there is a need to quantitatively define and measure the trustworthiness of the agent so that metrics can be used for planning and policy design. Second, in highly connected networks, constant monitoring and implementing defense with maximum security at all times can cause a time delay and degrade the performance of the system [8]. Hence, strategic zero trust needs to be employed for the sake of balancing system performance and security. Third, the mobility and the changing topology of IoT networks create a dynamic environment. Based on the baseline defense policy, the security decisions also need to accommodate the environmental change promptly and design adaptive policies using online learning.

In this chapter, we introduce a quantitative design framework to provide a formal design methodology to address these challenges in zero-trust design. We propose the strategic zero-trust principle:***"Never trust, verify (defense) strategically."*** To formalize the zero-trust design, game theory has been a natural and successful framework for modeling the interactions between the system and the potential attacker [9–11]. Many problems in cybersecurity are fundamentally decision-making problems under complex, uncertain, multi-agent conditions. For example, game-theoretic frameworks have been used to model intrusion detection and response [8, 12, 13], moving target defense [14–16], cyber deception [17–21], cyber warfare [22] and adversarial learning problems [23–25]. Game-theoretic equilibrium analysis not only provides a way to quantitatively assess the security posture of the network but also enables a formal methodology to design best-effort zero-trust policies. The optimal security policy aims to maximize the non-myopic well-being of the system by looking multiple steps ahead into the horizon. With the resort to the game-theoretic approach, the system can achieve automated zero-trust security with improved efficiency.

The chapter is organized as follows. Section 5.2 introduces the general framework of zero-trust defense and compares it with traditional perimeter-based defense. We elaborate on the design of two zero-trust core components, TE and policy engine (PE), in Sections 5.3 and 5.4, respectively. Section 5.5 discusses how zero trust contributes to cyber resilience. Then, we propose our strategic zero-trust design in Section 5.6 and introduce several works that apply game theory to cybersecurity. Section 5.7 concludes the chapter.

5.2 From Traditional Security to Zero Trust

Zero-trust security is a natural evolution of traditional perimeter-based security. It pushes the trust boundary down to every stage of digital interaction, offering granular access control and better security. A comprehensive zero-trust approach encompasses not only users but also devices and applications inside the network. For users, the system should apply strong authorization and authentication processes to ensure user identity. For devices (e.g., routers, controllers, end-point devices, etc.), the system should ensure that the devices are securely managed. For applications, a zero-trust system needs to remove implicit trust and enforce appropriate in-app permissions. Considerable efforts have been invested in research and implementation of zero-trust security. The National Institute of Standards and Technology (NIST) report [6] outlines the basic architecture and deployment of the zero-trust model. It has been applied to enterprise security (e.g., Google Beyond-Crop [26], cloud computing security [27], big data [28], etc.).

Zero trust takes a holistic view of network security and establishes access policies based on the trustworthiness of each network component. The goal of zero

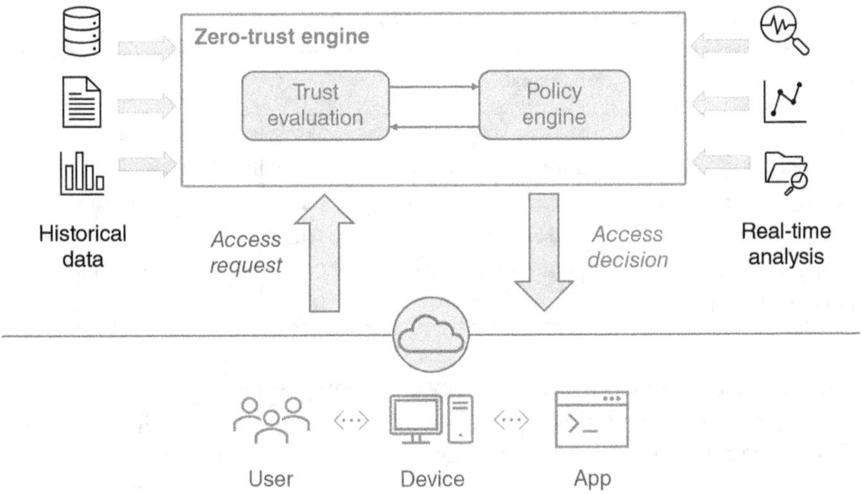

Figure 5.3 A generic zero-trust workflow: Every access request is sent to the zero-trust engine for approval. The engine evaluates the trustworthiness of the involved entities based on historical data and real-time analysis. The policy engine (PE) makes access decisions based on the trust evaluation (TE).

trust is to ensure that every stage of the digital data flow is trusted. The primary question to consider is who is requesting what under which conditions. Only when all the entities involved are trusted, the zero-trust engine allows permission for the request. To this end, a continuous and dynamic access control system is required. This system should not solely depend on the IP address of the request, but also on the historical behavior and real-time analysis of the components involved.

The workflow of a generic zero-trust system is depicted in Figure 5.3. The zero-trust engine is primarily comprised of two components: TE and PE. Upon receiving a request for access, the zero-trust engine first assesses the trustworthiness of the entities involved at TE. This assessment is based on historical data and observed footprints, which are obtained through continuous monitoring. Based on the evaluation result, PE makes access decisions for the request and enforces various policies for network resources.

Zero trust refers to a security framework that is guided by a set of principles [29], rather than a single technology or application. It aims to tackle modern cyber threats through the use of existing network management tools, taking into consideration the trustworthiness of network components in decision-making. Zero-trust security provides fine-grained access control that can be adapted to varying conditions.

Table 5.1 compares traditional perimeter-based security and zero-trust security. It highlights various key features that differentiate the two security models. It is

Table 5.1 Comparison between traditional and zero-trust security.

Features	Traditional	Zero trust
Principle	Trust but verify	Never trust, always verify
Trust boundary	Entire infrastructure	Individual component
Security consideration	Device and location	User, device, and application
Access control	IP-based access control	Trust-based access control
Authentication	One-time at initial access	Continuous authentication
Implementation cost	Low	High

worth noting that while zero-trust security offers comprehensive protection, it also entails higher implementation costs and network complexity. Therefore, it is crucial to strike a balance between security and costs when deploying a zero-trust system.

5.3 Trust Evaluation Design

Trust plays a pivotal role in zero-trust security policies. It has been extensively studied in various fields such as psychology, economics, political science, sociology, and computer science [30]. Essentially, trust refers to the degree of confidence an entity has in the expected behavior of another entity [31]. The trust-based decision-making is significant when there is a possibility of deception by the adversary, as in the case of cybersecurity. In such scenarios, attackers may intentionally mislead or conceal information to gain a strategic advantage. Therefore, it is essential to understand the definition, metrics, and evaluation techniques of trust to create an efficient TE in a zero-trust network. Refer to Table 5.2 for the necessary attributes to design a TE in computer networks.

5.3.1 Target

Different from transitional perimeter-based security, zero trust expands the target of trust to every component in the network. Trust decisions will be based not only on the trustworthiness of the requester but also on the device and environment where the data flow takes place. The granularity of the target in TE defense depends on the computational capability and the needs of the system.

5.3.2 Metric

TE adopts a metric to measure the trustworthiness of the entity and provide risk analysis for policy decisions. In this chapter, we refer to this metric as the trust

Table 5.2 Trust definition attributes in computer networks.

Attributes	Explanation
Target	Who is the entity that will be evaluated
Metric	What is the metric that is used to measure trust
Collection	What information is collected to calculate trust
Evaluation	How to evaluate trust
Purpose	How trust will be used in decision-making
Management	How to manage the trust information in the system

score (TS). To be specific, we formalize the TS of an entity at the current time as the probability that the entity is nonadversarial to the system. Let $\theta \in \Theta$ be the attributes of the entity i and denote the nonadversarial attributes set as Θ_T. Formally,

Definition 5.1 *(Trust Score)* The TS of the entity i at time t is defined as the probability that the entity is nonadversarial to the system:

$$\mathrm{TS}^t(i) := \Pr(\theta_i^t \in \Theta_T) \in [0, 1], \tag{5.1}$$

where θ_i^t is the attributes of entity i at time t.

It should be noted that in practice, trust is multifaceted and the attribute θ can be a multidimensional vector where each entry represents different trust attributes.

5.3.3 Collection and Evaluation

We adopt the categories from Bonatti et al. [32] and discuss two common approaches to trust collection and evaluation: policy-based and reputation-based trust management. Then, we propose our approach of Bayesian trust evaluation, which is a combination of policy- and reputation-based methods.

5.3.3.1 Policy-based Method

Policy-based methods enable the system to manage trust based on a set of predefined policies. These policies may include rules that specify the types of users or devices that are allowed to access certain resources, the level of access that is granted, and the conditions under which access is granted or denied. The trust is established based on collected hard evidences, e.g., credentials, access tokens, and certificates. The evaluation process is relatively simple as the trust engine only needs to determine whether the collected data satisfies the predefined conditions.

However, it is important to tailor the security policy to the needs of the system. We provide several examples under this category.

- **Network credential:** The access request can be granted based on the given credentials of the entity. The trust information of the entity is encrypted in the credential, as we assume only the trusted entity will process the credential. Kerberos [33] is one example of authenticating service requests between trusted hosts across an untrusted network, such as the Internet. The underlying requirement for this method is that the system needs to ensure that the credential is private and not revealed to the attacker.
- **Ad-hoc attributes check:** The system can configure a set of qualified attributes that must be met before access is allowed. These attributes may include the device configuration, network environment security, application permission, etc. Identifying the necessary security attributes requires extensive knowledge of the system vulnerabilities. Poor security checks can result in inaccurate estimation of TS, along with unresolved security vulnerabilities.
- **Promise and incentive compliance:** Trust can be influenced by promises and penalties. To encourage desirable safe behaviors of the entity, the system can create a set of rules or contracts that promote incentive-compatible actions. A reward and penalty mechanism can also be strategically designed to elicit such behaviors. For instance, trust-based collaborative IDS use incentive-compatible mechanisms to ensure no free-riding and facilitate cooperative network defense [34, 35]. Similarly, strategic trust frameworks based on evaluating the incentives of the opponents are used to guide the integration of IoT into communication networks [36, 37].

5.3.3.2 Reputation-based Method

Reputation-based methods estimate the trustworthiness of an entity and adjust access permissions based on interactions or observations from past experiences, either directly (e.g., using historical behaviors) or indirectly (e.g., using third-party recommendations). What information we need to collect depends on the availability of corresponding data and the needs of the system. This method can integrate more information, but is also more vulnerable to false positives or false negatives. The system needs to consider the reliability of the source of reputation during TE. We provide some examples under this category.

- **Historical behaviors:** If the system has had direct interactions with the entity, the TS of the entity at this request can be developed based on the history of their encounters. The behavior characteristics of the entity can be multidimensional, which involve login information, operational habits, abnormal behavior records, etc. The system needs to find proper risk measures that achieve the security goals. In addition, expired experiences should be excluded from the TE due to the dynamic features of modern networks. The out-of-date interaction record contributes little to the current trustworthiness of the entity, and it is important to consider the attenuation in the data history.

- **Social reputation:** Reputation from third parties or society can also serve as a source for TE. Reputation may be defined as the global perception of the entity as being trustworthy. In other words, it is a collective trust opinion of other systems about the behavior of a subject node. The system prefers to grant access to a well-reputed entity. This information is helpful when the entity aims to enter the system for the first time.
- **Recommendation:** Recommendation is the simplest case of trust propagation. For instance, a recommendation from a trusted neighbor will increase the TS of the new entity. Reliable recommendation reduces information overload, uncertainties, and the risk of access attempts. It is important to provide a trust inference model to find a reliable recommendation that could improve TE accuracy.
- **Supply chain:** Supply chain contains interorganizational relationships among interdependent companies contributing to the final components in the target system. The trust in the suppliers also influences the TE of the device they provided. This type of trust propagation is multi-hop due to the multi-tier structure in the supply chain. Accountability investigation and cyber insurance in the supply chain [38] could encourage truth-telling and information transparency to support TE.
- **Third-party evaluation:** Besides the trust information propagated from others, the security system can also leverage third-party evaluation results (e.g., IDS [34], Security Information and Event Management [SIEM] [39], etc.) to develop a more reliable measure of TS of the entity. The trace of the user provides a sequence of events that can be used for security analysis. It should be noted that the reliability of the side evidence largely impacts trust propagation. The system needs to incorporate reliable side evidence for an accurate trust measure.

5.3.3.3 Our Approach – Bayesian Trust Evaluation

Under the dynamic network environment, it is important for zero-trust security to continuously adjust the TS after the initial TE. The system needs to respond to changes in trust by investigating and orchestrating responses to potential incidents. The dynamic update should take account of previous knowledge about the entity as well as currently observed behaviors. In this work, we propose a Bayesian trust model to update the TS. This model offers a quantitative way to combine policy-based trust with reputation-based evidence and update the TS subject to the perceived strategies of the entity.

Definition 5.2 ***(Bayesian Trust Update)*** The TS of the entity i at time $t+1$ is the probability that the entity is nonadversarial ($\theta_i^{t+1} \in \Theta_T$) based on the prior knowledge, side evidence, and observed strategies of the entity:

$$\begin{aligned}\mathrm{TS}^{t+1}(i) &= Pr(\theta_i^{t+1} \in \Theta_T | a^t, e^t, \pi^t) \\ &= \frac{h(e^t|a^t, \theta_i^t \in \Theta_T)\sigma(a^t|\theta_i^t \in \Theta_T)\pi^t(\theta_i^t \in \Theta_T)}{\sum_{\hat{\theta}_i \in \Theta} h(e^t|a^t, \hat{\theta}_i)\sigma(a^t|\hat{\theta}_i)\pi^t(\hat{\theta}_i)}\end{aligned} \tag{5.2}$$

where $a^t \in \mathcal{A}$ is the observed action of the entity, $e^t \in \mathcal{E}$ is the received side evidence, and π^t is the system's prior knowledge about the entity up to time t. σ is the observed strategy of the opponent, and h is the evidence-generating function given by the third party. Note that the relationship between TS and π is $\mathrm{TS}^t(i) = \pi^t(\theta_i^t \in \Theta_T)$.

- **Prior knowledge** π^t**:** Prior knowledge is the ex-ante likelihood of the entity being nonadversarial before taking into consideration any new (posterior) information. This information can be collected through various sources through policy-based methods or reputation-based methods. The initial trust score $\mathrm{TS}^0(i) = \pi^0$ is usually constructed based on some kind of experience with, or firsthand knowledge of, the other party. For instance, attributes check, historical behaviors, reputation, etc., can all contribute to the prior computation. The system can establish an initial trust estimation of the entity at $t = 0$ and compute the probability of the agent being trusted, i.e., $\mathrm{TS}^0(i) \in [0, 1]$.
- **Side evidence** $e^t \in \mathcal{E}$**:** The system can also incorporate side security evidence during trust updates. The side evidence may involve real-time network detection, system monitoring information, intelligent risk analysis, security alerts, etc. Reliable evidence helps establish a fast and accurate TE [29].

  For instance, the external evidence is additional information taking binary value $e^t \in \mathcal{E} = \{0, 1\}$, where $e^t = 1$ indicates a security alarm, and $e^t = 0$ means no alarm. The security alarm warns the defender when the agent is more likely to be malicious. In general, the evidence is generated based on the probability that the agent with type θ^t takes an action a^t at the current time t. Observing the evidence e^t, the defender can further update the trust of the agent via Bayes' rule.
- **Observed strategies** $\sigma(a^t|\theta^t)$**:** The trustworthiness of an agent is determined by various factors, with their observed strategies playing a major part in trust updates. A strategy is a plan of actions that an agent intends to take to achieve its objectives. It also takes into account how an agent with a different type

would behave in the current security state. Abnormal behaviors of the agent, such as attempting to access sensitive or restricted information in the system, could indicate that the agent has been compromised by an attacker. In such cases, the TS of the agent should be decreased. To ensure the security of the system, it is essential to monitor the agent's behavior regularly and update or re-evaluate its trustworthiness as needed.

5.3.4 Purpose

In the zero-trust model, the TS is used to obtain trust-based access policies. It plays a key role in establishing secure communication between different systems, networks, and individuals. Depending on the needs of the system, each situation places different requirements on trust. For instance, in data communication, the trust requirements would focus on the security level of the transmission environment. In contrast, in supply chain security, the trust of the supplier depends more on the supplier's reputation and compliant behaviors. To ensure an effective TE, it's crucial to determine the purpose of the TE and design the trust system accordingly.

5.3.5 Management

Two major approaches to managing trust in cybersecurity are centralized and distributed trust management. Centralized trust management involves a central authority or entity that is responsible for managing and enforcing trust policies across a system or network [40, 41]. It is typically used in environments where there is a clear hierarchy of trust relationships. Distributed trust management, on the other hand, involves a decentralized network of entities that are responsible for managing and enforcing trust policies. In this approach, trust decisions are made based on consensus among multiple entities, rather than by a single central authority. Each entity in the network may have its own trust policies and evaluation criteria, and trust decisions are made based on the collective evaluation of these policies and criteria.

Both centralized and distributed trust management approaches have their advantages and disadvantages. Centralized trust management can provide a clear hierarchy of trust relationships and centralized enforcement of trust policies, but it may also be vulnerable to single points of failure and may require significant resources to maintain. Distributed trust management can be more resilient and adaptable to changing trust relationships, but it may also be more difficult to manage. The choice between centralized and distributed trust management in zero trust depends on the specific needs and requirements of the system or network.

5.4 Policy Engine Design

Zero trust is a holistic security model that provides additional layers of mitigation against sophisticated attacks. It forfeits the assumption that everything behind the security perimeter is safe, and thus requires continuous monitoring and validation of the identity and privilege associated with each network component. The key components of zero-trust security are identity verification, privilege management, and network segmentation. The fine-grained authentication and authorization process, along with network policy enforcement configuration, form comprehensive zero-trust security throughout the environment. Zero-trust architecture adds additional trust layers on top of the perimeter-based defense. It provides a multi-dimensional mitigation compared to traditional perimeter-based security. Based on this point of view, we provide our interpretation of zero trust from a trust layer perspective, as illustrated in Figure 5.4.

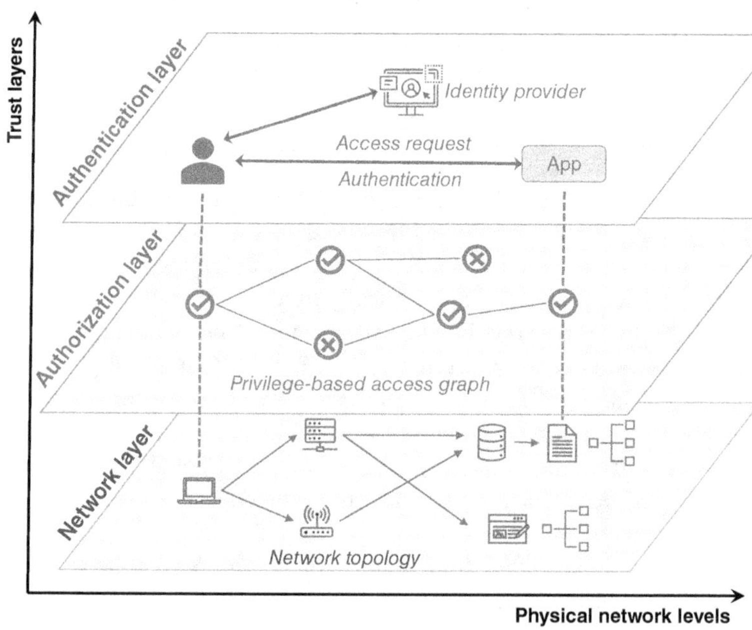

Figure 5.4 The figure illustrates a three-tiered security framework composed of the authentication layer (identity verification), authorization layer (privilege-based access control), and network layer (topology-aware data transmission). Each layer dynamically evaluates access conditions, and a request is only granted if all three requirements are satisfied. This layered approach enables adaptive, context-sensitive enforcement and enhances resilience against unauthorized access across both logical and physical domains.

5.4.1 Authentication Layer: Continuous Authentication

The authentication layer is a critical supporting component for realizing zero-trust security. It answers the question *"Who you are?"* in access decision-making. Zero trust security applies identity-based instead of location-based access policies, which require the system to conduct strict identity verification. The authentication process ensures that the attributes of the users/devices/applications coincide with the identity of who they claim to be. Under a zero-trust policy, the system continuously monitors the behaviors of the components and adjusts policies dynamically based on observations. Different authentication methods can be utilized to support this layer. The multifactor authentication (MFA) is preferred for security as it grants access only after successfully presenting two or more pieces of evidence to the zero-trust engine. However, the system also needs to balance cybersecurity and system efficiency, as it is time-consuming to conduct constant verification.

5.4.2 Authorization Layer: Least Privilege Access

This layer provides the zero-trust engine with the access graph based on the privilege level. It answers the question *"Where can you go?"* before granting any access. One fundamental principle of zero-trust security is least privilege access, which grants the least amount of privilege necessary, depending on who is requesting access and the context of the request. This approach mitigates the lateral movement of an attacker who compromises an existing user account and attempts to penetrate deeper into the system. To improve policy creation and enforcement, the system needs to have a thorough knowledge of the security postures inside the network as well as network topology and the context of the request.

5.4.3 Network Layer: Microsegmentation

The last layer is the network layer, which configures the network topology at the software level and virtually divides the network into multiple smaller segments. It answers the question *"How to get there?"* for any access request. Microsegmentation techniques enable the system to break the network and cloud environment into secure zones at the application workload level. This approach reduces the attack surface, prevents lateral movement and data breach, and achieves regulatory compliance. It provides a method to create granular access policies and helps visualize the vulnerabilities associated with applications.

In summary, zero trust enables multiple layers of defense from a holistic network system view. Traditional authentication, authorization, and network segmentation policies usually focus on IP-based local decisions and fail to consider the incentives of the access request. In zero-trust security, the policies on each trust layer of the zero-trust architecture would depend on the TE and risk assessment of the request, along with the global access policy for the whole network. The access attempt will be allowed only when it satisfies the requirements for all three layers.

5.5 Zero Trust for Cyber Resilience

5.5.1 How Zero Trust Contributes to Cyber Resilience

For a given attack, resilience is generally understood as the ability of the system to recover from an external disruptive event [42–44]. It involves actions before and after the incident [45]. Figure 5.5 illustrates the general performance transition when considering cyber resilience. We say the zero-trust system is (T, D)-resilient if the system can recover from the attack within $T = t_4 - t_2$ units of time and maintain a maximum loss of performance D [46].

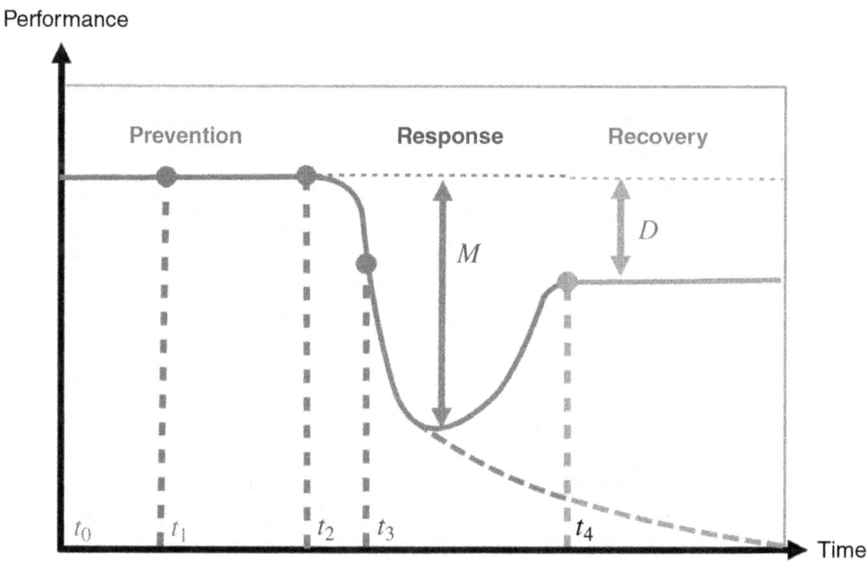

Figure 5.5 Resilience profile of a zero-trust system across prevention, response, and recovery phases. This figure illustrates how system performance evolves over time in the presence of a cyberattack. The timeline is divided into three phases: **prevention** (t_0 to t_2), where zero-trust mechanisms proactively deter threats; **response** (t_2 to t_4), where detection and containment mechanisms are activated, with M indicating the maximum performance degradation; and **recovery** (post-t_4), where the system restores functionality, with D representing residual performance loss. The solid line shows enhanced resilience due to zero-trust implementation, while the dashed line represents a system without such controls. This demonstrates how zero trust improves resilience by minimizing both impact and recovery time.

Zero trust plays a major role in building cyber resilience, as it provides additional layers of protection to prevent unpredictable threats, respond to the attacks, and limit impact if an unauthorized entity does gain access. Through this section, we explain how zero trust helps to build a resilient security ecosystem.

5.5.1.1 Prevention

Prevention in cyber resilience includes the ability to identify the risk and protect the system from potential threats. The first core function of cyber resilience is the ability to **identify** risks. Zero-trust security forfeits the assumption that everything behind the security perimeter is safe. The continuous TE process provides visibility to the system so that organizations can identify vulnerabilities of potential threats related to users' trustworthiness.

Where identity focuses primarily on baselining and monitoring, **protect** is when the framework becomes more proactive. The zero-trust model encourages the system to proactively establish strict security controls and comprehensive incident response plans. Based on the zero-trust assumption, the systems will always be prepared for any system compromises so that they can respond to the threats effectively.

5.5.1.2 Response

Response in cyber resilience includes the ability to detect cyber events and respond accordingly. The **detect** function is a critical step to a robust cyber program – the faster a cyber event is detected, the faster the repercussions can be mitigated. By continuously verifying the user's activity, zero-trust security provides organizations with greater visibility of network security [47]. Any changes in the user's behavior (e.g., unusual login attempts and unauthorized access requests) would lead to a TS update, informing the organization of any suspicious activity in the system.

Moreover, it is important to establish a **respond** function that supports the ability to contain the impact of a potential cybersecurity incident. Zero trust helps to improve cyber resilience by providing a multidimensional incident response to deter an attacker from a holistic system view [48].

5.5.1.3 Recovery

Finally, the **recover** function helps to reconfigure defense plans and restore any impaired capabilities or services after attacks. Zero-trust security solutions often include automated response capabilities, which can help to quickly contain security incidents and adapt to sudden changes in the network [49]. We will show in a later section that game theory provides the analytical basis for establishing effective automated zero-trust security responses.

5.5.2 A Running Example

With the aforementioned three trust layers, zero trust provides multidimensional mitigation against comprehensive cyberattacks and plays a major role in building cyber resilience. We provide an example to illustrate how zero-trust security helps the system build a resilient security model against insider threats and internal lateral movement at each layer.

5.5.2.1 Traditional Architecture

Consider an attacker stealthily gaining access to the victim's system through phishing attacks or account compromise, as shown in Figure 5.6. Traditional defense tends to focus on the boundaries of the network. However, traffic within the trusted zone is usually only lightly monitored because users inside the firewall are assumed to be trusted. With traditional perimeter-based defense, once inside the trusted zone, the attacker can disguise as an insider with stolen credentials and move laterally in the network toward the primary target. This one-dimensional protection is inadequate when dealing with sophisticated attacks such as APTs.

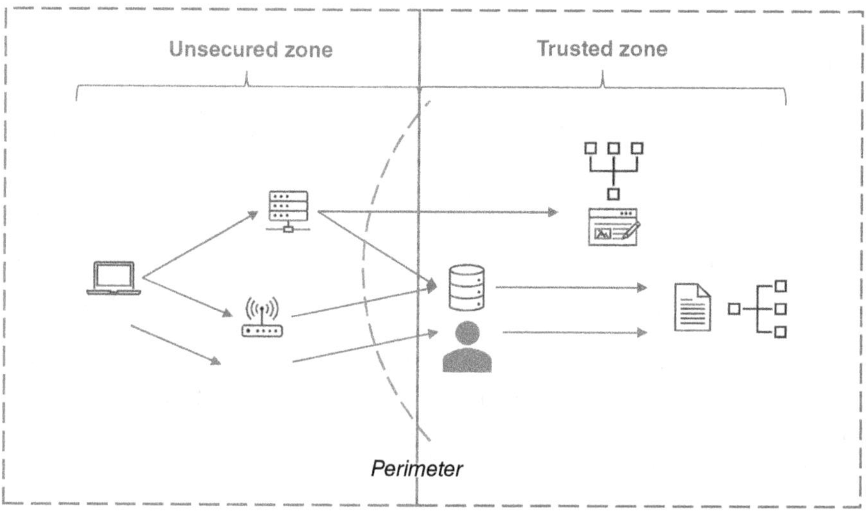

Figure 5.6 Illustration of an attack under traditional perimeter-based defense. The network is divided into an unsecured zone and a trusted zone, separated by a static perimeter. Once an attacker breaches this perimeter, they are treated as a trusted entity and can move laterally to access sensitive assets without further verification. This highlights a major vulnerability in legacy security architectures, where trust is implicitly granted based on network location, making it difficult to contain insider threats or sophisticated external breaches.

5.5.2.2 Cyber Resilience with Authentication Layer

Due to the zero-trust principles, network systems are required to continuously monitor the behavior of the user and adjust access decisions accordingly. After penetrating the system as an insider, the attacker still needs to go through constant authentication processes at each step before reaching the final destination, as illustrated in Figure 5.7. Continuous authentication creates extra effort for the attacker, especially when the system applies strict authentication methods like MFA or biometric authentication. The access request is denied if the attacker fails the authentication; thus, the critical asset is protected. Dynamic policy adjustment and continuous authentication help the system recover from existing compromises and prevent further damage to the system.

5.5.2.3 Cyber Resilience with Authorization Layer

Zero-trust security enforces the least privilege access as the fundamental principle and ensures that a user is given the minimum levels of permissions to perform legitimate functions at a bounded period. This principle mandates strict

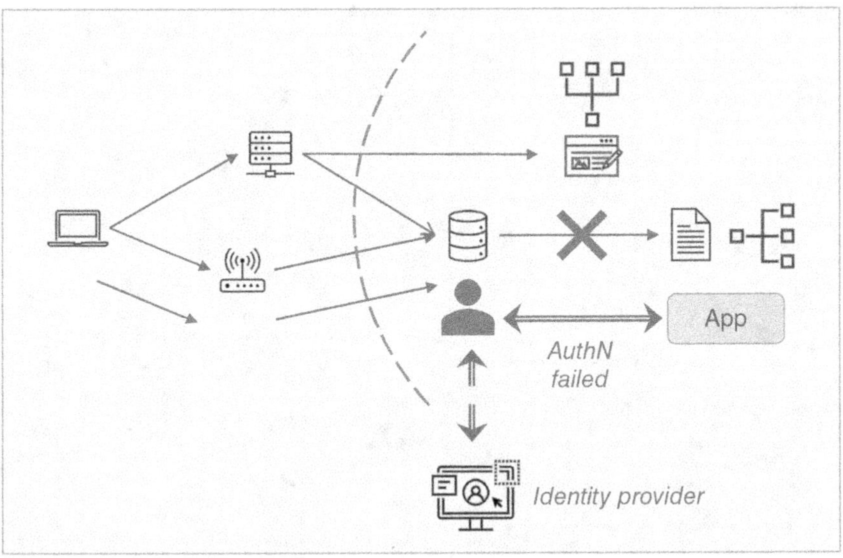

Figure 5.7 Cyber resilience through continuous authentication. Even after an attacker breaches the traditional perimeter, a zero-trust architecture enforces ongoing identity verification at multiple points before allowing access to critical assets. The figure shows that failure at any authentication checkpoint, facilitated by an identity provider and monitored by the application, halts the attack progression. This layered verification mechanism disrupts lateral movement and significantly enhances the resilience of the system by reducing reliance on a single point of defense.

policies and permissions for all accounts. With the help of TE mechanisms and user behavior analytics, the system could downgrade the privilege level of the compromised user account based on abnormal observations, thus stopping the attacker from accessing the critical assets, as in Figure 5.8. This layer again provides cyber resilience after the security measures at the traditional perimeter fail.

5.5.2.4 Cyber Resilience with Network Layer

Finally, microsegmentation in the network layer limits the attack impact if an external or insider breach does occur. As illustrated in Figure 5.9, the protection at the network layer restricts the influence radius of the data breach within only one network segment and prevents further damage to the system. By isolating the workloads, zero trust limits the effect of malicious lateral movement and ensures the security of other parts of the system after the attack. Microsegmentation offers granular security as network administrators can strengthen and pinpoint security by creating specific policies for critical applications. The segmentation policy can be expressed in terms of workload identities or attributes rather than physical network constructs. Thus, it offers dynamic protection that is adaptive to topology changes, especially in dynamic IoT environments.

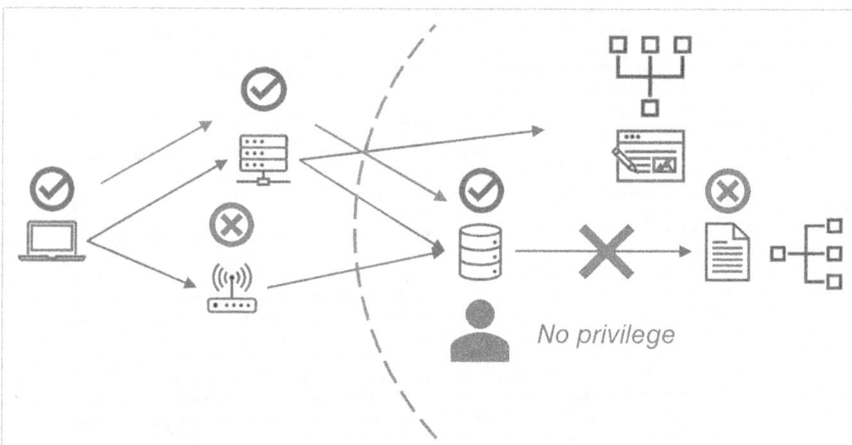

Figure 5.8 Cyber resilience through authorization control. Even after breaching the internal network boundary, an attacker must possess explicit privileges to access sensitive assets. In this scenario, the absence of proper authorization prevents lateral movement and access escalation, thereby halting the attack. The enforcement of least-privilege access policies adds a critical layer of defense that complements authentication and strengthens overall system resilience.

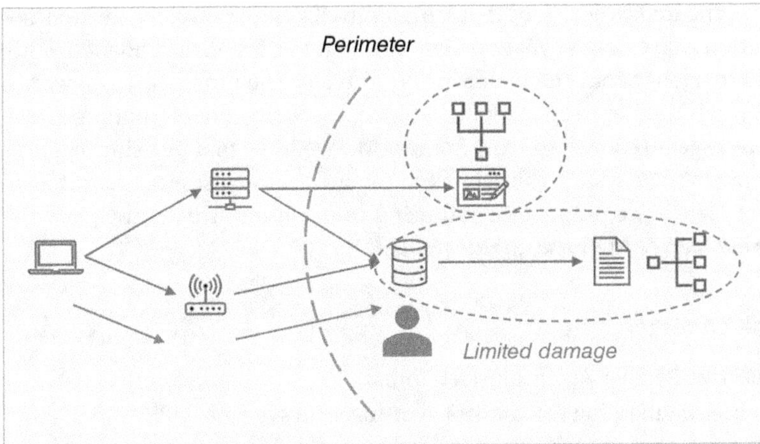

Figure 5.9 Cyber resilience through network-layer segmentation. Microsegmentation at the network layer limits the blast radius of a successful intrusion by confining the attacker's movement and isolating critical subsystems. Even if some nodes are compromised, the segmentation ensures the rest of the system remains operational and protected. This containment strategy is essential for sustaining system functionality and minimizing the overall impact of attacks.

5.6 Strategic Zero-trust Implementation

5.6.1 A Game-theoretic Approach

The interdependency between TE and PE is critical in zero trust as it helps ensure that trust policies are effective, appropriate, and adaptive to changing threats and risks. To formalize the zero-trust design, game theory has been a natural and successful framework for modeling the interactions between the system and the potential attacker. Many problems in cybersecurity are fundamentally decision-making problems under complex, uncertain, multi-agent conditions [9]. The optimal security policy aims to maximize the non-myopic well-being of the system by looking ahead to multiple steps into the horizon. The TS of an agent is evaluated under a given security policy, and the optimal security policy is computed using the Bellman principle based on the TS of an agent. The game theory equilibrium analysis not only provides a way to quantitatively assess the security posture of the network but also enables a formal methodology to design best-effort zero-trust policies. The optimal security policy aims to maximize the non-myopic well-being of the system by looking ahead multiple steps into the horizon.

In this section, we introduce several works that apply game theory to cybersecurity and achieve cyber resilience with autonomous and proactive zero-trust security responses. The autonomous defense depends on constant monitoring of user activities and makes decisions that are adaptive to online situation awareness. The automation also enables cyber resilience so that the system can adapt to sudden changes in agent behaviors under insider threats. The proposed frameworks consolidate traditional protections with zero-trust security models and provide a guide for a next-generation zero-trust framework. We hope that by using a game-theoretic approach, the system can achieve automated zero-trust security with better efficiency. Hence, we propose the following strategic zero-trust principle:

"Never trust, verify (defense) strategically."

5.6.2 Case Studies

5.6.2.1 Proactive Defense Against Insider Threat

APTs are a class of emerging threats for cyber-physical systems (CPS) due to their stealthy, dynamic, and adaptive nature. The deceptive behaviors of the attacker are captured by the multistage game of incomplete information, where each player has their private information unknown to the other [50]. Both players act strategically according to their beliefs about the type of opponent, which are formed by multistage observation and learning. It is important to develop a proactive and adaptive defense mechanism based on the trust estimation of the user.

Consider a two-player Markov game with incomplete information played on finite stages, $k \in \{0, 1, \dots, K\}$. Each player ($i \in \{1, 2\}$) has a set of possible types Θ_i, which is private information unrevealed to the opponent. The user's type θ_2 is either adversarial θ_2^b or legitimate θ_2^g, and the defender's type is either sophisticated θ_1^H or primitive θ_1^L. Based on the current state $x^k \in X^k$, the defender evaluates the trustworthiness of the user (forms a belief $b_1^k \in \Delta(\Theta_2)$) and takes action $a_1^k \in A_1^k$ according to his behavioral strategy $\sigma_1(\cdot) \in \Delta(A_1^k)$. Similarly, the user computes her belief on the defender's sophistication level $b_2^k \in \Delta(\Theta_1)$ and makes a move $a_2^k \in A_2^k$ according to her strategy $\sigma_2(\cdot) \in \Delta(A_2^k)$. The state x^k transfers to the next state $x^{k+1} \in X^{k+1}$ through a known state transition function f^k, i.e., $x^{k+1} = f^k(x^k, a_1^k, a_2^k)$. Both players update their beliefs using a Bayesian approach based on observed information:

$$b_i^{k+1}(\theta_j | x^{k+1}, \theta_i) = \frac{\Pr[x^{k+1} | \theta_j, x^k, \theta_i] b_i^k(\theta_j | x^k, \theta_i)}{\sum_{\bar{\theta}_j \in \Theta_j} \Pr[x^{k+1} | \bar{\theta}_j, x^k, \theta_i] b_i^k(\bar{\theta}_j | x^k, \theta_i)} \qquad i, j \in \{1, 2\}, j \neq i. \tag{5.3}$$

With the conditional independence of the player's strategies σ_1^k and σ_2^k,

$$\Pr[x^{k+1} | \theta_j, x^k, \theta_i] = \sum_{a_1^k \in A_1^k, a_2^k \in A_2^k} f^k(x^k, a_1^k, a_2^k) \sigma_1^k(a_1^k | x^k, \theta_1) \sigma_2^k(a_2^k | x^k, \theta_2). \tag{5.4}$$

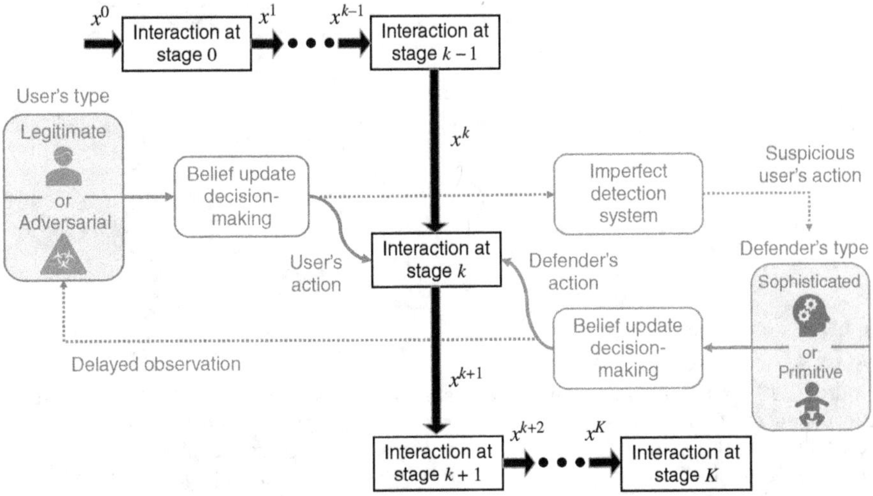

Figure 5.10 A detailed illustration of a proactive defense strategy against multistage APT attacks. The diagram models the sequential interaction between a user, a defender, and system states (in standard rectangle), forming a dynamic multistage game. The user may be legitimate or adversarial and chooses actions at each stage based on observed defender responses and inferred beliefs. Meanwhile, the defender utilizes an imperfect detection system to classify the user's behavior as suspicious or benign and updates its own beliefs accordingly. Both parties engage in belief-driven decision-making to optimize their objectives across a sequence of interactions from stage 0 to stage K. Each interaction results in a system transition $x^k \rightarrow x^{k+1}$, and the outcome at each stage informs future decisions. This framework captures the uncertainty, adaptivity, and strategic deception underlying cyber conflicts and emphasizes the need for continual situational awareness and belief updates in resilient security architectures.

Under this setting, the TS of the user at stage k can be interpreted as the defender's belief that the user is legitimate to the system, i.e., $TS^k = b_1^k(\theta_2 = \theta^g)$ (Figure 5.10).

Both players at each stage should optimize their expected cumulative utilities concerning the updated beliefs at the future stages, which leads to the perfect Bayesian Nash equilibrium (PBNE). A PBNE consists of two conditions: belief consistency and sequential rationality. The belief consistency emphasizes that when strategic players make long-term decisions, they have to consider the impact of their actions on their opponent's beliefs at future stages. Sequential rationality guarantees that unilateral deviations from the equilibrium at any state do not benefit the deviating player. Huang and Zhu [50] provide a computational algorithm to find the relaxed ϵ-PBNE.

Figure 5.11 illustrates the Tennessee Eastman process as a benchmark case study of industrial control systems. The initial stage $k = 0$ contains two states to

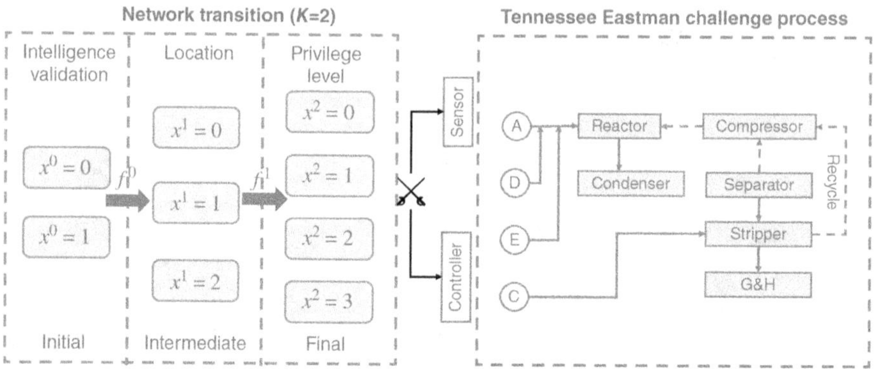

Figure 5.11 A case study combining cyber state transition modeling with the physical consequences of a cyberattack on the Tennessee Eastman process, a benchmark industrial control system (ICS). The left panel depicts a staged cyber access model where a user advances through a series of states based on successful validations (e.g., intelligence, location, privilege level). The adversary aims to escalate privilege through network transitions ($K = 2$), with each state encoding increasing access to system functionalities. The right panel shows the corresponding physical process flow in the Tennessee Eastman plant, which includes critical components such as the reactor, compressor, condenser, and separator. A successful cyber compromise could manipulate control logic or sensor readings, triggering cascading disruptions across physical units. This figure highlights the cyber-physical risk propagation and emphasizes the importance of zero-trust principles and stagewise authentication to restrict unauthorized access and maintain system integrity.

show whether the reconnaissance is effectual $x^0 = 1$ or not $x^0 = 0$. The defender could choose to conduct different levels of security training to increase employees' security awareness and protect them from web phishing. The user (potential attacker) can send emails with nonexecutable attachments and shortened URLs to the accounts of entry-level employees, managers, or avatars. The state at the intermediate stage $k = 1$ can be interpreted as the location of the user. The user can choose to escalate their privileges or perform no operation. On the other hand, the defender decides whether to permit the privilege escalation or not based on their assessment of the trustworthiness of the user. The decision is based on the trust estimation of the user via Bayesian updates in Eq. (5.3). At the final stage $k = 2$, the state represents the privilege levels of the user. Based on the types of both players (θ_1, θ_2), their action choices (a_1^k, a_2^k), and the underlying state x^k, we estimate the utilities by considering command injection attacks at supervisory control and data acquisition (SCADA) systems in the Tennessee Eastman process.

Experimental results illustrate that the private types of players would affect their policies and utilities under different information structures. It is important to establish a reliable trust assessment mechanism so that the defense policy remains effective. Besides, the Bayesian belief update leads to a more accurate estimate

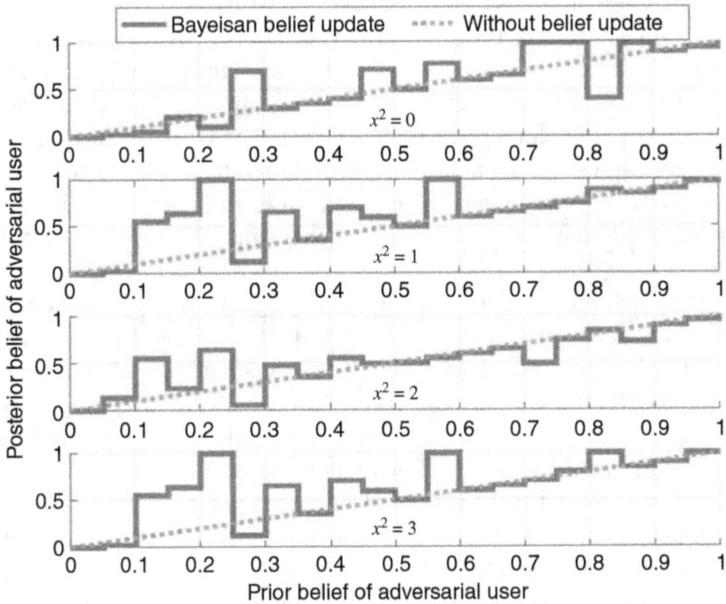

Figure 5.12 Posterior belief of the defender regarding whether a user is adversarial, given different system states $x^2 \in \{0, 1, 2, 3\}$. Each subplot compares the Bayesian belief update (solid line) with a static linear update baseline (dashed line), plotted as a function of the defender's prior belief. The Bayesian update incorporates new observations such as user actions and side-channel evidence, allowing for abrupt, information-sensitive adjustments. In contrast, the static update reflects no learning or adaptation. These plots demonstrate how Bayesian inference enables defenders to either amplify or dampen suspicion based on contextual cues, particularly in the midrange of prior belief values (e.g., 0.2–0.6), where decision uncertainty is greatest. This dynamic update mechanism is essential for adaptive and strategic zero-trust authentication, empowering the defender to refine access control policies in real time as the system evolves.

of users' types. By considering the prior knowledge, side evidence, and observed strategies, the defender effectively discovers the true type of user. As illustrated in Figure 5.12, Bayesian update helps to correct the inaccurate static prior belief and allows the defense strategies to remain effective. One interesting observation is that the defender benefits from introducing defensive deception, e.g., a primitive defender can disguise himself as a sophisticated one to confuse the attacker. Interested readers can refer to [17] for more examples and applications.

5.6.2.2 Strategic Trust in Cloud-enabled Cyber-physical Systems

Zero-trust security is important in CPS [51]. The integrated physical and computational capabilities in CPS have created a new generation of systems. However, the heterogeneous components in such systems enlarge the attack surface and leave multiple vulnerabilities that the attacker could explore. Trust in devices and signals becomes a critical factor in decision-making. Each device must decide whether to trust other components that may be compromised. In Pawlick and Zhu [37], we use a game-theoretic approach to evaluate the trust of the cloud service based on the potential consequence of the trust. The trust is based on the game-theoretic assessment of the attack and defense strategies. The trust game and the defense games are consolidated into a meta-game framework, as shown in Figure 5.13, to jointly design trust and defense mechanisms to achieve a zero-trust architecture.

Each agent in a CPS must decide whether to trust signals from the vulnerable cloud that may be compromised. We refer to this trust as strategic trust, which is a positive belief about the perceived reliability of, dependability of, and confidence in the signal. The trust of the signal is estimated using the FlipIt game $\mathbf{G_F}$ [52], in which an attacker ($\mathcal{A}$) and a defender ($\mathcal{D}$) are competing to control the cloud service. The players choose how often to move based on their incentives to control the cloud and the cost that they pay to capture it. Nash equilibrium of $\mathbf{G_F}$ reveals the probability with which the cloud is compromised in the steady state of the game. In equilibrium, the attacker $\mathcal{A}$ controls the cloud service with probability $p \in [0, 1]$. Then, the trustworthiness of the cloud signal can be written as $TS^0 = 1 - p \in [0, 1]$, which serves as the prior belief in the following signaling game between the cloud and the device ($\mathcal{R}$).

In the following signaling game $\mathbf{G_S}$, the sender may be an attacker with type θ_A or a defender with type θ_D. The device $\mathcal{R}$ determines who controls the cloud (the type of the sender). Thus $\mathcal{R}$ needs to decide whether to trust the received command (message m) based on his belief (trust) about the unknown type of the sender. This posterior belief is computed in a Bayesian fashion by considering the prior trust TS^0 from the FlipIt game and the sender's strategies under the equilibrium of $\mathbf{G_S}$.

The trust-based decision is vital, especially in CPS related to critical infrastructures, vehicle networks, personal health products, etc. The consequence of wrongly trusting an attacker could be severe as it could involve public operations or human safety. The Gestalt Nash Equilibrium (GNE) [53] of the overall macro-game ($\mathbf{G_F}, \mathbf{G_S}$) characterizes the steady state and risk assessment in CPS. It helps to study the strategic trust of vulnerable network components and contributes to the design of zero-trust security in CPS.

5.6.2.3 Strategic Zero-trust Authentication for 5G Networks

The recent trends in remote work and bring your own device (BYOD) exacerbate the need for a trustworthy 5G network system to provide proper authentication mechanisms for external connections from unknown or uncertain environments. 5G network can be divided into a public network that is open to any connection

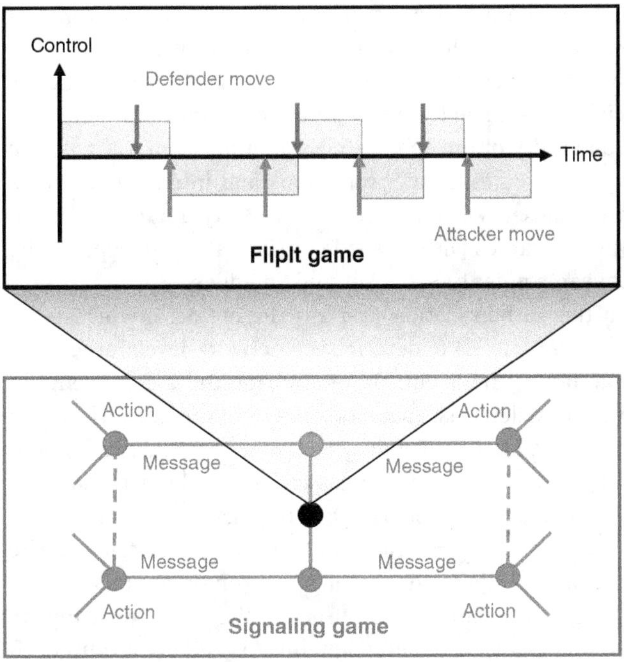

Figure 5.13 Conceptual model of the combined cloud control game. The attacker ($\mathcal{A}$) and defender ($\mathcal{D}$) play the FlipIt game for control of the cloud. Then, the winner sends a command to the device ($\mathcal{R}$) in the signaling game. The top panel illustrates the FlipIt game, a stealthy timing game where both the attacker and defender attempt to seize and maintain control of a cloud-based resource by making covert moves at random or strategic intervals. Control of the cloud alternates based on who has made the most recent move, and the resulting fraction of time each player maintains control determines the real-time trustworthiness of the cloud. In the bottom panel, the current controller, either $\mathcal{A}$ or $\mathcal{D}$, acts as a sender in a signaling game, transmitting a message to the device $\mathcal{R}$. The receiver must interpret this message without knowing the sender's true identity, relying instead on a prior belief informed by the outcome of the FlipIt game. The device must strategically decide whether to trust and act on the received command, weighing the potential risk of adversarial manipulation. This composition of the FlipIt and signaling games captures the interplay between long-term stealthy control dynamics and short-term trust decisions, forming the basis for a dynamic and game-theoretically grounded zero-trust framework. It supports rigorous analysis of how control over infrastructure influences downstream communication security and policy enforcement under uncertainty.

and a private network that is fully controlled by industrial infrastructure or government. Although the private network is composed of trusted devices, it still needs to exchange information with the public network due to external access or cloud services. If a remote agent from a public network is trying to access a critical node in the private network, it is essential to evaluate the trust of the agent before granting access. An attacker may utilize the stored credentials in the already compromised nodes and penetrate the system to reach some critical assets. To prevent such lateral movements of the potential attacker, the zero-trust system should strategically make authentication decisions based on the TE of the agent. Since the system cannot fully observe the true identity of the agent, the system needs to estimate the trustworthiness of the agent based on past observations and interactions. In Ge and Zhu [29, 54], we have proposed a formal zero-trust security framework called GAZETA, building on Markov games with one-sided information, to capture the dynamic interactions between a potential attacker and defender.

The game is played on the authentication graph in Figure 5.14, which is an agent-centric directed graph $G = \langle V, E \rangle$ to describe the network-level authentication activities and reachability of the agent. By monitoring the logon events or processes that search for user credentials, each node $v \in V$ in the network can be labeled by an indicator function $L(v) = \mathbb{1}$ (node v has been visited). The authentication graph and labeling function over all nodes consist of the game state at each stage $k = \{1, 2, \ldots, K\}$. A binary type set $\Theta = \{0, 1\}$ is considered for the agent, where $\theta = 0$ is a legitimate user and $\theta = 1$ represents a malicious attacker. The TS of the agent is defined as the belief the agent is legitimate at stage k, i.e., $TS^k = b^k(\theta = 0)$. At each stage, the agent attempts to access the next node using the stored credentials in the visited nodes. The defender aims to validate the authentication of the agent and reject potential lateral movement from malicious attackers. The identity validation may require alternative authentications (e.g., MFA), which would create difficulty for the attacker with only stored credentials. However, this additional authentication process is resource- and time-consuming. The defender needs to discover attacks while minimizing resource consumption for the sake of balancing system performance and security. The game is played until the finite game horizon K, which represents the maximum time span for the agent to exist in the network without credential renewal. The attacker will lose his foothold in the network if he cannot reach the target within K steps.

The game commits to one-sided ϵ-PBNE, which is a refined ϵ-PBNE when there is only one player (the defender) who cannot fully observe the type of the opponent (attacker) (Figure 5.15). To improve cyber robustness and resilience to unexpected environmental changes, Ge and Zhu [29] proposed a moving-horizon algorithm to approximately compute the optimal strategies online. The online zero-trust defense enables the system to integrate side evidence into TE, identify the attacker quicker, and eliminate the potential risks of a persistent attack.

Experiments on the 5G network case study in Figure 5.14 show that the strategic zero-trust defense outperforms other access control methods by providing the shortest access time for the benign user and the longest access time for the malicious attacker. It has been corroborated that the defense mechanism can efficiently

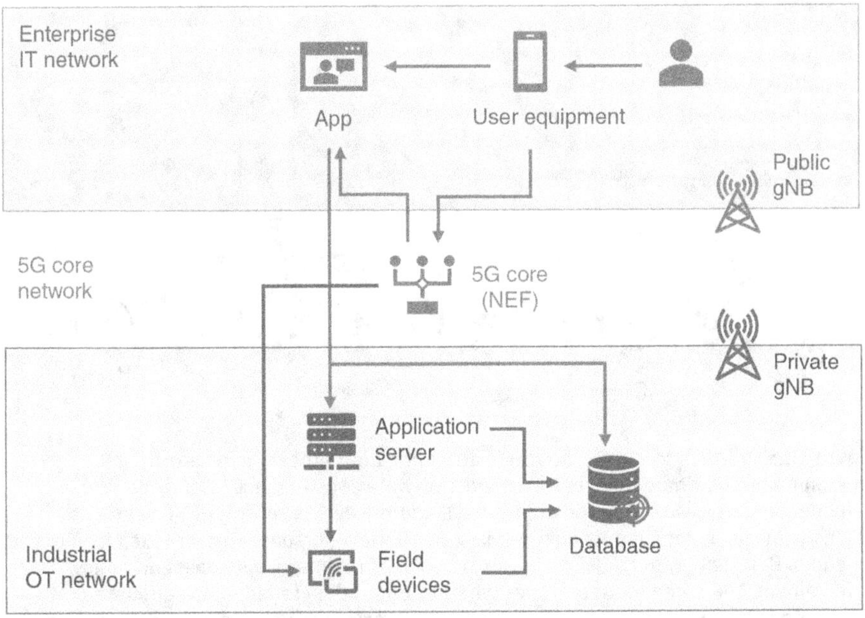

Figure 5.14 Example architecture of a hybrid 5G-enabled industrial network integrating enterprise IT, 5G core, and operational technology (OT) domains. The user initiates access through user equipment, such as a smartphone or IoT device, connected via either public or private 5G base stations (gNBs). These access requests are processed through the 5G Core Network Exposure Function (NEF), which facilitates secure communication between the application layer and 5G core services. The 5G core mediates interactions between the enterprise application and downstream OT systems, including an application server and field devices within the industrial control environment. Access to critical assets, such as the central database, is governed through coordinated policy enforcement across domains. This setup highlights key security challenges: cross-domain trust propagation, low-latency control over field devices, and potential lateral movement risks across interconnected segments. The figure underscores the need for dynamic, context-aware authentication and access control mechanisms that span both IT and OT environments, aligning with zero-trust principles to safeguard industrial cyber-physical infrastructure.

correct erroneous prior trust and provide a more reliable TE. With moving-horizon computation, GAZETA has created a robust security model that can adapt to unexpected environmental changes and account takeover. Experimental results show that the online defense scheme can quickly discover account takeover and deter the lateral movement of the attacker successfully. The proposed mechanism provides a guide for the development of next-generation secure and resilient 5G zero-trust networks.

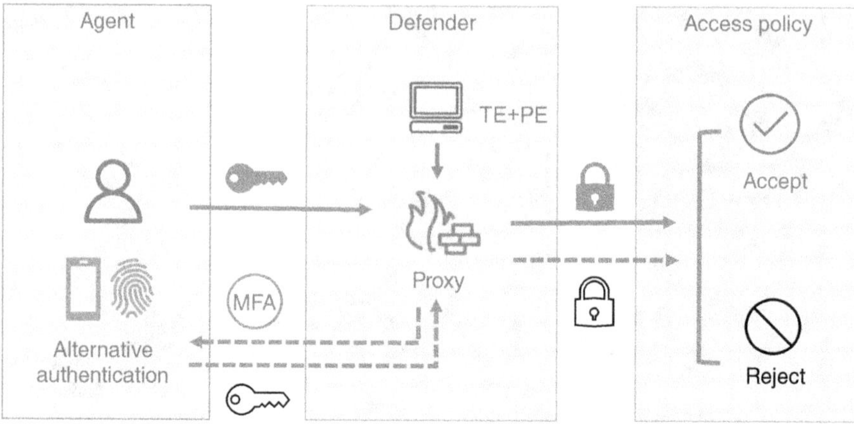

Figure 5.15 Illustration of the strategic authentication process in a zero-trust environment. The figure depicts the interaction between an agent (user or device), a defender (acting as an authentication proxy), and the access control PE. The process begins with the agent submitting a primary credential (e.g., password or token key) to the defender. Based on internal TE mechanisms, such as telemetry evidence and policy enforcement, the defender determines whether the initial credential is sufficient or whether additional verification is required. If uncertainty or risk is detected, the defender challenges the agent with an alternative or MFA mechanism, such as biometric data or a one-time passcode. This decision is conditional and context-aware, depending on factors such as device posture, location, behavioral signals, or historical TS. Upon successful validation, the defender proxies the access request to the access control system, which ultimately accepts or rejects the request based on defined policies. The diagram illustrates a key component of zero-trust security: authentication is dynamic and adaptive, not static. Every access request is evaluated independently, with risk-sensitive escalation paths that balance usability and security. This architecture enhances cyber resilience by ensuring that access decisions respond to evolving threat conditions in real time.

5.7 Conclusion

Zero trust represents a paradigm shift in cybersecurity, moving beyond traditional perimeter-based defenses toward a dynamic, identity- and behavior-centric security model. In contrast to legacy systems that grant implicit trust based on network location, zero trust enforces continuous verification of all users, devices, and processes, regardless of their position within the network. This chapter examined how zero-trust principles can be formalized and operationalized to achieve autonomous cyber resilience, particularly in adversarial and complex environments.

We began by tracing the evolution from perimeter-based models to zero-trust architectures, emphasizing architectural distinctions such as microsegmentation, identity-centric controls, and policy enforcement points. Central to the proposed framework are two core components: TE and PE. TE performs real-time, probabilistic assessments of user and system trustworthiness using Bayesian inference and behavioral cues. PE leverages these dynamic TS to implement context-aware, risk-adaptive security decisions, thus forming a closed control loop that adapts to threats over time.

This chapter highlighted how the interplay between TE and PE contributes to end-to-end cyber resilience by allowing the system to proactively detect, contain, and recover from attacks. We formalized this adaptive decision-making process using game-theoretic models, including signaling games, Stackelberg games, and multistage Bayesian games that enable strategic reasoning under uncertainty. These models capture key challenges such as information asymmetry, adversarial deception, and resource allocation, and they serve as the analytical backbone for zero-trust policy design.

To ground these concepts in practice, we presented several illustrative examples, including a detailed case study involving a 5G-enabled industrial network. This example demonstrated how an adversary may attempt lateral movement across a dynamic authentication graph and how the defender, guided by trust assessments and policy strategies, can effectively halt attack progression. Further, we discussed a cyber-physical attack scenario on the Tennessee Eastman Process, showing how privilege escalation in cyberspace can lead to real-world consequences. These case studies bridge abstract theory with real-world deployment challenges in modern industrial systems.

This chapter complements and extends the discussion in Chapter 2, which focused on cyber resilience in transportation infrastructure [55], an example of OT. While Chapter 2 examined resilience from the perspective of sensing, routing, and system dynamics, this chapter centers on information technology (IT) resilience through access control and policy enforcement. Given the growing convergence of IT and OT environments, our work demonstrates how zero-trust principles can provide a unified framework for protecting large-scale, interconnected CPS. Notably, game theory emerges as a common analytical language for both domains, enabling integrated strategies that account for adversarial dynamics, decision-making under uncertainty, and strategic defense.

Together, these chapters chart a coherent roadmap that connects theoretical models with practical defense architectures. By combining adversarial reasoning, probabilistic trust modeling, and real-time policy enforcement, we lay the groundwork for next-generation zero-trust systems that are autonomous, adaptive, and resilient by design. Future directions include the integration of reinforcement learning for personalized and evolving trust inference, federated policy coordination across organizational boundaries, and defense mechanisms against strategic deception and misinformation, which are further elaborated in subsequent chapters.

References

1 Quanyan Zhu, Stefan Rass, Bernhard Dieber, and Victor Mayoral Vilches. Cybersecurity in robotics: Challenges, quantitative modeling, and practice. *arXiv preprint arXiv:2103.05789*, 2021.

2 Tim Weil and San Murugesan. It risk and resilience—cybersecurity response to COVID-19. *IT Professional*, 22(3): 4–10, 2020.

3 Linan Huang and Quanyan Zhu. Duplicity games for deception design with an application to insider threat mitigation. *IEEE Transactions on Information Forensics and Security*, 16: 4843–4856, 2021.

4 Quanyan Zhu and Stefan Rass. On multi-phase and multi-stage game-theoretic modeling of advanced persistent threats. *IEEE Access*, 6: 13958–13971, 2018.

5 Yunfei Ge and Quanyan Zhu. MEGA-PT: A meta-game framework for agile penetration testing. In *International Conference on Decision and Game Theory for Security*, pages 24–44. Springer, 2024.

6 V. A. Stafford. Zero trust architecture. *NIST Special Publication*, 800: 207, 2020.

7 Carl Colwill. Human factors in information security: The insider threat–who can you trust these days? *Information Security Technical Report*, 14(4): 186–196, 2009.

8 Quanyan Zhu and Tamer Başar. Dynamic policy-based IDS configuration. In *Proceedings of the 48h IEEE Conference on Decision and Control (CDC) held jointly with 2009 28th Chinese Control Conference*, pages 8600–8605. IEEE, 2009.

9 Charles A. Kamhoua, Christopher D. Kiekintveld, Fei Fang, and Quanyan Zhu. *Game theory and machine learning for cyber security*. John Wiley & Sons, 2021.

10 Mohammad Hossein Manshaei, Quanyan Zhu, Tansu Alpcan, Tamer Bacşar, and Jean-Pierre Hubaux. Game theory meets network security and privacy. *ACM Computing Surveys (CSUR)*, 45(3): 1–39, 2013.

11 Quanyan Zhu and Stefan Rass. Game theory meets network security: A tutorial. In *Proceedings of the 2018 ACM SIGSAC Conference on Computer and Communications Security*, pages 2163–2165. 2018.

12 Saman A. Zonouz, Himanshu Khurana, William H. Sanders, and Timothy M. Yardley. Rre: A game-theoretic intrusion response and recovery engine. *IEEE Transactions on Parallel and Distributed Systems*, 25(2): 395–406, 2013.

13 Yinan Hu and Quanyan Zhu. Evasion-aware Neyman-Pearson detectors: A game-theoretic approach. In *2022 IEEE 61st Conference on Decision and Control (CDC)*, pages 6111–6117. IEEE, 2022.

14 Sushil Jajodia, Anup K. Ghosh, V. S. Subrahmanian, Vipin Swarup, Cliff Wang, and X. Sean Wang. *Moving target defense II: application of game theory and adversarial modeling*, Vol. 100. Springer, 2012.

15 Linan Huang and Quanyan Zhu. Strategic learning for active, adaptive, and autonomous cyber defense. In *Adaptive autonomous secure cyber systems*, pages 205–230. Springer, 2020.

16 Quanyan Zhu and Tamer Başar. Game-theoretic approach to feedback-driven multi-stage moving target defense. In *International conference on decision and game theory for security*, pages 246–263. Springer, 2013.

17 Jeffrey Pawlick and Quanyan Zhu. *Game theory for cyber deception: from theory to applications*. Springer Nature, 2021.

18 Tao Zhang and Quanyan Zhu. Hypothesis testing game for cyber deception. In *Decision and Game Theory for Security: 9th International Conference, GameSec 2018*, Seattle, WA, USA, 29–31 October 2018, *Proceedings 9*, pages 540–555. Springer, 2018.

19 Kimberly Ferguson-Walter, Sunny Fugate, Justin Mauger, and Maxine Major. Game theory for adaptive defensive cyber deception. In *Proceedings of the 6th Annual Symposium on Hot Topics in the Science of Security*, pages 1–8, 2019.

20 Jeffrey Pawlick, Edward Colbert, and Quanyan Zhu. A game-theoretic taxonomy and survey of defensive deception for cybersecurity and privacy. *ACM Computing Surveys (CSUR)*, 52(4): 1–28, 2019.

21 Ya-Ting Yang and Quanyan Zhu. When to deceive: A cross-layer stackelberg game framework for strategic timing of cyber deception. *arXiv preprint arXiv:2505.21244*, 2025.

22 Ya-Ting Yang and Quanyan Zhu. A multi-resolution dynamic game framework for cross-echelon decision-making in cyber warfare. *arXiv preprint arXiv:2507.03021*, 2025.

23 Yan Zhou, Murat Kantarcioglu, and Bowei Xi. A survey of game theoretic approach for adversarial machine learning. *Wiley Interdisciplinary Reviews: Data Mining and Knowledge Discovery*, 9(3): e1259, 2019.

24 Ling Huang, Anthony D. Joseph, Blaine Nelson, Benjamin I. P. Rubinstein, and J. Doug Tygar. Adversarial machine learning. In *Proceedings of the 4th ACM workshop on Security and Artificial Intelligence*, pages 43–58. 2011.

25 Lijun Gao, Zheng Yan, Xueqin Liang, Xi Xu, Jie Wang, Wenxiu Ding, and Laurence Tianruo Yang. Taxonomy and recent advance of game theoretical approaches in adversarial machine learning: A survey. In *ACM Transactions on Sensor Networks*, 2022.

26 Rory Ward and Betsy Beyer. Beyondcorp: A new approach to enterprise security. *; login:*, 39(6): 6–11, 2014.

27 Jianxin Li, Bo Li, Tianyu Wo, Chunming Hu, Jinpeng Huai, Lu Liu, and K. P. Lam. Cyberguarder: A virtualization security assurance architecture for green cloud computing. *Future Generation Computer Systems*, 28(2): 379–390, 2012.

28 Yang Tao, Zhu Lei, and Peng Ruxiang. Fine-grained big data security method based on zero trust model. In *2018 IEEE 24th International Conference on Parallel and Distributed Systems (ICPADS)*, pages 1040–1045. IEEE, 2018.

29 Yunfei Ge and Quanyan Zhu. Mufaza: Multi-source fast and autonomous zero-trust authentication for 5g networks. In *MILCOM 2022-2022 IEEE Military Communications Conference (MILCOM)*, pages 571–576. IEEE, 2022.

30 J-Hee Cho, Kevin Chan, and Sibel Adali. A survey on trust modeling. *ACM Computing Surveys (CSUR)*, 48(2): 1–40, 2015.

31 Zheng Yan and Silke Holtmanns. Trust modeling and management: From social trust to digital trust. In *Computer security, privacy and politics: current issues, challenges and solutions*, pages 290–323. IGI Global, 2008.

32 Piero Bonatti, Claudiu Duma, Daniel Olmedilla, and Nahid Shahmehri. An integration of reputation-based and policy-based trust management. In *W9: The Semantic Web and Policy Workshop (SWPW)*, page 136. Citeseer, 2007.

33 B. Clifford Neuman and Theodore Ts'o. Kerberos: An authentication service for computer networks. *IEEE Communications Magazine*, 32(9): 33–38, 1994.

34 Quanyan Zhu, Carol Fung, Raouf Boutaba, and Tamer Basar. Guidex: A game-theoretic incentive-based mechanism for intrusion detection networks. *IEEE Journal on Selected Areas in Communications*, 30(11): 2220–2230, 2012.

35 Carol J. Fung and Quanyan Zhu. Facid: A trust-based collaborative decision framework for intrusion detection networks. *Ad Hoc Networks*, 53: 17–31, 2016.

36 Jeffrey Pawlick, Juntao Chen, and Quanyan Zhu. iSTRICT: An interdependent strategic trust mechanism for the cloud-enabled internet of controlled things. *IEEE Transactions on Information Forensics and Security*, 14(6): 1654–1669, 2018.

37 Jeffrey Pawlick and Quanyan Zhu. Strategic trust in cloud-enabled cyber-physical systems with an application to glucose control. *IEEE Transactions on Information Forensics and Security*, 12(12): 2906–2919, 2017.

38 Yunfei Ge and Quanyan Zhu. Accountability and insurance in iot supply chain. *arXiv preprint arXiv:2201.11855*, 2022.

39 David R. Miller. *Security information and event management (SIEM) implementation*. McGraw-Hill Higher Education, 2011.

40 Yunfei Ge and Quanyan Zhu. Trust threshold policy for explainable and adaptive zero-trust defense in enterprise networks. In *2022 IEEE Conference on Communications and Network Security (CNS)*, pages 359–364. IEEE, 2022.

41 Yunfei Ge, Tao Li, and Quanyan Zhu. Scenario-agnostic zero-trust defense with explainable threshold policy: A meta-learning approach. *arXiv preprint arXiv:2303.03349*, 2023.

42 Devanandham Henry and Jose Emmanuel Ramirez-Marquez. Generic metrics and quantitative approaches for system resilience as a function of time. *Reliability Engineering & System Safety*, 99: 114–122, 2012.

43 Quanyan Zhu. Foundations of cyber resilience: The confluence of game, control, and learning theories. *arXiv preprint arXiv:2404.01205*, 2024.

44 Quanyan Zhu and Tamer Başar. Disentangling resilience from robustness: Contextual dualism, interactionism, and game-theoretic paradigms. *IEEE Control Systems Magazine*, 44(3): 95–103, 2024.

45 Quanyan Zhu and Zhiheng Xu. *Cross-layer design for secure and resilient cyber-physical systems*. Springer, 2020.

46 Yuhan Zhao, Craig Rieger, and Quanyan Zhu. Multi-agent learning for resilient distributed control systems. *arXiv preprint arXiv:2208.05060*, 2022.

47 Hans de Bruijn and Marijn Janssen. Building cybersecurity awareness: The need for evidence-based framing strategies. *Government Information Quarterly*, 34(1): 1–7, 2017.

48 Christoph Buck, Christian Olenberger, André Schweizer, Fabiane Völter, and Torsten Eymann. Never trust, always verify: A multivocal literature review on current knowledge and research gaps of zero-trust. *Computers & Security*, 110: 102436, 2021.

49 Linan Huang and Quanyan Zhu. Adaptive strategic cyber defense for advanced persistent threats in critical infrastructure networks. *ACM SIGMETRICS Performance Evaluation Review*, 46(2): 52–56, 2019.

50 Linan Huang and Quanyan Zhu. A dynamic games approach to proactive defense strategies against advanced persistent threats in cyber-physical systems. *Computers & Security*, 89: 101660, 2020.

51 Jiong Jin, Zhibo Pang, Jonathan Kua, Quanyan Zhu, Karl H. Johansson, Nikolaj Marchenko, and Dave Cavalcanti. Cloud-fog automation: The new paradigm towards autonomous industrial cyber-physical systems. *IEEE Journal on Selected Areas in Communications*, 43(9): 2917–2937, 2025.

52 Marten Van Dijk, Ari Juels, Alina Oprea, and Ronald L. Rivest. Flipit: The game of "stealthy takeover". *Journal of Cryptology*, 26(4): 655–713, 2013.

53 Juntao Chen and Quanyan Zhu. Security investment under cognitive constraints: A gestalt nash equilibrium approach. In *2018 52nd Annual Conference on Information Sciences and Systems (CISS)*, pages 1–6. IEEE, 2018.

54 Yunfei Ge and Quanyan Zhu. Gazeta: Game-theoretic zero-trust authentication for defense against lateral movement in 5g iot networks. *IEEE Transactions on Information Forensics and Security*, 19: 540–554, 2023.

55 Y-Ting Yang, Haozhe Lei, and Quanyan Zhu. Prada: Proactive risk assessment and mitigation of misinformed demand attacks on navigational route recommendations. *arXiv preprint arXiv:2409.00243*, 2024.

6

Cyber Insurance for Cyber Resilience

Shutian Liu and Quanyan Zhu*

Tandon School of Engineering, New York University, Brooklyn, NY, USA

*Corresponding Author: sl6803@nyu.edu

6.1 Introduction

Cyber resilience refers to the abilities of a cyber system or a cyber-physical system (CPS) to be resistant to potential harms, be repairable from cyberattacks and system failures, and be sustainable after a pause of services or a shutdown of networked communications. Cyber resilience [1, 2] extends the notion of cybersecurity, as resiliency accounts for post-damage restorations, while traditional security notions aim at securing systems at the ex-ante stage to defend against interim harms. Possible ways to enhance the level of system security include setting up antivirus software and firewall, deploying intrusion detection systems (IDSs) [3–5], adopting moving target defense systems [6, 7], and using cyber deception [8–10] and autonomous defense [11, 12]. These traditional techniques build on increasing system security against possible attack vectors including phishing, cryptojacking, and advanced persistent threats (APTs). However, not all attacks can be successfully defended, and many system failures are unavoidable.

Cyber insurance is a unique approach to enhance cyber resilience among the other traditional defense mechanisms. As illustrated in Figure 6.1, it is a complementary mechanism to further reduce the financial impact on the systems (e.g., critical infrastructure operators, autonomous system users, and enterprise network owners) after their efforts in defending against cyberattacks and implementing resilience mechanisms to maintain the system-level operation despite the fact that the attacker is already in the system. The perfect defense and resilience

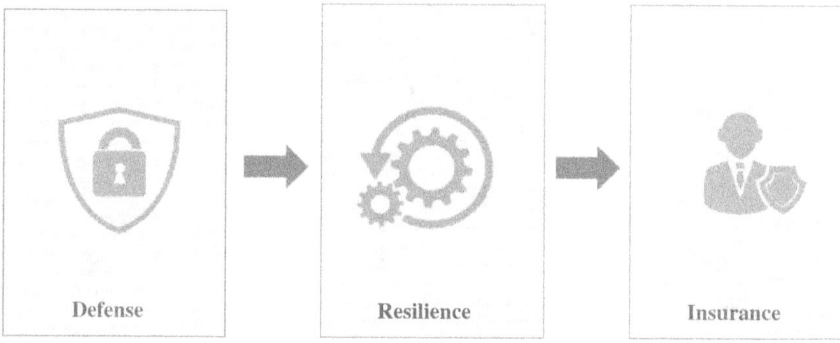

Figure 6.1 Insurance is a complementary mechanism to provide a socioeconomic layer of resilience to the system protected under a technical security and resilience mechanism.

mechanisms that can prevent or deter the attacker from inflicting significant damages are either cost-prohibitive or impossible to attain without compromising usability. There exist residual cyber risks even though the system has deployed sophisticated defense mechanisms. Cyber insurance is one last resort to mitigate the damage on individual systems through financial means so that business or operational continuity of the system can be ensured, and further recovery is economically feasible. It is particularly important for individuals or small or midsize businesses that do not have sufficient cybersecurity expertise and cannot afford a significant investment in cybersecurity for their systems.

From the user's perspective, cyber insurance is not a direct security investment. It is an agreement initiated by payments from the users to the insurer and followed by the insurer's promises of covering the costs of cyber losses to be encountered by the users. Cyber insurance functions through risk sharing. Risk sharing exists between the users and the insurer, as can be observed from how a cyber insurance contract is established. A prominent use case of cyber insurance where the users benefit from risk sharing is ransomware, which has recently spread and affected many victims, including large corporations (e.g., Colonial Pipeline ransomware attack [13] and Honda ransomware attack [14]), and many small businesses, including local high schools and hospitals. Attackers are financially motivated to gain by cryptoviral extortion. The victims would face the to-pay-or-not-to-pay dilemma. Without paying the ransom, the services and the businesses supported by the system will be disrupted. However, by paying the ransom, the victims will suffer financially and experience irrevocable damage to the system and their reputation. Cyber insurance is a risk-sharing mechanism that can transfer the residual risks to a third party (the insurers) to mitigate the loss due to the ransom payment as well as the disruptions caused by the attack. Besides, there is also risk sharing among the users, as the existence of the cyber insurance markets depends on the population of the insured users.

Cyber insurance adds to the users' strategy pools for defending their systems, since users can invest in system security and purchase cyber insurance at the same time. While security investments can stochastically reduce cyber risks, contracting cyber insurance protects users against potential severe losses from low-probability yet fatal attacks or failures. For mid- and small-scale businesses and companies, cyber insurance may be the only feasible way to defend their systems. The reason lies in that, with the advances of the attack vectors, there is a need to involve experienced and sophisticated cybersecurity expertise or professional teams to build protection systems or to form security consulting departments. These approaches may be too costly for mid- to small-scale business owners. Cyber insurance comes more handy, since the expensive procedure of hiring and training of individuals is taken care of by the insurance company. What the owners need to do is to choose a reliable third party and contract with it to obtain reasonable coverage for future cyber losses. Cyber insurance creates a win-win situation for the insurers and the users. A successful cyber insurance contract not only benefits the users by reducing their financial losses but also produces profits for the insurance companies. Therefore, it is beneficial to create cyber insurance markets to enable an ecosystem in which system users and operators can further mitigate their cyber risks.

To this end, there is a need to understand the challenges in the ecosystem that prohibit the implementation of cyber insurance. These challenges arise because of the influences on the ecosystem, which include the technologies for understanding cyber losses to enable insurance plans, the agents (customers) in the cyber insurance, and the economic relations between the insurer and the agents that affect the incentives for purchasing the insurances and the agents' behaviors when they are insured. From the aspect of the technologies, the coverage plan of the insurance is challenging to determine because of the difficulties in cyber risk assessment. The reason is twofold. First, due to the existence of different types of cyberattacks (such as human-layer attacks due to cognitive vulnerabilities and human errors, cyber-layer attacks targeting the IT, and physical-layer attacks), it is impossible for the network users to locate the actual cause of cyber risks. In other words, the origin of cyber risks is mixed, as attacks from different layers are interdependent. Second, the insurer has no incentive to cover the cyber threats that are likely to be successfully defended by common defense mechanisms. Therefore, it is crucial for the insurer to figure out the feasible cyber defense actions of their customers and design coverage plans keyed to those defenses that are not included. From the lens of human vulnerabilities [15–17], risk preferences play an essential role in establishing insurance contracts. On the one hand, the users are often risk-averse, since they wish to mitigate the uncertainty they are facing and aim to avoid severe fatal outcomes despite their low possibilities. On the other hand, the insurer needs to be risk neutral, since their assessment of the risk should be rational in order to provide revenue-maximizing risk-sharing insurance services. Due to the challenges of risk assessments [18] caused by the aspect of technologies, the risk preferences of the users and the insurer add one dimension of difficulty in the quantification of the perceived cyber losses. From a practical viewpoint, elicitation techniques can aid the calibration of human risk preferences [19]. However, there is no universal agreement on a specific mathematical description for representing a risk attitude. Moreover, cyber risks are more challenging to evaluate since immaterial resources in the informational technology (IT) systems such as data and information are often involved. Hence, choosing a proper and convenient model to assess the risks is still an obstacle sitting in front of the implementation of cyber insurance. From an economic perspective, insurance design is challenging since dilemmas may occur when the insurer and the insured agents are asymmetric in terms of knowledge about the environment and information about the actions. The adverse selection situation and the moral hazard issue, among others, are the most common phenomena [20–22]. While the former appears due to information asymmetry before establishing an insurance contract, the latter occurs when the insurer cannot observe the real action taken by the insurers after the contract has been signed. They both create challenges for designing and implementing cyber insurance, since the insurance contract may not be profitable anymore for the insurer in the presence of these dilemmas.

This chapter presents a review of the quantitative cyber insurance design framework and discusses how the challenges mentioned previously can be overcome with the help of modern techniques. Figure 6.2 illustrates the framework by depicting the interactions among the three players: the insurer, the insuree, and the attacker. The insuree defends its IT system and protects its operational technology (OT) systems (e.g., smart buildings, smart grids, and autonomous vehicles) from damage. The attacker can exploit vulnerabilities in the IT system to take over the OT resources. The insurer determines the level of coverage as well as the premium to reduce the total risk in the system and maximize revenue.

This chapter aims to analyze the potential of cyber insurance to enhance cyber resilience and to synthesize traditional and modern techniques that promote a systematic upgrade of cyber insurance design for cyber resilience. Different from traditional cybersecurity, cyber resilience approaches the security issues of cyber systems from a unique perspective, which includes resistance, repairability, and sustainability of cyber systems. Cyber insurance is suitable for these cyber resilience notions, since it tries to achieve post-threat system restoration and damage mitigation through financial means.

While traditional cyber defense techniques primarily focus on preventing cyberattacks or system failures to increase security levels, cyber insurance aims to provide financial support to users in case of cyber threats that are difficult to defend

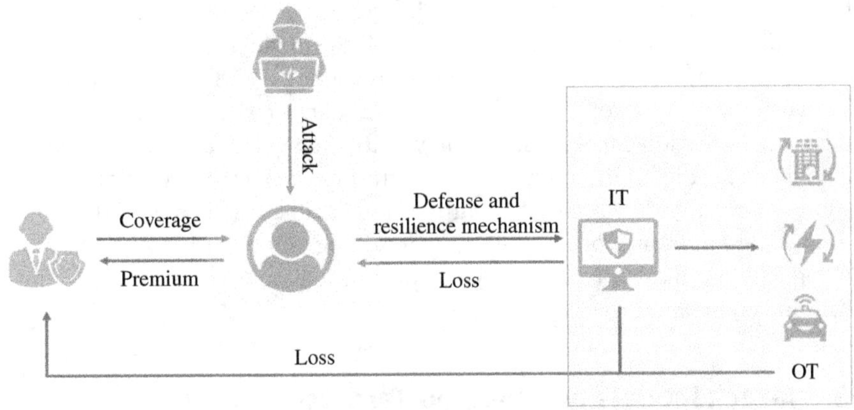

Figure 6.2 Interaction among a cyber insurer, a system user, and an attacker in the context of IT/OT operations. The user operates integrated IT and OT systems and is exposed to potential cyberattacks. In response, the user employs defense and resilience mechanisms to mitigate losses. The cyber insurer evaluates the user's risk profile and determines both the insurance premium and the coverage offered. In the event of a successful attack, resulting losses are partially transferred to the insurer based on the agreed coverage.

against. These cyber threats are capable of bypassing cyber defenses, and they can be fatal for system users. We refer to them as residual risks in our chapter and explain their complexity by elaborating on the existing attack vectors and defense mechanisms. Mitigating residual risk involves reducing harm resulting from successful cyberattacks and system failures, which ultimately leads to enhanced cyber resilience.

We have developed a framework that unifies the design of cyber insurance contracts and incentives for cyber defense efforts by users. This framework uses a type of principal-agent (P-A) problem to address residual risk, which is the potential damage from cyber threats that users may face despite their security investments. By designing cyber insurance contracts properly, businesses of all sizes can enjoy enhanced cyber resilience, which frees them from the concerns associated with consecutive cyber threats. The framework's mathematical modeling of residual risks allows for modern risk preference calibration techniques. These techniques enhance the design of P-A problems and improve the overall system performance and practicality of the resulting insurance contracts. As a result, our upgraded cyber insurance design framework takes into account both cybersecurity and cyber resilience, while also ensuring practicality.

We explicitly introduce several popular and state-of-the-art attack models with the corresponding insured targets in Section 6.2. We discuss the potential defense mechanisms in accordance with the attack models in Section 6.3. The quantitative cyber insurance design framework will be introduced in Section 6.4 after we elaborate on the insurer's observations necessary for the modeling of the cyber insurance contracts. The review of risk preference modeling and the relation between risk preferences and system security in cyber insurance contracts are included in Section 6.5. In Section 6.6, we discuss a novel situation where human perceptions can be shaped using information. The economic impact of this perception manipulation is linked with the moral hazard issue. Possible extensions of the cyber insurance design framework to the dynamic setting will be discussed in Section 6.7. Regulations on cyber insurance will appear in Section 6.8, including accountability and compliance issues.

6.2 Attack Models and Insured Targets

The user can also be referred to as the defender of a system. The defender aims to protect their system against potential harm from the attacker, who acts strategically and stealthily to achieve their attack objectives. The goal of the attacker can be categorized using CIA triad (i.e., confidentiality, integrity, and availability). For example, ransomware attackers often aim to compromise the availability of the data for critical services, and they choose the amount of ransom depending on the wealth and the willingness to pay of the victims. The Target data breach is another attack that aims at data confidentiality. The attacker gained access to Target servers through the credentials of a third-party vendor in 2013. It has been reported that Target claimed a total loss of $290 million as a result.

This section introduces several types of popular and state-of-the-art attack models and the corresponding targets to insure. We divide the discussion into three parts, namely, the human-layer attacks caused by or through insiders, the cyber-layer attacks that target the IT, and the physical-layer attacks that can harm physical devices and equipment. We not only discuss cyber threats that mainly fall into one of the three layers, but also, and more importantly, mention the interdependencies among the layers. For example, an attack vector targeting the cyber layer can be initiated using a phishing email, meaning that this attack can be successfully defended if the employees are well-trained. The connections among the layers make it challenging for the insurer to conduct risk assessment. They also complicate the deployment of cyber defense mechanisms and make it challenging to determine the insurance coverage plan.

6.2.1 Human-layer Attacks

The human-layer attack is a special type of attack where the attacks are not directly aimed at the cyber systems. On the contrary, human-layer attacks are those attacks that influence the cyber systems through the actions of the targeted individuals. A phishing attack is one of the most common examples, since phishing emails and text messages aim to utilize the lack of awareness of individuals to either steal private information or harm the networked system through a trusted user. We focus on the insider threats [23, 24], where the attacks are performed by so-called insiders, that is, individuals who are advantageous or privileged in accessing certain systems. The notion of an insider is fairly general. An employee of a company or a business can be referred to as an insider. A software development engineer who has knowledge about the coding of an IT system can create insider threats. Any individual who has physical access to the computer terminals can also be considered an insider.

Insider threats, compared to other cyber losses caused by an arbitrary individual, can be more severe and sometimes fatal to the IT systems. The reason lies in, but is not limited to, the following three points. First, insiders may have extra knowledge about the weaknesses of an IT system compared to other people. This advantage can be utilized to directly target the attacks at the system vulnerabilities, causing massive losses to the IT systems. Second, insiders can act more stealthily, since they are classified as authorized or trusted users. The behavior of an employee accessing documents and resources from the intranet is common. Hence, it is more challenging to detect it as a malicious behavior when an authorized individual manipulates or collects certain data. Third, insider threats can happen at any time due to the advantage of access. Unless the IT system is constantly monitored, it is difficult to identify malicious behaviors. However, monitoring and verifying all behaviors happening at all times is costly and may not be a feasible approach for many businesses and companies.

Several taxonomies of insiders and insider threats have been discussed in the literature [25, 26]. According to the survey [23], one taxonomy partitions insiders into masqueraders, traitors, and unintentional perpetrators. While traitors and unintentional perpetrators mainly create insider threats, including data exfiltration, violations against data integrity or availability, and sabotage of information and communication technology (ICT) systems [27], masqueraders contribute to a richer domain of insider threats. The reason lies in that the kill chain of a masquerader involves several phases, where different threats can be posed [28]. Examples of threats posed by masqueraders include network and database vulnerability scans, email spam and phishing, and distributed denial-of-service attacks [29].

On the one hand, since the insiders are already in the system, the aforementioned threats cannot be avoided by setting up firewalls or antivirus software. On the other hand, businesses and companies can turn to cyber insurance to mitigate the financial risk of these insider threats. Although cyber insurance is a feasible solution to insider threats, the targets to insure need further investigation. Indeed, the insured targets in this scenario can vary from individual computers in the ICT system to datasets that contain essential information. The reason lies in that insiders may adopt any attack vector to achieve their goals. The threats caused by APTs [29] can target arbitrary entry points of a networked system.

6.2.2 Cyber-layer Attacks

There are many attack vectors that can be classified as directly targeting IT systems, for example, cryptojacking, viruses and worms, and payment fraud. We focus on two types of attacks, namely APTs and data breaches, as the nominal ones to represent the state-of-the-art strategies of the attackers. Both of them can lead to fatal consequences for businesses and companies. The APTs have been proven to be one of the most dangerous attacks, since the hackers are directly targeting the systems or the business. They will not give up before they manage to achieve their malicious goals. Data breaches often occur in a stealthy way that the defenders will not be aware of the stolen or manipulated data until they have somehow realized that their business secrets have been taken advantage of by their opponents in the market.

6.2.2.1 Advanced Persistent Threats

APTs are the most dangerous cyber threats that can involve various state-of-the-art attack methods and can last for a sufficiently long period until the attackers achieve their goals [30]. Perhaps the most infamous example of an APT is the Stuxnet virus [31]. Initially infected through the universal serial bus devices in June 2010, the Stuxnet computer worm eventually caused damage to the control systems of a nuclear-enrichment plant in Iran. Due to the effectiveness of Stuxnet, many variances of Stuxnet started to emerge, including Duqu, Shamoon, Triton, etc. [32]. These APTs are challenging to detect or notice, for they often involve a lateral movement phase in their attacks [33]. Hence, it is insufficient to merely rely on defense systems to avoid being infected by APTs. Furthermore, since APTs often have specific attack targets, they can cause the most deadly damage to a system. Therefore, businesses and companies should be prepared, to a reasonable level, to recover from potential attacks in the form of APTs.

Insuring against APTs is generally a challenging task since APTs can be sophisticated enough to stealthily target the most essential components in a system. Nevertheless, feasible insurance targets include, but are not limited to, the following. The dataset containing sensitive information is a reasonable target since the market strategies or business plans of companies are determined based on it. It is also necessary to insure the main communication links in an ICT system, for the interconnections between subnetworks and information flows for maintaining synchronous functions rely heavily on these links. From the example of the Stuxnet attack, we know that critical infrastructures can also be the target of APTs. Therefore, the functionality of these physical components in the OT system should also be guaranteed. Companies are highly recommended to purchase cyber insurance for their base stations or networked computer systems to obtain compensation under unavoidable APTs.

6.2.2.2 Data Breaches

Data breaches can happen every day at any place [34, 35]. Confidentiality is the main concern regarding stolen data or missing information. The data stolen can contain private information, including personal contact information, identification information, and even individual medical history. This information can not only be used in marketing and advertising but can also be taken advantage of for malicious purposes. Hence, to avoid severe consequences caused by data breaches, there is a need to understand the value of the stolen data and how the data can be utilized. However, it is challenging to do so in practice.

There are two possible scenarios of data breaches. In the first scenario, data is stolen or missing, and the users are aware of it. Hence, the user can quantify the amount of stolen data and verify its usage in the system. Then, the user can estimate the potential loss based on the performance degradation without the stolen data. In other words, since the users know what data is stolen, they can approximately determine the corresponding losses to their businesses because of the data breaches. In the second scenario, data is duplicated by malicious attackers. In this case, the users still hold the data duplicated by the attacker. Hence, it is more challenging for the user to verify what data has been leaked. Accordingly, it is more difficult to quantify the loss because of the leakage. The only way to infer the loss is to compare the system's performance with potential competitors in the market. Take an advertising company as an example. When data breaches take place, the company's dataset containing customer preferences can be duplicated by another advertising company. The company being attacked is not aware of the data breach. But advertisement designers of the company can conjecture about the data breach if they observe advertisements that target their potential customers.

The insured targets for data breaches should be distinguished according to the two scenarios discussed previously. For the first scenario, since the value of the stolen data can be quantified by the users, the insured target can be simply the data. For the second scenario, since the users can only be aware of the duplication from exogenous responses, quantification of the value of the duplicated data is challenging. Therefore, an alternative insurance target could be the performance. For example, the effectiveness of an advertisement can be calibrated as the value of the duplicated data. If an advertising company is assured that its opponents have duplicated its customer preference information, then the decreased number of customers can be considered as the effect of the data breach. Hence, the loss due to the data breach can be determined.

Securing data or system performance can be adaptable for insurance contracts covering data breaches. Since the insured targets are immaterial, it is more convenient to deceive them. Indeed, when users are not honest or have incentives to misreport missing data or system performance degradation, the risk sharing between users and insurers may be compromised. Nevertheless, dishonesty can be considered a consequence of informational asymmetry between users and insurers. We will elaborate on how to mitigate this asymmetry with the help of insurance contract modeling in Section 6.4.

6.2.3 Physical-layer Attacks

We have mentioned previously that some APTs can target the critical infrastructures and the physical components in the OT system. Here, we use the ransomware as a representative of physical-layer attacks.

Ransomware originally refers to a class of malware that exploits security mechanisms to hijack user files and documents in computer systems for asking ransoms [36]. With the advances of the hackers, ransomware can also target the user ends in networked computer systems or even robots and unmanned vehicles in autonomous systems. Conceptually, the attack target of ransomware is making the systems unavailable to their users. Therefore, we use it as an example of physical-layer attacks.

Dating back to at least the floppy disk Trojan in 1989, ransomware has been advancing to extend the set of targets to infect and update the encrypting methods to secure the hacker's profits. Some variants include CryptoLocker [37] and Petya [38]. It is predicted that the ransomware damage costs will exceed $265 billion by the year 2031 [39].

One feature of ransomware is that it spreads over communication networks or communication links in Internet-of-Things (IoT) systems [40]. The monetary exchanges the attackers ask for are dependent on the number of disabled units in the system. In this scenario, the cyber loss can be normalized to be the number of disabled computers. Accordingly, an intuitive approach is to design the insurance to cover the ransoms for a fraction of the disabled units.

The insured targets for cyber insurance against ransomware depend on the strategies for protecting the networked system. If the individual units in the network are federated, that is, they have independent firewalls and anti-malware software, then the insured targets are the individual computers. In this scenario, individual users become the insurees. They have the choice to determine whether or not to participate in a cyber insurance contract. If units in the networked system share the same protection technique, then the insured target should be the whole networked system. In this scenario, the owner of the whole networked system is the insuree. The owner's decision to purchase the cyber insurance ensures the capability of financially recovering from availability issues at the users' end.

6.3 Defense Mechanisms and Residual Risks

Aiming at defending the security of the systems, the users adopt various defense mechanisms keyed to individual attack vectors from the attackers. In this section, we first introduce generic models for describing the relationships between the defenders and the attackers to understand how to react to different types of attacks from the defender's perspective. Then, we review different types of security investments that can aid the defenders in protecting against the attacks mentioned in Section 6.2. Elaborating these investments reveals the potential uncovered cyber threats of certain systems used by various users, especially those from small- to midscale businesses and companies, and aids the design of the coverage plan of the cyber insurance. Finally, we turn to the resiliency aspect of the systems by discussing the residual risks from cyber threats after the defense mechanisms have been set up.

6.3.1 Modeling of Defense Mechanisms

To efficiently and successfully defend their systems, the defenders need to be prepared for all kinds of attacks from all possible attackers. This adversarial environment brings the necessity of figuring out potential malicious ones from a population of users. Game theory is one of the emerging modeling techniques that digs into the rationality and strategic behaviors of individuals [41]. The Nash equilibrium (NE) of a game characterizes the status of players' strategies where no one can benefit by deviating from the equilibrium. The strategic relations can be utilized to analyze the actions taken by rational agents when they face adversaries. In particular, a simple two-player zero-sum game can explain the mental combat between an attacker and a defender. For example, the work [42] uses zero-sum games to model the relation between a system defender and an intruder in a networked IDS. The intruder aims to scan the host machine for vulnerabilities while the defender monitors the suspicious behavior taking place across the network and tries to detect any intruder. The relation between a malicious attacker and an IDS has also been investigated under the two-person zero-sum game framework in earlier work, such as Refs. [43–45].

One of the most recognized applications of game-theoretic tools in the domain of security is the Stackelberg security game [46]. As a game with a special leader–follower structure, the Stackelberg game [47] models the system defender as the leader who takes the defending action first and models the attacker as the follower who best responds to the action of the defender. Compared to a common simultaneous game where the players take actions at the same time without observing others' actions, a Stackelberg game adapts well to the scenarios of cyber threats and system attacks. The reason lies in that all the investments of a defender to increase the security levels of the IT and OT are performed before the attacks. Hence, the attackers can leverage the knowledge of the first-mover's action to determine their plays in the game. Stackelberg games elaborate on this timing. Therefore, Stackelberg security games have been applied to many scenarios, such as moving target defense [48–50], infrastructure security [51–53], proactive defense [54–56], etc.

Information plays an important role in the strategic relations between the defender and the attacker. When the defender has to figure out the true target of the attacker or to find the stealthy malicious user from a population of users before adopting any defensive action, Bayesian games offer the tools to deal with the incompleteness of information in the environment. Instead of the scenario described by the common-knowledge assumption of complete-information games, what we are dealing with in real life is a slightly more complicated scenario where the information about the game or about other players is incomplete. Harsanyi's Bayesian game [57] introduces the notion of types, which describes the player's state of mind when one constructs beliefs about the state of the game using observable information. Due to the modeling power, Bayesian games have been applied to defensive cyber deception [8, 58, 59], defenses against APTs [60–62], CPS security [61, 63, 64], etc.

Apart from game theory, another meaningful model suitable for applications involving informational incompleteness is the partially observable Markov decision process (POMDP). While Markov processes naturally apply to dynamic environments, such as encrypting probabilities for attackers to appear in the transition kernel, the decision-maker's partial observation can model the defender's knowledge about whether a user is classified as benign or malicious. For example, the authors in Miehling et al. [65] adopt POMDP to study the dynamic defense of cyber networks where the defender has partial observation of the security state of the system and has to construct a belief of the security state using information from security alerts. In Kurt et al. [66], the authors use POMDP models to investigate the dynamic detection of cyber threats where the defender has partial information about the security of the environment. Related modeling techniques can also be found in Refs. [67–69].

6.3.2 Types of Security Investments

In the popular game models for characterizing the strategic relations between the system defender and the attackers mentioned in Section 6.3.1, the defenders' defending strategies vary according to the attack models. From the user's perspective, this variety captures the difficulty in finding a unified approach to strengthen system security. In the following, we elaborate on the possible security investments for the attack models discussed in Section 6.2. Due to the differences in the expenses and the deployment difficulty of the security investments, network users are recommended to invest a reasonable amount that is feasible for them to protect against corresponding attacks. If certain security investments are too expensive for the users, they can resort to cyber insurance to make their systems resilient.

6.3.2.1 Against Insider Threats

At first glance, employee training may be an effective investment to defend against insider threats. However, it can only benefit businesses and companies when the insiders are unintentional perpetrators. The reason lies in that the other two types of insiders, namely the masqueraders and the traitors, possess malicious intentions. Hence, they can be well-behaved according to certain employee behavior standards, but they can still stealthily harm the system.

The intricacy of insider threats lies in the fact that we can hardly trust anyone in the system [70]. In fact, several game-theoretic frameworks to address insider threats have utilized a probabilistic way to model insiders. That is, any player in a game can become an insider and create insider threats to the system with some probability. Examples of these frameworks include [71–74].

This consequence of insider threats brings the notion of zero trust [75]. The zero-trust architecture is a cybersecurity paradigm that emphasizes that trust must be evaluated continuously [76]. This infers, for example, that even when an individual has been granted access to certain enterprise data or resources, the system will not trust this person anymore as soon as the one-time access expires. The zero-trust architecture contains basic tenets that benefit the cyber systems in the protection of privacy, the allocation of resources and computation power, the authorization of individuals or entities, etc. [77].

Adopting the zero-trust security paradigm will increase the overall security level of cyber systems. However, as a more sophisticated and comprehensive security structure, the zero-trust architecture certainly costs much more to implement. A simple reason is that to enforce zero trust, every action in the ICT needs to be monitored. The dynamic nature requires more expenses to be invested. Therefore, despite the advances of zero-trust security, efforts are still needed to enable its implementability in practice and compatibility with the investment power of small-scale businesses.

6.3.2.2 Against APTs

Defending against APTs is a challenging task since APTs combine different attack vectors and can last for a reasonably long period. The APT defense method can be divided into mainly three types [30] due to the many-phased attack process APTs possess. The three types include monitoring, detection, and mitigation.

The monitoring can be classified as a screening or filtering of relative data prior to the detection of threats. Business owners may need to build large-scope monitoring systems that cover the entire ICT and monitor all the areas from the memory to the codes. This comprehensive approach will certainly generate an enormous amount of expenses. However, since APTs can perform their initial invades at arbitrary entry points of a system, this type of monitoring is necessary.

While the monitoring utilizes traditional techniques, the detection of APTs benefits more from recent technical advances. For example, machine learning-based APT detection systems [78–80], reinforcement learning-based APT detection [60, 81], and game-theoretic detection frameworks [61, 62, 82, 83].

In recent years, proactive methods for mitigating damages caused by APTs have emerged. The engagement of defensive deception techniques and moving target defense systems, among the other proactive methods, have proved their effectiveness [84]. Implementation of honeypots, as an example of defensive deception, can have the chance to trap the hackers into a carefully designed trap, so that the defender is able to learn the invading strategies and attack targets of the hacker [50, 72, 85, 86]. Moving target defenses, as a dynamically changing mechanism, protect systems by creating an ever-changing view for the attacker. Dynamic game is one of the promising tools for designing moving target defense systems [6, 50].

Investments in novel technologies can improve the successful detection rates and enhance cybersecurity by mitigating potential harms. However, technologies update very rapidly. Knowing how to choose the correct and compatible method can sometimes become a challenging task for businesses.

6.3.2.3 Against Data Breaches

Although there exist efforts in the research of data breach incident predictions [87], data breaches are hard to avoid because of the various initiatives that can lead to the leak of information. One factor that serves as the starting point of many data breach incidents is phishing. Hence, employee training is the very first investment businesses and companies can think of to defend against data breach threats. The training can simply contain content such as methods to recognize phishing emails or messages, so that even if some of the emails pass through the automatic classification system, they can be considered malicious by human eyes.

The second straightforward investment is maintaining backups of data and information or separating the storage into partitions and saving them in a disjoint fashion. Since the data backups are often saved on certain devices that are offline or disconnected from the main communication networks, they can be unreachable to hackers. Though keeping backups cannot stop the data stored or used in the ICT from being stolen, they can at least secure the normal functionality of the systems when data breaches happen. Partition of storage is also a way to reduce the amount of data being hacked. Hence, it reduces the losses due to data breaches to the least.

In recent years, multifactor authentication methods [88] have emerged to replace traditional authentication methods which contain only a single factor. It is realized that single-factor authentication is not adequate against many threats [89]. Instead, by coupling one factor of identification data such as usernames and passwords with another factor of personal belongings such as smartphones, the two-factor authentication methods have already enriched the authentication procedure and have enhanced the accuracy and security of authentication. In multifactor authentication methods, biometric factors enabled by modern technologies such as natural language processing and facial recognition systems have become reliable data sources for authentication purposes. These biometric factors include, but are not limited to, personal voice characteristics, facial information, fingerprints, and hand geometry [88].

Encryption of data provides an additional layer of protection which adds to the previous security investments. By encrypting the sensitive information, even when the previous security mechanisms fail, the hackers may be unable to read the encrypted data and may have to stop before harming the system further.

6.3.2.4 Against Ransomware Attacks

Ransomware, as a special malware that can spread through the ICT and other networks connecting autonomous systems, can be successfully blocked by generic antivirus software and firewalls [90]. As it is a more fatal malware that can completely shut down the services of businesses or stop the functionality of companies, more detection systems and defense frameworks explicitly designed for it have appeared in recent years [40, 91–93].

6.3.3 Residual Risk and Its Connection with Cyber Insurance

Despite the effectiveness of the defense mechanisms introduced in Section 6.3.2, hoping to gain complete invincibility against cyber threats through security investments is impossible. Indeed, attackers can always seek the vulnerabilities in current defense mechanisms and try designing specific attacks targeting these weaknesses. Therefore, cyber risks always exist in the long run. That being the case, addressing the challenges in cyber risk assessment will be crucial for building a resilient ecosystem.

Due to the sophistication in the interdependency among the attack vectors in different layers and the uncertainties present in the quantification of the reduction of cyber risks caused by defense methods, a probabilistic description of the relationship between the security investment and cyber risks is plausible. Namely, security investment can reduce cyber risks but can never eliminate them. The remaining risk passing through the functions of defending mechanisms is referred to as the residual risk. The residual risk is one of the central concerns of cyber resilience, as enhancing cyber resilience can be equivalently understood as mitigating the residual risk.

In a practically meaningful stochastic relation between the security investment and the residual risk, a parametric probability distribution is one of the most concise and convenient descriptions. Intuitively, increased security investment should be able to at least reduce the probability that cyberattacks successfully harm the system. This relation can be precisely described by the notion of stochastic dominance [94].

Consider two random variables Z_1 and Z_2. Let ϕ_1 and ϕ_2 denote the probability density functions (PDFs) of Z_1 and Z_2, respectively. Let Φ_1 and Φ_2 denote the cumulative distribution functions (CDFs) of Z_1 and Z_2, respectively. Then, Z_1 stochastically dominates Z_2 in the first order if $\Phi_1 \leq \Phi_2$. Consider Z_1 and Z_2 to be the residual risks of a cyber system under different amounts of security investments. Then the stochastic dominance relation can be intuitively understood as that, compared to Z_2, Z_1 contains a greater likelihood for more severe cyber losses to happen. In this scenario, the investment that leads to Z_2 should be higher than the investment that leads to Z_1. An example of the relations between the CDFs Φ_1 and Φ_2 is illustrated in Figure 6.3.

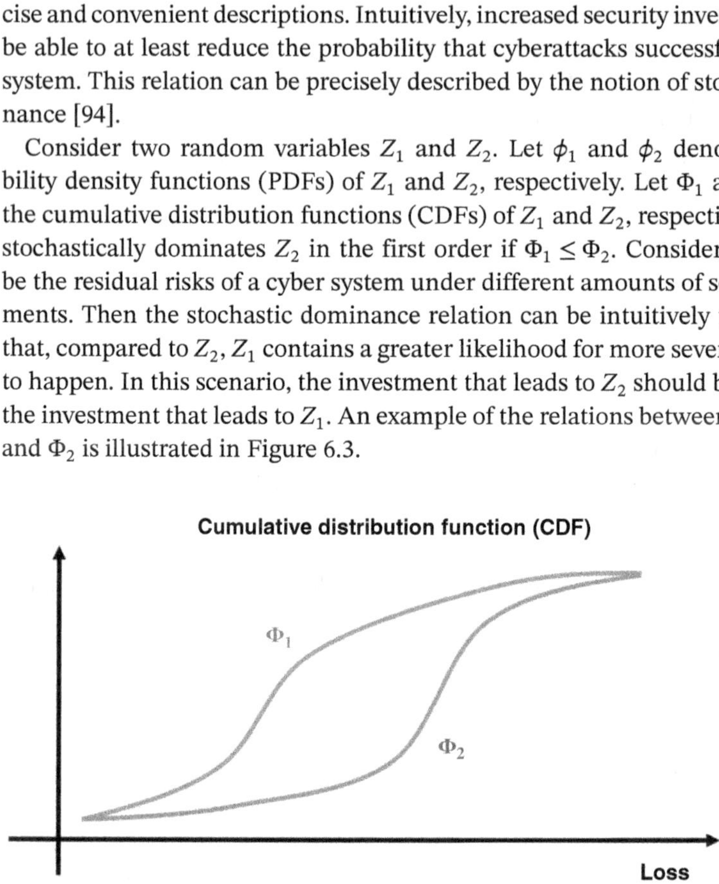

Figure 6.3 Illustration of first-order stochastic dominance (FSD) using CDFs. The x-axis represents the level of loss, increasing from left to right, while the y-axis denotes the cumulative probability that the loss is less than or equal to a particular value. Two CDFs, Φ_1 and Φ_2, are shown. Distribution Φ_1 is said to first-order stochastically dominate Φ_2 if $\Phi_1(x) \leq \Phi_2(x)$ for all loss values x, with strict inequality for some x. This condition implies that Φ_1 corresponds to a risk profile with generally lower losses and would therefore be preferred by all risk-averse decision-makers. FSD is a fundamental concept in decision theory and risk analysis, allowing for comparisons between uncertain outcomes without requiring assumptions about specific utility functions.

Parameterized probability distributions and the stochastic dominance relations enable the insurer to calibrate the residual risk when the users' security investments on protecting their cyber systems are observable to them. Using these mathematical tools, the effects of defense mechanisms described in Section 6.3.2 can be holistically described in a formal way. Combining the modeling of the users' monetary utilities or costs, these relations enable the insurer to evaluate the profits from claiming a cyber insurance contract with certain premiums and coverage.

In the sequel, we will elaborate on the available observations of the insurer, based on which they aims to design cyber insurance contracts. Then, we will introduce the cyber insurance design framework.

6.4 Insurer's Observations and the P-A Model

6.4.1 User Behavior Monitoring

Users obtain financial support and gain protection against cyber losses from cyber insurance because of risk sharing. However, the loss coverage provided by the insurance contract is not effective until the user makes a prior payment to the insurer as the premium. That is, an insurance company is essentially a business organization. This means that the existence of the cyber insurance market depends on whether insurance contracts produce profits.

Since a cyber insurance contract is offered to the users by the insurer, the insurer can carefully design the insurance plan to maximize their profits. One essential reference for designing the insurance contract is the insurer's observation of the users' security investments. The calibration of the relation between the coverage and the premium is often performed using historical data on the users' willingness to invest in system protection and the successes of cyberattacks targeting the systems. While these data cannot predict what the users will do after they purchase the insurance plan, they can, to some extent, help the insurance company learn the effectiveness of various security investments against different cyber threats. Utilizing models such as the parameterized probability distributions introduced in Section 6.3.3, the insurer can obtain a clear picture of the potential cyber risks. Hence, they can design the proportion of losses to cover and the expense to charge the users.

The behavior of the users can change after they are insured. This makes the monitoring of the users' behaviors very important. For example, consider an owner of a networked system. Suppose that there is an offer of a cyber insurance contract that fully covers the losses due to cyber threats with a reasonable amount of monetary charge. Then, if the owner purchases this insurance plan, they will not have any incentive to invest in system protection. Since whether or not they update the firewalls or deploy IDSs, the losses will be fully covered by the insurance company.

The aforementioned phenomenon is referred to as the moral hazard issue in the economic literature [95]. More formally, moral hazard describes a situation where individuals tend to behave more recklessly when they do not fully bear the risk. It appears when there is information asymmetry between the users and the insurer. Insurance contracts are severely affected by moral hazard. The reason lies in that if the users do not follow the statistical pattern of historical behaviors and become reckless after they are insured, the design of the contract can fail to function and can lead to negative profits for the insurer. In the following, we will formally describe the standard framework for insurance design and how a variation of the framework addresses the moral hazard issue.

6.4.2 Principal-agent Problems

A suitable framework for cyber insurance design is a class of P-A problems [96]. The P-A problem can be viewed as a bilevel optimization problem [97], where the principal solves the upper-level optimization problem and the agent solves the lower-level problem. P-A problem has been applied to the modeling of the relations between, for example, employers and employees, buyers and sellers, citizens and elected officials, etc. Prior works using the P-A framework to design insurance contracts include [98–102].

We proceed to formally introduce two types of P-A problems, as shown in Figure 6.4. The first one corresponds to the scenario where the insurer can perfectly observe the action of the user after they are insured. The second one deals

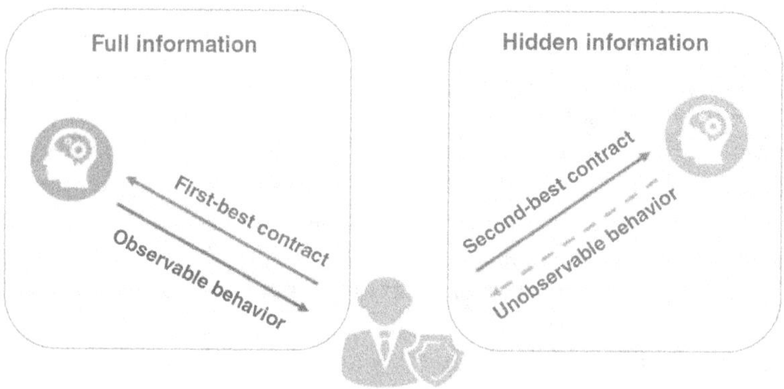

Figure 6.4 Comparison between full-information and hidden-information P-A problems in cyber insurance contract design. Under full information, the insurer observes the user's behavior and can implement a first-best contract. In contrast, with hidden information, the user's actions are unobservable, leading to a second-best contract that addresses moral hazard through incentive-compatible mechanisms.

with the opposite situation where the moral hazard issue occurs and a calibration of the user's action is required.

Let $x \in X$ denote the security investment from the user. In practice, x can refer to any type of investment (as described in Section 6.3.2) depending on the potential cyberattacks that can occur. Let ξ denote the residual risk under certain deployed defense mechanisms. The residual risk is a random outcome from a probability space $(\Xi, \mathcal{F})$. The stochasticity of the residual risk is described by the parameterized probability distribution $P(\xi, x)$, which depends on the security investment. The insurer's profit by designing the insurance contract $w : \Xi \to \mathbb{R}$ is described by the utility function $V : \Xi \times \mathbb{R} \to \mathbb{R}$, which also depends on the residual risk ξ. The user's cost from the security investments and loss due to the residual cyber risks after enrolling in the insurance contract is described by the disutility function $U : X \times \mathbb{R} \to \mathbb{R}$.

When the insurer has perfect observation of the user's actions of security investments, the full-information P-A problem can be formulated as:

$$\begin{aligned} &\max_{w(\cdot),x} \int_{\Xi} V(\xi, w(\xi))dP(\xi, x) \\ &\text{s.t.} \quad \int_{\Xi} U(w(\xi), x)dP(\xi, x) \leq \bar{U}, \text{(IR)}, \end{aligned} \tag{6.1}$$

where $\bar{U}$ denotes the minimum cost of the user when they are not enrolled in the cyber insurance contract. In the optimization problem (6.1), the IR constraint refers to individual rationality [103], which guarantees beneficial participation. The reason why the insurer in problem (6.1) possesses full information about the user's action lies in that the security investment is fully controlled by the insurer. That is, as long as an investment satisfies IR, it is feasible for the optimization problem (6.1). The insurer can choose a security investment for the user to obtain optimal profit. This can also be observed from the single-level structure of the problem (6.1).

When the insurer cannot observe the action of the user, a moral hazard issue may occur. In this scenario, to design a profitable insurance contract, it is necessary for the insurer to calibrate the user's action. The hidden-information P-A problem, also referred to as the hidden-information moral hazard problem, can be formulated as:

$$\begin{aligned} &\max_{w(\cdot),x} \int_{\Xi} V(\xi, w(\xi))dP(\xi, x) \\ &\text{s.t.} \quad \int_{\Xi} U(w(\xi), x)dP(\xi, x) \leq \bar{U}, \text{(IR)}, \\ &\qquad x \in \arg\min_{x' \in X} \int_{\Xi} U(w(\xi), x')dP(\xi, x'), \text{(IC)}. \end{aligned} \tag{6.2}$$

The difference between problem (6.2) and problem (6.1) lies in the additional IC constraint in problem (6.2), which refers to incentive compatibility [103]. By adding the IC constraint, problem (6.2) takes into account the user's rationality. In other words, since the insurer cannot observe the action of the user and has no control over their security investment, the insurance plan that the insurer designs has to stand in the user's place and minimize the monetary cost of the user. Furthermore, the IC constraint introduces an additional layer of decision-making and makes problem (6.2) a bilevel optimization problem.

From an optimization-theoretic perspective, the optimal insurance contract obtained by solving problem (6.1) is referred to as the first-best contract, and the optimal insurance contract obtained by solving problem (6.2) is referred to as the second-best contract. The insurer's profit under the first-best contract cannot be worse than the profit produced by the second-best contract. The reason lies in that the feasible set of (6.2) is a subset of the feasible set of (6.1).

From a practical perspective, the first-best contract suffers from the moral hazard issue. Hence, problem (6.2) is a more reasonable choice for the design of a cyber insurance contract in practice. The practicality of problem (6.2) is obtained at the cost of a deduction in the insurer's profit.

As a bilevel optimization problem, problem (6.2) is challenging to solve both analytically and numerically [97]. One approach to characterize the optimal insurance contract of problem (6.2) is to use the first-order optimality condition of the IC constraint and transform the bilevel optimization problem into a single-level optimization problem. Critical factors that enable the first-order approach include the shapes of the utility functions U and V, or the risk sensitivities of the insurer and the user, which we are going to elaborate on in Section 6.5.

In practice, the insurance contract $w(\cdot)$ is often restricted to the class of linear insurance plans consisting of a premium payment $\mathfrak{p} > 0$ and a coverage rate $\mathfrak{c} \in (0, 1)$. The linear insurance plan is commonly used since it is convenient and intuitive.

6.5 Modeling of Risk Preferences

Risk preference refers to the decision-maker's perception of losses or gains in an environment with uncertainties. This perception influences whether one quantifies probabilistic events as valuable or not. There are three common types of risk preferences, namely, risk-neutral, risk-averse, and risk-seeking. Risk-neutral decision-makers evaluate probabilistic events purely according to their law. That is, they consider a certain event and an uncertain event as equivalent when they are equal in the average sense. A risk-averse decision-maker tends to dislike or avoid uncertain events. Sometimes, they prefer a certain event to an uncertain

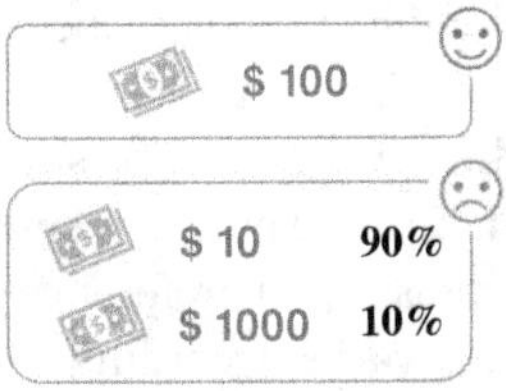

Figure 6.5 Illustration of risk aversion in decision-making. A risk-averse individual prefers the guaranteed payoff of $100 (top) over a probabilistic gamble (bottom) that offers a 90% chance of receiving $10 and a 10% chance of receiving $1000, even though the expected value of the gamble ($109) is higher. This preference reflects the individual's aversion to uncertainty and potential loss.

event even when the former benefits them less than the latter in the expected sense (see Figure 6.5). A risk-seeking decision-maker holds the opposite preference compared to a risk-averse decision-maker.

One of the most consequential impacts risk preferences have on cyber insurance is the existence of the cyber insurance markets. It has been discovered that the cyber insurance market only exists when the insurer is risk-neutral and the users are risk-averse [98–100].

In the sequel, we will briefly introduce the modeling of risk preferences. Then, we will explain how risk preferences can help enhance cyber resilience.

6.5.1 Risk Modeling

The modeling of risk preference has a long history. It dates back at least to the expected utility theory of John Von Neumann and Oskar Morgenstern [104]. According to the hypothesis of expected utility theory, rational agents make choices based on the expected utility they perceive. The risk appetite of agents is captured by the utility functions associated with the agents. When the utility functions are concave, a profit-maximizing agent exhibits risk aversion. The famous Arrow–Pratt measure of absolute risk aversion [105, 106] extends the definition of risk aversion merely based on the second derivative by involving the first-order information of the utility function to make the risk preferences invariant with respect to affine transformations. The choice of utility functions heavily affects the properties of the contracts obtained by solving the P-A model. For example, risk aversion is essential in proving the monotonicity of optimal contracts [107].

Risk preferences appear because of the uncertainties in the environment. The expected utility expression mainly evaluates how the randomness in the uncertainties affects the decision-maker's choice when the subjective probability rule is fixed. The cumulative prospect theory in Tversky and Kahneman [108] introduces an additional layer in the quantification of randomness, which is the perception of probabilities. In particular, Tversky and Kahneman [108] use experimental and psychological evidence to show that the perception of probability is also objective. Hence, in addition to agent-specific utility functions, Tversky and Kahneman [108] consider probability weightings when the expected utilities of decision-makers are specified. This comprehensive expression of preference enriches the original approach, where only the utility function varies according to individuals. The idea of probability weightings can be influential to cyber insurance design. For example, the stochastic relation between the security investments from the users and the law of cyber loss can be equivalently understood as a probability distortion. Then, with the probability weighting associated with individual risk perceptions, the physical impact of the investments on cyber losses and the psychological impact of individual preference on cyber losses may be unified and expressed holistically.

A modern approach to modeling individual risk preferences is the use of risk measures. In the seminal work [109], the authors have introduced the notion of coherent risk measures (CRMs) to quantify uncertainty. The coherency refers to the four axioms a risk measure has to satisfy, namely, monotonicity, subadditivity, translation invariance, and positive homogeneity. These axioms not only rigorously define how to order or compare different random quantities, but also take into account the practicality that CRMs need to adapt to in scenarios such as investment and asset management. For example, the subadditivity axiom is closely related to the hedging effect in finance, which states that an investment position can be used to offset the potential losses by an adverse one. Since the introduction of CRMs, there has been a trend in studying both the theoretical properties and the applications of CRMs [110–115].

Among the popular CRMs, average value-at-risk (AVaR) [116], which also bears the name of the conditional value-at-risk (CVaR), the expected shortfall risk, and the expected tail loss, is one of the most investigated. The reasons lie in but are not limited to the following. First, it is a direct extension of the popular noncoherent value-at-risk (VaR) measure. VaR has been used as the industrial standard before the introduction of coherency. Second, the Kusuoka representation [117] indicates that any law-invariant CRM can be represented by a class of AVaRs. Third, the computation of AVaR can be equivalently cast into a convex optimization problem [116].

Adopting CRMs also adds robustness to the agents' decisions. This can be seen from the dual representation of a CRM [118]. In particular, the dual representation of a CRM coincides with a distributionally robust stochastic programming problem [119]. The distributional robustness can be inferred from the fact that, by adopting a CRM, the decision-maker is actually making decisions under the worst-case scenario probability distribution.

The modern CRM approach to risk modeling has advances in both the convenience of mathematical expressions and the richness of describing objective preferences. We will introduce how CRMs can be applied to the design of cyber insurance contracts and how CRMs contribute to cyber resilience in the next section.

6.5.2 Enhancing Cyber Resilience

As we have mentioned in Section 6.4 that the cyber insurance market only exists when the insurer is risk-neutral and the user is risk-averse. The existence of the market does not necessarily mean that it is a beneficial market. In the literature, researchers have discovered the phenomenon that the cyber insurance market will decrease the security level of networked cyber systems [98–100]. The reason lies in that the market disincentivizes the users to invest in system protections. This phenomenon leads to worse-off social welfare, though individual users receive reduced overall costs with the help of cyber insurance. Note that the cause of this phenomenon is not the moral hazard issue, since the insurance models considered in Refs. [98–100] do contain incentive compatibility constraints. This drawback of the cyber insurance market has prevented its practical implementation.

Among the other approaches, the recent work [120, 121] circumvents this challenge by enriching the risk perceptions considered in the classic cyber insurance frameworks that build on the P-A model (see Figure 6.6). The authors of [120]

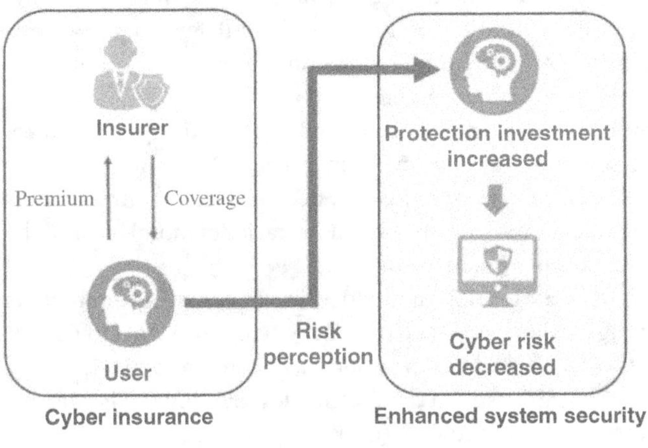

Figure 6.6 The role of risk perception in aligning cyber insurance with improved cybersecurity outcomes. The user pays a premium to the insurer in exchange for coverage, but it is the user's perception of cyber risk that drives additional investments in protective measures. This heightened protection response reduces overall cyber risk, demonstrating how cyber insurance, when coupled with elevated risk awareness, can enhance both cyber resilience and system-level security.

have shown analytically that, with properly specified risk perceptions, purchasing cyber insurance can enhance the security level of cyber systems by incentivizing the users to increase their security investments. In particular, Shutian Liu and Quanyan Zhu [120] require that the insurer's risk perception should be more sensitive to the stochastic dominance shift induced by the user's action than the user's risk perception is. This investigation into the evolution of risk attitudes according to the variation in the user's investment action is enabled by adopting the risk measures.

While the work of Shutian Liu and Quanyan Zhu [120] has shown that cyber insurance, as a means to increase cyber resilience, can also enhance the level of cybersecurity, it only considers linear cyber insurance plans. In the next section, we will investigate the position of risk preferences in cyber insurance with a generic insurance contract and consider cybersecurity and cyber resilience holistically.

6.6 Insurance Design with Preference Manipulation

We have discussed previously that defense mechanisms are deployed for potential cyberattacks to increase the level of cybersecurity, while cyber insurance is the means to enhance the resilience of systems to guarantee post-damage recovery. On the one hand, cyber insurance is an independent consideration for businesses whose security investment is fixed or takes a long time to upgrade. On the other hand, companies that update their system protection methods constantly will more likely consider the investment in insurance and defense mechanisms as a whole. In this scenario, a prominent phenomenon that may occur and affect investment decisions is the moral hazard issue.

When a moral hazard issue happens, users tend to invest less in system protection after their cyber losses are covered by cyber insurance. While this pattern is out of the rationality of the users, it can significantly decrease security investments and lead to poor system protection. Furthermore, in scenarios of moral hazard, the first-best insurance contract is not practical anymore.

As we have discussed in Section 6.4.2, the hidden-information P-A problem is one approach to designing a cyber insurance contract when moral hazard cannot be ignored. Although the second-best contract obtained from problem (6.2) does not suffer from the moral hazard issue, it generates a lower profit to the insurer than that of the first-best contract of problem (6.1).

Recently, in [122], the authors have proposed using risk preference design to mitigate the moral hazard issue. The notion of risk preference design is motivated by the fact that human risk preferences are not stable [123, 124]. In particular, the authors suggest using approaches such as information distributing and nudging to shape the risk preferences of potential insurees. This preference manipulation can help the insurer in obtaining a special state of a population where individual risk preferences benefit the insurer in their design of the insurance contract at a certain monetary cost. The main benefit that the insurer can obtain through risk preference design is the mitigation of the intensity of the moral hazard issue, which is measured by the difference from the user's action solving the full information P-A problem to the one the user actually chooses given the first-best contract.

One of the most significant consequences of the mitigation of the moral hazard issue is that the first-best insurance contract becomes more applicable in practice. Since, by designing the risk preferences, the users may not deviate from the actions specified by the full-information P-A problem after they have been covered by the cyber insurance, the insurer has a better chance to obtain the first-best profit than the second-best one. This advantage creates motivations for the insurer to expand the cyber insurance markets to cover potential cyber losses of various classes and types.

Another notable contribution of [122] is the proposed holistic framework for the joint design of cyber insurance and risk preferences. Built on the classic P-A problems, the framework of [122] provides a convenient way to analyze the effect of risk design and insurance design. What the insurers need to do other than design a traditional cyber insurance contract is to calibrate the monetary cost of preference shaping. This cost could include the expenses in distributing certain information, advertising, and hiring expertise to elicit users' risk preferences.

Preference manipulation benefits cyber resilience in the following ways. First, the insurer can directly design the risk preferences of the users so that they become more careful in taking actions and more risk-averse in planning their defense strategies. Then, these users are less likely to behave recklessly, and hence cyber resilience is enhanced due to upgraded defense methods and increased security investments. The cautiousness in the users' preferences can help maintain a reasonable level of cyber resilience even under misassessed cyber risks, since it is likely that these users have set up necessary security devices and strategies in the ex-ante stage. Second, the reduction of moral hazard enhances cyber resilience for the following reasons. As we have mentioned in Section 6.4.2, the hidden-action P-A problem is challenging to solve due to its bilevel structure. Therefore, an approximation of the second-best contract is often a more feasible anticipated solution. This fact indicates that an insurance contract obtained by taking into account the exact incentives of the users is hard to obtain. However, due to the mitigation of moral hazard, the incentives of the user and the insurer become more aligned. Hence, even though we only have access to an approximate second-best insurance contract, it still characterizes, to a reasonable extent, the incentive of the users. Therefore, the users' actions will not deviate too much from the anticipated actions of the insurer, which leads to a resilient design of cyber insurance. Third, risk

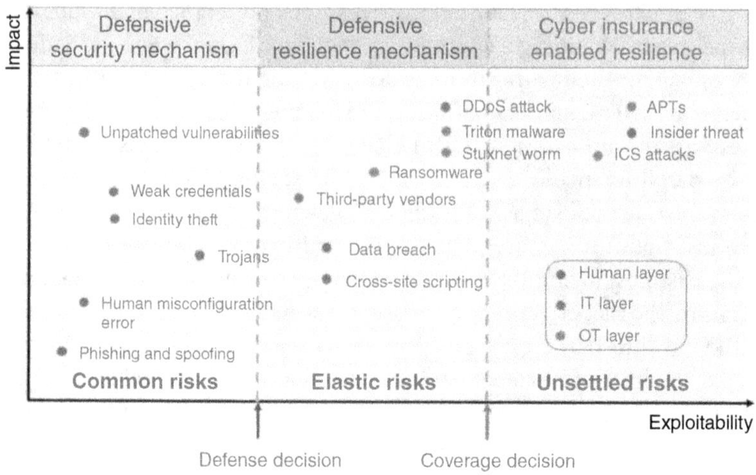

Figure 6.7 Classification of cyber threats based on their exploitability and impact, highlighting the layered approach to cyber resilience. The x-axis distinguishes threats by their exploitability, transitioning from common risks (e.g., phishing, weak credentials) that can be mitigated through preventive security mechanisms, to elastic risks (e.g., ransomware, data breaches) requiring adaptive resilience strategies, and finally to unsettled risks (e.g., APTs, ICS attacks) where preventive and resilient measures may fall short. The y-axis captures the potential impact of these threats. The diagram also distinguishes risks by operational layer (human, IT, and OT). Cyber insurance complements traditional security by covering high-impact, low-predictability threats in the unsettled region, enabling recovery and continuity after damage has occurred. This delineation underscores the importance of integrating security, resilience, and insurance as coordinated layers of defense.

design enhances cyber resilience by pushing the borders of the coverage. Since an increased level of risk aversion makes users invest more in system protection and security, common threats can be taken care of by the users themselves. This leaves more space for the insurer to focus on those attacks that require more expertise to defend against, which results in a higher level of resiliency (see Figure 6.7).

6.7 Dynamic Insurances

In previous sections, we have focused on the scenario where participation in a cyber insurance contract is modeled as a single-stage decision problem. In other words, the users only decide once whether or not to purchase cyber insurance. However, in practice, cyber threats always exist, and they upgrade themselves constantly. For example, one of the features of an APT is that the attacker will always adopt state-of-the-art methods to achieve their targets. This evolving environment motivates the consideration of dynamic cyber insurance contracts, whose coverage plans are not fixed but changing according to both the security states of the networked environment and the types of attacks of cyber threats.

The frequency of updating the cyber insurance contracts should depend on the cyber landscape. In particular, the future landscape of IT systems can be influenced by advances of both attack vectors and defense techniques. When the upgrades of the attack vectors lead to the updates of the defense techniques, we would more likely set a higher premium for the insurance. When the defense mechanisms are more advanced, we can probably deploy a high coverage since the residual risk is not severe. In both cases, recalibrations of the probabilities and the severities of cyber losses are needed, as they provide necessary statistics for the execution of insurance contracts.

The extension of the P-A problem to its dynamic setting can aid the design of dynamic insurances [125]. One of the foundations of dynamic insurance design is dynamic cyber risk assessment [126]. In Zhang and Zhu [127], the authors have adopted a Markov decision process to capture the dynamic correlations between the cyber risks and the users' decisions. The Markov decision process was later incorporated into a P-A problem to aid the design of dynamic cyber insurance. In Papastergiou and Polemi [128], the authors have considered dynamic supply chain cyber risk assessment from an experimental perspective. While they have focused on the mitigation of supply chain cyber risks, the methodology of [128] can be utilized for the dynamic calibration of cyber risks as a pre-screening method before the design of cyber insurance contracts. The work [129] has investigated dynamic contract design to provide hints for asset owners and cyber risk managers regarding the cyber risk management of enterprise networks.

Apart from dynamic risk assessment, dynamic contract problems are themselves challenging. It is straightforward to obtain a stochastic game problem when we consider the extension of the P-A problem to the dynamic setting. One common approach to analyzing and solving a dynamic P-A problem is to reformulate it to stochastic control problems and utilize dynamic programming. This method is adopted, for example, in Refs. [129, 130]. The approach of [127] digs into the structures of some representative problem forms to find the optimal dynamic insurance plan. More generally, dynamic insurance design is closely related to dynamic mechanism design, which we refer to in [131–133] and the references therein.

The notion of cyber resilience naturally extends to its dynamic version. The reason lies in the following. First, resilience itself involves a two-stage perspective toward cyber threats. As we have discussed in Section 6.3.3, cyber resilience accounts for the mitigation of residual risk, which is captured by the cyber risk that remains after the effect of defense mechanisms. Hence, from the perspective of cyber resilience, cyber threats are no longer static. Second, one of the consequences of enhancing cyber resilience is the restoration of a system from the damage induced by cyberattacks. While this recovery represents that the system has survived the previous cyber threats, it also puts the system in front of future attacks. Hence, users and insurers naturally commit consecutive efforts to either invest in system protection or update the insurance contract.

In conclusion, there is a need for future cyber insurance markets to consider dynamic insurance contracts to cope with the ever-changing cyber threats and to reach a reasonable level of cyber resilience.

6.8 Regulations on Cyber Insurance

Cyber insurance is a relatively recent product, developed in response to the escalating cyber risk landscape. Due to its novelty, many users remain unfamiliar with its structure, benefits, and limitations. In this context, regulatory frameworks are essential to help standardize the market, enhance transparency, and mitigate speculative or opportunistic behaviors on the part of both insurers and insurees.

6.8.1 Mandatory Cyber Insurance

Insurance contracts are usually based on the idea that people make rational choices and join voluntarily if it benefits them. This makes sense in markets that work well. However, when it comes to cyber insurance, assuming it should always be optional may not be the best approach. In some cases, making cyber insurance mandatory can be important. Many small- and medium-sized enterprises (SMEs) lack the cybersecurity expertise and institutional infrastructure necessary to assess and manage their cyber risks effectively. Without the ability to conduct thorough risk assessments or to implement comprehensive security controls, these firms often misjudge the value of insurance coverage. As noted by Jan Martin Lemnitzer [134], even in regions with extensive awareness campaigns and frequent high-profile cyber incidents, such as in parts of Europe, many companies remain uninsured. This suggests a widespread underestimation of risk among firms that are arguably the most vulnerable.

In addition, many businesses act as intermediaries that store, process, or transmit sensitive customer data, often making decisions on behalf of users. In such cases, insurance is not solely about protecting the business itself; it becomes a critical instrument for safeguarding user privacy and rights [98]. Risk-taking by service providers, particularly when customer data or resources are leveraged for competitive advantage, can pose significant threats to individuals. The issue of whether service providers have the authority to expose users to such risks raises not only questions of economic rationale but also of ethical responsibility and legal accountability.

To normalize participation in cyber insurance markets, one possible approach is to mandate enrollment for service providers, particularly those who collect or manage personal data. This requirement helps internalize the residual risks that might otherwise be transferred to customers. A notable example of such regulation is found in California, where legislation requires businesses handling private user data to maintain cyber insurance coverage [135]. The availability of insurance compensation ensures that even when firms fall victim to cyberattacks, users are not left without recourse, and essential services are not abruptly suspended. Mandating coverage is especially crucial in environments where service providers display low levels of risk aversion.

Another viable regulatory strategy is to bundle cyber insurance products with widely used IT infrastructure such as operating systems or networking devices. By embedding insurance within the product ecosystem rather than tying it to specific individuals or businesses, this approach may lower the barrier to adoption. Moreover, it offers a platform for educating users about cyber insurance coverage, its benefits, and the terms of use. Such education could gradually foster greater awareness and literacy about cyber risk management, further strengthening market participation.

6.8.2 Insurance Policy Elaboration

Beyond mandatory participation, regulatory oversight of insurance policy elaboration is critical to the development of a fair and effective cyber insurance market.

Policy elaboration refers to the requirement that insurers provide clear and detailed information about the scope and limits of coverage, including cybersecurity protocols, budget allocations, risk qualifications, and incident response provisions [136]. With the increasing interconnectivity of modern CPSs, cyber risks are often correlated and cascading, making it imperative that policies are precisely defined and transparent. This need is also reflected in recent case law in the United States, which has called for clearer policy language [137].

In addition to specifying coverage terms, regulations can enforce minimum coverage standards based on security controls implemented by the insuree [138]. These externally imposed baselines allow insurers to compete on additional features rather than undercutting one another on fundamental coverage. Europe's insurance oversight authorities have supported such regulatory guidance [134].

Policy elaboration thus functions as a cornerstone for establishing trust and setting shared norms across the industry [139]. It can help foster a more mature insurance ecosystem by clearly delineating rights, responsibilities, and acceptable risk levels.

6.8.3 Designing Accountability Mechanisms

Accountability is essential in ensuring that all parties to an insurance contract act in good faith. Violations of agreed-upon terms must trigger meaningful consequences. Of particular concern are opportunistic behaviors, actions that may appear beneficial in the short term but carry hidden or misrepresented risks.

Such actions often arise from risk-seeking tendencies, where decision-makers overemphasize best-case scenarios while neglecting average or worst-case outcomes. In cybersecurity, an example would be running a complex system with outdated firewall protection to save costs. While this may seem advantageous in the short run, it exposes the organization to significant threats.

Modern risk measures, such as CVaR or mean-downside deviation, can be integrated into an accountability design to penalize such opportunistic behaviors. These tools naturally incorporate both the value and likelihood of outcomes, encouraging more balanced and responsible decision-making.

6.8.4 Insurance Market Monitoring

To ensure a well-functioning cyber insurance market, ongoing regulatory monitoring is essential. This includes both macro-level oversight and micro-level data collection.

Market regulation begins with user education, raising awareness of cyber threats and the resilience benefits that insurance can provide. Informed users are more receptive to enrolling in insurance products and sharing risk across a wider pool. Education initiatives may even include controlled perception management to help users appreciate the severity and frequency of cyber threats. In some cases, it may be useful to assess and categorize users' risk preferences before they become service providers.

What sets the cyber insurance market apart is the speed with which it evolves. The dynamic nature of cyber threats demands that regulatory frameworks remain agile and up-to-date. Regulators should require periodic reporting from insurers on premiums collected, types of policies offered, claims frequency, and loss metrics [136]. This continuous flow of information enables adaptive regulation and facilitates the co-evolution of policy and market dynamics [138].

Ultimately, market monitoring helps promote fairness, transparency, and sustainability. It ensures that prices reflect actual risk, standards are upheld, and insurers remain accountable [135, 139]. Such oversight helps build a resilient insurance infrastructure that can evolve alongside the threats it is designed to mitigate.

6.8.4.1 National Implementations and Regulatory Penalties

The regulatory landscape surrounding cyber insurance is deeply influenced by national and regional legal frameworks, especially those governing data protection and privacy. These frameworks not only define the liability exposure of organizations but also shape the design and demand for cyber insurance contracts. As discussed in Section 6.1, cyber insurance plays a crucial role in enhancing cyber resilience by transferring residual risks that persist even after robust technical defenses are deployed.

A prominent example is the European Union's General Data Protection Regulation (GDPR), which imposes stringent requirements on organizations handling personal data. These include obligations for breach notification, lawful processing, and the implementation of adequate security controls. Failure to comply may result in administrative fines of up to €20 million or 4% of a company's global annual turnover, whichever is higher [140].

Recent enforcement actions demonstrate how seriously these penalties are taken. For instance, Amazon received a €746 million fine in 2021, Meta was fined €1.2 billion in 2023, and British Airways and Marriott were penalized by the UK Information Commissioner's Office for data protection failures [141–143]. These cases underscore the financial and reputational consequences of noncompliance.

As noted in Section 6.3.3, cyber insurance provides a vital backstop for high-impact, low-probability events. Although policies often exclude direct coverage of criminal fines, they frequently include legal defense costs, forensic investigation, breach response, crisis communications, and business interruption [144]. This is particularly important for SMEs that lack the resources to absorb such shocks.

The insurability of GDPR fines is jurisdiction-dependent. Some EU member states allow limited coverage if the fines are not due to gross negligence or willful misconduct, while others prohibit coverage outright to preserve deterrence [145]. Many cyber insurance policies contain clauses stating that coverage applies only "where insurable by law" [146]. As insurers navigate this legal uncertainty, they increasingly require proof of regulatory compliance and baseline cybersecurity controls before underwriting or renewing coverage [147].

As described in Section 6.5, the economic rationale for cyber insurance relies on user risk aversion and insurer risk neutrality. Regulatory requirements reinforce this market by providing structured incentives for organizations to comply and invest in better security. Insurance underwriting reinforces this behavior, aligning risk transfer with responsible cyber hygiene. The coevolution of legal enforcement and insurance design supports a robust cyber ecosystem. Regulatory penalties drive demand for insurance, and insurance mechanisms incentivize compliance, creating a virtuous cycle that enhances resilience [148].

6.9 Conclusion

This chapter has examined cyber insurance as a strategic instrument for managing residual risks in modern CPSs. We have presented a comprehensive framework that incorporates both incentive-driven and perception-sensitive elements into the design of cyber insurance contracts. Central to this framework is the concept of residual risk, those threats that persist despite optimal deployment of technical defense mechanisms, which cyber insurance is uniquely positioned to address.

Through the exploration of insurer monitoring capabilities, we introduced the notion of *moral hazard intensity*, emphasizing how different observability conditions impact the alignment between insuree actions and socially desirable outcomes. By integrating models of individual risk preferences and perceptual distortions, we showed how cyber insurance can be jointly optimized with user behavior and awareness to improve overall system resilience.

In particular, our findings underscore the importance of balancing incentive compatibility with perception-aware contract design, especially in environments where perfect monitoring is infeasible. Moreover, we discussed how regulatory mechanisms and national implementations, such as those under the GDPR, further shape the structure and viability of cyber insurance markets.

Looking forward, future research may explore more dynamic and networked models of cyber risk, the co-evolution of adversarial behavior and insurance strategies, and the integration of cyber insurance with real-time security monitoring and adaptive defense systems. As cyber threats continue to grow in sophistication, a robust cyber insurance ecosystem, supported by sound policy, technological foresight, and economic rigor, will be critical to ensuring resilient digital infrastructures.

References

1 Quanyan Zhu and Tamer Basar. Disentangling resilience from robustness: Contextual dualism, interactionism, and game-theoretic paradigms. *arXiv preprint arXiv:2403.06299*, 2024.

2 Quanyan Zhu. Foundations of cyber resilience: The confluence of game, control, and learning theories. *arXiv preprint arXiv:2404.01205*, 2024.

3 Carol J. Fung and Quanyan Zhu. FACID: A trust-based collaborative decision framework for intrusion detection networks. *Ad Hoc Networks*, 53: 17–31, 2016.

4 Tao Zhang and Quanyan Zhu. Distributed privacy-preserving collaborative intrusion detection systems for vanets. *IEEE Transactions on Signal and Information Processing over Networks*, 4(1): 148–161, 2018.

5 Ansam Khraisat, Iqbal Gondal, Peter Vamplew, and Joarder Kamruzzaman. Survey of intrusion detection systems: Techniques, datasets and challenges. *Cybersecurity*, 2(1): 1–22, 2019.

6 Quanyan Zhu and Tamer Başar. Game-theoretic approach to feedback-driven multi-stage moving target defense. In *International Conference on Decision and Game Theory for Security*, pages 246–263. Springer, 2013.

7 Sushil Jajodia, Anup K. Ghosh, Vipin Swarup, Cliff Wang, and X. Sean Wang. *Moving Target Defense: Creating Asymmetric Uncertainty for Cyber Threats*, volume 54. Springer Science & Business Media, 2011.

8 Jeffrey Pawlick and Quanyan Zhu. *Game Theory for Cyber Deception*. Springer, 2021.

9 Sushil Jajodia, V. Subrahmanian, Vipin Swarup, and Cliff Wang. *Cyber Deception*. Cham, Switzerland: Springer, 2016.

10 Ya-Ting Yang and Quanyan Zhu. When to deceive: A cross-layer Stackelberg game framework for strategic timing of cyber deception. *arXiv preprint arXiv:2505.21244*, 2025.

11 Linan Huang and Quanyan Zhu. Strategic learning for active, adaptive, and autonomous cyber defense. In *Adaptive Autonomous Secure Cyber Systems*, pages 205–230. Springer, 2020.

12 Ehab Al-Shaer, Jinpeng Wei, W Kevin, and Cliff Wang. *Autonomous Cyber Deception*. Springer, 2019.

13 Allegra Hobbs. The colonial pipeline hack: Exposing vulnerabilities in US cybersecurity. In *SAGE Business Cases*. SAGE Publications: SAGE Business Cases Originals, 2021.

14 Qian Chen and Robert A. Bridges. Automated behavioral analysis of malware: A case study of WannaCry ransomware. In *2017 16th IEEE International Conference on Machine Learning and Applications (ICMLA)*, pages 454–460. IEEE, 2017.

15 Linan Huang and Quanyan Zhu. *Cognitive Security: A System-scientific Approach*. Springer Nature, 2023.

16 Shuo Huang, Fred Jones, Nikolos Gurney, David Pynadath, Kunal Srivastava, Stoney Trent, Peggy Wu, and Quanyan Zhu. Psyborg+: Modeling and simulation for detecting cognitive biases in advanced persistent threats. In *MILCOM 2024-2024 IEEE Military Communications Conference (MILCOM)*, pages 1–6. IEEE, 2024.

17 Anh Tung Nguyen, Quanyan Zhu, and André Teixeira. Bilateral cognitive security games in networked control systems under stealthy injection attacks. *arXiv preprint arXiv:2505.01232*, 2025.

18 Ya-Ting Yang, Haozhe Lei, and Quanyan Zhu. PRADA: Proactive risk assessment and mitigation of misinformed demand attacks on navigational route recommendations. *arXiv preprint arXiv:2409.00243*, 2024.

19 Colin Camerer and Martin Weber. Recent developments in modeling preferences: Uncertainty and ambiguity. *Journal of Risk and Uncertainty*, 5: 325–370, 1992.

20 Arnold Chassagnon and Pierre-André Chiappori. Insurance under moral hazard and adverse selection: The case of pure competition. *Delta-CREST Document*, 1997. https://www.parisschoolofeconomics.com/chassagnon-arnold/acpac95.pdf

21 Yanfen Zhang, Qi Xu, and Guoqing Zhang. Optimal contracts with moral hazard and adverse selection in a live streaming commerce market. *Journal of Retailing and Consumer Services*, 74: 103419, 2023.

22 Shutian Liu and Quanyan Zhu. Mitigating moral hazard in insurance contracts using risk preference design. *Operations Research Letters*, 62: 107322, 2025.

23 Liu Liu, Olivier De Vel, Qing-Long Han, Jun Zhang, and Yang Xiang. Detecting and preventing cyber insider threats: A survey. *IEEE Communications Surveys & Tutorials*, 20(2): 1397–1417, 2018.

24 Jeffrey Hunker and Christian W Probst. Insiders and insider threats-an overview of definitions and mitigation techniques. *Journal Wireless Mobile Networks Ubiquitous Computing Dependable Applications*, 2(1): 4–27, 2011.

25 Matt Bishop, Sophie Engle, Sean Peisert, Sean Whalen, and Carrie Gates. Case studies of an insider framework. In *2009 42nd Hawaii International Conference on System Sciences*, pages 1–10. IEEE, 2009.

26 Shari Lawrence Pfleeger, Joel B. Predd, Jeffrey Hunker, and Carla Bulford. Insiders behaving badly: Addressing bad actors and their actions. *IEEE Transactions on Information Forensics and Security*, 5(1): 169–179, 2009.

27 George J. Silowash, Dawn M. Cappelli, Andrew P. Moore, Randall F. Trzeciak, Timothy Shimeall, and Lori Flynn. Common sense guide to mitigating insider threats. Technical report, 2012.

28 Eric M. Hutchins, Michael J. Cloppert, Rohan M. Amin. Intelligence-driven computer network defense informed by analysis of adversary campaigns and intrusion kill chains. *Leading Issues in Information Warfare & Security Research*, 1(1): 80, 2011.

29 Malek Ben Salem, Shlomo Hershkop, and Salvatore J. Stolfo. A survey of insider attack detection research. In *Insider Attack and Cyber Security*, pages 69–90. Springer, 2008.

30 Adel Alshamrani, Sowmya Myneni, Ankur Chowdhary, and Dijiang Huang. A survey on advanced persistent threats: Techniques, solutions, challenges, and research opportunities. *IEEE Communications Surveys & Tutorials*, 21(2): 1851–1877, 2019.

31 James P. Farwell and Rafal Rohozinski. Stuxnet and the future of cyber war. *Survival*, 53(1): 23–40, 2011.

32 Sumayah Al-Rabiaah. The “stuxnet” virus of 2010 as an example of a “apt” and its “recent” variances. In *2018 21st Saudi Computer Society National Computer Conference (NCC)*, pages 1–5. IEEE, 2018.

33 Yunfei Ge and Quanyan Zhu. GAZETA: Game-theoretic zero-trust authentication for defense against lateral movement in 5g IoT networks. *IEEE Transactions on Information Forensics and Security*, 19: 540–554, 2023.

34 Liyuan Liu, Meng Han, Yan Wang, and Yiyun Zhou. Understanding data breach: A visualization aspect. In *International Conference on Wireless Algorithms, Systems, and Applications*, pages 883–892. Springer, 2018.

35 R. Barona and EA Mary Anita. A survey on data breach challenges in cloud computing security: Issues and threats. In *2017 International Conference on Circuit, Power and Computing Technologies (ICCPCT)*, pages 1–8. IEEE, 2017.

36 Bander Ali Saleh Al-rimy, Mohd Aizaini Maarof, and Syed Zainudeen Mohd Shaid. Ransomware threat success factors, taxonomy, and countermeasures: A survey and research directions. *Computers & Security*, 74: 144–166, 2018.

37 Kevin Liao, Ziming Zhao, Adam Doupé, and Gail-Joon Ahn. Behind closed doors: Measurement and analysis of cryptolocker ransoms in bitcoin. In *2016 APWG Symposium on Electronic Crime Research (eCrime)*, pages 1–13. IEEE, 2016.

38 Jagmeet Singh Aidan, Harsh Kumar Verma, and Lalit Kumar Awasthi. Comprehensive survey on petya ransomware attack. In *2017 International Conference on Next Generation Computing and Information Systems (ICNGCIS)*, pages 122–125. IEEE, 2017.

39 David Braue. Global ransomware damage costs predicted to exceed 265 billion by 2031, 2022. https://cybersecurityventures.com/global-ransomware-damage-costs-predicted-to-reach-250-billion-usd-by-2031/.

40 Yuhan Zhao, Yunfei Ge, and Quanyan Zhu. Combating ransomware in internet of things: A games-in-games approach for cross-layer cyber defense and security investment. In *International Conference on Decision and Game Theory for Security*, pages 208–228. Springer, 2021.

41 Tamer Başar and Geert Jan Olsder. *Dynamic noncooperative game theory*. SIAM, 1998.

42 Quanyan Zhu, Hamidou Tembine, and Tamer Başar. Heterogeneous learning in zero-sum stochastic games with incomplete information. In *49th IEEE Conference on Decision and Control (CDC)*, pages 219–224. IEEE, 2010.

43 Quanyan Zhu and Tamer Başar. Dynamic policy-based ids configuration. In *Proceedings of the 48h IEEE Conference on Decision and Control (CDC) held jointly with 2009 28th Chinese Control Conference*, pages 8600–8605. IEEE, 2009.

44 Tansu Alpcan and Tamer Basar. An intrusion detection game with limited observations. In *12th International Symposiumon Dynamic Games and Applications, Sophia Antipolis, France*, volume 26, 2006.

45 Karin Sallhammar, Bjarne E. Helvik, and Svein J. Knapskog. On stochastic modeling for integrated security and dependability evaluation. *Journal Networks*, 1(5): 31–42, 2006.

46 Arunesh Sinha, Fei Fang, Bo An, Christopher Kiekintveld, and Milind Tambe. Stackelberg security games: Looking beyond a decade of success. IJCAI, 2018.

47 Heinrich von Stackelberg. *Theory of the Market Economy*. University of California, 1952.

48 Fei Fang, Albert Xin Jiang, and Milind Tambe. Protecting moving targets with multiple mobile resources. *Journal of Artificial Intelligence Research*, 48: 583–634, 2013.

49 Xiaotao Feng, Zizhan Zheng, Prasant Mohapatra, and Derya Cansever. A Stackelberg game and Markov modeling of moving target defense. In *International Conference on Decision and Game Theory for Security*, pages 315–335. Springer, 2017.

50 Jeffrey Pawlick, Edward Colbert, and Quanyan Zhu. A game-theoretic taxonomy and survey of defensive deception for cybersecurity and privacy. *ACM Computing Surveys (CSUR)*, 52(4): 1–28, 2019.

51 James Pita, Manish Jain, Janusz Marecki, Fernando Ordóñez, Christopher Portway, Milind Tambe, Craig Western, Praveen Paruchuri, and Sarit Kraus. Deployed armor protection: The application of a game theoretic model for security at the los angeles international airport. In *Proceedings of the 7th International Joint Conference on Autonomous Agents and Multiagent Systems: Industrial Track*, pages 125–132, 2008.

52 Manish Jain, Jason Tsai, James Pita, Christopher Kiekintveld, Shyamsunder Rathi, Milind Tambe, and Fernando Ordónez. Software assistants for randomized patrol planning for the LAX airport police and the federal air marshal service. *Interfaces*, 40(4): 267–290, 2010.

53 Bo An, Eric Shieh, Milind Tambe, Rong Yang, Craig Baldwin, Joseph DiRenzo, Ben Maule, and Garrett Meyer. PROTECT–A deployed game theoretic system for strategic security allocation for the United States coast guard. *Ai Magazine*, 33(4): 96–96, 2012.

54 Quanyan Zhu, Husheng Li, Zhu Han, and Tamer Başar. A stochastic game model for jamming in multi-channel cognitive radio systems. In *2010 IEEE International Conference on Communications*, pages 1–6. IEEE, 2010.

55 Quanyan Zhu, Hamidou Tembine, and Tamer Başar. Hybrid learning in stochastic games and its application in network security. In *Reinforcement Learning and Approximate Dynamic Programming for Feedback Control*, pages 303–329. Wiley, 2012.

56 Quanyan Zhu, Carol Fung, Raouf Boutaba, and Tamer Basar. A game-theoretical approach to incentive design in collaborative intrusion detection networks. In *2009 International Conference on Game Theory for Networks*, pages 384–392. IEEE, 2009.

57 John C. Harsanyi. Games with incomplete information played by "Bayesian" players, i–iii part i. the basic model. *Management Science*, 14(3): 159–182, 1967.

58 Linan Huang and Quanyan Zhu. Dynamic bayesian games for adversarial and defensive cyber deception. In *Autonomous Cyber Deception*, pages 75–97. Springer, 2019.

59 Quanyan Zhu. Game theory for cyber deception: A tutorial. In *Proceedings of the 6th Annual Symposium on Hot Topics in the Science of Security*, pages 1–3, 2019.

60 Linan Huang and Quanyan Zhu. Adaptive strategic cyber defense for advanced persistent threats in critical infrastructure networks. *ACM SIGMETRICS Performance Evaluation Review*, 46(2): 52–56, 2019.

61 Linan Huang and Quanyan Zhu. A dynamic games approach to proactive defense strategies against advanced persistent threats in cyber-physical systems. *Computers & Security*, 89: 101660, 2020.

62 Quanyan Zhu and Stefan Rass. On multi-phase and multi-stage game-theoretic modeling of advanced persistent threats. *IEEE Access*, 6: 13958–13971, 2018.

63 Jeffrey Pawlick, Sadegh Farhang, and Quanyan Zhu. Flip the cloud: Cyber-physical signaling games in the presence of advanced persistent threats. In *International Conference on Decision and Game Theory for Security*, pages 289–308. Springer, 2015.

64 Jeffrey Pawlick and Quanyan Zhu. Strategic trust in cloud-enabled cyber-physical systems with an application to glucose control. *IEEE Transactions on Information Forensics and Security*, 12(12): 2906–2919, 2017.

65 Erik Miehling, Mohammad Rasouli, and Demosthenis Teneketzis. A pomdp approach to the dynamic defense of large-scale cyber networks. *IEEE Transactions on Information Forensics and Security*, 13(10): 2490–2505, 2018.

66 Mehmet Necip Kurt, Oyetunji Ogundijo, Chong Li, and Xiaodong Wang. Online cyber-attack detection in smart grid: A reinforcement learning approach. *IEEE Transactions on Smart Grid*, 10(5): 5174–5185, 2018.

67 Quanyan Zhu and Zhiheng Xu. *Cross-layer Design for Secure and Resilient Cyber-physical Systems*. Springer, 2020.

68 Carlos Sarraute, Olivier Buffet, and Jörg Hoffmann. Pomdps make better hackers: Accounting for uncertainty in penetration testing. In *Twenty-Sixth AAAI Conference on Artificial Intelligence*, 2012.

69 Sara Marie Mc Carthy, Arunesh Sinha, Milind Tambe, and Pratyusa Manadhata. Data exfiltration detection and prevention: Virtually distributed pomdps for practically safer networks. In *International Conference on Decision and Game Theory for Security*, pages 39–61. Springer, 2016.

70 Carl Colwill. Human factors in information security: The insider threat–who can you trust these days? *Information Security Technical Report*, 14(4): 186–196, 2009.

71 Chaitanya Joshi, Jesus Rios Aliaga, and David Rios Insua. Insider threat modeling: An adversarial risk analysis approach. *IEEE Transactions on Information Forensics and Security*, 16: 1131–1142, 2020.

72 Linan Huang and Quanyan Zhu. Duplicity games for deception design with an application to insider threat mitigation. *IEEE Transactions on Information Forensics and Security*, 16: 4843–4856, 2021.

73 Quanyan Zhu, Carol Fung, Raouf Boutaba, and Tamer Basar. GUIDEX: A game-theoretic incentive-based mechanism for intrusion detection networks. *IEEE Journal on Selected Areas in Communications*, 30(11): 2220–2230, 2012.

74 William Casey, Jose Andre Morales, Evan Wright, Quanyan Zhu, and Bud Mishra. Compliance signaling games: Toward modeling the deterrence of insider threats. *Computational and Mathematical Organization Theory*, 22(3): 318–349, 2016.

75 Jason Garbis and Jerry W. Chapman. *Zero Trust Security: An Enterprise Guide*. Springer, 2021.

76 Scott Rose, Oliver Borchert, Stu Mitchell, and Sean Connelly. Zero trust architecture. Technical report, National Institute of Standards and Technology, 2020.

77 VA Stafford. Zero trust architecture. *NIST Special Publication*, 800: 207, 2020.

78 Sana Siddiqui, Muhammad Salman Khan, Ken Ferens, and Witold Kinsner. Detecting advanced persistent threats using fractal dimension based machine learning classification. In *Proceedings of the 2016 ACM on International Workshop on Security and Privacy Analytics*, pages 64–69, 2016.

79 Ibrahim Ghafir, Mohammad Hammoudeh, Vaclav Prenosil, Liangxiu Han, Robert Hegarty, Khaled Rabie, and Francisco J. Aparicio-Navarro. Detection of advanced persistent threat using machine-learning correlation analysis. *Future Generation Computer Systems*, 89: 349–359, 2018.

80 Saranya Chandran, P. Hrudya, and Prabaharan Poornachandran. An efficient classification model for detecting advanced persistent threat. In *2015 International Conference on Advances in Computing, Communications and Informatics (ICACCI)*, pages 2001–2009. IEEE, 2015.

81 Yunhan Huang and Quanyan Zhu. Deceptive reinforcement learning under adversarial manipulations on cost signals. In *International Conference on Decision and Game Theory for Security*, pages 217–237. Springer, 2019.

82 Yunhan Huang, Juntao Chen, Linan Huang, and Quanyan Zhu. Dynamic games for secure and resilient control system design. *National Science Review*, 7(7): 1125–1141, 2020.

83 Stefan Rass and Quanyan Zhu. GADAPT: A sequential game-theoretic framework for designing defense-in-depth strategies against advanced persistent threats. In *International Conference on Decision and Game Theory for Security*, pages 314–326. Springer, 2016.

84 Quanyan Zhu and Stefan Rass. Game theory meets network security: A tutorial. In *Proceedings of the 2018 ACM SIGSAC Conference on Computer and Communications Security*, pages 2163–2165, 2018.

85 Linan Huang and Quanyan Zhu. Adaptive honeypot engagement through reinforcement learning of semi-Markov decision processes. In *International Conference on Decision and Game Theory for Security*, pages 196–216. Springer, 2019.

86 Yunhan Huang, Linan Huang, and Quanyan Zhu. Reinforcement learning for feedback-enabled cyber resilience. *Annual Reviews in Control*, 53: 273–295, 2022.

87 Armin Sarabi, Parinaz Naghizadeh, Yang Liu, and Mingyan Liu. Risky business: Fine-grained data breach prediction using business profiles. *Journal of Cybersecurity*, 2(1): 15–28, 2016.

88 Aleksandr Ometov, Sergey Bezzateev, Niko Mäkitalo, Sergey Andreev, Tommi Mikkonen, and Yevgeni Koucheryavy. Multi-factor authentication: A survey. *Cryptography*, 2(1): 1, 2018.

89 Nancie Gunson, Diarmid Marshall, Hazel Morton, and Mervyn Jack. User perceptions of security and usability of single-factor and two-factor authentication in automated telephone banking. *Computers & Security*, 30(4): 208–220, 2011.

90 Ömer Aslan Aslan and Refik Samet. A comprehensive review on malware detection approaches. *IEEE Access*, 8: 6249–6271, 2020.

91 Ahmed El-Kosairy and Marianne A. Azer. Intrusion and ransomware detection system. In *2018 1st International Conference on Computer Applications & Information Security (ICCAIS)*, pages 1–7. IEEE, 2018.

92 Yu-Lun Wan, Jen-Chun Chang, Rong-Jaye Chen, and Shiuh-Jeng Wang. Feature-selection-based ransomware detection with machine learning of data analysis. In *2018 3rd International Conference on Computer and Communication Systems (ICCCS)*, pages 85–88. IEEE, 2018.

93 Ahmad O. Almashhadani, Mustafa Kaiiali, Sakir Sezer, and Philip O'Kane. A multi-classifier network-based crypto ransomware detection system: A case study of locky ransomware. *IEEE Access*, 7: 47053–47067, 2019.

94 Haim Levy. Stochastic dominance and expected utility: Survey and analysis. *Management Science*, 38(4): 555–593, 1992.

95 Mark V. Pauly. The economics of moral hazard: Comment. *The American Economic Review*, 58(3): 531–537, 1968.

96 Sanford J. Grossman and Oliver D. Hart. An analysis of the principal-agent problem. In *Foundations of Insurance Economics*, pages 302–340. Springer, 1992.

97 Stephan Dempe. *Foundations of bilevel programming*. Springer Science & Business Media, 2002.

98 Angelica Marotta, Fabio Martinelli, Stefano Nanni, Albina Orlando, and Artsiom Yautsiukhin. Cyber-insurance survey. *Computer Science Review*, 24: 35–61, 2017.

99 Mohammad Mahdi Khalili, Parinaz Naghizadeh, and Mingyan Liu. Designing cyber insurance policies: The role of pre-screening and security interdependence. *IEEE Transactions on Information Forensics and Security*, 13(9): 2226–2239, 2018.

100 Rainer Böhme, Galina Schwartz. Modeling cyber-insurance: Towards a unifying framework. In *WEIS*, 2010. https://informationsecurity.uibk.ac.at/pdfs/BS2010_Modeling_Cyber-Insurance_WEIS.pdf

101 Rui Zhang, Quanyan Zhu, and Yezekael Hayel. A bi-level game approach to attack-aware cyber insurance of computer networks. *IEEE Journal on Selected Areas in Communications*, 35(3): 779–794, 2017.

102 Rui Zhang and Quanyan Zhu. `FlipIn` : A game-theoretic cyber insurance framework for incentive-compatible cyber risk management of internet of things. *IEEE Transactions on Information Forensics and Security*, 15: 2026–2041, 2019.

103 Bengt Holmström. Moral hazard and observability. *The Bell Journal of Economics*, pages 74–91, 1979.

104 John Von Neumann and Oskar Morgenstern. Theory of games and economic behavior. In *Theory of games and economic behavior*. Princeton University Press, 2007.

105 Kenneth J. Arrow.The theory of risk aversion. In *Essays in the theory of risk-bearing*, pages 90–120, Pennsylvania State University, 1971.

106 John W. Pratt. Risk aversion in the small and in the large. In *Uncertainty in economics*, pages 59–79. Elsevier, 1978.

107 Lars Stole. Lectures on the theory of contracts and organizations. *Unpublished paper, University of Chicago, Booth School of Business,* 2001.

108 Amos Tversky and Daniel Kahneman. Advances in prospect theory: Cumulative representation of uncertainty. *Journal of Risk and Uncertainty*, 5(4): 297–323, 1992.

109 Philippe Artzner, Freddy Delbaen, Jean-Marc Eber, and David Heath. Coherent measures of risk. *Mathematical Finance*, 9(3): 203–228, 1999.

110 Hans Föllmer and Alexander Schied. Stochastic finance. In *Stochastic finance*. de Gruyter, 2016.

111 Andrzej Ruszczyński and Alexander Shapiro. Optimization of convex risk functions. *Mathematics of Operations Research*, 31(3): 433–452, 2006.

112 Georg Ch Pflug and Alois Pichler. *Multistage stochastic optimization*, volume 1104. Springer, 2014.

113 Dimitris Bertsimas and Akiko Takeda. Optimizing over coherent risk measures and non-convexities: A robust mixed integer optimization approach. *Computational Optimization and Applications*, 62(3): 613–639, 2015.

114 Shutian Liu and Quanyan Zhu. Robust and stochastic optimization with a hybrid coherent risk measure with an application to supervised learning. *IEEE Control Systems Letters*, 5(3): 965–970, 2020.

115 Erfaun Noorani and John S Baras. Embracing risk in reinforcement learning: The connection between risk-sensitive exponential and distributionally robust criteria. In *2022 American Control Conference (ACC)*, pages 2703–2708. IEEE, 2022.

116 R. Tyrrell Rockafellar, Stanislav Uryasev. Optimization of conditional value-at-risk. *Journal of Risk*, 2: 21–42, 2000.

117 Shigeo Kusuoka. On law invariant coherent risk measures. In *Advances in Mathematical Economics*, pages 83–95. Springer, 2001.

118 Alexander Shapiro, Darinka Dentcheva, and Andrzej Ruszczynski. *Lectures on Stochastic Programming: Modeling and Theory*. SIAM, 2021.

119 Hamed Rahimian and Sanjay Mehrotra. Distributionally robust optimization: A review. *arXiv preprint arXiv:1908.05659*, 2019.

120 Shutian Liu and Quanyan Zhu. On the role of risk perceptions in cyber insurance contracts. *arXiv preprint arXiv:2210.15010*, 2022.

121 Shutian Liu and Quanyan Zhu. Stackelberg risk preference design. *Mathematical Programming*, 209(1): 785–823, 2025.

122 Shutian Liu and Quanyan Zhu. Mitigating moral hazard in cyber insurance using risk preference design. *arXiv preprint arXiv:2203.12001*, 2022.

123 Hannah Schildberg-Hörisch. Are risk preferences stable? *Journal of Economic Perspectives*, 32(2): 135–54, 2018.

124 Lisa R. Anderson and Jennifer M. Mellor. Are risk preferences stable? Comparing an experimental measure with a validated survey-based measure. *Journal of Risk and Uncertainty*, 39(2): 137–160, 2009.

125 Vincent P. Crawford. Dynamic games and dynamic contract theory. *Journal of Conflict Resolution*, 29(2): 195–224, 1985.

126 Raj Badhwar. Dynamic measurement of cyber risk. In *The CISO's Next Frontier*, pages 327–334. Springer, 2021.

127 Rui Zhang and Quanyan Zhu. Optimal cyber-insurance contract design for dynamic risk management and mitigation. *IEEE Transactions on Computational Social Systems*, 5: 1087–1100, 2021.

128 Spyridon Papastergiou and Nineta Polemi. MITIGATE: A dynamic supply chain cyber risk assessment methodology. In *Smart Trends in Systems, Security and Sustainability*, pages 1–9. Springer, 2018.

129 Juntao Chen, Quanyan Zhu, and Tamer Başar. Dynamic contract design for systemic cyber risk management of interdependent enterprise networks. *Dynamic Games and Applications*, 11(2): 294–325, 2021.

130 Jakša Cvitanić, Dylan Possamaï, and Nizar Touzi. Dynamic programming approach to principal–agent problems. *Finance and Stochastics*, 22(1): 1–37, 2018.

131 Dirk Bergemann and Juuso Välimäki. Dynamic mechanism design: An introduction. *Journal of Economic Literature*, 57(2): 235–74, 2019.

132 Alessandro Pavan, Ilya Segal, and Juuso Toikka. Dynamic mechanism design: A myersonian approach. *Econometrica*, 82(2): 601–653, 2014.

133 Tao Zhang and Quanyan Zhu. On incentive compatibility in dynamic mechanism design with exit option in a Markovian environment. *Dynamic Games and Applications*, 12(2): 701–745, 2022.

134 Jan Martin Lemnitzer. Why cybersecurity insurance should be regulated and compulsory. *Journal of Cyber Policy*, 6(2): 118–136, 2021.

135 Sasha Romanosky, Lillian Ablon, Andreas Kuehn, and Therese Jones. Content analysis of cyber insurance policies: How do carriers price cyber risk? *Journal of Cybersecurity*, 5(1): tyz002, 2019.

136 Aviva Abramovsky and Peter Kochenburger. Insurance online: Regulation and consumer protection in a cyber world. In *The "Dematerialized" Insurance: Distance Selling and Cyber Risks from an International Perspective*, pages 117–142. Springer, 2016.

137 Bernold Nieuwesteeg, Louis Visscher, and Bob de Waard. The law and economics of cyber insurance contracts: A case study. *European Review of Private Law*, 26(3), 2018.

138 Daniel Woods and Andrew Simpson. Policy measures and cyber insurance: A framework. *Journal of Cyber Policy*, 2(2): 209–226, 2017.

139 Nir Kshetri. The evolution of cyber-insurance industry and market: An institutional analysis. *Telecommunications Policy*, 44(8): 102007, 2020.

140 Paul Voigt and Axel Von dem Bussche. *The EU General Data Protection Regulation (GDPR)*. Springer, 2017.

141 European Data Protection Board. Meta fined €1.2 billion for GDPR violations, 2023. https://edpb.europa.eu. Press release.

142 Information Commissioner's Office. ICO fines British Airways £20 million for data breach, 2020. Regulatory announcement.

143 Information Commissioner's Office. ICO fines Marriott £18.4 million for GDPR failings, 2020. Regulatory announcement.

144 EDUCAUSE and URMIA. FAQ: What does cyber insurance cover?, 2025. https://www.educause.edu. White paper.

145 DLA Piper. The price of data security—A guide to the insurability of GDPR fines across Europe, 3rd, 2020. https://www.dlapiper.com.

146 Pillsbury Law. Massive GDPR fine a wake-up call for compliance and cyber insurance, 2020. https://www.pillsburylaw.com. Legal bulletin.

147 RevOps HQ. Managing cyber liability in revops teams, 2024. White paper.

148 Stimson Center. *Market incentives: The insurance industry and cyber accountability*. Policy brief, 2024.

7

Enhancing Cyber Resiliency: Assessing the Effectiveness of Deploying Honeypots in Different Network Topologies

7.1 Introduction

Cyber deception has been effectively used to mislead and misinform attackers to slow them down and waste their resources to mitigate attacks on critical infrastructure [1], thereby enhancing cyber resilience. Defenders could use deception to delay attackers by invalidating the information collected during the reconnaissance phase. Cyber deception could be achieved by information dissimulation or information simulation [2]. Dissimulation strategy consists of partially or fully concealing the true state of reality. For example, masking, which attempts to hide or erase crucial information to escape detection. On the other hand, simulation strategies exhibit false information. For example: decoying, where network defenders deploy honeypots or other kinds of decoys to lure attackers. Honeypots and similar types of decoys represent the most rudimentary uses of deception in the protection of information systems [3]. In fact, deception through honeypots (systems that pretend to be real) has been a prominent technique for the detection, prevention, and response to cyber exploits [4–8]. In the real world, such honeypots can be created by using fake patches or placing fake content on computer systems [9]. Deception through honeypots has also been used in cutting-edge technologies such as the Internet of Things (IoT) to defend against modern cyber exploits [10].

The effectiveness of honeypots can be influenced by their design, including the way misleading information is presented, the plausibility and consistency of the information, the level of detail, and the vagueness of the information [11, 12]. Research efforts have also been devoted to quantitative measurement and systematic planning of honeypot deception [13]. Researchers have also investigated behavioral aspects of cyber deception [7, 14, 15]. Defenders are still unaware of the effective proportion of honeypots in a network, the role of network topology, and the effective features of honeypots. Honeypots are often deployed on a network scale with multiple honeypots mixed with real hosts. It is difficult for cyber defenders to decide how to allocate honeypots within the network structure. Stephan Achleitner et al. [16] proposed a reconnaissance-deceptive virtual network topology (layered topology) that can be generated based on Software Defined Networks (SDN). However, prior research has investigated the effectiveness of network topology in reconnaissance performance by executing common scanning techniques in the simulated test environment, but it is not clear how network topology influences the performance of human attackers.

In this research, we conducted human-in-the-loop experiments using a tool called "HackIT" [17] to study the effectiveness of deploying honeypots in different network topologies. As a first step, we used two network topologies (layered and star) for the network structure and randomly selected nodes to assign as honeypots within these networks. Then, the human participants were randomly assigned to one of the network topology conditions. Human participants, i.e., attackers, attempt to exploit nodes in their network by interacting with the HackIT tool. The experiment results suggest that deploying honeypots in the layered topology was successful in luring more attackers and led them to launch exploits on honeypots compared to the star topology. Since deception strategies accomplish defense purposes by causing adversaries to have false beliefs, their effectiveness is innately determined by the cognitive status of deceivers, which evolves dynamically and differs for individual attackers. Defenders should be aware of that when enhancing cyber resilience through maximizing the advantages of deception strategies.

It is very difficult to find human participants (attackers) with expertise in cybersecurity, so to fill this gap, we developed an instance-based learning (IBL) theory model to capture human attacker actions in such complex tasks. Therefore, in the absence or shortage of human attackers, IBL models can play the role of the attacker and could be useful in testing novel defense algorithms.

7.1.1 Contribution

The primary objective of this research is to understand the influence of network topology on human attacker decision-making. We developed a cybersecurity game that manipulates the network topology using HackIT [18]. We perform human experiments to evaluate human decision-making processes. In addition, we replicate human actions using an IBL model and explain human decision-making using the cognitive model of an attacker.

In what follows, first, we detail a HackIT experiment on the network topology. Next, we evaluate the experimental data of human participants. Furthermore, we model human decisions in the HackIT game using IBL. Finally, we compare the behavior of human and IBL models and highlight their implications for using deception for cyber resilience in the real world.

7.2 Task Description

Using an experimentation testbed called HackIT, i.e., an experimental testbed to conduct human-in-the-loop cybersecurity experiments, we test the effectiveness of honeypots in different network topologies. In this task, the defenders create two network topologies and deploy the honeypots in different networks, which are then presented to attackers. Human participants in the role of attackers perform the task in two phases: network reconnaissance, i.e., gather information about the network using tools such as nmap and network exploitation, i.e., attackers exploit the nodes and exfiltrate the data. In the network reconnaissance phase, attackers could gather information using network scanning tools, i.e., nmap. Once they are satisfied with the network scan, attackers exploit the nodes and exfiltrate the data.

7.2.1 Experiment Conditions

In this experiment, we considered a network of 40 nodes where 10 of the nodes are real and 30 nodes are honeypots. We manipulate the network topology at two levels: star topology and layered topology. In both conditions, the allocation of honeypots was pre-generated randomly and kept the same for all participants. The actual allocation of honeypots in each condition is provided in Table 7.1 of the Appendix.

7.2.1.1 Layered Topology

As shown in Figure 7.1, in the layered topology (left) the network is divided into two layers, at layer 1, we have 10 nodes, each of these 10 nodes is further connected to a subnet of 3 nodes at layer 2. Therefore, the attacker could only access any of the

Table 7.1 The configuration of the easy-to-attack and difficult-to-attack nodes.

Category	Operating systems/services and ports
Easy	Windows Server 2003, Windows XP, HP-UX 11i, Solaris
	21/tcp – FTP, 25/tcp – SMTP, 80/tcp – HTTP,
	111/tcp – RPCBind, 135/tcp – MSRPC
Difficult	OpenBSD, Linux, MacOSX, Windows 8
	22/tcp – SSH, 53/tcp – DNS, 139/tcp – NetBIOS,
	443/tcp – HTTPS, 445/tcp – Microsoft-DS, 3306/tcp – MySQL

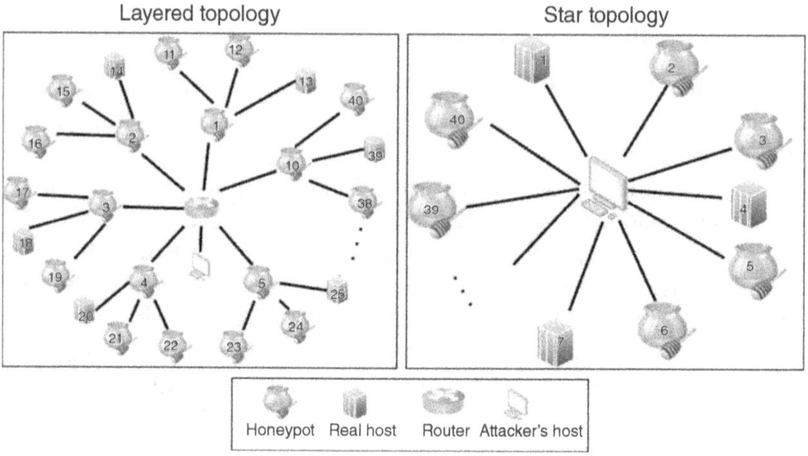

Figure 7.1 Network topologies: layered topology (left) and star topology (right).

10 nodes in layer 1 after entering the network. The nodes in layer 2 subnet could be accessed only after exploiting the layer 1 nodes. The nodes in the first layer are honeypots, and in layer 2, the honeypots are randomly assigned.

7.2.1.2 Star Topology

Figure 7.1 (right) represents the star topology where the 40 nodes are within one hop away from the attacker's location. The network is not divided into subnets. Attackers may have access to all 40 nodes in the first layer itself. The honeypots are randomly assigned among the real nodes.

7.2.1.3 Honeypot Features

The observable features of the nodes in the network were manipulated so that some nodes are "easy to attack" and some nodes are "difficult to attack." The assumption is that honeypots are typically easier to attack compared to real nodes. Table 7.1 shows the information on the configuration of the easy-to-attack and difficult-to-attack nodes. For example, a system with the Windows XP operating system, port 80/tcp, and http service will be easily exploitable. However, a system with the Linux operating system, port 22/tcp, and service ssh will be difficult to attack [19]. In the experiment, the participants were unaware of the assumptions of easy-to-exploit and difficult-to-exploit in the system configuration in Table 7.1.

We expect that attackers would take more time to detect real nodes within the layered topology compared to the star topology. Furthermore, we expect that attackers would attack easily exploitable systems compared to those that are hard to exploit.

7.2.2 Experiment Scenario

In this experiment, participants played the role of attackers and their goal is to score maximum points by "exploiting" network nodes and stealing confidential information from a file named "pin.txt" located inside the node. If the player exfiltrates data from a honeypot, they lose 100 points, but if the system exploited is a real node, then they win 300 points. Players are given 5 minutes for one practice round before the 15-minute-long main round, where they could exploit as many systems as they want. The practice round provides a sample network with 5 systems for participants to get familiar with the HackIT testbed. The configurations of the practice round were different compared to those of the main round, and the participants did not receive any points for their actions in the practice round. The main round simulated a network of 40 nodes (10 real nodes and 30 honeypot nodes). Players were allowed to scan, exploit, and fetch data from as many systems as they liked.

Figure 7.2 shows the step-by-step HackIT task procedure. To start, participants get information about their goals, network, and steps involved in the task. For example, in step 1 of Figure 7.2, participants get the information that they can exploit any of the nodes from node 1 to node 40. The first step for human participants was to investigate the network to collect information. Participants were advised to use the *help* command to view a list of available commands throughout

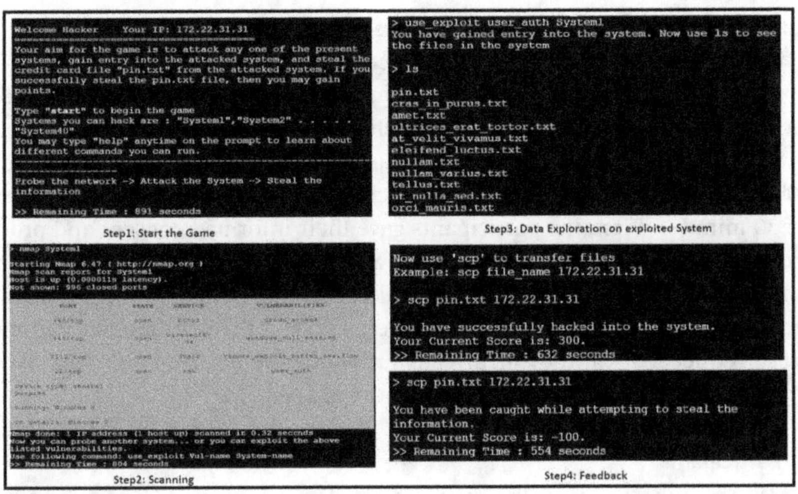

Figure 7.2 Steps involved in the HackIT task: (1) Description of the game that includes available systems, stages involved in the task, and instructions to start the task. (2) Exploring the network using the Nmap command. (3) Exploitation and searching for the credential file. (4) Exfiltration of data and feedback.

the task. In Figure 7.2 step 2, the hacker probes systems using the nmap command and observes the operating system, open ports, services, and vulnerabilities associated with the system. For example, probing system 1 gives the information to the hacker that the operating system is Windows 8 and the open ports on system 1 are 443, 445, 6112, and 22, each associated with an exploit. Once the attackers collect information about open ports and services on one or various systems, they could select a system for exploitation and launch an attack on the system by using the "use_exploit" command. The use_exploit command exploits the vulnerabilities of a system and helps the hacker gain access to that system. For example, in Figure 7.2 step 3, the hacker used the use_exploit command to gain access to system 1 using the user_auth vulnerability. After exploiting and gaining access to the system, attackers could list all files by using the "ls" command. The attacker transfers the required file, i.e., "pin.txt," using the "scp" command (Figure 7.2, step 4). After the file transfer, the human attackers were informed whether they were successful or not in stealing a credential file from a real host. If the file was transferred from a real node, the attacker would get 300 points, and if the file was transferred from the honeypot, the attacker would lose 100 points. Attackers could explore the other connected neighbors (if any) of the current system or logout directly. Nodes can be exploited only once and only if the attacker logs out from a node in the layered topology, the connected nodes are no longer accessible.

7.2.2.1 Procedure

Participants were recruited through advertisements in various university email groups, social media platforms, and cybersecurity-targeted groups. To be qualified to participate in the experiment, participants were required to pass an online cybersecurity knowledge screening test, which included questions on basic security, network scanning, different vulnerabilities, etc. The passing criterion was to score 70% in the screening test. Qualified participants were scheduled for an online study of 30 minutes. First, the participants gave their informed consent and provided demographic information. Then, they were asked to read the text instructions on the goal of the test and the general procedure. The instructions were followed by a brief quiz to assess their comprehension of the instructions. Participants received feedback if they incorrectly answered the questions on the quiz. After the quiz, the participants were directed to the task.

7.2.2.2 Participants

After a prescreening test on cybersecurity knowledge, we selected 58 participants for the main study (54% males, age mean: 27, SD: 8). Participants were randomly assigned to star topology ($N = 25$) or layered topology ($N = 33$) condition. About 47% reported having or pursuing master's degrees, 41% reported having a bachelor's degree, and the rest reported having PhD degrees. About 76% of the participants had a degree in computer science, 21% had other STEM degrees, 3% a degree in electrical engineering, and 3% reported other forms of education. Among all participants, about 84% participants took a cybersecurity course. After successful completion of the experiment, all participants received a base payment of $5 and could earn a bonus up to $6. The average time taken to complete this experiment was 30 minutes.

7.2.3 Results

We analyzed the attackers' actions in the practice round as well as in the main round. In the practice round, we observed that participants spent 1.05 minutes in the layered topology and 1.28 minutes in the star topology on average. We observe that the participants scanned and exploited at least one system to become familiar with the task. Next, we measure the exploration and exploitation rate, the honeypot attack rate, host detection rate (HDR), and their attack strategies in the main rounds.

7.2.4 Scanning and Exploitation Behavior

We present the average proportion of scans and exploits of participants acting as attackers in Figure 7.3. The scanning behavior was evaluated by calculating the number of systems they scanned using the nmap command. We also analyzed the exploitation behavior by calculating the number of systems exploited by participants using the "use_exploit" command. We observed that the proportions of scanning and exploitation were similar in the layered and the star topologies.

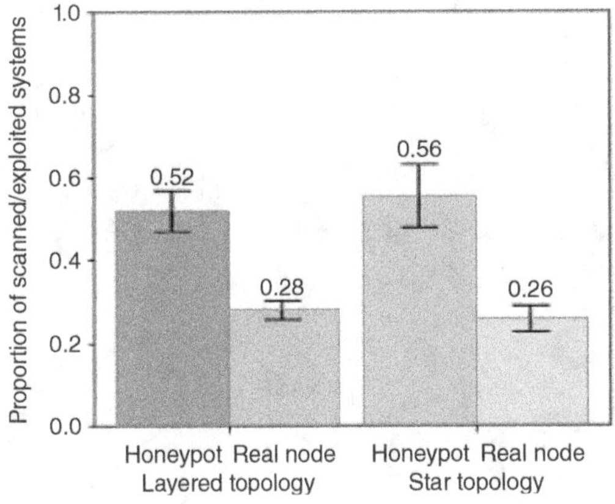

Figure 7.3 Scans and exploits behavior of participants in star and layered topology.

As shown in Figure 7.3, participants scanned 56% systems out of 40 systems on average throughout the experiment in the star topology and 52% systems in the layered topology. The percentage of exploits is much smaller, with 26 and 28% in star and layered topology, respectively. This difference was significant in both layered topology ($F(1, 32) = 4.4738$, $p < 0.001$) and star topology ($F(1, 24) = 6.7819$, $p < 0.001$).

Next, we observed that, despite the capability and permission to scan all systems, most attackers did not fully use their reconnaissance capabilities. Figure 7.4 is the histogram of the proportion of systems scanned and exploited in the layered and star topologies. The attackers were allowed to scan the systems within one hop, i.e., 10 nodes from the starting position and 3 nodes after exploiting a node. In the star topology, there is only one "layer" and the attackers could scan all 40 systems at once. As shown in Figure 7.4, attackers explore less than 16 systems in layered topology and 19 systems in star topology ($\text{Median}_{\text{layered}} = 16$, $\text{Median}_{\text{star}} = 19$). We observed that attackers did not exploit every system on the network. Figure 7.4 shows that the total number of exploits launched per attacker throughout the task and the exploit count rarely exceeds 20 ($\text{Median}_{\text{layered}} = 10$, $\text{Median}_{\text{star}} = 9$).

7.2.4.1 Proportion of Honeypot Scans and Attacks

We analyze the proportion of honeypot scans and exploits of the total scans or attacks in each network in Figure 7.5. In accordance with our hypothesis, we observe that both the proportion of scans as well as attacks on the honeypots are

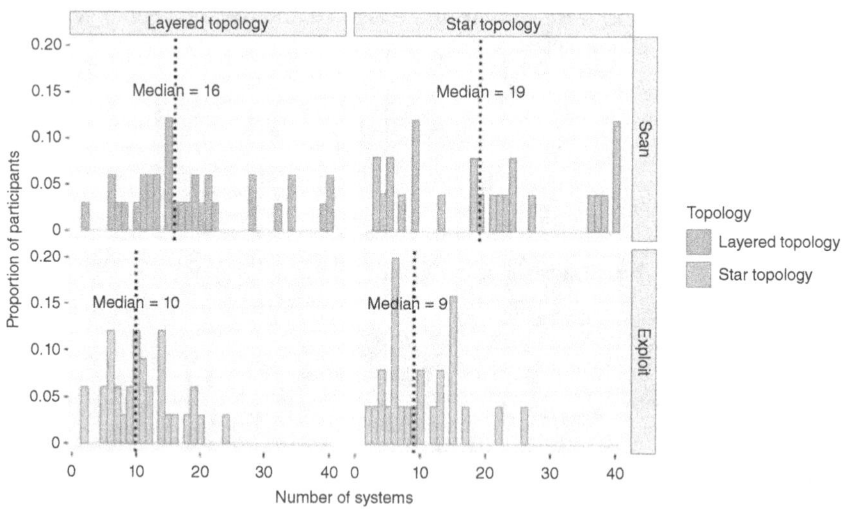

Figure 7.4 Exploration and exploitation distribution before each launching an exploit in both layered and star topology.

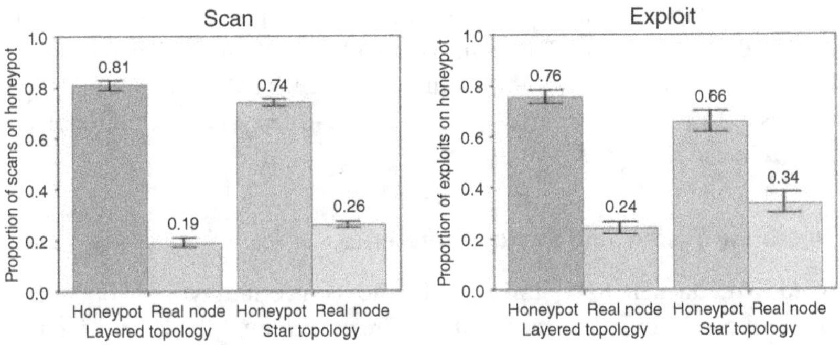

Figure 7.5 The proportion of scan/attack on honeypots in the star and layered topology.

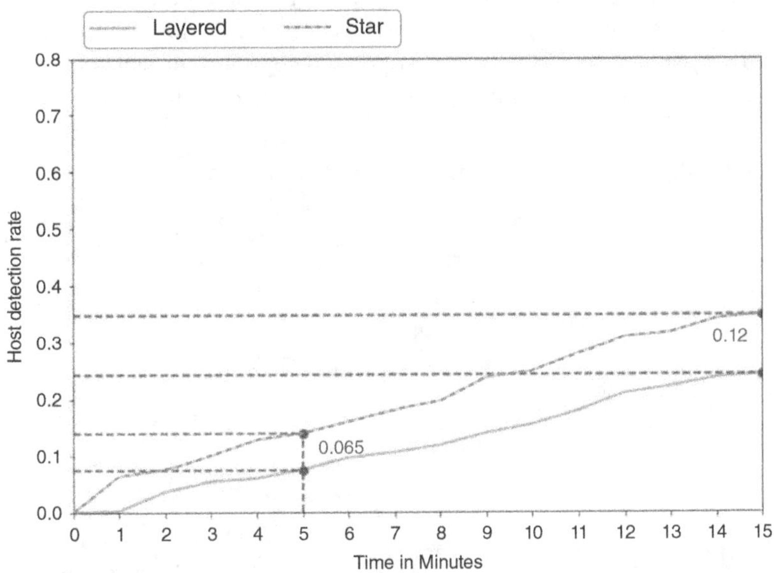

Figure 7.6 Host detection time.

higher in the layered topology compared to star topology. This difference is statistically significant ($F(1, 63)$=3.74, $p = 0.05$).

7.2.4.2 Host Detection Rate

To analyze the effect of network topology in delaying the detection of valued assets, that is, real hosts, we calculated the HDR in each condition, which means the percentage of real hosts detected based on the time spent in the task. The timestamp is derived from the time passed since the start of the round, i.e., the first command executed in the main round. As shown in Figure 7.6, overall HDR is higher for star topology compared to layered topology, and this difference between topologies increases over time. For example, HDR is 7.5% in the layered topology and 14% in the star topology after 5 minutes in the task, a difference of 0.065. At 15 minutes of task, the gap increases to 12% (0.10–0.15). The layered topology successfully reduced the speed of attackers.

7.2.5 Operating System and Exploit Preference

We observed that attackers have similar preferences on certain types of operating systems in both conditions. The radius of the circles in Figure 7.2 is linear to the percentage of the corresponding operating system being attacked. The most frequently chosen operating system, HP-UX 11i, is an easy-to-attack honeypot operating system in our assumption (Tables 7.1 and 7.2). Furthermore, we analyzed the proportion of an exploit being chosen when it is available on the target system. We observe in Figure 7.3 that in both the layered topology and the star topology, attackers prefer SQL injection, remote_auth and user_auth exploits (Table 7.3).

Table 7.2 Exploit distribution and corresponding operating systems.

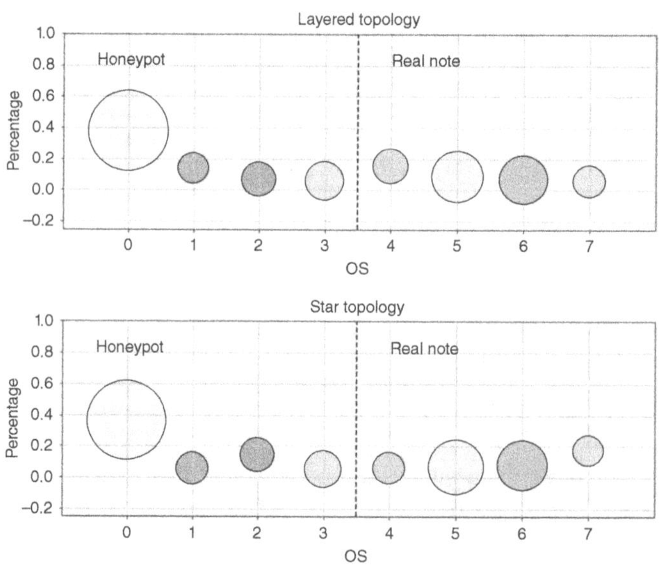

Index	OS
0	HP-UX 11i
1	Windows 2003
2	Solaris
3	Windows XP
4	Windows 8
5	OpenBSD
6	Mac OS X
7	Linux

Table 7.3 Exploit preferences.

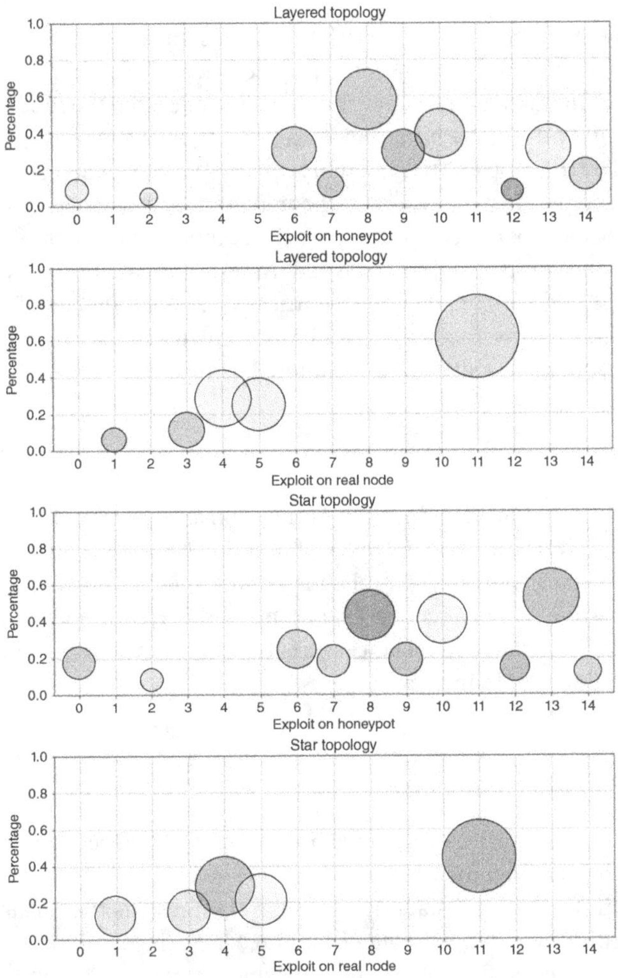

Index	Exploit
0	DCOM_buffer_overrun
1	DDoS_attack
2	DNS_zone_transfer
3	DoS_attack
4	brute_force
5	directory_harvest
6	drown_attack
7	pop3_version
8	remote_auth
9	Buffer overflow
10	remove_auth
11	SQL injection
12	url_decoder
13	user_auth
14	Windows null session

7.3 A Cognitive Model of Attackers in HackIT

7.3.1 IBL Theory

We developed a cognitive model of the attacker in the HackIT scenario using instance-based learning theory (IBLT) [20]. According to IBLT, a human makes decisions by generalizing past decision experiences that are similar to the present decision situation. Each experience (i.e., an instance) is represented as a triplet, including the contextual features of the selected target, the decision, and the outcome.

An IBL model accumulates the decision experiences in instances. During the recognition process, the model computes the similarity between the current situation and the existing instances in memory. For each possible decision, the model computes an expected utility using the *blending* – mechanism: an average across past outcomes weighted by the probability of memory retrieval, which depends on the contextual similarity to past instances and on the frequency and recency with which an instance has been experienced in the past (i.e., an *activation* memory mechanism). The decision with the highest expected utility is executed. Finally, the expected utility is updated with an experienced utility once the outcome of a decision made is known. These instances are reused for future decisions.

The blended value $V_{k,t}$ of option k at trial t is computed using:

$$V_{k,t} = \sum_{i=1}^{n} P_{i,k,t} * X_{i,k,t}, \tag{7.1}$$

where $X_{i,k,t}$ represents the outcome of an instance i for option k at trial t and $P_{i,k,t}$ represents the probability of retrieval of an instance i for option k at any trial t (the value of k is the options in each round). The probability of retrieval of an instance i is the activation ratio of the i_{th} instance corresponding to the activation of all instances (1, 2, ..., n; where n is the total instances) created within the option k at trial t. The retrieval probability is defined as:

$$P_{i,k,t} = \frac{e^{A_{i,k,t}}/\tau}{\sum_{i=1}^{n} e^{A_{i,k,t}}/\tau}. \tag{7.2}$$

Here, $\tau = \sigma * \sqrt{2}$ and τ is a free noise parameter. Noise captures the inaccuracy of remembering past experiences from memory.

At each trial t, the activation of an instance i on option k represents the linear aggregation of three cognitive elements: frequency and recency, the similarity of the instance to past experiences, and the noise that introduces stochasticity in the activation value. Based on ACT-R theory of cognition [21], the activation value represents how readily available an instance is in memory: the higher the activation, the easier and faster it would be to retrieve such an instance from memory.

The activation is computed as follows:

$$A_{i,k,t} = ln \sum_{t_i=1..t-1} (t - t_i)^{-d} + \text{MP} \sum_{k} \text{Sim}(v_k, c_k) + \sigma * ln\left(\frac{1-\gamma_{i,k,t}}{\gamma_{i,k,t}}\right) \tag{7.3}$$

The first term reflects the power law of experience and forgetting. t_i represents all previous trials in which instance i was either created or its activation was reinforced due to its recurrence. t_j is the time since the jth occurrence of instance

i and d is the decay rate of each occurrence, which is set to the default ACT-R value of 0.5. The activation of an instance can increase with the frequency of observing that outcome, as well as with the recency of observing that outcome (i.e., by small differences in $t - t_i$). This term represents the frequency and recency of events in memory. The decay parameter accounts the rate of forgetting the experienced events: the higher the decay, the faster the rate of forgetting the past events, and the reliance on recent events will increase.

The second term is a partial matching process that reflects the similarity between the current situation (c_k) and the instances that are stored in memory(v_k), scaled by a mismatch penalty (set to 2.5). Similarities between numerical slot values are computed on a linear scale of 0.0–1.0. The value close to 0.0 refers to the minimum similarity, and values toward 1.0 represent highest similarity. Symbolic values are either an exact match or maximally different.

The third term represents the Gaussian noise mechanism for capturing the variability in individual choices and $\gamma_{i,k,t}$ is a random number drawn uniformly between 0 and 1. The σ i.e., the variance in the noise term is set to the default ACT-R value of 0.50.

7.3.2 IBL Model for Attacker

7.3.2.1 IBL Process

Figure 7.7 represents the IBL decision process for the human attacker model in HackIT. The cognitive procedure of attackers is modeled by simulating two phases of the experiment: scanning and exploitation using the IBL architecture in Python, called PyIBL [22]. Exfiltration of the data file is a necessary step in the experiment settings, but it is an automatic step after exploitation, and thus it was not simulated in this model.

For each decision, instances are represented by the contextual features of the system, their decisions, and the outcome. The first decision is to pick a target to

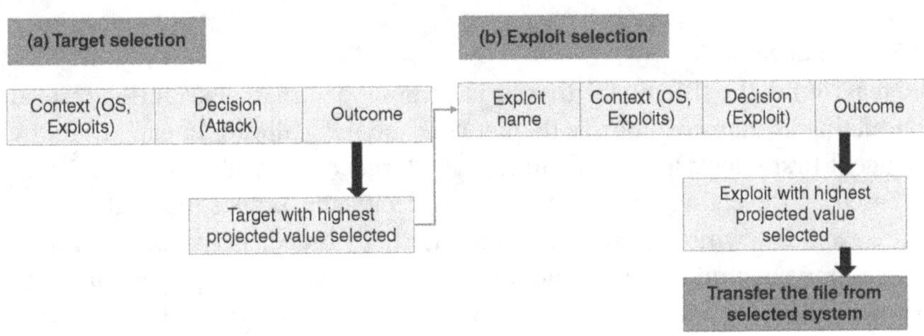

Figure 7.7 IBL process: (a) Target selection decision and (b) Exploit selection decision.

exploit. Human participants use the nmap command to collect information about different targets. Similar to humans, we simulated the scanning using the nmap command by the model agent and store the information in instances (hereafter, "nmap" instances). The nmap instance stores the context features, i.e., the operating system and a list of available exploits along with the decision and the outcome. The exploit decision is to select the exploit to launch for exploiting the selected system. The exploit instance stores the selected exploit name, operating system, and the exploit list. Both instances were given the same payoff determined by the type of the exploited system: 300 points if the decision is to exploit the real system and −100 points if the decision is to exploit a honeypot.

The similarity between the slots of the exploit list is determined by the proportion of set intersection, i.e., $(A \cap B)/|A|$, $(|A| = |B| = 4)$. For example, an instance with exploit list $DoSattack$, $DDoSattack$, $directoryharvest$, $sql\_injection$ and an instance with $exploit\_list$ $DoSattack, DDoSattack, sql\_injection,$ $directoryharvest$ have exploit list fully intersected, thus have $similarity = 1$. Slot os and $exploit\_name$ are both slots with symbolic values matched exactly by default with a binary similarity value. The weight of every slot is the same.

7.3.2.2 Pre-populated Memory

To begin the task, the model is initialized with five instances to simulate either successful or failed exploits experienced during the practice round. The nmap agent is populated with five instances with slots os and $exploit\_list$, while the exploit agent of that model is populated with five instances generated from the same five system configurations. Their values of the $exploit\_name$ slot are randomly selected from the corresponding list of exploits. Different from the payoff expectations during the practice round in the actual experiment, the payoff in pre-population stage is set as 330 for both honeypot and real nodes to induce more exploration on other systems instead of conservatively sticking to the safe choices reviewed in the practice round, which is possible since the system configurations in the practice round is a subsection of that in real round.

7.3.2.3 Real Exploitation

In the real round, the IBL model draws trials from the human distribution instead of conducting as many exploits as the network topology allows. In each trial, the nmap agent first selects a target to attack. The targets change dynamically across trials based on the actions in previous trials. Specifically, targets no longer accessible are excluded, while newly added systems are included. The select space is at the same time constrained by a random number of systems the players prefer to scan before choosing a target, sampled from the experimental data distribution.

After selecting a target system, the context is augmented with an exploit name (i.e., one option for each exploit in the available exploits list, that is, four options), and the exploit agent decides which exploit to launch. We assumed that humans base their choice of exploit not only on the exploit name itself, but also on the full context information of the target system. Therefore, the features considered by the exploit agent include the operating system, the list of exploits, and the name of the exploit.

Once the model has calculated the expected utility (blended values) of all options, the model selects the option with the highest blended value to attack. The actual experienced option is then stored in using the actual experienced outcome.

The exploration and exploitation process is repeated for N rounds in the task. N is determined by an upper bound sampled from the empirical exploit count distribution of human data and the exhaustion of the target select space. We run 1000 simulated agents acting as attackers and evaluated the model's performance against the empirical results of the two experimental conditions, layered and star, explained above. For the sake of result stability, the IBL model runs 1000 iterations for each condition, simulating 1000 participants, much larger than the number of human participants.

Next, we present the results from the model's simulation against empirical data in the layered and star topology conditions.

7.3.3 IBL Model Results

We compute the root mean square error (RMSE) to evaluate the performance of the IBL model against human performance. The proportions of human actions are compared to the proportion of model actions: scanning and exploits.

$$\text{RMSE} = \sqrt{\frac{1}{n}\sum_{i=1}^{n}(\text{Human}_i - \text{Model}_i)^2} \tag{7.4}$$

7.3.3.1 Proportion of Attacks on Honeypot

We compare the proportion of attacks on the honeypot from the IBL model and human data. We observe that the proportion of attacks on honeypots is higher in the layered topology compared to the star topology for both humans and the IBL model. The RMSE value for the average proportion of honeypot attacks is 0.042. The correlation value is 1.

Furthermore, we compare the honeypot exploitation distribution of the IBL model with the human data in Figure 7.8. The distribution plot indicates that the IBL model attacks more honeypots compared to human participants in the layered topology. The correlation values of the layered topology and the star topology for the honeypot attack distribution are 0.65 and 0.74, respectively.

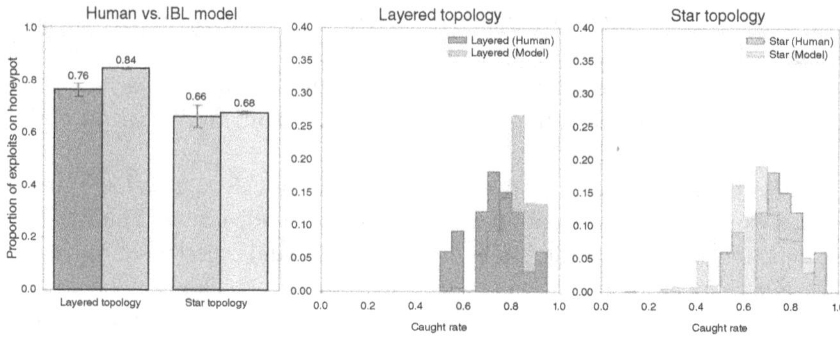

Figure 7.8 Honeypot exploit percentage.

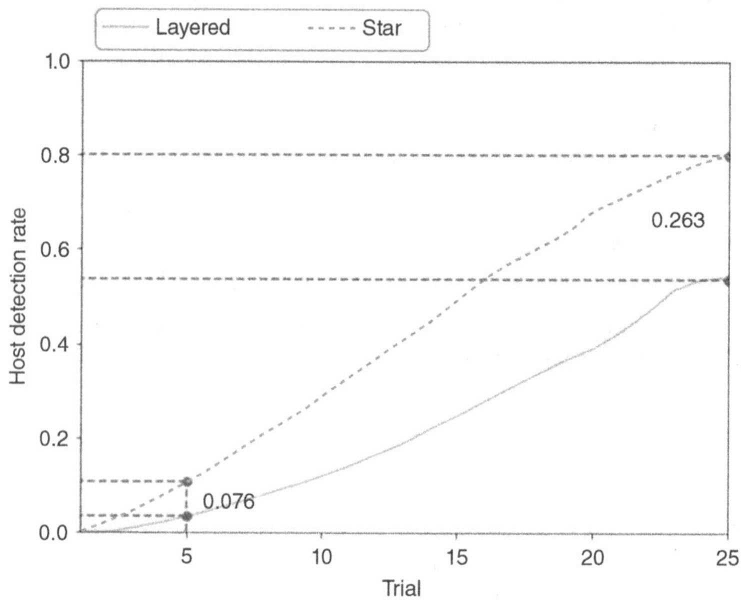

Figure 7.9 Host detection rate per trial for IBL model (layered vs. star topology).

7.3.3.2 Host Detection Rate

Similar to human data, we calculated the HDR in each condition for model, which means the percentage of real hosts detected based on the time spent in the task. The timestamp is derived from the time passed since the start of the round, i.e., the first command executed in the main round. Figure 7.9 presents the trial-wise HDR of model runs, respectively. The HDR of IBL model in layered and star topology aligns with our assumption, the layered topology performs better in delaying the progress of attackers. The advantage of layered topology in human data is not as obvious compared to time-wise HDR. One possible explanation is that the improvement of proficiency for human attackers is reflected also on the time it takes for them to launch an exploitation, while the concept of time is missing for the IBL model.

7.4 Discussion

Consistent with our hypothesis, the layered topology, similar to the reconnaissance deceptive network topology proposed by Stephan Achleitner et al. [16] was more effective in slowing down the attackers and downgrading their attack performance. Participants in the layered topology condition detected real hosts at a lower speed and got a negative average score, which means the defenders were at advantage.

The fictitious first layer in the layered topology seems to be the major factor contributing to the effectiveness gap between the two conditions. Confronted with a honeypot in their first attack, approximately 45% attackers decided not to attack further, logged out directly, and gave up the entire subnet with the acknowledgment that the second entrance to that same host is not allowed. To verify this deduction, we conducted IBL model simulation to see the impact of the first layer honeypot proportion on the caught rate. With a fixed honeypot proportion consistent with the experimental setting (75%), we vary the percentage of honeypot on the first layer and measure the performance of "simulated attackers." The caught rate in Figure 7.10 is calculated by averaging the honeypot attack proportion of 1000 simulated attackers. As shown in the figure, the average catching rate is positively correlated with the first layer honeypot proportion.

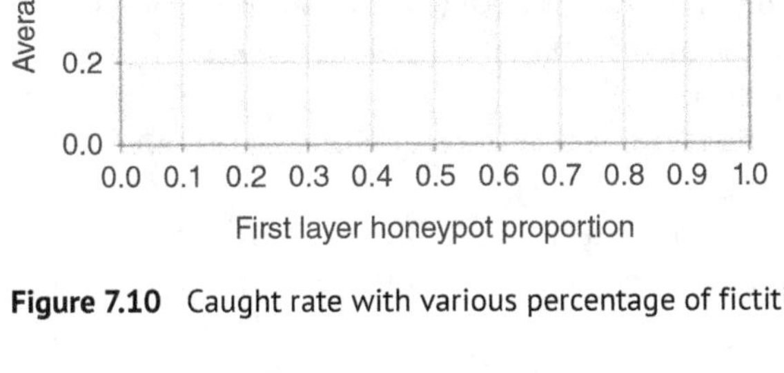

Figure 7.10 Caught rate with various percentage of fictitious node on first layer.

Apart from the findings above, we also observed some valuable characteristics of attackers' behavior. Given the randomness of the honeypot allocation of the second layer of the layered network and the star network, there is no optimal sequence of targets to follow. However, we see that participants were inclined to launch attacks in index order. Approximately 25% of the participants have a consecutive attack sequence length of 5. Approximately 90% of them attack two adjacent hosts in a row. This laziness might be exploitable with several consecutive honeypots in a network. Before being driven away by continuous failure, the attackers will leave considerable traces that can be used by the defenders.

Along with the valuable insights from the model, there are several limitations of the IBL model developed for this task. First, currently, the model relies on human data to decide how many systems to scan before deciding the attack node. In the future, we will improve the performance of this model by implementing the stopping point in the exploration process [23]. Next, human participants were provided continuous time and had a time limit to perform the task. For the IBL model, we discretized the time into trial, which might not be an accurate representation of the task environment. We plan to address this limitation by considering the reaction time in the IBL model or discretizing the time for human participants as well. We will address these limitations in the future. Moreover, this work can be extended to different network topologies available in other datasets, such as the recent work in [24].

References

1 Mohammed H. Almeshekah and Eugene H. Spafford. Planning and integrating deception into computer security defenses. In *Proceedings of the 2014 Workshop on New Security Paradigms Workshop*, pp. 127–138. ACM, 2014.

2 Zhuo Lu, Cliff Wang, and Shangqing Zhao. Cyber deception for computer and network security: Survey and challenges. *arXiv preprint arXiv:2007.14497*, 2020.

3 Fred Cohen. The use of deception techniques: Honeypots and decoys. *Handbook of Information Security*, 3(1): 646–655, 2006.

4 Neil C. Rowe and E. John Custy. Deception in cyber attacks. In *Cyber Warfare and Cyber Terrorism*, pp. 91–96. IGI Global, 2007.

5 Palvi Aggarwal, Cleotilde Gonzalez, and Varun Dutt. Cyber-security: Role of deception in cyber-attack detection. In *Advances in Human Factors in Cybersecurity*, pp. 85–96. Springer, 2016.

6 Mohammed H. Almeshekah and Eugene H. Spafford. Cyber security deception. In *Cyber Deception*, pp. 25–52. Springer-Verlag, 2016.

7 Kimberly J. Ferguson-Walter, Dana S. LaFon, and T. B. Shade. Friend or faux: Deception for cyber defense. *Journal of Information Warfare*, 16(2): 28–42, 2017.

8 Palvi Aggarwal, Omkar Thakoor, Shahin Jabbari, Edward A. Cranford, Christian Lebiere, Milind Tambe, and Cleotilde Gonzalez. Designing effective masking strategies for cyberdefense through human experimentation and cognitive models. *Computers & Security*, 117: 102671, 2022.

9 Timothy Shimeall and Jonathan Spring. *Introduction to Information Security: A Strategic-based Approach*. Newnes, 2013.

10 Quang Duy La, Tony Q.S. Quek, Jemin Lee, Shi Jin, and Hongbo Zhu. Deceptive attack and defense game in honeypot-enabled networks for the internet of things. *IEEE Internet of Things Journal*, 3(6): 1025–1035, 2016.

11 M. Stellar and G. Kohnken. Criteria-based content analysis. In *Psychological Methods for Criminal Investigation and Evidence*, pp. 217–245. Springer Publishing Company, 1989.

12 Aldert Vrij. Detecting lies and deceit: The psychology of lying and the implications for professional practice, 2007.

13 Ahmed H. Anwar, Charles A. Kamhoua, Nandi Leslie, and Christopher D. Kiekintveld. Honeypot allocation games over attack graphs for cyber deception. In *Game Theory and Machine Learning for Cyber Security*, pp. 62–76, 2021.

14 Kimberly J. Ferguson-Walter, Maxine M. Major, Chelsea K. Johnson, and Daniel H. Muhleman. Examining the efficacy of decoy-based and psychological cyber deception. In *30th USENIX Security Symposium (USENIX Security 21)*, pp. 1127–1144, 2021.

15 Maxine Major, Brian Souza, Joseph DiVita, and Kimberly Ferguson-Walter. Informing autonomous deception systems with cyber expert performance data. *arXiv preprint arXiv:2109.00066*, 2021.

16 Stefan Achleitner, Thomas F. La Porta, Patrick McDaniel, Shridatt Sugrim, Srikanth V. Krishnamurthy, and Ritu Chadha. Deceiving network reconnaissance using SDN-based virtual topologies. *IEEE Transactions on Network and Service Management*, 14(4): 1098–1112, 2017.

17 Palvi Aggarwal, Aksh Gautam, Vaibhav Agarwal, Cleotilde Gonzalez, and Varun Dutt. Hackit: A human-in-the-loop simulation tool for realistic cyber deception experiments. In *International Conference on Applied Human Factors and Ergonomics*, pp. 109–121. Springer, 2019.

18 Palvi Aggarwal, Cleotilde Gonzalez, and Varun Dutt. Hackit: A real-time simulation tool for studying real-world cyberattacks in the laboratory. In *Handbook of Computer Networks and Cyber Security*, pp. 949–959. Springer, 2020.

19 Tony Bradley. 65% of port vulnerabilities target just three ports, Jun 2021.

20 Cleotilde Gonzalez, Javier F. Lerch, and Christian Lebiere. Instance-based learning in dynamic decision making. *Cognitive Science*, 27(4): 591–635, 2003.

21 John R. Anderson, Daniel Bothell, Michael D. Byrne, Scott Douglass, Christian Lebiere, and Yulin Qin. An integrated theory of the mind. *Psychological Review*, 111(4): 1036, 2004.

22 Cleotilde Gonzalez and Don Morrison. *PyIBL: A Python Implementation of Instance-based Learning Theory.* Dynamic Decision Making Laboratory, Carnegie Mellon University. Version 4.1. Accessed Jan. 2026. https://www.cmu.edu/dietrich/sds/ddmlab/downloads.html

23 Cleotilde Gonzalez and Palvi Aggarwal. Sequential decisions from sampling: Inductive generation of stopping decisions using instance-based learning theory. In *Sampling in Judgment and Decision Making*, pp. 289–310. Cambridge University Press, 2021.

24 Quanyan Zhu. Guarding against malicious biased threats (GAMBiT) experiment 1, 2025.

Part 2

Resilient Machine Learning

8

Computational Game Theory for Security

Yevgeniy Vorobeychik

Department of Computer Science and Engineering, Washington University in Saint Louis, St. Louis, MO, USA

8.1 Introduction

Security, or protection from harm, is a central social good, crucial for thriving organizations and communities. In security, harm comes not spontaneously, but as a result of deliberate vicious acts by a malicious party or parties. For example, home security protects residents against unwanted intrusions, security in an airport entails protection against threats of violence by organized terror groups, while cybersecurity in an organization means protection against sabotage by parties who may aim to reduce the organization's competitiveness or harm its reputation. The interaction between the *defender*, who strives to protect a collection of assets, and an *attacker*, who aims to achieve some malicious goal that likely leads to direct or indirect harm to these assets, is thus endemic in security encounters. Game theory, which is a mathematical framework for modeling interactions among strategic (self-interested) agents whose actions impact one another, has emerged as an important framework for modeling such defender–attacker interactions in security.

An important conceptual step in game-theoretic modeling for security is to frame the interaction between the defender and attacker as sequential, with the defender first deploying ("committing" to) its defense strategy, and the attacker then responding to deployed defense in deciding on the attack strategy. A formal representation for this structure of interaction is as a Stackelberg game, in which a leader (in our case, the defender) chooses a strategy first, and the follower (the attacker) chooses thereafter, upon observing the leader's strategy. While alternative modeling frameworks abound, the Stackelberg model has had considerable practical impact [1–3] and will therefore be the primary focus of this chapter.

We begin this chapter by describing a formal model first of Stackelberg games (Section 8.2) and then their particular variations common in security settings, *Stackelberg security games* (Section 8.3), along with solution techniques for these. Subsequently, we consider a particular class of security problems in which the defender aims to *interdict* a path taken by an attacker through a network (Section 8.4). We broaden this first to consider attackers as decision makers in a dynamic setting and, finally, study security interactions in dynamic environments in which the defender commits to a *policy*, formalized as *stochastic Stackelberg games*, with adversarial patrolling problem providing a concrete application of this modeling framework (Section 8.5).

8.2 Stackelberg Games

Let us start with Stackelberg games in general. Consider two players, a leader (L) and a follower (F). Both L and F have sets of actions, A_L and A_F, respectively, along with their respective utility functions $u_L(a_L, a_F)$ and $u_F(a_L, a_F)$. Throughout, we assume that $A_L \cup A_F$ is finite. Let σ_L be a probability distribution over A_L, with $\sigma_L(a) \geq 0$ the associated probability of $a \in A_L$. Thus, $\sum_{a\in A_L} \sigma_L(a) = 1$. It is common to refer to σ_L as the leader's *mixed strategy*. We can extend utility functions to be functions of σ_L by taking the expectations with respect to this distribution, i.e.,

$$u_L(\sigma_L, a_F) = \sum_{a\in A_L} \sigma_L(a)u_L(a, a_F) \quad \text{and} \quad u_F(\sigma_L, a_F) = \sum_{a\in A_L} \sigma_L(a)u_F(a, a_F).$$

The follower is presumed to observe σ_L, but, crucially, *not the actual realization of random draws a from it*, and then respond by choosing a strategy $b \in A_F$. In particular, we assume that the follower chooses a strategy that is a *best response* $\phi(\sigma_L)$ to σ_L, that is,

$$\phi(\sigma_L) \in \arg\max_{b\in A_F} u_F(\sigma_L, b). \tag{8.1}$$

Our notation here already makes explicit that a best response strategy of the follower explicitly depends on the observed leader strategy σ_L; indeed, this dependence is what makes this game Stackelberg in nature, and the full strategy space of the follower in this game is the space of all functions that map σ_L to follower actions b.

At this point, one may observe that our formalization of the best response in Eq. (8.1), we have effectively assumed that the follower need not consider randomized strategies. Indeed, it is not difficult to show that in the game model we consider here, there always exists a deterministic best response. Intuitively, if a randomized strategy puts nonzero weight on multiple follower actions, we can do no worse than shifting all of this weight to the action that yields the highest follower utility.

A common solution concept for Stackelberg games is a *Stackelberg equilibrium (SE)*, in which the follower chooses a best response strategy $\phi(\sigma_L)$, while the leader chooses σ_L to maximize its strategy *given the follower's best response* ϕ. Formally, (σ_L^*, ϕ) is an SE if ϕ is the follower's best response in the sense of Eq. (8.1), and $\sigma_L^* \in \arg\max_{\sigma \in \Delta_L} u_L(\sigma, \phi(\sigma))$, where Δ_L is the simplex (i.e., the set of all probability distributions) over A_L.

A limitation of an SE is that the follower may have many ways to break ties, and the particular choices could be somewhat arbitrary. It is common, therefore, to make use of a refinement, referred to as the *Strong Stackelberg equilibrium (SSE)*, in which the follower breaks ties in the leader's favor (commonly justified using the argument that the leader can induce this to be a strict best response for the follower by simply slightly changing the strategy σ_L). Specifically, (σ_L^*, ϕ) form an SSE if

$$\sigma_L^* \in \arg\max_{\sigma \in \Delta_L; \phi(\sigma) \in \arg\max_{b \in A_F} u_F(\sigma, b)} u_L(\sigma, \phi(\sigma)). \tag{8.2}$$

It turns out that computing SSE amounts to solving a collection of linear programs (LPs). The idea is this. Let us fix a follower strategy $b \in A_F$ and ask the following question: how can the leader maximize utility while at the same time incentivizing the follower to choose b (i.e., while b is constrained to be the follower's best response)? The solution to this problem can be formulated as the following LP:

$$\max_{\sigma \geq 0} \sum_{a \in A_L} \sigma(a) u_L(a, b) \tag{8.3a}$$

$$\text{subject to:} \tag{8.3b}$$

$$\sum_{a \in A_L} \sigma(a) = 1 \tag{8.3c}$$

$$\sum_{a \in A_L} \sigma(a) u_L(a, b) \geq \sum_{a \in A_L} \sigma(a) u_L(a, b') \quad \forall b' \in A_F \backslash b. \tag{8.3d}$$

Of course, there may be no solution to the LP (8.3) for particular choices of b, but that simply means that it is not possible for the leader to have b be the follower's best response (e.g., if b is dominated by other choices the follower has). However, suppose we solve it for every possible strategy $b \in A_F$, with the associated solution σ^b and leader utility $u_L(\sigma^b, b)$. Whenever LP (8.3) is infeasible, define σ^b arbitrarily and $u_L(\sigma^b, b) = -\infty$. Then $\sigma^* = \sigma^{b^*}$, where $b^* \in \arg\max_b u_L(\sigma^b, b)$. In other words, we simply choose the solution to the LP corresponding to the opponent strategy b for which the leader's solution yields the highest leader utility.

The Stackelberg game model above presumes that the leader has complete information about the follower, and vice versa. An important generalization is to consider a leader's uncertainty about the follower's utility function, u_F, which we refer to as a *Bayesian Stackelberg game*. Specifically, suppose that there is a finite set of follower *types*, Θ. Each type $\theta \in \Theta$ is a parameter of the follower's utility function, which now takes the form $u_F(a_L, a_F; \theta)$ (with the extension to $u_F(\sigma_L, a_F; \theta)$ exactly as above). Let p_θ be the probability that the follower is of type θ; we suppose that although the leader does not know the actual type, the distribution itself is common knowledge. Let $\phi(\sigma; \theta)$ be the follower's *best response* strategy, which is now parametrized by θ and is characterized by $\phi(\sigma; \theta) \in \arg\max_{b \in A_F} u_F(\sigma, b; \theta)$. The leader then maximizes its expected utility, $\sum_{\theta \in \Theta} p_\theta u_L(\sigma, \phi(\sigma, \theta))$, over randomized strategies σ. Now, we can again seek a SSE solution to this problem. However, the approach above, where we solve multiple LPs, one for each possible follower action, no longer works: since each follower type can take any of the actions, we must solve $|\Theta|^{|A_F|}$ LPs in the worst case!

Instead, we can compute an SSE of a Bayesian Stackelberg game using the following mixed-integer linear program (MILP):

$$\max_{\sigma \geq 0} \sum_{\theta \in \Theta} p_\theta u_\theta \tag{8.4a}$$

$$\text{subject to:} \tag{8.4b}$$

$$\sum_{a \in A_L} \sigma(a) = 1 \tag{8.4c}$$

$$\sum_{b \in A_F} x(b, \theta) = 1 \quad \forall \theta \in \Theta \tag{8.4d}$$

$$u_\theta - \sum_{a \in A_L} \sigma(a) u_L(a, b) \leq (1 - x(b, \theta))Z \quad \forall b \in A_F, \theta \in \Theta \tag{8.4e}$$

$$0 \leq v_\theta - \sum_{a \in A_L} \sigma(a) u_F(a, b) \leq (1 - x(b, \theta))Z \quad \forall b \in A_F, \theta \in \Theta. \tag{8.4f}$$

In this MILP, u_θ denotes the expected utility of the leader when the follower's type is θ, while v_θ denotes the corresponding expected utility for the follower. Since the leader does not actually know the follower's type, the objective also takes the expectation with respect to the probability distribution over the follower types. Turning to constraints, their main role is to compute the best response strategy $\phi(\sigma; \theta)$ of the follower. We encode it using a binary vector $x(b, \theta)$ such that $x(b, \theta) = 1$ whenever b is the follower's *actual* best response. Note that it depends on σ implicitly insofar as the strategy σ of the leader is itself being computed by the MILP. Constraints (8.4f) actually do the work of computing the follower's best response for each type θ, while Constraints (8.4e) use the best response strategies

x of the follower to compute the leader's associated expected utility. In both of the sets of constraints above, Z is a large constant that we take conceptually to be $Z = \infty$.

8.3 Stackelberg Security Games

The Stackelberg game model can be applied to security settings directly as follows. Let the leader be the defender, with A_L the set of defender strategies, and the follower the attacker, with A_F the set of possible attacks. The machinery we developed goes through directly. As it turns out, however, there is more to say here.

Let us make the sets of strategies for the defender and attacker more concrete. In particular, let T be the set of targets that need to be defended from a possible attack. Suppose that the defender can defend – or *cover* – at most K targets at a time; that is, the defender has K protection resources (e.g., security guards). Then a defender strategy is a subset $C \subset T$ such that $|C| \leq K$, and the strategy set A_L is the set of all possible such subsets of targets. Similarly, if the attacker has L resources to attack the targets in T, the set of attack strategies A_F is the set of all subsets of T of size at most L. Even if we suppose that both players saturate their resource use, both A_L and A_F grow exponentially in the number of targets. Consequently, the approaches developed above, which require us to enumerate the entire A_L and A_F, will not scale. This means that we must exploit problem structure to develop effective approaches to practical security game models.

Let us add some structure to the utility functions. Let U_t^c be the utility the defender receives when a target t is attacked while it is covered by the defender, and V_t^c the associated utility of the attacker. Similarly, define U_t^u and V_t^u to be the utilities of the defender and attacker, respectively, when target t is attacked while it is not covered by the defender. Next, suppose that the attacker can only attack a single target; that is, $L = 1$, and the attacker strategy set is just the set of targets T. Furthermore, suppose that instead of a hard constraint K on the number of defense resources, the defender incurs a cost c for each time it uses a resource to cover a target. Let us also represent the defender's choice as a coverage vector $d \in \{0, 1\}^n$, where $n = |T|$ is the number of targets, and let σ be the probability distribution over d (i.e., the defender's mixed strategy). The defender's expected utility is then

$$u_D(\sigma, t) = \sum_d \sigma(d) \left((d_t U_t^c + (1 - d_t) U_t^u) - c \sum_t d_t \right).$$

If we define $q_t \in [0, 1]$ as the probability of covering target t induced by the mixed strategy σ, we can rewrite the utility as

$$u_D(q, t) = q_t U_t^c + (1 - q_t) U_t^u - c \sum_t q_t.$$

Consequently, we no longer need to explicitly reason about the mixed strategy over all possible coverage vectors, but just over target-specific coverage probabilities q_t, aggregated into a vector q. This means that despite the combinatorial underlying strategy space of the defender, we can actually compute a SSE of the Stackelberg security game of this form in polynomial time using multiple LPs just as above, where each LP corresponding to a particular target t of an attack has the following form:

$$\max_{q} \quad q_t U_t^c + (1 - q_t) U_t^u - c \sum_t q_t \tag{8.5a}$$

$$\text{subject to:} \tag{8.5b}$$

$$0 \leq q_t \leq 1 \quad \forall t \in T \tag{8.5c}$$

$$q_t V_t^c + (1 - q_t) V_t^u \geq q_{t'} V_{t'}^c + (1 - q_{t'}) V_t^u \quad \forall t' \in T \setminus t. \tag{8.5d}$$

The key idea above is that we replace a hard constraint on the defender's resource use with a soft cost function that in principle allows unlimited resources. This approach can be adapted in a straightforward way to consider a constraint that the number of resources used *in expectation* is bounded by K instead of the soft cost function. What does not work, however, is a hard constraint that *in every realization* of coverage vectors we can use at most K resources. In fact, imposing such a constraint effectively prevents us from using this compact representation of the problem, and we now must again enumerate all coverage vectors d.

But what if we do wish to impose a hard constraint that we can use at most K resources? It is often the case that there is little flexibility on this account: for example, we cannot hire new security staff if it happens that our utilization exceeds the current staff. The problem of inducing the attacker to choose a particular target t to attack then becomes

$$\max_{\sigma \geq 0} \quad \sum_d \sigma(d) u_D(d, t) \tag{8.6a}$$

$$\text{subject to:} \tag{8.6b}$$

$$\sum_d \sigma(d) = 1 \tag{8.6c}$$

$$\sum_d \sigma(d) \Delta V(d, t, t') \geq 0 \quad \forall t' \in T, \tag{8.6d}$$

where $\Delta V(d, t, t') = d_t V_t^c + (1 - d_t) V_t^u - d_{t'} V_{t'}^c - (1 - d_{t'}) V_{t'}^u$ and the consideration set of vectors d is restricted to those that involve the use of K resources (since we always wish to saturate resource use in this context, there is no need to include those using fewer than K resources). This set is exponential in the number of targets $|T|$. Nevertheless, we can make use of the problem structure here to avoid explicitly enumerating all variables $\sigma(d)$. Specifically, since the number of constraints is linear in the number of targets, we actually know that the support of the solution σ (i.e., the set of configurations d with $\sigma(d) > 0$) is also going to be linear in $|T|$ [4]; the trick is just to find it. To do this, we can use a technique called *column generation*, in which we begin with an arbitrary small subset of l resource assignments $\hat{D} = \{d_1, \ldots, d_l\}$ and solve the LP (8.6) considering only these. Suppose $\hat{\sigma}(\hat{D})$ is the resulting optimal solution. We can use this solution to compute the *reduced cost* of the standard form analog of this LP [4]. We now construct this standard form analog and derive the expression for reduced cost. First, we add slack variables $\lambda_{t'}$ to each of the inequality constraints to turn these into equality constraints, obtaining

$$\sum_{d} \sigma(d)\Delta V(d, t, t') - \lambda_{t'} = 0 \quad \forall\, t' \in T.$$

Let $u(t)$ be a vector associated with the security resource configurations in $\hat{D}$, and let $\Delta V(t, t')$ be a vector of $\Delta V(d, t, t')$ for all $d \in \hat{D}$. Turning each constraint into matrix-vector notation, we obtain

$$1^T\sigma = 1$$

for the first constraint, where 1^T is a row vector of 1s, and

$$\Delta V(t, t')^T \sigma - \lambda_{t'} = 0$$

for the rest. Let λ be a vector of all slack variables $\lambda_{t'}$. Define a matrix A as follows. Let the first row be $a_1 = [1^T, 0]$, where the number of 1s is the number of variables, and let each subsequent row be $a_{t'} = [\Delta V(t, t'), -1]$. Finally, define $b = [1, 0^T]^T$, where 0^T is a vector of $|T|$ 0s. The problem can then be rewritten as

$$\min_{\sigma, \lambda \geq 0} \quad -u(t)^T\sigma \tag{8.7a}$$

$$\text{subject to:} \tag{8.7b}$$

$$A[\sigma, \lambda]^T = b. \tag{8.7c}$$

From this standard form, we can then derive the expression for reduced cost associated with an arbitrary resource assignment d' that is not in $\hat{D}$ as follows. First, an optimal solution to the LP (8.7) over variables in $\hat{D}$ will compute the set of variables d for which $\sigma(d) > 0$. Let B be the submatrix of A with the associated columns, and let $u_B(t)$ be the associated components of $u(t)$. Let $[\alpha, \beta] = u_B(t)^T B$, where α is a scalar and β is a vector with one element for each target t'.

$$\bar{c}_{d'} = -d'_t U^c_t - (1 - d'_t)U^u_t - \alpha - \sum_{t'} \beta_{t'}(d'_t V^c_t + (1 - d'_t)V^u_t - d'_{t'} V^c_{t'} - (1 - d'_{t'})V^u_{t'}).$$

Let $\bar{\beta} = \sum_{t'} \beta_{t'}$. Then this expression can be slightly simplified to

$$\bar{c}_{d'} = -d'_t(U^c_t + \bar{\beta}V^c_t) - (1 - d'_t)(U^u_t + \bar{\beta}V^u_t) - \alpha + \sum_{t'} \beta_{t'}(d'_{t'} V^c_{t'} + (1 - d'_{t'})V^u_{t'}).$$

Our goal is now to minimize the reduced cost, which is equivalent to solving the following integer linear program (ILP):

$$\min_{d'} \quad d'_t(U^u_t - U^c_t + \bar{\beta}(V^u_t - V^c_t)) - \sum_{t'} d'_{t'}\beta_{t'}(V^u_{t'} - V^c_{t'}) \tag{8.8}$$

$$\text{subject to:} \tag{8.9}$$

$$\sum_t d'_t = K \tag{8.10}$$

$$d'_t \in \{0, 1\} \quad \forall t \in T. \tag{8.11}$$

Moreover, if for an optimal solution d' of this optimization problem we find that $\bar{c}_{d'} \geq 0$, we know that the solution we obtained in the last iteration is in fact optimal, and we can stop the column generation process. The power of this approach is that while ILPs are NP-hard to solve in general, in practice we can often solve them effectively and quickly using state-of-the-art ILP solvers.

8.4 Security Games on Networks

So far, we have studied both the rather general Stackelberg game model, and its specialization to security games with independent targets. One important class of problems in security entails preventing, or *interdicting*, the flow of malicious activity on networks. In its classical form, this problem is known as *network interdiction* [5, 6]. Many variations of this problem have been explored; here, I describe one of the first, *deterministic network flow interdiction* [7], which well illustrates the main idea.

Consider a network $G = (V, E)$, where V is the set of nodes and E the set of (directed) edges, with a particular edge denoted by $(i, j) \in E$. Additionally, we associate each edge (i, j) with a capacity u_{ij}. Suppose that a malicious actor aims to solve the *network flow* problem over this network, maximizing the total amount of flow (of goods, malicious activity, etc.) between a source node $s \in V$ and a target node $t \in V$. Assume for the moment that both s and t are known. The problem of maximizing total flow from s to t can be represented as the following LP [4, 7]:

$$\max_{x} \quad x_{ts} \tag{8.12a}$$

$$\text{subject to:} \tag{8.12b}$$

$$\sum_j x_{sj} - \sum_j x_{js} - x_{ts} = 0 \tag{8.12c}$$

$$\sum_j x_{ij} - \sum_j x_{ji} = 0 \quad \forall i \in V \setminus \{s, t\} \tag{8.12d}$$

$$\sum_j x_{tj} - \sum_j x_{jt} + x_{ts} = 0 \tag{8.12e}$$

$$0 \leq x_{ij} \leq u_{ij} \quad \forall (i, j) \in E \tag{8.12f}$$

$$x_{ts} \geq 0, \tag{8.12g}$$

where x_{ij} represents flows along edges $(i, j) \in E$ and x_{ts} is an artificial edge added to the network, going from t to s.

The network interdiction problem involves removing a subset of edges S from E, subject to a budget constraint, so as to minimize the maximum network flow as computed by the above LP with edges restricted to $E \setminus S$. Suppose that removing an edge (i, j) incurs a cost c_{ij}, and let C be the total budget on cutting edges. We can encode this network interdiction problem as follows:

$$\min_{y} \max_{x} \quad x_{ts} \tag{8.13a}$$

$$\text{subject to:} \tag{8.13b}$$

$$\sum_j x_{sj} - \sum_j x_{js} - x_{ts} = 0 \tag{8.13c}$$

$$\sum_j x_{ij} - \sum_j x_{ji} = 0 \quad \forall i \in V \setminus \{s, t\} \tag{8.13d}$$

$$\sum_j x_{tj} - \sum_j x_{jt} + x_{ts} = 0 \tag{8.13e}$$

$$0 \leq x_{ij} \leq u_{ij}(1 - y_{ij}) \quad \forall (i, j) \in E \tag{8.13f}$$

$$\sum_{ij} c_{ij} y_{ij} \leq C \tag{8.13g}$$

$$x_{ts} \geq 0 \tag{8.13h}$$

$$y_{ij} \in \{0, 1\} \quad \forall (i, j) \in E, \tag{8.13i}$$

where y_{ij} represents the choice of edges that are cut. Finally, we can note that the inner maximum flow problem admits a dual LP, and after taking the dual and linearizing the objective, we obtain the following integer LP for network interdiction:

$$\min_{y,\alpha,\beta} \sum_{ij} u_{ij}\beta_{ij} \tag{8.14a}$$

$$\text{subject to:} \tag{8.14b}$$

$$\alpha_i - \alpha_j + \beta_{ij} + y_{ij} \quad \forall (i,j) \in E \tag{8.14c}$$

$$\alpha_t - \alpha_s \geq 1 \tag{8.14d}$$

$$\sum_{ij} c_{ij} y_{ij} \leq C \tag{8.14e}$$

$$y_{ij}, \alpha_i, \beta_{ij} \in \{0,1\} \quad \forall i \in V, (i,j) \in E. \tag{8.14f}$$

The problem of network interdiction has received a great deal of attention over the years, with many variations of the setting above explored, including problems that are not zero-sum (that is, when the interdictor's goals are not necessarily in opposition to the adversary) [8], uncertainty (e.g., about the s, t source and destination nodes) [5, 9], etc. In the end, the general problem structure tends to closely resemble the basic network flow interdiction problem above.

One substantive variation of network interdiction is *plan interdiction*, in which the goal of the defender is to prevent the attacker from achieving its goals, which the latter attempts to accomplish by solving a dynamic decision problem. A number of variations of this problem have been explored [10–13]; here, we describe a very general setting – Markov decision process (MDP) initial state interdiction problem (MDPSI) – which admits a relatively simple solution approach.

Formally, the MDPSI is defined by (1) an MDP $\mathcal{M} = \{X, A, r(x,a), \gamma\}$, where $X, A, r(x,a)$, and γ are the state space, action space, reward function, and the discount factor of an infinite-horizon discounted MDP which the attacker is solving, respectively, and (2) interdiction costs $\rho(x_0', x_0) = \sum_i \rho_i |x_{i0}' - x_{i0}|$ of modifying an initial state x_0 into x_0', where ρ_i is the cost of modifying variable i. Note that this cost can also capture inability to modify specific state variables (the corresponding $\rho_i = \infty$). We assume that the game is zero-sum (modulo interdiction costs), so that the defender aims to minimize the sum of discounted attacker rewards. Define $V(x_0, \pi)$ as the attacker's value function for a policy π starting at state x_0 in MDP $\mathcal{M}$. Let Π be the set of deterministic stationary policies of the MDP. The defender then solves

$$\min_{x_0' \in X} V(x_0') + \rho(x_0', x_0), \tag{8.15}$$

where $V(x)$ is the optimal value function of the MDP. The key observation is that the optimal policy is *independent* of the interdiction decision x_0', since the optimal policy of an MDP is independent of starting state. Consequently, we can decompose this problem into two parts: first, we compute or approximate the value function $V(x)$, and second, we fix $V(x)$ and solve the optimization problem (8.15). The former can be done using standard reinforcement learning techniques, while the latter can subsequently be done using, for example, gradient-based methods (if the value function is differentiable in input state x).

8.5 Stochastic Stackelberg Games and Adversarial Patrolling

Stackelberg game models we had discussed thus far assume that the attacker knows the probability that each target is covered by the defender, but is oblivious to the actual sequence of defender moves. For example, the defender may in fact visit targets according to some fixed (but randomly generated) patrolling schedule, but the attacker is presumed to be unable to observe the defender's location at any point during the patrol. In many realistic settings, such as the US Coast Guard [14], it is likely that the attacker can in fact observe the patrol while it is in progress (e.g., the coast guard ships can be quite overt). Thus, a more plausible model in such a setting would allow the attacker to observe both the randomized policy of the defender (i.e., probability distribution over moves) and current defender location. We can model this setting as an *adversarial patrolling game*, or APG. APGs, in turn, are a special case of *discounted stochastic Stackelberg games (DSSGs)*. We begin by discussing DSSGs generally and then describe the APG model.

8.5.1 Stochastic Discounted Stackelberg Games

Two-player infinite-horizon DSSGs involve one player who is a "leader" and the other who is a "follower," just as in general Stackelberg games. The leader commits to a *policy* that becomes known to the follower who plays a best-response policy. These games have a finite state space S, finite action spaces A_L for the leader and A_F for the follower, payoff functions $R_L(s, a_l, a_f)$ and $R_F(s, a_l, a_f)$ for leader and follower, respectively, and a transition function $T_{ss'}^{a_l a_f}$, where $s, s' \in S$, $a_l \in A_L$, and $a_f \in A_F$. The discount factors are $\gamma_L, \gamma_F < 1$ for the leader and follower, respectively. Finally, $\beta(s)$ is the probability that the initial state is s.

The history of play at time t is $h_t = \{s_1 a_{l,1} a_{f,1} \cdots s_{t-1} a_{l,t-1} a_{f,t-1} s_t\}$, where t denotes time. Let Π and Φ be the set of nonstationary and non-Markov policies (i.e., mappings from histories to distributions over actions) for the leader and follower, respectively. Let U_L and U_F denote the utility functions for leader and follower, respectively. For arbitrary policies $\pi \in \Pi$ and $\phi \in \Phi$,

$$U_L(s, \pi, \phi) = \mathbb{E}\Big[\sum_{t=1}^{\infty} \gamma_L^{t-1} R_L(s_t, \pi(h_t), \phi(h_t)) | s_1 = s\Big],$$

where the expectation is over the stochastic evolution of the states, and where (abusing notation)

$$R_L(s_t, \pi(h_t), \phi(h_t)) = \sum_{a_l \in A_L} \sum_{a_f \in A_F} \pi(a_l|h_t)\phi(a_f|h_t)R_L(s_t, a_l, a_f),$$

with $\pi(a_l|h_t)$ the probability of leader-action a_l in history h_t under policy π, and $\phi(a_f|h_t)$ the probability of follower-action a_f in history h_t under policy ϕ. The utility of the follower, $U_F(s, \pi, \phi)$, is defined analogously.

For any leader policy $\pi \in \Pi$, the follower plays the best-response policy defined as

$$\phi_\pi^{BR} \in \arg\max_{\phi \in \Phi} \sum_s \beta(s)U_F(s, \pi, \phi).$$

The leader's optimal policy is then

$$\pi^* \in \arg\max_{\pi \in \Pi} \sum_s \beta(s)U_L(s, \pi, \phi_\pi^{BR}).$$

Together $(\pi^*, \phi_{\pi^*}^{BR})$ constitute a SE. If, additionally, the follower breaks ties in the leader's favor, these are a SSE.

A natural question arises: is the leader's optimal policy in a DSSG guaranteed to be Markov stationary (that is, only depend on current state)? Turns out, it is not, as the following example illustrates. Suppose that the DSSG has three states, i.e., $S = \{1, 2, 3\}$, and the leader and the follower have two actions each, $A_L = \{U, D\}$ for the leader and $A_F = \{L, R\}$ for the follower. Let the initial state be $s = 1$ and suppose that the following transitions happen deterministically and independently of either player's decisions: $T_{12} = 1, T_{23} = 1, T_{33} = 1$, that is, the process starts at state 1, then moves to state 2, and then, finally, to state 3, which is an absorbing state. In state $s = 1$ only the follower's actions have an effect on payoffs, which is as follows: $R_L(1, \cdot, L) = -M, R_L(1, \cdot, R) = 0, R_F(1, \cdot, L) = \epsilon, R_F(1, \cdot, R) = 0$, where M is an arbitrarily large number and $\epsilon << M$. In state $s = 2$, in contrast, only the leader's actions have an effect on payoffs: $R_L(2, U, \cdot) = R_L(2, D, \cdot) = 0$, $R_F(2, U, \cdot) = -M$, $R_F(2, D, \cdot) = 0$. Suppose that the discount factors $\gamma_L = \gamma_F$ are close to 1. First, note that a Markov stationary policy for the leader would be independent of the follower's action in state 2, and, consequently, the follower's best response is to play L, giving the leader a payoff of $-M$. On the other hand, if the leader plays the following non-Markov policy: play U when the follower plays L and D otherwise, the follower's optimal policy is to play R, and the leader receives a payoff of 0. Since M is arbitrarily large, the difference between an optimal and best stationary policy is arbitrarily large.

The consequence of the fact that the leader's optimal policy can have arbitrary dependence on history is that DSSGs are extremely difficult to solve, except in special cases, such as when the game is zero-sum (in which case it is equivalent to a stochastic game, which can be solved in polynomial time [15]).

Next, we consider the important special case of APGs [16, 17] and present solution techniques for these.

8.5.2 Adversarial Patrolling Games

Formally, an *APG* can be described by the tuple $\{T, U_d^c(i), U_d^u(i), U_a^c(i), U_a^u(i), \gamma, G\}$, where T is the set of n targets patrolled by the defender, $U_d^c(i)$ and $U_d^u(i)$ are the utilities to the defender if an attacker chooses a target $i \in T$ when it is patrolled and not, respectively, while $U_a^c(i)$ and $U_a^u(i)$ are the corresponding attacker utilities, $\gamma \in (0, 1)$ is the discount factor (in some cases, we also allow $\gamma = 1$), and $G = (T, E)$ is a graph with targets as vertices and E the set of directed edges constraining defender patrolling moves between targets. It is useful to consider the representation of this graph as an adjacency matrix A, where $A_{ij} = 1$ if and only if there is an edge from target i to target j.

The game proceeds in a (possibly infinite) sequence of steps in which the defender moves between targets (subject to the constraints imposed by G), while the attacker chooses the time and target of attack. The defender's (stochastic) patrolling policy is a schedule π, which can in general be an arbitrary function from all observed history (i.e., the sequence of targets patrolled in the past) to a probability distribution over the targets patrolled in the next iteration. The attacker is presumed to know the defender's policy π at the time of decision. At each time step t, the attacker observes the defender's current location i and may choose to wait or to attack an arbitrary target $j \in T$. If an attacker waits, he receives no immediate utility, while attacking a target j gains the attacker $U_a^c(i)$ if it is covered by the defender at time $t + 1$ and $U_a^u(i)$ if it is not. We denote the attacker's policy by ϕ. We say that a policy (π or ϕ) is *Markovian* if it only depends on the current location of the defender, and we call it *stationary Markovian* if it additionally has no dependence on time.

US Coast Guard's patrolling problem as an APG: US Coast Guard (USCG) safeguards important infrastructure at US coasts, ports, and inland waterways. Given a particular port and a variety of critical infrastructure that an adversary may choose to attack, USCG conducts patrols to detect an adversary and protect this infrastructure. However, while the adversary has the opportunity to observe patrol patterns, limited security resources imply that USCG patrols cannot be at every location at all times [14]. In the APG framework, USCG is the defender, while a terrorist group (for example) is an attacker who can conduct surveillance and can both observe the current location of the patrols and obtain a good estimate of the stochastic patrolling policy deployed.

We now observe that APGs can be naturally represented as DSSGs. Specifically, states in APGs correspond to the set of targets T, as well as an absorbing state s. Defender actions in each state are the targets j that he can move to in a single time step, while attacker actions are to wait or to attack (for the moment, we will assume that we can compute expected utilities when attacker chooses to attack; we deal with the issue of which targets are attacked below). The state transitions are actually deterministic, conditional on player actions: if the attacker chooses to attack, the system always transitions to the absorbing state s; otherwise, the next target is completely determined by the defender's action. Finally, if the attacker waits, our baseline model involves zero reward accruing to both players. Figure 8.1 offers a schematic illustration of APG as a stochastic game.

8.5.3 Solving Zero-sum APGs

Consider a special case of zero-sum APGs, where $U_d^c(i) = -U_a^c(i)$ and $U_d^u(i) = -U_a^u(i)$. In this case, APGs (and associated DSSGs) become equivalent to *stochastic games*, since the order of player moves is no longer important. A particularly important consequence is that while in general SSE solutions to DSSGs need not be

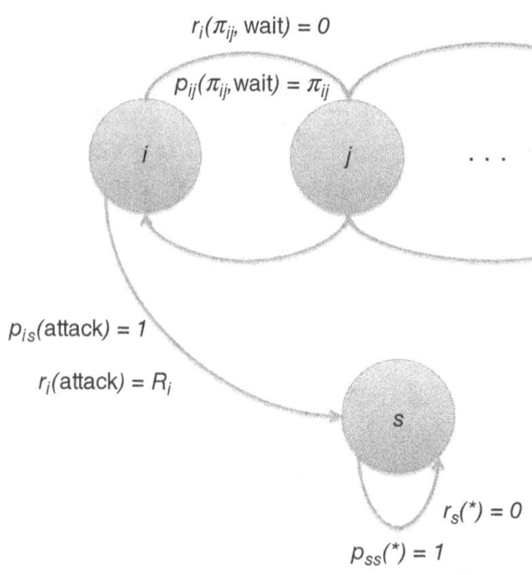

Figure 8.1 Schematic illustration of APG as a DSSG, showing example targets-states i and j, as well the absorbing state s. $p_{ij}(\cdot)$ denotes the transition probability, as a function of the probability π_{ij} that the defender moves from i to j and whether or not the attacker chooses "wait" or "attack." Note that if the attacker attacks, the DSSG transitions to the absorbing state with probability 1, independent of π_{ij}.

in Markov stationary policies (as our example above illustrated), stochastic games always have equilibria that are Markov stationary [18]. Thus, for zero-sum APGs, we can focus exclusively on stationary policies and denote by π_{ij} the (stationary) probability that the defender moves from target i to j.

Since APG is a special case of a stochastic game, we can adapt the nonlinear programming formulation for computing a Nash equilibrium in general zero-sum stochastic games by Filar and Vrieze [18] to our setting. One minor addition to their formulation that we find useful below is to represent the constraints on the defender's action imposed by the graph G as a set of constraints

$$\pi_{ij} \leq A_{ij} \quad \forall\, i, j \in T. \tag{8.16}$$

Let v_i be the expected attacker value of starting in state i. We can formulate the defender's problem as the following mathematical program:

$$\min_{\pi, v} \sum_i v_i \tag{8.17a}$$

s.t.:

$$\pi_{ij} \geq 0 \qquad \forall\, i, j \in T \tag{8.17b}$$

$$\sum_j \pi_{ij} = 1 \qquad \forall\, i \in T \tag{8.17c}$$

$$\pi_{ij} \leq A_{ij} \qquad \forall\, i, j \in T \tag{8.17d}$$

$$v_i \geq (1 - \pi_{ij}) U_a^u(j) + \pi_{ij} U_a^c(j) \quad \forall\, i, j \in T \tag{8.17e}$$

$$v_i \geq \gamma \sum_j \pi_{ij} v_j \qquad \forall i \in T. \tag{8.17f}$$

Constraints (8.17b) and (8.17c) simply constrain defender policy to be a valid probability distribution. The key constraints (8.17e) and (8.17f) are easiest to think about if we fix defender policy π and just consider the MDP faced by the attacker. The right-hand side of Constraint (8.17e) corresponds to expected utility of attacking (since attack moves the MDP into an absorbing state s and no further earnings follow), while the right-hand side of Constraint (8.17f) is the expected value of waiting (immediate reward is 0 for a waiting action). The constraints then arise because the state v_i must be the expected utility of making the best action choice, and minimizing the objective ensures that these values bind to *some* action in every state. While this formulation is a nonconvex nonlinear program, it turns out that all local optima are also global optima [18].

8.5.4 Solving General-sum APGs

The approach above for effectively computing equilibria in zero-sum APGs relies strongly on the particular structure of the zero-sum game. We now present a general formulation of the problem of computing SSE in APGs, which does not require the game to be zero sum. First, let $\beta(i)$ be the distribution over the initial location of the defender (which in many cases may simply be a fixed initial location). Let $v_d(i)$ be the defender's value (expected discounted cumulative reward) of the defender being in location i, and let $v_a(i)$ be the attacker's value when defender is at location i. For the attacker, we now also need to explicitly represent their policy best response. We again use ϕ to denote the attacker's policy, but our notation for it will be somewhat different than earlier. Specifically, we use ϕ_{ij} to denote the decision of the attacker whether or not to attack a location (target) j when the defender is at location i, and ϕ_{iw} to indicate whether the attacker chooses to wait when seeing the defender in location i (treating the decision to wait as effectively an artificial target w). The full mixed-integer nonlinear program (MINLP) for solving general-sum APGs can be represented as follows:

$$\max_{\pi,\phi,v_a,v_d} \sum_i \beta(i) v_d(i) \tag{8.18a}$$

s.t.:

$$\pi_{ij} \geq 0 \quad \phi_{ij} \in \{0,1\}, \phi_{iw} \in \{0,1\} \qquad \forall\, i,j \in T \tag{8.18b}$$

$$\sum_j \pi_{ij} = 1 \quad \sum_j \phi_{ij} + \phi_{iw} = 1 \qquad \forall\, i \in T \tag{8.18c}$$

$$\pi_{ij} \leq A_{ij} \qquad \forall\, i,j \in T \tag{8.18d}$$

$$v_i \geq (1-\pi_{ij})U_a^u(j) + \pi_{ij}U_a^c(j) \quad \forall\, i,j \in T \tag{8.18e}$$

$$v_i \geq \gamma \sum_j \pi_{ij} v_j \qquad \forall i \in T \tag{8.18f}$$

$$0 \leq v_a(i) - [(1-\pi_{ij})U_a^u(j) + \pi_{ij}U_a^c(j)] \leq (1-\phi_{ij})Z \qquad \forall i,j \in T \tag{8.18g}$$

$$v_a(i) - \gamma \sum_j \pi_{ij} v_a(j) \leq (1-\phi_{iw})Z \qquad \forall\, i \in T \tag{8.18h}$$

$$v_d(i) - [(1-\pi_{ij})U_d^u(j) + \pi_{ij}U_d^c(j)] \leq (1-\phi_{ij})Z \qquad \forall i,j \in T \tag{8.18i}$$

$$v_d(i) - \gamma \sum_j \pi_{ij} v_d(j) \leq (1-\phi_{iw})Z \qquad \forall\, i \in T. \tag{8.18j}$$

Note that this representation echoes back to our solution of Bayesian Stackelberg games in Section 8.2; in particular, the nature of the constraints used to compute the attacker's best response has very much the same structure.

Much as we can represent the general-sum APGs equilibrium computation as a MINLP, that is of only marginal help: such problems are extremely challenging to solve in practice. Even if we were to discretize the defender's policy π, turning this into a mixed-integer LP, the resulting problems are still difficult to solve. Indeed, scalable approaches for solving general-sum APGs – and all the more so, DSSGs – remain elusive.

8.6 Conclusion

Computational game theory for security has been a very active field of research for a number of years now, and the volume of both modeling and computational approaches far exceeds what can be reasonably covered in a short chapter. Consequently, this chapter was scoped somewhat narrowly on a collection of models and computational methods for several classes of Stackelberg security games. It is nevertheless worth specifically mentioning two important paradigms that the chapter has ignored entirely. First, there is now a considerable and important line of work on game-theoretic models of deception in security settings. Some of this work pertains to the strategic deployment of honeypots [19–21], while other efforts consider problems involving choosing configurations of devices on a network as well as deceptive presentation of such configurations [22–25]. Second, there is much work that aims to relax the assumption of perfectly rational behavior by adversaries. In this line of work, a common consideration is the merging of behavioral game-theoretic models with Stackelberg-style approaches for computing optimal defender strategies [1, 26, 27].

References

1 A. E. Abbas, M. Tambe, and D. Von Winterfeldt. *Improving Homeland Security Decisions*. Cambridge University Press, 2017.
2 F. Fang, T. Nguyen, B. Ford, N. Sintov, and M. Tambe. Introduction to green security games. In *International Joint Conference on Artificial Intelligence*, 2015.
3 M. Tambe. *Security and Game Theory: Algorithms, Deployed Systems, Lessons Learned*. Cambridge University Press, 2011.
4 D. Bertsimas and J. N. Tsitsiklis. *Introduction to Linear Optimization*. Athena Scientific, 1997.
5 K. J. Cormican, D. P. Morton, and R. K. Wood. Stochastic network interdiction. *Operations Research*, 46(2): 184–197, 1998.
6 J. C. Smith and Y. Song. A survey of network interdiction models and algorithms. *European Journal of Operational Research*, 283(3): 797–811, 2020.
7 R. K. Wood. Deterministic network interdiction. *Mathematical and Computer Modelling*, 17(2): 1–18, 1993.

8 M. Jain, D. Korzhyk, O. Vaněk, V. Conitzer, M. Pěchouček, and M. Tambe. A double oracle algorithm for zero-sum security games on graphs. In *International Conference on Autonomous Agents and MultiAgent Systems*, pp. 327–334. Citeseer, 2011.

9 B. S. Pay, J. R. Merrick, and Y. Song. Stochastic network interdiction with incomplete preference. *Networks*, 73(1): 3–22, 2019.

10 J. Letchford and Y. Vorobeychik. Optimal interdiction of attack plans. In *International Conference on Autonomous Agents and MultiAgent Systems*, pp. 199–206, 2013.

11 S. Panda and Y. Vorobeychik. Near-optimal interdiction of factored MDPs. In *Conference on Uncertainty in Artificial Intelligence*, 2017.

12 S. Panda and Y. Vorobeychik. Scalable initial state interdiction for factored MDPs. In *International Joint Conference on Artificial Intelligence*, 2018.

13 Y. Vorobeychik and M. Pritchard. Plan interdiction games. In *Adaptive Autonomous Secure Cyber Systems*, pp. 159–182. Springer, 2020.

14 B. An, J. Pita, E. Shieh, M. Tambe, C. Kiekintveld, and J. Marecki. Guards and protect: Next generation applications of security games. In *SIGECOM*, vol. 10, pp. 31–34, 2011.

15 M. L. Littman. Markov games as a framework for multi-agent reinforcement learning. In *International Conference on Machine Learning*, pp. 157–163, 1994.

16 Y. Vorobeychik, B. An, and M. Tambe. Adversarial patrolling games. In *2012 AAAI Spring Symposium Series*, 2012.

17 Y. Vorobeychik, B. An, M. Tambe, and S. Singh. Computing solutions in infinite-horizon discounted adversarial patrolling games. In *International Conference on Automated Planning and Scheduling*, 2014.

18 J. Filar and K. Vrieze. *Competitive Markov Decision Processes*. Springer-Verlag, 1997.

19 A. H. Anwar and C. A. Kamhoua. Cyber deception using honeypot allocation and diversity: A game theoretic approach. In *Annual Consumer Communications & Networking Conference*, pp. 543–549, 2022.

20 N. Garg and D. Grosu. Deception in honeynets: A game-theoretic analysis. In *IEEE SMC Information Assurance and Security Workshop*, pp. 107–113, 2007.

21 C. Kiekintveld, V. Lisý, and R. Píbil. Game-theoretic foundations for the strategic use of honeypots in network security. In *Cyber Warfare: Building the Scientific Foundation*, pp. 81–101. Springer, 2015.

22 A. Schlenker, O. Thakoor, H. Xu, F. Fang, M. Tambe, L. Tran-Thanh, P. Vayanos, and Y. Vorobeychik. Deceiving cyber adversaries: A game theoretic approach. In *International Conference on Autonomous Agents and MultiAgent Systems*, pp. 892–900, 2018.

23 Z. R. Shi, A. D. Procaccia, K. S. Chan, S. Venkatesan, N. Ben-Asher, N. O. Leslie, C. Kamhoua, and F. Fang. Learning and planning in the feature deception

problem. In *International Conference on Decision and Game Theory for Security*, pp. 23–44, 2020.

24 O. Thakoor, M. Tambe, P. Vayanos, H. Xu, C. Kiekintveld, and F. Fang. Cyber camouflage games for strategic deception. In *International Conference on Decision and Game Theory for Security*, pp. 525–541, 2019.

25 J. Wu, C. Kamhoua, M. Kantarcioglu, and Y. Vorobeychik. Learning generative deception strategies in combinatorial masking games. In *International Conference on Decision and Game Theory for Security*, pp. 98–117, 2021.

26 T. Nguyen, R. Yang, A. Azaria, S. Kraus, and M. Tambe. Analyzing the effectiveness of adversary modeling in security games. In *AAAI Conference on Artificial Intelligence*, vol. 27, pp. 718–724, 2013.

27 R. Yang, A. X. Jiang, M. Tambe, and F. Ordonez. Scaling-up security games with boundedly rational adversaries: A cutting-plane approach. In *International Joint Conference on Artificial Intelligence*, 2013.

9

Privacy and Robustness Trade-offs of Artificial Intelligence Models with Federated Learning

Kemal Davaslioglu[1], Yi Shi[2], and Yalin E. Sagduyu[1,3]

[1] *Nexcepta, Inc., Gaithersburg, MD, USA*
[2] *Virginia Tech, Commonwealth Cyber Initiative, Arlington, VA, USA*
[3] *Virginia Tech, National Security Institute, Arlington, VA, USA*

9.1 Introduction

Artificial intelligence (AI) and machine learning (ML) applications are increasingly used in privacy-sensitive applications such as medical diagnosis, health analytics, pharmacogenomics, location services, finance records, personal records, cybersecurity, and facial recognition. Despite their success, AI models are susceptible to privacy and security attacks. While most of the research in the literature has focused on evasion attacks (i.e., fooling ML models with tapered inputs), privacy attacks are equally important. Maintaining data privacy and model security is critical for many ML applications. Specifically, computer vision systems increasingly rely on ML to automatically detect, identify, and predict potential targets. Traditional systems use template matching. A critical problem is when an adversary can off-load the templates and determine the list of targets that the system is designed to identify. ML applications are susceptible to three types of privacy-related attacks that pose serious risks, and the performance limits are not yet fully characterized: (1) model inversion (ModInv) attacks, (2) training data membership inference (MI) attacks, and (3) attribute inference attacks.

Model inversion (ModInv) attacks aim to reconstruct an average sample given a model [1–3]. ModInv attacks can be launched by an adversary with a black-box access to the prediction models to estimate/reveal aspects of a feature of a class (e.g., genotype of an individual or face of an employee). ModInv attacks exploit the confidence values revealed along with predictions and pose serious privacy risks [3].

Training data MI attacks aim to determine whether a given data point was present in the training data [4]. Consider a target recognition system that uses satellite imagery, where membership status could reveal information specific to locales surveyed in the training data and target types. Another example is in health analytics where the distinction between case and control groups can reveal an individual's sensitive information.

Attribute inference attacks use an ML model together with incomplete information about a data point to infer the missing information for that point. Consider an adversary with partial information about an individual's medical record can infer the individual's genotype by using a model trained on similar medical records. Another example is that an adversary can use partial/occluded images of a target to determine if a model is trained using that target.

The current state-of-the-art systems rely on the black-box nature of ML models that are in general, hard to reverse engineer. However, the recent studies have shown that ML models are vulnerable against ModInv and MI attacks [5–10]. This necessitates research to preserve and maintain the privacy and security of ML models and the data they are trained on. In addition, as ML models are increasingly trained on personal data, anonymization of data alone is not sufficient. To protect the data privacy in deep learning (DL) applications, federated learning (FL) is a recently proposed framework that ensures user data privacy [11]. In this context, participating nodes (users) use a baseline model, make their local training, and send their gradient updates to a trusted centralized node that aggregates the updates from participants. This enables participants to jointly construct a DL model without sharing their private training data with each other.

This chapter investigates key data privacy challenges, as illustrated in Figure 9.1. First, we investigate the privacy vulnerabilities of DL models against ModInv and MI attacks using appropriate metrics. The algorithms and measures defined in the literature so far account for exact inference of the image. However, these algorithms and measures do not fully capture the privacy of the training data and models. These pose serious risks for privacy-sensitive applications in the computer vision domain. We use metrics such as Structural Similarity Index (SSIM) to evaluate the approximate adversary inferences and fully characterize privacy vulnerabilities of DL models.

Second, while **image transformations** are commonly employed for data augmentation and to reduce overfitting, their impact on data confidentiality remains underexplored. It is not yet well understood which transformations obscure sensitive training information and which inadvertently preserve features that can be exploited to identify the original data. In this chapter, we systematically evaluate the influence of various image transformations on the effectiveness of

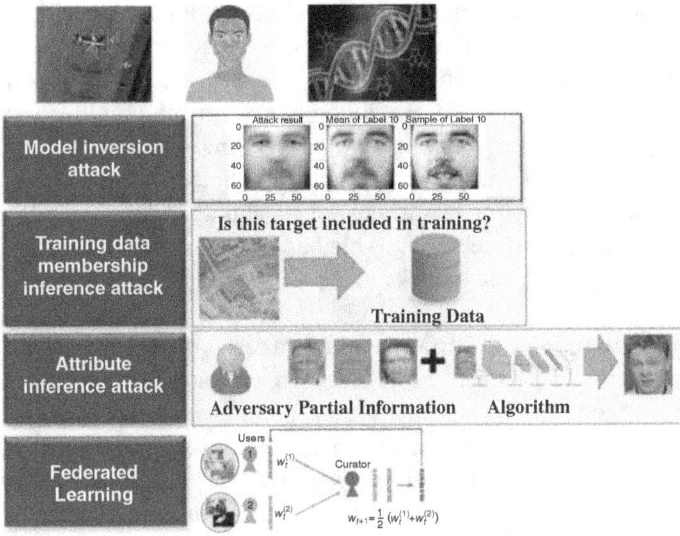

Figure 9.1 Privacy vulnerabilities of DL models.

ModInv attacks, providing new insights into their role in protecting (or exposing) training data.

Finally, we study **the resilience of FL systems** for deep convolutional neural networks (CNNs) against the ModInv, MI, and attribute inference attacks at different levels of the privacy budget. Specifically, we focus on the **differential privacy** (DP) method as a well-known and commonly used defense mechanism, which bounds each participant's influence over the joint model. DP often comes at the expense of global model's accuracy, and we evaluate the model performance for different privacy budgets to characterize the performance versus privacy tradeoff. All the datasets used in this chapter are publicly available.

Relevance to cyber resiliency: This chapter contributes directly to the cyber resiliency of autonomous systems that rely on ML models for perception, decision-making, and control. In such systems, maintaining confidentiality, integrity, and availability of both models and data is paramount. The chapter investigates how adversarial privacy attacks, including ModInv, MI, and attribute inference, can compromise the trustworthiness of ML. These vulnerabilities are particularly critical for autonomous systems, which often operate in untrusted environments and must make decisions with minimal human oversight.

We consider three types of privacy-related attacks, namely, (1) ModInv Attacks, (2) training data MI attacks, and (3) attribute inference attacks, and use image transformations as one approach to mitigate ModInv Attacks. These attacks can compromise the confidentiality and integrity of both the data and the model outputs, which can critically undermine the cyber resilience of a system.

To enhance autonomous cyber resilience, we explore defense mechanisms such as privacy-preserving image transformations, differentially private training, and FL. These methods provide adaptive protection and help maintain operational capabilities under attack. FL, in particular, supports distributed model training without data centralization, enabling privacy-aware collaboration between edge nodes and reducing the attack surface. DP adds further protection by limiting any single participant's influence on the global model, thereby impeding inference attacks.

We apply FL utilizing its unique properties to achieve a certain level of resilience even if no explicit defense mechanism is in place. In FL, participating nodes (clients) use a baseline model, perform local training, and transmit their gradient updates to a trusted centralized node that aggregates the updates from participants. This enables the participants to collaboratively construct a DL model without having to share their private training data with each other. The benefits of FL are the followings:

- Client-level redundancy: Even if some clients are compromised, others can still provide correct local models, allowing the global model to function reliably.
- Temporal robustness: Since FL proceeds over multiple rounds, short-term attacks can be diluted over time if not persistent.
- Potential for fault isolation: If clients exhibiting anomalous behavior can be detected, their contributions could be excluded to protect the global model, which highlights a promising direction toward resilient FL.

Thus, we study the resilience of FL systems for deep CNNs against the ModInv, MI, and attribute inference attacks at different levels of the privacy budget. In particular, we focus on DP as a well-known and commonly used defense mechanism that bounds each participant's influence over the joint model. While DP often comes at the expense of model accuracy, we evaluate its impact across different privacy budgets to characterize the trade-off between model utility and privacy protection.

While this chapter spans multiple techniques and attack surfaces, including ModInv, MI, and FL, this breadth is intentional. Our objective is to present an integrated view of privacy threats and defense mechanisms that collectively shape the cyber resiliency of AI-enabled systems. Rather than isolating these topics, we structure the chapter to build a progressive narrative: first by characterizing attack vectors that compromise data confidentiality and model integrity, then by analyzing the limitations of conventional training, and finally by advancing federated and differentially private learning as resilient design choices. This unified treatment is especially relevant for autonomous and distributed systems, where privacy, robustness, and trust must be addressed jointly.

The rest of this chapter is organized as follows: Sections 9.2 and 9.3 consider ModInv and MI attacks, respectively. Section 9.4 presents FL as a defense mechanism. Section 9.5 offers a discussion of key findings and implications, while Section 9.6 concludes with final remarks and directions for future work.

9.2 Model Inversion Attacks

To develop appropriate measures and algorithms based on membership advantage to account for *approximate* inferences of partial image information, we consider the ModInv attacks in [2]. We demonstrate these attacks using the facial recognition models and use the Olivetti faces from AT&T dataset [12]. We investigate different learning models, starting from a simple Softmax regression model (SRM) to a deeper CNN. We perform ModInv attacks with different parameters and characterize the effects of learning models and parameters on the attack results. The Olivetti faces dataset has 40 classes (distinct subjects) and consists of 400 samples [12]. Each sample is of 64 × 64 dimensions. For some subjects, images were taken at different times in varying lighting, facial expressions (open or closed eyes, smiling or not smiling), and facial details (glasses or no glasses). All the images were taken against a dark homogeneous background with the subjects in an upright frontal position. We divided the dataset into 75% for training (300 samples) and 25% for testing (100 samples). The attacker uses an objective loss that consists of two components. The first component of the attacker's loss is to minimize the distance between the target class and the predicted class of attacker's test sample. The second component of the loss minimizes the cross-entropy between X_t and the population mean (excluding the images of the target class). We also used two additional losses that incorporate (1) total-variation (TV) regularization term and (2) L_p-norm for regularization, both of which were not included in the original experiments in [2].

9.2.1 Softmax Regression Model Training

To train the facial recognition model, we first trained a simple Softmax regression model (SRM). This classifier is a generalization of logistic regression that allows the class variable to take more than two values. As the Olivetti dataset includes 40 individuals, the classifier needs to distinguish between 40 labels. Softmax regression is commonly used in the output layer of neural networks, so on its own, the classifier can be seen as a neural network with no hidden layers. As noted in [2], on this dataset, plain Softmax regression outperforms, or performs as well as, more complicated models (when tested against one hidden layer, deep convolutional). The validation accuracy of the SRM is **92%**.

The adversary attacks the victim model and defines a new loss function. The first component of the attacker's loss is to minimize the distance between the target class and the predicted class of attacker's test sample. The second component of the loss minimizes the cross-entropy between X_t and the population mean (excluding the images of the target class). We also developed the two optional losses that include (1) TV regularization term and L_p-norm for regularization, both of which were not included in the original experiments in Ref. [2].

The pseudocode of the algorithm is presented in Table 9.1. The parameters α denotes the number of gradient descent iterations, β represents number of iterations to limit the attack, γ is the cost improvement threshold, and λ stands for gradient step size. The cost function is defined as $c(x)$. The algorithm starts with an all-zeros image and applies gradient descent for up to α iterations with a step size of λ. After each step of the gradient descent, the function Process performs various image manipulations such as denoising and sharpening for the given attack. If the cost of the candidate did not improve in β iterations or the cost improvement from one iteration to another is less than some tolerance δ, the gradient descent terminates, and the best candidate is returned. We performed the ModInv attack presented in Table 9.1. The attacker determines if individual 10 (target label 10) is used in the training model or not. We considered $\alpha = 10,000$, $\beta = 100$, $\lambda = 10^{-3}$, and $\delta = 10^{-10}$.

In general, the best attack results are achieved using the TV regularization of 2.0 and L_p regularization with $p = 6$. Table 9.2 illustrates the attack result (ModInv image), mean face of the attacked label, and a random sample of a label for six selected classes. With these attack parameters, we observe that the face image that ModInv attack synthesizes visually a very close image to the mean image (and to the samples) of the target class.

Table 9.1 Pseudocode for the ModInv attack for facial recognition.

```
Function face model-inversion (target label, α, β, γ, δ):
c(x) = 1 − f_label(x) + AuxTerm(x)
x_0 = 0
for ii = 1, ..., α do:
   x_i = Process(x_{i−1} − λ∇c(x_{i−1}))
   If c(x_i) − c(x_{i−1}) ≥ max(c(x_{i−1}), ..., c(x_{i−β})) :
      Break
   If c(x_i) − c(x_{i−1}) ≤ δ :
      Break
Return [argmin_{x_i}(c(x_i)), min_{x_i}(c(x_i))]
```

Table 9.2 Attack result, mean face, and sample for all faces in the Olivetti dataset where the model under attack is a sigmoid layer.

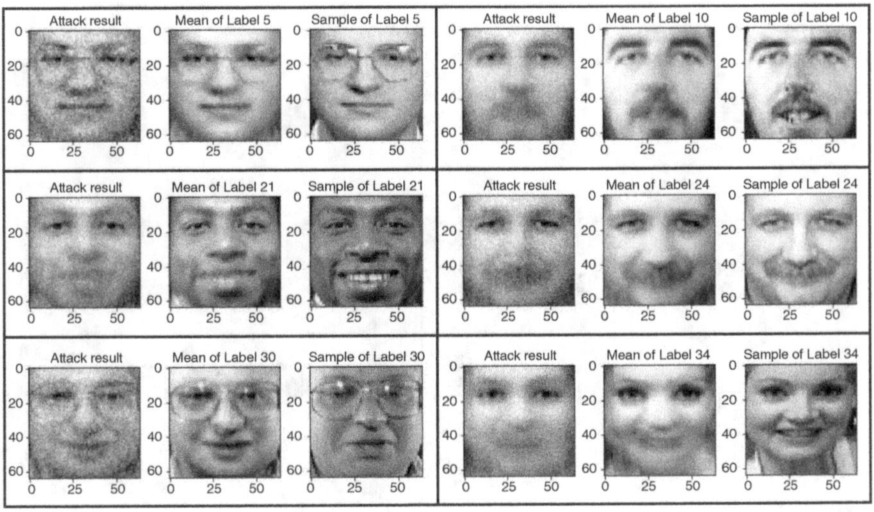

9.2.2 ModInv Attacks Against a Single-layer Convolutional Neural Network (CNN)

We extend the model under attack to a single-layer CNN using 32 filters with a size of (3, 3). The outputs of the convolutional layer are fed into a fully connected layer with 40 neurons. This final layer uses the Softmax activation for predictions. It is trained with categorical cross-entropy. The test accuracy of this model is 95%. We performed an extensive hyperparametrization attack with various TV and L_p regularizer, none of them were able to reconstruct meaningful faces. Then, we removed these regularization losses and increased the number of iterations to 50,000, while keeping the tolerance to 100 iterations and the same ADAM optimizer with step size of 10^{-4}. This time the attack was able to reconstruct the faces successfully for each label. In Table 9.3, we provide these results.

9.2.3 ModInv Attacks Against a Four-layer CNN

We build and train a deeper CNN model with four convolutional layers. This deeper CNN resembles a more realistic scenario, as real-life systems include several cascaded convolutional layers. The test accuracy is 95%. The four-layer CNN model using the same attack configuration as the single-layer CNN model described in Section 9.2.2. Table 9.4 presents the corresponding results.

Table 9.3 Attack result, mean face, and sample for faces in the Olivetti dataset where the model under attack is a single-layer CNN.

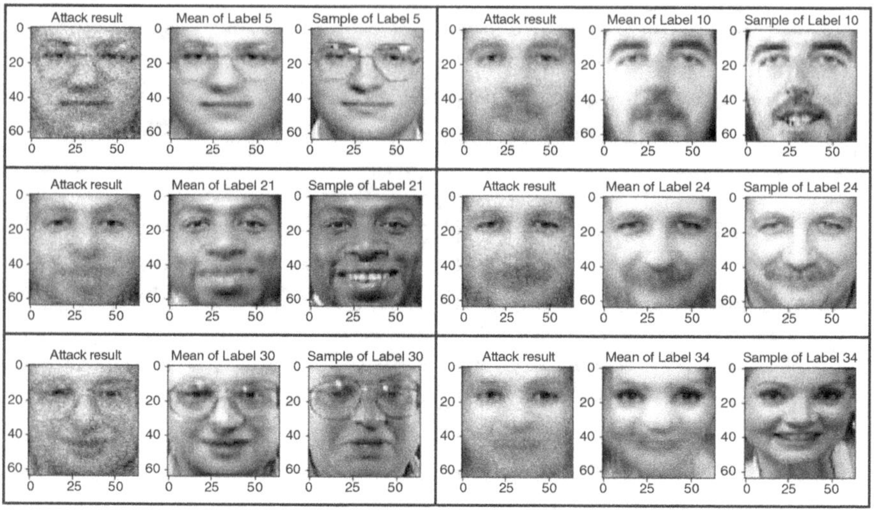

Table 9.4 Attack result, mean face, and sample for all 40 faces in the Olivetti dataset where the model under attack is a four-layer CNN.

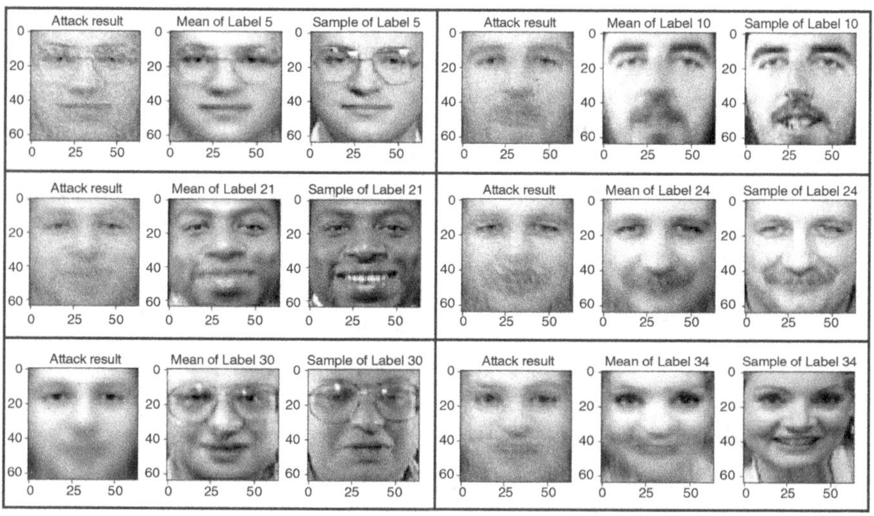

9.2.4 Comparison of the Three Types of Models Under Attack

We observe that the ModInv attack generates an image that is very similar to the mean face of the target label. Comparing all models, we observe that the reconstructions of the four-layer CNN are visually closer to the mean face than the single-layer CNN does. An example of three models of attack for target label 10 is as shown in Table 9.5.

9.2.5 Privacy Preservation Evaluation of Image Transformations Against ModInv Attacks

Now, we extend the ModInv attacks and apply different image transformations in the training time and evaluate the reconstructions obtained with the ModInv attack.

9.2.5.1 Structural Similarity Index Evaluation

To quantify the success in reconstructions, we can use different metrics such as the SSIM, mean-squared error (MSE), mean absolute error (MAE), and relative error (RelErr). The SSIM [13, 14] is calculated using the following equation:

- $$\text{SSIM}(\boldsymbol{x}, \boldsymbol{y}) = \frac{(2\mu_x\mu_y + C_1)(2\sigma_{xy} + C_2)(\sigma_{xy} + C_3)}{(\mu_x^2 + \mu_y^2 + C_1)(\sigma_x^2 + \sigma_Y^2 + C_2)(\sigma_{xy} + C_3)},$$

Table 9.5 ModInv reconstructions for models that are under attack.

Model	Reconstructions
1. A sigmoid layer	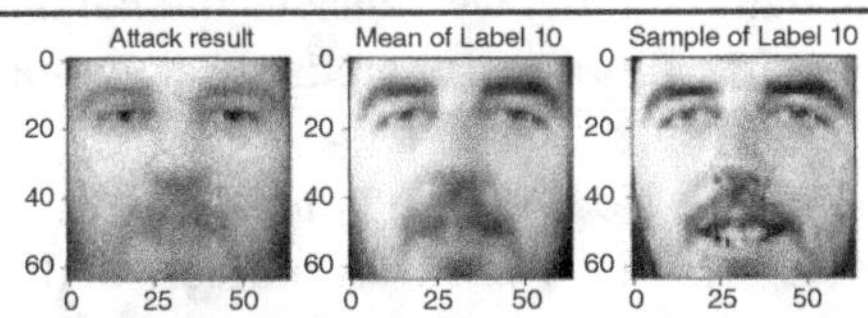
2. Single-layer CNN	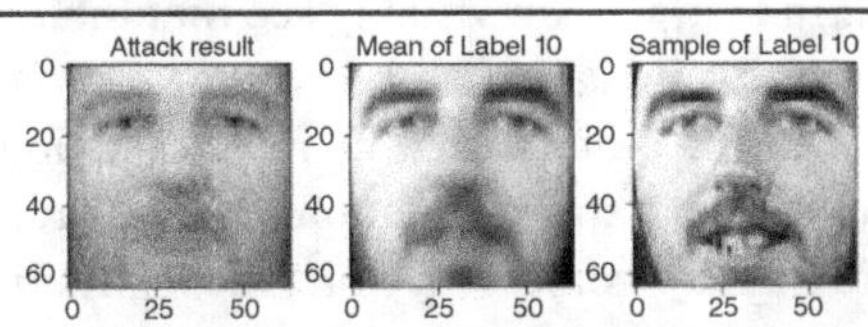
3. Four-layer CNN	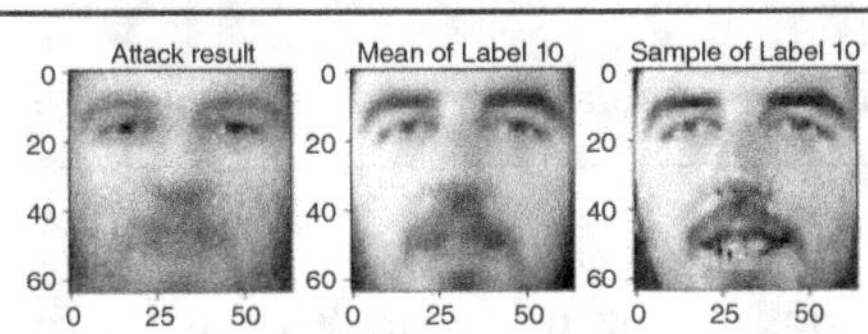

SSIM provides a robust metric to measure the difference between similar images, for example, $D(x, f(x))$, where x is the image and $f(x)$ is a classical image transformation, and $D(x, y)$ measures the difference between two images x and y in terms of the metric under test. We use the following steps to evaluate the privacy-preserving properties of image transformations against ModInv attacks (Table 9.6).

We train a four-layer CNN composed of sequential 2D convolutional layers, each with a kernel size of 3, stride of 1, and valid padding. All convolutional layers use the LeCun Uniform initializer and ReLU activation functions. Following the convolutional stack, a flattening layer is applied, which is then connected to a fully connected output layer consisting of 40 neurons with a Softmax activation, corresponding to the number of target classes. We used the ADAM optimizer with a learning rate of 0.001 and trained via the categorical cross-entropy function over 200 epochs with a batch size of 32.

In this experiment, we evaluate the impact of several common image transformations on ModInv attacks. The applied transformations include vertical and horizontal flips, each with a probability of 50%, as well as brightness adjustment, vertical shift, and rotation, each applied within a range of $\pm 20°$. These transformations are intended to explore how data augmentation techniques affect the model's ability to retain or obscure sensitive training information.

Also, we evaluate the case where no augmentation is used and use it as a benchmark. As the success of ModInv attack depends on the regularization and blurring effects during the attack time, we consider the combination of parameters presented in Table 9.7. Results when there is no defense (no image transformation) are presented in Figure 9.2.

Figures 9.3–9.7 show ModInv results for different image transformations. We observe that transformations such as horizontal flips are not robust against ModInv attacks. In fact, we can visually see that the reconstruction of the model trained on augmented images with horizontal flips is sharper compared to the original dataset. On the other hand, the reconstructions against the models augmented with other image transformations, such as rotations, vertical shifts, and vertical flips, are slightly worse. The worst reconstructions or most privacy-aware

Table 9.6 Algorithm to evaluate privacy-preserving image transformations.

1. For each transformation $f(\cdot)$:
   - **a.** Train a classifier using the original data and augmented samples using the transformation $f(\cdot)$.
   - **b.** Apply the ModInv attack for a given target class C_t.
   - **c.** Obtain the reconstruction x'.
   - **d.** Measure the distance between the reconstruction x' and mean face of class C_t.

Table 9.7 Attack parameters.

Attack name	Blurring	L_p-norm	Total-variation (TV) regularization
A1	False	None	None
A2	False	6	3
A3	False	6	2
A4	True	None	None
A5	True	6	3
A6	True	6	2

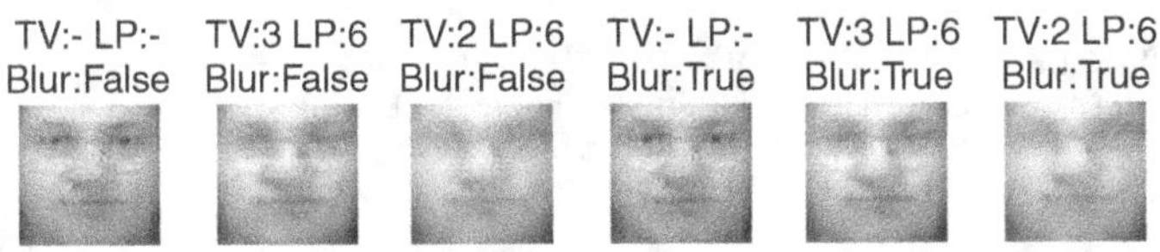

Figure 9.2 ModInv reconstructions (no image transformation).

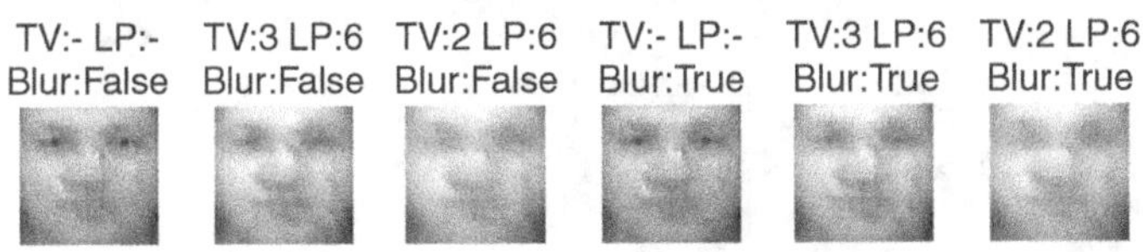

Figure 9.3 ModInv reconstructions for vertical flip transformations.

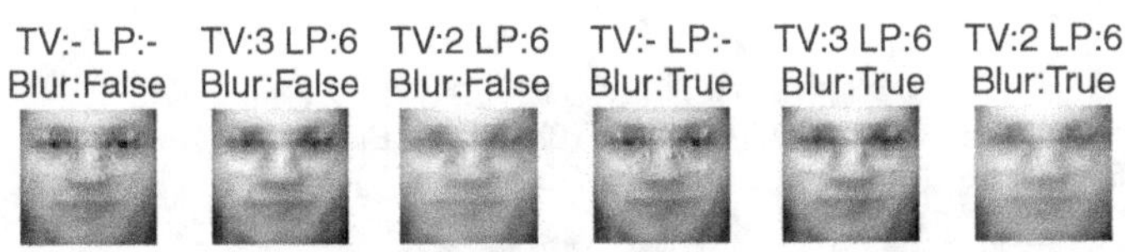

Figure 9.4 ModInv reconstructions for horizontal flip transformation.

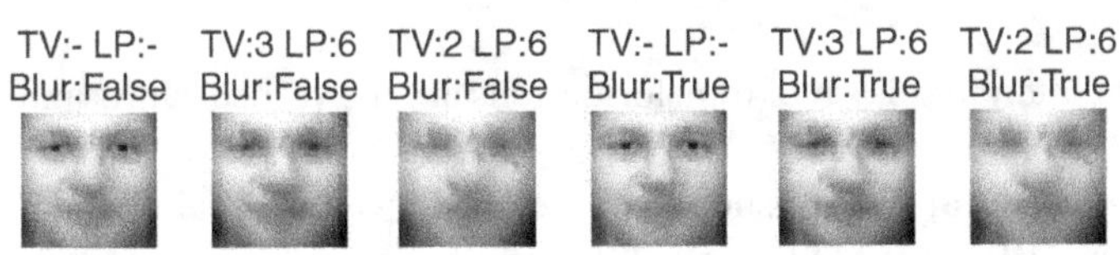

Figure 9.5 ModInv reconstructions for brightness transformation.

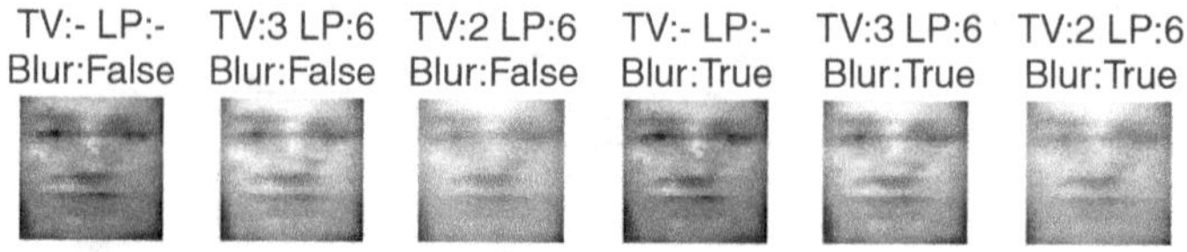

Figure 9.6 ModInv reconstructions for vertical shifts.

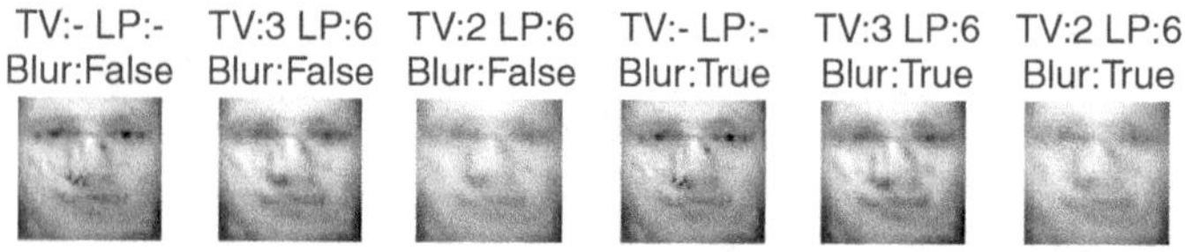

Figure 9.7 ModInv reconstructions for rotations.

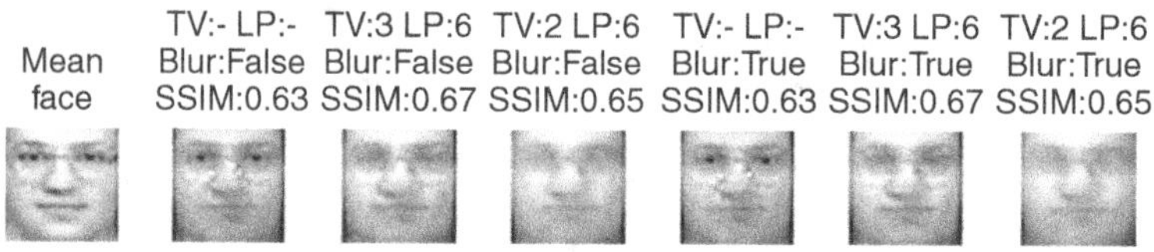

Figure 9.8 Structural Similarity Index (SSIM) distances (no image transformation).

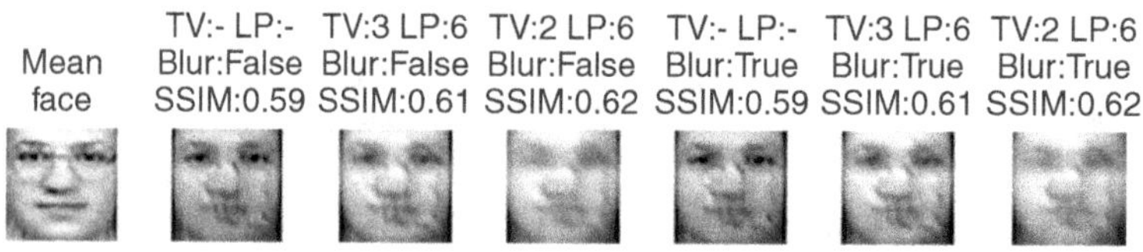

Figure 9.9 SSIM distances for vertical flip transformations.

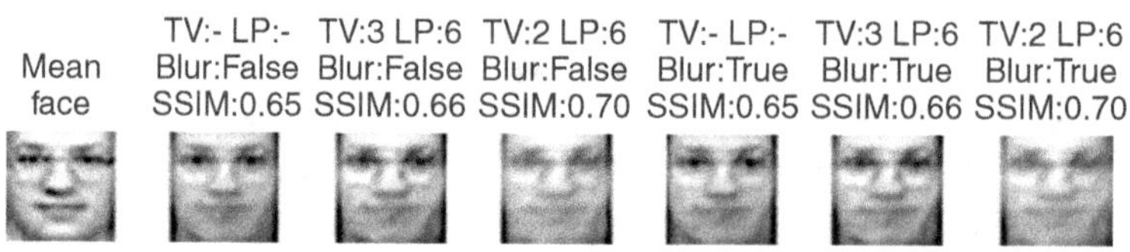

Figure 9.10 SSIM distances for horizontal flip transformation.

and robust transformation in this set of transformations are the vertical shifts and brightness.

Now, we quantitatively evaluate the success of the ModInv attack against these image transformations. We use the SSIM and MSE distance between the mean face and reconstructions, see results in Figures 9.8–9.13, respectively.

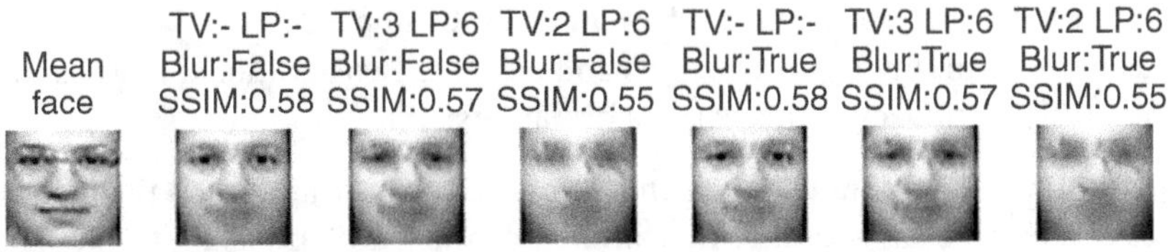

Figure 9.11 SSIM distances for brightness transformation.

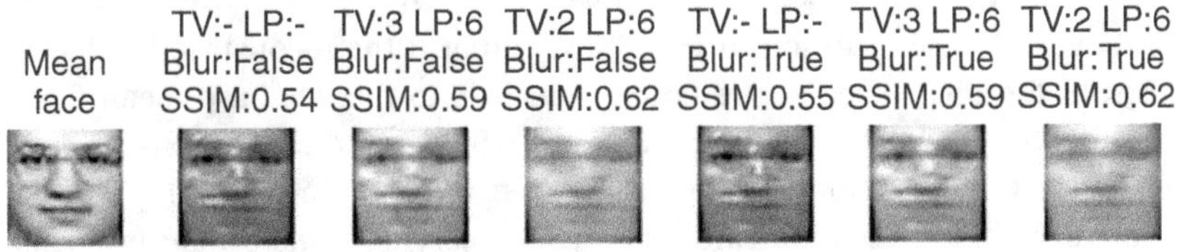

Figure 9.12 SSIM distances for vertical shifts.

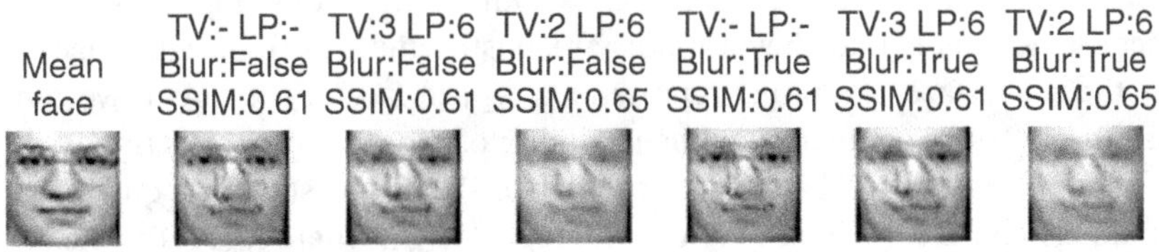

Figure 9.13 SSIM distances for rotations.

In our quantitative assessment in terms of SSIM, we make the following observations:

1. The model trained on augmented images with horizontal flips leaked more information compared to the original dataset. This confirms our visual assessment that these reconstructions against the model trained on horizontal flips are sharper.
2. The other image transformations such as rotations and vertical flips are slightly more robust against ModInv attacks.
3. The most robust transformations are brightness and vertical shifts.
4. All the reconstructions are able to achieve an SSIM score above 54%. This quantitative assessment demonstrates an important vulnerability against ModInv attacks.

9.2.5.2 Diff-SSIM and Peak Signal to Noise Ratio Evaluation

We focus on the ModInv reconstructions and evaluate two additional metrics to better quantify the privacy of image transformations:

- **Diff-SSIM:** Let us denote the mean face of the database as x_m and the mean face of a target class L_t as $x_m^{L_t}$. We can then define Diff-SSIM as the SSIM difference between the mean face of the target class $x_m^{L_t}$ and the ModInv reconstruction $\hat{x}$ and the mean face of the database x_m and the reconstruction $\hat{\boldsymbol{x}}$. Mathematically, this can be expressed as $\text{Diff}_{\text{SSIM}} = \text{SSIM}\left(\hat{\boldsymbol{x}}, \boldsymbol{x}_m^{L_t}\right) - \text{SSIM}\left(\hat{\boldsymbol{x}}, \boldsymbol{x}_m\right)$. The intuition in Diff-SSIM is that if the reconstruction looks closer to the mean face of the target than it is to the database mean face, then Diff-SSIM will be positive value (and will also indicate a non-privacy-preserving transformation), and if it is closer to x_m, then Diff-SSIM will be negative (and will also indicate a privacy-preserving transformation). This provides us with a clear indication of the success of the attack as well as the privacy-preserving properties of the transformation.
- **Peak signal-to-noise ratio (PSNR):** Another way of treating the ModInv reconstructions is that they are noisy reconstructions of the original faces. As the mean face of a target represents a typical face of the target, we can use the PSNR to compare the image quality of ModInv reconstruction with respect to the mean face of the target label. PSNR measures the quality of an image and is defined as $\text{PSNR} = -10 \log_{10}\left(\frac{e_{\text{mse}}}{s^2}\right)$, where e_{mse} is the mean-squared error between two similar images and s measures the maximum pixel value. PSNR is measured in decibels (dB). A high PSNR indicates a good reconstruction and a non-privacy-preserving transformation. Note that PSNR is a good measure to compare the similarity of the same image (original image and its restoration), but not an ideal metric to measure for between-image comparisons.

We utilize the same classifier employed in the SSIM evaluations and apply the following image transformations: vertical flip and horizontal flip, each with a 50% probability, as well as brightness adjustment, vertical shift, and rotation, all within a range of ±20°. These transformations are used to assess their influence on the model's susceptibility to inversion attacks and the extent to which they affect the preservation or obfuscation of training data features.

As the success of ModInv attack depends on the regularization and blurring effects during the attack time, we consider the combination of parameters presented in Table 9.7. First, we present the results when there is no defense (no image transformation) (see Figure 9.14).

As Figures 9.15–9.19 show us, different transformations yield different privacy-preserving or non-preserving properties. For example, on one hand, Diff-SSIM values for brightness, vertical flips, and vertical shifts are negative values. This shows

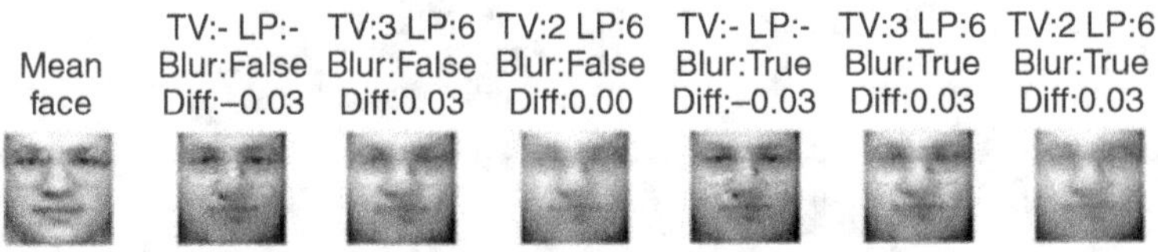

Figure 9.14 Diff-SSIM comparison of the ModInv reconstructions (no image transformation).

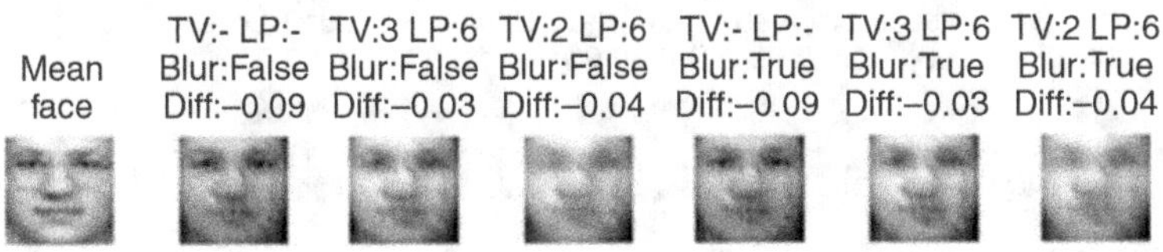

Figure 9.15 Diff-SSIM comparison of ModInv reconstructions for vertical flip transformations.

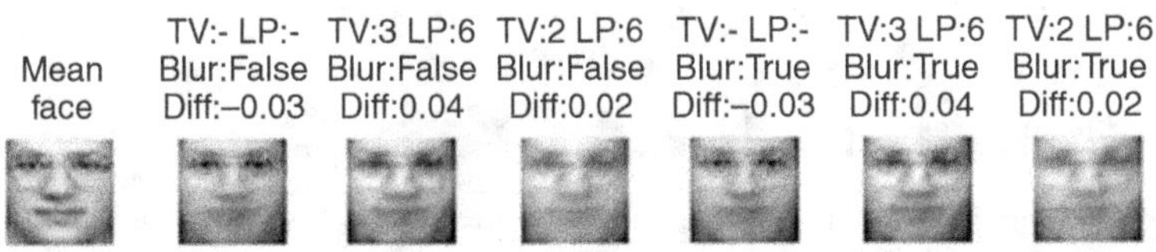

Figure 9.16 Diff-SSIM comparison of ModInv reconstructions for horizontal flip transformation.

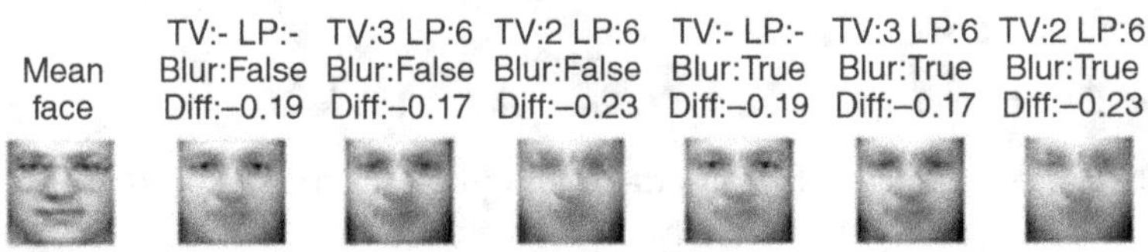

Figure 9.17 Diff-SSIM comparison of ModInv reconstructions for brightness transformation.

that these transformations can provide privacy-preserving properties. On the other hand, most Diff-SSIM values for horizontal flip and rotations are positive, which indicates a non-privacy-preserving property.

Next, we present PSNR between the mean face of the target class and the ModInv reconstruction from Figures 9.20–9.25 for different image transformations. A high PSNR indicates a low privacy–preserving property.

The highest PSNR that is achieved using these ModInv attack parameters is 19.3 using vertical shifts transformations and (TV: 2, LP: 6, and Blur: True) parameters. The lowest PSNR is 11.5 also achieved with vertical shifts and (TV: -, LP: -, and

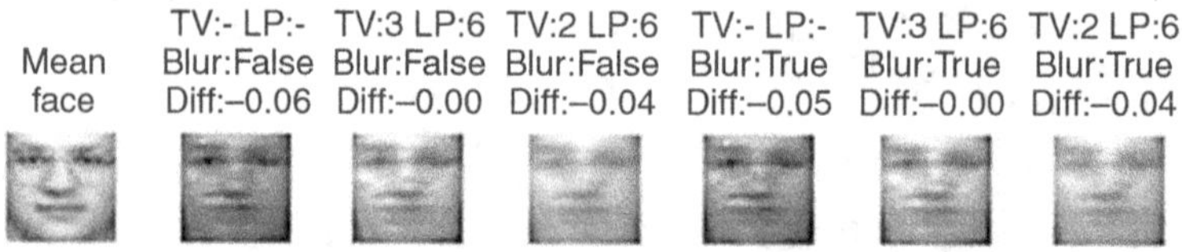

Figure 9.18 Diff-SSIM comparison of ModInv reconstructions for vertical shifts.

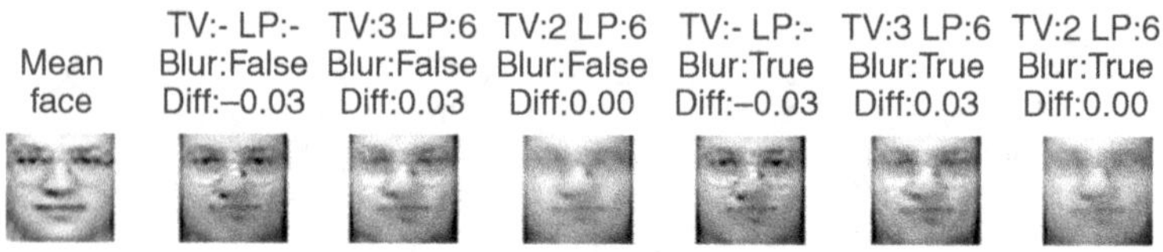

Figure 9.19 Diff-SSIM comparison of ModInv reconstructions for rotations.

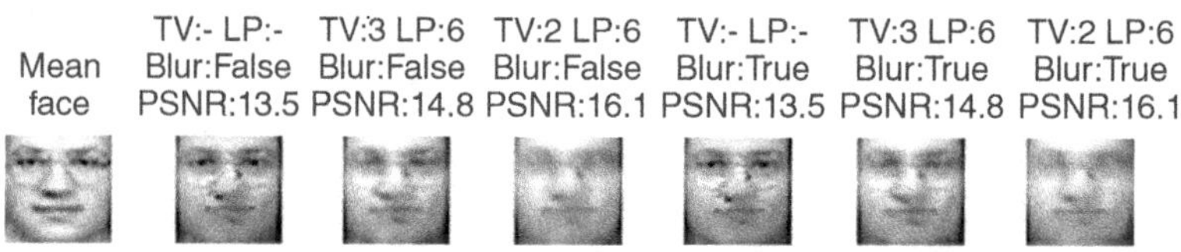

Figure 9.20 PSNR against different ModInv attacks (no image transformation).

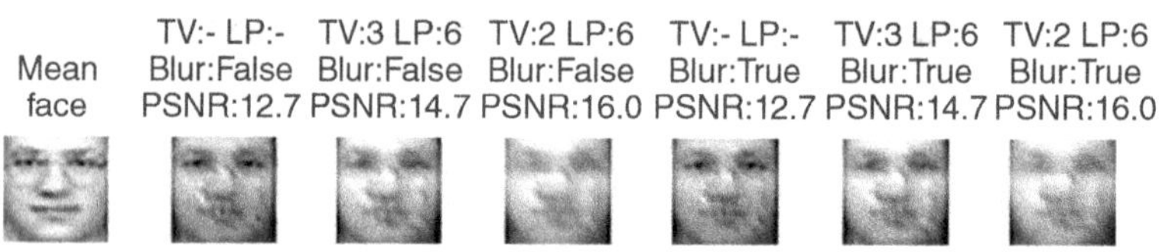

Figure 9.21 PSNR against different ModInv attacks for vertical flip transformations.

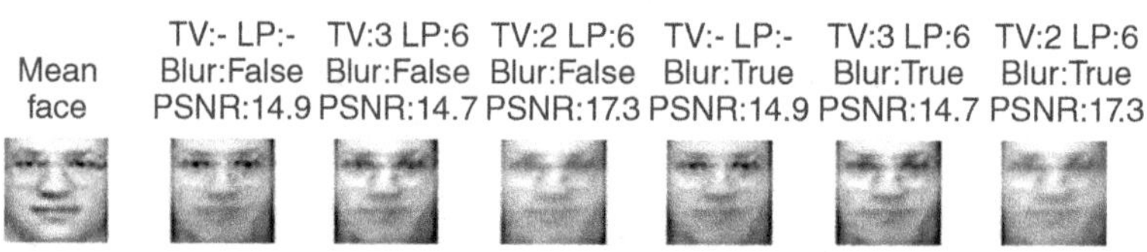

Figure 9.22 PSNR against different ModInv attacks for horizontal flip transformation.

Blur: False) parameters. Thus, PSNR may not be the best metric to use in determining the privacy-preserving properties of a transformation as PSNR values change drastically and they are not consistent. Checking the PSNR of the transformation – PSNR of the benchmark (with no transformation), results are more consistent

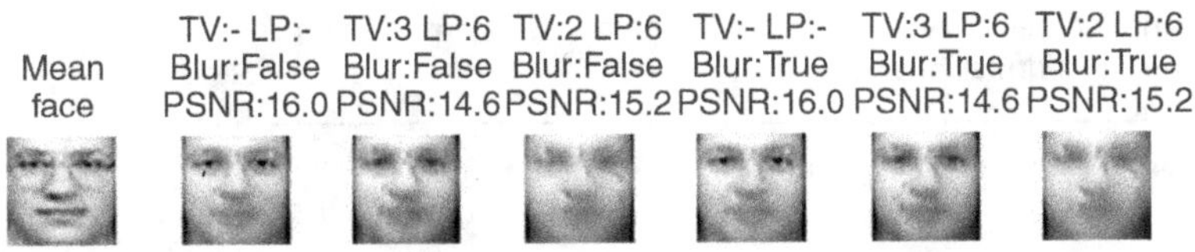

Figure 9.23 PSNR against different ModInv attacks for brightness transformation.

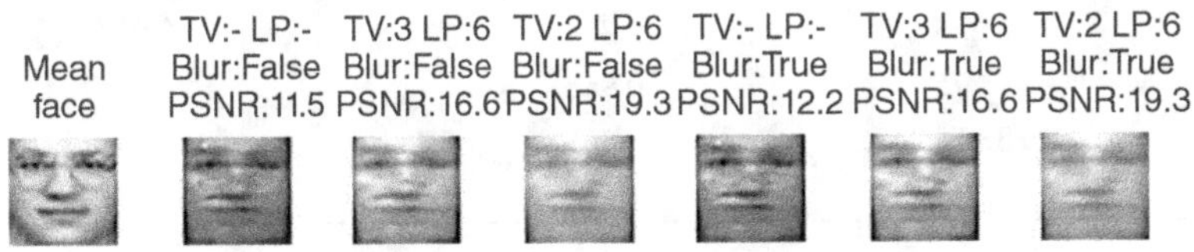

Figure 9.24 PSNR against different ModInv attacks for vertical shifts.

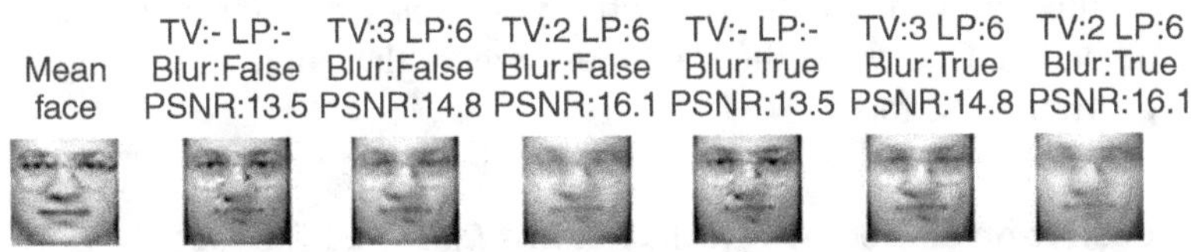

Figure 9.25 PSNR against different ModInv attacks for rotations.

with previous observations. If the difference between the PSNRs of the transformation and the benchmark (with no transformation) is positive, this indicates a low-quality image, a bad reconstruction, and a privacy-preserving transformation. Negative PSNR difference indicates positive diff-SSIM and low privacy-preserving transformation.

9.2.6 Accuracy of These Privacy-preserving Image Transformations in ModInv Attacks

We present the accuracy of the classifiers using each transformation. Consider the following classifiers: Classifier 1 (Vanilla classifier): No augmentation. Classifier 2: Training samples are augmented using vertical flips. Classifier 3: Training samples are augmented using a horizontal flip. Classifier 4: Training samples are augmented using brightness [−20°, 20°]. Classifier 5: Training samples are augmented using a vertical shift [−20°, 20°]. Classifier 6: Training samples are augmented using rotation [−20°, 20°]. In all cases, test samples are not augmented. The validation losses and accuracies of the respective classifiers are presented in Table 9.8. The vanilla classifier achieves 80% validation accuracy. The image transformation

Table 9.8 Validation accuracy and loss of classifiers augmented using different image transformations.

Classifier name	Validation accuracy (%)	Validation loss
Classifier 1	80.00	1.164
Classifier 2	90.00	0.483
Classifier 3	81.25	1.304
Classifier 4	83.75	0.968
Classifier 5	88.75	0.761
Classifier 6	73.75	1.866

that provides the most improvement in descending order are rotations, horizontal flip, vertical flip, and width shifts, respectively. The only transformation that reduces the validation accuracy is the brightness, where the validation accuracy slightly goes down from 80 to 73.75%.

9.2.7 Demonstration of ModInv Attacks Against CIFAR-10 Dataset

Next, we perform ModInv attack against the CIFAR-10 dataset [15] using extended versions or the algorithms presented in [2] that exploits confidence values revealed along with predictions and [16] "invertibility interference," where a highly invertible model quickly becomes highly non-invertible by adding little noise. In the CIFAR-10 dataset, there are ten classes, namely airplane, automobile, bird, cat, deer, dog, frog, horse, ship, and truck. The size of each image is 32×32 with 3 RGB channels. There are 6,000 images per class and a total of 60K images. The training set includes 50K samples, and the test set includes 10K samples. We consider an extensive set of attacks. The parameters of these attacks are listed in Table 9.9.

The model reconstructions are presented in Table 9.10. We attacked the label of dogs. Some parameters failed to be successful (non-recognizable targets). Some of them, such as Attack 3 (TV 2, LP 2, Blur False) and Attack 5 (TV 2, LP 2, Blur True), reconstructed a very good image that looks like a Terrier dog.

Next, we perform a quantitative assessment of the ModInv attack where we use the attack evaluation metric proposed in [17]. This approach uses an evaluation model f_{eval} that has the same network architecture as the one that is under attack f_{attacked}. The reconstructed images that are extracted from the classifier under attack f_{attacked} are evaluated using the evaluation classifier f_{eval} that returns its predictions (either in the form of a likelihood score or most likely target). If the returned label (or the argmax of the likelihood score) is equal to the target label used in the ModInv, then the reconstructed image is considered as *recognizable*.

Table 9.9 ModInv attack parameters against the CIFAR-10 dataset.

	TV regularization	LP-norm regularization	Blur
Attack 1	None	None	False
Attack 2	2	None	False
Attack 3	2	None	True
Attack 4	2	6	False
Attack 5	2	2	True
Attack 6	2	6	True
Attack 7	3	None	False
Attack 8	3	None	True
Attack 9	3	2	False
Attack 10	3	6	False
Attack 11	3	2	True
Attack 12	3	6	True

The evaluation results are presented in Table 9.11. As we see from the results, the best model reconstruction is achieved using Attack 3.

9.3 Membership Inference Attacks

9.3.1 Introduction

A DL classifier is built using a training dataset. Each sample is represented by a set of features F and is labelled as one of the classes, i.e., supervised learning. The deep neural network model is tuned to minimize the classification error probability on the training dataset. DL classifiers have shown to be very effective in many applications, in particular in the image domain. Compared with other ML-based classifiers, DL classifiers usually have better accuracy. Moreover, other ML may have strong requirements on selected features (to represent samples), e.g., a naïve Bayes classifier requires independence among features to achieve good performance in theory. On the other hand, DL-based classifier does not have a strong requirement on selected features. The only requirement is that these features should include all (or most) useful information for classification. DL has the capability to extract this information and then to use this information for classification.

MI attack for a DL-based classifier aims to identify if a given sample is in the training dataset for building the classifier or not. This attack can be a *white-box attack*, i.e., the target classifier is available to the adversary, or a *shadow attack*,

Table 9.10 ModInv reconstructions using different attack parameters against the CIFAR-10 dataset.

<table>
<tr><td>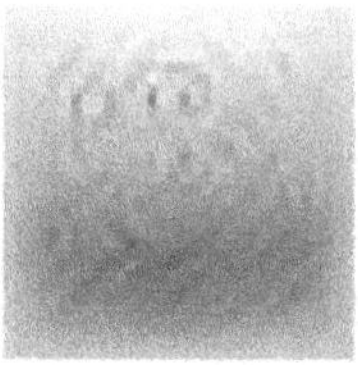
TV None, LP None, Blur False</td><td>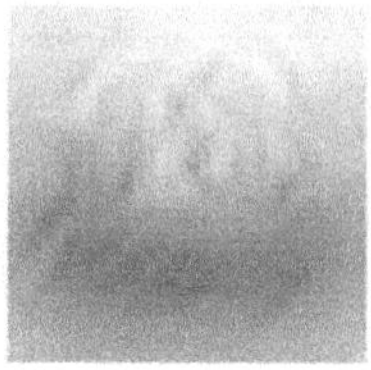
TV 2, LP None, Blur False</td><td>
TV 2, LP None, Blur True</td><td>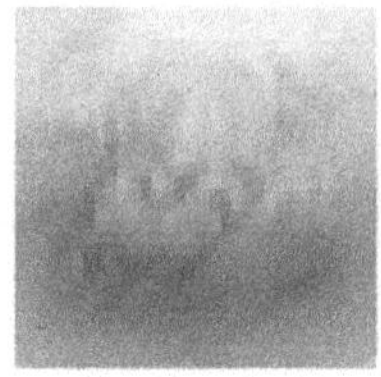
TV 2, LP 6, Blur False</td></tr>
<tr><td>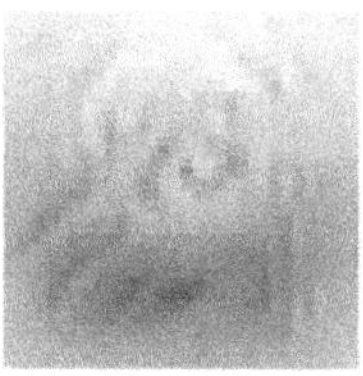
TV 2, LP 2, Blur True</td><td>
TV 2, LP 6, Blur True</td><td>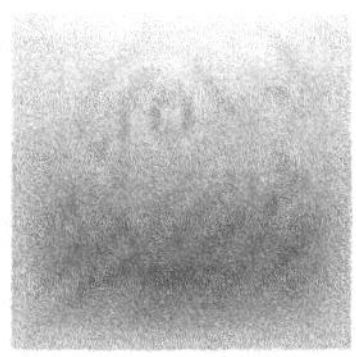
TV 3, LP None, Blur False</td><td>
TV 3, LP None, Blur True</td></tr>
<tr><td>
TV 3, LP 2, Blur False</td><td>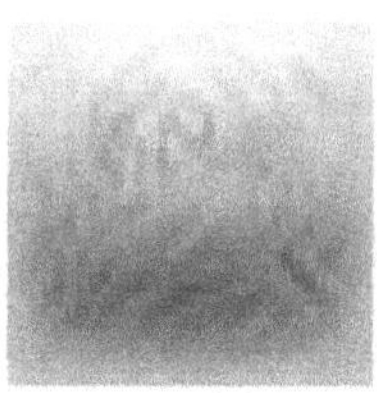
TV 3, LP 6, Blur False</td><td>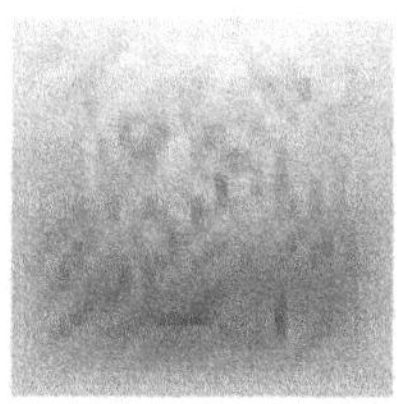
TV 3, LP 2, Blur True</td><td>
TV 3, LP 6, Blur True</td></tr>
</table>

Table 9.11 ModInv success rate via the evaluation method.

	TV regularization	LP-norm regularization	Blur	Success rate
Attack 1	None	None	False	2/10
Attack 2	2	None	False	1/10
Attack 3	**2**	**None**	**True**	**3/10**
Attack 4	2	2	False	1/10
Attack 5	2	6	False	1/10
Attack 6	2	2	True	1/10
Attack 7	2	6	True	1/10
Attack 8	3	None	False	1/10
Attack 9	**3**	**None**	**True**	**2/10**
Attack 10	**3**	**2**	**False**	**2/10**
Attack 11	**3**	**6**	**False**	**2/10**
Attack 12	**3**	**2**	**True**	**2/10**
Attack 13	**3**	**6**	**True**	**2/10**

Source: Adapted from Ref. [17].

i.e., the adversary built a classifier that is similar to the target classifier in an exploratory attack and thus analyze this inferred classifier for MI attack. Previous methods for MI attack are not successful for either white-box or shadow attack and have similar performance as a naïve attack. The adversary applies the target or inferred classifier to predict a label for a given sample. If the predicted label is correct, the adversary claims that this sample is a member of the training data. Otherwise, the adversary claims that this sample is not a member. In short, these attacks inherit the primary limitation of the naïve attack, i.e., there is little useful information to characterize the confidence of classification and no way to effectively calibrate for greater confidence in the results.

To launch an effective MI attack, we consider a general approach as follows. Suppose that features include all (useful, biased, and noisy) information, where useful information in F_u can be used to identify class, biased information F_b is due to the different distributions of training data and general test data, and noisy information F_n is other information with no statistical significance. Note that to simplify the discussion, we assume each feature includes only one type of information. For the general case that one feature includes multiple types of information, we can divide it into multiple features to meet our assumption. DL has the capability to extract useful and biased information and ignore noisy information. Then a classifier is optimized to fit on useful and biased information (F_u and F_b). While fitting on F_u can provide correct classification on general test data, fitting on F_b is called *overfitting*, which provides correct classification on the given training data but wrong classification on general test data.

For both white box attack and shadow attack on MI, overfitting leads to privacy issues as the classifier (or the inferred classifier) "memorizes" certain aspects of the training data in F_b and reflects it in the model's output behavior. Thus, we can infer membership based on overfitting. In particular, if overfitting exists in the training data, some features that are not related to a class may be used for classification. Therefore, a sample with such a feature is likely in the training data. By identifying such features in F_b, we can predict membership and provide a confidence score on such predictions. However, the distribution of training data may not be available, and distribution of general test data is unknown. Thus, features related to overfitting cannot be obtained directly for MI. Since DL models are sensitive to training data, we can study parameters in the target (or inferred) classifier based on local linear approximation for each layer and the combination of all layers. This approach builds a classifier for MI. Unlike the naïve attack, where only an inference result is obtained, the built classifier can also provide a confidence score on the inferred results. The impact of F_b will be examined to verify its impact on MI attack. If a feature is identified in F_b or is likely in F_b, we will study its impact on MI attack. Suppose the normal value of such feature is small. We can either increase the number of samples with a large feature value or increase feature values for these samples with a large feature value. By defining a level for such changes, we can examine the MI attack accuracy as a function of such a level to see the impact of a feature. With the MI attack, we can also design defense schemes by using the built classifier. The first approach aims to fix the distribution in training data such that it has a similar distribution as a general test data. Once the distribution is fixed, there is no overfitting issue, and thus MI attack based on overfitting will not work. The second approach aims to remove biased features F_b. Then a DL classifier will be built on features F_u with useful information only, which does not have overfitting issues either.

9.3.2 General MI Attack Model

In order to rigorously define MI attack, we use a formulation similar to that of Ref. [1]. First, a value, b, is chosen uniformly at random from $\{0, 1\}$. The adversary is then given a point, $(x;\ y)$, sampled from the training set, if $b = 1$, or from the general population, if $b = 0$. Finally, the adversary, given the additional knowledge determined by the threat model, predicts either 1 ($(x;\ y)$ is a member of S) or 0 ($(x;\ y)$ is not a member of S). The accuracy of the MI attack is the probability that the adversary's prediction is equal to b. In simpler terms, we can think of the accuracy of the attack as the fraction of correct inferences on equal-sized samples of the training set and the general population. Because an adversary that guesses randomly would achieve an accuracy of 50%, the literature on MI has occasionally measured the efficacy of a MI attack using advantage, which adjusts for the 50% baseline. The goal of the attacker is primarily to achieve the highest accuracy possible. However, while the accuracy of the attack is an indicator of the degree to which private information is leaked by the model, we also consider precision as a key desideratum for the attacker, as in a practical setting, the attacker may want to assume a high degree of confidence in instances identified by the attack.

9.3.3 Logistic Attack Models

For high-precision inference, it is desirable not only to obtain a binary prediction, but also an associated confidence score that quantifies the certainty of the inference. In this light, we can think of MI as an instance of binary logistic regression, in which we use a logistic, or sigmoid, function to model our confidence with respect to a binary dependent variable (i.e., membership or nonmembership). The sigmoid function, $s\,(x)$, is given as follows: $s\,(x) = \frac{1}{1 + e^{-x}}$. It can be thought of as converting the log-odds of the dependent variable to a probability. The use of the sigmoid function for binary classification is standard in ML.

9.3.4 Overview of the MI Attack

Intuitively, overfitting leaks information about the training data because the model "memorizes" aspects of the training data. Consider how this memorization is manifested in the model. At a high level, the model uses features to distinguish between classes; some features may be discriminative in general, while some may be discriminative only on the training data. The latter can be thought of as evidence for overfitting, because while they may activate and be useful for classifying training examples, they do not generalize to unseen test examples. Similarly, there may also be features that are discriminative on the data in general, but not on the training data.

Consider, for example, a model that learns to recognize the faces of a set of celebrities. Suppose that in reality, each celebrity is wearing sunglasses in exactly 10% of his or her respective pictures. Thus, the presence of sunglasses does not further inform us as to the identity of the celebrity. However, suppose that in the training set used to construct the model, Brad Pitt happened to be wearing sunglasses in 15% of his pictures. The model might then learn to use the presence of sunglasses when predicting that an image is of Brad Pitt. Knowing that the presence of sunglasses is not predictive on the general distribution, we would infer that Brad Pitt must have been more likely to be wearing sunglasses in the model's training set; thus, a picture of Brad Pitt wearing sunglasses would be more likely to be a member of the training set, all other things equal. This highlights the intuition that membership information is leaked via a target model's idiosyncratic use of features. Essentially, features that are distributed differently in the training data from how they are distributed in the general population provide evidence for or against membership.

9.3.5 Naïve Attacks

Surprising efficacy of a naïve attack: By far the simplest and most direct MI attack, which we dub the "naïve" attack, follows from the fact that generalization error necessarily leads to membership vulnerability [18]. Given a data point and its true label, the attacker runs the model and observes whether its predicted label is correct. If it is, the attacker concludes that the point was in the training data; otherwise, the point is presumed to be a nonmember. Surprisingly, in many cases, this works as well as the shadow model attack.

9.3.6 The Threat Models

The adversary in an MI attack must attempt to determine whether a given data point was in the training set, S, of target model, $\hat{g}$. The threat model determines what information is available to the adversary in order to make this determination. We consider two similar threat models, namely, the *white-box* threat model, and the *black-box* threat model. In both threat models, we assume that the adversary has access to a dataset, $\check{S}$, which is also drawn from $\theta^\star$, but is disjoint from S. In other words, the attacker has no a priori knowledge of the training set but has access to a set of points drawn from its underlying distribution. Furthermore, we assume the adversary has knowledge of the training algorithm, A, i.e., the adversary knows the architecture, training routine, and hyperparameters used to train $\hat{g}$. In the white-box threat model, the adversary additionally has knowledge of the learned parameters, W, of the target model. By contrast, the black-box threat model assumes that the adversary only has access to the final outputs of the model, but not the learned parameters (nor the internal activations, when the target model is a deep network).

9.3.7 Naïve Bayes MI

To motivate our formalized intuition, consider two Gaussian distributions, $\theta^\star = \mathcal{N}(\mu^\star, \sigma^\star)$ and $\widehat{\theta} = \mathcal{N}(\mu', \sigma')$. For a real x, x is more likely to have been generated by $\widehat{\theta}$ than by $\theta^\star$ when $\mathcal{N}(x|\mu', \sigma') > \mathcal{N}(x|\mu^\star, \sigma^\star)$. Assuming an equally likely prior probability of being drawn from either distribution, we can then construct a simple model that predicts whether x was drawn from $\hat{\theta}$ rather than $\theta^{\star}$ by solving for x in this inequality. When the variances, $\sigma^{\star}$ and $\hat{\sigma}$ are the same, this produces a linear decision boundary.

Proposition 1: For a linear Softmax model $\hat{g}$ with weights $\widehat{W}$ and intercept $\hat{b}$ and a proxy model $\breve{g}$ with weights $\breve{W}$ and intercept $\breve{b}$, the Bayes optimal MI model m on data that satisfies the Naïve Bayes assumptions is approximately $m^y = s\left(W^{y^T} + b^y\right)$, where $w^y = \widehat{W} - \breve{W}$ and $b^y = \hat{b}_y - \breve{b}_y$.

This proposition gives the weights and intercepts of m^y in terms of only the observable parameters of the target and proxy models, and can be used when the distributions of $\theta^{\star}$ and $\hat{\theta}$ are unknown.

9.3.8 MI in Deep Models

9.3.8.1 MI Attack Algorithm

Suppose a DL-based classifier is used for image classification, e.g., face recognition. MI attack aims to analyze any given sample and predicts whether this sample is within the training file or not. A fundamental assumption is that the training data and the general data have different distributions. Suppose the general distribution is $\theta^{\star}$ and the training data distribution is $\hat{\theta}$. For a given sample x', we can determine the probability of x' is generated by $\theta^{\star}$ (or by $\hat{\theta}$). If $P_{\hat{\theta}}(x') > P_{\theta^{\star}}(x')$, then x' is likely generated by $\hat{\theta}$. Moreover, we can calculate a confidence value for such MI attack result by $\frac{P_{\hat{\theta}}(x')}{P_{\hat{\theta}}(x') + P_{\theta^{\star}}(x')}$. This analysis provides a prediction on any sample if it is in training data or not, along with a confidence value for this prediction. We have the following two observations:

- Although the example is for Gaussian distributions, this analysis holds for any distributions.
- If $\theta^{\star} = \hat{\theta}$, the confidence value is always 0.5, i.e., we cannot make any better prediction than blindly guessing. Thus, the basis of MI attack is the difference between $\theta^{\star}$ and $\hat{\theta}$.

The analysis in the above example, although simple, assumes the knowledge on training data distribution and general data distribution, while the distribution of training data is usually unknown. To launch MI attack, we should not assume the training data distribution. Since the DL classifier is trained on training data, it somehow characterizes the distribution of training data. Similarly, we can build a proxy classifier based on a general dataset, which characterizes the distribution of general data. Then, instead of comparing two distributions, we compare two classifiers to predict if a sample is in the training data or not.

DL-based classifiers can be very complex. We use the following three-step approach to analyze such classifiers:

- Suppose the classifiers are simple linear models. We can have a closed formula for the confidence value on MI attack prediction.
- Suppose the classifiers have only one layer. We can approximate them as linear models to make MI attack predictions.
- For general multilayer (deep) models, we develop an approach to combine the analysis on each layer.

Due to the approximation in the second step, there is an error on the obtained confidence value for the entire process. However, our preliminary results for face recognition show that this approach achieves high accuracy in MI attack, i.e., our approximation is very accurate.

9.3.8.2 Local Linear Approximations of Deep Models

A slice, $\langle g, h \rangle$, is a decomposition of a deep network, f, into two functions, g and h, such that $f = g \circ h$. In layer i of the network, h computes the input to layer i, and g computes the output, beginning at layer i. When we select the slice corresponding to the top layer, g is simply a linear model acting on features, $h(x)$ for $x \in \mathcal{X}$. For arbitrary layers, we use an *influence measure* to get a local linear approximation of g at each point. For a given model, f, and feature, x_j, the *influence*, χ_j, of x_j on f is a quantitative measure of x_j's contribution to the output of f. In the literature, there is a growing body of work on the influence measure (e.g., Refs. [19–21]) that provides many choices for χ, each with different properties. Here, we consider the *internal influence* definition in Ref. [19] as it generalizes to internal variables. Internal influence for a *distribution of interest P* specifies a distribution of points that the measure is evaluated on $x_j(g \circ h, P) = \int_{x \in \mathcal{X}} \left.\frac{\partial g}{\partial h(x)_j}\right|_{h(x)} P(x)dx$. When h is used as a preprocessing step such that $z = h(x)$, in this case, P' is a distribution over the internal points z that can be expressed as $x_j(g \circ h, P) = \int_{z \in h(\mathcal{X})} \left.\frac{\partial g}{\partial z_j}\right|_{z} P'(z)dz$.

There are two properties of internal influence that we leverage:

1. **Linear agreement:** For linear models, the influence of feature x_j is simply the corresponding weight, W_j. Linear agreement allows us to use influence in place of the weights in equations defined in Proposition 1 while obtaining the same result.
2. **Efficient influence score:** For an internal point, $z = h(x)$, when we set P' to $P^z(z_0)$, the uniform distribution over the linear interpolation from baseline, z^0, to z, internal influence is efficient with respect to baseline, z^0, that satisfies $\sum_j \chi_j(g \circ h, P')\left(z_j - z_j^0\right) = g(z) - g(z^0)$.

This property helps locally approximate $\overline{g}$ at z as $\overline{g}(z) = \overline{W}^T z + \overline{b}$, where $\overline{W} = \chi\left(g \circ h, P_0^z\right)$ and $b = g(0)$. We can approximate an arbitrary layer of a deep network by approximating the remainder of the network as a linear model.

9.3.8.3 Deep Bayesian MI Attack

We present the deep Bayesian MI attack in Table 9.12. The algorithm can be applied to an arbitrary layer of a DNN by replacing the weights with their *natural generalization influence*. As influence allows to create a local linear approximation of the model at a point z, the results in a generalized attack. When we combine the influences of multiple layers in a DNN, the resulting attack utilizes the information form all the layers of a DNN and is much stronger.

9.3.8.4 MI Attack on All Layers

We combine the influences of multiple layers in a DNN. We make use of a meta model, which learns how to combine the confidences of an individual attack on each layer. Essentially, the meta model takes the confidences of the attack on each layer as input and outputs a single decision. To train a meta model, m', to attack target model, f, we partition $\widehat{S}$ into two parts, $\widehat{S}_{\text{in}}$ and $\widehat{S}_{\text{out}}$. We train a target model, f_{in}, on $\widehat{S}_{\text{in}}$, and a proxy model, f_{out}, on $\widehat{S}_{\text{out}}$. For each layer, i, in f, we train an attack model, m_i, on the ith layer of f_{in} using f_{out} as a proxy model for the attack. For each class, c, in $\widehat{S}$, we construct a training set, $\widehat{S}'^c = \widehat{S}'^c_{\text{in}} \cup \widehat{S}'^c_{\text{out}}$, such that $(x', y') \in \widehat{S}'^c_{\text{in}} = \left(m_j^c(x), 1\right)$ for $(x, c) \in \widehat{S}_{\text{in}}$, and $\left(x'_j, y'\right) \in \widehat{S}'^c_{\text{out}} = \left(m_j^c(x), 0\right)$ for $(x, c) \in \widehat{S}_{\text{out}}$. We can increase the size of $\widehat{S}'$ by creating multiple random partitions of $\widehat{S}$. Finally, we train m'^c on $\widehat{S}'^c$. The resulting attack utilizes the information from all the layers of a DNN and is much stronger.

Table 9.12 The deep Bayesian membership attack algorithm.

def create_attack_model $\left(\widehat{g} \circ \widehat{h}, \widehat{S}\right)$:
$\widehat{S}' = [(h(x), y) \text{ for } (x, y) \in \widehat{S}]$
$\widehat{g} = trainProxy\left(\widehat{S}'\right)$
$w^y = \lambda(z) : \chi\left(\widehat{g} \circ \widehat{h}, P_0^z\right)_y - \chi\left(\widehat{g} \circ \widehat{h}, P_0^z\right)_y$ for all $y \in C$
$b^y = \widehat{g}(0)_y - \widehat{g}(0)_y$ for all $y \in C$
return $\lambda(x, y) : s\left(w^y \left(\widehat{h}(x)\right)^T \widehat{h}(x) + b^y\right)$
def predict_membership (m, x, y) :
return 1 if $m^y(x) > 1/2$ else 0.

9.3.9 Differentially Private Stochastic Gradient Descent for Privacy

The privacy concern on DL is whether we can analyze a DL model and obtain some knowledge on the training data to build such a DL model. DP is a framework to ensure privacy, which requires that the trained DL model should not be changed a lot by any single sample (or a small number of samples). Stochastic gradient descent (SGD) is a widely used approach to update a DL model, which considers a batch of training samples and updates the DL model by the gradient of the loss. It has the following steps:

1. Sample a minibatch of training points $(x,\ y)$, where x is an input and y is a label.
2. Compute loss (i.e., error) $L_\theta\ (x, y)$ between the model's prediction $f_\theta\ (x)$ and label y, where θ represents the model parameters.
3. Compute gradient of the loss $L_\theta\ (x, y)$ with respect to the model parameters θ.
4. Multiply these gradients by the learning rate and apply the product to update model parameters θ.

To achieve DP, we need to make two changes in the above procedure: (1) gradients should be bounded to avoid large change on model due to a small number of samples, and (2) some random noise should be added to gradients to make it statistically impossible to determine whether a sample is in training data. Therefore, the above procedure is revised as follows [22]:

1. Sample a minibatch of training points $(x,\ y)$, where x is an input and y is a label.
2. Compute loss (i.e., error) $L_\theta\ (x, y)$ between the model's prediction $f_\theta\ (x)$ and label y, where θ represents the model parameters.
3. Compute the gradient of the loss $L_\theta\ (x, y)$ with respect to the model parameters θ.
4. Clip gradients, per training example included in the minibatch, to ensure each gradient has a Euclidean norm no more than a given upper bound.
5. Add random noise to the clipped gradients.
6. Multiply these gradients by the learning rate and apply the product to update model i.

There are three important metrics for DP, which are defined as follows:

- δ bounds the probability of our privacy guarantee not being held. It does not need to be too small. We can set it to be less than the inverse of the training data size.

- ϵ measures the strength of our privacy guarantee. In the case of differentially private ML, it gives an upper bound on how much the probability of a particular model output can vary by including (or removing) a single training example.
- σ denotes the standard deviation of the Gaussian noise that is added to the clipped gradients in the DP-SGD algorithm to ensure DP.

For different values of δ and σ, we calculate ϵ that measure our privacy guarantee. The results are given in Table 9.13.

9.3.10 Design Defense Approaches for MI Attack

We aim to design defense schemes by using the built classifier for MI attack. Since MI attack is based on overfitting, our defense scheme aims to remove overfitting by changing either training data or deep neural network. Note that the reason for overfitting is the different distributions in training data and a general test data. The first approach aims to fix the distribution in training data such that it has a similar distribution as a general test data. We can apply the MI attack classifier on all training data. If a sample is identified as a member with high confidence $m^y(x)$, it is likely that this sample contributes overfitting in the training data. We can set a threshold τ on confidence and remove any samples with confidence larger than τ to make the training data similar to a general test data. Once the distribution is fixed, there is no overfitting issue and thus MI attack based on overfitting will not work. The second approach aims to remove biased information in F_b. As we discussed, we can analyze the input to any layer and identify features that play an important role in F_b. We can limit that the DL classifier will be built on features not in these features and thus remove the impact of overfitting. We apply the above two approaches and then check whether MI attack is still successful with such defense schemes.

Table 9.13 DP performance under different noise levels.

$\delta = 10^{-5}$		$\delta = 5 \cdot 10^{-6}$		$\delta = 10^{-6}$	
σ	ϵ	σ	ϵ	σ	ϵ
2	1.33	2	1.37	2	1.45
4	0.62	4	0.64	4	0.68
6	0.41	6	0.42	6	0.45

9.3.11 Membership Privacy in ML

With ML as a service (MLaaS), owners of models and training data are considered intellectual property, and their copyright should be protected. In this problem, the models or the training procedures need to be trusted so that no secret information about the training data is leaked into the model; when the model is deployed, an adversary cannot retrieve the training membership information. The data owner tries to minimize the accuracy of the best black-box MI attack against the model, while trying to maximize the model's classification accuracy as a utility. This problem can be formalized as a min–max game such that for a given membership privacy guarantee, we can find a model that achieves the highest accuracy level. Nasr et al. [23], proposed a mechanism to mitigate the membership leakage through training with provable guarantees. They defined an optimization problem to jointly maximize the privacy (or minimization of the inference attack) and classification accuracy. Their results on CIFAR100 and other datasets show that privacy can be achieved at a small degradation in accuracy. The goal is to make the model's predictions on its training data to be indistinguishable from its predictions on other data points from the same data distribution. Their approach relies on training a ML model with provable guarantees on membership privacy.

Defender: Let $f : X \rightarrow Y$ denote the classifier that we want to protect, where X denotes the data distribution and $y \in Y$ denotes a label. The classifier f is trained using a training dataset $D : D \subset X \times Y$ using an expected empirical loss $L_D(f) = \frac{1}{|D|} \sum_{(x,y) \in D} l(f(x), y)$, where $l(f(x), y)$ denotes a real-valued loss function. A typical loss function is the cross-entropy function that is defined as $l(f(x), y) = \sum_i \beta_i \log y_i$, where β_i is a binary indicator function that is 1 if the sample x_i belongs to the class β_i, and y_i is the neural network's prediction.

Attacker: The attacker has access to some of the training dataset. The attacker also has a black-box access to the classifier. The attacker wants to maximize the inference on membership. The attacker compares the released statistics from the dataset and the same statistics computed on random samples from the population, to see which one is closer to the target data record. The attacker defines an inference model h, $h : X \times Y^2 \rightarrow [0, 1]$. For any data point (x, y) and model's prediction vector $f(x)$, the inference model outputs the probability of (x, y) being a member of the training dataset D. Consider two disjoint datasets D^A and D'^A, which are sampled according to the probability distribution of the data points inside the training dataset and outside the training dataset, respectively. For example, the dataset of the attacker D^A could be a subset of the target training dataset D known to the adversary.

The empirical calculation of the inference attack gain is then mathematically represented as $G_{f,D^A,D'^A}(h) = \frac{1}{2|D^A|} \sum_{(x,y) \in D^A} \log(h(x, y, f(x))) +$

$\frac{1}{2|D'^A|}\sum_{(x',y')\in D'^A} \log(h(x', y', f(x')))$. Thus, the optimization problem for the MI attack is to maximize the empirical gain as follows: $\max_h G_{f,D^A,D'^A}(h)$, for a target classification model f. In a black-box access type for the attacker, the attacker can train on a shadow model with the same model type, architecture, and objective function as the model f using data records sampled from $\Pr(X, Y)$. The inference attack model is presented in Figure 9.26.

Min–max membership privacy game: In this framework, the objective of the data owner (defender) is to develop and protect a ML system that anticipates the best attacker that wants to infer if a training sample is used in the training or not. As the defender wants to provide a protection mechanism and the attacker, on the other hand, wants to infer the membership privacy, this problem is cast as a *min–max game* where the final model achieves the highest accuracy level for a given protection. The privacy objective of the classification model is to minimize the privacy loss with respect to the worst-case (maximum inference gain) attack. The joint privacy and classification objectives can be formulated as the following min-max problem:

$$\min_f L_D(f) + \lambda \max_{\mathrm{h}} G_{f,D,D'}(h),$$

where h is the attacker's inference model, D is the training dataset, and D' is the attacker's dataset. The inner maximization finds the strongest inference model h against a given classification model f, while the outer minimization finds the strongest defense classification model f against a given inference model h. The inference attack term is multiplied by λ that acts as a regularizer for the classification model. This way, the classifier model prevents itself from adapting to the

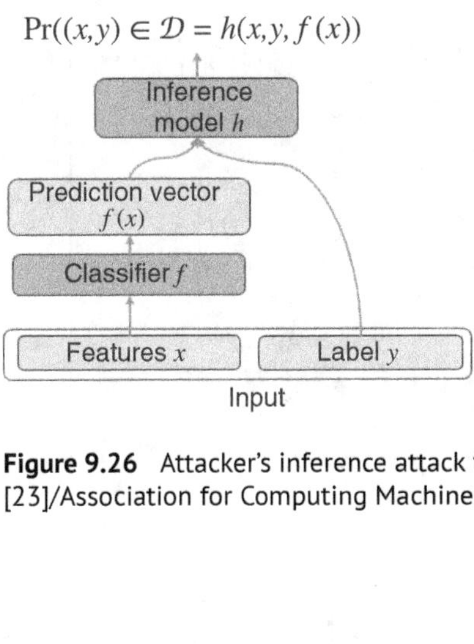

Figure 9.26 Attacker's inference attack to build the inference model ***h***. *Source*: [23]/Association for Computing Machinery/Public Domain.

training data at the cost of leaking information about the training data. These two conflicting optimizations need to be solved jointly to find the equilibrium point. The training involves two datasets: the training set D and a disjoint reference set D' that is similar to D but different and contains samples form $\Pr(X, Y)$. The proposed approach in [23] is presented in Table 9.14. The parameters of the classification model f and inference model h are represented with θ and w, respectively. Each training epoch includes k steps of finding the beset inference attack model h and finding the best defensive classification model against h.

For a given classification model f, let p_f denote the probability distribution of its output (prediction vector) on its training data D and p'_f denote that of any data points outside the training dataset. Using this notation, given that the training set is samples from the underlying probability distribution $\Pr(X, y)$ to build an attack that only depends on the predictions of the model, the optimal inference model can be represented as $h_f(x, f, f(x)) = \frac{p_f(f(x))}{p_f(f(x)) + p'_f(f(x))}$.

We can interpret this equation as the best strategy of the adversary is to determine the membership by comparing the probability of the prediction $f(x)$ that comes from the distribution p_f or alternatively from p'_f. The defense strategy is presented in Figure 9.27. The game-theoretic framework allows explicitly incorporate accuracy explicitly into the min-max optimization such that the cost of achieving privacy in the defense is minimized. In such a framework, the privacy loss is minimized against the strongest attacker. There are two deep neural network

Table 9.14 Training algorithm for ML with membership privacy.

For number of training epochs do

For k steps do

Randomly sample a mini-batch of m training data points $\{(x_i, y_i)\}_{i=1}^m$ from the training dataset D.

Randomly sample a mini-batch of m reference data points $\{(x'_i, y'_i)\}_{i=1}^m$ from the reference dataset D'.

Update the inference model h by ascending its stochastic gradient of its parameters w using

$$\nabla_w \frac{\lambda}{2m}\left(\sum_{i=1}^{m} \log(h(x_i, y_i, f(x_i))) + \sum_{i=1}^{m} \log\left(1 - h\left(x'_i, y'_i, f\left(x'_i\right)\right)\right)\right).$$

End For

Randomly sample a new mini-batch of m training points $\{(x_i, y_i)\}_{i=1}^m$ from D.

Update the classification model f by descending its stochastic gradients over its parameters.

$$\nabla_\theta \frac{1}{m}\sum_{i=1}^{m} (l(f(x_i, y_i)) + \lambda \log(h(x_i, y_i, f(x_i)))).$$

End For

architectures to consider. The first network is the defender's network (the classifier under attack) and the latter is the inference attack model. For the defender's network, we consider a DenseNet architecture [24], with bottleneck layers of Refs. [6, 12, 16, 19] and growth rate of $k = 12$. Note that in the DenseNet architecture, $H_l(\cdot)$ denotes a composite function of three consecutive operations: (1) Batch normalization, (2) Rectified linear unit (ReLU) activation, and (3) 3×3 convolution. If each function $H_l(\cdot)$ produces k feature maps, it follows that the lth layer has $k_0 + k(l-1)$ input feature maps, where k_0 is the number of channels in the input layer. The DenseNet architecture can have narrow layers, $k = 12$, and this is referred to as the *growth rate* of the network. To train the network, we used the ADAM optimizer with a learning rate of $1e^{-4}$ and utilized the categorical cross-entropy function as the objective function. For the inference model, attacker uses the model in Figure 9.28. The inference model network h is trained using the MSE loss and ADAM optimizer with a step size of 10^{-4}.

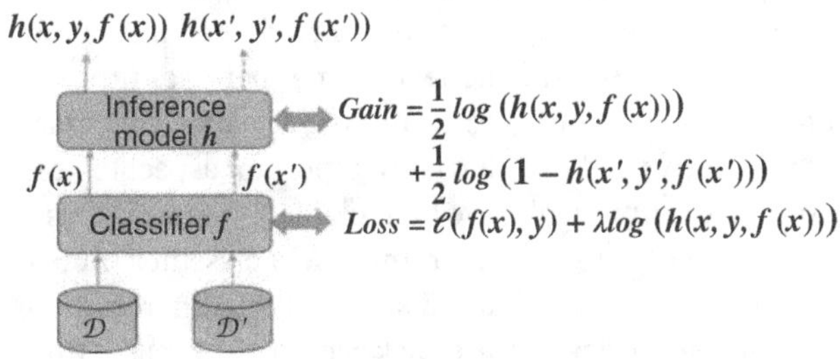

Figure 9.27 Classification loss and inference gain in the min–max defense strategy. *Source*: [23]/Association for Computing Machinery/Public Domain.

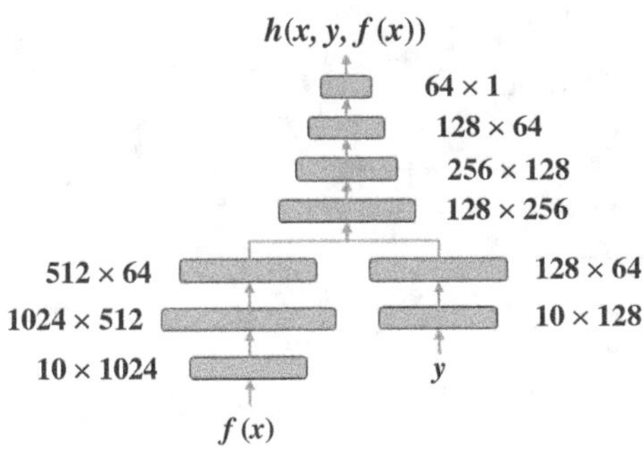

Figure 9.28 Attacker's inference attack to build the inference model ***h***.

9.3.11.1 Evaluation Results Using CIFAR-10 Dataset

The MI attack and defense approaches are evaluated using the CIFAR-10 dataset [15]. The CIFAR-10 dataset consists of 10 labels, namely, the categories of plane, car, bird, cat, deer, dog, frog, horse, ship, and truck. The training set consists of 50K samples, and it is divided into two sets, one for training the classifier D and one for the adversary to train on D'. The test set consists of 10K samples. We investigate different membership privacy regularization factors. In particular, we focused on $\lambda = [0,\ 0.1,\ 0.5,\ 1,\ 5,\ 10]$ in order to understand and characterize the trade-offs. Our results, presented in Table 9.15, demonstrate that as λ increases, test accuracy decreased, which comes at the benefit of decrease of the attacker's gain. We emphasize these take-away messages from the above results as follows:

1. **Attacker's gain depends on the dataset:** The attacker's gain is 67.6% on Purchase100, 63% on Texas100, and 54.5% on the CIFAR100 dataset, respectively.
2. **Attacker's gain depends on the references set size:** Depending on the size of the reference set size, the accuracy of the attacker changed. As more samples are added to the reference set, the model becomes better at properly representing the underlying distribution. For this reason, the attack accuracy converges to 50%, which is purely random. This is an important aspect to keep in mind while testing our algorithms against MI attacks such that more data does not mean a better classifier for the attacker. Instead, a classifier trained on a smaller dataset is better as its underlying distribution is different than the population's distribution. Numerically, the attack accuracy decreases from 59.2% down to 50.6% as the reference set size is increased from 1,000 samples to 30,000 samples.
3. **Attacker's gain depends on the regularization parameter λ:** As expected, the privacy regularization parameter λ determines the trade-off between the test accuracy of the defender and attacker's accuracy (as the price

Table 9.15 Highest test accuracy versus regularization parameter λ.

Regularization parameter λ	Test accuracy
0	69.32
0.1	69.93
0.5	69.54
1	69.66
5	68.13
10	67.13

to be paid for privacy). For example, for $\lambda = 0$, the test accuracy is 80.1% and attack accuracy is 67.6%. As λ increases to 10, the test accuracy goes down to 70.1% and attacker's gain becomes 50.6%. This means that privacy (of random guess) came at the cost of 10% drop in the accuracy.

9.3.11.2 Demonstration of MI Attack on a Classifier Trained on the xView Dataset

Next, we train an aircraft classifier using the xView dataset [25] with the labels of Fixed-wing Aircraft, Small Aircraft, Cargo Plane, Helicopter, and Helipad targets, which are cropped from the xView dataset and rescaled them to 64 × 64. We split the data into 80% for training and 20% for testing. On the training set, we performed classical image transformations of rotations, noise, brightness, and contrast adjustments. This augmentation step helped improve the classifier performance and increased the samples for training. Example aircraft images are in Figure 9.29.

We trained a CNN with the architecture presented in Table 9.16. For the MI test, the training set was divided into private training that the defender used for training and reference dataset that the attacker used for training. The test set was the hold-out set where we evaluated the results. We used 4,707 samples for training and 293 test samples. We use a small set of samples for the attacker (242 samples) and used the remaining (4,465 samples) to train the defender network. For training the neural network, we used categorical loss. We used the ADAM optimizer using a learning rate of 10^{-3}. We measured the test accuracy of the classifier and the attacker's gain. When $\lambda = 0$, the classifier did not have any regularization. For $\lambda \geq 0$, classifiers used different regularization values. We expect that as the

Figure 9.29 Sample images from each label in the Aircrafts.

Table 9.16 CNN classifier for aircrafts.

For ii: 1 – 5:
1. 2D-Conv layer with 32*ii filters, kernel size: 4 × 4, stride of 2 × 2, and Padding. 2. Batch normalization 3. ReLU activation
Linear layer connecting 2048 neurons to 64 neurons ReLU activation Linear layer connecting 64 neurons to 5 neurons

regularization parameter λ increases, the test accuracy incurred a penalty and decreased, but it also decreased the attacker's advantage.

Table 9.17 presents the results when the attacker uses 10% of the training data and the defender uses 90% of the training data. We observe that when there is no regularization, the test accuracy is 98.43%, but the MI attack is 90.23% that indicates a very critical vulnerability. As we increase the regularization to $\lambda = 10$, the test accuracy of the defender slightly decreases down to 92.18 while the attacker's gain significantly reduces to 59.95%. The last parameter that we investigated was the portion of the data that the attacker uses. For this study, we increased the attacker's training data size to 20% of the training data and measured the same parameters. Table 9.18 presents the results when the attacker used a larger dataset of 20% of the training population. As we expected, when the reference set size is increased, the difference between the classifier and underlying population decreases, which reduced the success of the attack. When $\lambda = 0$ (no defense), the attacker's gain was 79.94%. As λ increases to $\lambda = 10$, the attacker's gain reduced to 58.07%.

9.3.11.3 Evaluation on MI Attacks Using the xView Dataset

We tested MI attack on aircrafts in the xView dataset. The empirical calculation of the inference attack gain is $G_{f,D^A,D'^A}(h) = \frac{1}{2|D^A|}\sum_{(x,y)\in D^A} \log(h(x,y,f(x))) + \frac{1}{2|D'^A|}\sum_{(x',y')\in D'^A} \log(h(x',y',f(x')))$, where datasets D^A and D'^A are sampled according to the probability distribution of the data points inside the training dataset and outside the training dataset, respectively. Given that training data is limited, and general data is unlimited, we can approximate D'^A by samples from general data. However, it is challenging to build D^A. Thus, we studied the impact of imperfect D^A on MI attack. For this study, we build D^A by adding noise to samples from training data. For each pixel, there is a vector of three numbers in [0, 1] for RBG colors. The noise level at each pixel is measured by the norm-2 distance between two vectors. Results for different noise levels are shown in Table 9.19. Larger noise level reduces classification accuracy. But it also increases attack accuracy.

Table 9.17 Attacker's gain for different λ values when attacker uses 10% of population.

λ	Attacker's gain (%)	Test accuracy (%)
0	90.23	98.43
1	66.21	98.43
5	58.79	95.31
10	59.96	92.18

Table 9.18 Attacker's gain for different λ values when attacker uses 20% of population.

λ	Attacker's gain (%)	Test accuracy (%)
0	79.94	95.31
1	63.08	96.09
5	60.48	89.06
10	58.07	83.59

Table 9.19 The impact of noise level.

Noise	Classification accuracy (%)	Attack accuracy (%)
0	61.33	50.00
0.01	80.47	64.00
0.10	73.05	74.00
0.20	39.45	87.00

9.3.11.4 Evaluation of MI Attack to Transformations

In the MI attack, the attackers ask the question if this sample (e.g., image) is used in the training of the classifier under attack. From the defender's perspective, being robust against such privacy attacks is important, it is also critical to understand what happens if the attacker queries an image that is similar but not exactly the same as a sample in the training set. Can the defense mechanism still provide privacy for such cases? From an operational perspective, if the classifier that we want to defend is trained on sensitive images (e.g., targets/objects of a red force), the attacker may query an image that is of the same target but collected at a slightly different angle, orientation, or light condition. Under this condition, the defender wants to know how privacy-aware its classifier is. To answer these questions, we used this defense framework and performed evaluations. In Section 9.3.11.5, we implemented different image transformations applied to the images in the training data and quantified how the MI attack result changed. From the operation point of view, if the attacker collected the image under different spatial conditions (brighter day, different angle, etc.), then how much privacy will leak about the model.

9.3.11.5 Demonstration of Robustness Evaluation of the MI Attacks Against Classical Image Transformations

Consider the classical image transformations listed in Table 9.20. We start with an image with a high confidence inferred by the attack that the image is in the training dataset. We then perform each image transformation and record the attacker model's output.

Figures 9.30–9.32 show the image transformations and the corresponding inference output at the attacker model. In particular, blurring, brightness, rotation, and contrast transformations are investigated. We also present the MI output of the attacker on the original image for comparison.

Our results summarized in Table 9.21 suggest the following:

- Blurring transformation has negligible effect on the attacker's model. This is an expected result, as the original image and blurred image can be very close to each other in the feature space.

Table 9.20 List of studied image transformations.

Image transformation
Blur
Brightness: 50%, 75%, 125%, 150%, 175%
Rotation: 5°, 10°, 15°, 45°, 90°, 135°
Contrast: 50%, 150%, 250%

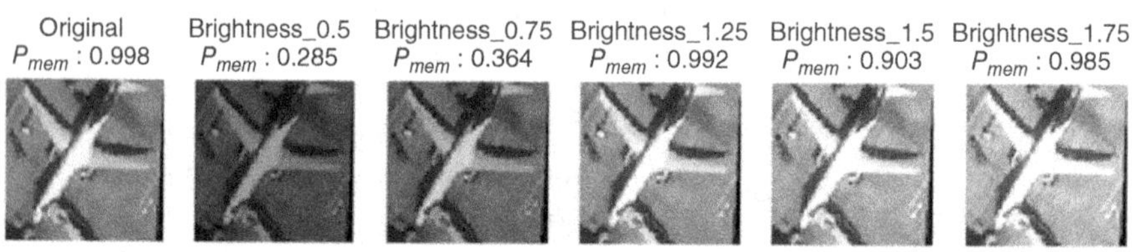

Figure 9.30 Different amounts of brightness transformation applied to an image in the training data and the corresponding MI attack outputs are shown.

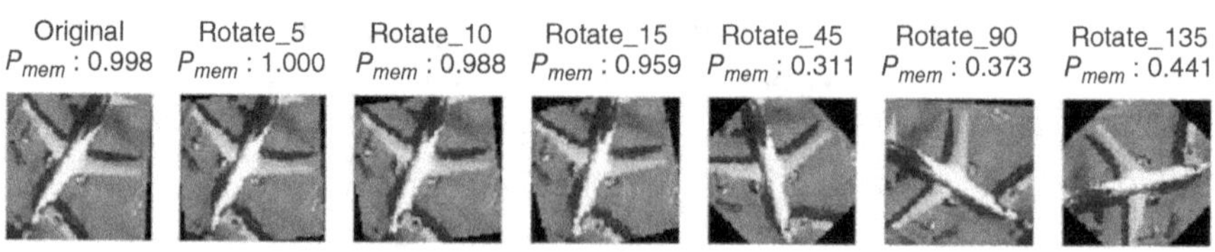

Figure 9.31 Different amounts of rotation applied to an image in the training data and the corresponding MI attack outputs are shown.

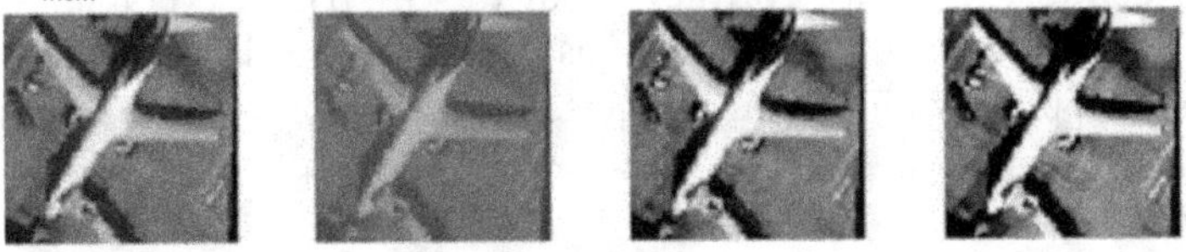

Figure 9.32 Different amounts of contrast transformation applied to an image in the training data and the corresponding MI attack outputs are shown.

Table 9.21 Image transformation factors and corresponding MI probability.

Transformation	Factor	Attacker's MI probability (%)
Original image		99.8
Blur		97.6
Brightness	50%	28.5
	75%	36.4
	125%	99.2
	150%	90.3
	175%	98.5
Rotation	5	100
	10	98.8
	15	95.9
	45	31.1
	90	37.3
	135	44.1
Contrast	50%	37.4
	150%	100
	250%	100

- For the brightness transformation, we observe that, on one hand, as the brightness of the image increases, so does the attacker's success. On the other hand, while the image gets darker, privacy risk decreases, and attacker's inference degrades.
- For the rotations, as the rotation increases, attacker's inference degrades significantly. From an operation perspective, this is an advantage for the defender such that the attacker needs to find the approximate rotation of the image to test; otherwise, the inference result would be misleading for the attacker. For example, at 90° rotation, membership probability reduces from 99.8 to 37.3%.

- For the contrast operation, we observe that those transformations that increase the contrast leak more privacy about the MI. This is very similar to brightness transformations such that as the image gets darker, model becomes more robust, while as image gets lighter, attacker gains more advantage.

9.4 Federated Learning

FL is a learning scheme that leaves the training data distributed on mobile devices to protect the privacy of users and learns a shared model by aggregating locally computed updates. The learning process improves the shared model in each round, by using update information from its clients (either aggregating from all clients or a subset of clients). FL is designed as follows:

- Each client updates the DL model based on its own training data. Denote the matrix of current model parameters as W_t and the matrix of updated model parameters by client i as W_t^i. Deep neural networks can be modeled as a matrix of parameters by letting parameters for each layer as one row (or column).
- Each client sends the update $H_t^i = W_t^i - W_t$ to a server.
- The server aggregates all updates H_t^i as H_t and updates the DL model as $W_{t+1} = W_t + \eta_t H_t$. Note that H_t can be an average or a weighted average of H_t^i and the learning rate η_t can be simple as 1.

Note that FL does not require a client to send its training data to the server, which reduces the communication overhead and ensures privacy. Moreover, an update H_t^i can be (or can be approximated as) a low-rank matrix. Thus, it can be compressed and transmitted with a lower communication overhead. The low-rank property can be explicitly exploited by specifying some random mask, i.e., we limit some elements to zero. This random mask changes over rounds such that all parameters can be updated eventually. Another approach to reduce communication overhead is quantization. That is, instead of transmitting floating numbers for each element in H_t^i, we can quantize them as some discrete values to reduce the number of bits for H_t^i. If we limit each element's values as one of the four values, each element can be described by two bits. FL protects privacy at three levels:

1. There is no local training data to be sent to the server. Thus, an attacker cannot get local data by overhearing.
2. Updated model W_t^i includes information on local data. However, W_t^i is not sending to the server. Thus, an attacker cannot get W_t^i by overhearing.

3. Even the difference H_t^i on previous and new models is not transmitted completely (due to the low-rank operation such as random mask). Thus, even if an attacker overhears the transmitted version of H_t^i and obtains the previous model W_t, it cannot recover W_t^i.

The earlier works of Abadi et al. [26] that showed DP-SGD provides theoretical DP guarantees to neural networks and is considered as a de facto algorithm to training neural networks with privacy guarantees. The random algorithm is the neural network training and guarantees will be measured with respect to the training data. This way, the DP guarantees that we provide measures the robustness against the membership attacks. An algorithm is said to be DP if its behavior is indistinguishable on two datasets that only differ by only one sample [27]. A training algorithm A is said to be (ϵ, δ)-DP if it satisfies the following property for two datasets (d, d') that differ by only one sample and all possible subsets $S \subset Range\,(A)$: $\Pr(A(d) \in S) \leq e^{\epsilon} \Pr(A(d') \in S) + \delta$, where δ is a small probability. The parameter ϵ stands for the privacy guarantee. A smaller ϵ indicates a stronger privacy guarantee. The DP-SGD algorithm uses the algorithm in Table 9.22.

9.4.1 Federated Learning Implementation

We use Google's TensorFlow Federated (TFF). Ideally, it would be best (in terms of accuracy and convergence) to use updates from all clients. However, the overhead of collecting updates from all clients is high, and the availability of the client updates may not be ready. Moreover, if the data collection time is large, the collected information may be outdated. Thus, the number of clients that provide updates in each round can be set as a parameter of federated learning (FL),

Table 9.22 Differentially private Stochastic Gradient Descent (DP-SGD) algorithm.

Input: Examples $\{x_1, \ldots, x_N\}$, loss function $\mathcal{L}(\theta) = \frac{1}{N}\sum_i \mathcal{L}(\theta, \boldsymbol{x}_i)$, learning rate η_t, noise scale σ, group size L, gradient norm bound C.
Output: θ_t and overall privacy cost (ϵ, δ) using a privacy accounting method

- Initialize θ_0 randomly.
- For t in [T] do
  - Take a random sample L_t with sampling probability L/N
  - Compute gradient for each $i \in L_t$, compute $\boldsymbol{g}_t(\boldsymbol{x}_i) = \nabla_{\theta_t}\mathcal{L}(\theta_t, \boldsymbol{x}_i)$
  - Clip gradient $\overline{\boldsymbol{g}}_t(\boldsymbol{x}_i) = \boldsymbol{g}_t(\boldsymbol{x}_i) + \max\left(1, \frac{\|\boldsymbol{g}_t(\boldsymbol{x}_i)\|_2}{C}\right)$
  - Add noise $\widetilde{\boldsymbol{g}}_t(\boldsymbol{x}_i) = \frac{1}{L}\left(\sum_i \overline{\boldsymbol{g}}_t(\boldsymbol{x}_i) + \mathcal{N}(0, \sigma^2 C^2 \boldsymbol{I})\right)$
  - Descent $\theta_{t+1} = \theta_t - \eta_t \widetilde{\boldsymbol{g}}_t$

in addition to other parameters in the training and in the optimizer. Thus, the number of clients that provide updates in each round can be set as a parameter of FL, in addition to other parameters in the training and in the optimizer. In terms of aggregation, there are two approaches:

- Local aggregation: This level of aggregation includes multiple batches of examples that are owned by the same client. The local statistics (e.g., the average loss, accuracy, etc.) will be updated locally as it iterates over the client's data stream.
- Federated aggregation: This level of aggregation includes the updates across multiple clients. The statistics include the model parameters that are being aggregated across clients as well as metrics in the model as a result of local aggregation.

In terms of parameters, the batch sizes, number of users that are collaborating, epochs, and learning rates in the federal learning training affect the system performance. We focus on the privacy aspects of FLwith DP when we have access to all the data available. Therefore, we compare the following two cases:

- Case 1: The central processor has access to all the available data and trains a model using these.
- Case 2: The system applies FL (with local aggregation and federated aggregation).

9.4.2 Aircraft Classification in the xView Dataset Using FL

We use the xView dataset and trained an aircraft classifier using FL. We consider five target types in aircrafts category, namely, the fixed-wing aircraft, small aircraft, cargo plane, helicopter, and helipad. In each tiff file, we crop the respective target out and rescale to a 64 × 64 image. We ended up with 1,457 samples. The class distributions are as follows: Fixed-wing Aircraft: 91 samples, Small Aircraft: 500 samples, Cargo Plane: 497 samples, Helicopter: 164 samples, and Helipad: 205 samples. Figure 9.33 shows a sample image from each label in the aircraft's category.

Figure 9.33 Sample images from each label in the aircraft category.

For the training-test data split, 80% of samples are allocated for training and 20% are reserved for test. For the training samples, we performed classical image augmentations to increase the classifier accuracy. In particular, rotations, brightness, and contrast augmentations are performed. This has increased training samples from 1,164 samples to 6,984 samples. Our hold-out test set includes 293 samples.

We used a deep CNN architecture for classification, consisting of multiple convolutional, pooling, and fully connected layers. The network begins with two convolutional layers, each with 128 filters of size (5 × 5), a stride of (1 × 1), and ReLU activation. This is followed by a max-pooling layer with a (2 × 2) filter. Next, two convolutional layers with 256 filters of size (3 × 3) and ReLU activation are applied, followed by another max-pooling layer. The network continues with two additional convolutional layers, each with 512 filters of size (3 × 3) and ReLU activation, followed by a final max-pooling layer. After flattening the output, a fully connected layer maps the features to 256 neurons, followed by a second fully connected layer reducing the dimensionality to 128 neurons with ReLU activation and a dropout of 0.25. A third fully connected layer projects back to 256 neurons, followed by another dropout layer with a probability of 0.25. Finally, the output layer maps to 5 neurons corresponding to target classes, using a Softmax activation function for classification. ADAM optimizer is used with a learning rate of 0.001 for 100 epochs. Early stopping is used if the validation accuracy does not improve for 10 epochs. The test accuracy is 86.35%.

During federated learning training, for each round, we perform the local updates using the client data and aggregate them. We pass the weights of the global model in the iterative process object to an evaluation model classifier to evaluate the performance at each round. For the parameters used in FL, we create 20 clients with 100 batches and train for 100 epochs. The client uses the ADAM optimizer with a learning rate of 0.001, and server uses the SGD with a learning rate of 0.1. For the FL framework, we consider 20 clients, each with a batch size of 20, and have performed FL for 400 epochs. The clients use SGD optimizer with a learning rate of 0.02. Figure 9.34 presents the classification accuracy of the FL model. We observe that the federated model quickly reaches 96.31% test accuracy in 30 epochs and oscillates around that level for a long time. The reason for sudden drops at epochs between 200 and 300 can be attributed to the fact that the training data is limited, such that some client updates overfit the training data rather than learning to generalize. However, updates from multiple clients help mitigate overfitting in the federated model in the long run such that the test accuracy goes back to >95%.

9.4.3 Effect of FL Parameters

In FL, there are several parameters to tune. For example, it would ideally be best to aggregate updates from all clients. However, when the number of clients is high, the overhead of model aggregation from all clients would be very high, and the availability of the client updates may not be ready. Moreover, if the data collection time is large, the collected information may even be outdated. Thus, the number of clients that provide updates in each round is a critical parameter. We evaluate FL performance on the EMNIST dataset and present the impact of the number of clients in Table 9.23. We can see that accuracy in general increases with the number of clients, since more clients can provide more update information. However, even for 2 clients, the accuracy is already 96.75% of the EMNIST dataset. The room for accuracy improvement with more clients is very limited. For example, the accurac using 100 clients per round is 97.70%, and the improvement of 2 clients per round is only 0.95%.

Another parameter that is studied is the number of client epochs per round. This parameter determines the number of local updates a client needs to make before the model is sent to the server. Table 9.24 presents the results on the number of client epochs per round. The accuracy of the global model slightly increases with more client epochs per round. In addition, more client epochs per round increases

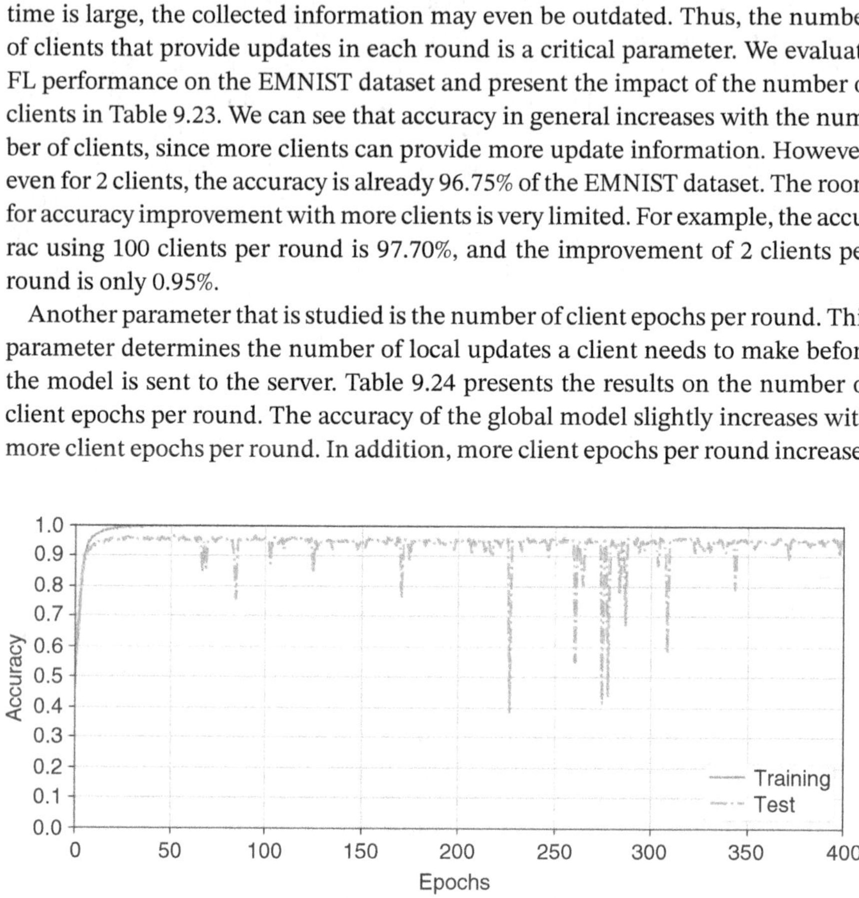

Figure 9.34 Classification accuracy using FL applied to xView dataset.

Table 9.23 The impact of the number of clients on accuracy.

No. of clients	2	3	4	5	6	7	8	9	10	100
Accuracy (%)	96.75	96.97	97.16	97.00	97.31	97.33	97.47	97.66	97.40	97.70

Table 9.24 The impact of the number of client epochs per round.

No. of client epochs per round	Accuracy (%)	Run time (second)
1	96.7452	8,527.08
2	97.0293	8,529.36
5	97.5411	8,630.18
10	97.5852	8,676.69
50	97.1199	9,293.23
100	97.4971	10,184.91

run time slightly. There are also other parameters for FL evaluation, which can be grouped in training parameters and optimizer parameters, respectively.

- **Training parameters** will include the total rounds in learning, the number of rounds per evaluation, the number of client epochs per round, the training batch size, and test batch size.
- **Optimizer parameters** will include server learning rate and client learning rate.

The impact of these parameters is given as follows:

1. The default value of total rounds in learning is 256. The accuracy increases with this parameter, while the complexity also increases.
2. The default value of the number of rounds per evaluation is 1. Increasing this may reduce complexity (since the number of evaluations is reduced). It may also reduce accuracy for given number of rounds.
3. The default value of the number of client epochs per round is 1. Increasing this parameter may improve accuracy, but the complexity also increases.
4. The default values of training batch size and test batch size are 20 and 100, respectively. In general, a large batch size may improve accuracy but needs a larger memory to process data.
5. The default values of server and client learning rates are 1.0 and 0.1, respectively. The larger learning rate can speed up the learning process. But the final accuracy may not be very good. Given that learning at the server has more data than learning at clients, we can set a larger learning rate at the server than that at clients.

FL is vulnerable to a variety of attacks and exploits such as (training data) poisoning attacks [28], communication disruption attacks [29–31], and selfish (free-rider) behavior [32]. In this chapter, we study ModInv attacks against FL.

9.4.4 Demonstration of ModInv Attack Against FL Models

Using the shared model that is updated using 100 clients, we performed ModInv attack. To evaluate the success of the attack, we use two approaches. The first approach is a qualitative assessment where we visualize the ModInv reconstructions. The second approach is a quantitative assessment where we use an attack-based evaluation method described in [17]. In the quantitative approach, we train an auxiliary evaluation classifier $f_{\text{eval}}(\cdot)$ using the test samples. The ModInv reconstruction is input to the evaluation model f_{eval} in the inference phase and the output of the evaluation model returns the most likely label. If the returned label is equal to the given attack target, then the reconstructed image is considered to be recognizable. We quantify the efficacy of the attack over all the reconstructed data using this evaluation process. Before presenting the ModInv results, let us reintroduce the ModInv attack parameters. There are three parameters that we consider: TV regularization, ℓ_p-norm, and Blur. In the analysis below, we consider TV = 3, LP = 6, and Blur = True. This set of parameters has shown to perform very well. Figure 9.35 presents the ModInv reconstruction for each target label. These reconstructions qualitatively demonstrate the ModInv reconstructions. The yellow areas in the reconstruction show the heat map of digit locations in the images. As we can see, the images are mostly centered around the digits. Inside the yellow regions, the dark blue silhouette reveals the digits.

Our results demonstrate that the ModInv attack can reconstruct labels when the model is trained using a FL framework. We note that this investigation did not study the dependence of the transformation of the dataset that can be applied to reduce ModInv reconstruction or the difficulty of the dataset. We had studied the effect of transformations in Section 9.3.11.3.

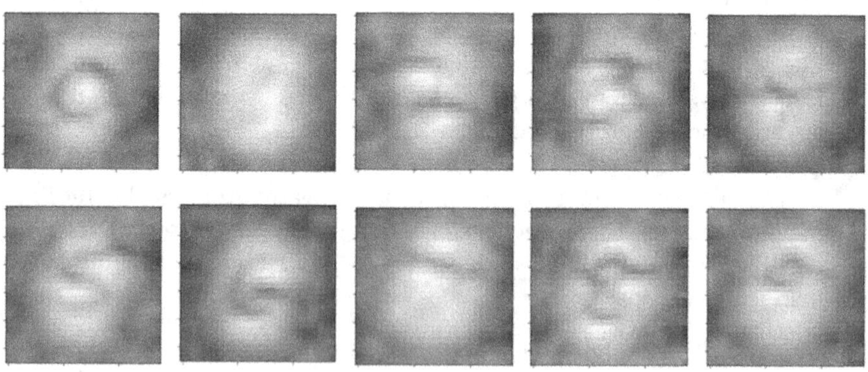

Figure 9.35 ModInv reconstruction for Target Labels 0–9.

9.4.5 Differentially Private Stochastic Gradient Descent

We revisit the character recognition task using the EMNIST dataset and adopt the following experimental configuration. Each client processes data in batches of 200, with 20 clients participating in each communication round. The number of local training epochs per client is varied across {1, 5, 10, 100} to examine the impact of local computation on global model performance. Model evaluation occurs after every round, and checkpoints are saved every 50 rounds. To study the effects of regularization, weight clipping is tested at two levels: 0.05 and 0.20, while no noise is added (i.e., the noise multiplier is set to None), resulting in a standard Federated Averaging (FedAvg) setup. The client optimizer is SGD with a learning rate of 0.1, and the server uses SGD with a learning rate of 1.0. The underlying CNN model consists of two convolutional layers, one with 32 filters of size (5×5) and another with 64 filters of the same size, both using a stride of (2×2) and padding, each followed by a 2D max-pooling layer with a (2×2) window. The network concludes with a fully connected layer of 512 neurons with ReLU activation and a final output layer with 10 neurons and Softmax activation for classification.

Figure 9.36 shows the test accuracy of different gradient clip and client epochs. Gradient clip limits the contribution of each client update in the federated aggregation, whereas the client epochs denote the number of local updates at each client per federated training round. First, we observe that the effect of gradient clip in the FedAvg is fairly limited. When we use a larger clip (clip = 0.20), we see that there are less ripples in the performance, but the slope of the accuracy increase is the same between clip = 0.05 and clip = 0.20. Next, we study the effect of different client epochs. We observe that while the test accuracy of different client epochs reaches similar values (~95–98%), the slope of increase strongly depends on the number of local updates (captured by the *client epochs* parameter). As more local client updates are taken per federated round, the higher the slope becomes. For example, when there are 100 local client updates are taken, the accuracy goes above 90% in 20 training rounds, whereas it takes 120 training rounds for the configuration with five client updates. We note that the configuration with 1 local update fluctuates significantly and takes a very long time to reach 90%. The same observation is noted in a recent paper published by the group at Google maintaining the Federated Learning repository [33], which shows that it takes 1,500 epochs to reach 85% accuracy with one local client epoch in the EMNIST dataset (c.f. Figure 2(c) in Ref. [33]).

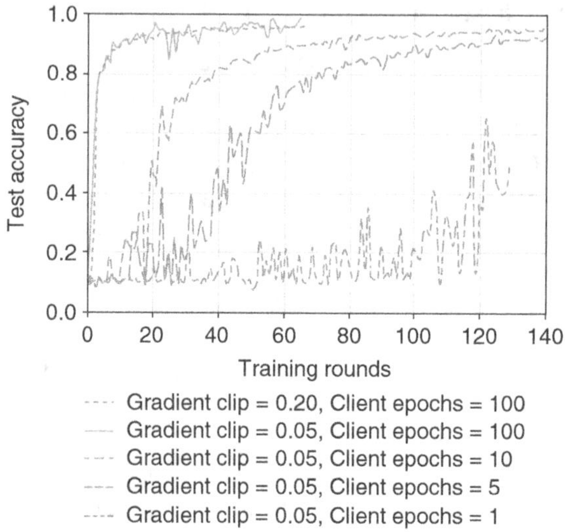

Figure 9.36 Test accuracy of FL with different gradient clip and client epochs.

9.4.6 Evaluate Effects of Different Parameters of DP-SGD

We investigated the effects of different parameters of DP-SGD and analyzed their effects. Our implementation builds up on Google's Federated Learning [34, 35]. Parameters are:

Number of clients: This parameter is related to the general FL framework and is used to generate the number of clients that will perform the FL task. In this analysis, we kept the number of clients constant.

Client epochs: This parameter is related to the general FL framework and is used to set the number of backpropagation updates at each client before their update is sent to the FL. The number of client epochs is kept constant.

Noise multiplier: This parameter is used to control how much noise is sampled and added to the gradients before they are used to update the optimizer. In general, higher noise multiplier provides more privacy, but it often comes at the cost of lower utility (accuracy or negative loss).

Initial gradient clip: This parameter sets the maximum Euclidean norm of each individual gradient computed on an individual training example from a minibatch (to bound the optimizer's sensitivity to individual training points).

Table 9.25 shows the effects of different DP-SGD and FL parameters. A prominent trend in all the curves is that after a certain training epoch, the models tend

Table 9.25 List of DP-SGD parameters and corresponding test accuracy.

Parameter setting	No. of clients	Client epochs	Initial gradient clip	Noise multiplier	Adaptive clip rate	Test accuracy
1	20	10	1.0	0.1	0.1	1.0
2	20	10	0.1	0.1	0.1	0.9816
3	20	10	0.01	0.9	0.1	0.8917
4	20	10	1.0	0.5	0.1	0.8750
5	20	10	0.05	1.0	0.1	0.8500
6	20	10	0.05	0.9	0.1	0.8342
7	20	10	0.05	1.1	0.1	0.6538
8	20	10	0.5	0.9	0.1	0.6199
9	20	10	1.0	0.5	0.9	0.4750
10	20	10	1.0	1.0	0.1	0.1750
11	20	10	1.3	1.3	0.1	0.0833

to memory rather than learn and start overfitting to the training data. This problem can be easily mitigated by applying an early stopping criterion and saving the model with the lowest test loss (or highest test accuracy). We observe that the parameter value for the noise multiplier closely affects the results. As the noise multiplier increases, the test accuracy decreases sharply. We can see this effect by observing parameter settings 1, 4, and 10, where the noise multiplier increases from 0.1, 0.5 to 1.0, while the test accuracy decreases from 1.0, 0.8750 to 0.1750, respectively. As the initial gradient clip increases, the test accuracy decreases. By observing parameter settings 1, 3, and 8, the initial gradient clip increases from 0.01, 0.05 to 0.5, the test accuracy decreases from 0.8917, 0.8342 to 0.6199. Next, we discuss the DP guarantee.

9.4.7 Demonstration of Renyi DP Evaluations

As discussed in previous sections, our implementation utilizes Google's Federated Learning library [34, 35] and extends it to apply the DP-SGD during FL training and calculate the epsilon privacy. We extend the same experiments to measure the privacy guarantee provided using the analysis tools included in TensorFlow Privacy [21]. This library provides a script to compute the value of ϵ for a given fixed value of δ. This script is called *compute_dp_sgd_privacy.py*, which calculates the Renyi DP (refer to Ref. [36] for more details). DP is usually quantified by two parameters:

- **Delta:** This parameter bounds the probability of the privacy guarantee not being held. A rule of thumb is to use the inverse of the population size (training data size). In the experiments below, δ is fixed to $\delta = 10^{-5}$.
- **Epsilon:** This parameter measures the strength of the privacy guarantee. For DP in ML, it bounds how much an output of model varies on removing or including a single training example. In general, a small epsilon is desired. However, this parameter is only an upper bound, and a large value of epsilon could still mean good practical privacy.

The Renyi DP [36–38] depends on the total number of points in the training data, denoted by n, the batch size, the noise multiplier, and the number of epochs in training. Table 9.26 shows the DP-SGD results.

Table 9.26 presents the trade-off between the noise multiplier and epsilon privacy. As a reminder, epsilon privacy denotes the privacy budget and measures the strength of the privacy guarantee by bounding the inference probability of a single training point to be included or excluded during the training of a model. A smaller value of ϵ indicates a better privacy guarantee. When we look at Experiment #1 that achieved a test accuracy of 100%, we observe that it achieves by far the lowest privacy guarantee of 7,403,493.030. This high number indicates that using such a low noise multiplier in the FL training, in fact, does not bring any privacy advantages. Experiment #3 and Experiment #5 demonstrate an effective compromise between maintaining high test accuracy and providing strong privacy protection.

Table 9.26 Results of different DP-SGD experiments.

Experiment	No. of clients	Client epochs	Initial gradient clip	Noise multiplier	Adaptive clip rate	Test accuracy	Epsilon Privacy
#1	20	10	1.0	0.1	0.1	1.0	7,403,493.030
#2	20	10	0.1	0.1	0.1	0.9816	7,403,493.030
#3	20	10	0.01	0.9	0.1	0.8917	1.488
#4	20	10	1.0	0.5	0.1	0.8750	8.843
#5	20	10	0.05	1.0	0.1	0.8500	1.208
#6	20	10	0.05	0.9	0.1	0.8342	1.488
#7	20	10	0.05	1.1	0.1	0.6538	1.050
#8	20	10	0.5	0.9	0.1	0.6199	1.488
#9	20	10	1.0	0.5	0.9	0.4750	8.843
#10	20	10	1.0	1.0	0.1	0.1750	1.208
#11	20	10	1.3	1.3	0.1	0.0833	0.773

They achieve 89.17 and 85.00% test accuracy while maintaining a low privacy ϵ (better for privacy) of 1.488 and 1.208, respectively.

9.5 Discussion

This chapter presented a comprehensive study of privacy vulnerabilities in DL models with a focus on ModInv and MI attacks. We evaluated the effectiveness of these attacks under different configurations, model depths, and training techniques, including FL and DP.

A key finding in this chapter is that even standard convolutional architectures are susceptible to inversion attacks that can reveal class-level representations. This vulnerability is exacerbated when data augmentations, such as horizontal flipping, preserve visual patterns that aid reconstruction. On the other hand, transformations such as brightness reduction and vertical shifting were found to hinder inversion, serving as lightweight privacy-preserving methods.

In the context of MI, we demonstrated that deep models can inadvertently memorize training data, and that overfitting or bias in data distributions can be exploited for privacy leakage. The proposed deep Bayesian MI method effectively generalized across layers using influence functions and local approximations. When applied to both structured datasets (e.g., CIFAR-10) and real-world overhead imagery (e.g., xView), the method exposed meaningful vulnerabilities with practical consequences for applications in surveillance and autonomous systems.

While our study began with the Olivetti face dataset, which is indeed a legacy dataset, its use allowed controlled, interpretable experimentation and side-by-side comparisons of different attack variants. To address realism, we extended the attacks to modern and large-scale datasets such as CIFAR-10 and xView, both of which reflect current operational environments. The consistent attack success across these datasets demonstrates that the vulnerabilities identified are not specific to any one dataset or domain but rather intrinsic to the model architecture and training procedure.

Moreover, our evaluation of FL under adversarial conditions highlighted its potential to support cyber resiliency. We found that even without added defense mechanisms, FL across distributed clients offers temporal robustness to short-lived attacks. However, the lack of built-in fault isolation, i.e., identifying and excluding malicious clients, remains an open challenge for future work. The integration of FL with DP was shown to further mitigate privacy risks, though this comes at a trade-off in model performance.

Overall, the findings underscore a critical insight: privacy leakage and resilience must be codesigned, particularly in autonomous and distributed systems where data exposure is difficult to control. Defense strategies must account not only for algorithmic guarantees but also for operational considerations such as adversary persistence, client diversity, and transformation invariance.

9.6 Conclusions

This chapter investigated the intersection of privacy, adversarial ML, and FL from a cyber resiliency perspective. We explored how ML models, particularly deep neural networks, can be vulnerable to privacy attacks such as ModInv, MI, and attribute inference. These attacks reveal sensitive information either by reconstructing training inputs or by exposing the membership status of individuals in the training set.

Our results demonstrate that DL models are prone to leaking recognizable class-level features under ModInv attacks, even in more complex architectures. Moreover, certain image transformations (such as horizontal flips) can inadvertently exacerbate inversion vulnerabilities, while others, such as vertical shifts and brightness adjustments, can mitigate them and offer lightweight privacy-preserving options. MI attacks, on the other hand, exploit model overfitting and biased feature representations, and we showed that their efficacy can be significantly enhanced through influence-based approximations across different network layers. FL, though inherently more private due to the decentralized nature of training, still requires additional mechanisms such as DP to provide robust protection against inference attacks. Importantly, the integration of privacy mechanisms into FL introduces a trade-off between privacy guarantees and model utility, which must be carefully managed in practical deployments.

The implications of these findings are particularly relevant for autonomous systems, where models are often deployed at the edge, operate in contested or untrusted environments, and must continue functioning under adversarial conditions. Building privacy-aware and resilient AI components is essential to ensure operational robustness, especially in mission-critical applications.

Future research directions include the development of fault-tolerant FL frameworks capable of detecting and isolating adversarial participants, extending the attack and defense methodologies to multimodal and vision-language models, and integrating real-time privacy monitoring capabilities into the ML deployment pipeline. By rigorously analyzing attack surfaces and quantifying the trade-offs involved in defense strategies, this chapter contributes to the broader effort to secure AI-enabled autonomous systems operating in adversarial environments.

9.7 Acknowledgment

Any opinions, findings, and conclusions or recommendations expressed in this material are those of the authors.

References

1 S. Yeom, M. Fredrikson, and S. Jha. Privacy risk in machine learning: Analyzing the connection to overfitting. In *2018 IEEE 31st Computer Security Foundations Symposium (CSF)*, pp. 268–282, 2018.

2 M. Fredrikson, S. Jha, and T. Ristenpart. Model inversion attacks that exploit confidence information and basic countermeasures. In *Proceeding 22nd ACM SIGSAC Conference Computer and Communications Security*, pp. 1322–1333. New York, NY, 2015.

3 M. Fredrikson, E. Lantz, S. Jha, S. Lin, D. Page, and T. Ristenpart. Privacy in pharmacogenetics: An end-to-end case study of personalized warfarin dosing. In *Proceeding 23rd USENIX Conference on Security Symposium*, pp. 17–32. USENIX, 2014.

4 R. Shokri, M. Stronati, C. Song, and V. Shmatikov. Membership inference attacks against machine learning models. In *2017 IEEE Symposium on Security and Privacy (SP)*, pp. 3–18. San Jose, CA, USA, 2017.

5 N. Papernot, P. McDaniel, S. Jha, M. Fredrikson, Z. B. Celik, and A. Swami. The limitations of deep learning in adversarial settings. In *2016 IEEE European Symposium on Security and Privacy (EuroS&P)*, pp. 372–387. Saarbruecken, Germany, 2016.

6 Y. Shi, Y. E. Sagduyu, K. Davaslioglu, and R. Levy. Vulnerability detection and analysis in adversarial deep learning. In *Guide to Vulnerability Analysis for Computer Networks and Systems. Computer Communications and Networks.* pp. 211–234. Cham: Springer International Publishing, 2018.

7 Y. Shi, Y. E. Sagduyu, K. Davaslioglu, and J. Li. Active deep learning attacks under strict rate limitations for online API calls. In *2018 IEEE International Symposium on Technologies for Homeland Security (HST)*, pp. 1–6. Woburn, MA, USA, 2018.

8 Y. Shi and Y. E. Sagduyu. Evasion and causative attacks with adversarial deep learning. In *IEEE Military Communications Conference (MILCOM)*, pp. 243–248. Baltimore, MD, USA, 2017.

9 Y. E. Sagduyu, T. Erpek, and Y. Shi. Adversarial machine learning for 5G communications security. In *Game Theory and Machine Learning for Cyber Security*. IEEE Press-Wiley, 2021.

10 Y. Shi and Y. E. Sagduyu. Membership inference attack and defense for wireless signal classifiers with deep learning. *IEEE Transactions on Mobile Computing*, 22(7): 4032–4043, July 2023.

11 Google AI Blog. *Federated learning: Collaborative machine learning without centralized training data*. https://ai.googleblog.com/2017/04/federated-learning-collaborative.html.

12 AT&T Labs Cambridge. *Database of faces*. https://www.cl.cam.ac.uk/research/dtg/attarchive/facedatabase.html.

13 Z. Wang, A.C. Bovik, H. R. Sheikh, and E. P. Simoncelli. Image quality assessment: From error visibility to structural similarity. *IEEE Transactions on Image Processing*, 13(4): 600–612, 2004.

14 Z. Wang and A. C. Bovik. Mean squared error: Love it or leave it? *IEEE Signal Processing Magazine*, 26(1): 98–117, 2009.

15 The CIFAR-10 dataset. https://www.cs.toronto.edu/~kriz/cifar.html.

16 X. Wu, M. Fredrikson, S. Jha, and J. F. Naughton. A methodology for formalizing model-inversion attacks. In *2016 IEEE 29th Computer Security Foundations Symposium (CSF)*, pp. 355–370. Lisbon, Portugal, 2016.

17 C. Park, D. Hong, and C. Seo. An attack-based evaluation method for differentially private learning against model inversion attack. *IEEE Access*, 7: 124988–124999, 2019.

18 N. Z. Gong and B. Liu. Attribute inference attacks in online social networks. *ACM Transactions on Privacy and Security (TOPS)*, 21(1): 1–30, 2018.

19 K. Leino, S. Sen, A, Datta, M. Fredrikson, and L. Li. Influence directed explanations for deep convolutional networks. *CoRR, abs/1802.03788*, 2018.

20 K. Simonyan, A. Vedaldi, and A. Zisserman. Deep inside convolutional networks: Visualising image classification models and saliency maps. *CoRR, abs/1312.6034*, 2013. https://arxiv.org/abs/1312.6034.

21 TensorFlow Privacy Github. https://github.com/tensorflow/privacy.

22 N. Papernot, I. Goodfellow, R. Sheatsley, R. Feinman, and P. McDaniel. Cleverhans v1.0.0: An adversarial machine learning library. *arXiv preprint arXiv:1610.00768*, 2016.

23 M. Nasr, R. Shokri, and A. Houmansadr. Machine learning with membership privacy using adversarial regularization. In *Proceedings of the 2018 ACM SIGSAC Conference on Computer and Communications Security*, pp. 634–646. New York, NY, USA: Association for Computing Machinery, 2018.

24 G. Huang, Z. Liu, L. van der Maaten, K. Q. Weinberger. Densely connected convolutional networks. In *Proceeding Computer Vision and Pattern Recognition*, 2017.

25 D. Lam, R. Kuzma, K. McGee, S. Dooley, M. Laielli, M. Klaric, Y. Bulatov, and B. McCord. xView: Objects in context in overhead imagery. *ArXiv preprints: arXiv: 1802.07856*, 2018. https://xviewdataset.org/#dataset.

26 M. Abadi, A. Chu, I. Goodfellow, H. B. McMahan, I. Mironov, K. Talwar, and L. Zhang. Deep learning with differential privacy. In *Proceedings of the 2016 ACM SIGSAC Conference on Computer and Communications Security*, pp. 308–318. New York, NY, USA: Association for Computing Machinery, 2016.

27 Z. Zaho, N. Papernot, S. Singh, N. Polyzotis, and A. Odena. Improving differentially private models with active learning. *ArXiv preprints: arXiv:1910.01177*, October 2019.

28 Y. E. Sagduyu, T. Erpek, and Y. Shi. Securing NextG systems against poisoning attacks on federated learning: A game-theoretic solution. In *2023 IEEE Military Communications Conference (MILCOM)*, 2023.

29 Y. E. Sagduyu, Y. Shi, and T. Erpek. Jamming attacks on decentralized federated learning in general multi-hop wireless networks. In *IEEE INFOCOM Wireless-Sec: 5G and Beyond Wireless Security Workshop*, 2023.

30 Y. Shi and Y. E. Sagduyu. How to launch jamming attacks on federated learning in NextG wireless networks. In *IEEE Globecom Workshops the Seventh IEEE Workshop on 5G and Beyond Wireless Securitys*, 2022.

31 Y. Shi and Y. E. Sagduyu. Jamming attacks on federated learning in wireless networks. *arXiv preprint arXiv:2201.05172*, 2022.

32 Y. E. Sagduyu. Free-rider games for federated learning with selfish clients in NextG wireless networks. In *IEEE Conference on Communications and Network Security (CNS): Cyber Resilience Workshop*, 2022.

33 S. J. Reddi, Z. Charles, M. Zaheer, Z. Garrett, K. Rush, J. J. Konecny, S. Kumar and H. B. McMahan. Adaptive federated optimization. In *International Conference on Learning Representations*, 2021.

34 Google TensorFlow. *TensorFlow federated: Machine learning on decentralized data*. https://www.tensorflow.org/federated.

35 Google TensorFlow Github. https://github.com/tensorflow/federated.

36 I. Mironov. Renyi differential privacy. In *Proceeding IEEE 30th Computer Security Foundations Symposium (CSF)*, 2017.

37 C. Dwork. Differential privacy. In *Proceeding ICALP*, 2006.

38 R. Shokri and V. Shmatikov. Privacy-preserving deep learning. In *Proceeding ACM CCS*, 2015.

10

Resilient Deep Neural Network Random Ensemble Against Adversarial Attacks

Kirsen Sullivan,[1] Yitao Li,[2] Charles A. Kamhoua,[3] and Bowei Xi[4]*

[1] *Oak Ridge National Laboratory, Tennessee, Oak Ridge, USA*
[2] *AstrumU Inc., Washington, Bellevue, USA*
[3] *Army Research Laboratory, Maryland, Adelphi, USA*
[4] *Department of Statistics, Purdue University, Indiana, West Lafayette, USA*

*Corresponding Author: xbw@purdue.edu

10.1 Introduction

This chapter specifically addresses how to improve the resilience of a cyber-physical system facing unexpected security incidents. One type of security incident is caused by the algorithms implemented in a cyber-physical system. There is an increasing use of DNN to process the signals received by the sensors in a cyber-physical system. When DNN fails to properly interpret the signals, there could be fatal consequences. For example, it has been observed that autonomous vehicles repeatedly crashed into parked cars. This is not a traditional cybersecurity problem, because the errors are not caused by a malicious attack. As of now, there does not exist any adversarial physical attack that could cause an autonomous vehicle to crash. Although it was called "adversarial attacks" in the existing literature, this type of security incident is caused by a fundamental deficiency in DNN itself. When the existing DNN models were developed, resilience was not taken into consideration. Hence, when DNN becomes a crucial part of a cyber-physical system operating in a complex environment, people started to notice the lack of resilience. This leads to a claim that fully autonomous systems are years away. The existing approaches believe that simply by running more road tests or running more simulations, the autonomous systems could become more resilient. Unfortunately, such simple solution will not completely solve the problem. This chapter emphasizes that to develop a resilient autonomous system, it requires a structural solution to address the unexpected security incidents.

In this chapter we develop a moving target defense through building random DNN ensembles as a starting point. The random DNN ensemble defense strategy begins with a DNN model trained through the standard training process. Then, a certain portion of the weights on the first convolutional layers are replaced by random numbers generated from a Gaussian distribution. The Gaussian parameters are determined through a bootstrap. Bootstrapping several DNN models with different network structures reveals that an increasingly large percentage of the bootstrap weight distributions and the bootstrap bias distributions become non-normal as the network size increases. In this chapter we describe the network architectures, bootstrapping strategies, and the results pertaining to the NN weight distribution properties. Since given one single trained network, we have infinitely many random ensembles, even the strongest attacks lose the target. In our experiments, the random DNN ensembles based on a large network are the most effective against adversarial attacks.

10.1.1 Related Work

Convolutional Neural Networks (CNNs) are a class of neural networks that have been used heavily in image analysis. CNN architecture includes a number of convolutional layers, as well as pooling and fully connected layers. In a convolutional layer, a grid is convolved across the width and height of an image. This grid, or filter, performs a dot product between the filter and the input. As the network learns, this kernel can extract features from images. The output feature maps can then be passed on to more convolutional layers for higher levels of feature extraction. Pooling layers are used to downsample the output feature map size as well as increase local translational invariance. Finally, the output feature map is flattened, and a fully connected layer is implemented to classify the images.

A convolution is ultimately a linear transformation. So even if many convolutions are stacked on top of each other, it would simply reduce to a linear transformation without some nonlinearity being introduced into the network. A nonlinear activation function after the convolutional layer achieves this and greatly increases the complexity of tasks the network can learn. One important activation function is the rectified linear unit, or ReLU. This function reassigns all negative values to 0. Since AlexNet won the ImageNet competition with a large margin, CNN regained its popularity over all other classifiers, leading to the third wave of AI.

10.1.1.1 Adversarial Attacks

DNN models are very sensitive to perturbations, as illustrated by the numerous adversarial attacks. Evasion attacks, e.g., [1–6], add targeted perturbations to the test samples that cause DNN to misclassify the objects at test time. Backdoor attacks, e.g., [7–10], which are also called poisoning attacks, perturb the training data so the resulting DNN misclassify certain test samples to cause significant damages. By now, there are numerous attacks against all the different types of AI models in different application areas.

The earliest evasion attack against DNN [11] was published in 2014, soon after NN regained its popularity. Since then, a large number of evasion attacks were quickly developed with some adding larger total amount of perturbations than others. Such a targetedly perturbed test sample is called the adversarial example. Fast Gradient Sign Method (FGSM) [12] is a one-step method, using the sign of the gradient of the cost function to generate adversarial examples. Afterwards, iterative FGSM attacks [13, 14] were developed. Projected Gradient Descent (PGD) attack [15] is also an iterative FGSM attack. With a different approach than FGSM, Carlini and Wagner (CW) attacks [16] are much improved version of L-BFGS attack [11]. CW attacks use different distance measures. The one based on L_2 distance is called CW L_2 (CW2) attack. CW attacks are stronger attacks than FGSM and PGD attacks since they add much smaller amount of perturbations to generate adversarial examples. Unfortunately, CW attacks require significantly longer computation time than FGSM and PGD attacks. DeepFool (DP) attack [17] is another strong attack that adds only a small amount of perturbation and is able to find a universal adversarial perturbation that causes almost all test samples to fool a classifier.

Many defense strategies were developed and quickly proved to be ineffective [16, 18], such as network distillation, several adversarial detection methods, and obfuscated gradients, etc. Image pre-processing, such as denoising, has some success to fend off adversarial examples, since a pre-processing method recalculates a different perturbation than the original adversarial perturbation. Image pre-processing methods simply generate a different perturbed test sample without addressing the weakness of DNN models. Adversarial training [13], now considered a baseline defense, achieves some success by iteratively training DNN with adversarial examples included in the training data. Unfortunately, only attacks that can quickly generate adversarial examples can be used in adversarial training, such as FGSM and PGD attacks. If an attack is not used for adversarial training, the performance of the adversarially trained DNN drops significantly. Given there are numerous known and unknown attacks, adversarial training is not likely to be the solution to the problem.

More recently, Tramer et al. [18] proposed adaptive attacks that evaluate a defense strategy by developing a customized attack for the defense. Many sophisticated defenses failed the test of the adaptive attacks. After nearly 10 years of the arms race between attacks and defenses, to robustify DNN remains a difficult unsolved problem.

Our approach is a moving target defense. We build random DNN ensembles given a single trained network. The ensemble of randomized learners requires a certain portion of the weights from a selected layer to be replaced with random numbers from a Gaussian distribution. There are infinitely many random DNN ensembles, thus even adaptive attacks lose the target to attack. The Gaussian parameters of the weights in a CNN are unknown, but can be estimated by bootstrapping. All networks in this chapter were trained using PyTorch, and with GPU computing resources.

10.1.1.2 CNN Parameter Distribution

The effort to understand the theoretical properties of CNN models can trace back to the late 1980s. However, there were limited work on bootstrap CNN models, e.g., [19–29]. There were also very limited work on understanding CNN parameter distributions [30–36].

Bootstrapping [37], is a resampling algorithm to study the parameter distributions of a model. In the literature, bootstrapped NNs were often used to build an ensemble to enhance the performance. Bootstrapping a NN was also conducted to quantify the uncertainty of NN output. Bootstrapping a NN was never intended to study NN parameter distribution. NN weights were believed to have heavy tails during the training process. These past works did not take into consideration the randomness of the training dataset nor the size of the network. We discovered that for NN models with smaller network structure, the bootstrap NN parameter distributions are mostly normal. For bigger and more complex NN, a significant percentage of the bootstrap NN parameter distributions are still normal. As the network size and complexity increases, more bootstrap parameter distributions become heavier tailed than normal.

In this chapter, we develop a moving target defense based on NN parameter distributions through bootstrapping NN. The chapter is organized as follows. Section 10.2 discusses the bootstrap experiment and the CNN bootstrap parameter distributions. Section 10.4 describes our strategy to build random ensembles of CNN models. Section 10.5 shows the CNN random ensemble accuracies over adversarial examples from four attacks. Section 10.6 concludes this chapter.

10.2 Data and Bootstrapped CNNs

Two datasets are utilized in the bootstrap experiments in this chapter. Modified National Institute of Standards and Technology (dataset) (MNIST) is a database of handwritten digits. There are a total of 70,000 black and white images of size 28 × 28. The database includes 60,000 training images and 10,000 test images. There are 10 classes, one for each of the digits 0–9, inclusive. CIFAR-10 [38] consists of 60,000 32×32 color images. There are a total of 10 classes, with 6,000 images per class. The images are divided as 50,000 training images and 10,000 testing images. The ten classes are airplane, automobile, bird, cat, deer, dog, frog, horse, ship, and truck.

In our experiments, we bootstrapped each CNN model 150 times, i.e., we trained 150 unique learners on bootstrapped training data for each of the three NN architectures considered. There is no shared information between the learners, and thus the computational cost scales linearly with the number of learners. The models were all trained on the Gilbreth cluster at Purdue University. Gilbreth is a community cluster optimized for communities running GPU-intensive applications such as machine learning. It has 66 Dell compute nodes with Intel Xeon processors and 136 Nvidia Tesla GPUs. Figure 10.1 shows the out-of-bag (OOB) images of the bootstrapped networks.

10.2.1 Bootstrap Three-layer CNN

Three networks were bootstrapped, on a total of two image datasets. Network architectures were selected for different datasets based on what is already known to work well for the datasets. The first network is a three-layer CNN, which we call CNN3. This model takes as input two-dimensional (2D), $n \times n$ black and white images. The input goes through a 2D convolution, followed by a ReLU activation function and a max pooling. This is repeated three times. After these three convolutional layers, there is a dropout layer and finally a fully connected layer. The output of the fully connected layer is that of a linear transformation, with each image being assigned a value for each of the classes. The image will be classified as whichever class has the maximum value.

The CNN3 network (Figure 10.2) was used to classify the MNIST dataset, described above. The images were preprocessed prior to training. Each image was transformed to a tensor image and normalized. Transformation to a tensor image takes the $28 \times 28 = 784$ input integer values within the range [0, 255] and outputs a three-dimensional tensor of size (1, 28, 28) with values in the range [0, 1). Normalization then occurs by subtracting the mean and dividing by the standard deviation, 0.1307 and 0.3081, respectively. With an image input size of only 28 by 28 pixels, it was determined that each of the convolutions in the network used the relatively small kernel size of 3, a stride of 1, and padding was set to 2. The max pooling was performed with a kernel size of 2 and a stride of 2. The dropout was performed during training at a rate of 0.5.

Training was performed by iterating through the training dataset 10 times. The data was randomly ordered during training, with a different randomization for each of the 10 epochs. Network parameters were initialized according to the Kaiming Uniform initialization. The data went through the model in batches of size 100.

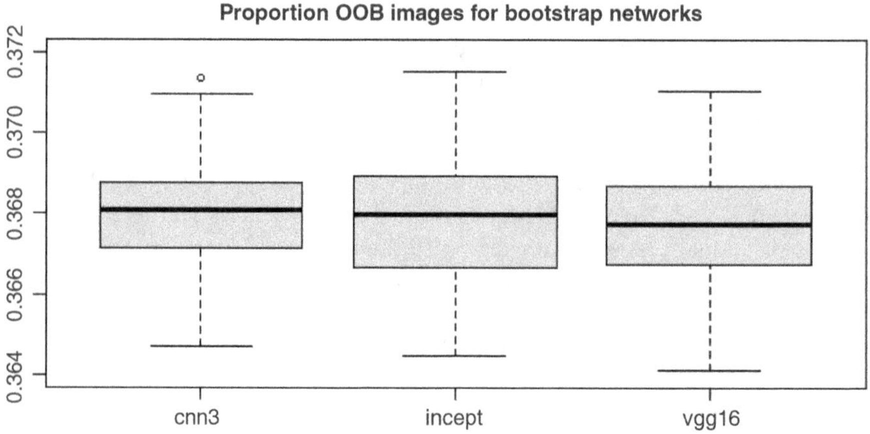

Figure 10.1 Proportion OOB images for bootstrap networks.

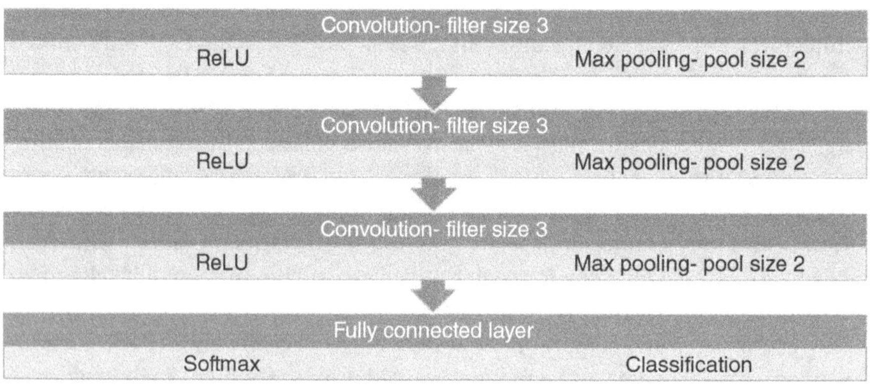

Figure 10.2 Network structure for CNN3.

Optimization was done via the Adam algorithm, with a learning rate of 0.001. This same training technique was performed 150 times using 150 distinct training datasets selected via bootstrap sampling – 60,000 images were selected with replacement from the available 60,000 images. All parameter values were stored for each of the 150 networks.

Bootstrap distribution of parameters was visualized via histograms. There were 320 parameters for the first convolutional layer, 18,496 for the second, 36,928 for the third, and 16,010 for the fully connected layer, for a total of 71,754 trainable parameters.

	Data	Models	Layers	Parameters	Epochs	Batch size
CNN3	MNIST	150	4	71,754	10	100
VGG16	CIFAR-10	150	16	27,828,042	180	256
Inception v3	CIFAR-10	150	42	21,806,058	180	64

10.2.2 Bootstrap VGG16

The second network is the VGG16 network as in Ref. [39]. This network is comprised of 13 convolution layers and three fully connected layers, followed by a softmax layer. The 13 convolutional layers, and their corresponding activation functions, are separated into 5 blocks. Each block is followed by a max pooling layer. Following the five blocks, an adaptive average pooling is performed, followed by the fully connected block. The fully connected block proceeds with two repetitions of: dropout layer, linear function, activation function. A final linear transformation is applied with softmax, resulting in one value for each of the classes, with all values summing to one.

The VGG16 network was used to train the CIFAR-10 image dataset, described above. The images were preprocessed prior to training. Random images were flipped horizontally at a rate of 50%. Each image was then padded with four pixels on every side and randomly cropped to back to 32×32. Each image was also transformed to a tensor image and normalized. Transformation to a tensor image takes the $3 \times 32 \times 32 = 3072$ input integer values within the range $[0, 255]$ and outputs a 3D tensor of size $(3, 32, 32)$ with values in the range $[0, 1)$. Normalization then occurs by subtracting the mean and dividing by the standard deviation, $[0.485, 0.456, 0.406]$ and $[0.229, 0.224, 0.225]$, respectively.

The convolutions all use a 3×3 kernel size, as in the CNN3 above. This small kernel size was necessary in order to achieve this network depth on a sequential CNN [39]. The number of trainable parameters is in the following chart. The first two convolutional layers have 1,792 and 36,928 trainable parameters. This value increases as the model progresses, with a maximum of 2,359,808 parameters seen in the last five convolutional layers. The first fully connected layer jumps to 12,845,568 trainable parameters, with the second containing 262,656, and the final fully connected layer including 5,130 trainable parameters. With a total of 27,828,042 trainable parameters, this is the slowest of the networks in the bootstrap experiments.

Prior to training on CIFAR-10, the weights were set to pre-trained values available in the Torchvision library. The weights were learned from the ImageNet database. PyTorch reports a Top-1 accuracy of 71.592% on the ImageNet dataset. However, ImageNet has 1,000 classes, whereas CIFAR-10 has 10 classes. Thus, the three fully connected layers must be reset to the correct size to accommodate the correct output size. Resizing the linear layers also loses the pretrained weights. Weights are then initialized via the Kaiming algorithm, described above. During training, all weights were updated, including both the pre-trained and newly initialized weights.

Training was performed by iterating through the training dataset 180 times. As with the training of the MNIST data on CNN3, the data was randomly assigned during training, with a different randomization for each of the 180 epochs. The data went through the model in batches of size 256. Optimization was done using stochastic gradient descent, with momentum 0.9, weight decay of 0.0005, and an initial learning rate of 0.05. The learning rate decayed by a factor of 0.1 every five epochs. The same hyperparameters were used to train 150 unique networks, each using a bootstrapped sampling of the CIFAR-10 training data. Fifty thousand images were selected with replacement from the 50,000 CIFAR-10 training image dataset. The 27,828,042 trainable parameters had their values stored for each of the 150 models.

The generation of plots for each of the 27.8 million parameters was not feasible. The plots of randomly selected weights and biases were generated, shown in Section 10.3.

10.2.3 Bootstrap Inception v3

The third network is the third iteration of the Inception framework [40], so named for the "network in network" set-up as well as a popular (at the time) meme based on the movie of the same name. Utilizing a "network in network" framework, called Inception modules, Inception v3 contains 42 layers, making it the most complex of the networks in the bootstrap experiments.

The motivation for the Inception modules is to have a sparsely connected architecture, even within the convolutional layers. The Inception modules make heavy use of 1×1 convolution filters. These 1×1 layers are applied before a larger filter size. The authors included these layers as a means of dimension reduction, as well as to increase the representational power of the network [40]. This allows for more layers with a fewer number of overall parameters. Inception v3 uses three Inception modules, labeled as modules A, B, and C. Module A consists of four parallel 1×1 convolution layers. The first of which is then passed to two 3×3 filters sequentially. The second is passed to a single 3×3 filter, the third undergoes max pooling before the 1×1 layer, and the final one is just a single 1×1 layer. The results of these four parallel networks are then placed into a single output filter bank and become the input for the next module. Thus, the subsequent modules focus on the local regions of interest from the previous module. The different layer types and filter sizes are designed to capture different parts of the input image.

The 1×1 filters focus on the correlation in local regions. The larger filter sizes are designed to identify features of higher abstraction.

The first six layers of Inception v3 are traditional convolution layers, each of which is followed by a batch normalization. The third and fifth are also followed by max pooling. After the first five convolution layers, there are three repetitions of Inception module A, five repetitions of Inception module B, and two repetitions of Inception module C. The output of these layers is input to an adaptive average pooling layer, followed by a dropout layer with rate 0.4 and finally a fully connected linear transformation with softmax.

The Inception v3 architecture also makes use of an auxiliary classifier after the final round of Inception module B, near the end of the model. The auxiliary classifier, used only during training, acts as a regularizer and helps with convergence in late training [40]. During training, the total loss is computed as loss1 + 0.4 × loss2, where loss1 is the loss associated with the full network, and loss2 is the loss associated with the auxiliary branch.

PyTorch's Inception v3 network has the constraint that the input image size must be 299×299 color images. This network was used to learn the CIFAR-10 dataset, with image size of 32×32 color images. In order to use this dataset, it was necessary to first increase the image size. This was performed by first resizing the images to 325×325 by padding the images on all sides, then taking the center crop of the required 299×299. The resultant images are surrounded by large black borders. Each image was also transformed to a tensor image and normalized. Transformation to a tensor image takes the $3 \times 299 \times 299 = 268{,}203$ input integer values within the range [0, 255] and outputs a 3D tensor of size (3, 299, 299) with values in the range [0, 1). Normalization then occurs by subtracting the mean and dividing by the standard deviation, [0.485, 0.456, 0.406] and [0.229, 0.224, 0.225], respectively.

The strategic filtering technique keeps the number of parameters in this network relatively small as compared to VGG16. Although there are over 2.5 times the number of layers, Inception v3 has 21,806,058 trainable parameters as compared with over 27.8 million for VGG16. Similarly, the computational efficiency is superior as compared with the more straightforward VGG framework. There is the additional benefit that the number of parameters remains unchanged for any image size up to 299×299 in the Inception v3 network. Meanwhile, the number of trainable parameters for VGG16 jumps to over 138 million for an image of 299×299.

Prior to training on CIFAR-10, the weights were set to pre-trained values available in the Torchvision library. The weights were ported in directly from the Inception v3 paper. PyTorch reports a Top-1 accuracy of 77.294% on the ImageNet dataset. As above, the number of parameters in the fully connected layer changes because the number of classes differs between the pretrained dataset and our dataset. After creating linear transformation layers of the correct dimension, weights are initialized via the Kaiming algorithm, described above. During training, all weights were updated, including both the pre-trained and newly initialized weights.

Training was performed by iterating through the training dataset 180 times. As with the training of the previously mentioned networks, the data was randomly assigned during training, with a different randomization for each of the 180 epochs. The data went through the model in batches of size 64. Optimization was done using stochastic gradient descent, with momentum 0.9, weight decay of 0.0005, and an initial learning rate of 0.05. The learning rate decayed by a factor of 0.1 every 5 epochs. The same hyperparameters were used to train 150 unique networks, each using a bootstrapped sampling of the full CIFAR-10 training data – 50,000 images were selected with replacement from the 50,000 CIFAR-10 training image dataset. The values of each of the 21,806,058 trainable parameters were stored for each of the 150 models.

As with the VGG16 results, only a random selection of weights and biases were plotted. A few examples of the weights and biases are shown in Section 10.3.

10.3 Bootstrapped Distributions

10.3.1 CNN3 Parameter

Majority of the bootstrap weight distributions of the first convolutional layer for the CNN3 model trained on MNIST data are mostly approximately symmetric, as shown in Figure 10.3 with selected ones. Majority of the bootstrap bias distributions of the first convolutional layer are approximately symmetric too, as shown in Figure 10.4. Both the weights and the biases are mostly in the ±0.4 range.

Majority of the bootstrap weight distributions of the fully connected layer for the CNN3 model trained on MNIST data are approximately symmetric, as shown in

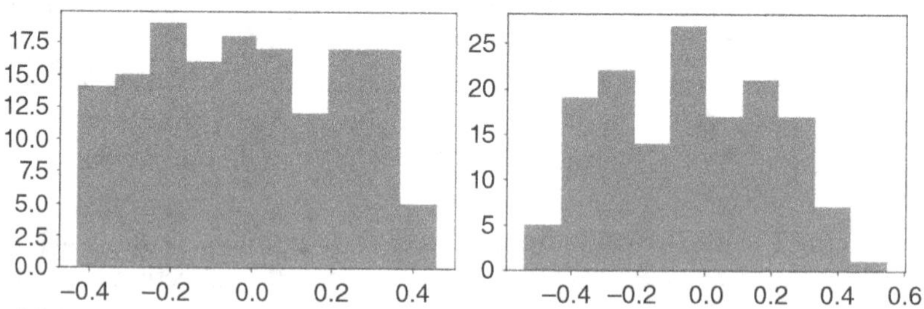

(a) (b)

Figure 10.3 Distribution of weights from bootstrap CNN3, first convolutional layer. (a) One representative weight distribution. (b) Another weight distribution from the same layer.

Figure 10.5 with selected ones. Majority of the bootstrap bias distributions of the fully connected layer are approximately symmetric too, as shown in Figure 10.6. Most of the weights are primarily in the ±0.15 range, while most of the biases are in the ±0.05 range.

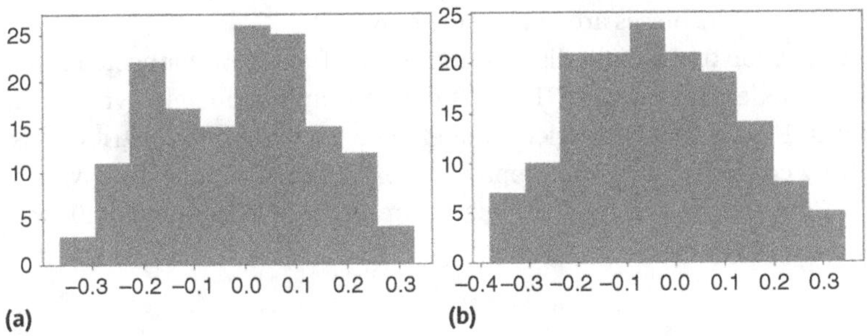

Figure 10.4 Distribution of biases from bootstrap CNN3, first convolutional layer. (a) One representative bias distribution. (b) Distribution of another bias from the same layer.

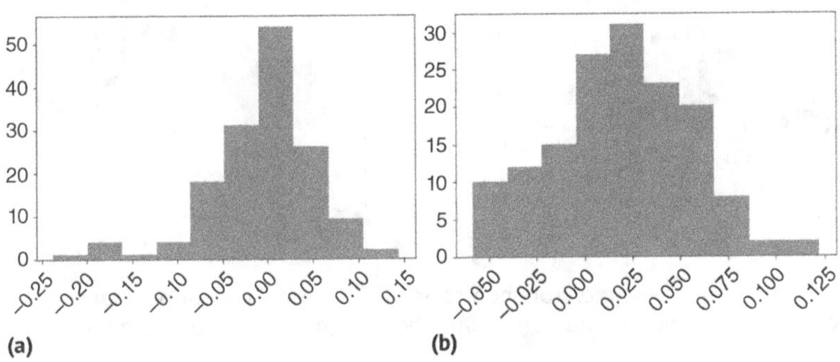

Figure 10.5 Distribution of weights from bootstrap CNN3, fully connected layer. (a) One representative weight distribution. (b) Another weight distribution from the same layer.

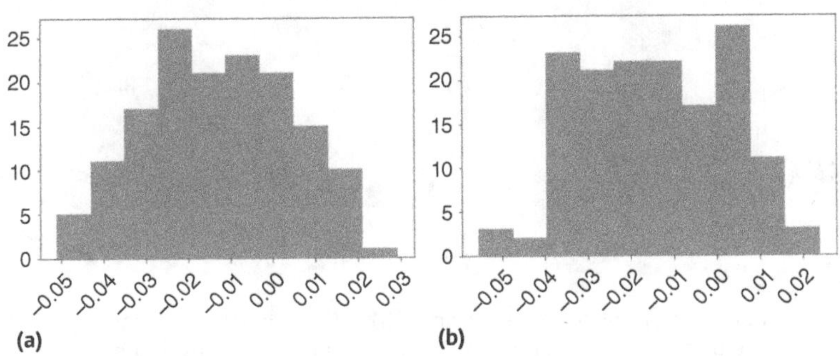

Figure 10.6 Distribution of biases from bootstrap CNN3, fully connected layer. (a) One representative bias distribution. (b) Distribution of another bias from the same layer.

10.3.2 VGG16 Parameters

Majority of the bootstrap weight distributions of the first convolutional layer for the VGG16 model trained on CIFAR-10 data are approximately symmetric, as shown in Figure 10.7 with selected ones. The bootstrap bias distributions of the first convolutional layer are approximately symmetric too, as shown in Figure 10.8. Both the weights and the biases are in the ±0.1 range.

Majority of the bootstrap weight distributions of the final fully connected layer for the VGG16 model trained on CIFAR-10 data are approximately symmetric too, as shown in Figure 10.9 with selected ones. The bootstrap bias distributions of the final fully connected layer are approximately symmetric too, as shown in Figure 10.10. Both the weights and the biases are in the ±0.15 range, with the exception of some heavy tails.

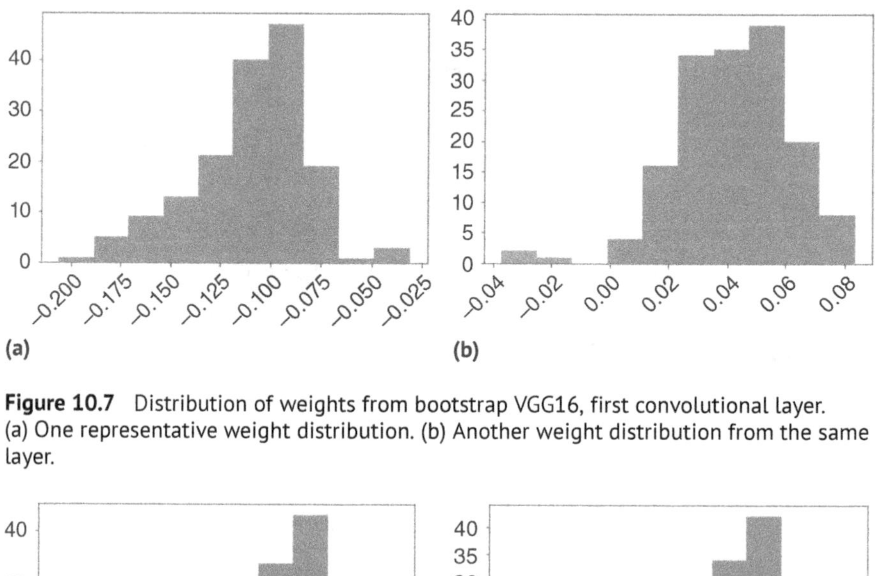

Figure 10.7 Distribution of weights from bootstrap VGG16, first convolutional layer. (a) One representative weight distribution. (b) Another weight distribution from the same layer.

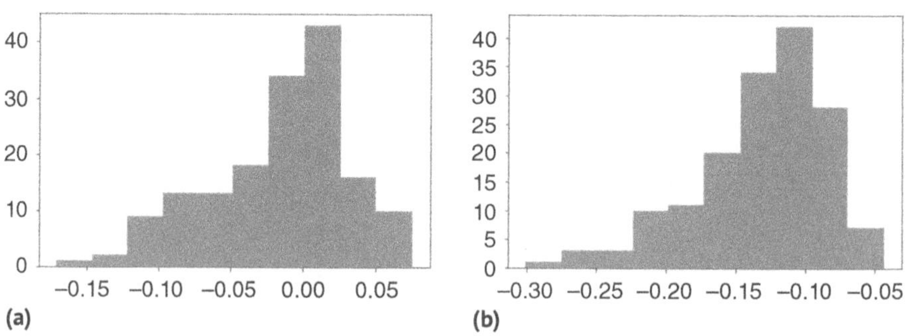

Figure 10.8 Distribution of biases from bootstrap VGG16, first convolutional layer. (a) One representative bias distribution. (b) Distribution of another bias from the same layer.

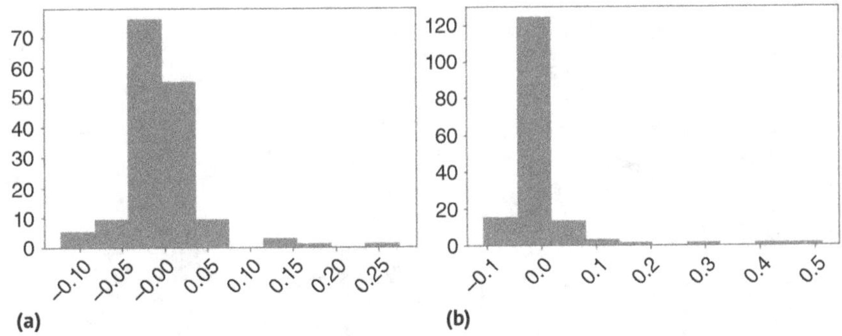

Figure 10.9 Distribution of weights from bootstrap VGG16, final fully connected layer. (a) One representative weight distribution. (b) Another weight distribution from the same layer.

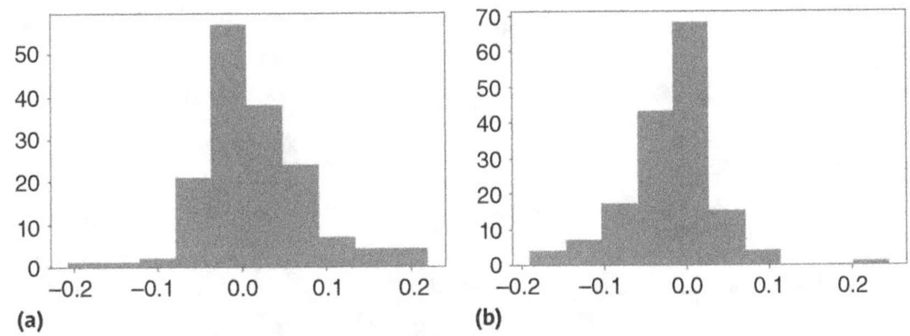

Figure 10.10 Distribution of biases from bootstrap VGG16, final fully connected layer. (a) One representative bias distribution. (b) Distribution of another bias from the same layer.

10.3.3 Inception v3 Parameters

Majority of the bootstrap weight distributions of the first convolutional layer for the Inception v3 model trained on CIFAR-10 data are approximately symmetric, as shown in Figure 10.11 with selected ones. Heavy tails are observed in some weight distributions. Weights without heavy tails are approximately in the ± 0.4 range, while the ranges of the heavy-tailed weights are sometimes smaller.

Majority of the bootstrap weight distributions of the second convolutional layer for the Inception v3 model trained on CIFAR-10 data are approximately symmetric, as shown in Figure 10.12 with selected ones. Heavy tails are also observed. Most of the weights range less than ± 0.01.

Majority of the bootstrap weight distributions of the third convolutional layer for the Inception v3 model trained on CIFAR-10 data are approximately symmetric, as shown in Figure 10.13 with selected ones. Heavy tails are observed in some weights. Weights are approximately in the ± 0.15 range.

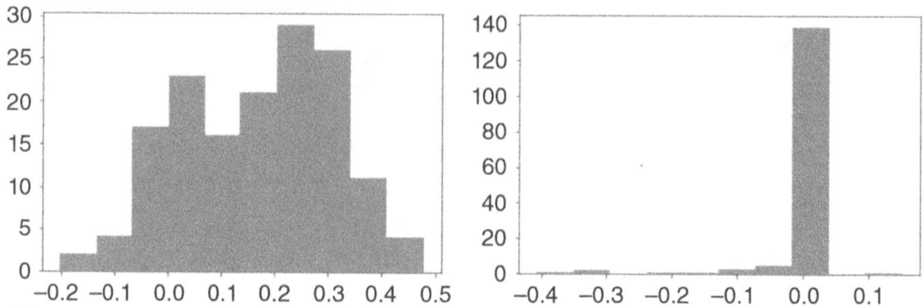

(a) (b)

Figure 10.11 Distribution of weights from bootstrap Inception v3, first convolutional layer. (a) One representative weight distribution. (b) Another weight distribution from the same layer.

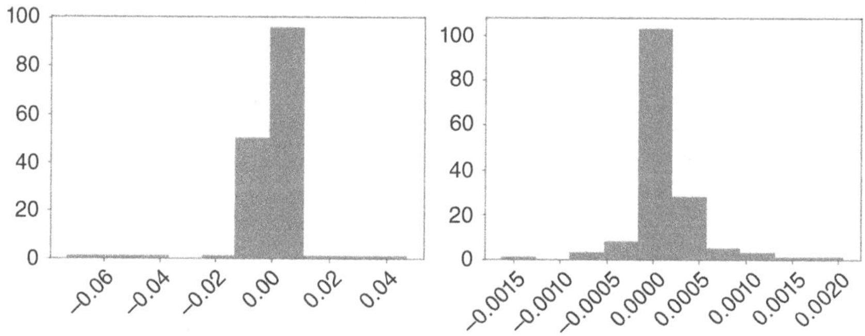

(a) (b)

Figure 10.12 Distribution of weights from bootstrap Inception v3, second convolutional layer. (a) One representative weight distribution. (b) Another weight distribution from the same layer.

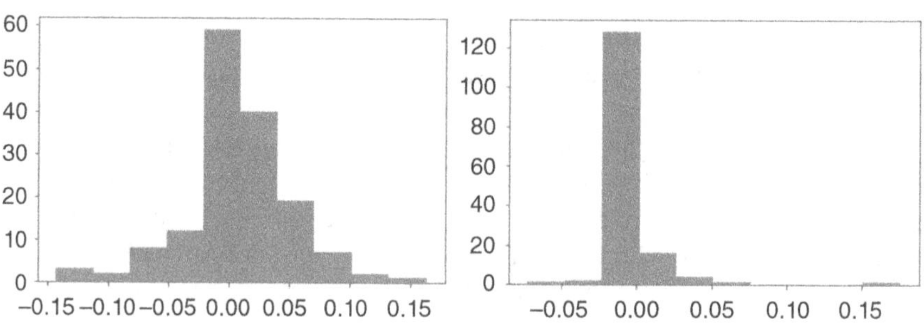

(a) (b)

Figure 10.13 Distribution of weights from bootstrap Inception v3, third convolutional layer. (a) One representative weight distribution. (b) Another weight distribution from the same layer.

Majority of the bootstrap weight distributions of the fourth convolutional layer for the Inception v3 model trained on CIFAR-10 data are approximately symmetric, as shown in Figure 10.14 with selected ones. Weights are approximately in the ±0.15 range, with the exception of some heavy tails.

Majority of the bootstrap weight distributions of the fifth convolutional layer for the Inception v3 trained on CIFAR-10 data are approximately symmetric, as shown in Figure 10.15 with selected ones. Weights are approximately in the ±0.05 range, with the exception of some heavy tails.

Majority of the bootstrap weight distributions of the sixth convolutional layer for the Inception v3 trained on CIFAR-10 data are approximately symmetric, as shown in Figure 10.16 with selected ones. Weights are approximately in the ±0.1 range, with the exception of some heavy tails.

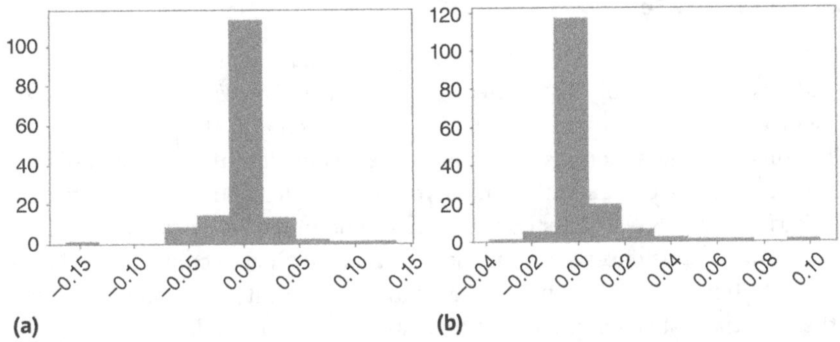

Figure 10.14 Distribution of weights from bootstrap Inception v3, fourth convolutional layer. (a) One representative weight distribution. (b) Another weight distribution from the same layer.

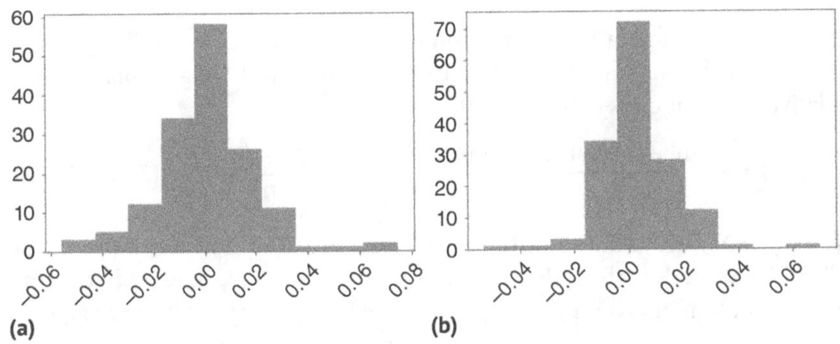

Figure 10.15 Distribution of weights from bootstrap Inception v3, fifth convolutional layer. (a) One representative weight distribution. (b) Another weight distribution from the same layer.

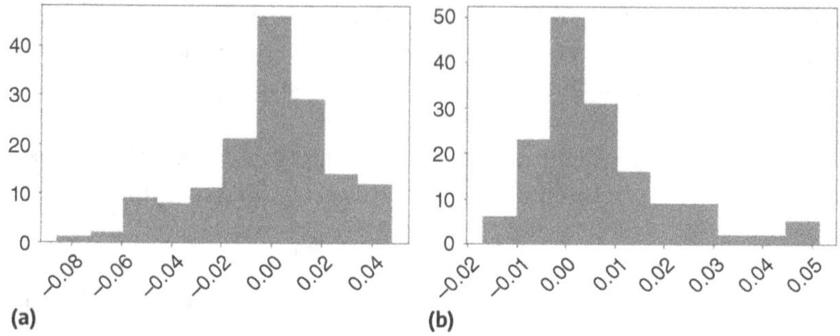

Figure 10.16 Distribution of weights from bootstrap Inception v3, sixth convolutional layer. (a) One representative weight distribution. (b) Another weight distribution from the same layer.

10.3.4 Normality Test

The Kolmogorov–Smirnov (KS) test [41] was performed to determine whether the weights/biases are normally distributed. The KS test statistic is a quantification of the distance between the empirical distribution of a sample and the cumulative distribution of a comparison distribution. The test statistic is the largest observed difference between the empirical cumulative distribution and the reference cumulative distribution. KS test statistics are therefore bounded between 0 and 1. Two identical distributions observe a value of 0. In this chapter we compare the bootstrap distributions of NN weights/biases with a univariate Gaussian. The null hypothesis of the test is that the bootstrap distribution is normal.

In the one sample case with sample size n, the Kolmogorov–Smirnov statistic, D_n, is computed as:

$$D_n = \sup_x |F_n(x) - F(x)|, \tag{10.1}$$

where $F(x)$ is the cumulative distribution function of the reference distribution, and $F_n(x)$ is the bootstrap cumulative distribution of NN weights/biases. The cumulative distribution is defined as follows:

$$F_n(x) = \frac{\text{number of elements in the sample} \leq x}{x} = \frac{1}{n}\sum_{i-1}^{n} 1_{(-\infty,x]}(X_i), \tag{10.2}$$

where $1_{(-\infty,x]}(X_i)$ is the indicator function, equal to 1 if $X_i \leq x$, otherwise equal to 0. The KS test rejects the null hypothesis that the sample comes from the reference distribution at level α if $\sqrt{n}D_n > K_\alpha$, where K_α is defined as the value at which the cumulative distribution of K is equal to $1 - \alpha$. All tests in this chapter are evaluated at level $\alpha = 0.05$.

For all bootstrapped networks, the KS test statistic was computed for 1,000 randomly selected weights and 1,000 randomly selected biases in all layers. Any layer with fewer than 1,000 weights (or 1,000 biases) has KS tests performed for all weights (or biases). For layers with more than 1,000 weights or biases, a random sampling of 1,000 was taken.

Below we summarize the KS test *p*-values for the weights and the front convolutional layers in three CNN models. *P*-values larger than 0.01 suggest the bootstrap parameter distributions are reasonably normal.

- CNN3 first convolutional (conv.): 95% of the KS tests have *p*-values greater than 0.054.
- VGG16 first conv.: 75% of the KS tests have *p*-values greater than 0.022.
- Inception v3 first conv.: 10% of the KS tests have *p*-values greater than 0.11.
- Inception v3 second conv.: 5% of the KS tests have *p*-values greater than 0.014.
- Inception v3 third conv.: 5% of the KS tests have *p*-values greater than 0.045.
- Inception v3 fourth conv.: 10% of the KS tests have *p*-values greater than 0.034.
- Inception v3 fifth conv.: 25% of the KS tests have *p*-values greater than 0.025.
- Inception v3 sixth conv.: 50% of the KS tests have *p*-values greater than 0.026.

Here we summarize the KS test *p*-values for the weights and of the last fully connected layers in the CNN models.

- CNN3 last fully connected: 95% of the KS tests have *p*-values greater than 0.027.
- VGG16 last fully connected: 1% of the KS tests have *p*-values greater than 0.014.

Here we summarize the KS test *p*-values for the biases of the front convolutional layers and the last fully connected layers in the CNN models.

- CNN3 first conv.: 99% of the KS tests have *p*-values greater than 0.156.
- CNN3 last fully connected: 99% of the KS tests have *p*-values greater than 0.253.
- VGG16 first conv.: 50% of the KS tests have *p*-values greater than 0.029.
- VGG16 last fully connected: 25% of the KS tests have *p*-values greater than 0.055.

We examined the shape of the nonnormal weights and biases from each layer of VGG16 and Inception V3. Unfortunately, we do not see a single distribution that can fit all the nonnormal weights or biases.

10.3.5 NNs by Varying Initial Random Seeds

Training an NN with cross entropy loss is a nonconvex optimization problem. When we use a different random initial seed, we obtain a different trained network. By having 150 different random initial seeds, we have 150 trained networks with the same training data. They all have nearly identical accuracy over the clean test data, but the weights and biases of the 150 trained networks are different. Interestingly, the distributions of the weights and the biases by varying the random initial seeds are similar to the bootstrap distributions.

Here we compute the distance between the trained and the bootstrapped values for the same parameter. Distances are evaluated using the Wasserstein 1 distance, as well as the two sample Kolmogorov–Smirnov test.

The Wasserstein distance [42] is a metric based on the real-world task of moving dirt. It is defined as the amount of earth that needs to be moved multiplied by the distance it would move, in order to turn one pile of earth into a different pile of earth. Here we use the one-dimensional metric to compare the distributions of weights and biases derived from bootstrapping neural networks with those derived from networks generated by varying initial seeds. The Wasserstein 1-distance, $W_1(u, v)$, for probability measures $u, v \in P_p(\mathbb{R})$ is:

$$W_1(u, v) = \inf_{\pi \in \Gamma(u,v)} \int_{\mathbb{R}\times\mathbb{R}} |x - y| \, d\pi(x, y), \tag{10.3}$$

where $\Gamma(u, v)$ is the set of probability distributions on $\mathbb{R} \times \mathbb{R}$ whose marginals are u and v. This definition is equivalent [43] to:

$$W_1(u, v) = \int_{\mathbb{R}} |U - V|, \tag{10.4}$$

where U and V are the cumulative distribution functions of u and v, respectively.

We select 1,000 weights and 1,000 biases from each layer. The selected weights and biases match those selected for plotting the bootstrap distributions. We compute Wasserstein-1 distances for CNN3 1st convolutional and last fully connected, and VGG16 1st convolutional and last fully connected. The 95th percentile of the distances between the weights are 0.056, 0.012, 0.044, and 0.011, respectively. The 95th percentile of the distances between the biases are 0.031, 0.004, 0.075, and 0.07, respectively.

Here we also perform the KS test to measure the distance between two empirical samples. The test statistic is a quantification of the distance between the empirical distributions of two samples. The test statistic is the largest observed difference between the two empirical cumulative distributions. KS test statistics are therefore bounded between 0 and 1. Two identical distributions observe a value of 0.

The null hypothesis of the test is that the two empirical samples are drawn from the same distribution. A cutoff of the largest allowable distance is defined for a given confidence level. If the largest distance exceeds that value, the null hypothesis is rejected. The Kolmogorov–Smirnov statistic, $D_{n,m}$, for two samples of sizes n and m, respectively, is computed as:

$$D_{n,m} = \sup_x \left| F_{1,n}(x) - F_{2,m}(x) \right|, \tag{10.5}$$

where $F_{1,n}(x)$ is the empirical cumulative distribution of the first sample, and $F_{1,m}(x)$ is the empirical cumulative distribution of second. The empirical cumulative distributions are defined as in Equation 10.2.

All tests in this work are evaluated at level $\alpha = 0.05$. For n and m sufficiently large, the null hypothesis that the two samples come from the same distribution is rejected if:

$$D_{n,m} > c(\alpha)\sqrt{\frac{n+m}{nm}}, \tag{10.6}$$

where $c(\alpha)$ is the inverse of the Kolmogorov distribution,

$$c(\alpha) = \sqrt{-\ln\left(\frac{\alpha}{2}\right) * \frac{1}{2}} \tag{10.7}$$

P-values greater than 0.01 suggest two distributions are reasonably similar to each other. For the weights of CNN3 first conv, 99% of the p-values are larger than 0.352. For the weights of VGG16 first conv, 90% of the p-values are larger than 0.038. For the biases of CNN3 1st conv, 99% of the p-values are larger than 0.50. For the biases of VGG16 first conv, 75% of the p-values are larger than 0.052.

The distributions of the weights and biases by bootstrap and by varying random initial seeds are similar to each other.

10.3.6 Regression for NN Parameters

Sometimes, it may not be practical to bootstrap a neural network. In some instances, bootstrapping a network may not converge. Using the distribution information obtained in our bootstrap experiments, we estimate the distribution parameters where we cannot bootstrap. We have a single distribution for the weights in a layer and estimate its parameters using a regression model. The weight distribution parameters are estimated with the number of weights in a layer being the predictor variable. Regression models below are for Gaussian weight distributions.

When we cannot bootstrap, for the Gaussian distribution, the mean is set to the average value of all trained weights in a given layer of the network. We only estimate the standard deviation using linear regression. Standard deviations of each weight were taken for the bootstrap experiments run on Inception v3 and VGG16. The bootstrap experiments from CNN3 were excluded from the analysis due to the small number of parameters in this neural network. The mean standard deviation was then taken for each layer. The formula for the regression model is in Equations 10.8, where Y is the average standard deviation of the weights in the layer and X is the number of weights in the layer.

$$Y = 0.048585 - 0.002251\log_2 X. \tag{10.8}$$

10.4 Randomized DNN Ensembles with Gaussian Random Weights

The goal of bootstrapping the network is to learn distribution information about the parameters in the convolutional layers and the fully connected layer. In particular, we estimate the percentiles, mean, and variance of the weights. Armed with this information, parameters for the weight distributions are estimated, and the weights in a network are randomized according to these distributions. With a portion of the weights randomized, the individual network is weakened. Since even a smaller CNN has a large number of parameters for each layer, replacing some weights by random numbers in a CNN model only slightly reduces the accuracy of the model on clean test data. Then an ensemble of CNN models with some random weights is able to achieve the same accuracy as the trained model without random weights on clean data. A random ensemble also achieves robust performance over adversarial examples.

Given one trained CNN model, we can have infinitely many CNN random ensembles that all maintain the same accuracy over the clean test data as the trained model itself, and achieve robust performance over adversarial examples. We design this strategy to address the adaptive attacks. An adaptive attack is customized to break a defense strategy itself. By having infinitely many random ensembles, we are able to frequently switch to a different ensemble without incurring additional training time. Thus, the adaptive attacks lose the target to attack. Although we cannot break the cycle of attacks and defenses, we are able to manage to stay ahead of the adversaries in the cycle.

10.4.1 Adversarial Examples Generation

We implement the ensemble strategy with CNN3, VGG16, and Inception v3. As in the bootstrap experiment, CNN3 is trained on MNIST. VGG16 is trained on CIFAR-10. Different from the bootstrap experiment, Inception v3 is trained on Tiny ImageNet database.

Tiny ImageNet is a subset of the ImageNet database. Tiny ImageNet training data consists of 100,000 images from 200 classes. Each class has 500 training images, 50 test images, and 50 validation images. The images are all 64×64 color images. The Tiny ImageNet database can be downloaded from "http://cs231n.stanford.edu/tiny-imagenet-200.zip."

Inception v3 was initialized using the pre-trained weights available on Python. After resetting the fully connected module to the number of output classes, the layer was initialized using Kaiming's uniform method. The Tiny ImageNet images were scaled to 299×299, as required by Torchvision's implementation of Inception v3. The full database of 100,000 training images was used in retraining. Tiny ImageNet is much larger than MNIST and CIFAR-10. The network was trained with a batch size of 64. There were 24 epochs of training. Optimization was performed with Stochastic Gradient Descent (SGD), with momentum of 0.9 and weight decay 0.0005. The initial learning rate was 0.05 and decayed by a factor of 0.5 every 30 epochs.

For each of the three networks, a set of 4,000 adversarial examples was generated. Four white-box attack methods were implemented, with 1,000 examples generated from each. Each attack generated adversarial examples based on the same 1,000 clean images, with an even distribution of examples from each class from the original datasets. This amounts to 100 images per class for MNIST and CIFAR-10 databases, and 5 images per class for Tiny ImageNet. The attacks used were FGSM, PGD, DP, and Carlini-Wagner L2 (CW2). Adversarial examples were generated using the "foolbox" Python library. The baseline accuracy of three NNs over the clean samples and the adversarial examples from four attacks are summarized in the chart. The average total amount of adversarial perturbations generated by CW2 and DP attacks is just one tenth of those generated by FGSM and PGD. Note PGD attack can be considered as an iterative version of FGSM attack.

Accuracy	Clean	PGD	FGSM	DeepFool	CW2
CNN3	0.993	0.016	0.044	0.004	0.002
VGG16	0.932	0.055	0.064	0.037	0.033
Inception v3	0.850	0.084	0.193	0.085	0.038

10.4.2 Randomization

We first train one network. The random ensembles are generated from that single network. One layer of the architecture is selected to be randomized. For ensemble size n, there are n copies of the network with the selected layer randomized. The weights to be randomized in the layer are also selected randomly. Thus, one copy of the randomized network differs from any other copy. The remainder of the parameters in the network remain unchanged. For each of the n copies of the selected layer, each weight in the layer is replaced by a random number with a predetermined probability p. The decision to replace a specific weight is made using a Bernoulli distribution. The selected layer and the replacement probability, p, remain constant for all the copies in the ensemble.

The distributions to generate the random numbers as weights have the parameters learned from bootstrap. CNN3 trained on MNIST and VGG16 trained on CIFAR-10 were used for both bootstrap and generating random ensembles. For these two networks, random numbers are directly generated from the bootstrap distributions to replace the weights. Ensembles with Gaussian weights are used in Section 10.5. The mean of a Gaussian distribution equal to the mean of the bootstrap parameter means. The standard deviation is the mean of the bootstrap parameter standard deviations.

For the networks without bootstrap parameter distributions, we learn from the bootstrap networks and build a linear model to estimate the Gaussian distribution parameter values. Details for the linear regression are given in Section 10.3.6. For those networks without bootstrap distributions, the Gaussian mean is set to the average of the trained weights in the selected layer.

Preliminary results indicated that randomization of the front convolutional layers demonstrated a greater robustness than randomizing later convolutional layers or fully connected layers. All ensembles presented here have layers selected from the beginning of the network. For every network presented here, we ran experiments with the replacement probabilities $p = 0.1, 0.2, \ldots 0.9$. Each setting was repeated five times. The accuracy reported in Section 10.5 is the average of five runs. Sometimes, additional values of p are included when the initial results suggest a more likely range for p to achieve higher accuracy.

10.5 Ensemble Experiment Results

Parameters for the Gaussian distributions were determined using the method described in Section 10.4.2. We achieved the best performance on randomizing Inception v3, which has the largest and most complex network structure. We randomize only one layer when building a random ensemble. We discovered that using random weights at the front of a network achieves the best results on correctly classify the adversarial examples and maintain the accuracy on the clean data. For smaller DNN models, the performance of the random ensemble on the adversarial examples with larger perturbations (i.e., FGSM and PGD) drop significantly. Every accurate result reported here is based on the average of five runs.

10.5.1 CNN3 Randomization Results

Figure 10.17 shows ensemble results for the first convolutional layer of CNN3, using Gaussian randomization. It includes four adversarial attacks, and ensemble sizes ranging from 3 to 8 randomized models. For the CW attack and DP attack, randomizing 10% of the weights of the convolutional layer achieves the highest accuracy. For both attacks, an ensemble of 7 randomized networks achieves the highest accuracy of 88.0 and 78.4%, respectively. For FGSM and PGD attacks, randomizing 80% of the weights of the convolutional layer achieves the highest accuracy. For both FGSM and PGD, an ensemble of 3 randomized networks has the highest accuracy of 23.1 and 24.9%. A smaller percentage (<10%) of randomized weights might improve the accuracy on CW2 and DP as Figure 10.17 suggests.

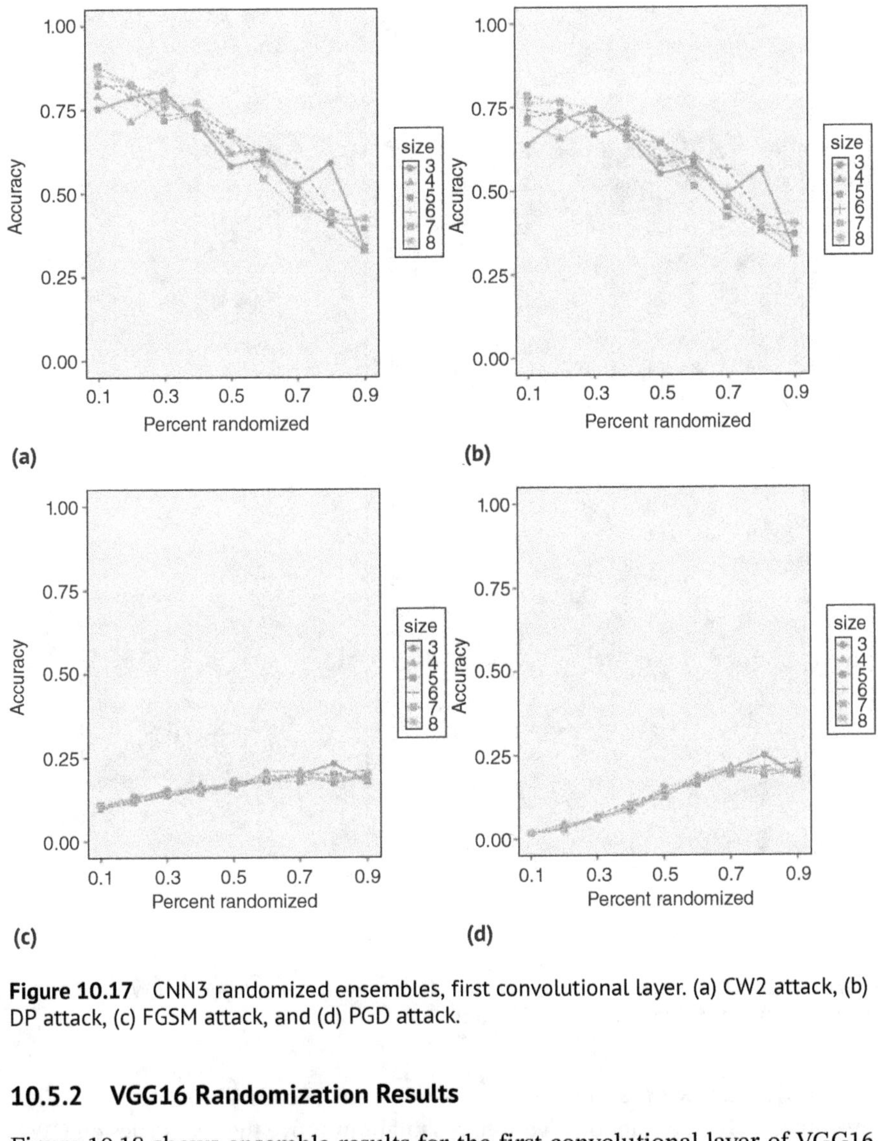

Figure 10.17 CNN3 randomized ensembles, first convolutional layer. (a) CW2 attack, (b) DP attack, (c) FGSM attack, and (d) PGD attack.

10.5.2 VGG16 Randomization Results

Figure 10.18 shows ensemble results for the first convolutional layer of VGG16, using Gaussian randomization. It includes four adversarial attacks, and ensemble sizes ranging from 3 to 8 randomized models. For the CW attack, randomizing 10% of the weights of the convolutional layer achieves the highest accuracy. Ensemble size 8 achieves the highest accuracy of 76.4%. For DP, randomizing 30% of weights with ensemble size 5 achieves accuracy 45.6%. For FGSM, randomizing 70% of weights with ensemble size 3 achieves accuracy 18.9%. For PGD, randomizing

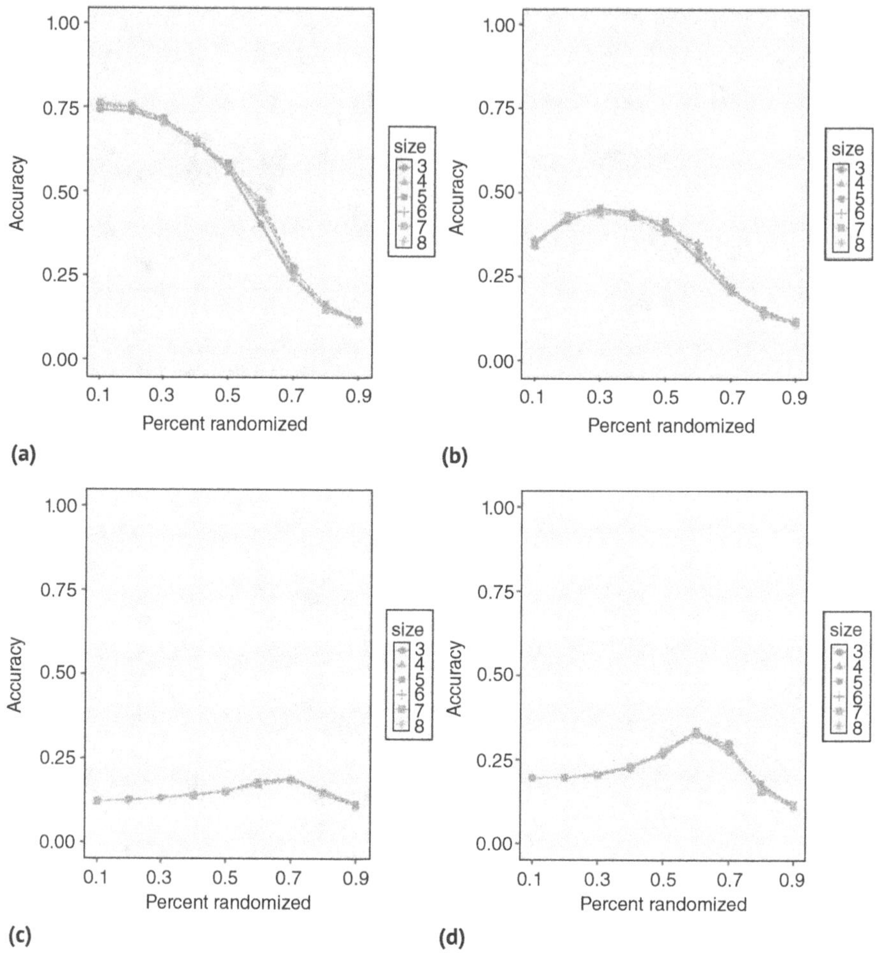

Figure 10.18 VGG16 randomized ensembles, first convolutional layer. (a) CW2 attack, (b) DP attack, (c) FGSM attack, and (d) PGD attack.

60% of weights with ensemble size 8 achieves accuracy 33.7%. A smaller percentage (<10%) of randomized weights might improve the accuracies on CW2 as Figure 10.18 suggests.

10.5.3 Inception v3 Randomization Results

Figure 10.19 shows ensemble results for the first convolutional layer of Inception v3, using Gaussian randomization. It includes four adversarial attacks, and ensemble sizes ranging from 3 to 8 randomized models. For the DP attack, randomizing 10% of the weights of the convolutional layer achieves the highest accuracy. Ensemble size 7 achieves the highest accuracy of 78.0%. For the CW attack, randomizing 20% of the weights of the convolutional layer achieves the highest accuracy. Ensemble size 3 achieves the highest accuracy of 77.0%. For FGSM, randomizing 60% of weights with ensemble size 7 achieves accuracy 47.2%. For PGD, randomizing 50% of weights with ensemble size 8 achieves accuracy 58.5%.

Figure 10.20 shows ensemble results for the second convolutional layer of Inception v3, using Gaussian randomization. It includes four adversarial attacks, and

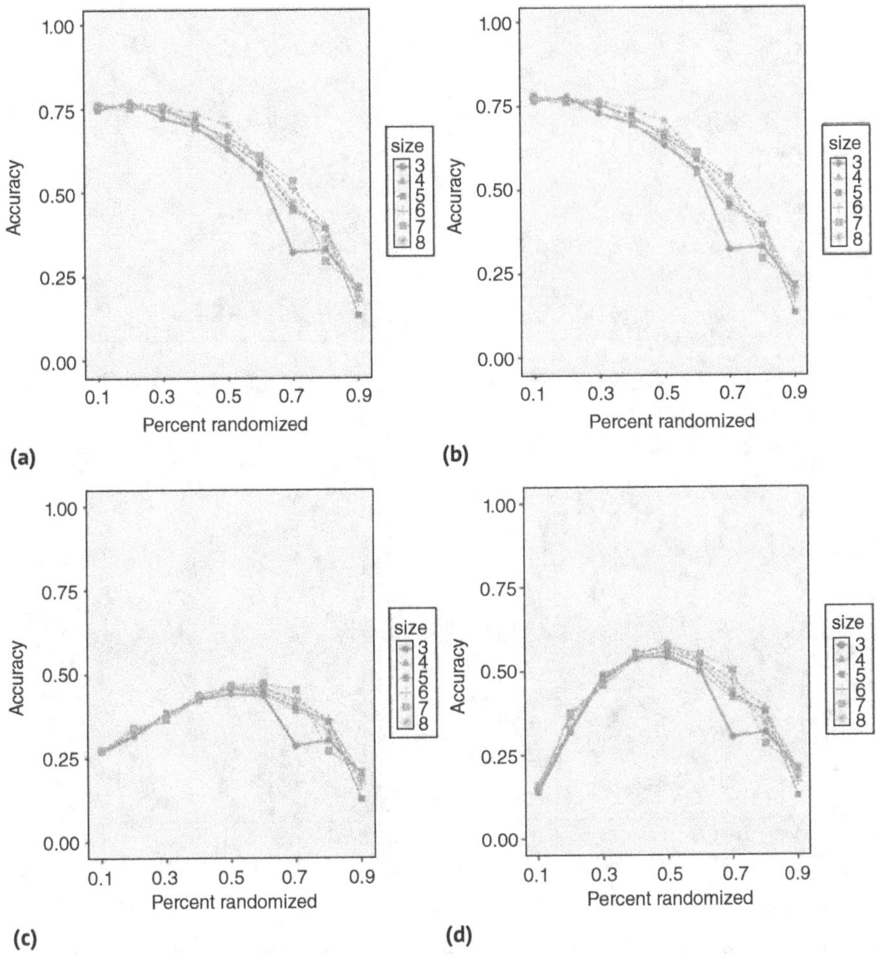

Figure 10.19 Inception v3 randomized ensembles, first convolutional layer. (a) CW2 attack, (b) DP attack, (c) FGSM attack, and (d) PGD attack.

ensemble sizes ranging from 3 to 8 randomized models. For the four attacks, randomizing 10% of the weights of the 2nd convolutional layer, and ensemble size 7 achieve the highest accuracy. For the DP attack the highest accuracy is 52.2%. For the CW2 attack, the highest accuracy is 51.9%. For FGSM and PGD attacks, the highest accuracies are 41.1 and 47%, respectively. For the second convolutional layer, we ran additional experiments. As Figure 10.20 shows, randomizing a smaller percentage of the weights of the second convolutional layer significantly increased the random DNN ensemble accuracies on the attacks. For the DP attack,

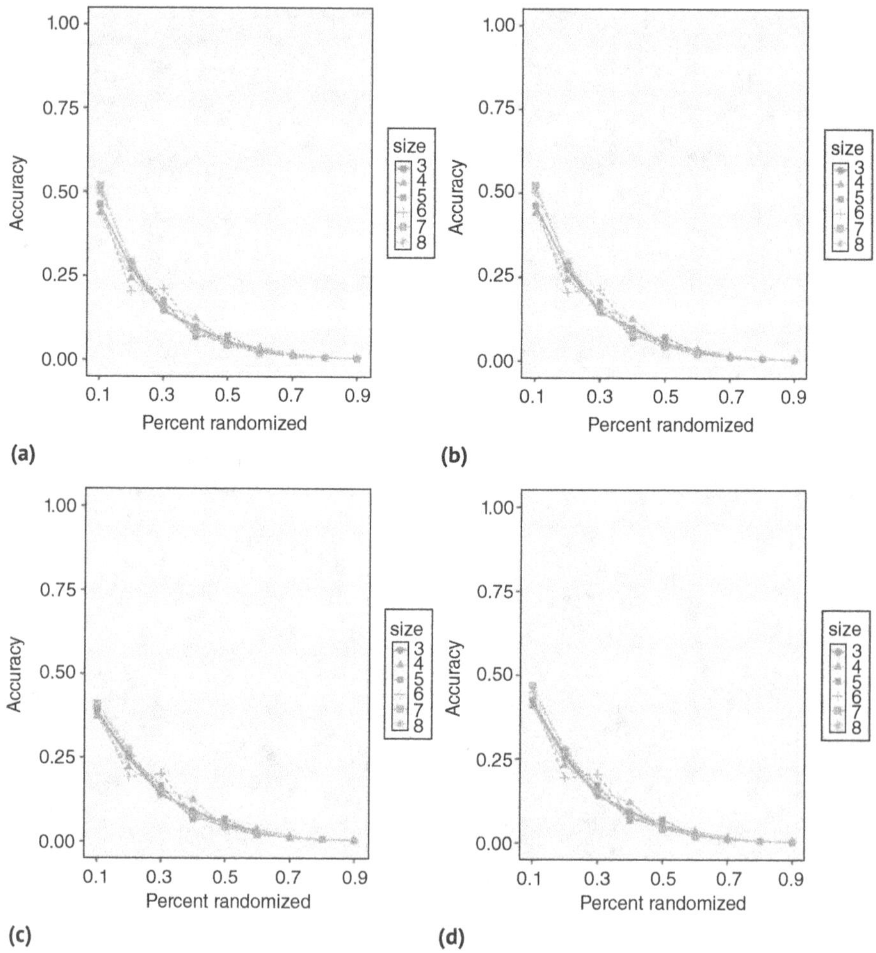

Figure 10.20 Inception v3 randomized ensembles, second convolutional layer. (a) CW2 attack, (b) DP attack, (c) FGSM attack, and (d) PGD attack.

randomizing 1% of the weights and ensemble size 7 achieve the highest accuracy 77.4%. For the CW2 attack, randomizing 1% of the weights and ensemble size 5 achieve the highest accuracy 76.3%. For FGSM and PGD attacks, randomizing 5% of weights with ensemble size 8 achieves the highest accuracy of 43.7 and 57.7%, respectively.

Figure 10.21 shows ensemble results for the third convolutional layer of Inception v3, using Gaussian randomization. It includes four adversarial attacks, and ensemble sizes ranging from 3 to 8 randomized models. For the CW and DP attacks, randomizing 10% of the weights of the convolutional layer achieves the

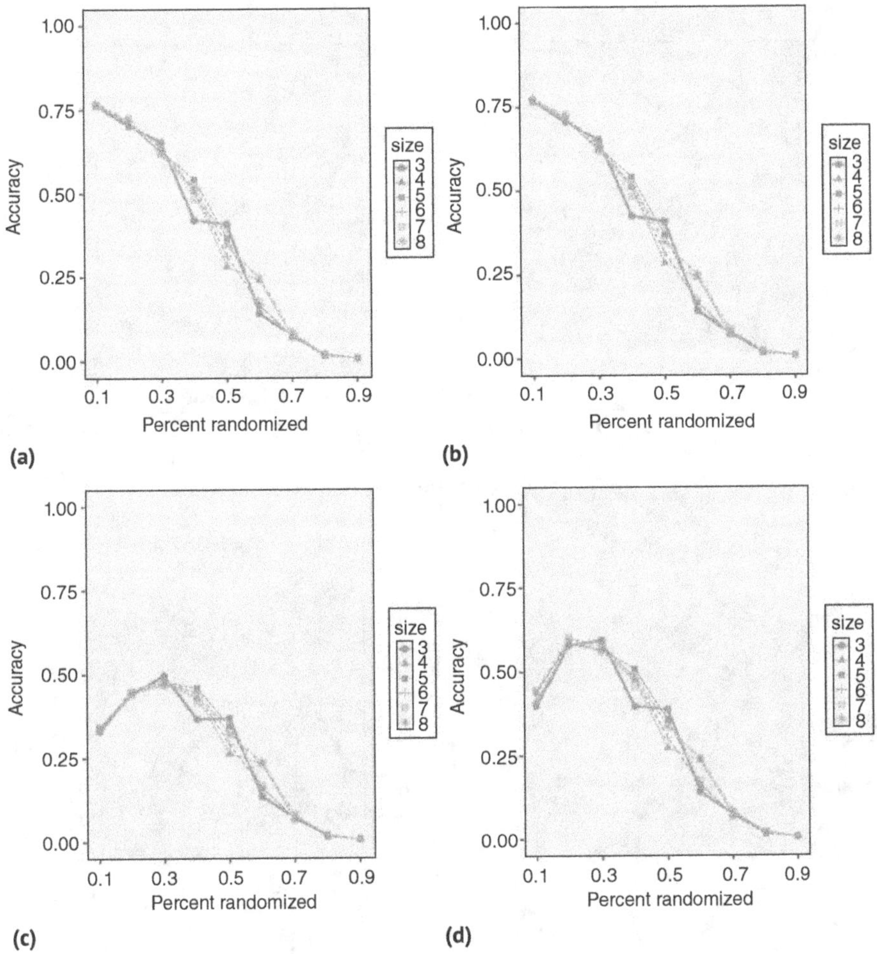

Figure 10.21 Inception v3 randomized ensembles, third convolutional layer. (a) CW2 attack, (b) DP attack, (c) FGSM attack, and (d) PGD attack.

highest accuracy. For both attacks, ensemble size 6 achieves the highest accuracy of 77.2 and 77.7%, respectively. For FGSM, randomizing 30% of weights with ensemble size 3 achieves accuracy 49.7%. For PGD, randomizing 20% of weights with ensemble size 7 achieves accuracy 60.4%. A smaller percentage (<10%) of randomized weights might improve the accuracies on CW2 and DP as Figure 10.21 suggests.

Figure 10.22 shows ensemble results for the fourth convolutional layer of Inception v3, using Gaussian randomization. It includes four adversarial attacks, and ensemble sizes ranging from 3 to 8 randomized models. For the CW and DP attacks, randomizing 10% of the weights of the convolutional layer achieves the

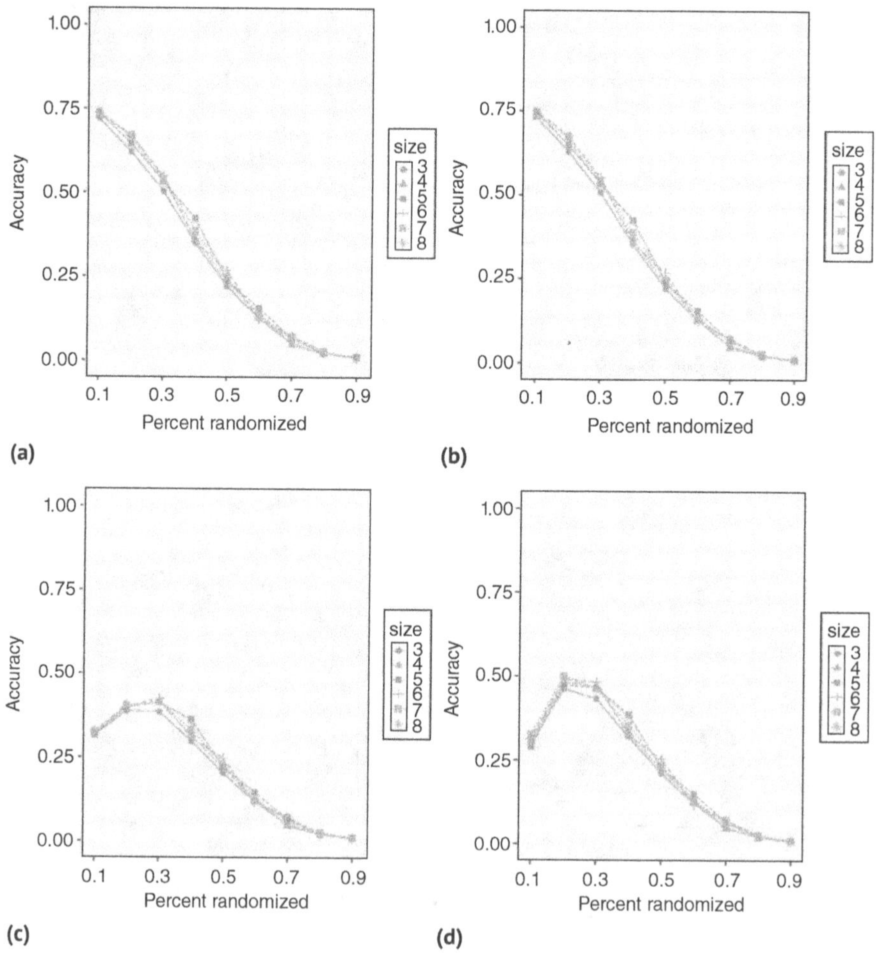

Figure 10.22 Inception v3 randomized ensembles, fourth convolutional layer. (a) CW2 attack, (b) DP attack, (c) FGSM attack, and (d) PGD attack.

highest accuracy. For both attacks, ensemble size 8 achieves the highest accuracy of 74.1 and 75.1%, respectively. For FGSM, randomizing 30% of weights with ensemble size 6 achieves accuracy 42.4%. For PGD, randomizing 20% of weights with ensemble size 7 achieves accuracy 50.0%. A smaller percentage (<10%) of randomized weights might improve the accuracies on CW2 and DP as Figure 10.22 suggests.

Figure 10.23 shows ensemble results for the fifth convolutional layer of Inception v3, using Gaussian randomization. It includes four adversarial attacks, and ensemble sizes ranging from 3 to 8 randomized models. For the CW and DP attacks, randomizing 10% of the weights of the convolutional layer achieves the

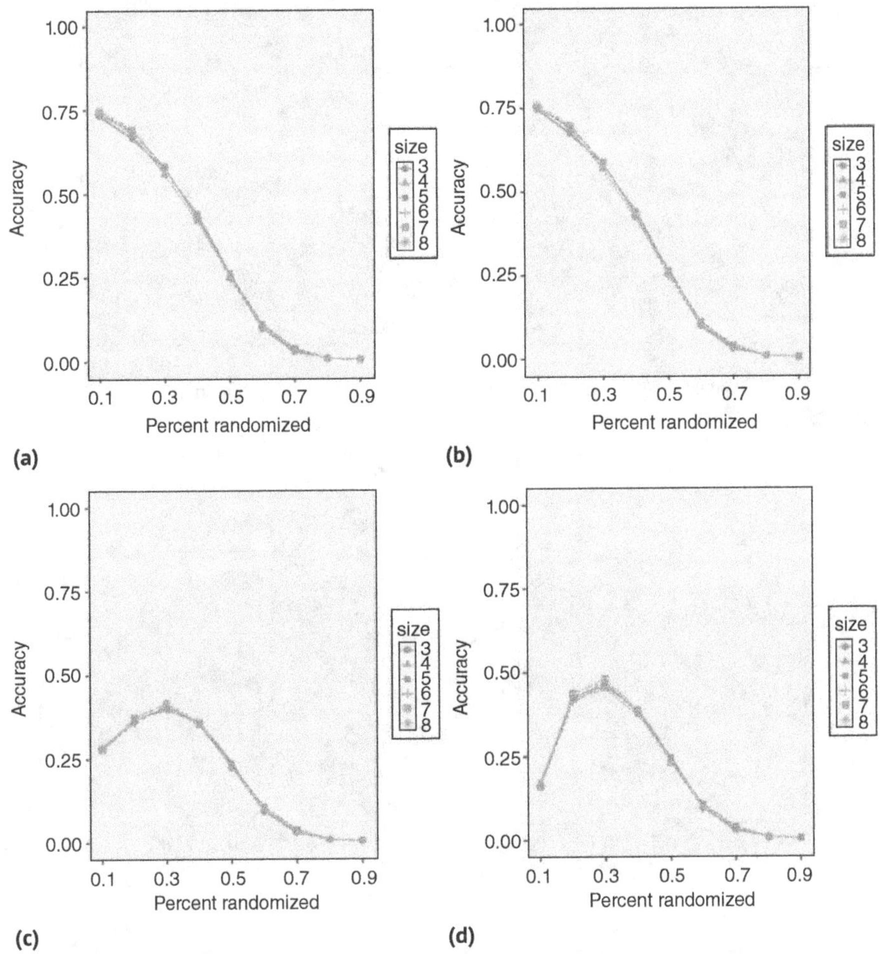

Figure 10.23 Inception v3 randomized ensembles, fifth convolutional layer. (a) CW attack, (b) DP attack, (c) FGSM attack, and (d) PGD attack.

highest accuracy. For both attacks, ensemble size 8 achieves the highest accuracy of 74.9 and 76.2%, respectively. For FGSM, randomizing 30% of weights with ensemble size 8 achieves accuracy 41.7%. For PGD, randomizing 30% of weights with ensemble size 7 achieves accuracy 48.2%. A smaller percentage (<10%) of randomized weights might improve the accuracies on CW2 and DP as Figure 10.23 suggests.

Figure 10.24 shows ensemble results for the sixth convolutional layer of Inception v3, using Gaussian randomization. It includes four adversarial attacks, and ensemble sizes ranging from 3 to 8 randomized models. For the CW2 and DP

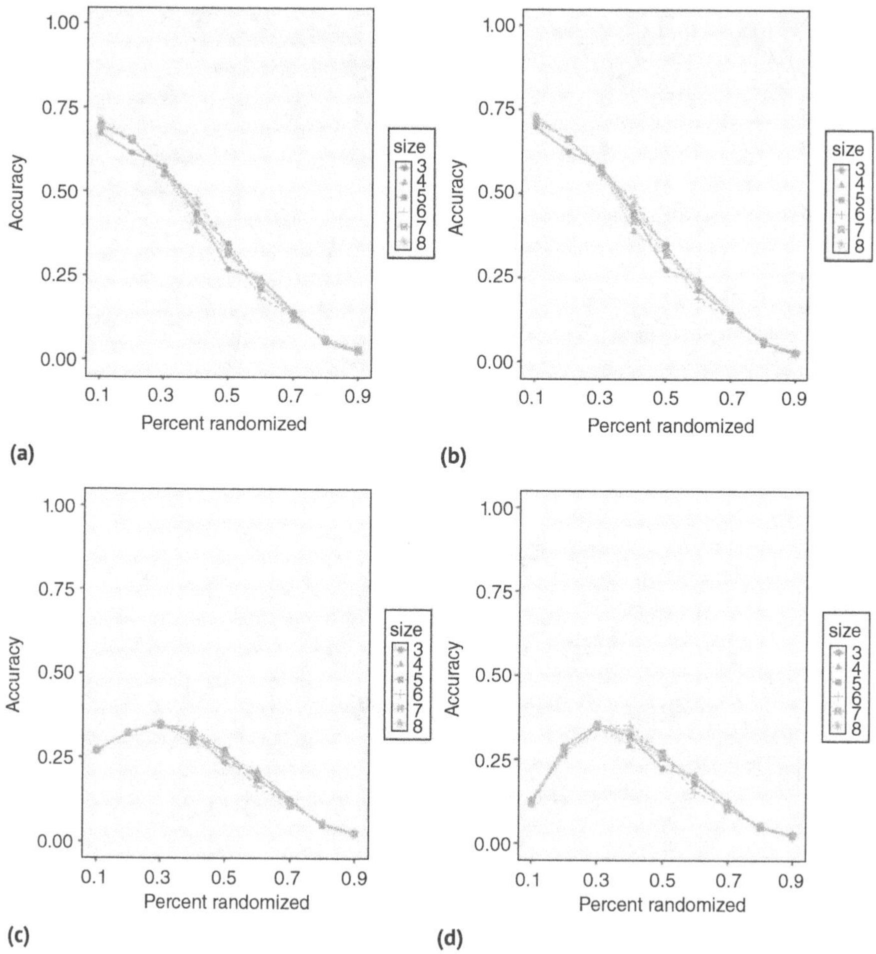

Figure 10.24 Inception v3 randomized ensembles, sixth convolutional layer. (a) CW attack, (b) DP attack, (c) FGSM attack, and (d) PGD attack.

attacks, randomizing 10% of the weights and ensemble size 8 achieve the highest accuracies of 71.2 and 73.1%, respectively. For FGSM and PGD, randomizing 30% of weights with ensemble size 8 achieves highest accuracies 35.1 and 35.5%, respectively. A smaller percentage (<10%) of randomized weights might improve the accuracies on CW2 and DP as Figure 10.24 suggests.

10.6 Conclusion

Although most of this chapter is devoted to the technical details of the DNN random ensemble, here we emphasize that a resilient DNN ensemble will enhance the safety of cyber-physical systems.

The most resilient random DNN ensembles are built upon randomizing the front convolutional layers of a network. As Inception v3 experiment shows, randomizing the sixth convolutional layer leads to a drop in the accuracies. For a smaller network, such as VGG16 and CNN3, only the very first convolutional layer should be randomized to obtain the best performance. The random DNN ensembles show the most robust results for the largest network in our experiments, Inception v3. We expect our moving target defense to show consistently robust performance for very large and complex networks.

Our moving target defense strategy has a key parameter – the percentage of random weights p in a front convolutional layer. From our experiments, the optimal p values are different for the four attacks. For the CW2 and DP attacks, which are strong attacks by adding a very small amount of adversarial perturbations, the optimal p should be smaller or equal to 10%. For FGSM and PGD attacks, which generate adversarial perturbations that are 10 times larger than CW2 and DP, the optimal p values are around 30%. The random DNN ensembles are not perfect, because their accuracies drop over weaker attacks which generate large adversarial perturbations. Hence, our moving target defense is still not an end of the game to defeat all the existing and future unknown attacks.

We first need to understand the distributions of DNN parameters. This is achieved by two different approaches: (1) Bootstrap each DNN model 150 times. We bootstrapped three increasingly larger DNN models; (2) Train each DNN model 150 times with different initial random seeds while using the same training data without bootstrap. We obtained another set of DNN parameter distributions by varying the initial random seeds. This is the first step towards building a DNN random ensemble.

This step is very computationally expensive. We have limited computing resources available in an academic department, as described in this chapter. In order to complete the computations within a reasonable timeframe, we had to use older and smaller datasets in the experiments.

For the commercial use cases, they have very large training data and potentially much bigger models, while a vast amount of computing power is also available. The state-of-the-art approach is to train the complex model once and obtain the parameters. This chapter points to the limitation of such approach. A trained model is only a point estimate, which is vulnerable under various adversarial attacks. Estimating the distribution of the model parameters is still important for today's complex systems, albeit a lot more computationally expensive. There is a moving target defense against adversarial attacks, armed with the knowledge of the model parameter distributions.

References

1 N. Papernot, P. McDaniel, I. Goodfellow, S. Jha, Z. B. Celik, and A. Swami. Practical black-box attacks against deep learning systems using adversarial examples. In *Proceedings of the 2017 ACM Asia Conference on Computer and Communications Security*, pp. 506–519, 2017.

2 X. Liu, H. Yang, Z. Liu, L. Song, H. Li, and Y. Chen. Dpatch: An adversarial patch attack on object detectors. In *The AAAI's Workshop on Artificial Intelligence Safety (SafeAI 2019)*, pp. 1–8, 2019.

3 A. Ilyas, L. Engstrom, A. Athalye, and J. Lin. Black-box adversarial attacks with limited queries and information. In *Proceedings of the 6th International Conference on Learning Representations (ICLR)*, pp. 1–10, 2018.

4 J. Su, D. V. Vargas, and K. Sakurai. One pixel attack for fooling deep neural networks. *IEEE Transactions on Evolutionary Computation*, 23(5): 828–841, 2019.

5 N. Papernot, P. McDaniel, S. Jha, M. Fredrikson, Z. B. Celik, and A. Swami. The limitations of deep learning in adversarial settings. In *2016 IEEE European Symposium on Security and Privacy (EuroS&P)*, pp. 372–387, 2016.

6 B. Xi. Adversarial machine learning for cybersecurity and computer vision: Current developments and challenges. *Wiley Interdisciplinary Reviews: Computational Statistics*, 12(5): e1511, 2020.

7 T. Gu, B. Dolan-Gavitt, and S. Garg. Badnets: Identifying vulnerabilities in the machine learning model supply chain. *arXiv 1708.06733,* 2017.

8 Y. Gao, B. G. Doan, Z. Zhang, S. Ma, J. Zhang, A. Fu, S. Nepal, and H. Kim. Backdoor attacks and countermeasures on deep learning: A comprehensive review. *arXiv preprint arXiv:2007.10760*, 2020.

9 A. Saha, A. Subramanya, and H. Pirsiavash. Hidden trigger backdoor attacks. In *Proceedings of the AAAI Conference on Artificial Intelligence*, vol. 34, pp. 11957–11965, 2020.

10 A. Shafahi, W. R. Huang, M. Najibi, O. Suciu, C. Studer, T. Dumitras, and T. Goldstein. Poison frogs! targeted clean-label poisoning attacks on neural networks. *Advances in Neural Information Processing Systems*, 31, 2018.

11 C. Szegedy, W. Zaremba, I. Sutskever, J. Bruna, D. Erhan, I. Goodfellow, and R. Fergus. Intriguing properties of neural networks. In *Proceedings of the International Conference on Learning Representations (ICLR)*, pp. 1–10, 2014.

12 I. Goodfellow, J. Shlens, and C. Szegedy. Explaining and harnessing adversarial examples. In *International Conference on Learning Representations*, pp. 1–12, 2015.

13 A. Kurakin, I. Goodfellow, and S. Bengio. Adversarial machine learning at scale. In *Proceedings of the 6th International Conference on Learning Representations (ICLR)*, pp. 1–10, 2017.

14 A. Rozsa, E. Rudd, and T. Boult. Adversarial diversity and hard positive generation. In *Proceedings of the IEEE Conference on Computer Vision and Pattern Recognition Workshops*, pp. 25–32, 2016.

15 A. Madry, A. Makelov, L. Schmidt, D. Tsipras, and A. Vladu. Towards deep learning models resistant to adversarial attacks. In *Proceedings of the 6th International Conference on Learning Representations (ICLR)*, pp. 1–10, 2018.

16 N. Carlini and D. Wagner. Adversarial examples are not easily detected: Bypassing ten detection methods. In *Proceedings of the 10th ACM Workshop on Artificial Intelligence and Security*, pp. 3–14. ACM, 2017.

17 S.-M. Moosavi-Dezfooli, A. Fawzin, and P. Frossard. Deepfool: A simple and accurate method to fool deep neural networks. In *Proceedings of the IEEE Conference on Computer Vision and Pattern Recognition (CVPR)*, pp. 2574–2582, 2016.

18 F. Tramer, N. Carlini, W. Brendel, and A. Madry. On adaptive attacks to adversarial example defenses. *Advances in Neural Information Processing Systems*, 33: 1633–1645, 2020.

19 M. Shin, H. Cho, H. Min, and S. Lim. Neural bootstrapper. *Advances in Neural Information Processing Systems*, 34: 16596–16609, 2021.

20 S. Reed, H. Lee, D. Anguelov, C. Szegedy, D. Erhan, and A. Rabinovich. Training deep neural networks on noisy labels with bootstrapping. In *ICLR Workshop*, 2015.

21 G. Paass. Assessing and improving neural network predictions by the bootstrap algorithm. *Advances in Neural Information Processing Systems*, 5, 1992.

22 J. Nixon, B. Lakshminarayanan, and D. Tran. Why are bootstrapped deep ensembles not better? In *"I Can't Believe It's Not Better!"NeurIPS 2020 Workshop*, 2020.

23 J. Franke and M. H. Neumann. Bootstrapping neural networks. *Neural Computation*, 12(8): 1929–1949, 2000.

24 J. Lee, Y. Lee, J. Kim, E. Yang, S. J. Hwang, and Y. W. Teh. Bootstrapping neural processes. *Advances in Neural Information Processing Systems (NIPS)*, 33: 6606–6615, 2020.

25 M. K. Tiwari and C. Chatterjee. Uncertainty assessment and ensemble flood forecasting using bootstrap based artificial neural networks (banns). *Journal of Hydrology*, 382(1–4): 20–33, 2010.

26 E. Zio. A study of the bootstrap method for estimating the accuracy of artificial neural networks in predicting nuclear transient processes. *IEEE Transactions on Nuclear Science*, 53(3): 1460–1478, 2006.

27 J. Ji, Y. Sun, F. Kong, and Q. Miao. A construction approach to prediction intervals based on bootstrap and deep belief network. *IEEE Access*, 7: 124185–124195, 2019.

28 H. Du, E. Barut, and F. Jin. Uncertainty quantification in cnn through the bootstrap of convex neural networks. In *Proceedings of the AAAI Conference on Artificial Intelligence*, vol. 35, pp. 12078–12085, 2021.

29 E. Nalisnick and P. Smyth. The amortized bootstrap. In *ICML 2017 Workshop on Implicit Models*, 2017.

30 B. Lakshminarayanan, A. Pritzel, and C. Blundell. Simple and scalable predictive uncertainty estimation using deep ensembles. *Advances in Neural Information Processing Systems*, 30, 2017.

31 C. Blundell, J. Cornebise, K. Kavukcuoglu, and D. Wierstra. Weight uncertainty in neural network. In *International Conference on Machine Learning*, pp. 1613–1622, 2015.

32 U. Simsekli, L. Sagun, and M. Gurbuzbalaban. A tail-index analysis of stochastic gradient noise in deep neural networks. In *Proceedings of the 36th International Conference on Machine Learning*, pp. 5827–5837, 2019.

33 G. Franchi, A. Bursuc, E. Aldea, S. Dubuisson, and I. Bloch. Tradi: Tracking deep neural network weight distributions. In *European Conference on Computer Vision*, pp. 105–121, 2020.

34 M. Mahoney and C. Martin. Traditional and heavy tailed self regularization in neural network models. In *International Conference on Machine Learning*, pp. 4284–4293. PMLR, 2019.

35 C. H. Martin and M. W. Mahoney. Implicit self-regularization in deep neural networks: Evidence from random matrix theory and implications for learning. *Journal of Machine Learning Research*, 22(165): 1–73, 2021.

36 M. Vladimirova, J. Arbel, and P. Mesejo. Bayesian neural networks become heavier-tailed with depth. In *NeurIPS 2018-Thirty-second Conference on Neural Information Processing Systems*, pp. 1–7, 2018.

37 B. Efron. Bootstrap methods: Another look at the jackknife. *The Annals of Statistics*, 7(1): 1–26, 1979. https://doi.org/10.1214/aos/1176344552.

38 A. Krizhevsky and G. Hinton. Learning multiple layers of features from tiny images. Technical Report 0, Toronto, Ontario: University of Toronto, 2009.

39 K. Simonyan and A. Zisserman. Very deep convolutional networks for large-scale image recognition. *arXiv 1409.1556*, 2015.

40 C. Szegedy, V. Vanhoucke, S. Ioffe, J. Shlens, and Z. Wojna. Rethinking the inception architecture for computer vision. *arXiv 1512.00567v3*, 2015.

41 F. J. Massey. The kolmogorov-smirnov test for goodness of fit. *Journal of the American Statistical Association*, 46(253): 65–78, 1951. https://doi.org/10.2307/2280095.

42 L. N. Vaserstein. Markov processes over denumerable products of spaces, describing large systems of automata. *Problems Information Transmission*, 5(3): 47–52, 1969.

43 A. Ramdas, N. Garcia, and M. Cuturi. On wasserstein two sample testing and related families of nonparametric tests, 2015. https://doi.org/10.48550/ARXIV.1509.02237.

Part 3

Game Theory for Network Resilience

11

Poisoning Attack and Defense Game for Federated Learning in Resilient NextG Networks

Yalin E. Sagduyu,[1] Tugba Erpek,[1] and Yi Shi[2]*

[1] *Nexcepta, Gaithersburg, MD, USA*
[2] *Commonwealth Cyber Initiative, Virginia Tech, Arlington, VA, USA*

*Corresponding Author: yalinsagduyu@ieee.org

11.1 Introduction

Federated learning for next-generation (NextG) communication systems: *NextG communication systems*, primarily referring to 6G and beyond, and in some contexts including advanced 5G systems, promise substantial performance improvements over current communication technologies. These enhancements are essential to meet the growing demands of emerging applications such as the Internet of Things (IoT), vehicle-to-everything (V2X) networks, and virtual/augmented reality (VR/AR). These advancements demand high throughput, low latency, and overall improvements in quality of experience. Traditional analytical methods, relying on domain subject expertise, often fall short in capturing the intricate nuances of NextG communications, including waveforms, channels, and resource dynamics. Therefore, the integration of *machine learning* techniques becomes crucial to support NextG communications by adapting to and learning from spectrum dynamics.

Deep learning, with its capacity to comprehend complex data characteristics of high dimensions that are inherent in wireless communications, surpasses traditional machine learning methods in performing tasks such as detection, classification, and prediction within NextG systems [1]. *Federated learning* emerges as a solution to train a global model using data collected by decentralized edge nodes, ensuring data privacy and avoiding excessive spectrum data exchange [2–4]. In federated learning, a group of clients collaborates to train a global machine learning model by sharing only model parameters with a central server instead of sharing their own individual training data sets. In addition to privacy, federated learning is useful for spectrum sensing applications, where communication load is reduced as the size of trained models is smaller than the size of training data samples, compared to sharing data between clients and server. In addition, edge devices whose training datasets or computing resources are typically limited can still contribute to the process of global model training. When federated learning is performed over a wireless network, there is a need to account for wireless communication characteristics such as channel and interference effects [5–9].

Federated learning application use case in NextG: Using spectrum sensors as clients, federated learning can be applied for distributed spectrum sensing over a wireless network [10]. One promising use case of federated learning is enhancing the Environmental Sensing Capability (ESC) within the Citizens Broadband Radio Service (CBRS) framework. CBRS refers to a 150 MHz radio frequency band ranging from 3550 to 3700 MHz (commonly known as the 3.5 GHz band) in the United States. This band is primarily occupied by incumbent users, most notably US Navy radar systems. CBRS Devices (CBSDs), which include Priority Access License (PAL) holders and General Authorized Access (GAA) users, are permitted to operate in the band only when there are no active incumbent users. When incumbent activity is detected, the Spectrum Access System (SAS) administrator is responsible for dynamically managing spectrum access, which may include deactivating certain CBSDs to ensure interference constraints are maintained and Navy radar systems are protected. To detect incumbent activities, ESC sensors are deployed in strategically selected locations, particularly along the coastline, to monitor the spectrum environment. Rather than having each ESC sensor independently train its own detection model or centralizing raw sensor data at the SAS for processing, federated learning offers a privacy-preserving and bandwidth-efficient alternative. Through federated learning, ESC sensors and the SAS can collaboratively train a robust incumbent user detector without sharing raw data, thereby improving detection performance while maintaining data confidentiality and reducing communication overhead. Similarly, federated learning can be applied to authenticate user equipment using the transmitted waveform in NextG communications.

Security vulnerabilities of federated learning for NextG: As deep learning becomes integral to NextG systems, concerns regarding its vulnerability to different exploits and attacks escalate. It is possible that clients exhibit selfish behavior [11, 12] by withholding their trained local models in federated learning scenarios, or conventional jamming attacks may disrupt communication between clients and the server. Additionally, adversaries may manipulate training or test inputs to compromise deep learning algorithms embedded in NextG communications, necessitating a study of adversarial machine learning [13–15]. Exploiting the shared wireless medium, adversaries like eavesdroppers and jammers pose significant threats by observing and manipulating data and control planes in NextG communications.

To address these challenges, understanding the attack surface due to *adversarial machine learning* attacks [16–18] and developing resilient operation modes become imperative and have received increasing attention in different data domains ranging from computer vision to natural language processing. Since the wireless medium is shared by different users, NextG communications become susceptible to adversarial actions. In particular, eavesdroppers and jammers have the ability to sense and tamper with the inputs of training and test phases over the air. Therefore, it is essential to comprehend the attack vector resulting from adversarial machine learning attacks on both data and control planes of wireless systems, and determining resilient operation modes [19–24]. To that end, it is important to develop defense mechanisms for resiliency by developing a mathematical framework to analyze the potential conflicting interactions of the attacker and the defender. *Game theory* offers an analytical framework to quantify the outcomes of interactions between attackers and defenders, applicable not only to conventional attacks like jamming [25–28] but also in the context of adversarial machine learning [29].

Poisoning attacks on federated learning for NextG: We examine the susceptibility of federated learning to *poisoning attacks*, where malicious participants (e.g., fake or compromised ESC sensors) inject false data to bias the model, potentially disrupting NextG communications. This attack can cause the model (and consequently the global model in the context of federated learning) to become biased or inaccurate, leading to incorrect predictions or decisions. The vulnerabilities to poisoning attacks have been studied for wireless systems with applications in spectrum access [24, 30], cooperative spectrum sensing [31, 32], and IoT [33, 34]. Poisoning attacks can be extended to backdoor (Trojan) attacks where the attacker adds a trigger to select training data samples and later activates them in test time. Such attacks have been considered for signal classification [35], task-oriented communications [36], and semantic communications [37]. In this setting, the goal of the attacker is to jam NextG communications based on learned transmit patterns when the sensors (e.g., user equipment) share their machine learning model parameters with the server (such as the base station), decrease the accuracy of the machine learning-based signal detection algorithm, and ultimately increase the interference from the NextG communications system to the incumbent system.

Defense to protect federated learning for NextG: To mitigate poisoning attacks, we propose resilience-boosting techniques to detect and mitigate the potential effects of poisoned data samples and ensure the integrity and reliability of the federated learning system. We adopt a proactive defense scheme, selecting clients for federated learning to enhance resilience against attacks. This defense becomes successful in providing resilience against the poisoning attack if it rejects poisoned clients and admits unpoisoned ones (the accuracy will improve as more unpoisoned clients admitted instead of the poisoned ones are admitted). This chapter studies the interactions between defenders and attackers in NextG communications in a *game-theoretic* setting, evaluating the resilience of machine learning algorithms used in NextG communications to adversarial machine learning to enhance *cyber resiliency*. Specifically, we focus on a deep learning-based wireless signal classifier for incumbent user detection for spectrum coexistence scenarios of NextG communications systems. Overall, this approach aims to enhance security, privacy, data sovereignty, and collaboration while reducing communication overhead and latency.

Attack–defense game: By formulating the relationship between the attacker and the defender as a *noncooperative game*, we derive Nash equilibrium strategies that correspond to resilient operation modes. The actions are to select which client to poison for the attacker, and which clients to admit for federated learning for the defender to support resilient operations. The payoff or the utility to maximize by the defender is the difference of the classification accuracy and the cost of admitting clients to federated learning (this cost is due to computing and communications for model exchanges). The payoff to maximize by the attacker is the classification error minus a cost when the attack is launched (this cost is due to eavesdropping, computing, and jamming operations). This chapter studies this game and identifies the (pure and mixed) *Nash equilibrium* strategies in forms of resilient operation modes, where each player (attacker and defender) cannot individually change its strategy and increase its payoff when the opponent's strategy is fixed. In this formulation, we derive the equilibrium payoffs as a function of the classification accuracy as well as the costs for the defender and the attacker.

Relevance to cyber resilience: This chapter provides methods for *cyber resilience* rather than only analyzing *cyber security* of NextG systems and delves into the novel attack surface of adversarial machine learning in NextG systems from a game-theoretic perspective. This chapter improves cyber resiliency since it allows the defender to assess the impact of a potential attack on the target system better and make more informed decisions in the presence of an attacker. As a result, the impact of the attack is minimized without disruption of the spectrum sensing task. Applying defense comes with a cost, so it cannot be applied all the time. A UE/sensor can optimize the probability of applying defense by taking the defense cost (i.e., accuracy of the universal deep learning model used for signal detection) into account.

The chapter is structured as follows: Section 11.2 discusses federated learning for wireless signal classification. Section 11.3 addresses security aspects of federated learning, describes the attack mechanisms, and presents defense mechanisms for resilient operation in NextG communications. Section 11.4 formulates the game solution for two clients available for federated learning. Section 11.5 studies the game for an arbitrary number of clients. Section 11.6 outlines future research directions. Section 11.7 concludes the chapter.

11.2 Federated Learning for Distributed Spectrum Monitoring

Federated learning is a distributed machine learning approach designed to safeguard user privacy by allowing multiple clients to collaboratively train a model while keeping their data localized. Instead of transmitting sensitive data to a central server, federated learning enables clients to retain their data locally and share only model parameters during the training process. Illustrated in Figure 11.1, this model involves clients maintaining local models (with weights w_i), while a global model (with weight w) is assembled at the server.

The federated learning workflow encompasses several key steps. Initially, the central server disseminates an initial model to participating clients. These clients then independently train their local models using their own data without disclosing it. Following local training, each client forwards an update (model parameters) to the central server that combines these updates to refine the global model, which is subsequently redistributed to the clients for further training. Federated averaging [4] can be used to update a global model by averaging input from multiple clients.

This iterative process continues until the model attains a satisfactory level of accuracy or reaches a predefined stopping criterion, such as a specified number of epochs. Federated learning presents notable advantages, including data privacy

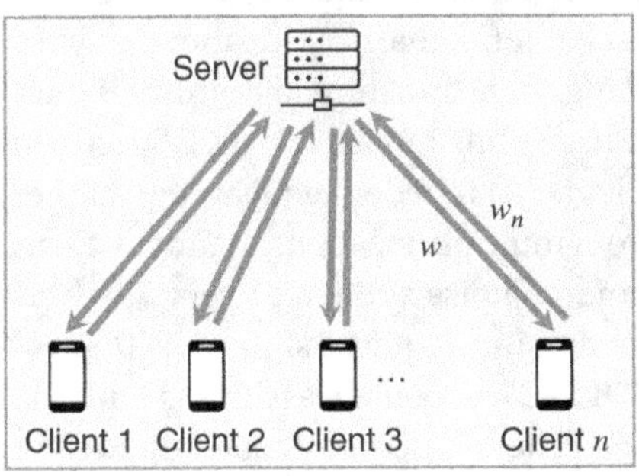

Figure 11.1 The client–server structure of federated learning.

preservation and reduced data transmission to a central server. This approach is especially useful in scenarios involving distributed data across multiple clients, such as IoT or mobile devices.

A formal description of the federated learning algorithm involves the following steps:

1. The central server disseminates the current shared model (w) to all participating clients.
2. Each client i uses its private data to train its local model (w_i).
3. Clients send their local models back to the central server.
4. The central server aggregates client updates to compute a new shared model (w) through averaging, which is then redistributed to clients.
5. Steps 2–4 are repeated by clients until convergence or a predefined stopping criterion.

Federated averaging ensures that the global model incorporates input from all participating clients while upholding data privacy and ensuring model consistency across diverse data distributions.

In the context of wireless applications, federated learning operates on data sourced from myriad edge devices, including ESC sensors, smartphones, tablets, or IoT devices, interconnected via wireless networks like those envisioned for NextG communication systems. Training occurs directly on edge devices, minimizing data transmission over wireless networks. Facilitating federated learning on wireless networks necessitates communication between edge devices and a central server, achievable via peer-to-peer protocols or communication through a wireless access point.

In spectrum sensing applications, federated learning involves training a model on numerous edge devices, each equipped with local (individual) spectrum data samples. Edge devices experience diverse channel conditions when collecting spectrum measurements in varied environments. Local models are aggregated by the central server to form a global model, which is then disseminated for collaborative signal detection and classification within specified frequency bands.

In the specified scenario considered in this chapter, signal classification serves as the machine learning task for federated learning. Data transmissions utilize Binary Phase Shift Keying (BPSK) or Quadrature Phase Shift Keying (QPSK). Spectrum sensors, representing the total number of clients (n) in federated learning, gather in-phase and quadrature-phase (I/Q) data from multiple locations. Random client distribution is assumed, with fixed-power random noise at the receivers. Analysis of I/Q data yields 32 features per sample, comprising 16 phase shifts and 16 powers. Each sample is labeled as "BPSK" or "QPSK." A robust classifier is built via federated learning to differentiate modulation schemes across signals collected at diverse locations.

11.3 Attack and Defense Mechanisms for Resilient Federated Learning

Federated learning can bolster privacy and security by enabling multiple edge devices to train a global model without disseminating raw data. Its potential applications in 5G and future communication networks, designed to accommodate massive connectivity, low latency, and high-speed data transmission, are significant. For instance, in 5G networks, federated learning can be instrumental in enhancing security measures. By leveraging machine learning models trained on data sourced from edge devices, network operators can swiftly detect and mitigate security threats [38]. These threats include anomaly detection in spectrum usage and network traffic, identification of malicious activities, and prompt detection of security breaches, even predicting them before occurrence. However, ensuring the integrity and confidentiality of federated learning systems for resilient operation requires addressing several security threats.

- **Model poisoning:** In this type of attack, malicious data is injected into the training process to bias the model toward a specific outcome, such as misclassifying certain data points. Techniques like differential privacy or data filtering can help identify and eliminate malicious data to mitigate this threat.
- **Data leakage:** In this type of attack, attackers intercept sensitive data during transmission, compromising data confidentiality. Encryption techniques can safeguard data during transmission, ensuring access is restricted to authorized parties only.
- **Model extraction:** In this type of attack, attackers attempt to extract the model from edge devices or the central server to make predictions independently, without needing access to the edge devices or the central server. Techniques like model encryption or obfuscation can prevent the model from being extracted.
- **Membership inference:** In this type of attack, attackers attempt to discern whether specific data points were part of the training process. This can reveal sensitive information about the training data and compromise user privacy. Differential privacy or randomized response techniques can protect against such inference attacks.

To evaluate federated learning's resilience against manipulation of training data, we consider a poisoning attack wherein attackers poison training data samples, altering their labels. The notation used in this chapter is shown in Table 11.1. This results in manipulated model updates contributing to global training. We assume an associated cost (c_A) for each client the attacker poisons.

Table 11.1 Notation table.

Symbol	Definition
n	Total number of clients
c_D	The cost of defender
c_A	The cost of attacker
$U_{k\|i}$	The utility of the server when i clients are admitted and k clients are poisoned
q_i	The probability of client i's contributing to the global model
p_i	The probability of attacking client i

To withstand and recover from poisoning attacks, a client admission policy serves as a defense for resilient operation. This policy allows clients to independently decide on participation or the server to select participants. The ideal setup would only admit clients with clean (unpoisoned) data, excluding those with poisoned data from the federated learning process. The cost to sustain resilience (c_D) is assumed for each admitted client. The system model for this attack and defense is depicted in Figure 11.2.

A feedforward neural network (FNN) architecture is adopted by the client and server. The properties of the FNN are outlined in Table 11.2. The FNN's local model is unique to each client. During the training process, each client offers 1000 samples, with an additional 1000 samples used to evaluate the global model's performance. The global model trained by federated learning is assessed in terms of its accuracy after 100 rounds.

The classification accuracy ($U_{k|i}$) of federated learning, given i admitted clients with k poisoned, is depicted in Figure 11.3. It is assumed that 50% of the training data is poisoned when a client is attacked. For a given i, $U_{k|i}$ decreases with k, as more clients are poisoned. Conversely, for a fixed k, $U_{k|i}$ rises with increasing i since there are more unpoisoned clients contributing to the training.

Similarly, the classification accuracy ($U_{k|i}$) of federated learning, given i admitted clients with k poisoned, is shown in Figure 11.4 where it is assumed that 25% of the training data is poisoned when a client is attacked. As expected, the impact on the classification accuracy decreases when the attacker poisons a smaller portion of the training data once it attacks a client.

Clients undergo either admission or rejection for participation in federated learning. The efficacy of this admission policy in sustaining resilience hinges on rejecting poisoned clients while accepting unpoisoned ones. Considering a total of n clients, with i admitted ($n - i$ rejected) and m poisoned, we denote by k the number of poisoned clients among those admitted. In the worst-case scenario, the

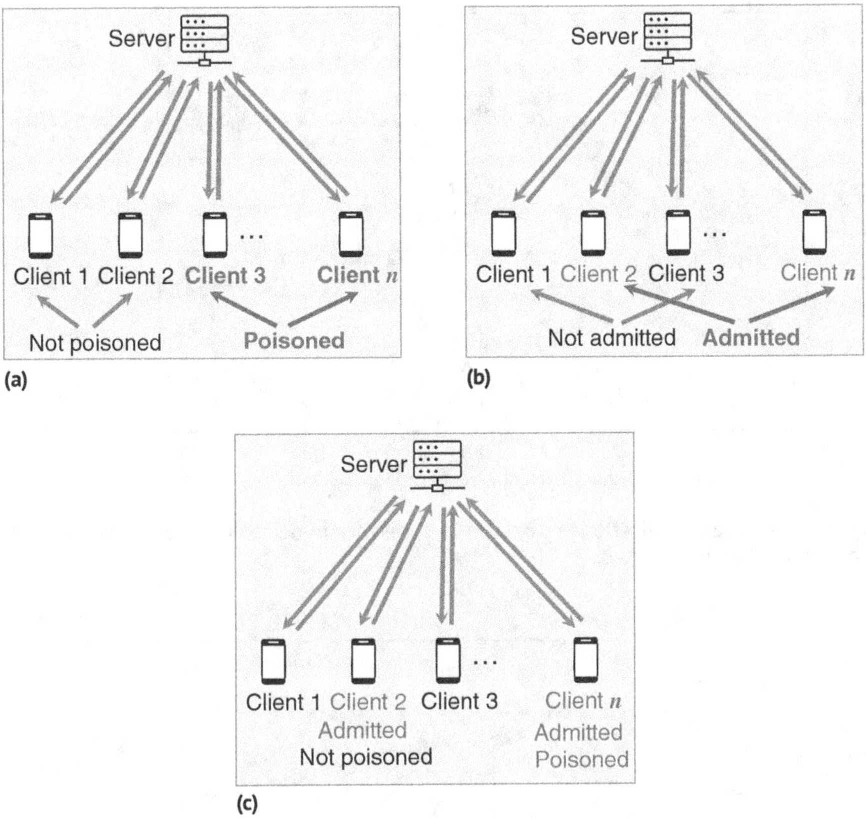

Figure 11.2 Poisoning attack and defense. (a) Poisoning attack; (b) Defense of admitting some clients and rejecting others; (c) Combined effect of attack and defense.

Table 11.2 The properties of the FNN used as the wireless signal classifier.

Input size	32
Output layer size	2
Hidden layer sizes	128, 64, 32
Dropout rate	0.2
Activation function	ReLU (hidden layer), Softmax (output layer)
Loss function	Crossentropy
Optimizer	RMSprop
Number of parameters	14,626

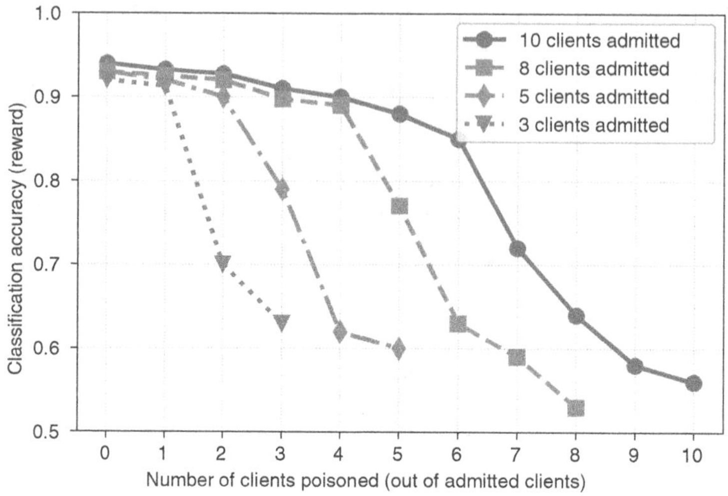

Figure 11.3 The classification accuracy in the presence of poisoning attack when 50% of the training data is poisoned.

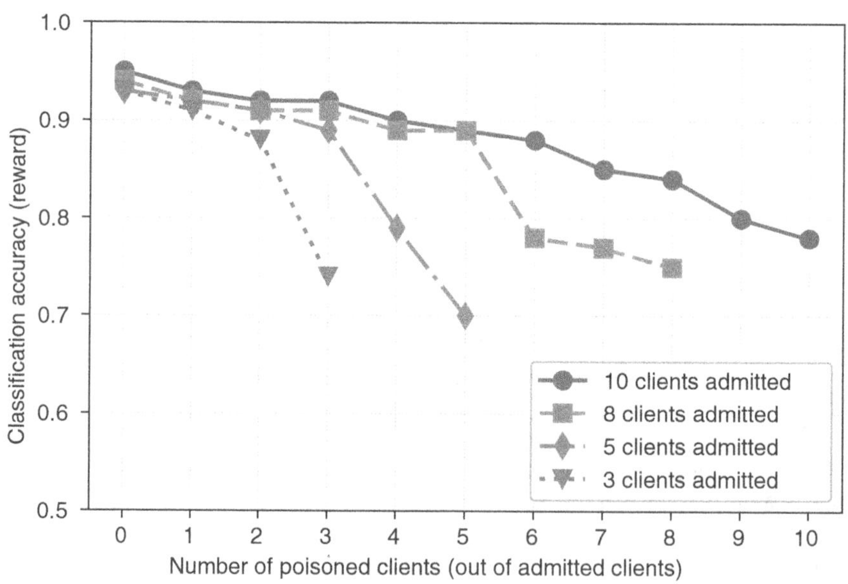

Figure 11.4 The classification accuracy in the presence of poisoning attack when 25% of the training data is poisoned.

defense strategy opts for admitting clients with poisoned members, resulting in $k = \min(m, i)$. Conversely, in the best-case scenario, unadmitted clients $(n - i)$ predominantly comprise poisoned clients (m), leading to $k = \max(m - (n - i), 0)$. Generally, the most and least effective defense strategies, involving the selection of admitted clients to regulate the number of poisoned members, are described by:

$$k = \begin{cases} \max(m - (n - i), 0), & \text{for best defense,} \\ \min(m, i), & \text{for worst defense.} \end{cases}$$

Figures 11.5 and 11.6 illustrate the defender utility $U_{k|i} - i\,c_A$, optimized over i and m for the best and worst defense strategies, given n (where c_A denotes the cost of admitting a client) when the attacker poisons 50% and 25% of the training data when it attacks a client, respectively. These outcomes delineate the upper and lower bounds for defender utility as resilient operation modes. Subsequent sections will study the game's performance within these bounds.

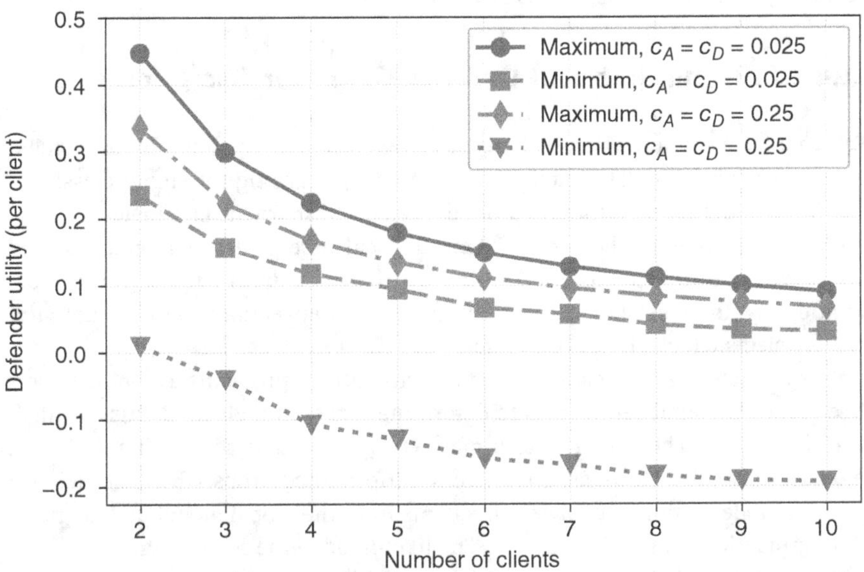

Figure 11.5 The best and worst defender utilities (optimized by selecting the admitted and poisoned clients) in response to the poisoning attack. The attacker poisons 50% of the training data when its decision is to attack a client.

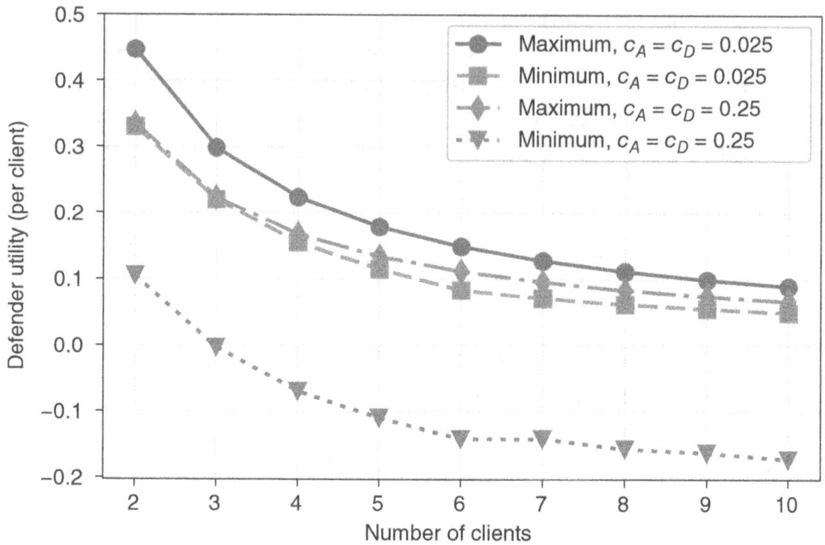

Figure 11.6 The best and worst defender utilities (optimized by selecting the admitted and poisoned clients) in response to the poisoning attack. The attacker poisons 25% of the training data when its decision is to attack a client.

11.4 Poisoning Attack–Defense Game for Two Clients

We begin with the scenario involving two clients that can potentially participate in federated learning. These clients employ deep learning for signal classification, independently train their neural networks, and share the parameters of their resulting models with the server. Then all local models are aggregated by the server, which further distributes the global model updates back to the clients. Additionally, there exists an attacker that decides between attacking or not, and further selects which client(s) to attack.

We formulate the application of defense and attack problems as a noncooperative game. The attacker's aim is to determine when and which clients to attack at a given time. The server determines which clients to accept or reject as a defensive measure. However, the system performance drops when the defense excludes model parameters of certain clients from the global model update, making it impractical for continuous use. The likelihood of the server admitting client i to participate in federated learning is denoted by q_i. Let $\mathbf{q}$ represent the vector containing the probabilities of admission. The probability that the attacker targets client i is p_i. Let $\mathbf{p}$ represent the vector containing the probabilities of attack. Let $U_{i|j}$ indicate the classifier accuracy of federated learning, where i is the total number of clients involved in the model update at a specific round, j signifies the number of clients whose models remain unaltered by the attacker, and $i \geq j$.

We presume that the server independently makes decisions of accepting or rejecting each client to ensure resilient operation. Likewise, each client can independently determine whether to engage in federated learning or not. If client $i = 1, 2$ chooses to participate in federated learning, its utility is defined as follows:

$$\begin{aligned} U_i^N(q_{-i}, \mathbf{p}) = q_{-i}(p_i p_{-i}(U_{2|2} - c_D) + p_i(1 - p_{-i})(U_{1|2} - c_D) \\ +(1 - p_i)p_{-i}(U_{1|2} - c_D) + (1 - p_i)(1 - p_{-i})(U_{0|2} - c_D)) \\ +(1 - q_{-i})(p_i(U_{1|1} - c_D) + (1 - p_i)(U_{0|1} - c_D)). \end{aligned} \tag{11.1}$$

If client $i = 1, 2$ opts out of participating in federated learning, its utility is as follows:

$$U_i^D(q_{-i}, \mathbf{p}) = q_{-i}(p_{-i}U_{1|1} + (1 - p_{-i})U_{0|1}) + (1 - q_{-i})U_{0|0} \tag{11.2}$$

where $-i$ corresponds to user other than i.

Based on Eqs. (11.1–11.2), the average utility of client i (averaged across its strategy q_i) is expressed as:

$$U_i(\mathbf{q}, \mathbf{p}) = q_i U_i^N(q_{-i}, \mathbf{p}) + (1 - q_i)U_i^D(q_{-i}, \mathbf{p}). \tag{11.3}$$

For given q_{-i} and $\mathbf{p}$, each client $i = 1, 2$ has the objective of maximizing its average utility at a given time, such as:

$$\max_{q_i\,:\,0 \le q_i \le 1} \quad q_i U_i^N(q_{-i}, \mathbf{p}) + (1 - q_i)U_i^D(q_{-i}, \mathbf{p}) \tag{11.4}$$

or, equivalently

$$\min_{q_i\,:\,0 \le q_i \le 1} \quad -\left(q_i U_i^N(q_{-i}, \mathbf{p}) + (1 - q_i)U_i^D(q_{-i}, \mathbf{p})\right). \tag{11.5}$$

The solution to the optimization in Eq. (11.5) should satisfy the Karush–Kuhn–Tucker (KKT) conditions to achieve a local minimum. The Lagrangian is expressed as:

$$\mathcal{L}(q_i; \mu_i^1, \mu_i^2) = -(q_i U_i^N(q_{-i}, \mathbf{p}) + (1 - q_i)U_i^D(q_{-i}, \mathbf{p})) - \mu_i^1 q_i + \mu_i^2(q_i - 1). \tag{11.6}$$

The KKT conditions for $i = 1, 2$ are given by

$$\begin{aligned} &-U_i^N(q_{-i}, \mathbf{p}) + U_i^D(q_{-i}, \mathbf{p}) - \mu_i^1 + \mu_i^2 = 0, \text{(stationarity)} \\ &0 \le q_i, q_i \le 1, \text{(primal feasibility)} \\ &\mu_i^1 \ge 0, \mu_i^2 \ge 0, \text{(dual feasibility)} \\ &\mu_i^1 q_i = 0, \mu_i^2(q_i - 1) = 0. \text{(complementary slackness)} \end{aligned} \tag{11.7}$$

The optimal selection of q_i should satisfy the KKT conditions. The solution when $\mu_i^1 = \mu_i^2 = 0$ is given by $U_i^N(q_{-i}, \mathbf{p}) = U_i^D(q_{-i}, \mathbf{p})$. Then, from Eqs. (11.1) and (11.2), we obtain,

$$\begin{aligned}
&q_{-i}(p_i p_{-i}(U_{2|2} - c_D) + p_i(1 - p_{-i})(U_{1|2} - c_D) + (1 - p_i)p_{-i}(U_{1|2} - c_D)\\
&+(1 - p_i)(1 - p_{-i})(U_{0|2} - c_D) - p_{-i}U_{1|1} - (1 - p_{-i})U_{0|1})\\
&+(1 - q_{-i})(p_i(U_{1|1} - c_D) + (1 - p_i)(U_{0|1} - c_D) - U_{0|0}) = 0.
\end{aligned} \tag{11.8}$$

If we assume the symmetric case with $p_i = p$ and $q_i = q, i = 1, 2$, Eq. (11.8) translates to

$$\begin{aligned}
&q(p^2(U_{2|2} - 2U_{1|2} + U_{0|2}) + p(2U_{1|2} - 2U_{0|2} - U_{1|1} + U_{0|1}) + U_{0|2} - c_D - U_{0|1})\\
&+(1 - q)(p(U_{1|1} - U_{0|1}) + U_{0|1} - c_D - U_{0|0}) = 0
\end{aligned} \tag{11.9}$$

The attacker has four options to choose from at any given time:

1. Attacking Clients 1 and 2 at the same time.
2. Attacking only Client 1.
3. Attacking only Client 2.
4. Not attacking any client.

For case 1, where the attacker makes the decision to attack both clients simultaneously, the utility of the attacker is given by

$$\begin{aligned}
U_A^2(q_1, q_2) = {} & q_1q_2(-U_{2|2} - 2c_A) + q_1(1 - q_2)(-U_{1|1} - 2c_A)\\
&+(1 - q_1)q_2(-U_{1|1} - 2c_A) + (1 - q_1)(1 - q_2)(-U_{0|0} - 2c_A).
\end{aligned} \tag{11.10}$$

For case 2, where the attacker makes the decision to attack only Client 1, the utility of the attacker is given by

$$\begin{aligned}
U_{A,1}^1(q_1, q_2) = {} & q_1q_2(-U_{1|2} - c_A) + q_1(1 - q_2)(-U_{1|1} - c_A)\\
&+(1 - q_1)q_2(-U_{0|1} - c_A) + (1 - q_1)(1 - q_2)(-U_{0|0} - c_A).
\end{aligned} \tag{11.11}$$

For case 3, where the attacker makes the decision to attack only Client 2, the utility of the attacker is given by

$$U_{A,2}^{1}(q_1, q_2) = q_1 q_2(-U_{1|2} - c_A) + q_1(1 - q_2)(-U_{0|1} - c_A) \\ +(1 - q_1)q_2(-U_{1|1} - c_A) + (1 - q_1)(1 - q_2)(-U_{0|0} - c_A). \tag{11.12}$$

For case 4, where the attacker decides not to attack, the utility of the attacker is given by

$$U_{A}^{0}(q_1, q_2) = q_1 q_2(-U_{0|2}) + q_1(1 - q_2)(-U_{0|1}) \\ +(1 - q_1)q_2(-U_{0|1}) + (1 - q_1)(1 - q_2)(-U_{0|0}). \tag{11.13}$$

By averaging over the utilities (11.10–11.13) for four cases, the attacker's average utility is given by

$$U_A(\mathbf{q}, \mathbf{p}) = p_1 p_2 U_A^2 + p_1(1 - p_2) * U_{A,1}^1 + p_2(1 - p1)U_{A,2}^1 + (1 - p_1)(1 - p_2)U_A^0. \tag{11.14}$$

Given the defender's strategy $\mathbf{q}$, the attacker pursues the objective of maximizing its total utility:

$$U_A^*(\mathbf{q}, \mathbf{p}) = \max_{\mathbf{p}:\, 0 \le \mathbf{p} \le 1} p_1 p_2 U_A^2 + p_1(1 - p_2)U_{A,1}^1 + p_2(1 - p_1)U_{A,2}^1 \\ +(1 - p_1)(1 - p_2)U_A^0. \tag{11.15}$$

Equation (11.15) can be expressed as minimizing:

$$U_A^*(\mathbf{q}, \mathbf{p}) = \min_{\mathbf{p}} -(p_1 p_2 U_A^2 + p_1(1 - p_2)U_{A,1}^1 + p_2(1 - p_1)U_{A,2}^1 \\ +(1 - p_1)(1 - p_2)U_A^0). \tag{11.16}$$

The solution to the optimization in Eq. (11.16) should satisfy the KKT conditions. The Lagrangian is expressed as:

$$\mathcal{L}(\mathbf{p}; \mu^1, \mu^2, \mu^3, \mu^4) = -(p_1 p_2 U_A^2 + p_1(1 - p_2) * U_{A,1}^1 + p_2(1 - p1)U_{A,2}^1 \\ + (1 - p_1)(1 - p_2)U_A^0) - \mu^1 p_1 + \mu^2(p_1 - 1) - \mu^3 p_2 \\ + \mu^4(p_2 - 1). \tag{11.17}$$

The KKT conditions are given by

$$-p_2U_A^2 - (1 - p_2) * U_{A,1}^1 + p_2U_{A,2}^1 + (1 - p_2)U_A^0 - \mu^1 + \mu^2 = 0 \text{ (stationarity)}$$

$$-p_1U_A^2 + p_1 * U_{A,1}^1 - (1 - p_1)U_{A,2}^1 + (1 - p_1)U_A^0 - \mu^3 + \mu^4 = 0 \text{ (stationarity)}$$

$$0 \leq p_1, 0 \leq p_2, p_1 \leq 1, p_2 \leq 1 \text{ (primal feasibility)}$$

$$\mu^1 \geq 0, \mu^2 \geq 0, \mu^3 \geq 0, \mu^4 \geq 0 \text{ (dual feasibility)}$$

$$\mu^1 p_1 = 0, \mu^2(p_1 - 1) = 0, \mu^3 p_2 = 0, \mu^4(p_2 - 1) = 0$$
$$\text{(complementary slackness)}. \tag{11.18}$$

The optimal choice of $\mathbf{p}$ should satisfy the KKT conditions. When $\mu^1 = \mu^2 = \mu^3 = \mu^4 = 0$, the solution for the symmetric case of $p_1 = p_2 = p$ and $q_1 = q_2 = q$ is given by

$$-pq^2U_{2|2} - q^2U_{1|2} - qU_{1|1} + q^2U_{1|1} - qU_{0|1} + q^2U_{0|1} - c_A - q^2U_{0|0} + 2pq^2U_{1|2}$$
$$+q^2U_{0|2} + 2qU_{0|1} - 2q^2U_{0|1} + q^2U_{0|0} - pq^2U_{0|2} = 0. \tag{11.19}$$

In Nash equilibrium, Eqs. (11.9) and (11.19) are satisfied. Figure 11.7 depicts the utilities for both the attacker and the defender as they vary with the costs incurred by each. The attacker poisons 50% of the training data when it decides to attack a client. Figure 11.8 shows the utilities for both the attacker and the defender when the attacker poisons 25% of the training data when it decides to attack a client. Defender utility remains higher with increasing attacker and defender costs when less training data is poisoned. On the other hand, attacker utility decreases with increasing cost. Figures 11.9 and 11.10 illustrate the strategies adopted by the attacker and the defender as a function of their respective costs when 50% and 25% of the training data is poisoned, respectively. We observe a trend where clients are less inclined to participate in federated learning, leading to a reduced contribution to the global model, especially as the defender's costs increase. Consequently, the defender's utility declines. This situation, in turn, prompts more attacks from the attacker's side, aimed at amplifying the impact of the attacks. Consequently, the attacker's utility does not decrease as the costs decrease for both 50% and 25% training data poisoning cases.

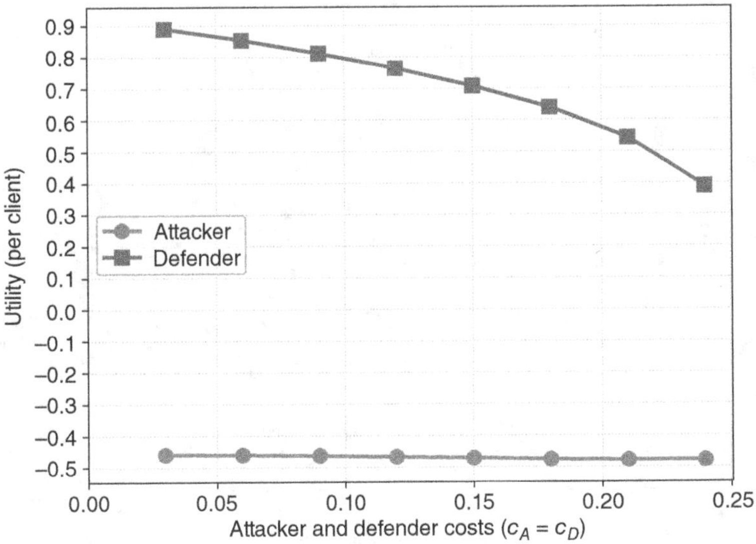

Figure 11.7 The utility per client with increasing attacker and defender costs. The attacker poisons 50% of the training data when its decision is to attack a client.

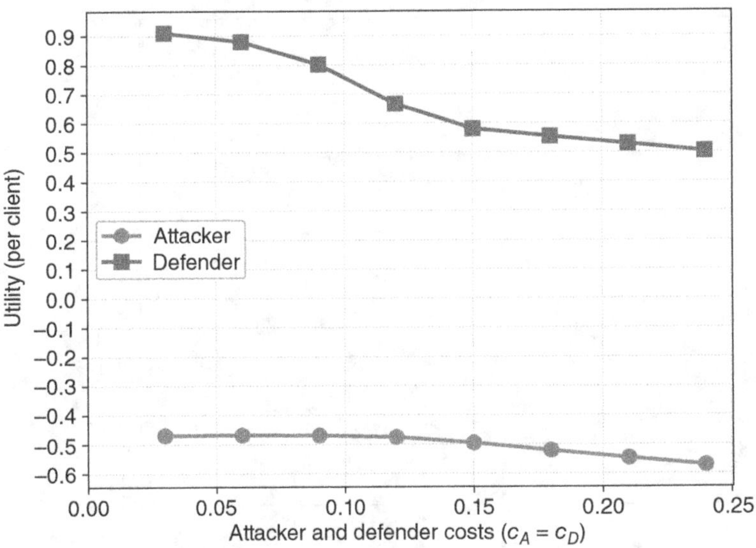

Figure 11.8 The utility per client with increasing attacker and defender costs. The attacker poisons 25% of the training data when its decision is to attack a client.

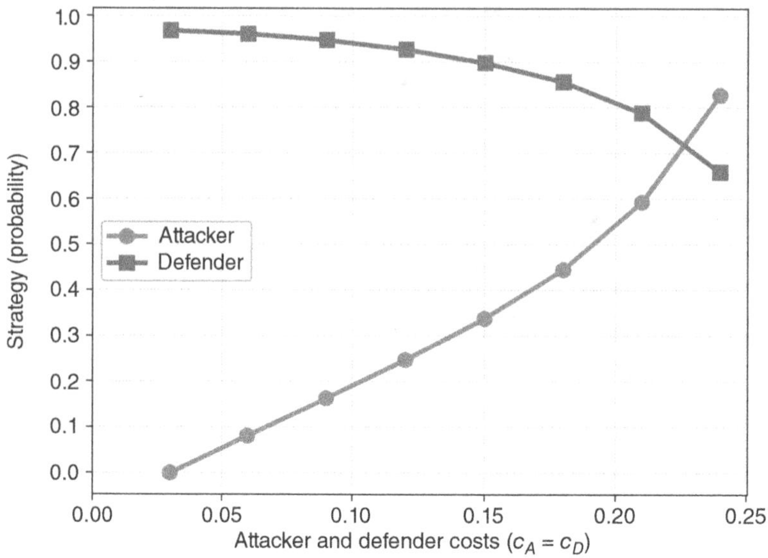

Figure 11.9 The attacker and defender strategies with increasing attacker and defender costs. The attacker poisons 50% of the training data when its decision is to attack a client.

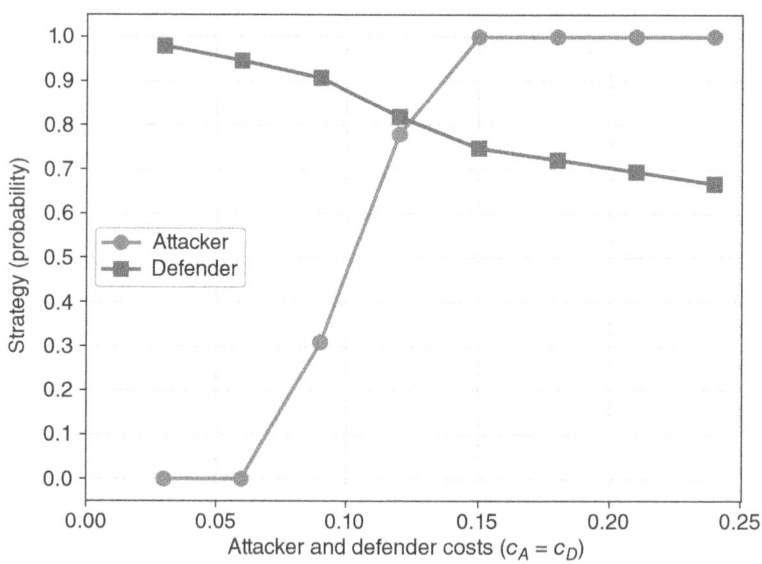

Figure 11.10 The attacker and defender strategies with increasing attacker and defender costs. The attacker poisons 25% of the training data when its decision is to attack a client.

11.5 Poisoning Attack–Defense Game for More than Two Clients

Next, we expand to consider the general case of n clients in total, each having the option to participate or not in federated learning. To ensure the resilience of federated learning, the defender chooses i out of n clients for participation in federated learning (resulting in $n - i$ clients being declined from federated learning). Simultaneously, the attacker chooses j clients out of n to poison (randomly chosen). The attacker's utility $U_A(i, j)$ encompasses two penalties:

- the penalty related to the federated learning reward, and
- the penalty accounting for the cost of poisoning j clients (with a cost of c_A per poisoned client), i.e., $j\ c_A$ (this cost pertains to each client being targeted individually in the data poisoning attack).

To calculate the first penalty, we need to evaluate the federated learning reward when i out of n clients are admitted and j out of n clients are poisoned, where $i, j \leq n$. When the attacker chooses j clients to poison, they do so uniformly and randomly from the n clients. Expressing this reward requires $U_{k|i}$, which signifies the federated learning reward when i out of n clients are admitted and k out of those i clients are poisoned (where $k \leq i$). Considering j clients chosen out of n, some are from the pool of i admitted clients, while the rest come from the remaining $n - i$ clients that are not admitted. Consequently, the contribution from $U_{k|i}$ to the first penalty $U_A(i, j)$ occurs with probability $\frac{\binom{i}{k}\binom{n-i}{j-k}}{\binom{n}{j}}$, since there are $\binom{n}{j}$ ways to select j poisoned clients from n clients, $\binom{i}{k}$ ways for k poisoned clients from the i admitted clients, and $\binom{n-i}{j-k}$ ways for the rest of the poisoned clients $(j - k\ )$ from the non-admitted clients. We can express the attacker's utility as:

$$U_A(i, j) = \sum_{k=0}^{j} -\frac{\binom{i}{k}\binom{n-i}{j-k}}{\binom{n}{j}} U_{k|i} - j\ c_A, \tag{11.20}$$

where $0 \leq j \leq i$.

On the other hand, the defender's utility $U_D(i, j)$ comprises one reward and one penalty:

- The reward linked to the federated learning reward (the first penalty for the attacker is the reward for the defender) when i clients participate in federated learning, and there are m out of these i clients that are poisoned.

- The penalty reflecting the cost of admitting i clients for federated learning (at a cost of c_D per admitted client), i.e., $i\,c_D$ (this cost is related to the server's information exchange requirement for each client).

In this setting, the defender's utility is expressed as:

$$U_D(i,j) = \sum_{k=0}^{j} \frac{\binom{i}{k}\binom{n-i}{j-k}}{\binom{n}{j}} U_{k|i} - i\,c_D. \tag{11.21}$$

The best response of the attacker when the defender admits i clients to federated learning is given by

$$B_A(i) = \arg\max_{0 \le j \le n} U_A(i,j), \quad 0 \le i \le n. \tag{11.22}$$

Similarly, the best response of the defender when the attacker poisons j clients is given by

$$B_D(j) = \arg\max_{0 \le i \le n} U_D(i,j), \quad 0 \le j \le n. \tag{11.23}$$

Then, from Eqs. (11.20) to (11.21), the Nash equilibrium strategies (i^*, j^*) are computed from

$$(i^*, j^*) \in (B_D(j^*), B_A(i^*)). \tag{11.24}$$

Figure 11.11 illustrates the attacker and defender utilities, $U_A(i^*, j^*)$ and $U_D(i^*, j^*)$, at Nash equilibrium as a function n. The attacker poisons 50% of the training data when it makes a decision to attack a client. Figure 11.12 illustrates the attacker and defender utilities as a function of n when the attacker poisons 25% of the training data when it makes a decision to attack a client. As n increases, the defender's utility per client decreases because it becomes easier to poison some of this increasing number of clients, and admitting more clients becomes costlier. As a response, the attacker's utility increases. When we raise the attack and defense costs, the attacker's utility decreases due to the higher costs associated with attacking. This decrease helps the defender offset its own cost increase and enhances its utility for more resilient federated learning.

11.6 Future Research Directions

In future research endeavors, several potential extensions can enrich the understanding of the attack surface and resilient operation modes in federated learning:

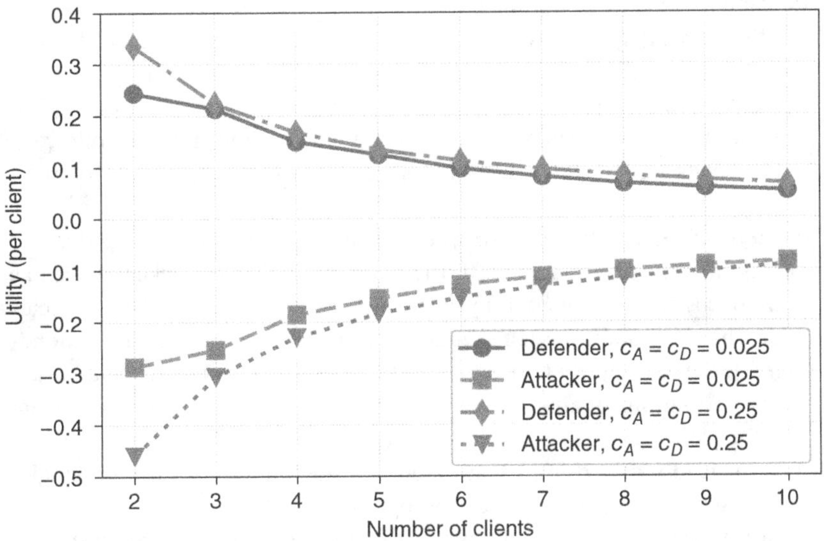

Figure 11.11 The attacker and defender utilities in Nash equilibrium as the number of clients is increased. The attacker poisons 50% of the training data when its decision is to attack a client.

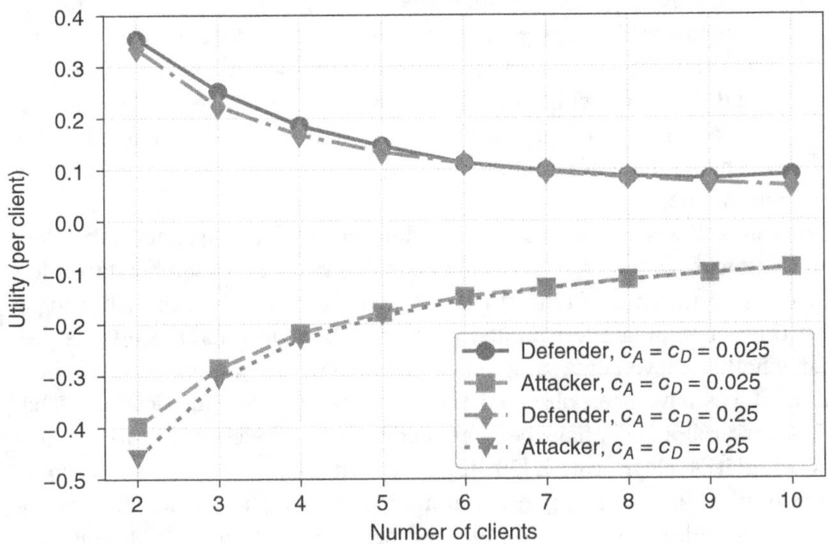

Figure 11.12 The attacker and defender utilities in Nash equilibrium as the number of clients is increased. The attacker poisons 25% of the training data when its decision is to attack a client.

1. Extension to other game settings:
   (a) **Stackelberg game dynamics:** Introducing a reactive attacker who follows the defender's actions rather than acting concurrently. A Stackelberg game framework can be explored, where the defender (leader) initiates moves, followed by sequential actions from the attacker (follower). Strategies aiming for subgame perfect Nash equilibrium can then be pursued.
   (b) **Bayesian game with incomplete information:** Recognizing that the classification accuracy of both the defender and the attacker, as well as their costs, may not be fully known beforehand due to dependencies on channel conditions. In scenarios of incomplete information, extending the game setting to a Bayesian framework allows for consideration of distributions of channel conditions rather than perfect channel state information.
   (c) **Repeated game dynamics:** Extending the game setup from a single-shot scenario to a repeated game spanning multiple rounds. This extension is pertinent, especially when the attacker's actions are limited by finite energy reserves, such as in cases involving computing and jamming operations. Strategies for subgame perfect Nash equilibrium can be pursued, with the attacker's available energy regarded as a state, potentially leading to the construction of a *Markov game*.
   (d) **Multi-player game scenarios:** Enriching the game framework to encompass multiple players, including multiple defenders (e.g., base stations) and attackers (e.g., rogue UEs). In such setups, players make individual decisions while their payoffs are interdependent. For instance, an attacker's payoff may escalate when another attacker joins the fray, or when a defender commits controlled errors, alleviating pressure on another defender.
2. Explorig additional attack vectors: In addition to poisoning attacks, there are other attacks such as adversarial (evasion) attacks and membership inference attacks that warrant investigation. Adversarial attacks, occurring during test time, manipulate test inputs, while membership inference attacks predict whether a given data sample was included in the training dataset. These attack types have been observed across various wireless applications. That is, adversarial attacks have been applied against wireless applications such as modulation classification [39–43], spectrum sensing [44–46], autoencoder communications [47], semantic communications [48], task-oriented communications [36], power control [49], and beam prediction [50]. Membership inference attacks have been applied against wireless signal classification and user equipment identification in [51, 52]. They can be further analyzed in conjunction with defense mechanisms within a game-theoretic framework.

3. Exploring additional federated learning schemes: In addition to the standard federated learning framework, where multiple clients collaboratively train a model under the coordination of a central server, several alternative federated learning schemes have been developed to address diverse application scenarios. Notable examples include clustered federated learning and decentralized federated learning. Clustered federated learning is designed for scenarios in which clients exhibit inherent structural similarities. In such cases, clients are grouped into clusters based on shared characteristics, and model training is first performed within each cluster before aggregating across all clusters to form a global model. Decentralized federated learning, on the other hand, is suitable for settings where no single entity can serve as a central server. Instead, each client acts as a local server, performing federated averaging with models received from neighboring clients in a peer-to-peer manner. These advanced federated learning paradigms significantly influence both attack strategies and defense mechanisms, introducing new challenges and opportunities for secure and robust model training.

11.7 Conclusion

In this chapter, we studied the poisoning attack on federated learning when the model is trained to classify signals for NextG communications. We formulated a game to analyze the interactions between the attacker and the defender and assessed resilient operation modes for federated learning. The poisoning attack manipulates the training data of clients to misguide the model training. On the other hand, the defender decides on whether to admit or reject clients with the goal of excluding poisoned clients from federated learning and improving its resiliency. We characterized it as a noncooperative game that is played by the attacker and the defender. This way, we quantified the performance subject to the conflicting interests of the attacker and the defender. To that end, we first derived the performance bounds for the attacker and defender utilities. Then we evaluated the attacker and defender strategies and the corresponding utilities in Nash equilibrium, first for two clients and then for an arbitrary number of clients. These results lead to novel modes of resilient operation, indicating how to secure federated learning against poisoning attacks that pose a major threat to NextG communications.

References

1 Tugba Erpek, Timothy O'Shea, Yalin E. Sagduyu, Yi Shi, and T. Charles Clancy. Deep learning for wireless communications. In *Development and Analysis of Deep Learning Architectures*. Springer, 2020.

2 Jakub Konečný, H Brendan McMahan, Felix X Yu, Peter Richtárik, Ananda Theertha Suresh, and Dave Bacon. Federated learning: Strategies for improving communication efficiency. *arXiv preprint arXiv:1610.05492*, 2016.

3 Tian Li, Anit Kumar Sahu, Ameet Talwalkar, and Virginia Smith. Federated learning: Challenges, methods, and future directions. *IEEE Signal Processing Magazine*, 37(3): 50–60, 2020.

4 Brendan McMahan, Eider Moore, Daniel Ramage, Seth Hampson, and Blaise Aguera y Arcas. Communication-efficient learning of deep networks from decentralized data. In *Artificial Intelligence and Statistics*, pages 1273–1282. PMLR, 2017.

5 Mingzhe Chen, Zhaohui Yang, Walid Saad, Changchuan Yin, H Vincent Poor, and Shuguang Cui. A joint learning and communications framework for federated learning over wireless networks. *IEEE Transactions on Wireless Communications*, 20(1): 269–283, 2020.

6 Mingzhe Chen, Deniz Gündüz, Kaibin Huang, Walid Saad, Mehdi Bennis, Aneta Vulgarakis Feljan, and H. Vincent Poor. Distributed learning in wireless networks: Recent progress and future challenges. *IEEE Journal on Selected Areas in Communications*, 39(12): 3579–3605, 2021.

7 Yi Liu, Jialiang Peng, Jiawen Kang, Abdullah M. Iliyasu, Dusit Niyato, and Ahmed A. Abd El-Latif. A secure federated learning framework for 5G networks. *IEEE Wireless Communications*, 27(4): 24–31, 2020.

8 Solmaz Niknam, Harpreet S. Dhillon, and Jeffrey H. Reed. Federated learning for wireless communications: Motivation, opportunities, and challenges. *IEEE Communications Magazine*, 58(6): 46–51, 2020.

9 Zhaohui Yang, Mingzhe Chen, Kai-Kit Wong, H. Vincent Poor, and Shuguang Cui. Federated learning for 6G: Applications, challenges, and opportunities. *Engineering*, 8: 33–41, 2022.

10 Yi Shi, Yalin E. Sagduyu, and Tugba Erpek. Federated learning for distributed spectrum sensing in NextG communication networks. In *Artificial Intelligence and Machine Learning for Multi-domain Operations Applications IV*, volume 12113, pages 472–478. SPIE, 2022.

11 Kate Donahue and Jon Kleinberg. Model-sharing games: Analyzing federated learning under voluntary participation. In *AAAI Conference on Artificial Intelligence*, volume 35, pages 5303–5311, 2021.

12 Yalin E. Sagduyu. Free-rider games for federated learning with selfish clients in NextG wireless networks. In *2022 IEEE Conference on Communications and Network Security (CNS)*, pages 365–370, 2022.

13 Yi Shi and Yalin E Sagduyu. Jamming attacks on federated learning in wireless networks. *arXiv preprint arXiv:2201.05172*, 2022.

14 Yi Shi and Yalin E. Sagduyu. How to launch jamming attacks on federated learning in NextG wireless networks. In *2022 IEEE Globecom Workshops (GC Wkshps)*, pages 945–950. IEEE, 2022.

15 Yi Shi, Yalin E. Sagduyu, and Tugba Erpek. Jamming attacks on decentralized federated learning in general multi-hop wireless networks. *arXiv preprint arXiv:2301.05250*, 2023.

16 Battista Biggio and Fabio Roli. Wild patterns: Ten years after the rise of adversarial machine learning. In *Proceedings of the 2018 ACM SIGSAC Conference on Computer and Communications Security*, pages 2154–2156, 2018.

17 Alexey Kurakin, Ian Goodfellow, and Samy Bengio. Adversarial machine learning at scale. *arXiv preprint arXiv:1611.01236*, 2016.

18 Yevgeniy Vorobeychik, Murat Kantarcioglu, Ronald Brachman, Peter Stone, and Francesca Rossi. *Adversarial Machine Learning*. Springer, 2018.

19 Damilola Adesina, Chung-Chu Hsieh,Yalin E Sagduyu, and Lijun Qian. Adversarial machine learning in wireless communications using RF data: A review. *IEEE Communications Surveys & Tutorials*, 25: 77–100, 2022.

20 Tugba Erpek, Yalin E. Sagduyu, and Yi Shi. Deep learning for launching and mitigating wireless jamming attacks. *IEEE Transactions on Cognitive Communications and Networking*, 5(1): 2–14, March 2019.

21 Jinxin Liu, Michele Nogueira, Johan Fernandes, and Burak Kantarci. Adversarial machine learning: A multilayer review of the state-of-the-art and challenges for wireless and mobile systems. *IEEE Communications Surveys & Tutorials*, 24(1): 123–159, 2021.

22 Yalin E. Sagduyu, Yi Shi, Tugba Erpek, William Headley, Bryse Flowers, George Stantchev, and Zhuo Lu. When wireless security meets machine learning: Motivation, challenges, and research directions. *arXiv preprint arXiv:2001.08883*, 2020.

23 Yalin E. Sagduyu, Tugba Erpek, and Yi Shi. Adversarial machine learning for 5G communications security. *Game Theory and Machine Learning for Cyber Security*, pages 270–288. Wiley-IEEE Press, 2021.

24 Yalin E. Sagduyu, Yi Shi, and Tugba Erpek. Adversarial deep learning for over-the-air spectrum poisoning attacks. *IEEE Transactions on Mobile Computing*, 20(2): 306–319, February 2021.

25 Andrey Garnaev, Athina P. Petropulu, Wade Trappe, and H. Vincent Poor. A jamming game with rival-type uncertainty. *IEEE Transactions on Wireless Communications*, 19(8): 5359–5372, 2020.

26 Yalin E. Sagduyu and Anthony Ephremides. A game-theoretic analysis of denial of service attacks in wireless random access. *Wireless Networks*, 15: 651–666, 2009.

27 Yalin E. Sagduyu, Randall Berry, and Anthony Ephremides. MAC games for distributed wireless network security with incomplete information of selfish and malicious user types. In *International Conference on Game Theory for Networks*, pages 130–139. IEEE, 2009.

28 Yalin E. Sagduyu, Randall A. Berry, and Anthony Ephremides. Jamming games in wireless networks with incomplete information. *IEEE Communications Magazine*, 49(8): 112–118, 2011.

29 Yalin E. Sagduyu. Adversarial machine learning and defense game for NextG signal classification with deep learning. In *IEEE Military Communications Conference (MILCOM)*, pages 1076–1081, 2022.

30 Yi Shi, Tugba Erpek, Yalin E. Sagduyu, and Jason H. Li. Spectrum data poisoning with adversarial deep learning. In *IEEE Military Communications Conference (MILCOM)*, pages 407–412, 2018.

31 Zhengping Luo, Shangqing Zhao, Zhuo Lu, Jie Xu, and Yalin E. Sagduyu. When attackers meet AI: Learning-empowered attacks in cooperative spectrum sensing. *IEEE Transactions on Mobile Computing*, 21(5): 1892–1908, 2020.

32 Zhengping Luo, Shangqing Zhao, Rui Duan, Zhuo Lu, Yalin E. Sagduyu, and Jie Xu. Low-cost influence-limiting defense against adversarial machine learning attacks in cooperative spectrum sensing. In *Proceedings of the 3rd ACM Workshop on Wireless Security and Machine Learning*, pages 55–60, 2021.

33 Zhengping Luo, Shangqing Zhao, Zhuo Lu, Yalin E Sagduyu, and Jie Xu. Adversarial machine learning based partial-model attack in IoT. In *Proceedings of the 2nd ACM Workshop on Wireless Security and Machine Learning*, pages 13–18, 2020.

34 Yalin E. Sagduyu, Yi Shi, and Tugba Erpek. IoT network security from the perspective of adversarial deep learning. In *2019 16th Annual IEEE International Conference on Sensing, Communication, and Networking (SECON)*, pages 1–9, 2019.

35 Kemal Davaslioglu and Yalin E Sagduyu. Trojan attacks on wireless signal classification with adversarial machine learning. In *IEEE International Symposium on Dynamic Spectrum Access Networks (DySPAN)*, pages 1–6, 2019.

36 Yalin E. Sagduyu, Sennur Ulukus, and Aylin Yener. Task-oriented communications for NextG: End-to-end deep learning and AI security aspects. *IEEE Wireless Communications*, 30(3): 52–60, 2023.

37 Yalin E. Sagduyu, Tugba Erpek, Sennur Ulukus, and Aylin Yener. Vulnerabilities of deep learning-driven semantic communications to backdoor (trojan) attacks. In *2023 57th Annual Conference on Information Sciences and Systems (CISS)*, pages 1–6, 2023.

38 Utku Demir, Yalin E. Sagduyu, Tugba Erpek, Hossein Jafari, Sastry Kompella, and Mengran Xue. Distributed federated learning for vehicular network security: Anomaly detection benefits and multi-domain attack threats, 2025. https://arxiv.org/abs/2505.23706.

39 Brian Kim, Yalin E. Sagduyu, Kemal Davaslioglu, Tugba Erpek, and Sennur Ulukus. Over-the-air adversarial attacks on deep learning based modulation classifier over wireless channels. In *2020 54th Annual Conference on Information Sciences and Systems (CISS)*, pages 1–6. IEEE, 2020.

40 Brian Kim, Yalin E. Sagduyu, Tugba Erpek, Kemal Davaslioglu, and Sennur Ulukus. Adversarial attacks with multiple antennas against deep learning-based modulation classifiers. In *IEEE Global Communications Conference (Globecom) Workshops*, pages 1–6, 2020.

41 Brian Kim, Yalin E. Sagduyu, Kemal Davaslioglu, Tugba Erpek, and Sennur Ulukus. Channel-aware adversarial attacks against deep learning-based wireless signal classifiers. *IEEE Transactions on Wireless Communications*, 21(6): 3868–3880, 2021.

42 Brian Kim, Yalin E. Sagduyu, Tugba Erpek, Kemal Davaslioglu, and Sennur Ulukus. Channel effects on surrogate models of adversarial attacks against wireless signal classifiers. In *IEEE International Conference on Communications (ICC)*, pages 1–6, 2021.

43 Meysam Sadeghi and Erik G. Larsson. Adversarial attacks on deep-learning based radio signal classification. *IEEE Wireless Communications Letters*, 8(1): 213–216, 2018.

44 Brian Kim, Yalin E. Sagduyu, Kemal Davaslioglu, Tugba Erpek, and Sennur Ulukus. How to make 5G communications "invisible": Adversarial machine learning for wireless privacy. In *Asilomar Conference on Signals, Systems, and Computers*, pages 763–767. IEEE, 2020.

45 Brian Kim, Tugba Erpek, Yalin E. Sagduyu, and Sennur Ulukus. Covert communications via adversarial machine learning and reconfigurable intelligent surfaces. In *IEEE Wireless Communications and Networking Conference (WCNC)*, pages 411–416, 2022.

46 Brian Kim, Yalin Sagduyu, Kemal Davaslioglu, Tugba Erpek, and Sennur Ulukus. Adversarial machine learning for NextG covert communications using multiple antennas. *Entropy*, 24(8): 1047, 2022.

47 Meysam Sadeghi and Erik G. Larsson. Physical adversarial attacks against end-to-end autoencoder communication systems. *IEEE Communications Letters*, 23(5): 847–850, 2019.

48 Yalin E. Sagduyu, Tugba Erpek, Sennur Ulukus, and Aylin Yener. Is semantic communication secure? A tale of multi-domain adversarial attacks. *IEEE Communications Magazine*, 61(11): 50–55, 2023.

49 Brian Kim, Yi Shi, Yalin E. Sagduyu, Tugba Erpek, and Sennur Ulukus. Adversarial attacks against deep learning based power control in wireless communications. In *IEEE Global Communications Conference (Globecom) Workshops*, pages 1–6, 2021.

50 Brian Kim, Y. Sagduyu, Tugba Erpek, and Sennur Ulukus. Adversarial attacks on deep learning based mmWave beam prediction in 5G and beyond. In *IEEE Statistical Signal Processing Workshop (SSP)*, pages 590–594, 2021.

51 Yi Shi and Yalin Sagduyu. Membership inference attack and defense for wireless signal classifiers with deep learning. *IEEE Transactions on Mobile Computing*, 22: 4032–4043, 2022.

52 Yi Shi, Kemal Davaslioglu, and Yalin E Sagduyu. Over-the-air membership inference attacks as privacy threats for deep learning-based wireless signal classifiers. In *ACM Workshop on Wireless Security and Machine Learning*, pages 61–66, 2020.

12

Self-adapting Quantum Network Provisioning Using Game Theory

Stefan Rass[1,2], Miralem Mehic[3], Sandra König[4], Stefan Schauer[5], and Miroslav Voznak[6]*

[1] *LIT Secure and Correct Systems Lab, Johannes Kepler University, Linz, Austria*
[2] *Institute of Artificial Intelligence and Cybersecurity, Universitaet Klagenfurt, Klagenfurt, Austria*
[3] *Department of Telecommunications, Faculty of Electrical Engineering, University of Sarajevo, Sarajevo, Bosnia and Herzegovina*
[4] *Research Driven Solutions Ltd., Greystones, Ireland*
[5] *Center for Digital Safety and Security, AIT Austrian Institute of Technology, Vienna, Austria*
[6] *Department of Telecommunications, VSB-Technical University of Ostrava, Ostrava, Czech Republic*

*Corresponding Author: stefan.rass@jku.at

12.1 Introduction

A practical challenge in using cryptography for secure communication (where secure means confidential, reliable, and with assured authenticity and integrity) is the proper management of keys. Public key infrastructures are well established but bear a strong human element in the management of certificates and keys on the user side, implied by the need to refresh (enlarge) keys from time to time. The deployment of secret keys for symmetric encryption likewise requires much manual labor and is hence error prone. Infrastructures to automatically deploy and refresh secret keys for symmetric encryption are thus attractive to reduce the manual share of workload in the key management, and hence also the risks of human error. Quantum key distribution (QKD) networks are candidates to handle such transparent management of keys, with an adjustable level of security and self-adaptation to changing environmental conditions. Such changes can range from incidents or exploits reported for certain nodes in the network, to changes in the working conditions of devices, up to the discovery of new vulnerabilities in already deployed systems.

In all these cases, self-adaptation is possible in different forms: whenever devices are under suspicion of being hacked, the routing layer can bypass them to keep the traffic confidential. Whenever temporarily elevated security is required, the encryption algorithms can be adapted to be leveraging stronger encryption methods (at the cost of consuming more key material). And finally, upon the discovery of new vulnerabilities, both the routing and the encryption methods may be designed adaptable to the new conditions to retain security.

12.2 Basics of Quantum Networks

A quantum network in the following will be any network in which nodes that are connected by a direct link are capable of producing arbitrary amounts of shared secret, with the help of QKD protocols. They were originally inspired by an idea of Wiesner's [1] and first proposed by Charles Bennett and Gilles Brassard in 1984 [2]. Ekert modified the idea to use entanglement [3], which would theoretically lend itself also to the construction of quantum repeaters [4–6]. The latter is interesting as it would – in theory – allow to overcome arbitrary distances, while all contemporary QKD protocols are length-limited by damping effects losses on the quantum channels or connections. If Alice and Bob are too far to communicate directly, they will need an intermediate node, e.g., Carol, to forward traffic between them. Without end-to-end shared secrets, Alice can only share a key with Carol, and Carol can share (another) key with Bob, and will need to decrypt and re-encrypt any payload between Alice and Bob.

Obviously, the critical moment is the messages appearing in plain inside an intermediate forwarding node, e.g., Carol, which induces the widely adopted "trusted relay assumption," which means that no attack on the relay (Carol or any other) must ever occur. While this instantly implies end-to-end confidentiality, it is practically satisfiable only under strong organizational and physical access control over the nodes. However, the relay nodes are essentially just conventional computers, running standard operating systems, and are as vulnerable as any other computer. They need regular updating, patching, and generally an interface for administration. Thus, physical and logical access control is a nontrivial matter to establish but a pillar of the overall end-to-end security. In fact, for an attacker to break the entire scheme, it is enough to conquer one node on the path between Alice and Bob. Any intermediate relay getting under the adversary's control would render all quantum physical proofs of security void, since these mostly refer only to the security of the transmission *line* (see, for example, Shor's argument [7]). An exception is device-independent security [8–12], which attempts to broaden the security guarantees beyond pure eavesdropping resilience and to establish robustness of devices against misconfigurations and imperfectness of physical components. However, these precautions may as well need continuous calibration and update, and are thus also subject to maintenance processes, and candidates for automatic adaption.

The resilience of the relay against active attacks adds to the required assumption of no denial-of-service (DoS) by eavesdropping to occur. The proven security, insofar as it shall rest on laws of quantum physics, does not cover resilience against outages of lines and relays, which gets back to classical arguments, involving redundancy among others. If the network layout is such that it offers some path redundancy between Alice and Bob, or more generally between any two nodes in the network, then the outage of a single connection leaves at least another line intact that Alice and Bob can switch to. Such redundancy is widely found in today's computer networks, which arrange connections in a ring in many cases, exactly for the purpose of bridging a temporary outage of one line in the network. While this is in most cases a reactive action, game theory can use the same redundancy to establish a proactive protection against eavesdropping and DoS events. Indeed, having more than one path to use for Alice and Bob, they can set up a communication game to optimally utilize the quantum network resources, while at the same time relaxing the trusted node assumption toward a threshold assumption on the network topology. That is, while a single node to get conquered is enough for trusted relay to fail, game-theoretic quantum network provisioning, in connection with network path redundancy, can help raising the bar to $k > 1$ nodes necessary to fail before the end-to-end confidentiality deteriorates. The remainder of the proposed chapter is thus about (i) formalizing confidentiality and availability as a joint notion of security, (ii) introducing game theory as a tool to model the transmission game between Alice and Bob toward optimizing their security in both, confidentiality and availability regards, and (iii) describing ways of changing the network configuration and topology upon noticing incidents in the network, which makes use of the QKD eavesdropping detection facility.

12.3 Game Theory to Orchestrate Cryptography

Similarly, as in Chapter 11, the goal of end-to-end confidentiality lends itself to a game-theoretic model, with an equilibrium that has a natural interpretation for the network provisioning. Since game mechanism's payoff will depend on the underlying cryptographic mechanisms, we first review the concept of perfectly secure transmission (without QKD) using secret sharing, from which all ingredients for our game model will naturally arise.

12.3.1 Basics of Perfectly Secure Message Transmission

QKD is an elegant but not the first technique to establish unconditionally secure transmission. In fact, techniques from threshold cryptography, most importantly secret sharing and multipath transmission [13–15], offer traditional methods of sending information in a provably secure fashion, void of computational intractability assumptions and even not relying on any quantum laws. The underlying assumption is a secure broadcast channel, so that nodes can securely communicate pairwise, and this assumption is exactly what QKD can satisfy.

An early information-theoretic study [16] of the possibility to communicate in perfect privacy is based on the assumption that from whatever location the attacker Eve is listening to the conversation between Alice and Bob, the channel between Eve and Alice (or between Eve and Bob) sure has physically different characteristics compared to the channel from Alice to Bob. Based on this difference, it is possible to quantify, in terms of mutual information, the amount of leakage from Alice to Eve (resp. from Bob to Eve), under certain assumptions on the noise. In essence, the argument is that the adversary will necessarily receive less information from Alice than what Bob receives, and it is this "residual" information that Bob gets but Eve does not get, that can be utilized to protect the conversation. More than three decades later, the concept was framed into modern cryptographic notions as semantic security [17], but operationalizing the idea is actually possible with techniques from threshold cryptography in connection with network redundancy.

Let us return to the physical observation behind the wiretap channel, saying that Eve may drain something, but not all of what Bob would receive from Alice. Can we "enforce" such a setting intentionally? And if so, how? An answer lies in the uncertainty for Eve about where to intercept the channel exactly, since her location "between" Alice and Bob will determine how much (or how little) information Eve can get from her attack. Many contemporary networks offer some connection redundancy to cope with temporary outages, but also to bridge periods of maintenance or repair, without disrupting the overall service. The simplest such redundant layout is the ring structure, which allows any segment of the ring to be temporarily unavailable. If so, the ring breaks up into a line, nonetheless leaving all nodes connected over the line until the ring can be recovered.

Putting the idea of the wiretap channel to operation, we may think of Alice and Bob, knowing that they are on a joint ring, using both their existing channels in a random yet alternating way to transmit parts of their secret conversation. If the adversary is able to intercept only one out of two channels, it will necessarily miss the "other half" of the conversation, which, under proper encodings of the packets, may bound the information flow to Eve, up to zeroing it in the best case. The security is, however, void at the instant where Eve manages to intercept both paths between Alice and Bob, in which case she has become the person-in-the-middle, and unless Alice and Bob have successfully exchanged some key before and without Eve's knowledge, there is no common secret between them, and hence no confidential information flow possible. The crucial assumption is thus discovered to be a bound on how many nodes Eve can intercept. This is a "threshold assumption" but imposes no restriction on Eve's computational power. Thus, we are in the same setting as with QKD, only having traded computational limits of the attacker (on which symmetric and public-key rely) by a limiting assumption on how many nodes can get under Eve's control. The important difference herein is the "verifiability" of such assumptions, which is a main selling point of QKD too: QKD rests on scientifically established and experimentally verified laws of physics. Corresponding computational intractability assumptions underneath symmetric or public-key cryptography do not lend themselves to experimental confirmations, despite the absence of reported success on solving some of the underlying problems. Despite the evidence for the difficulty of the Diffie–Hellman problem and many others is strong, the verifiability remains an issue. Threshold assumptions like "Eve cannot intercept more than one node at a time" can be, on the contrary, much easier to argue, since we have regular maintenance routines that may clean nodes from malware (even without knowing so when it happens), intrusion detection systems, physical access protection, and many other technical and non-technical means to substantiate the assumption. In fact, trusted relay, as outlined above, is also a threshold assumption, namely stating that "Eve cannot intercept any node on the path between Alice and Bob." If this assumption is justified by technical and non-technical precautions on the classical parts, and likewise technical protection of the quantum parts (e.g., by using measurement-device-independent QKD [8, 9, 11]), end-to-end security is assured and verifiably so.

However, since no protection is ultimately perfect, it remains to deal with whatever residual information may get into Eve's hands despite all protection efforts. And this is the point where cryptographic protocols can help out, in connection with a suitable network topology. If we let all nodes be arranged in an (undirected) graph, the ring structure would be called a "2-vertex-connected" network, since any two nodes on the ring have two node-disjoint paths connecting them (the respective "halves" of the ring). Generalizing this idea, a network is said to be *k-vertex-connected*, if there are at least k pairwise non-intersecting paths between any two nodes. The conceptual simplicity is in contrast to practical circumstances, since hardly any real-life network would offer, say, 10 non-intersecting paths between any two nodes, although empirical studies found that many networks admit about four disjoint paths indeed [18, 19].

If we allow paths to intersect, the number of paths in a graph between two arbitrary (but fixed) nodes is generally exponential in the number of nodes in the network. This exponentially long list would necessarily contain many paths that not only intersect but widely overlap with one another, and the natural question is whether there is a reasonable "middle ground" between what a real-life network can offer in terms of connectivity and what we can use for secure communication. Threshold cryptography offers a refined view on what an adversary can do or cannot do, for the sake of designing (hierarchical) access structures. We will now walk through an introduction example, to end up connecting this to perfectly secure message transmission.

12.3.2 Hierarchical Secret Sharing and Access Structures

In the following, we will let all calculations be done in some finite field. Let a person P be the owner of some secret s, and assume that P is not all time available, and hence seeks the possibility of replacement by a group of n subordinate persons $P_1, \ldots, P_n$. Then P can distribute parts of its secret to $P_1, \ldots, P_n$, giving each of them a random number $r_1, \ldots, r_n$, chosen such that the representation $s = r_1 + r_2 + \ldots + r_n$ holds. In that role P is called the "dealer" in the vocabulary of secret sharing, and the values $r_1, \ldots, r_n$ are called the "shares." Having distributed its shares to $P_1, \ldots, P_n$, no colluding subset $C \subset \{P_1, \ldots, P_n\}$ will be able to recover the secret s on their own, since the single equation for s will contain at least one unknown r_i corresponding to the missing "player" $P_i \in \{P_1, \ldots, P_n\} \setminus C$, which admits a multitude (up to including all possible elements in the underlying finite field) of solutions, hence perfectly concealing the secret to any coalition of $< n$ players. The "threshold" is herein fixed to be the number n of shares to the secret s. A more general form is using interpolation, in which case the dealer P sets up a polynomial of degree $k-1$ with random coefficients, e.g., $f(x) := s + \alpha_1 x + \alpha_2 x^2 + \ldots + \alpha_{k-1} x^{k-1}$, and let the share for P_i be $s_i = f(i)$, if i is a value that one-to-one corresponds P_i's identity. Under the condition of all players using different values, at least k or more players can uniquely recover the polynomial f by interpolation, and recover f by evaluating $s = f(0)$.

Now, iterating the scheme (either sum- or interpolation-based), each player P_i can itself become a dealer and distribute its share s_i to its own subordinate players and so on. Thus, each player will accumulate a set of shares and can be involved in different groups to reconstruct secrets accordingly to the respective sharing technique. The scheme provides confidentiality only but is vulnerable against any form of actively dishonest behavior, such as manipulations to shares, blocking of shares, and others. We shall hereafter not be concerned with countermeasures against such manipulations, except mentioning that the threshold scheme above is equivalent to Reed–Solomon error-correcting encoding, and using the Welch–Berlekamp algorithm, the players seeking to reconstruct the secret s that was "threshold-shared" by polynomial interpolation can detect up to $k-1$ manipulated shares and can repair up to $\left\lfloor \frac{n-k}{2} \right\rfloor$ shares from errors (even if caused by an active adversary) [20].

Let us suppose that a secret has been shared along one or a combination of the techniques mentioned above. The collection of all sets of players that shall be able to recover the secret is an *access structure*, denoted as $\mathcal{A}cc = \{X \subseteq \{P_1, \ldots, P_n\} :$ the coalition X can reconstruct the secret$\}$. For the sum-based sharing of above, we would have $X = \{P_1, \ldots, P_n\}$, and for the interpolation-based scheme of above, we would have X as any subset of k or more players. The complement set, w.r.t. all players, is the set of coalitions that shall not be capable of learning information about the secret and is hence called the *adversary structure* $\mathcal{A}dv = 2^{\{P_1,\ldots,P_n\}} \setminus \mathcal{A}cc$. The adversary structure would thus contain all subsets of $\{P_1, \ldots, P_n\}$ of cardinality $< n$ (for the sum-based sharing), or cardinality $< k$ for interpolation-based sharing.

12.3.3 Using Secret Sharing for Perfectly Secure Multipath Transmission (Defense Strategies)

The application of this access control technique to secure transmission is then straightforward along the following steps:

1. We let Alice take her secret message m, and compute shares $s_1, \ldots, s_n$ from it.
2. These shares are then sent to Bob over distinct channels, depending on how many such (possibly node disjoint) channels the network permits (in case of a ring structure, there would be two channels only, but more are of course possible if the network is sufficiently meshed).
3. Bob receives all shares and reconstructs the secret accordingly by interpolation or summation.

Multipath transmission protocols such as [13, 15, 21] run along these lines, with details differing mostly in the particular sharing scheme (possibly other than the ones described above), and error correction phases for resilience against active adversaries. Security holds under the assumption that the adversary is constrained to conquer only parts of the network that are also included in $\mathcal{A}dv$, meaning that no region of the network possibly under the attacker's control is good enough to breach the confidentiality. Classical symmetric encryption is indeed a special case of the above scheme, since it assumes two paths (threshold would be $k = 2$), that are not simultaneously intercepted (the adversary structure would be $\mathcal{A}dv = \{\{P_1\}, \{P_2\}, \ldots, \{P_n\}\}$), and send the secret key sk over one path and the ciphertext c over the other path. The sharing and reconstruction would then both be based on the equation $c = m + sk$, which is in a finite field, and if sk is used only once, it is as good as a one-time pad.

12.3.4 How to Define or Identify Adversary Structures (Attack Strategies)?

The definition of the adversary structure depends on reasonable hypotheses on what devices the attacker can bring under its control. The use of measurement-device-independent QKD lets us simplify this matter by taking out all quantum devices from the consideration, leaving only the "classical" parts of a quantum network as relevant here. These classical parts then include operating systems, Internet ports and connections, and all software and non-quantum hardware stack. On this level, a quantum network is not fundamentally different to any other computer network and, as such, open for network vulnerability scanning and hardening along standard processes and workflows.

An adversary structure can then be defined by collecting nodes that share common possible vulnerabilities, based on the same configuration, device characteristics, firmware, etc. For example, one can put all nodes running on the same operating system into a set A_{OS}, while collecting nodes under maintenance of the same administrative team #1 into another set $A_{\text{team\#1}}$, put the nodes of the same subnet X as possibly be all exposed ot the same threats into a third set $A_{\text{subnet}-X}$, and so on. The adversary structure would then at least be $\mathcal{A}dv = \{A_{OS}, A_{\text{team\#1}}, A_{\text{subnet}-X} \ldots\}$. Eventually, the adversary structure may thus contain all sets that are *jointly exposed* to some threat, and the size and form of $\mathcal{A}dv$ may thus correspond to a prior threat analysis conducted along the regular risk management activities. We can even put whole subnets as their own elements into $\mathcal{A}dv$, for example, in cases where we outsource the transmission itself to an external vendor, from which we rent the fiber-optic cables and transmission devices. If we let this externally provisioned subnet be possibly compromised, we would include the entire set of nodes $A_{\text{external}-\text{subnet}}$ as a member in $\mathcal{A}dv$.

12.3.5 Quantum Cryptography in Combination with Multipath Transmission

Note that the definition of access and adversary structures are based on nodes only, but do not consider the possibility to eavesdropping at the time when the shares are transported from the dealer to the players. Why would the adversary not try getting the shares from eavesdropping on their transmission? If this is feasible, the assumption that the adversary is not one of the players is satisfiable, but the scheme is nonetheless insecure, since player P_i's share is no longer just known to this player, but also to the adversary. Classical threshold cryptography tackles this by assuming a secure broadcast channel, but quantum networks naturally provide perfectly secure links already. This makes quantum networks natural candidates to implement multipath transmission for end-to-end security, if we can afford building a network with sufficiently strong vertex-connectivity to meet the assumptions on the adversary structures. We will postpone a deeper discussion of this issue until Section 12.5.

Two questions remain for practical purposes:

1. How to deal with "mobile" adversaries, i.e., cases where more and more nodes become conquered over time, or if nodes become conquered and released at random (where the release could be due to some malware being washed away by a scan or reconfiguration, or because the attacker has lost access upon a change of access credentials, or similar)?
2. How to deal with situations in which the network connectivity is low, but the adversary structure is such that a person-in-the-middle attack would be possible in at least one scenario?

As we will show in the next subsection, game theory can provide answers to both of these questions. Moreover, it also lets us quantify the chances for a data leakage, or similarly, quantify the loss upon a confidentiality breach, which is important information for the design of cyber insurances (Chapter 6).

12.3.6 Game-theoretic Orchestration of Perfectly Secure Message Transmission

Let us make our assumptions for a showcase on how to accomplish quantifiably perfect end-to-end security in a quantum network explicit:

- Eve has unlimited computational power; specifically, she could break all forms of public-key encryption.
- Alice and Bob do not possess any pre-shared secrets for communication. We do, however, assume that Alice and Bob are mutually authenticated by some means (usually using a pre-shared secret, but not allowed to use this same secret also to communicate in secrecy), following a zero-trust principle (Chapter 5).

Eavesdropping in quantum networks is convertible into a two-player game, with Alice as player 1 trying to deliver her message to Bob in a way such that the opponent player 2, Eve, has only a minimal gain of information. The strategies for the second player are already known by the adversary structure $\mathcal{A}dv$, which is the hostile second's player's *action set* $AS_2 = \mathcal{A}dv$. We hereafter assume that the attacker is "limited" to conquering subsets of nodes only according to which possibilities are listed in AS_2, and makes a strategic choice from that set. Likewise, Alice can choose from her own list of transmission paths $\pi_1, \pi_2, \ldots$, all of which connect her to Bob, and some of which, depending on the adversary's choices, may be intercepted. Alice's problem is choosing the right path (or path-bundle as a whole set of paths) so that Eve does not intercept her message packets, but she has only a partial indication about Eve's presence due to the eavesdropping facility of the quantum network. That is, Eve can effectively "cut" certain links by eavesdropping and hence make certain paths unavailable to Alice. However, in doing so, she may reveal her activity and Alice, in the worst case for Eve, may stop her communication at all. So, we hereafter assume that Eve strives to remain stealthy and eavesdrop only on nodes to avoid detection by Alice. We let Alice's choices be made from a list of possible transmission configurations, abstractly called $TC_1, TC_2, \ldots$ and collected in an *action set* AS_1 for Alice. Each such configuration includes the full specification of how Alice's message is delivered to Bob. This includes transmission paths over the network, as well as routing information and other signals to intermediate nodes. The particular contents of each such configuration are hereafter of no deeper interest, except for the question of whether the transmission initiated by Alice involves nodes under the attacker's control, and if so, whether Eve gets enough information to reconstruct the secret.

Remark: The symbols AS_1 and AS_2 will hereafter be taken as finite and with an arbitrary but fixed ordering on their elements. That is, whenever we refer to the i-th, resp. j-th, strategy of a player, this will always point to some fixed element(s) from the list.

For illustration, let the network be a graph $G = (V, E)$, where V is the set of nodes, and E is a set of all QKD-secured bidirectional communication links. Alice and Bob both have their nodes contained in V. The graph G is undirected (the directed case is conceptually no different). In the simplest instance of a game-theoretic security analysis, we may let Alice choose single paths to deliver her message over, and use only these paths as her transmission configuration, which makes $AS_1 = \{TC_1 = \pi_1 \subseteq V, TC_2 = \pi_2 \subseteq V, \ldots\}$ each an Alice-to-Bob path in the network. Note that we let a path here be a *set of consecutive nodes* from V. The adversary structure is an arbitrary collection of subsets, constrained only to not contain an Alice-Bob-Cut, because otherwise, Eve could place herself as the person-in-the-middle and thereby rule out all possibilities for Alice to communicate with Bob in privacy (since they do not share the necessary encryption key). To exclude this trivial (and for Alice impossible to solve) case, we thus assume that the adversary structure $\mathcal{A}dv = AS_2 \subseteq 2^{V\setminus\{\text{Alice,Bob}\}}$ is such that all $C \in AS_2$ are such that C contains less than V elements, excluding Alice and Bob's nodes in all cases, since this would correspond to an impersonation attack of Eve pretending to be Bob to Alice, or pretending to be Alice when she communicates with Bob (this assumption hence supports the previous hypothesis on Alice and Bob to be authenticated, or at least can rely on the authenticity of their messages).

If Alice uses only a single transmission path π, and Eve can conquer any set $C \in \mathcal{A}dv$, then Alice's message remains confidential if and only if

$$\pi \cap C = \emptyset, \tag{12.1}$$

That is, Eve has not intercepted any node on the path. Observe that this condition is *nothing else than the trusted relay assumption*. Writing (12.1) as a indicator function that we can consider as a "utility function" for Alice that actually counts messages that she lost to the adversary. We can define

$$u(\pi, C) = \begin{cases} 1 & \text{if condition (12.1) holds;} \\ 0 & \text{otherwise (messagewas lost to the attacker).} \end{cases} \tag{12.2}$$

and evaluate (12.2) on all possible combinations of transmission paths $\{\pi_1, \ldots \pi_i, \ldots, \pi_n\} = AS_1$ and adversarial sets $\{C_1, \ldots, C_j, \ldots, C_m\} = AS_2$, to generate an $(n \times m)$-tableau of all 0/1 values.

Example Let the quantum network be as in Figure 12.1.

An exhaustive enumeration of all paths from Alice to Bob reveals a total of 29 possible strategies for Alice to transmit her message. Since this number is worst-case exponential in the number of nodes, let her thus reduce her set of strategies to using only shortest paths. This brings down the number of strategies to only three that constitute $AS_1 = \{\pi_1 = A \to 3 \to 6 \to B, \pi_2 = A \to 4 \to 5 \to B, \pi_3 = A \to 1 \to 2 \to B\}$. Under trusted relay, Alice can choose any of them, only perhaps subject to quality of service (QoS) criteria, e.g., selecting the path with the

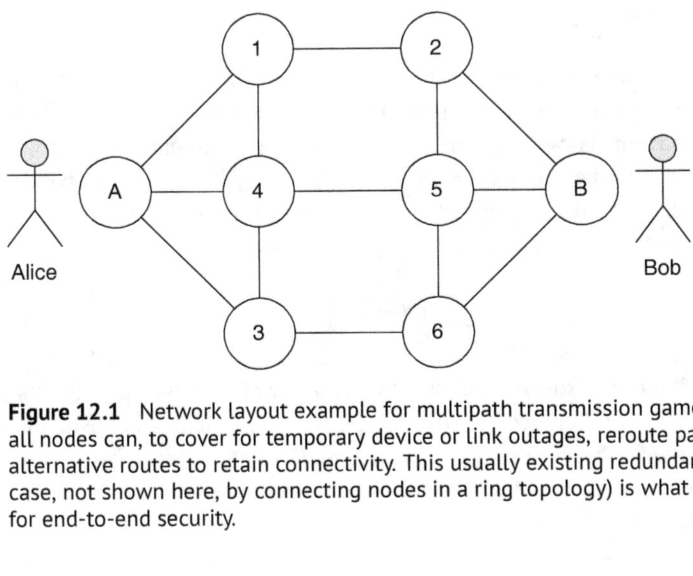

Figure 12.1 Network layout example for multipath transmission game. We assume that all nodes can, to cover for temporary device or link outages, reroute packets over alternative routes to retain connectivity. This usually existing redundancy (in the simplest case, not shown here, by connecting nodes in a ring topology) is what we can dual-use for end-to-end security.

highest bandwidth. If we relax the trusted node assumption and admit the adversary's power to conquer one node, this makes $AS_2 = \{1, 2, \dots, 6\}$ for its strategies. The matrix for the game is hence 3×6 in size, and given by evaluating (12.1) for all $\pi_i \in AS_1$ versus $C_j \in AS_2$:

	$C = \{1\}$	$C = \{2\}$	$C = \{3\}$	$C = \{4\}$	$C = \{5\}$	$C = \{6\}$
$\pi_1 = A \to 3 \to 6 \to B$	1	1	0	1	1	0
$\pi_2 = A \to 4 \to 5 \to B$	1	1	1	0	0	1
$\pi_3 = A \to 1 \to 2 \to B$	0	0	1	1	1	1

Obviously, to intercept path π_1, it makes no difference from the attacker's perspective whether node 1 or node 2 was conquered, so we can drop either column (but not both) without changing the possibilities. Practically, the attacker would target the "easier" node among the two. For the game theoretic analysis, we can (in a simplification of real matters where the difficulty of attacking node 1 or attacking node 2 would play a role), cross out either of the two strategies from the attacker's actions set as being "weakly strategically dominated." This means that a strategy is "as good as some other," and hence can be substituted by whatever action has the same (or better) effect. In this way, we can further reduce the tableau to a 3×3 matrix, such as for example,

	$C = \{2\}$	$C = \{3\}$	$C = \{4\}$
$\pi_1 = A \to 3 \to 6 \to B$	1	0	1
$\pi_2 = A \to 4 \to 5 \to B$	1	1	0
$\pi_3 = A \to 1 \to 2 \to B$	0	1	1

Now, let Alice's random choice rule be a probability distribution over her set of actions, generally being some set AS_1, and let the attacker likewise randomly but strategically choose from its own action set AS_2. Taking the tableau from above as a matrix A, and letting the vectors $x = (x_1, \dots, x_n)$, $y = (y_1, \dots, y_m)$ be probability distributions (i.e., have all nonnegative values that sum up to 1 within x and within y), the vector-matrix-vector product

$$u(x, y) = x^\top \cdot A \cdot y = \sum_{i=1}^{n} \sum_{j=1}^{m} x_i \cdot y_j \cdot u\left(\pi_i, C_j\right) \tag{12.3}$$

is just the expectation of the success indicator variable, w.r.t. the joint probability distribution of both players' choices, assuming that they are made stochastically independent (otherwise, the product $x_i \cdot y_j$ would need to be replaced by a more general expression for $\Pr\left(X = x_i \wedge Y = y_j\right)$ if X, Y are random variables expressing the choices made by both players).

Expression (12.3) is, by construction, a probability and interpretable based on the definition of the function u. If u is defined by (12.1), we have

$$\Pr(\text{message remains confidential} \mid \text{Alice randomly chooses the transmission path with distribution } x, \text{ and Eve randomly chooses nodes to intercept with probabilities } y) = u(x, y). \tag{12.4}$$

Therefore, this conditional probability quantifies the probability of eavesdropping, given *specific* attacks. Game theory then proceeds by letting both players, Alice and the attacker, simultaneously optimize their strategies toward maximizing or minimizing, respectively, the chances for a confidential delivery. Formally, Alice thus seeks

$$x^* \in \underset{x \in AS_1}{\operatorname{argmax}}\, u(x, y^*)$$

while the attacker computes

$$y^* \in \underset{y \in AS_2}{\operatorname{argmin}}\, u(x^*, y),$$

that is, Alice seeks the transmission configuration to maximize the chances of secure transmission by making a random choice according to x^*, while the adversary does its best to eavesdrop at random positions, chosen according to y^*. The simultaneous max/min optimization is accomplishable with standard (even open source) software tools, such as [22]. For the example above, the result would be $x^* = \left(\frac{1}{3}, \frac{1}{3}, \frac{1}{3}\right)$, $y^* = \left(\frac{1}{3}, \frac{1}{3}, \frac{1}{3}\right)$, leading to $u(x^*, y^*) = 2/3$. This appears rather trivial, since it just tells that Alice should – in a moving target fashion – choose her paths to avoid Eve's interception. Without any further information on the hardness to exploit some nodes or the QoS parameters that additionally impact possible choices, the result is just an equiprobable choice. Nontrivial choice rules will naturally arise under a more informed setup, such as probabilistic success ratings under different scenarios; we will come to this below.

The analysis so far used the same goals for both players, but if the attacker has other incentives than eavesdropping, e.g., just disrupting the communication, (12.4) merely changes into an upper bound:

$$\Pr(\text{message remains confidential} \mid \text{Alice randomly chooses the transmission path with distribution } x^*, \text{ and } \textit{Eve acts anyhow random but inside her action space } AS_2) \geq u(x^*, y^*). \tag{12.5}$$

In terms of our example from above, this would mean that Alice has a 66.6% chance to get her message to Bob without trusted relay, but under the weaker assumption that Eve controls no more than one node in the network. Increasing this chance further is a matter of changing the protocol as such, e.g., using a longer sequence of packets that all travel over randomly chosen paths, with error corrections done by Bob, or changing the network topology. In our case, condition (12.1) is very specific for the transmission technique to use (i) only a single path, and (ii) assume that the attacker can break the trusted node assumption. Using more than one path and threshold secret sharing, such as the protocol in [13], for example, does, condition (12.1) becomes more complicated, but nonetheless remains a decidable predicate on when Alice succeeds or loses her secret message to the adversary. Doing the likewise game-theoretic analysis by simultaneous optimization, leads to a likewise valid lower bound (12.5) for the probability of a confidentiality breach.

There is no conceptual barrier stopping us from replacing the predicate (12.1) by a condition about recoverability of the message by the receiver Bob. That is, if the channel encoding is known, and the attacker's action space is defined with the goal of blocking the message or making it otherwise irrecoverable by Bob, the likewise analysis toward an optimal lower bound (12.5) will give the minimum chance of a reliable delivery.

Armed with game theory as a tool to quantify the chances of confidential delivery or correct delivery, the final question is whether the two goals are "combinable." At this point, it is imaginable to define a conjunctive predicate to indicate a correct and confidential delivery, depending on the underlying protocol.

In a more general setting, and toward self-adaption, we can also replace (12.1) by a probability that the delivery was successful and/or confidential. The eavesdropping mechanism of QKD networks can help here to decide about correct delivery: imagine that the network operational layer keeps record of how often a link was disrupted by an eavesdropping attempt that the QKD devices detected, or by other reasons. Based on such information, we can assign a probability to each link and, for a chosen path, can determine the QoS and quality of security parameters accordingly. This changes the matrix from 0/1-valued to a continuous scale between 0 and 1. Again, for the example from above, the change would be assigning the three paths different reliabilities depending on how likely we suspect the eavesdropper to "cut" a line or how hard we think a penetration of a node would be. Filling in example numbers (in reality to be justified on the concrete network configuration and state), the game matrix could look like the following, in which we (arbitrarily) assumed that node 2 is "weakest" and allows for a 20% chance to be conquered, whereas nodes 3 and 4 are harder to attack and will become compromised with a chance of 10% and 15%, respectively. The cells with a 1 here mean that Eve simply missed the transmission as a whole; hence, Alice was 100% successful.

The likewise analysis as above by running the equilibrium computation (e.g., using [22]), now delivers a different result, namely saying that the chances

	$C = \{2\}$	$C = \{3\}$	$C = \{4\}$
$\pi_1 = A \to 3 \to 6 \to B$	1	Pr (conquer node 2) = 0.1	1
$\pi_2 = A \to 4 \to 5 \to B$	1	1	Pr (conquer node 2) = 0.15
$\pi_3 = A \to 1 \to 2 \to B$	Pr (conquer node 2) = 0.2	1	1

for Alice to get her message through have come to $x^* \approx (0.314, 0.333, 0.353)$, $y^* = (0.353, 0.314, 0.333)$, and $u^* \approx 0.717$, which shows that Alice's chances by hardening the three nodes 2, 3 and 6 would have increased to 0.717. This reasoning, however, would be falsified by Eve instantly, since the original game had 6 strategies for her, and Alice did not yet harden the previous alternative nodes 1, 5, and 6. So, it is generally advisable for Alice, upon every change to the network, to reconsider the whole game with all previously abandoned strategies, to avoid missing out an attack vector of Eve. To really get her chances of a confidential delivery up to 71.7%, she would have to consider all strategies that are available to Eve.

Based on that, a self-adaptation mechanism of a QKD network is possible by letting the network control layer maintain a transmission (game) matrix between any two peers in the network and updating the numbers (reliabilities of paths in terms of eavesdropping) accordingly based on the reported state of the QKD links. For each transmission from (some) "Alice" to (some other) "Bob" node in the network, it is then a matter of solving a finite matrix game (boiling down to the solution of a linear program internally) to compute a best transmission configuration for the current network state.

Another trigger of change to the numbers can be a (permanent) change in the network topology or the transmission game, which can be, for example, hardening parts of the network to delete strategies from the attacker's set AS_2, or open up new transmission paths for Alice to enlarge her set AS_1. We will come back to this in more detail in Section 12.6.

12.4 Self-adaption of QKD Devices to Environmental Conditions

The eavesdropping facility of a QKD protocol requires reliable information about how much error to expect in an undistorted channel, which means to first establish a "baseline" under environmental conditions in absence of an attacker.

Some experimental studies [23] provide information about how temperature, radiation, and other factors impact the expected quantum bit error rate, and using copula theory, we can let QKD devices self-adapt their thresholds to changes of the environment [24] using predictive distributions, to make the device resilient against unstable working atmosphere.

To operationalize the current environmental state to adjust the devices to conditions, we will consider the experimental measurements conducted on the SECOQC network in Vienna [25], which has been statistically evaluated in [23]. The dataset collected in this latter reference had $n = 276$ samples of the following quantities that we will abbreviate in the following:

- The qubit error rate in percentage terms (QBER)
- Air temperature (TEMP)
- Relative humidity (HUM)
- Sunshine duration in seconds (DUR)
- Global radiation in watt/m^2 (RAD)

The entire data behind the descriptions to follow is thus a 276×5 matrix, hereafter abbreviated as the *data matrix* $\mathbf{D}$.

Our goal is to make predictions about QBER based on the current configuration of the other variables. To this end, we first need to statistically model the interdependence between these variables, since assuming stochastic independence would be an oversimplification of matters. Copula theory allows to separate out the dependence structure from the marginal distributions of each variable by letting us write the joint distribution $F_{\text{QBER,TEMP,HUM,DUR,RAD}}(x) = C\left(F_{\text{QBER}}(x), F_{\text{TEMP}}(x), F_{\text{HUM}}(x), F_{\text{DUR}}(x), F_{\text{RAD}}(x)\right)$, in which C is a copula function, and the inner functions $F_{\text{QBER}}, F_{\text{TEMP}}, \ldots$ are the marginal distributions. The copula is itself just an n-dimensional (multivariate) distribution function whose marginals are all uniform. Sklår's theorem tells that the function C that creates the joint from the marginal distribution is essentially unique if the marginals are continuous. This applies for the setting outlined above, so that we can safely look for an estimate of the function C based on data. As for standard parametric statistical models (like Gaussian distributions, Poisson distributions, or similar), copula theory provides us with various parameterizable choices for copula functions, such as Archimedean copulas and others. A simple example is the independence copula, which is just $C(x_1, \ldots, x_n) = x_1 x_2 \ldots x_n$, or the two-dimensional Gumbel copula, whose density is given by

$$C(u, v) = \exp\left[-\left((-\ln u)^{\theta} + (-\ln v)^{\theta}\right)^{\frac{1}{\theta}}\right]$$

for a parameter $\theta \geq 1$. To account for several dimensions via more than one parameter to adjust the copula fit, Archimedean copulas allow for a systematic way of nesting the functions. We briefly outline the construction here to shed light on the parameters that an automated fitting in statistical software environments like R would give as results. Let a generator function $\phi : [0, 1] \to [0, \infty]$ be given such that $\phi(1) = \phi(\infty) = 0$, and let it be n-monotone, i.e., differentiable up to order $n - 2$ with $(-1)^{n-2}\phi\hat{}((n-2)(t)$ being nondecreasing and convex and $(-1)^i \phi^{(i)}(t) \geq 0$ for $0 \leq i \leq n-2$ and for all $0 \leq t < \infty$. Then, an Archimedean copula is definable from ϕ as the function $C(x_1, \dots, x_n) = \phi^{-1}(\phi(x_1) + \dots + \phi(x_n))$. As an example, the Gumbel copula (also in the higher-dimensional case) is generated by $\phi(t) = (-\ln t)^\theta$. Taking a set of different generators $\phi_1, \dots, \phi_{n-1}$, e.g., from the literature [26], a nested copula is defined by $C(x_1, \dots, x_n) = \phi_{n-1}^{-1}\left[\phi_{n-1}(\dots\left[\phi_2(\phi_1^{-1}[\phi_1(x_1) + \phi_1(x_2)] + \phi_2(x_3)\right] + \dots + \phi_{n-2}(x_{n-1})) + \phi_{n-1}(x_n))\right]$. This formula refers to a fully nested copula, but it is not difficult to rearrange terms to produce an arbitrary nesting structure. Thus, part of the nested copula estimation problem is also to define, or better to estimate as well, the structure of the nesting itself. The reason to buy this additional complexity is flexibility to allow for a good fit. Practically, the R environment [27] offers the HAC ("hierarchical Archimedean copula") package [28] to directly fit an Archimedean copula to given data using maximum likelihood methods, and does both, i.e., it gives the parameters and nesting structure in one blow. The result comes as a nicely displayed graphical representation of the copula, showing the individual parameters, such as Figure 12.2 shows.

The fitting algorithm assumes nonnegative correlations between the variables, which is easy to verify as not given in the data collected about the Vienna network. The authors of [29] therefore gave a simple method to re-correlate the data accordingly to satisfy the assumptions necessary for the fitting. Let Σ be the (empirical) covariance matrix of the data, and let us Cholesky-decompose it as $\Sigma = \boldsymbol{U}^\top \boldsymbol{U}$. Then, choose any matrix A that is invertible and has all positive entries that shall be the "new" correlations, and define the transformed data matrix as

$$\boldsymbol{D}' = \boldsymbol{D} \cdot \underbrace{\boldsymbol{U}^{-1} \cdot \boldsymbol{A}}_{=:\boldsymbol{M}} \tag{12.6}$$

The matrix $\boldsymbol{A}$ is free to choose to improve the goodness of fit, and at the same time, the numeric stability of the linear transformation $\boldsymbol{M}$ and its inverse by looking for a good condition number $\|\boldsymbol{M}^{-1}\|_2 \cdot \|\boldsymbol{M}\|_2$. In [29], the choice of $\boldsymbol{A}$ was made with Gamma-distributed values (to assure non-negativity), taking a total of 200 trials to pick the result whose goodness of fit was best, based on the p-value.

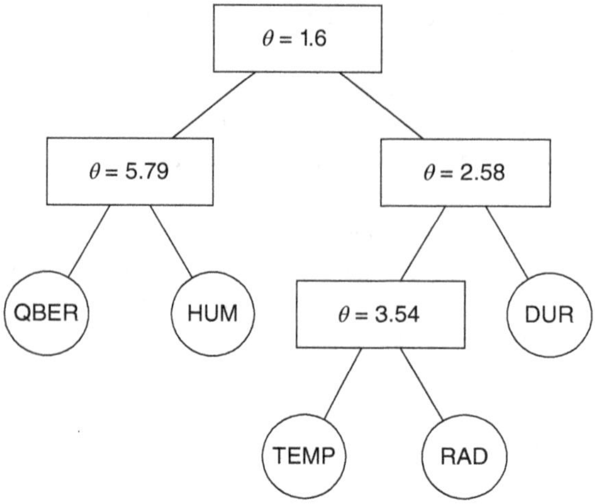

Figure 12.2 Example of hierarchical Archimedean copula fit (from [29]). The diagram shows how the different variables are combined best in the copula to explain the data. Nodes that appear together (in groups) hereby thus have a "joint" impact on the final variable, thus providing a qualitative indication of how sensitive a system would respond to changes in some or more parameters.

The final result obtained for the data as given with a bootstrap fit of the nested copula (using the HAC package) was $p \approx 0.613$, with the matrix $\boldsymbol{A}$ given as

$$\boldsymbol{A} = \begin{pmatrix} 0.122 & 4.444 & 0.378 & 1.634 & 4.384 \\ 0.650 & 0.870 & 1.321 & 0.941 & 2.293 \\ 0.606 & 3.326 & 0.763 & 2.172 & 2.102 \\ 2.534 & 0.415 & 2.055 & 1.969 & 1.659 \\ 2.668 & 2.031 & 3.590 & 2.241 & 1.015 \end{pmatrix}$$

and the condition number of $\boldsymbol{M}$ being ≈ 24.4945, which indicates that we can transform and back-transform the data without much risk of numerical inaccuracies. We stress that the matrix $\boldsymbol{A}$ given above was specifically obtained for the data at hand and essentially comes out of a random number generator. Thus, the practical way of finding $\boldsymbol{A}$ is repeating this trial and error method, looking for a good fit and good condition number. The data transformation is to be applied before fitting the copula, so that we actually fit the copula to the random variable $\boldsymbol{Y} := \boldsymbol{M} \cdot \boldsymbol{X}$, with $\boldsymbol{X} = (\text{QBER, TEMP, HUM, DUR, RAD})^{\top}$. With the copula model fitted as f_Y, and subsequently verified to be a good fit (based on the p-value of a statistical test), the density for the original data is recovered as

$$f(\boldsymbol{x}) = f_Y(\boldsymbol{M} \cdot \boldsymbol{x}) \cdot |\det \boldsymbol{M}| . \tag{12.7}$$

Ultimately, we are interested in the predictive density, which is obtained as the conditional

$$f(x_1|x_2, \dots, x_{n-1}) = \frac{f_X(x_1, \dots, x_n)}{\int_{\mathbb{R}} f_X(x_1, \dots, x_n)\, dx_1},$$

in which $x_1 = \text{QBER}$ and $(x_2, \dots, x_n) = (x_2, \dots, x_5) = (\text{HUM, TEMP, DUR, RAD})$. In this context, the (general) structure of the copula comes is again convenient, as for the case of an Archimedean copula, we can rewrite the predictive density as

$$f(x_1|x_2, \dots, x_n) = f_1(x_1) \cdot \frac{c_n(u_1, \dots, u_n)}{c_{n-1}(u_2, \dots, u_n)}$$

for $u_i = F_i(x_i)$ for all variables i of interest (five in our example case). In simple, non-nested models, the copula density c_n is directly obtainable from the generator function as $c_n(u_1, \dots, u_n) = (\phi^{-1})^{(n)}(\phi(u_1) + \dots + \phi(u_n)) \cdot \prod_{i=1}^{n} \phi'(u_i)$, which can be worked out even analytically for a large class of functions. For the general nested case, we no longer have analytical expressions in general, but can give the following formula that can be evaluated numerically: let the i-th variable x_i (e.g., HUM, TEMP, DUR, and RAD in our example) range in the interval $\left[\underline{x}_i, \bar{x}_i\right]$, and define

$$\Delta(x) := \frac{\partial^{n-1}}{\partial x_1 \cdots \partial x_{n-1}} C_n(F_1(x_1), \dots, F_{n-1}(x_{n-1}), F_n(x)),$$

where the inner distributions $F_1, \dots, F_n$ and the function C_n are directly obtained from fitting a nested copula to the data. Knowing the algebraic form of each of them (as we prespecified them for the fit), one can use computer algebra systems to work out the derivatives or otherwise, numerically approximate them.

Then the predictive density is computable as

$$f(x_1|x_2, \dots, x_n) = f_1(x_1) \cdot \frac{c_n(F_1(x_1), \dots, F_n(x_n))}{\Delta(\bar{x}_i) - \Delta\left(\underline{x}_i\right)} \tag{12.8}$$

and can, for example, look like shown in Figure 12.3.

The overall process for feedback-based calibration of a QKD device is illustrated by the workflow in Figure 12.4.

We refer to [29] for a fully worked example and instead discuss a few possible applications, since the method in general is not restricted to predicting the QBER only, but also possible during the key reconciliation phase [30], privacy amplification [31], or error correction [32], where different and extended methods have

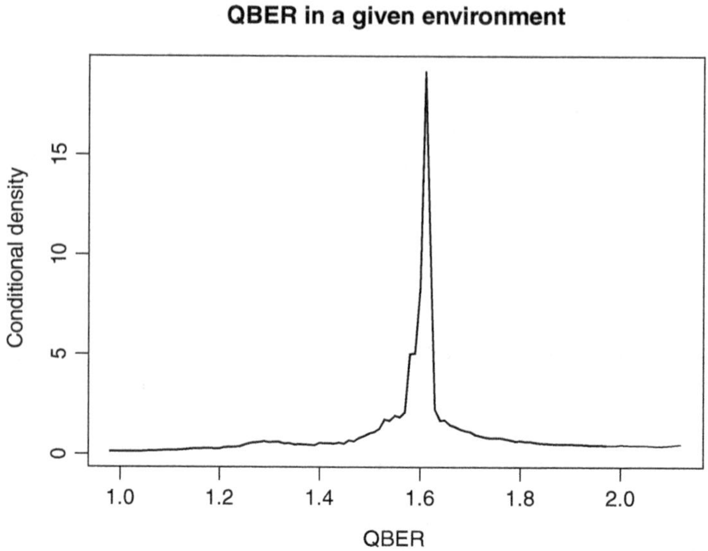

Figure 12.3 Probability density of QBER in a known environment (example plot of hierarchical copula density), from which the expected QBER is computable under the current environmental conditions. The variance of the distribution is an auxiliary indicator of how "accurate" the QBER estimate is (showing only small likely fluctuation around the mean).

been proposed. To illustrate the added value of self-adaptation during the error correction, let us briefly recall how this process works:

Alice and Bob start with their raw keys k_A and k_B distilled from the QKD protocol. These are strings that widely, but not entirely, match, so that Alice and Bob need to delete or correct the mismatching positions in their bitstrings k_A, k_B to equalize the two. Doing so without leaking information to the adversary makes the corrected key usable as a secret for later communication.

To this end, Alice and Bob both partition their keys into blocks $k_{A,1}, \dots, k_{A,m}$ and $k_{B,1}, \dots, k_{B,m}$ of substrings, such that the blocks are of the same length and contain not too many errors. Then, they start to publicly exchange parities of each sub-block, with a parity mismatch pointing to an error in the block and a parity match supporting the hypothesis that there was no error in the block. For blocks that apparently contain errors, they bisectively search for the error until it is located and the bit can be deleted from the raw key; see Figure 12.5 for an illustration. This process leaks out a logarithmic number of bits depending on the size of the blocks.

Since there is still the possibility of an even number of bit errors that a parity check would miss, Alice and Bob repeat the process after shuffling their strings to scatter the errors accordingly. Equipped with a predictive model of how many

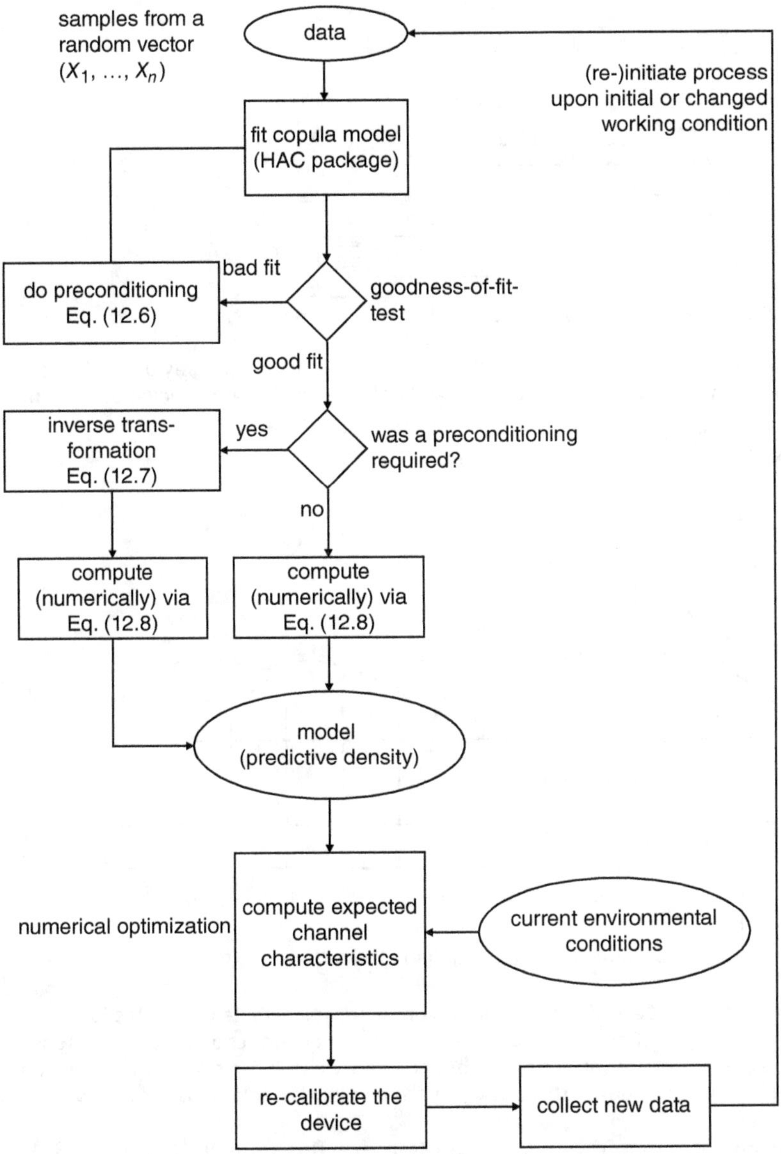

Figure 12.4 Workflow to automatically calibrate devices using predictive distributions, according to [29]. The input to the workflow is the current environmental working conditions of the device (temperature, humidity, etc.), which can then self-adapt (last step) to retain the optimal working point.

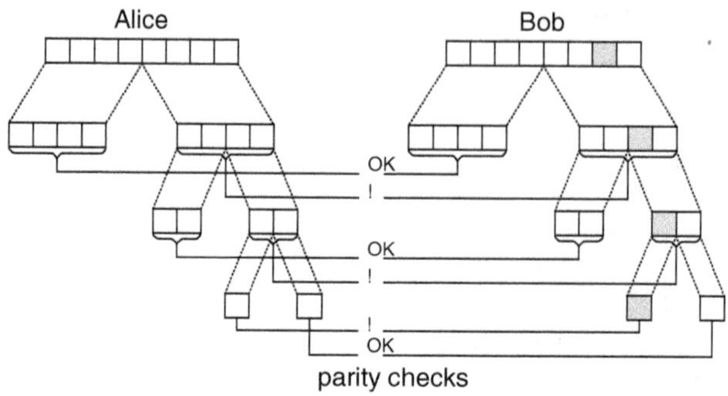

Figure 12.5 Illustration of bisective error correction in Cascade (the gray box indicates the location of the unknown error that Alice and Bob iteratively narrow down using parity checks).

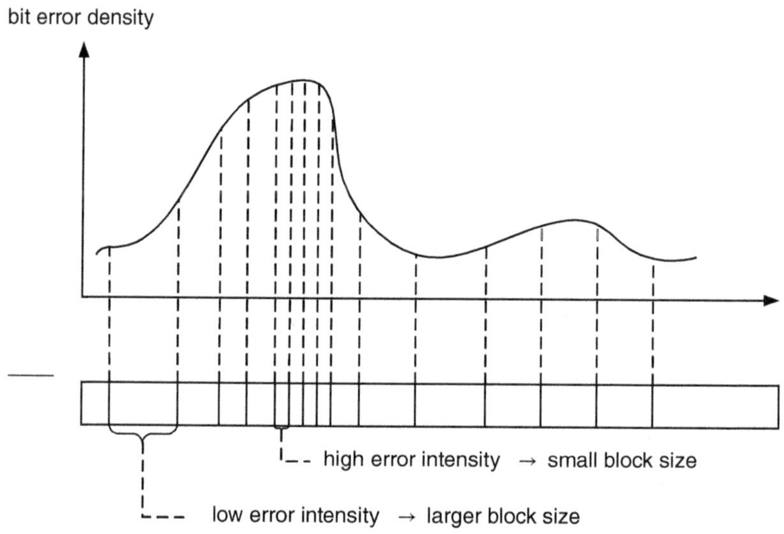

Figure 12.6 Adapting Cascade's block size on predicted expectable error rates [33]. During temporal peaks of errors, the block size for the error correction may be shortened to retain the average of 1 error per block so that a parity check can discover it (correctly). When the error rate goes down, the block size can be likewise enlarged.

errors to expect in the raw key, Alice and Bob can, theoretically, bring down the whole process to a single run of the bisective search: there is no conceptual need to have an equi-partitioning of the raw key, and protocols were proposed to adaptively change the block size to expect no more than a single bit error per block. Predictive distributions can help determine how many errors to expect over a given number of bits, and from this, adapt the block size accordingly and adaptively for efficiency. Figure 12.6 shows the concept, proposed first in [32].

It comes natural to think about improving the prediction by more powerful AI models to predict time series; however, we need to bear in mind that the prediction system may itself become subject to manipulation and attacks. Hence, the design of AI models needs to be robust against an attacker injecting errors in patterns crafted with methods from adversarial AI (see Part 2 of the book). Statistical methods like the above make attacks more difficult and the prediction at the same time explainable; combining such statistical models with the approximative power of deep networks is an interesting further route to explore.

12.5 Adapting the Level of Service to Traffic Changes

Typical QKD networks run their protocols endlessly to regenerate key material for potential demand, but DoS by eavesdropping will make the protocols stop, and the peers will then live off their previously stored key resources. Sooner or later, depending on the traffic, the key stores may run dry, and again, we can extend the communication games for the goal of an optimal randomization, coming as an equilibrium, to randomly switch between perfect confidentiality (using QKD) and computational confidentiality (to save resources) [34–36].

If the key buffers refill at rate λ (see [37]) and key is consumed at a different rate μ, a standard application of queuing theory shows that the key buffer will handle the traffic properly if $\mu < \lambda$. The key generation and consumption rates are standardized parameters (see [38]), and thus available over the API of the QKD device itself. In case of a temporary unusually high key consumption, e.g., due to an attack, the device may fix a threshold upon which it switches from a one-time pad encryption to a classical symmetric encryption to avoid further consumption of key material and keep the link running on standard symmetric encryption using a fixed-size key (note that, as of the time of writing this text, symmetric encryption is even resilient against quantum computing attacks if the key size is sufficient to escape brute-force attacks by Grover's algorithm to search the key space. Other attacks exploiting a quantum advantage and tailored to the structure of symmetric primitives have not been found so far).

The device may thus strategically choose to switch between AES and OTP encryption. Letting the "OTP transmission mode" utilize single-path transmission with trusted relay, or multipath transmission without trusted relay, we may abstractly describe this configuration as the transmission protocol Π_1, whose probability of a correct delivery is, by an analysis like sketched in Section 12.3 quantified by a transmission game with equilibrium value v_1 that assures Pr (confidential delivery of the message m via the protocol Π_1) $\geq v_1$. Similarly, we may abstractly consider another protocol Π_2 that, for example, utilizes symmetric encryption with a fixed key size. As for the (perhaps multipath, OTP-based) encryption, let us assign a quality of security value v_2 with a likewise semantic, i.e., Pr (confidential delivery of the message m via the protocol Π_2) $\geq v_2$. Depending on how "confident" we are in the confidentiality of Π_2, we may assign some value $v_2 > 0$, or, assuming a computationally unlimited adversary, set $v_2 = 0$ to express either that Π_2 provides no particular protection by itself (i.e., the message is just sent unencrypted), or the adversary is so powerful that it would certainly break the encryption that Π_2 uses.

For example, we could use

- Π_1: OTP-based transmission under trusted relay or over multiple paths.
- Π_2: AES-based encryption using a fixed (reserved) portion of key in the QKD device buffer.

Why would we even need to choose between the two? The reason is to be adaptive to the current conditions, for example, if the adversary causes key buffers to empty faster than they refill, thus rendering OTP-based transmission impossible over a longer run.

With the two protocols, we can set up another transmission game that lets Alice randomly, and in a way to be optimized, choose between Π_{OTP} and Π_2, to send her message. Using secret sharing again, but now in a sequential manner, she starts by expanding her message $m = s_1 \oplus s_2 \oplus \cdots \oplus s_n$ such that m is (information-theoretically) irrecoverable for an eavesdropper even with unbounded computational capabilities, unless all shares $s_1, \ldots, s_n$ are known. The $\oplus$ operation is herein the bitwise XOR. Now, she (sequentially) transmits $s_1, \ldots, s_n$ to Bob, each share being delivered either with the protocol Π_1 or with the protocol Π_2, in case of a temporary bottleneck of key material, an otherwise broken link, etc. To quantify the overall security of the protocol, we can conduct a similar analysis as in Section 12.3, making use of the following result (adapted from [39] and proven in [40]):

Lemma: Let Alice transmit a sequence of messages $m_1, \ldots, m_n$ using a fixed protocol Π with random coin flips and define the indicator variable $L_i := 1$ if and only if Π fails to deliver m_i in confidentiality to Bob (i.e., Eve has gained knowledge about the plaintext M_i). Let v be such that $\Pr(L_i = 1) \leq v$, for example, from a game-theoretic analysis as in Section 12.3. Then,

$$\Pr\left(\min_{i=1,\ldots,n} L_i \geq v + \varepsilon\right) \leq \exp\left(-\frac{n \cdot \varepsilon^2}{2}\right) \tag{12.9}$$

We remark that this result does not assume stochastic independence of the messages. Its proof is essentially an application of Hoeffding's inequality, but in a generalized version that allows for some dependence among the L_i (given by [41]). The analysis of the security when we randomly switch between protocols is a simple application of the lemma to the case of transmitting a sequence of shares sequentially over the channel, and by virtue of (12.9) upper bounding the chances for Eve to catch all the necessary shares (since in that, and only in that, case, we have $\min L_i = 1$).

So, letting Alice send her shares $s_1, \dots, s_n$ sequentially at random, switching between the perfectly secure Π_{OTP} and the (possibly insecure) Π_2, where she chooses Π_{OTP} with probability $0 < p \leq 1$ and Π_2 with probability $1 - p$. The overall probability for the attacker to catch a share in plain is thus $0 \leq q = p \cdot \Pr(\Pi_1 \text{ fails}) + (1-p) \cdot \Pr(\Pi_2 \text{ fails}) < 1$, if $\Pr(\Pi_1 \text{ fails}) < 1$. Note that even the OTP-based protocol Π_1 is herein assumed to possibly fail, either if the attacker can breach the trusted relay, or if the threshold assumption underlying the adversary structure was invalid (i.e., the attacker managed to conquer more nodes than assumed).

The combination of secret sharing for a sequential transmission, together with (12.9) implies that Alice's chances of losing a message to Eve are bounded by $2^{-O(n)} \to 0$ as n grows, where the constant in the big-O is determined by $\varepsilon = 1 - \upsilon_1$. Now, she can use this to adapt to the current conditions easily: suppose that the key buffer status is such that the bandwidth for OTP transmission is cut down to allow only a (small) fraction of at most p_0 percent of the traffic to use OTP, while the remaining traffic needs to use conventional encryption. Then, since the OTP protocol Π_1, under the trust assumptions encoded in the adversary structure $\mathcal{A}dv$, has a chance of $\geq \upsilon$ to deliver the message confidentially, Alice can compute the value $\varepsilon_0 = 1 - p_0 \cdot (1 - \upsilon) + (1 - p_0)$ under the worst-case assumption that the alternative AES encryption is not trusted to be broken (otherwise, we would have the second term be $(1 - p_0) \cdot (1 - \upsilon_2)$ for υ_2 as the chances for AES to withstand the attacker). Given this ε_0 and choosing an acceptably small chance $\delta > 0$ to still lose her content to the eavesdropper, she can compute the number of necessary shares as $n > \varepsilon^{-2} \cdot 2 \cdot \log \delta$. This number makes (5) = $\Pr(\text{Eve gets all shares}) \leq \delta$ (in a slight abuse of notation), provided that Alice first splits her message into a total of $n - 1$ random values $s_1, \dots, s_{n-1}$, and a final value $s_n = m \oplus s_1 \oplus \dots \oplus s_{n-1}$.

This self-adaptation to keeping up an arbitrary level of secrecy against possibly disrupted channels or emptying key buffers is bought at a high price, since the overall traffic load over the network scales by the same factor of n. So, the practical choice will here be on the utilization of alternative routes, i.e., to employ quality-of-service aware routing, which determines routes based on the current link characteristics by virtue of adapted "shortest path" algorithms or others [37].

12.6 Adapting the Network Topology

When a network is composed as a join of multiple heterogeneous vendors, each of which runs its infrastructure but not letting a centralized instance take control over the entire routing layer, a core question is how to unify different networks while retaining security, or how to assure one's own level of service in regards of security for others (customers, other networks, etc.).

Let us look at how to design a network to let messages bypass possibly vulnerable nodes that we cannot physically secure for any reason, but we can also try to set up the original network for heterogeneity so as to reduce the attack surface and hence make the elements of $\mathcal{A}dv$ smaller in size. Such a reduction would be possible by letting devices run on different operating systems so as to make it harder to conquer several nodes or apply strong physical and logical access protection to devices, to effectively remove a node from the list of possible eavesdropping spots for the attacker. Candidates for such strong protection would be "bottleneck nodes" in the graph, i.e., nodes that several paths between Alice and Bob traverse. Figure 12.7 shows such a graph, in which the "inner" node 3 is a choke point and hence the best spot for the attacker to target. In a game theoretic analysis, if 3 is part of the adversary structure and hence its action set, attacking node 3 would be found as an optimal attack strategy, leaving zero chance for Alice to route her message privately toward Bob. In pure graph-theoretic terms, the network would be 1-vertex connected, since taking out node 3 would decompose the graph into two non-connected components.

"Taking out" node 3, however, may also mean to secure it physically against Eve's interceptions, so that all traffic running over node 3 is secure by trusted relay, and attacks can only happen at other locations. Such information can, for example,

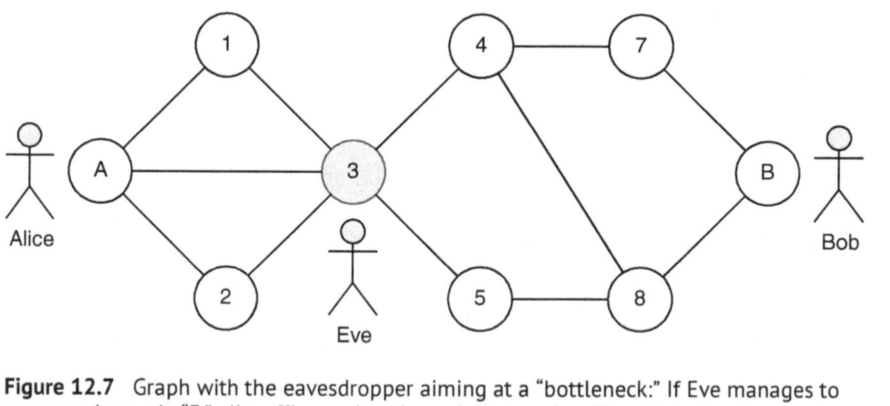

Figure 12.7 Graph with the eavesdropper aiming at a "bottleneck:" If Eve manages to compromise node "3," all traffic passing through that node will get into her hands, thus breaking end-to-end confidentiality of the system.

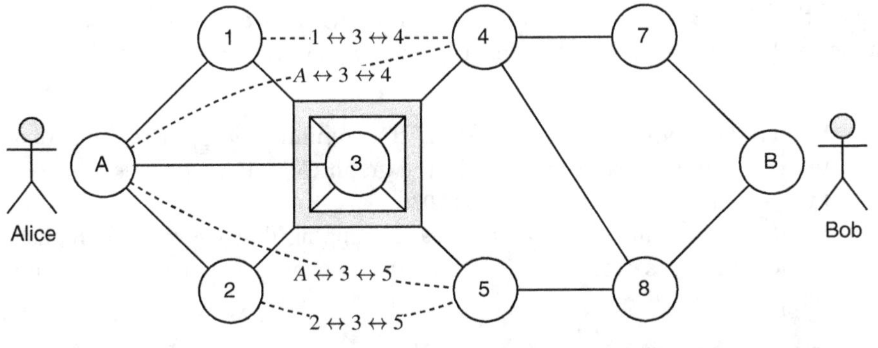

Figure 12.8 Graph with now "protected" bottleneck node and hence "increased" connectivity. Here, the previously "weak" (or compromised) node "3" has been cleaned from eavesdroppers (e.g., malware) and hardened to avoid future compromise along the same (or other known) attack vectors. Conditional on this assumption, node "3" can be taken out from the network model and replaced by "virtual" links between the neighbors of node "3." This is nothing else than a (strongly justified) "trusted relay" assumption imposed on node "3."

be obtained by strategically placed honeypots (Chapter 7), or suspected based on reports of new vulnerabilities that have been discovered. Formally, we would here delete "attack node 3" from the adversary's strategy set, and the transmission game as of Section 12.2 changes accordingly. In terms of vertex connectivity, we may even think of "virtual" connections between all of 3's neighbors, which increases the vertex connectivity of this example graph from one to 2, enabling multi-path transmission with perfect secrecy against any adversary that can conquer no more than 1 node (during a full transmission). Figure 12.8 shows the accordingly modified graph.

Generalizing this idea, we have the following result on the connection of two networks, both of which are k-vertex connected: let $G_1 = (V_1, E_1), G_2 = (V_2, E_2)$ be two graphs that are k-vertex connected. Choose k distinct nodes $u_1, \dots, u_k \in V_1$ and $v_1, \dots, v_k \in V_2$. Then the graph $G = (V_1 \cup V_2, E_1 \cup E_2 \cup \{(u_i, v_i) : i = 1, \dots, k\})$ is again k-vertex connected. This fact (see [40] for a proof) allows to build a network for multipath transmission from respectively smaller networks that are themselves suitable for multipath transmission.

This concept allows a "bottom-up" design of large networks. The respective "top-down" design would start from a given network with insufficient vertex connectivity and ask for an optimal extension in one of two flavors: let a graph $G = (V, E)$ be given, and let there be possible new edges to be chosen from E'

(such that $E' \cap E = \emptyset$), all of which have a known cost $c(e)$ for $e \in E'$. Then, a network design problem for security can be formulated as two different optimizations:

- What is the "optimal" selection $E'' \subseteq E'$ that minimizes $\sum_{e \in E''} c(e)$, such that the probability of eavesdropping in the graph $G' = (V, E \cup E'')$ is no more than a fixed (acceptable) chance $\upsilon > 0$?
- What is the minimal chance υ of eavesdropping that we can accomplish by adding edges from $E'' \subseteq E'$ such that we obey a fixed budget limit $\sum_{e \in E''} c(e) \leq L$?

Both problems have been studied in [42], where υ was quantified in terms of transmission games for information theoretic security, as laid out in Section 12.3. Unfortunately, by a reduction to the bi-connectivity augmentation problem (see [43]), the two problems could both be shown to be computationally equivalent but intractable in the sense that even an approximate solution would imply $P = NP$. This nonetheless also implies a positive conclusion, since either:

- $P = NP$, in which case we are capable of efficiently building quantum networks by augmenting existing fiber-optic infrastructures toward being admissible for perfectly secure multipath transmission,
- Or $P \neq NP$, in which case existing cryptographic systems built on NP-hard problems such as McEliece encryption will continue to provide a sufficient secrecy level.

Irrespectively of how P-vs-NP may eventually be settled, the "bottom-up" method of network design remains available, and the analysis in [42] only established worst-case intractability, still allowing for efficient constructions "from scratch" [44].

A noteworthy middle ground is a "partial mitigation" of the winning strategy, if one is found for the attacker. For example, let us return to the game matrix from before, and let us assume that the adversary exhibited some unexpected behavior that turned out as a winning strategy, and hence as a matrix of all 0s for the game with Alice:

	$C = \{2\}$	$C = \{3\}$	$C = \{4\}$	**New/unexpected strategy**
$\pi_1 = A \to 3 \to 6 \to B$	1	0	1	0
$\pi_2 = A \to 4 \to 5 \to B$	1	1	0	0
$\pi_3 = A \to 1 \to 2 \to B$	0	1	1	0

The fourth column in this matrix strategically dominates all others, since the attacker's sure best move is to use the "unexpected" strategy to win regardless of how Alice transmits her message. An equilibrium analysis would give Alice an expectation of $v = 0$ to deliver her message in privacy, meaning that zero messages go uncaught by Eve on average. However, it turns out that Alice can restore security by hardening only one of her strategies against Eve's new attack. Suppose that she manages to "win" in any of the three strategies, but not necessarily in the other two; for example, let Alice succeed in defeating the "new attack" only in case of transmitting over π_1, but still fail in the other two cases:

	$C = \{2\}$	$C = \{3\}$	$C = \{4\}$	**New/unexpected strategy**
$\pi_1 = A \to 3 \to 6 \to B$	1	0	1	0
$\pi_2 = A \to 4 \to 5 \to B$	1	1	0	1
$\pi_3 = A \to 1 \to 2 \to B$	0	1	1	0

The attack in the fourth column has thus been "partially mitigated," so the new attack was not thwarted in all cases, and neither is strategy π_2 now a winning case for Alice (it would still be defeated if the adversary conquers node 4), but the chances for Alice to get her message secretly to Bob have gone up to $v = 1/2$ again. And from there, using the same methods as in Section 12.5 Alice can again bring down the eavesdropping chances exponentially fast toward any acceptably small threshold.

This observation allows for more cost-aware risk mitigations, since the advent of new attacks that possibly defeat all existing security precautions does not necessarily require an equally powerful countermeasure. It is actually sufficient to turn the new strategy into no longer being a winning strategy in the sense that it must not strategically dominate all other strategies (see [39] for the formal statement and proof). Practically, one can thus simply "try" which scenarios in the above matrix could be changed such that the game gives Alice a value $v > 0$, which is a matter of analyzing the game under different hypothetical scenarios of hardening, identifying the easiest option, and practically applying additional security to accomplish the change in the game matrix as desired.

A randomized transmission offers the advantage of needing to be hardened only in one or a few cases, so that the overall saddle point success rate of the transmission game becomes positive. At this point, cryptographic techniques such as secret sharing, together with general results as (12.9), can restore security up to any desired level, at the cost of increased traffic load (this is the price we have to pay).

12.7 Conclusions, Outlook, and QKD in Today's Networks

QKD has been practically implemented to work with IPSec, the internet key exchange (IKE), and point-to-point (PPP) protocols [45–48]. Further implementations in multi-protocol label switching (MPLS) and overlay networks have also been reported [49]. The main advantage gained from the integration of QKD in contemporary protocols is the degree to which it lets key management be automated, or alternatively said, how much it reduces matters of certificate management by administrative parties. While QKD does not ultimately resolve the key generation issue since it does require a small amount of pre-shared secrets for authentication purposes, the key management itself is, compared to public-key infrastructures, more transparent and less dependent on the user's capabilities. Since quantum keys are generally a scarce resource, significant efforts to integrate QKD in the key management and network control layers have been made, partially integrating self-adaptive mechanisms in quality-of-service-aware routing schemes, for example [50]. Most notable for practical matters before rolling out a QKD network in practice is the possibility to simulate the network first, to support later design decisions. The work of [51] provides such an integration for the network simulator NS-3. Self-adaptation mechanisms in the sense as explained above have, however, not yet seen wide adoption in practice. Indeed, the routing itself can be its own attack vector: in a network graph, imagine the attacker having identified some node x that it may be able to conquer, but Alice's routing will not frequently use this node. However, if the attacker can manipulate the QoS parameters for a set of links such that a QoS-aware routing layer is forced to redirect traffic over node x under the attacker's control, then all security guarantees of trusted relay or randomized routing (using game theory) can become void. Somewhat ironically, this manipulation is even possible by exploiting the eavesdropping detection mechanism itself, since a QKD link may "shut down for security reasons," if the QBER exceeds a threshold due to the adversary's presence. In that case, the attack would not be for eavesdropping, but rather for traffic redirection. This possibility has first been described theoretically in [52], and has been simulated in [37], finding the possibility confirmed under QoS aware routing strategies. This generally indicates that self-adaptiveness can itself be turned against the network. Standard means of network intrusion detection systems (IDS) and intrusion prevention systems (IPS) are thus equally (if not more) important in QKD networks than elsewhere.

The level of secrecy provided by the technology, compared to the efforts for integrating a QKD key exchange in real-life networks, call for a careful cost-benefit balance consideration. However, having QKD available in a network, even if it is only on some links, allows for QoS-aware routing to make preferred use of these strong links, and the protocol switching methods from Section 12.4 are indeed directly applicable to make use of (expensive) QKD and (cheap) classical transmissions in an optimized balance.

The remaining issue to keep in mind about QKD, regardless of whether one adopts trusted relay or multipath transmission, is ethics: a perfectly secure transmission is generally to be considered with care in cases of law enforcement. While conventional encryption is under intensive discussions about legal regulations to apply on the key management, to perhaps "open" encrypted content upon court orders or similar, QKD networks are again special due to their natural support of such demands. Trusted relay naturally means that all traffic is readable in plain inside a node, and multipath transmission extends this merely to the need of sniffing on more than one node. Regulating such access on legal grounds is in fact even simpler for QKD networks than it is for transmissions using conventional encryption, since the QKD key management layer is part of the network. Self-adapting to not only technical, but perhaps also ethical needs is thus its own dimension of complexity and, to the best of our knowledge, under-investigated area of research.

References

1 S. Wiesner. Conjugate Coding, *SIGACT News*, Bd. 15, Nr. 1, S. 78–88, 1983.

2 C. Bennett and G. Brassard. Public key distribution and coin tossing. *gehalten auf der IEEE International Conference on Computers, Systems, and Signal Processing*, S. 175–179, 1984.

3 A. Ekert, Quantum cryptography based on bell's theorem. *Physical Review Letters*, 67(6): 661–663, 1991.

4 H.-J. Briegel, W. Dür, J. I. Cirac, and P. Zoller, Quantum repeaters for communication, *ArXivquant-Ph9803056*, März 1998, Zugegriffen: 17. Oktober 2019. [Online]. Verfügbar unter: http://arxiv.org/abs/quant-ph/9803056

5 Z.-D. Li, R. Zhang, X. F. Yin, L. Z. Liu, Y. Hu, Y. Q. Fang, Y. Y. Fei, X. Jiang, J. Zhang, J. Li, and N. L. Liu. Experimental quantum repeater without quantum memory. *Nature Photonics*, 13(9): 644–648, 2019. https://doi.org/10.1038/s41566-019-0468-5.

6 Z.-S. Yuan, Y.-A. Chen, B. Zhao, S. Chen, J. Schmiedmayer, and J.-W. Pan. Experimental demonstration of a BDCZ quantum repeater node. *Nature*, 454(7208): 1098–1101, 2008. https://doi.org/10.1038/nature07241.

7 P. W. Shor and J. Preskill. Simple proof of security of the BB84 quantum key distribution protocol. *Physical Review Letters*, 85: 441–444, 2000.

8 A. Acin, N. Brunner, N. Gisin, S. Massar, S. Pironio, and V. Scarani. Device-independent security of quantum cryptography against collective attacks. *Physical Review Letters*, 98(23): 230501, 2007. https://doi.org/10.1103/PhysRevLett.98.230501.

9 X.-L. Hu, Y. Cao, Z.-W. Yu, and X.-B. Wang. Measurement-device-independent quantum key distribution over asymmetric channel and unstable channel. *Scientific Reports*. 8(1): 17634, 2018. https://doi.org/10.1038/s41598-018-35507-z.

10 Y. Liu, T. Y. Chen, L. J. Wang, H. Liang, G. L. Shentu, J. Wang, K. Cui, H. L. Yin, N. L. Liu, L. Li, and X. Ma. Experimental measurement-device-independent quantum key distribution. *Physical Review Letters*, 111(13): 130502, 2013.

11 L. Zhou, Y.-B. Sheng, and G.-L. Long. Device-independent quantum secure direct communication against collective attacks. *Science Bulletin*, 65(1): 12–20, 2020. https://doi.org/10.1016/j.scib.2019.10.025.

12 S. Sajeed, A. Huang, S. Sun, F. Xu, V. Makarov, and M. Curty. Insecurity of detector-device-independent quantum key distribution. *Physical Review Letters*, 117(25): 250505, 2016. https://doi.org/10.1103/PhysRevLett.117.250505.

13 M. Fitzi, M. K. Franklin, J. Garay, and S. H. Vardhan. Towards optimal and efficient perfectly secure message transmission. In *TCC 2007: Theory of Cryptography*, 2007, Bd. 4392, pp. 311–322. [Online].

14 Y. Desmedt, S. Erotokritou, and R. Safavi-Naini. Simple and communication complexity efficient almost secure and perfectly secure message transmission schemes. *gehalten auf der Proceedings of the Third international conference on Cryptology in Africa*, 2010, pp. 166–183. https://doi.org/10.1007/978-3-642-12678-9_11.

15 Y. Wang and Y. Desmedt. Perfectly secure message transmission revisited. *IEEE Transactions on Information Theory*, 54(6): 2582–2595, 2008.

16 S. K. Leung-Yan-Cheong and M. Hellman. The gaussian wire-tap channel. *IEEE Transactions on Information Theory*, 24(4): 451–456, 1978.

17 M. Bellare, S. Tessaro, and A. Vardy. Semantic security for the wiretap channel. In *Advances in Cryptology – CRYPTO 2012*. Berlin, Heidelberg, 2012, pp. 294–311. https://doi.org/10.1007/978-3-642-32009-5_18.

18 R. Teixeira, K. Marzullo, S. Savage, and G. M. Voelker. Characterizing and measuring path diversity of internet topologies. In *Proceedings of the 2003 ACM SIGMETRICS International Conference on Measurement and Modeling of Computer Systems*. New York, NY, USA, 2003, pp. 304–305. https://doi.org/10.1145/781027.781069.

19 B. Augustin, T. Friedman, and R. Teixeira. Measuring multipath routing in the internet. *IEEE/ACM Transactions on Networking*, 19(3): 830–840, 2011. https://doi.org/10.1109/TNET.2010.2096232.

20 R. J. McElice and D. V. Sarwate. On sharing secrets and reed-solomon codes. *Communications of the ACM*, 24(9): 583–584, 1981.

21 M. V. N. Ashwin Kumar, P. R. Goundan, K. Srinathan, and C. Pandu Rangan. On perfectly secure communication over arbitrary networks. In *gehalten auf der PODC '02: Proceedings of the Twenty-first Annual Symposium on Principles of Distributed Computing*, pp. 193–202, 2002. https://doi.org/10.1145/571825.571858.

22 R. D. McKelvey, A. M. McLennan, and T. L. Turocy. *Gambit: software tools for game theory, Version 16.0.1*. 2016. [Online]. Verfügbar unter: http://www.gambit-project.org.

23 K. Lessiak, C. Kollmitzer, S. Schauer, J. Pilz, and S. Rass. Statistical analysis of QKD networks in real-life environments. In *Proceedings of the Third International Conference on Quantum, Nano and Micro Technologies*, pp. 109–114. 2009. https://doi.org/10.1109/ICQNM.2009.30.

24 S. König and S. Rass. Self-adaption of quantum key distribution devices to changing working conditions. In *Proceedings of the International Conference on Quanum-, Nano- and Microtechnology (ICQNM)*, 2014.

25 M. Peev, C. Pacher, R. Alléaume, C. Barreiro, J. Bouda, W. Boxleitner, T. Debuisschert, E. Diamanti, M. Dianati, J. F. Dynes, and S. Fasel. The SECOQC quantum key distribution network in Vienna. *New Journal of Physics*, 11(7): 075001, 2009. https://doi.org/10.1088/1367-2630/11/7/075001.

26 P. Embrechts, F. Lindskog, and A. McNeil. Modelling dependence with copulas and applications to risk management. *Handbook of Heavy Tailed Distributions in Finance*, 8(1): 329–384, 2003.

27 R Core Team. *R: A Language and Environment for Statistical Computing*. Vienna, Austria: R Foundation for Statistical Computing, 2018. [Online]. Verfügbar unter: https://www.R-project.org/.

28 O. Okhrin and A. Ristig. Estimation, simulation and visualization of hierarchical archimedean copulae (HAC). *Journal of Statistical Software*, 2014.

29 S. König and S. Rass. Stochastic models for quantum device configuration and self-adaptation. *International Journal on Advances in Systems and Measurements*, 8(1): 124–134, 2015.

30 D. Elkouss, J. Martinez-Mateo, and V. Martin. Analysis of a rate-adaptive reconciliation protocol and the effect of leakage on the secret key rate. *Physical Review A*, 87(4): 042334, 2013. https://doi.org/10.1103/PhysRevA.87.042334.

31 S.-S. Yang, Z.-L. Bai, X.-Y. Wang, and Y.-M. Li. FPGA-based implementation of size-adaptive privacy amplification in quantum key distribution. *IEEE Photonics Journal*, 9(6): 1–8, 2017. https://doi.org/10.1109/JPHOT.2017.2761807.

32 S. Rass and C. Kollmitzer. Adaptive cascade. In *Applied Quantum Cryptography*. Springer, 2010, pp. 49–69.

33 M. Mehic, S. Rass, P. Fazio, and M. Voznak. *Quantum Key Distribution Networks: A Quality of Service Perspective*. Cham: Springer International Publishing, 2022. https://doi.org/10.1007/978-3-031-06608-5.

34 P. Schartner and S. Rass. Quantum key distribution and Denial-of-Service: Using strengthened classical cryptography as a fallback option. In *Computer Symposium (ICS), 2010 International*, 2010, pp. 131–136.

35 I. Devetak and P. Shor. The capacity of a quantum channel for simultaneous transmission of classical and quantum information. *Communications in Mathematical Physics*, 256(2): 287–303, 2005.

36 S. König and S. Rass. On the transmission capacity of quantum networks. *International Journal of Advanced Computer Science and Applications*, 2(2): 9–16, 2011.

37 M. Mehic, S. Rass, E. Dervisevic, and M. Voznak. Tackling denial of service attacks in software-defined quantum key distribution networks. *IEEE Access*, 10: 110512–110520, 2022. https://doi.org/10.1109/ACCESS.2022.3214511.

38 European Telecommunications Standards Institute, Quantum Key Distribution (QKD); Control Interface for Software Defined Networks. Standard ETSI GS QKD 015, V2.1.1 (2022-04), 2022. [Online]. Verfügbar unter: https://www.etsi.org/deliver/etsi_gs/QKD/001_099/015/02.01.01_60/gs_QKD015v020101p.pdf.

39 S. Rass and P. Schartner. Information-leakage in hybrid randomized protocols. In *Proceedings of the International Conference on Security and Cryptography (SECRYPT)*, 2011, pp. 134–143.

40 S. Rass. *On information-theoretic security: contemporary problems and solutions*. Klagenfurt University, Institute of Applied Informatics, 2009. Zugegriffen: 1. Januar 2009. [Online]. Verfügbar unter: \documents\dissertation\diss_DRUCKVERSION.pdf.

41 W. D. Smith. *Tail bound for sums of bounded random variables*, 2005. [Online]. Verfügbar unter: https://rangevoting.org/WarrenSmithPages/homepage/works.html.

42 S. Rass. Complexity of network design for private communication and the P-vs-NP question. *International Journal of Advanced Computer Science and Applications*, 5(2): 148–157, 2014.

43 M. R. Garey and D. S. Johnson. *Computers and intractability*. New York: Freeman, 1979. [Online]. Verfügbar unter: \documents\eBooks\Garey M.R., Johnson D.S. Computer and intractability.. a guide to the theory of NP-completeness (1979)(L)(T)(175s).djvu.

44 R. Alleaume, F. Roueff, E. Diamanti, and N. Lütkenhaus. Topological optimization of quantum key distribution networks. *New Journal of Physics*, 11: 075002, 2009.

45 C. Elliott, D. Pearson, and G. Troxel. Quantum Cryptography in Practice. In *Proceedings of the 2003 Conference on Applications, Technologies, Architectures, and Protocols for Computer Communications*, pp. 227–238, 2003.

46 S. Ghernaouti-Hélie, M. A. Sfaxi, G. Ribordy, and O. Gay. Using quantum key distribution within IPSEC to secure MAN communications. gehalten auf der MAN 2005 Conference, 2005. [Online]. Verfügbar unter: http://citeseerx.ist.psu.edu/viewdoc/summary?doi=10.1.1.132.2333.

47 T. M. T. Nguyen, M. A. Sfaxi, and S. Ghernaouti-Helie. Integration of Quantum Cryptography in 802.11 Networks. *gehalten auf der Proceedings of the first*

International Conference on Availability, Reliability and Security (ARES'06), pp. 116–123, 2006. [Online]. Verfügbar unter: http://dx.doi.org/10.1109/ares.2006.75.

48 S. Ghernaouti-Hélie and M. A. Sfaxi. Upgrading PPP security by quantum key distribution. *gehalten auf der NetCon 2005 Conference*, 2005. [Online]. Verfügbar unter: C:\Users\stefan\Documents\Citavi 5\Projects\Literaturdatenbank\Citavi Attachments\Ghernaouti-Hélie, Sfaxi 2005 - Upgrading PPP security by Quantum.pdf.

49 M. Mehic, M. Niemiec, S. Rass, J. Ma, M. Peev, A. Aguado, V. Martin, S. Schauer, A. Poppe, C. Pacher, and M. Voznak. Quantum key distribution: a networking perspective. *ACM Computing Surveys*, 53(5): 1–41, 2020. https://doi.org/10.1145/3402192.

50 M. Mehic, P. Fazio, S. Rass, O. Maurhart, M. Peev, A. Poppe, J. Rozhon, M. Niemiec, and M. A. Voznak. A novel approach to quality-of-service provisioning in trusted relay quantum key distribution networks. *IEEE/ACM Transactions on Networking*, 1–10, 2019. https://doi.org/10.1109/TNET.2019.2956079.

51 M. Mehic, O. Maurhart, S. Rass, and M. Voznak. Implementation of quantum key distribution network simulation module in the network simulator NS-3. *Quantum Information Processing*, 16(10): 7, 2017. https://doi.org/10.1007/s11128-017-1702-z.

52 S. Rass and S. König. Turning quantum cryptography against itself: How to avoid indirect eavesdropping in quantum networks by passive and active adversaries. *International Journal on Advances in Systems and Measurements*, 5(1): 22–33, 2012.

13

Conclusion and Future Works

*Quanyan Zhu**

Tandon School of Engineering, New York University, Brooklyn, NY, USA

*Corresponding Author: qz494@nyu.edu

13.1 Overview

This book provides an extensive exploration of cyber resilience, emphasizing the need for cyber networks to possess cognitive abilities that allow them to perceive, analyze, and respond to a spectrum of online events. These events may range from anticipated occurrences to unanticipated attacks. Effectively minimizing the impact and consequences of abnormalities and attack behaviors emerges as a central theme in the pursuit of cyber resilience.

The book systematically divides its discussions into three distinct parts. The first part revolves around establishing the foundation of cyber resilience. It delves into the methodologies for achieving cyber resilience through fundamental concepts such as zero-trust frameworks, tactical machine learning (ML), cyber insurance, and other pivotal components. Within this context, the creation of feedback loops is highlighted in many chapters in the book as a fundamental aspect. These chapters emphasize the necessity of feedback loops to facilitate learning, adaptation, and autonomy, which are essential for the dynamic nature of cyber resilience.

Moving into the second part, the focus shifts toward the vulnerabilities inherent in ML algorithms. While these algorithms hold the potential to improve resilience, they are equally susceptible to threats. The critical challenge addressed in this section is how to defend ML algorithms against attacks, ensuring their resilience and robustness. Establishing trustworthy ML algorithms becomes paramount for their effective integration into the broader landscape of cyber resilience.

The third part of the book introduces game-theoretic techniques, elucidating their significance in crafting strategic responses in the cyber realm. Strategic decision-making, as discussed in the first part, forms a cornerstone for building cyber resilience. Game-theoretic tools offer a means to develop mechanisms that consider adversarial behaviors, creating redundancies and other strategic measures in adversarial environments. The application of game theory has been extended to critical infrastructures like power systems, manufacturing, and supply chain networks. Dynamic games, in particular, emerge as crucial tools, equipping solutions with the capacity to adapt to uncertain environments and fostering continuous learning capabilities.

13.2 Summary

Chapter 1 explores the concepts of cyber resilience and cybersecurity, emphasizing the evolving definitions and distinctions between these terms. The definitions of security, resilience, and risk are discussed, highlighting the difference between preventing damage (security) and recovering from difficulties (resilience). The importance of both cybersecurity and cyber resilience is acknowledged, with a caution against conflating the two, as applying the wrong approach can lead to costly failures.

Chapter 1 delves into the concept of autonomous cyber resilience, defining it as a system's ability to adapt to cyber compromises without human control. The autonomous system is expected to perceive, analyze, and interpret events, formulate response plans, assess potential outcomes, and execute actions while anticipating counteractions from hostile malware. Various autonomous actions for cyber resilience are explored, including absorption, deflection, discarding and replacement, reconfiguration, obfuscation, dynamic generation of information, and dynamic restrictions. Two broad approaches to implementing autonomous cyber resilience are outlined: resilience by design, where resilience is inherent in the system structure, and resilience by intervention, where external services provide monitoring and support.

The benefits and risks of autonomous cyber resilience are discussed. The benefits include rapid response, reduced reliance on human personnel, and the ability to prevent damaging ramifications of cyberattacks. Risks include potential damage from autonomous actions, and developers are advised to mitigate these risks through controlled rules, modeling, simulation, and continuous monitoring.

Chapter 1 emphasizes the growing importance of autonomous cyber resilience, particularly in the context of the increasing presence of autonomous systems in society. While acknowledging the risks, the benefits of autonomous cyber resilience are deemed to outweigh the potential drawbacks, given the limitations of human-based cyber defense.

13.2.1 Summary and Synthesis of Part 1 on Foundations of Cyber Resilience

The first part of this book extensively focuses on laying the foundation for cyber resilience. Establishing cyber resilience demands the creation of innovative mechanisms and quantitative frameworks aimed at creating a trustworthy cyberspace. ML emerges as a pivotal tool to equip systems with the essential capabilities for adaptation and real-time decision-making. Additionally, the strategic and predictive reasoning capabilities afforded by game theory play a crucial role, enabling systems to harness knowledge effectively to achieve resilience goals within the constraints of available resources. Thus, ML and game theory jointly serve as the backbone engines powering diverse cyber resilience mechanisms.

This section explores several mechanisms to strengthen cyber resilience. One such mechanism is the zero-trust approach, which mandates continuous and dynamic monitoring of networks coupled with an adaptive framework for access control and network management. By integrating game theory and ML, a zero-trust mechanism can evolve into an adaptive trust management system within network environments. Another significant mechanism discussed in this section is cyber insurance. In the face of escalating threats, such as ransomware, capable of causing substantial disruptions to production and services, cyber insurance becomes increasingly vital. This mechanism allows systems to recuperate from financial losses incurred post-attack. Establishing incentive-compatible frameworks among stakeholders becomes a critical step in providing assurance to network operators and users, particularly in small- and medium-sized businesses. Again, leveraging game theory and ML, this mechanism assesses risks comprehensively and formulates optimal policies for resilience.

The section not only explores the foundations of these resilience mechanisms but also delves into the design frameworks that intricately rely on the synergistic application of game theory and ML. By comprehensively addressing these aspects, the book aims to equip readers with a holistic understanding of the multifaceted strategies essential for bolstering cyber resilience in today's complex and dynamic cyber landscape.

Chapter 2 explores how game theory can enhance cyber resilience in Intelligent Transportation Systems (ITS) against deceptive information attacks. These attacks, such as data poisoning, spoofing, and phishing, exploit vulnerabilities in ITS, targeting vehicles, communication networks, and human operators. The chapter highlights the interconnected nature of ITS, where an attack on one component, like an autonomous vehicle or traffic management system, can ripple through the system, causing widespread disruptions. By leveraging game theory, control mechanisms, and learning models, the chapter proposes strategies to model attacker–defender dynamics and improve system resilience. A key example is the Proactive Risk Assessment and Mitigation of Misinformed Demand Attacks (PRADA) framework, which integrates trust mechanisms and learning processes to counter threats like GPS spoofing and misdirected traffic recommendations.

The chapter also emphasizes the importance of cross-domain and holistic resilience strategies. It details how intra-vehicle, inter-vehicle, and transportation domains, along with human interactions, must be secured collectively to prevent cascading failures. Game-theoretic frameworks are presented as powerful tools to anticipate and mitigate risks, offering solutions like dynamic control adjustments and predictive modeling. Case studies, including the PRADA framework, demonstrate how strategic modeling and trust-based systems can counter both localized and system-wide attacks. The chapter concludes by advocating for integrated, adaptive mechanisms to address emerging ITS threats, ensuring safety, reliability, and public trust in transportation systems.

Chapter 3 describes the development of a framework called CYBER-MIRA for assessing the cyber mission impact resilience of a tactical ML-based mission system. The framework aims to evaluate the system's effectiveness in the face of adversarial attacks, considering fault tolerance, adaptability, recoverability, and transformability. CYBER-MIRA incorporates hypergame theory to represent attack–defense interactions and subjective Bayesian networks to account for uncertainty in the system's resilience. The framework also considers resource consumption and overhead while ensuring seamless services in contested network environments. The goal is to measure and enhance cyber resilience, emphasizing the system's ability to deliver expected outcomes despite cyber threats.

The concept of cyber resilience is explained as the capacity of a system to consistently deliver expected outputs in the presence of unfavorable cyber occurrences. Unlike cybersecurity, which focuses on preventing attacks, cyber resilience assumes that attacks will occur and aims to understand how effectively the system performs under those circumstances. The chapter highlights the importance of studying both attackers and defenders in assessing mission impact and introduces the CYBER-MIRA framework as a solution.

Chapter 3 introduces the CYBER-MIRA framework, which utilizes subjective logic for uncertainty-aware resilience modeling, introduces a hypergame model for attacker and defender interactions, and addresses the efficiency of mission completion under resource constraints. The chapter also discusses the limitations of CYBER-MIRA and outlines future work, including the extension of mission impact assessment to consider security, trust, and agility, as well as practical implementation and evaluation of the framework in an Internet of Things (IoT)-based object detection mission system setup.

Chapter 4 delves into the challenges and methods for modeling autonomous network resilience in adversarial environments. The chapter highlights the growing difficulty in maintaining secure and reliable network systems amidst increasingly sophisticated cyberattacks, especially in environments with interconnected devices like IoT. The discussion introduces the use of ML and topological data analysis (TDA) as tools to analyze network vulnerabilities and resilience.

By examining network structures as weighted graphs and leveraging TDA concepts such as simplicial complexes and persistent homology, the chapter explores how these techniques can better characterize network robustness, identify attack impacts, and measure recovery dynamics. Despite their potential, ML approaches for anomaly detection face challenges such as false alarms, prompting further research into refining data preprocessing and feature extraction.

The chapter also emphasizes the importance of understanding network topology in resilience modeling, specifically during the avoidance and survival phases of disruptions. TDA tools, such as persistent homology, provide insights into the shape and structure of networked data, enabling the identification of patterns and vulnerabilities. Techniques such as Vietoris–Rips complexes and Betti numbers offer ways to analyze high-dimensional data for resilience assessments. The chapter concludes with a discussion of network resilience in terms of recovery from disruptions, contrasting it with robustness, which focuses on maintaining functionality during attacks. By integrating TDA and ML, the chapter presents a framework for advancing autonomous resilience modeling and enhancing cybersecurity measures.

Chapter 5 focuses on the zero-trust security model as a response to the vulnerabilities of traditional network defenses in the face of increased connectivity and evolving cyber threats, especially with the rise of the IoT. The zero-trust model, in contrast to the traditional perimeter-based security, scrutinizes every incoming request, verifying it before granting access. The chapter emphasizes the evolution from traditional security to zero trust, highlighting two key components: trust evaluation (TE) and policy engine (PE). The TE assesses the trustworthiness of entities based on historical data, while the PE enforces access policies. The interaction between TE and PE is crucial for achieving cyber resilience within the zero-trust framework.

Chapter 5 discusses the application of dynamic game theory and learning to quantitatively approach automated zero-trust cyber resilience. Several case studies illustrate the benefits of this security model in addressing the challenges posed by the increasing connectivity, heterogeneous devices, and potential insider threats. The strategic zero-trust design principle of "never trust, verify strategically" is proposed to address challenges like defining trustworthiness metrics, balancing system performance, and adapting to the dynamic environment of IoT networks. The chapter concludes by highlighting the contributions of zero trust to cyber resilience, offering a comprehensive guide for developing secure and resilient networks in the face of modern cyber threats.

In Chapter 6, the importance of cyber insurance as a complementary mechanism for enhancing cyber resilience is discussed. The framework for designing quantitative cyber insurance is explored, focusing on the correlation between attack vectors and defense mechanisms. The concept of residual risks is introduced, emphasizing the role of cyber insurance in mitigating damages even when advanced defense mechanisms are in place. The framework considers the insurer's observations and various monitoring scenarios, addressing the intensity of moral hazard issues. The integration of risk perceptions and economic impacts into cyber insurance design is highlighted, emphasizing the potential enhancement of cyber resilience.

Chapter 6 emphasizes cyber resilience, defining it as the ability of a system to resist, repair, and sustain itself after cyberattacks or system failures. Traditional defense mechanisms, such as antivirus software and intrusion detection systems, are discussed, acknowledging that not all attacks can be prevented. Cyber insurance is positioned as a unique approach to enhance resilience, especially for individuals and small businesses lacking cybersecurity expertise. The user's perspective on cyber insurance as a risk-sharing mechanism is detailed, particularly in scenarios like ransomware attacks, where financial losses are shared with insurers, enabling business continuity.

The role of cyber insurance in users' defense strategies is highlighted, emphasizing its compatibility with security investments. For smaller businesses, cyber insurance may be a more feasible option than investing in costly cybersecurity measures. The challenges hindering cyber insurance implementation are discussed, including difficulties in cyber risk assessment, user risk preferences, and economic relations between insurers and agents. The need for dynamic cyber insurance contracts to adapt to evolving cyber threats is proposed, linking it to the broader concept of cyber resilience.

Regulations on cyber insurance are deemed essential for standardizing the market and addressing speculative behaviors. Voluntary participation is suggested, with considerations for mandatory participation for service providers or bundling insurance with IT products. Regulations are also seen as crucial for education and awareness, shaping user risk preferences, and ensuring accountability through penalties for violations. The chapter concludes by stressing the importance of dynamic insurance contracts in adapting to evolving cyber threats for a more resilient cyber insurance market.

Chapter 7 examines the role of honeypots in enhancing cyber resilience by assessing their effectiveness across different network topologies. The researchers conducted experiments using a tool called "HackIT," involving human participants acting as attackers to explore two network setups: layered and star topologies. Honeypots, which act as decoy nodes, were strategically placed in these networks to lure attackers. The results revealed that the layered topology was more effective at delaying attackers and protecting real assets compared to the star topology. In the layered setup, attackers encountered honeypots early, leading many to abandon further attacks, which slowed their progress and minimized their success in exploiting valuable nodes.

The study also utilized an instance-based learning (IBL) model to simulate attacker behavior when human participants were unavailable, offering insights into defense strategies and attacker decision-making processes. This cognitive model mimicked human attackers' actions and provided predictive insights into the effectiveness of honeypot deployment. Key findings showed that honeypots in layered topologies not only misled attackers more effectively but also left traces of attacker behavior that defenders could exploit. These findings highlight the importance of topology design and strategic honeypot placement in cybersecurity, emphasizing that layered networks provide a significant advantage in mitigating attacks.

13.2.1.1 Synthesis: Foundation of Cyber Resilience

Across Chapters 1 through 7, a recurring and unifying theme emerges: cyber resilience is not merely a function of technical capability, but an evolving convergence of autonomous adaptation, structural robustness, and intelligent decision-making. Resilience, in this view, is not reactive but inherently proactive, driven by systems capable of self-monitoring, self-assessing, and self-correcting in response to an increasingly dynamic threat landscape.

Chapter 1 lays the conceptual groundwork by distinguishing between cybersecurity and cyber resilience, and crucially, it introduces autonomy as a defining characteristic of next-generation defense systems. It articulates the need for cyber systems to independently perceive, reason, and act upon threats without relying solely on human oversight. Chapters 2 and 3 extend this foundation by embedding autonomy within cyber-physical environments. Through the PRADA and CYBER-MIRA frameworks, they show how systems can use game-theoretic and probabilistic models not only to detect and mitigate risks but to anticipate adversarial behaviors and adapt in mission-critical settings. These models exemplify how autonomous systems can operate with situational awareness and foresight, enabling them to make resilient decisions in the face of incomplete or deceptive information.

Chapters 4 and 5 deepen the exploration of autonomous cyber resilience by focusing on self-aware network architectures. They introduce ML and TDA as tools for autonomous anomaly detection and resilience quantification. These chapters demonstrate how networks can evolve and reconfigure themselves in response to disruptions, embodying autonomy through adaptive feedback and structural learning. Meanwhile, Chapters 6 and 7 highlight complementary mechanisms, economic and cognitive in nature, that reinforce system autonomy. Cyber insurance is positioned not just as a financial buffer but as a dynamic risk-sharing mechanism that incentivizes autonomous resilience practices across organizations. Honeypots, on the other hand, showcase deception as an autonomous tactic, misleading adversaries while gathering intelligence without human intervention.

Taken together, these chapters present a layered and multifaceted vision of autonomous cyber resilience. From strategic modeling and real-time learning to economic incentives and behavioral defenses, the integration of autonomous functions spans across technical, organizational, and adversarial domains. Central to all contributions is the notion of feedback loops, which are mechanisms through which systems sense, evaluate, and evolve in response to their environment. This feedback-driven adaptability, when embedded within systems at design time, empowers them to operate independently, intelligently, and resiliently in complex cyber terrains. As the chapters collectively show, autonomous cyber resilience is not a singular capability but an emergent property arising from the orchestration of sensing, learning, strategic reasoning, and adaptive response.

13.2.2 Summary and Synthesis of Part 2 on Resilient ML

The second part of this book delves into resilient ML, a crucial facet of modern information technology. While ML has experienced notable success in diverse applications, from malware detection to health diagnosis, it is imperative to acknowledge and address the vulnerabilities that may surface at various stages of development and deployment. The chapters in this section highlight the critical need for ML algorithms embedded within our systems to exhibit resilience against potential attacks. Recognizing that the security landscape is ever evolving, understanding and mitigating vulnerabilities in ML algorithms become paramount for the sustained effectiveness of these intelligent systems. This part of the book explores several attack models targeting ML algorithms, including decision-time attacks, model inversion, and membership inference attacks. By formalizing these attack models, the book provides readers with a nuanced understanding of potential threats to ML systems. This understanding serves as a foundational step toward developing resilient solutions with the goal of developing ML algorithms that possess the intelligence and adaptability necessary to counteract adversarial attempts effectively.

Chapter 8 delves into the realm of adversarial ML, a domain focused on understanding the threats faced by ML algorithms in terms of prediction integrity or confidentiality. The two main types of algorithmic problems addressed in this context are attacks, aiming to compromise integrity or confidentiality, and defenses, working to mitigate such violations. The overarching interest lies in defense, making research on attacks instrumental for evaluating defense mechanisms. Despite this, there is a notable gap in exploring the optimal threat model to serve the instrumental goal of defense.

The chapter narrows its focus to decision-time attacks, involving deliberate changes to inputs for a deployed ML model. It explores two prediction problems within this scope: malware detection (binary classification) and image classification. The discussion primarily centers on the crucial issue of realizable attacks, where the underlying entity is modified, and the feature vector arises as a consequence. The chapter evaluates the efficacy of feature-space attacks in defending against realizable attacks in the domains of PDF malware detection and image classification. Counterintuitively, it finds that feature-space attacks are surprisingly efficacious in the former but have little value in the latter, shedding light on the intricate dynamics between feature-space and realizable attacks in different domains.

Chapter 9 underscores the escalating integration of AI and ML in privacy-sensitive domains such as medical diagnosis, health analytics, and facial recognition. While AI models exhibit success in these applications, their susceptibility to privacy and security attacks, particularly model inversion, training data membership inference, and attribute inference attacks, poses significant concerns. Model inversion attacks, where adversaries reconstruct average samples from a model, exploit confidence values to reveal sensitive features like an individual's genotype or facial attributes. Training data membership inference attacks aim to discern if a given data point was part of the training data, potentially exposing locale-specific information in applications like satellite imagery-based target recognition or sensitive health conditions. Attribute inference attacks leverage ML models and incomplete data to deduce missing information, such as inferring an individual's genotype from partial medical records.

The chapter highlights the vulnerability of current state-of-the-art ML systems to model inversion and membership inference attacks, necessitating further research to ensure data privacy and model security. It proposes federated learning (FL) as a framework to safeguard user data privacy, wherein participants collaboratively construct a deep learning (DL) model without sharing individual training data. The research challenges identified include investigating privacy vulnerabilities of DL models, studying the impact of image transformations on model inversion attacks, and evaluating the resilience of FL systems against various privacy attacks. The article concludes by emphasizing the critical need for robust solutions to mitigate vulnerabilities in AI models, particularly in applications with sensitive data, such as health analytics, finance, and cybersecurity.

Chapter 10 focuses on improving the resilience of deep neural networks (DNNs) against adversarial attacks by introducing a "random ensemble" approach. Traditional DNNs are vulnerable to adversarial perturbations, which can cause misclassification of inputs. The chapter proposes a strategy to address this vulnerability by bootstrapping DNNs to study parameter distributions and then randomizing portions of the weights in specific layers. By replacing certain weights with values generated from Gaussian distributions, the authors create randomized ensembles of DNNs that act as moving targets for attackers, rendering adaptive attacks ineffective. This technique is scalable and maintains accuracy on clean data while significantly improving resistance to adversarial attacks, such as those generated by methods like FGSM, PGD, and CW2.

The approach is tested on three DNN architectures: CNN3, VGG16, and Inception v3, using datasets like MNIST, CIFAR-10, and Tiny ImageNet. Results show that randomizing weights in the early convolutional layers achieves the best balance between robustness against adversarial attacks and performance on clean data. Larger and more complex networks like Inception v3 benefit the most from this method, as their ensemble configurations can better handle adversarial perturbations. While the strategy is not a complete solution to adversarial attacks, it demonstrates significant progress in building robust DNNs by effectively leveraging randomness to disrupt attack patterns.

13.2.2.1 Synthesis: Resilient ML

Chapters 8 through 10 form a cohesive narrative around the vulnerabilities of ML systems and the innovative methods being developed to fortify them in adversarial environments. At the heart of this section lies the challenge of constructing intelligent systems that are not only accurate but also robust, adaptive, and autonomous in their defense mechanisms. Each chapter offers a distinct but complementary lens on this overarching challenge, contributing to the broader goal of enabling autonomous cyber resilience.

Chapter 8 delves into decision-time adversarial attacks, highlighting how subtle, real-world perturbations can mislead ML models and degrade system performance. By analyzing the differences between realizable and feature-space attacks across domains such as malware detection and image classification, this chapter underscores the need for models that can autonomously detect and neutralize manipulations in real time. In the context of cyber resilience, this capacity for real-time adversarial awareness and response is foundational to building self-defending systems.

Chapter 9 turns the spotlight to privacy-focused adversarial threats, including model inversion and membership inference attacks. These attacks expose sensitive training data, posing significant risks in domains like healthcare and finance. The chapter introduces FL as a promising defense, one that not only protects user data but also distributes intelligence across the edge. This decentralized, privacy-preserving architecture is inherently aligned with autonomous cyber resilience, as it enables learning and adaptation to occur locally without centralized control, thereby enhancing both scalability and survivability in contested environments.

Chapter 10 shifts focus to architectural robustness, exploring how randomized ensemble methods can create moving targets for attackers. By injecting uncertainty into model parameters, particularly in DNNs, these ensembles disrupt adversarial strategies and make it harder for attackers to generalize successful exploits. Importantly, these randomized defenses are not hard-coded rules but emergent behaviors generated through algorithmic diversity. This reflects a key trait of autonomous resilience: the ability of systems to dynamically reconfigure and self-harden in the face of threats, without requiring manual intervention.

Together, these chapters highlight that achieving true cyber resilience requires embedding autonomy deep within ML models, not only in their ability to learn from data but also in their capacity to sense attacks, protect information, and adapt strategies independently. The cross-cutting insight is that robustness must be an intrinsic property of both the algorithm and its deployment context. Moreover, there are unavoidable trade-offs among performance, interpretability, and resilience, which must be navigated thoughtfully in the design of resilient AI systems. By integrating privacy, robustness, and adaptability as first-class design principles, the research in this section pushes the frontier of what it means to develop ML systems that are not only intelligent but autonomously resilient in adversarial cyber landscapes.

13.2.3 Summary of Part 3 on Game Theory for Network Resilience

Part 3 of this book focuses on game theory for network resilience in next-generation communication systems. As we navigate the evolution of communication technologies, the next generation of systems is poised to harness the power of ML to establish automated intelligence for signal classification. Simultaneously, quantum technologies, such as quantum key distribution (QKD), are central to next-generation network technologies. Part 3 delves into how game-theoretic methods can be employed to fortify these next-generation networks against emerging threats. For instance, it explores potential attacks that may target the training processes integral to the ML systems in NextG communication. A game-theoretic approach is proposed to enhance security by strategically incorporating redundancy into the layout of network architectures.

The section further delves into the intricacies of game theory by examining the joint consideration of confidentiality and availability as pivotal facets of network security. Emphasis is placed on the adaptability of network configurations in response to incidents detected through QKD's eavesdropping detection capabilities. The integration of game-theoretic principles into network resilience strategies becomes a crucial component in effectively addressing the evolving threat landscape of next-generation communication systems. Through this exploration, the book aims to equip readers with insights and methodologies essential for ensuring the robustness and security of cutting-edge communication infrastructures.

Chapter 11 explores the dynamics of poisoning attacks and defense interactions in FL applied to wireless signal classification for NextG communications. FL allows multiple clients, acting as spectrum sensors, to collaboratively train a global model without sharing raw data. The focus is on defending against malicious clients that can poison the training process and compromise the global model. The interactions between attackers injecting false data and defenders implementing a proactive admission strategy are formulated as a non-cooperative game.

NextG communications, promising significant performance improvements, rely on ML, particularly DL, to adapt to spectrum dynamics. FL facilitates collaborative training while maintaining data privacy and reducing communication load. However, it is vulnerable to poisoning attacks, prompting the need for defense mechanisms. The chapter employs game theory to model the strategic decisions of attackers and defenders, seeking Nash equilibrium strategies that maximize their respective payoffs.

The chapter emphasizes the susceptibility of NextG communications to adversarial ML attacks due to the shared and open nature of the wireless medium. It proposes a proactive defense mechanism for FL, where the defender selects clients to admit, aiming to reject poisoned ones. The game-theoretic formulation provides insights into novel operation modes for safeguarding FL in NextG communication systems, considering both two-client scenarios and extensions to arbitrary numbers of clients. The study contributes to understanding the attack surface in adversarial ML and quantifying its impact on NextG communication performance.

Chapter 12 primarily addresses the challenge of ensuring end-to-end security in quantum networks, focusing on the practical limitations and vulnerabilities associated with QKD. While QKD offers unparalleled confidentiality based on the laws of quantum physics, its current practical implementation is constrained to direct connections without intermediate hops. This limitation necessitates the "trusted relay assumption," which assumes that relay nodes in the network are secure and not vulnerable to cyber threats. The challenge lies in the vulnerability of relay nodes, which are essentially conventional computers with standard operating systems, making them susceptible to attacks. The chapter explores the risks associated with this assumption, emphasizing the potential compromise of the entire quantum network if even one relay node is compromised. The discussion delves into the need for robust physical and logical access control over relay nodes, highlighting the difficulty of establishing and maintaining such controls.

The chapter introduces a game-theoretic approach to enhance security by leveraging redundancy in network layouts. It explores the joint consideration of confidentiality and availability as crucial aspects of security, emphasizing the importance of adapting network configurations based on incidents detected through QKD's eavesdropping detection capabilities. The chapter revolves around establishing and maintaining the security of quantum networks, considering the vulnerabilities associated with relay nodes, the limitations of current QKD implementations, and the need for adaptive mechanisms to address both technical and ethical requirements.

13.2.3.1 Synthesis: Game Theory for Network Resilience

Part 3 (Chapters 11 and 12) demonstrates how game-theoretic reasoning is foundational to achieving autonomous cyber resilience, particularly in complex, distributed communication environments where threats are dynamic and adversarial behavior is strategic. These chapters emphasize that autonomous defense is not just about automation – it is about strategic foresight, self-adjusting mechanisms, and learning-enabled decision-making in the face of incomplete or deceptive information.

Chapter 11 explores an FL framework for wireless spectrum sensing in NextG communication systems, where malicious participants attempt to poison the shared learning model. The system must operate without centralized control, making autonomous operation essential. By formulating a non-cooperative game between adversarial clients and the defender, the chapter derives adaptive admission control strategies that allow the system to autonomously select trustworthy participants while filtering out potential attackers. This is a clear manifestation of autonomous cyber resilience, where defense strategies are not statically configured but emerge from strategic reasoning embedded within the system's operational loop.

Chapter 12 extends this strategic autonomy into the quantum realm, addressing the challenge of securing QKD networks under the assumption of vulnerable trusted relays. Here, redundancy, dynamic reconfiguration, and adaptive trust management are modeled through a game-theoretic lens to preserve confidentiality and availability. The ability of a network to autonomously reconfigure itself based on signals of compromise embodies a core capability of resilient autonomous systems. It reflects how resilience and security can be co-designed through mechanisms that anticipate attacker strategies and restructure the system's posture in real time.

Across both chapters, game theory emerges as a critical enabler of decision autonomy, bridging the gap between design-time guarantees (e.g., protocol correctness, redundancy planning) and run-time adaptability (e.g., admission decisions, relay selection). Strategic modeling empowers systems not only to react to threats but also to anticipate, influence, and shape adversarial behavior in data-driven and decentralized contexts. Moreover, these game-theoretic frameworks support learning over time, allowing systems to refine their strategic policies through interaction histories, thus enhancing resilience as experience accumulates.

Taken together, Chapters 11 and 12 exemplify how autonomous cyber resilience is not a static property but a dynamic capability, rooted in the ability to reason about future uncertainties, adversarial goals, and system interdependencies. Through game-theoretic foundations, cyber defense can evolve from rule-based automation to strategic autonomy, equipping systems to operate securely and effectively in adversarial, complex, and ever-changing networked environments.

13.3 Future Directions: Charting the Path Toward Autonomous Cyber Resilience

Cyber resilience, at its core, hinges upon the ability of systems to learn, adapt, and respond in the face of evolving, complex threats. As autonomous systems become more deeply integrated into our digital infrastructure – from self-driving vehicles to distributed control networks – cyber resilience must evolve from reactive defense into proactive, strategic autonomy under adversarial conditions. This next-generation resilience requires new computational paradigms, systemic design principles, and strategic intelligence grounded in interdisciplinary research.

Several key directions emerge from the synthesis of this volume, offering a roadmap for advancing both the science and practice of cyber resilience in increasingly autonomous and contested environments.

13.3.1 Learning Autonomy: From Reactive Defense to Strategic Adaptation

The evolution of cyber resilience hinges increasingly on the development of learning systems that do more than merely respond to known threats. Instead, future autonomous cyber defense must be capable of anticipating adversarial strategies, adapting to previously unseen scenarios, and evolving continuously in dynamic environments. This vision calls for a paradigm shift away from conventional supervised learning approaches, which depend on labeled data and static training sets, toward a suite of more flexible, autonomous learning paradigms. These include unsupervised learning, self-supervised learning, continual learning, meta-learning, and reinforcement learning under uncertainty.

Unsupervised and self-supervised learning techniques allow systems to discover patterns, correlations, and anomalies in raw, unlabeled data streams. Such capabilities are crucial in real-world cybersecurity environments where threats are not always labeled or even known in advance. For instance, a self-supervised learning agent could learn robust feature representations from encrypted traffic or network telemetry and detect subtle deviations that indicate early stages of an attack. These models can autonomously infer structure from data, making them more resilient to rapidly changing threat landscapes and minimizing dependency on expensive manual annotation processes.

Continual learning further enhances autonomy by enabling systems to adapt incrementally without forgetting previously acquired knowledge, a phenomenon known as catastrophic forgetting. In cyber defense scenarios where adversaries continually change tactics, techniques, and procedures, a continual learning framework allows the system to update its defense posture while retaining competence across prior attack classes. The ability to update in situ, without retraining from scratch, supports low-latency adaptation, energy efficiency, and longer system lifespans in resource-constrained environments.

Meta-learning, or "learning to learn," equips cyber-resilient agents with the ability to quickly generalize from limited experiences. In highly dynamic or low-data environments, such as responding to a zero-day attack, meta-learned policies can infer optimal countermeasures by leveraging structural similarities with prior attack–defense interactions. Coupled with model-based reinforcement learning, these systems can simulate and evaluate action sequences to determine optimal responses under uncertainty, balancing exploitation of known defenses with exploration of novel counterstrategies.

Central to the deployment of such learning systems is the need for transparency and explainability. As autonomous cyber agents increasingly assume control over high-stakes decisions, such as isolating devices, initiating deception maneuvers, or shutting down critical subsystems, their decision-making processes must remain intelligible and accountable to human operators and regulators. The integration of explainable AI (XAI) is not merely a technical enhancement; it is a foundational requirement for operational trust, legal compliance, and ethical assurance. Explainability bridges the cognitive gap between algorithmic inference and human reasoning, enabling analysts to understand, challenge, and refine the behavior of autonomous systems.

Interpretable ML techniques, such as attention mechanisms, saliency maps, counterfactual reasoning, and symbolic regression, offer means to audit algorithmic behavior and diagnose failure modes. In hybrid control settings, where human and machine share decision authority, explainability also facilitates collaborative human–AI teaming, allowing experts to supervise, calibrate, or override autonomous actions when necessary. This collaboration is especially critical in adversarial contexts, where trust must be earned not only from system users but also from defenders coordinating across organizational or national boundaries.

As learning autonomy advances, a crucial design challenge will be the reconciliation of adaptability and safety. Highly adaptive systems must be equipped with mechanisms to assess confidence, monitor behavioral drift, and enforce policy constraints. Failing to do so risks producing brittle or erratic behaviors under adversarial manipulation or unanticipated inputs. Safeguards such as confidence-based triggering mechanisms, adversarial training, and robust optimization can help ensure that learning systems degrade gracefully and avoid catastrophic failure.

13.3.2 Multiscale Resilience: Tailoring Autonomy Across Layers and Contexts

Cyber resilience is not a monolithic capability; rather, it is a layered and distributed property that must manifest coherently across a spectrum of technological, operational, and organizational levels. From embedded edge devices that perform real-time sensing and actuation to mission-critical cyber-physical platforms such as autonomous vehicles or medical systems, and further up to large-scale interconnected infrastructures such as smart grids, supply chains, and national defense networks, each layer presents distinct operational tempos, threat models, and resource constraints. Consequently, building effective cyber resilience demands not only robust mechanisms at each scale but also seamless integration and coordination across them.

Designing autonomy that is resilient across such heterogeneous scales introduces profound challenges. Techniques that are effective at the node or device level, such as local dynamic reconfiguration, lightweight anomaly detection, or redundant signal paths, may not translate directly to larger networked settings, where coordination, data consistency, and collective behavior matter more. For example, an edge node may autonomously isolate itself upon detecting an anomaly, but without system-wide awareness, such an action could inadvertently disrupt higher-level services or cause cascading failures in tightly coupled systems.

To bridge this gap, future cyber resilience research must focus on scalable autonomy: the ability of systems to self-organize and adapt at multiple levels of granularity while preserving global coherence. This calls for frameworks in which local intelligence, including observations, decisions, and adaptations, can be meaningfully aggregated, propagated, or modulated to inform broader situational awareness and control policies. Achieving such coordination entails the development of architectural blueprints that support hierarchical learning, where insights and policies learned at one layer are contextualized and integrated across others.

At the architectural level, multiscale resilience necessitates cross-layer control protocols that can regulate interactions between low-level and high-level decision-making processes. For instance, a low-level controller detecting abnormal packet loss may trigger mid-level re-routing policies or engage high-level risk assessment functions depending on its context within the network. These vertical interactions must be complemented by horizontal coordination mechanisms that facilitate collaboration among peer nodes, such as FL across distributed sensors or decentralized trust negotiation among autonomous agents.

A particularly promising approach lies in distributed consensus mechanisms and multi-agent coordination algorithms. These enable resilient agreement on shared state, intent, or trust, even when nodes are compromised or operating under partial observability. Techniques such as Byzantine fault-tolerant consensus, gossip protocols, and blockchain-inspired state synchronization can help enforce global consistency while preserving the decentralized, self-healing properties critical to resilience. Such consensus schemes must be lightweight and adaptive to suit the resource and latency constraints characteristic of edge and embedded systems.

Importantly, these multiscale frameworks must be designed with resilience-by-design principles in mind. Resilience must be embedded from the outset as a fundamental architectural requirement, rather than layered post hoc, by accounting for both functional dependencies and failure propagation paths within and across system layers. This requires tight collaboration between system architects, control theorists, cybersecurity engineers, and AI researchers to co-design protocols, data structures, and control policies that jointly satisfy safety, performance, and resilience guarantees.

Another crucial dimension of multiscale resilience is the organizational and human-in-the-loop context. At the operational scale, autonomous subsystems must be able to escalate decisions, provide interpretable situational reports, or defer to human operators when thresholds are met. Meanwhile, at the enterprise or national scale, policy and risk management decisions depend on actionable insights distilled from massive volumes of heterogeneous data. Building autonomy that can adaptively translate low-level signals into high-level strategic assessments remains a critical research frontier, requiring novel work in multi-resolution knowledge representation, causal inference, and context-aware alerting systems.

13.3.3 Game-theoretic Intelligence: Strategic Reasoning for Resilience

Game theory is uniquely suited to address the strategic and adversarial dynamics of cyber resilience. As illustrated throughout this book, autonomous cyber defense is not only a technical endeavor but a deeply strategic one, requiring systems to reason about opponent intent, anticipate counter-responses, and understand the potential consequences of escalation or deterrence. In adversarial settings, where threats are intelligent, adaptive, and often deceptive, purely reactive or rule-based systems fall short. Instead, cyber resilience must incorporate mechanisms that emulate human-like strategic reasoning, planning, and anticipation, which are capabilities naturally modeled through game-theoretic frameworks.

Future research in this area should advance the development of multi-agent game-theoretic models, which can capture the interactions among multiple defenders, attackers, neutral entities, and stakeholders with varying goals and information asymmetries. These models go beyond simple attacker–defender dyads to reflect real-world complexity, where coalitions may form, deception may be employed, and long-term incentives shape short-term actions. Meta-games, or games of games, provide a higher-order lens to analyze how systems adapt over time, learn opponent strategies, and escalate or de-escalate conflicts based on changing objectives and constraints. Such frameworks are essential for equipping autonomous systems with the ability to reason about strategic depth, anticipate opponent adaptation, and select robust actions under uncertainty.

A particularly salient application is the formalization of algorithmic deception and counter-deception. Game-theoretic models such as signaling games, Bayesian persuasion, and dynamic Stackelberg games enable defenders to simulate and deploy misinformation, honeypots, or misleading signals in a calculated way to misdirect attackers, force early resource expenditure, or provoke behavior that reveals adversarial intent. These tactics must be carefully balanced with the risks of unintended side effects and require predictive models of adversary cognition, areas where game-theoretic reasoning provides valuable structure.

Adversarial learning, another critical frontier, can also benefit from game-theoretic analysis. In adversarial ML scenarios, the interaction between attacker and learner can be modeled as a repeated or sequential game, where each player adapts based on observed outcomes. The design of robust classifiers, generative defenses, and strategic randomization methods can be grounded in equilibrium concepts such as minimax strategies, correlated equilibria, or regret-based learning. The inclusion of bounded rationality, exploration constraints, and partial observability further increases the realism of these models, allowing for resilient decision-making under limited knowledge.

Moreover, game-theoretic techniques offer powerful tools for strategic adaptation at scale. In distributed and federated systems, where learning or control is shared among many autonomous agents, coordination and alignment are nontrivial. Game theory can model the competitive and cooperative dynamics that arise when multiple agents seek to optimize their local objectives while contributing to global resilience. For example, in FL under adversarial conditions, game theory informs the design of client selection policies, aggregation rules, and incentive-compatible protocols that discourage data poisoning or model manipulation.

Beyond defense mechanisms, game theory is also instrumental in shaping cybersecurity economics and policy. Mechanism design and contract theory provide a basis for engineering incentive-compatible interactions among infrastructure owners, service providers, insurers, and regulators. For instance, cyber insurance as a market-driven risk management tool can be optimized through Stackelberg or principal-agent models to ensure that insured parties invest adequately in security, while insurers accurately price risk and promote systemic resilience. These models can internalize externalities such as contagion risk or shared vulnerabilities, leading to more stable and efficient ecosystems.

Another emerging domain is the game-theoretic analysis of systemic cyber risks and critical infrastructure interdependencies. Using models from network games and mean-field games, researchers can assess how local failures propagate through interdependent systems, and how incentives at one layer (e.g., the enterprise level) interact with broader system-wide vulnerabilities (e.g., in power or logistics networks). Game-theoretic tools can thus inform both microscale decision-making (e.g., patching strategies, authentication protocols) and macroscale resilience planning (e.g., investment in redundancy, information sharing, or joint incident response).

Ultimately, the promise of game-theoretic intelligence lies in its ability to imbue autonomous systems with a principled, adaptable, and strategic worldview. Rather than relying on static rules or heuristic optimization, resilient autonomous agents must be able to simulate future consequences, reason under uncertainty, learn opponent models, and adapt behavior in real time, which are all core competencies of strategic reasoning. As adversarial threats continue to evolve, it is imperative that cyber defense evolves with them, not as a passive shield, but as an active, learning, and strategically informed adversary in its own right.

13.3.4 Holistic and Integrative Approaches: Building a Converged Resilience Architecture

The next frontier of cyber resilience lies in the synthesis of diverse methodologies and technologies into coherent, converged architectures that support real-time, intelligent, and autonomous defense. No single technique, be it ML, cryptography, or control theory, can independently ensure resilience in today's complex, multilayered digital ecosystems. Instead, resilience must emerge from the deliberate integration of heterogeneous capabilities, orchestrated across systems, layers, and organizational boundaries.

To this end, converged resilience architectures must be designed to support adaptability, verifiability, explainability, and security simultaneously. This involves harmonizing ML for adaptive intelligence, game theory for strategic reasoning, blockchain and decentralized ledgers for trustworthy coordination, and quantum technologies for future-proof security guarantees. Such integration enables the creation of cyber-physical systems that are not only autonomous but also robust under adversarial pressure, auditable under regulatory scrutiny, and interpretable under operational uncertainty.

One critical component of these architectures is quantum resilience. As quantum computing matures, the threat landscape will shift dramatically, with traditional public-key cryptographic systems rendered vulnerable to quantum algorithms such as Shor's and Grover's. To mitigate these risks, systems must transition toward quantum-resistant cryptographic protocols, including lattice-based, hash-based, and multivariate polynomial schemes. In parallel, the adoption of QKD, which leverages the principles of quantum mechanics to detect eavesdropping and guarantee secure communications, can enhance confidentiality in high-assurance environments. While current QKD implementations are limited by physical infrastructure and trust assumptions, ongoing research into post-quantum trust frameworks will be essential to operationalizing quantum-secure communication at scale.

Complementing this are decentralized systems, particularly those based on blockchain and distributed ledger technologies, which offer tamper-resistant record-keeping, decentralized consensus, and verifiable provenance. These systems can play a pivotal role in establishing distributed trust for autonomous agents operating in partially trusted or adversarial environments. By embedding consensus protocols, identity management, and immutable logging into the operational backbone, blockchain-enhanced architectures can reduce the risk of single points of failure and provide auditable trails for incident response and post-mortem forensics. Moreover, decentralized smart contracts can serve as programmable policies that autonomously enforce access controls, conditional triggers, and cross-domain coordination among agents.

A further architectural advance lies in neurosymbolic systems, which combine the statistical adaptability of ML with the logical precision of symbolic reasoning. Neurosymbolic AI offers a promising foundation for introspective and generalizable autonomous agents that can reason abstractly, explain their decisions, and revise their internal models in the face of novelty or conflict. These hybrid systems support causal inference, hierarchical abstraction, and compositional learning, all of which are essential for strategic decision-making in uncertain and adversarial settings. As cyber defense agents become more embedded in complex sociotechnical environments, the ability to reconcile data-driven inference with rule-based reasoning will become increasingly important for both operational effectiveness and compliance transparency.

The true power of these technologies, however, is only realized through system-level integration and orchestration. Building a converged resilience architecture requires not only technical compatibility but also unified semantics, interoperable protocols, and a shared trust framework across domains. For example, an intelligent cyber-physical system might use neurosymbolic reasoning to plan a defensive response, ML to predict attacker behavior, game theory to evaluate tradeoffs, blockchain to coordinate distributed agents, and QKD to secure control messages – all while maintaining auditability and explainability for human oversight.

In such architectures, interoperability and modularity are key design principles. Systems should be constructed as composable microservices or resilience modules, each responsible for a specific aspect of the defense pipeline – such as anomaly detection, trust scoring, deception planning, or threat attribution. These modules can communicate via well-defined interfaces and operate under a common policy language or mission objective. Moreover, dynamic orchestration mechanisms can allocate computational, sensing, and control resources in real time, based on evolving threat conditions and system states.

Finally, building converged resilience architectures is not solely a technical challenge; it is also an organizational and policy imperative. These systems must align with governance structures, regulatory frameworks, and ethical guidelines to ensure responsible autonomy. As resilience capabilities become increasingly embedded in critical sectors such as healthcare, transportation, finance, and defense, cross-sector coordination, standards development, and risk-informed policy design will be essential to ensuring both the safety and legitimacy of autonomous operations.

13.3.5 Research and Policy Translation: From Innovation to Implementation

In parallel with rapid technical advances, it is imperative to build translational pathways that bridge the gap between academic research and real-world deployment. Innovation in cyber resilience will only achieve its intended impact if it is successfully operationalized within mission-critical environments, scaled across sectors, and aligned with governance frameworks. As resilience becomes increasingly synonymous with autonomy, new challenges arise around verification, accountability, workforce readiness, and interorganizational coordination. Meeting these challenges requires a comprehensive strategy that spans technology, policy, education, and collaboration.

A key enabler for implementation is the operationalization of autonomy in controlled and evaluative settings. Research-driven prototypes must be validated through testbeds, digital twins, and high-fidelity simulation environments that faithfully represent adversarial conditions, infrastructure constraints, and human–machine interactions. These environments allow developers to assess not only the functional correctness of autonomous systems but also their behavior under stress, failure modes, and strategic adversary models. Digital twins, virtual replicas of physical systems, are particularly valuable in enabling real-time, closed-loop experimentation with minimal risk. By simulating attacks, recovery protocols, and cascading failures, researchers and operators can jointly iterate on system designs and resilience strategies in advance of deployment.

In tandem, regulatory frameworks and assurance mechanisms must evolve to govern the certification and accountability of autonomous cyber defense systems. Traditional notions of software testing and compliance are insufficient for systems that learn, adapt, and make decisions independently. New models of assurance are required: ones that accommodate non-determinism, adaptive behavior, and evolving threat landscapes. This calls for the development of resilience metrics, behavioral verification tools, and explainability benchmarks tailored to autonomous systems operating under adversarial and uncertain conditions. Certification processes must incorporate not only technical evaluations but also assessments of human–machine transparency, mission impact, and failure containment strategies.

Another foundational pillar of implementation is education and workforce development. The rise of autonomous resilience demands a new generation of practitioners fluent in multiple disciplines: AI, control theory, cybersecurity, policy, and systems engineering. Universities and training institutions must design curricula that go beyond siloed expertise, equipping students with the integrative mindset and skills necessary to build, audit, and operate resilient autonomous systems. This includes not only technical competencies but also ethical reasoning, regulatory literacy, and system-level thinking. Short-term, scalable education models such as stackable credentials, bootcamps, and cross-sector fellowships will also play a critical role in upskilling the current cybersecurity workforce.

Equally important is the promotion of public–private partnerships, which can align incentives, foster information sharing, and standardize best practices across sectors. Critical infrastructure resilience depends on collaboration among stakeholders with diverse risk profiles, capabilities, and regulatory environments. Governments can play a catalytic role by funding joint R&D, facilitating testbed access, and establishing procurement frameworks that reward innovation aligned with resilience objectives. Industry, in turn, can contribute domain-specific insights, deployment infrastructure, and feedback loops for iterative improvement. Multi-stakeholder consortia can help standardize shared taxonomies, metrics, and protocols for resilience, enabling interoperability and collective defense.

Moreover, policy translation should aim to embed resilience into economic and legal structures, ensuring that innovation is not only technologically feasible but also societally sustainable. This includes developing liability frameworks for autonomous agents, privacy-preserving compliance schemes, and international norms for cyber conflict deterrence. Mechanisms such as incentive-compatible regulation, cyber insurance models, and risk-adjusted subsidies can promote the adoption of resilience-enhancing technologies without mandating uniform prescriptions.

Finally, researchers must embrace new models of engaged scholarship, wherein academic work is co-designed with end-users and contextualized by real-world constraints. This entails working closely with policymakers, industry partners, and civil society to ensure that research agendas reflect actual operational needs and ethical concerns. Open-source platforms, participatory design workshops, and living labs are all examples of translational mechanisms that can accelerate the co-production of resilient technologies and practices.

13.4 Concluding Remarks

This concluding chapter has charted the conceptual, methodological, and operational landscape of cyber resilience in the age of intelligent and adversarial threats. Across its three interrelated parts, foundational frameworks, resilient ML, and game-theoretic strategies, the book has collectively argued that resilience is no longer a static property or an afterthought to system design. It is a dynamic, multilayered capability that must be designed, learned, and reasoned, often autonomously, under conditions of uncertainty, deception, and strategic adversarial behavior.

The rise of autonomous systems, coupled with the increasing complexity of cyber-physical environments, demands a redefinition of cyber resilience as an emergent property of intelligent, adaptive, and context-aware defense. To this end, the book has advanced a cohesive narrative that integrates ML for perception and adaptation, game theory for strategic interaction, and systemic tools such as zero-trust architectures, cyber insurance, and quantum-secure communication for operational hardening. Together, these dimensions offer a roadmap for achieving cognitive cyber resilience – a form of resilience characterized not only by robustness and recovery, but also by foresight, learning, and coordination.

The volume has also highlighted a growing need to operationalize resilience across multiple scales – from embedded sensors and tactical mission systems to cloud-based federated infrastructures and globally interconnected networks. This requires modular and composable architectures capable of integrating resilience-by-design with real-time adaptation. It also demands systems that can learn safely under pressure, explain their decisions to human stakeholders, and coordinate their actions with both allies and adversaries in complex sociotechnical ecosystems.

Crucially, this book emphasizes that cyber resilience is not merely a technical pursuit; it is a sociotechnical and institutional challenge. Translating research into practice requires engaged governance, policy innovation, ethical foresight, and cross-sector collaboration. Whether through public–private partnerships, standardization consortia, or regulatory frameworks for certifying autonomous systems, the broader ecosystem must evolve to support the deployment, auditing, and accountability of next-generation resilient technologies.

As a final reflection, the book underscores that building autonomous cyber resilience is not a one-time engineering effort but a continuing process of adaptation and co-evolution. Threat actors are intelligent, evolving, and often unpredictable. So too must be the systems that defend against them. By embedding strategic reasoning, adaptive learning, and systemic coordination into the fabric of digital infrastructure, we can begin to shift the paradigm from fragile systems that react, to resilient systems that understand, withstand, and adapt.

This transformation is not only possible but also necessary. The insights and frameworks presented in this volume aim to inspire the next generation of researchers, engineers, and policymakers to take up this challenge, forging pathways toward resilient, secure, and intelligent systems that can thrive in an increasingly adversarial digital world.

Index

Note: Page numbers in *italics* and **bold** refers to figures and tables respectively.

o

p

q

Z

www.ingramcontent.com/pod-product-compliance
Lightning Source LLC
LaVergne TN
LVHW011531200926
848484LV00001B/234
* 9 7 8 1 3 9 4 2 1 5 3 8 6 *